Apollonius' *Argonautica* and the *Homeric Hymns*

Mnemosyne Supplements

MONOGRAPHS ON GREEK AND
LATIN LANGUAGE AND LITERATURE

Executive Editor

J.J.H. Klooster (*University of Groningen*)

Editorial Board

K.M. Coleman (*Harvard University*)
R. Gagné (*University of Cambridge*)
C.C. de Jonge (*Leiden University*)
C. Pieper (*Leiden University*)
T. Reinhardt (*Oxford University*)

VOLUME 489

The titles published in this series are listed at *brill.com/mns*

Apollonius' *Argonautica* and the *Homeric Hymns*

A Study in Hymnody, Hero Cult, and Homeric Reception

By

Brian D. McPhee

BRILL

LEIDEN | BOSTON

The Library of Congress Cataloging-in-Publication Data is available online at https://catalog.loc.gov
LC record available at https://lccn.loc.gov/2024052447

Typeface for the Latin, Greek, and Cyrillic scripts: "Brill". See and download: brill.com/brill-typeface.

ISSN 0169-8958
ISBN 978-90-04-71510-3 (hardback)
ISBN 978-90-04-71538-7 (e-book)
DOI 10.1163/9789004715387

Copyright 2025 by Brian McPhee. Published by Koninklijke Brill BV, Leiden, The Netherlands.
Koninklijke Brill BV incorporates the imprints Brill, Brill Nijhoff, Brill Schöningh, Brill Fink, Brill mentis, Brill Wageningen Academic, Vandenhoeck & Ruprecht, Böhlau and V&R unipress.
Koninklijke Brill BV reserves the right to protect this publication against unauthorized use. Requests for re-use and/or translations must be addressed to Koninklijke Brill BV via brill.com or copyright.com.

This book is printed on acid-free paper and produced in a sustainable manner.

To my parents
Finis ab origine pendet

Contents

Acknowledgments   XI
Note on Texts, Translations, and Abbreviations   XIII

Introduction   1
1   Topic and *Status Quaestionis*   2
2   The *Homeric Hymns*: An Overview   6
   2.1   *The Collection*   6
   2.2   *Structure*   9
   2.3   *Performance Context*   16
   2.4   *Attribution of Authorship*   18
   2.5   *The Appeal of the* Homeric Hymns *in Third-Century Alexandria*   24
3   Method and Terminology   27
4   A Survey of Exemplary Intertexts from the *Homeric Hymns*   31
   4.1   *The* Homeric Hymns *as Sources for Myth*   32
   4.2   *Epic World-Building*   45
   4.3   *The Reception of the Homeric Gods*   49
   4.4   *Allusive Characterization*   51
   4.5   *Allusions to the* Hymns *as Metacommentary*   53
   4.6   *Thematic Allusions: Apollonius' Programmatic Allusion to the Homeric Hymn to Selene*   56
5   Outline of Chapters   78

PART 1
The Argonautica *as Epic Hymn*

1 A Diachronic Reading of the *Argonautica*'s Hymnic Frame   83
   1   The Introit   86
      1.1   *What Kind of Hymn?*   86
      1.2   *The "Hymnic Proem" Interpretation*   91
      1.3   *The Ambiguity of "Beginning with You, Phoebus"*   96
      1.4   *The Case for the "Hymnic Proem" Interpretation*   104
      1.5   *Excursus: A Hymnic Proem or a Hymn to Apollo?*   114
   2   The Envoi   118
      2.1   *The Rhetorical Structure of the Envois of the* Argonautica *and the Homeric Hymns*   118

	2.2	*Further Parallels for the Envoi from the* Homeric Hymns 126
	2.3	*Apollonius' Envoi and* HH *3.165–176* 130
	2.4	*The Text and Significance of* Arg. *4.1773* 133
3	Rereading the Introit in Light of the Envoi 137	
4	Conclusion 142	

2 Heroization and Generic Hybridity   145
    1 The Duality of the Concept of the Hero in Greek Culture   148
    2 Hero Cult and Immortalization in the *Argonautica*   156
        2.1 *Explicit References to Hero Cult*   157
        2.2 *Ambiguous Cases of Hero Cult*   165
        2.3 *Hesiodic Heroization*   169
        2.4 *Apotheosis*   172
    3 The Duality of the Hero and Generic Hybridity   177
        3.1 *Idmon and Agamestor*   180
        3.2 *Polydeuces in Bebrycia*   184
        3.3 *The Syrtis and the Envoi*   189
    4 Literary Precedents for Apollonius' Generic Experiment   198
        4.1 *Callimachus'* Hecale   199
        4.2 *Theocritus'* Idyll *22*   201
        4.3 *Simonides' Platea Elegy*   203
        4.4 *The* Homeric Hymn to Heracles *(15)*   206
    5 In the Footsteps of *Heracles*   212
        5.1 *Correspondences between* Arg. *1.1–22 and* HH *15.4–6*   212
        5.2 *The Teleology of Heroism*   218
    6 Conclusion   226

PART 2
The Apollonian Narrator's Hymnic Voice

3 Narratological Features with Precedent in the *Homeric Hymns*   231
    1 The Overt Narrator   233
    2 The Narrator's Piety   237
        2.1 *Pious Similes*   239
        2.2 *Pious Silences*   244
        2.3 *Apologies to the Gods*   250
    3 Etiology   254
    4 Further Hymnic Techniques   266
    5 Conclusion   270

CONTENTS   IX

4 Hymnic Moments within the Epic 272
  1 Contagious Hymnody 273
  2 Other Apostrophes 281
    2.1 *Apostrophes to Mortals* 281
    2.2 *Other Hymnic Addresses* 286
  3 Hymnic Narratization 291
  4 Orpheus' Hymn to Apollo: The Thynias Episode (*Arg.* 2.669–719) 305
    4.1 *Summary of the Episode* 306
    4.2 *Allusions to Apolline Hymns* 309
    4.3 *Representing Hymnic Speech* 318
  5 Conclusion 328

Conclusion 331
  1 Major Findings and Directions for Future Research 331
  2 Final Reflections 335
    2.1 *The Ptolemaic Context* 335
    2.2 *Heroization and Heroism* 343

Appendix: Divine Epithets in the *Argonautica* 351
Glossary of Hymnic Terminology 357
Bibliography 361
Index of Greek Terms 412
Index Locorum 413
Index Rerum 431

Acknowledgments

This book began its life as a 2020 doctoral dissertation at the University of North Carolina at Chapel Hill. For all of their generous guidance and criticism, I must in the first instance thank the members of my doctoral committee: Patricia Rosenmeyer, Bill Race, Jim O'Hara, Jim Clauss, and Suzanne Lye. I owe especial debts of gratitude to Patricia, who was a wonderful supervisor and who remains my constant supporter, and to Bill, a most judicious second reader and the man who first kindled my love for Apollonius. There are many other professors beyond my committee members who deserve to be acknowledged for contributing to my formation both as a scholar and as a human being. Of these, I would like to single out for mention Sharon James, Susan MacManus, Dell deChant, Ava Chitwood, Hip Kantzios, and Casey Moore. This book would not exist without the mentorship I received from each and every one of them.

I presented papers relating to the research for this book at many venues over the years, including in Chapel Hill, London, Kitchener, Groningen, Rome, Seattle, Durham, İstanbul, and London, ON. To all of the colleagues who attended these talks and helped to sharpen my thinking with their questions, comments, and conversation, I extend my warmest thanks.

For sharing copies of their work with me, whether forthcoming or just difficult for me to access, I would like to thank Jackie Murray, Aniek van den Eersten, Thanasis Vergados, and Martin Korenjak. In addition, I would be remiss if I did not thank all the librarians—the real unsung heroes of our profession—and all the other colleagues whose bibliographical assistance made my work possible, especially in the face of the obstacles posed by the COVID-19 pandemic.

As a PhD student, my research was supported by fellowships from the Royster Society at UNC-Chapel Hill as well as the American Academy in Rome. I then undertook the process of revising and expanding my thesis into a book for the most part during a Loeb Classical Library Foundation Postdoctoral Fellowship hosted at Durham University. I am hugely grateful to all of these institutions for facilitating the research that went into this monograph. The LCLF in particular deserves tremendous plaudits for creating a postdoctoral fellowship for the express purpose of supporting early career researchers in what continues to be such a difficult post-pandemic job market. Truly, to borrow an image from the *Argonautica*, their intervention was like a radiant burst of Apolline light piercing a shroud of darkness over the Cretan main.

Finally, I come to the sweetest portion of the task of acknowledgment, thanking my friends and family. Through all the trials and tribulations and twists and turns of a burgeoning academic career, I could always count on their unconditional support and encouragement. To my best friend Max; my sisters, Laura and Sarah; my amazing wife Gamze; and our delightful feline companions Defne and Hermes: thank you all so much. You will never know what having each of you in my life has meant to me. Above all, I would like to thank my parents, Susan and David. Whatever success I might enjoy in this life, it can all be traced back to the values you instilled in us and the sacrifices you made so that we could follow our dreams—whatever they were and wherever they took us. With every passing year and every ounce of wisdom I glean therein, the more I realize how lucky I am to be your son. Mom and Dad, this book is dedicated to you.

Note on Texts, Translations, and Abbreviations

Unless otherwise noted, all Greek and Latin texts and their English translations are taken from the most current editions of the Loeb Classical Library. Translations are sometimes adapted, especially in the case of the *Homeric Hymns*. For these, I have consulted both Evelyn-White 1914 and West 2003a, often updating the archaizing language of the former and modifying certain idiosyncrasies in the latter.

Abbreviations for ancient authors and works follow the conventions of the fourth edition of the *Oxford Classical Dictionary*, with two exceptions. First, I do not abbreviate the major *Homeric Hymns* (1–5) differently from the rest of the collection, preferring instead to identify each hymn by its conventional number (as, e.g., in West 2003a). Thus:

HH 1   The major *Homeric Hymn to Dionysus* ("*HH Dion.*")
HH 2   The major *Homeric Hymn to Demeter* ("*HH Dem.*")
HH 3   The major *Homeric Hymn to Apollo* ("*HH Ap.*")
HH 4   The major *Homeric Hymn to Hermes* ("*HH Herm.*")
HH 5   The major *Homeric Hymn to Aphrodite* ("*HH Aph.*")

Second, I have adopted the following shorthand for some oft-repeated terms:

AR narrator   Apollonian narrator (i.e., the narrator of the *Argonautica*)
Arg.   *Argonautica*
HE   Homeric epic (referring to the *Iliad* and *Odyssey*)
HH   Homeric Hymn

Bibliographical Abbreviations

Periodicals are abbreviated according to the conventions of L'année philologique. The following additional abbreviations are also used:

AHS   Allen, T.W., W.R. Halliday, and E.E. Sikes. 1936. *The Homeric Hymns*. 2nd ed. Oxford: Clarendon.
FVS   Faulkner, Andrew, Athanassios Vergados, and Andreas Schwab, eds. 2016. *The Reception of the Homeric Hymns*. Oxford: Oxford University Press.
HG   *Hellenistica Groningana* series ([vol. 1–3] Groningen: Egbert Forsten; [vol. 4–present] Leuven: Peeters; editors: [vol. 1–23] M.A. Harder, R.F. Regtuit, and G.C. Wakker; [vol. 24] J.J.H. Klooster, M.A. Harder, R.F. Regtuit, and G.C. Wak-

ker; [vol. 26] M.A. Harder, J.J.H. Klooster, R.F. Regtuit, and G.C. Wakker; [vol. 27] A. Harder, J.J.H. Klooster, R.F. Regtuit, G.C. Wakker, and C.L. Caspers). Vol. 1 = *Callimachus*; Vol. 3= *Genre in Hellenistic Poetry*; Vol. 4 = *Apollonius Rhodius*; Vol. 7 = *Callimachus II*; Vol. 16 = *Gods and Religion in Hellenistic Poetry*; Vol. 21 = *Past and Present in Hellenistic Poetry*; Vol. 23 = *Drama and Performance in Hellenistic Poetry*; 24 = *Callimachus Revisited*; 26 = *Women and Power in Hellenistic Poetry*; 27 (forthcoming) = *Crisis and Resilience in Hellenistic Poetry*.

SAGN   *Studies in Ancient Greek Narrative* series (Leiden: Brill). Vol. 1 = Jong, Irene J.F. de, René Nünlist, and Angus Bowie (eds.), *Narrators, Narratees, and Narratives in Ancient Greek Literature* (2004); Vol. 2 = Jong, Irene J.F. de, and René Nünlist (eds.), *Time in Ancient Greek Literature* (2007); Vol. 3 = Jong, Irene J.F. de (ed.), *Space in Ancient Greek Literature* (2012); Vol. 4 = De Temmerman, Koen, and Evert van Emde Boas (eds.), *Characterization in Ancient Greek Literature* (2018); Vol. 5 = Bakker, Mathieu de, and Irene J.F. de Jong (eds.), *Speech in Ancient Greek Literature* (2022).

Introduction

This book seeks to shed new light on Apollonius of Rhodes' third-century BCE epic poem, the *Argonautica* (hereafter, *Arg.*), by investigating his engagement with the corpus of hexametric hymns attributed in antiquity to Homer, the so-called *Homeric Hymns* (hereafter, *HH*s). Apollonius occupies a key position in literary history as the author of the only Greco-Roman epic to survive from the centuries separating Homer and Vergil. Accordingly, it is only natural that the scholarship on his poem has long been devoted to tracing the patterns of imitation, transformation, and allusive interaction that mark his place in the epic tradition. The present study significantly expands this inquiry, opening new vistas onto the *Argonautica* by examining the poem's relationship with another body of poetry attributed to Homer in antiquity, namely, the *Homeric Hymns*, whose rich history of reception has only recently begun to attract critical attention. This monograph constitutes the first in-depth investigation of Apollonius' profound engagement with the hymnic Homer, which, I argue, is fundamental to understanding such major features of his work as its conception of heroism, its innovative narratological strategies, and even its very generic affiliations. My findings also have ramifications for the recent effort to set the *Arg.* in its historical context in third-century Alexandria, as the *Arg.*'s unique experiments with hymnody resonate not just with the Archaic practice of hero cult, but with the contemporary institution of the Ptolemaic ruler cult as well. The opening words of the *Arg.* already flag the programmatic importance of the *HH*s for Apollonius' project. It is my hope that a book dedicated to his reception thereof will help to restore this hymnic corpus from the margins of Apollonian studies to their rightful place alongside the *Iliad* and the *Odyssey* themselves as models of the utmost consequence for our reading of the Hellenistic epic.

This introduction contextualizes the study from a number of angles. Section 1 defines the research question and situates the inquiry at the crossroads of an enduring scholarly interest in Apollonius' reception of the Homeric epics (hereafter, HEs) and a more recent interest in the reception that Homer's other hexameter poems, the *HH*s, enjoyed in antiquity. Section 2 establishes some of the basic facts about the *HH*s, especially vis-à-vis Apollonius: the contents of the hymnic collection itself, the structural features of the individual hymns, the likelihood that they were originally recited as "Hymnic Proems" to epic performances,[1] the *HH*s' attribution to Homer in antiquity, and the appeal that

---

[1] I capitalize "Hymnic Proems" and other terms related to hymnody to distinguish them as

these hymns manifestly held for Alexandrian poets in the first century of the Hellenistic period. Section 3 is devoted to the question of methodology. The theory of allusion and intertextuality provides the primary lens of analysis for this study, and in addition to explaining what I mean by these terms, in this section I discuss the role that hypothetical "readers" play in staging my arguments. Section 4 moves us from the abstract to the concrete, as I offer a select survey of Apollonian allusions to individual *HH*s. In addition to demonstrating my method, this survey is intended to showcase the great range of uses to which Apollonius could put allusions to the *HH*s. I conclude in section 5 by outlining the contents of the remainder of this book.

1 Topic and *Status Quaestionis*

The primary objective of this study is, in a word, to establish the nature of Apollonius' reception of the *HH*s in his Alexandrian epic. There are several forms that such a project might take, ranging from a comprehensive investigation of the *HH*s' influence on Apollonius' poetic technique, complete with indices listing parallel passages,[2] to a survey of the major episodes of the epic and hymns and their verbal and typological interconnections,[3] to a collection of more loosely united literary-interpretative essays that each broach this relationship in a different way.[4] All of these methods are valuable and will find moments of exemplification at various points in this project, but as we will see, the state of research on the relationship between these particular texts is still so embryonic at present as to necessitate a more broad-based approach that focuses on Apollonius' engagement with the *HH*s at the most general level. My focus will thus fall primarily on the *Arg.*'s "hymnic frame," the poem's generic hybridity, the role of the Greek conception of the "hero" in mediating the interrelationship between epic and hymnody, and the narratological reflexes of the narrator's "hymnic voice." By attending to these macroscopic features of the relationship between the *Arg.* and the *HH*s, I hope to establish a firm context in which future studies that investigate this relationship may be grounded.

For well over a century, the poetic antecedents that have received the lion's share of Apollonian scholars' attention are undoubtedly the HEs.[5] Numerous

---

technical terms, which are defined for the reader's convenience in the Glossary as well as in section 2.2 below.
2   Knauer 1964 is the classic example of this approach.
3   E.g., as one finds in much of Knight 1995 or Nelis 2001.
4   E.g., see many of the chapters in Faulkner, Vergados, and Schwab (FVS) 2016.
5   By "Homeric epic" I mean the *Iliad* and the *Odyssey* as distinct from the *HH*s, though this

studies are devoted solely to this topic,[6] while many more use HE intertextuality as a primary method of analysis.[7] This is, on the whole, as it should be. Apollonius was himself a Homeric scholar of such stature as to succeed Zenodotus as head of the Royal Library of Alexandria. Indeed, one of his few treatises of which we know the name is an "Against Zenodotus" (Πρὸς Ζηνόδοτον), recording its author's disagreements with his predecessor's critical edition of the HEs; hence, presumably, Apollonius' philological judgments are sometimes recorded in the Homeric scholia.[8] As a poet, Apollonius worked in multiple genres, including epigram[9] and hexameter narratives treating the foundation legends of cities (Κτίσεις);[10] he also wrote a poem in choliambics called *Canobus*, which seems to have told the story of the death of Menelaus' helmsman in Egypt.[11] But these poems and his philology notwithstanding, Apollonius was best remembered in antiquity as the author of the *Arg.*, which is his only work that survives entire today.[12] Homer is inevitably the chief generic exemplar for any ancient epic poet, and in Apollonius' case, every page of his work announces its author as a creative adapter of the HE tradition. Accordingly, I would hardly dispute Beye's declaration that "the first and most important ele-

---

category could in principle embrace the Cycle poems, which were sometimes attributed to Homer in antiquity (see, e.g., Burgess 2001: 129–131; West 2013: 26–40). When I wish to refer to the Cycle poems, however, I will denote them as such. Note that while the *Margites* is sometimes described as a "mock-epic," its mixed hexameter and iambic meter distinguishes it from the other epic poems attributed to Homer. As for the *Batrachomyomachia*, I believe that it postdates Apollonius and, indeed, alludes to him in places, as I touch upon in 1.1.3.

6   Important entries in the vast bibliography include: Seaton 1890; Carspecken 1952; Händel 1954; Garson 1972; Lennox 1980; Dufner 1988; Fantuzzi 1988, 2008a; Knight 1995; Fantuzzi and Hunter 2004: 89–132, 266–282.
7   E.g., Clauss 1993; Hunter 1993; Clare 2002.
8   For Apollonius' scholarly activities, see the overviews in: Pfeiffer 1968: 140–148; Montana 2020: 183–184. The fragments and testimonia are collected in Michaelis 1875: 16–23, 40–56. For the evidence for Apollonius' philological scholarship from his own poetry, see, e.g.: Michaelis 1875: 23–40; Erbse 1953; Giangrande 1967, 1970: 56–61; Livrea 1972; Nelis 1992; Rengakos 1993, 1994, 2002, 2008.
9   See fr. 50 *SH*. The one epigram attributed to Apollonius that we possess (fr. 13 Powell = *AP* 11.275) is of dubious authenticity, reflecting as it does the questionable ancient biographical tradition that Apollonius feuded with his "teacher" Callimachus. Lefkowitz 2008 is a good starting place within the substantial bibliography on this controversy.
10 Frr. 4–12 Powell. For introductions to these fragmentary poems, see: Levin 1962; Krevans 2000; Smith 2001; Sistakou 2008b.
11 Frr. 1–3 Powell. For some different reconstructions of this poem, see McPhee (forthcoming, a), with earlier bibliography. Curiazi 1979 proposes Apollonian authorship for an anonymous choliambic fragment as well.
12 See, e.g., Levin 1962: 161–162.

ment in the criticism of the *Argonautica* ... must be a pervasive knowledge of the *Iliad* and the *Odyssey*."[13]

The *Iliad* and *Odyssey* represent the *Arg.*'s most important poetic models, bar none, but it is curious that in pursuing the question of Apollonius' engagement with "Homer," scholars have largely left the *HH*s out of consideration. Apollonius himself signals their programmatic importance for the *Arg.* by beginning his epic (1.1–2) with an unmistakable allusion to the *Homeric Hymn to Selene* (32.18–19),[14] and his poem ends with a hymnic Envoi addressed to the Argonauts marked by several points of contact with the *HH*s (*Arg.* 4.1773–1781).[15] But beyond a great number of almost perfunctory acknowledgments of the *Arg.*'s "hymnic frame,"[16] the *HH*s do not occupy anything like the prominent place in Apollonian scholarship that these programmatic allusions would seem to recommend. A number of studies adduce particular hymns in passing, especially with reference to certain well-known *loci*.[17] The hymns also comprise part of the repertory of early Greek ἔπος with which Apollonius' phraseology is regularly compared, particularly in the commentaries; Campbell has done an especial service to students of Apollonius in cataloging a huge number of "echoes and imitations" of early Greek epic, including the *HH*s, in the *Arg*.[18] But to my knowledge, only two full-scale articles (let alone books) wholly devoted to Apollonius' engagement with a *HH* had appeared by the time I first embarked on the research for this project as a graduate student.[19] While both represent valuable contributions, clearly much work remains to be done.[20]

---

13   Beye 1982: 11; for similar pronouncements, see further: Händel 1954: 7; Lloyd-Jones 1984: 70; Nelis 2005a: 354.
14   Cf. Clauss 1993: 16, who interprets this allusion not as flagging the importance of the *HH*s specifically as poetic models but rather as Apollonius' way of "mak[ing] it clear that he will not be restricted in the exposition of his epic theme by considerations of genre." See further in this vein: Schaaf 2014: 36; Llanos 2017a: 2, 2017b: 7. For the pre-Apollonian date of *HH* 32, see below, introduction 4.6.1.
15   I discuss this Envoi, and its connections with the *HH*s, particularly in 1.2.
16   For this term, see the introductory section of chapter 1.
17   For examples beyond the hymnic frame, see, among others: Boesch 1908: 3–4, 39–42; Richardson 1974: 69–70; Campbell 1977; Zumbo 1978; Janko 1979; Nelis 1991: 101; Clauss 1993: 69–74, 83–84, 2016: 62–65; Hunter 1996: 144; Vergados 2013: 113–117. A cluster of allusions in Book 4 to the *Homeric Hymn to Demeter* is particularly well-recognized; see 177n159.
18   Campbell 1981.
19   The first is Pace 2004, who demonstrates that Apollonius' brilliant portraits of the petulant Eros and put-upon Aphrodite at the beginning of Book 3 are partly modeled on Hermes and Maia in the *Homeric Hymn to Hermes*; see further Campbell 1983a: 18–19, 1994 ad *Arg.* 3.129 f.; Vergados 2013: 115. The second is Clayton 2017, who builds on Hunter 1993: 40–41

The neglect of the *HH*s by Apollonian critics is part of the much larger story of neglect suffered by these "sub-epic" poems until the past thirty years or so,[21] when Clay's *Politics of Olympus* revitalized the hymns as poems worthy of study in their own right.[22] More recently, the *HH*s' rich history of reception by later authors and artists has inspired the publication of a 2016 collection of essays on this topic;[23] the editors themselves trace scholarly interest in the afterlife of the *HH*s to a 1999 article on Ovid's adaptations thereof in the *Metamorphoses* by Barchiesi, who first pointed out what fertile but untilled ground this area represented for future research.[24] My project thus stands at the intersection of two major trends in classical scholarship: a long-standing interest in Apollonius' engagement with "Homer" and a newfound interest in the reception of the *HH*s.[25] Above all, I take seriously Apollonius' programmatic allusions to the hymns, most clearly signaled in his hymnic frame, and argue accordingly that these poems served alongside the *Iliad* and *Odyssey* as equally authoritative and authorizing "Homeric" models for the *Arg*.

---

to offer a sensitive reading of the Hylas episode in light of the abduction of Persephone in the *Homeric Hymn to Demeter*. As the same intertext has been put forward for Theocritus' rendition of the Hylas episode in *Id*. 13 (Gutzwiller 1981: 26–27), we may be dealing here with a two-tier allusion (for this term, see 29*n*147).

20 I am pleased to report, however, that some promising signs have since appeared. One new article has come out and another is forthcoming: the former is a piece of my own (McPhee 2021a), on Apollonius' characterization of Medea in light of models from the *HH*s, and the latter is a chapter by Athanassios Vergados, which investigates the relationship between Apollonius' etymologizing in the Thynias episode and that of the *Homeric Hymn to Apollo*. In addition, Manolis Tsakiris has now written a dissertation (2022) that tackles the phenomenon of generic layering in the *Arg*., including the presence of the *HH*s in Books 1–2 and 4; and at Trinity College Dublin, Jeremy Lam is currently working on a dissertation on the reception of the *HH*s in Hellenistic poetry, including the *Arg*. It seems that "Apollonius' *Argonautica* and the *Homeric Hymns*" is an idea whose time has finally come.

21 The term "sub-epic," from Hoekstra 1969, was not intended as a value judgment, but it naturally carried with it a negative connotation (Clay 2006: 4).

22 Clay 2006, first published in 1989.

23 FVS 2016. The volume focuses on Roman and Imperial Greek receptions, but Apollonian interactions with the *HH*s are cataloged on pp. 10–12 and figure in Clauss's chapter as well; see further Faulkner 2011c: 193–195.

24 FVS 2016: 2, referring to Barchiesi 1999.

25 I might also point to the marked interest in the past few decades in Hellenistic poets' revival of and allusion to a great variety of Archaic forms; see, e.g.: Hunter 1996; Acosta-Hughes 2010a. The *Arg*.'s engagement with tragedy represents a longstanding interest in Apollonian scholarship, but recent years have also seen increased attention paid to the epic's engagement with other non-hexameter genres, including historiography; see 147*n*9.

2   The *Homeric Hymns*: An Overview

2.1   *The Collection*

It will be useful to review some of the basic facts concerning the hymns to establish the context for analyzing Apollonius' allusions thereto.[26] The *HH*s are a collection of thirty-three hexameter hymns whose "formal elements of diction, style, and narrative technique link the hymns to *epos*, of which they form a subset."[27] They are, in other words, "Rhapsodic Hymns," whose relatively impersonal manner and consistent set of formal features distinguish them from "Cultic Hymns," with their more intimate tone and flexible structure.[28] The *HH*s range in length considerably—from 3 lines to 580—and are often divided into "major," "midlength," and "minor" subgroups on this basis.[29] Many of the hymns, including all of the major ones, include mythical narratives, which are marked by certain recurrent themes such as a god's birth or appearance in epiphany.[30] Clay has argued that the major hymns, which she considers a subgenre unto themselves, are especially concerned with the gods' acquisition of new divine prerogatives (τιμαί), which results in each case in a permanent reordering of relations within the pantheon and between gods and humanity. On the temporal continuum of mythological poetry, she sees the major hymns as filling the gap between Hesiod's *Theogony*, which describes the earliest origins of Zeus' reign, and the HEs, which take for granted a fully developed and permanent Olympian order.[31]

---

26   Good introductions to the *HH*s can be found in Clay 1997 and the chapters in Faulkner 2011a. The introduction of Allen, Halliday, and Sikes (AHS) 1936 remains valuable as well, especially as regards the manuscript tradition and ancient testimonia.

27   Clay 2006: 15. For all hexameter poetry as belonging to one "super-genre" in ancient conceptions of genre, see Hutchinson 2013: 20–24; cf. the earlier use of the term by Martin 2005: 17. For the likelihood that many more Homeric-style hymns, including longer hymns, once existed than have survived, see Parker 1991: 1.

28   For the distinction between Rhapsodic and Cultic Hymns, see: Meyer 1933: 2–7; Lenz 1975: 10–13; Miller 1986: 1–5; Race 1992: 19–31. Wünsch (in *RE* 9.1. s.v. "Hymnos") uses the terms "objektiv" and "subjektiv" (142).

29   The major category includes *HH*s 1–5; the first of these is now fragmentary, but probably contained as many as 411 lines (West 2001: 1). Of the remaining hymns, two are noticeably longer (7, 19) than the rest, but the line dividing the mid-length and short examples is rather hazy. Fröhder 1994, a study devoted exclusively to the mid-length hymns, sets the boundary at about twenty lines (see pp. 14–15 with n. 1).

30   See, e.g., Janko 1981: 13–14. For common epic and folkloric themes in the narratives of the *Hymns*, see Sowa 1984, with a summary of results on pp. 281–284; see further the schematic index of themes in Pavese 1993. Miller (1986: 5–9) applies the encomiastic terminology of ancient rhetorical theory to the contents of the *HH*s.

31   Clay 2006; this thesis is summed up on p. 15. Clay's approach is anticipated somewhat

INTRODUCTION   7

The hymns' dates of composition are difficult to determine, especially for the shorter pieces, though one recent study has concluded that there is no compelling reason to date any of them later than the early Classical period.[32] Some seem to fit in particularly well in this period; for instance, the *Homeric Hymn to Hephaestus* (20), with its narrative of cultural progress, has often been associated with the philosophical and poetic speculations on this subject in Classical Athens.[33] But the collection also includes some of the oldest extant works in all of Greek literature. Indeed, according to Janko's statistical analysis of archaisms in the language of early Greek hexameter, the major *Homeric Hymn to Aphrodite* (5) predates even the *Odyssey* and the Hesiodic corpus.[34] One hymn, however, is manifestly much later than the rest—*Hymn 8, to Ares*. Somehow this hymn found its way into the Homeric collection from another source—perhaps the *Hymns* of the fifth-century CE Neoplatonist philosopher Proclus, as West argues.[35] In any case, it can safely be disregarded for the purposes of this study. As for places of composition, we are wholly reliant on internal evidence from the hymns themselves; for instance, the mention of Salamis in the tenth *Homeric Hymn* (10.4) suggests that it was originally performed in the Cypriot town of that name.[36]

It is unknown when the hymns were collected into an edition approximating the one that we have today.[37] Van der Valk speculates that rhapsodes might have collected these poems themselves in the Archaic period to serve as a handbook for performance.[38] Most scholars, however, assume that the *HH*s were collected

---

    by Rudhardt 1978. For the major hymns as their own genre, see further Clay 1997: 494–498, 2011: 240; cf. Haubold 2001: 23–24. Felson (2011: 262–271, 278–279, on *HH* 28) and Hall (2023: 88–90, on *HH* 33) demonstrate that the thematic concerns identified by Clay are operative in some of the minor hymns as well. See further de Hoz 1998: 64–65.

32   Hall 2012: ch. 2. For the date of *HH* 31–32, see introduction, 4.6.1. For late datings that have been proposed for *HH* 9 and 26, see Hall 2023: 80 n. 9.

33   See, e.g., Haubold 2001: 32–33.

34   Janko 1982, whose results (summarized p. 200) are revisited and defended in Janko 2012. For a summary of earlier attempts at dating on the basis of linguistic criteria, see Clay 1997: 490. The only major *HH* whose early date has been doubted is the fragmentary *Homeric Hymn to Dionysus* (1), but the arguments raised by Dihle (1987: 51–55, 2002) are open to doubt (Faulkner 2010b: 2; 2011b: 9–10; West 2011; Bernabé 2017: 22–23). The hymn's rhetoric is more traditional than Dihle grants (see Race 1982b: 43–45), and note as well that its geography is compatible with an Archaic dating (see Mazzarino 1989: 142–144).

35   West 1970; see further: Faulkner 2011c: 176 n. 4; van den Berg 2016. Van der Valk (1976: 438–445) went against the grain in considering the hymn authentically Archaic, but cf. Bona 1978: 226.

36   Shackle 1915: 164; West 2003a: 17; Olson 2012: 291 and n. ad loc.; cf. AHS 1936: 391.

37   Hall 2012: 4–12 provides a useful survey of theories.

38   Van der Valk 1976: 445. Càssola (1975a: lix–lxv) would date the emergence of such a profes-

and edited in the Hellenistic period as part of the work of the Alexandrian philologists. The earliest datable reference to "the hymns" of Homer is in the first-century BCE historian Diodorus Siculus (τὸν Ὅμηρον ... ἐν τοῖς ὕμνοις, 4.2.4; see also 1.15.7, 3.66.3), though there is evidence that he may be drawing on the third-century mythographer Dionysius Scytobrachion.[39] Though less explicit, allusions in Callimachus' own Rhapsodic Hymns provide precious evidence that he knew a collection beginning with the longer hymns in the order 1, 2, 3, 4, 5, 7, at least.[40] Given Apollonius' extensive allusions to individual *HH*s from throughout the corpus, it is likely that he knew a collection very similar to our own in terms of content, and perhaps, in light of the evidence from his older contemporary Callimachus, even in order.

The ordering of the hymns in the collection as it has come down to us is idiosyncratic, but general patterns are recognizable, especially a principle of organization according to length.[41] The collection begins with the major hymns (1–5); one of the shorter hymns to Aphrodite (6) has been attracted to its major counterpart (5),[42] but then the longest of the midlength hymns follows (7). After the interloper hymn to Ares (8), a subgroup of short hymns for goddesses

---

sional handbook to sometime between the mid-fourth and second centuries BCE. Cf. Hall's (2023) recent theory that Cynaethus and his circle were responsible for the initial stages of assembling (and, in part, composing) the corpus of *HH*s, first in the form of a "proto-collection" emerging on Polycratean Samos, with the later addition of an "appendix" transpiring on Sicily in the early fifth century. On Cynaethus, see 19*n*97 below.

39 See AHS 1936: lxvii–lxix; Faulkner 2011c: 176. Dionysius belongs to the middle of the third century (Rusten 1982: ch. 6), if not earlier (cf. D'Alessio 2000: 100–102). In fact, Diodorus' citation of Homer's "hymns" at 1.15.7 could be derived from his source in this section, Hecataeus of Abdera (Stephens 2003: 84), who wrote during the reign of Ptolemy I.

40 See Faulkner 2011c: 180–181, 205; see further Acosta-Hughes and Cusset 2012, who argue that the *HH*s qua edited collection inspired Callimachus' own curation of his hymnic sextet. Notably, Callimachus' imitation already privileges the "major" *HH*s, but see also Hall 2012: 68–71, who surveys evidence for the poet's knowledge of some of the minor *HH*s (13, 15 and/or 20, 21, 24) and concludes that the collection known to the Cyrenian contained at least some of the shorter hymns as well. See further Vamvouri Ruffy 2004: 121 n. 45 for a probable Callimachean allusion to *HH* 30 as well. For the likelihood that Callimachus arranged his own hymnic collection, see, e.g.: Henrichs 1993; Haslam 1993: 115; Boychenko 2013.

41 This paragraph is substantially based on van der Valk 1976, though I am not convinced of his overarching thesis that the organization of the collection reflects an "archaic" mindset; for critique, see Bona 1978: 225–227. For slightly different accounts of the collection's arrangement, see Torres-Guerra 2003 (adducing narrative content and strategies in addition to length as organizational principles), and Hall 2021 (adducing closural formulas that demarcate subgroupings within the collection).

42 In fact, in two manuscripts these hymns to Aphrodite have actually been merged into one continuous poem; see Clay 1997: 495 n. 27. See further Hall 2021: 25.

commences (9–14) and is itself succeeded by a subgroup of hymns for deified heroes (15–17). Another subgroup of short hymns for gods comes next (18, 20–23), punctuated by the midlength *Hymn to Pan* (19), which has apparently been attracted to the eighteenth hymn, to Pan's father Hermes. After two odd hymns (24–25), the collection ends with a series of hymns that are a bit longer, each 13–22 lines long (26–33); this series may conclude with a sort of celestial subgroup dedicated to the Sun (31), Moon (32), and the Dioscuri, whose epiphany at sea takes the form of St. Elmo's Fire (33).[43] Some manuscripts then append a Homeric epigram (Εἰς Ξένους, "To Strangers"), which is titled using the same conventions employed for the other *HH*s (εἰς + the name of the Hymnic Subject in the accusative case), as though it were another hymn. Pfeiff has plausibly interpreted this poem as a sort of *sphragis* sealing the collection, because this epigram is associated with the composition of the *Homeric Hymns* in the *Life of Homer* attributed to Herodotus.[44]

2.2 Structure

Greek hymns are possessed of the most consistent rhetorical structure of any brand of Archaic poetry, and in its basic form it persisted as long as Greek religion itself. This structure is perhaps best described by the tripartite schema *invocatio—laudatio—preces*:[45] contact with the god is established immediately, praise is offered in order to incline the deity to be propitious, and finally a request is made for a divine boon. This structure is eminently logical, in that the *laudatio* is intended to lay the groundwork for the hymnist's petition by securing the god's goodwill.[46] This schema is keyed, in other words, to the ulti-

---

43   Other scholars would include the thirtieth hymn, to the Earth, within this subgroup, which they understand as "cosmic" in scope; see 60n28.

44   Pfeiff 2002: 196–197; cf. Càssola (1975b: 216), who argues that the epigram was included in the collection by an accident of transmission. In *Vita Homeri* 2.9 West, this epigram represents the first verses that Homer ever recited, and with it he wins the hospitality of a cobbler named Tychius in the city of Neonteichos, near Smyrna. At Tychius' workshop he then performs (ἐπεδείκνυτο) "Amphiaraus' Expedition to Thebes, and the Hymns that he had composed to the gods" (Ἀμφιάρεώ τε τὴν ἐξελασίαν τὴν ἐς Θήβας, καὶ τοὺς ὕμνους τοὺς ἐς θεοὺς πεποιημένους αὐτῷ); evidently we are to understand that Homer had begun work on these poems while still in Smyrna (2.8), but that their first public display was at Neonteichos. The author claims that the Neonteichians still show the spot where Homer would recite.

45   I here follow Furley and Bremer 2001: 1.50–64 (esp. p. 51), who provide plentiful bibliography on earlier attempts to label these parts of Greek hymns.

46   For the hymn as a kind of pleasing dedication to the god on a par with material offerings or sacrifices, see, e.g.: Pulleyn 1997: 49–55; Depew 2000; and (with reference to the *HH*s) Petrovic 2012.

mate aim of any Greek hymn, which is to establish χάρις between the speaker and the addressee—that "relationship ... of reciprocal pleasure and goodwill"[47] that ties hymnist and god together in a mutual bond of gratitude and grace.[48]

Rhapsodic Hymns like the *HH*s abide by even more standardized formal principles—indeed, they are the only type of Archaic ἔπος (cf. theogonic, heroic, and didactic hexameter poetry) with a definite structure, of which the opening and closing formulas are especially invariable.[49] This rigidity is particularly useful for the alluding poet (as for the scholar studying such allusions), for it means that in the right context even a single word can be distinctive enough to serve as a "system reference" to the rhetoric of the *HH*s, as I argue, for instance, for the verb μνήσομαι (*Arg.* 1.2) in chapter 1.[50] I would also observe that, in light of these formal distinctions, it makes sense for the purposes of this study to use the anachronistic category of "genre" to distinguish the *HH*s from the HEs,[51] for while these two corpora share many salient characteristics, including the hexameter,[52] Archaic poets evidently knew to shape their compositions according to a different set of formal criteria when hymning a god than they would observe in composing another type of song.[53] And besides, from the perspective of a philologist like Apollonius in third-century Alexandria, "hymns" (ὕμνοι) had become a recognized (if capacious) generic term denoting songs dedicated to the gods, including several Cultic subtypes such as processional hymns (προσόδια), hymns performed beside an altar (παραβώμια), and so on.[54]

---

47   Race 1982a: 8.
48   On this fundamental concept in Greek hymnody, see, e.g.: Keyssner 1932: 131–135; Bundy 1972: 49–54; Race 1982a: 8–10; Furley 1995: 45–46; Furley and Bremer 2001: 1.61–63; Calame 2005: 26–29.
49   See, e.g.: Janko 1981: 23; Clay 1997: 493; 2011: 235. Haubold (2001: 24–25) emphasizes the *HH*s' fixed closural formulas as their most distinctive element, because, as we will see, heroic epic shares its own opening formulas with Rhapsodic Hymnody.
50   Edmunds (2001: 143–150) defines "system references" as allusions (or "quotations," in his terminology) to "verbal categories, literary and nonliterary, larger than single texts" (143)—e.g., legal discourse, the Oenotropae myth, Roman love elegy, etc.
51   For the idea that performance context, not formal features, distinguished different types of song in the Archaic period, see, e.g., Ford 2002: 10–13, with earlier bibliography.
52   Farrell (2003: 384) notes that in antiquity, meter was "the primary marker of generic identity." For the *HH*s as belonging to the super-genre of ἔπος, see 6n27.
53   So Fowler 1987: 95: "'Hymn' as a general term for poetry that is sung is not itself the name of a genre, but it is reasonable to suppose that the praises of gods were recognized as a genre by archaic poets. At least these compositions had elaborate characteristics to which the poets adhered."
54   See the discussion of the term ὕμνος in 2.3.2.

Like Greek hymns generally, the *HH*s can be divided into three major sections, each of which is characterized by its own typical conventions.[55] In this study I capitalize the names for the constituent parts of these hymns in order to mark them off from ordinary usage as technical terms relating to hymnody; moreover, all of these terms are defined in the Glossary. Following Miller, I will call the first section of *HH*s the Exordium,[56] which functions to identify by name the Hymnic Subject, that is, the god to be honored in the hymn. Whereas Cultic Hymns tend to invoke the god in the second person, Rhapsodic Hymns can be said to evoke the god in the third person.[57] If metrically feasible, the god's name will normally occur as the first word of the hymn, typically in the accusative case as the direct object of a first-person Evocatory Verb of singing, as in "Of Hermes I sing" (Ἑρμῆν ἀείδω, *HH* 18.1).[58] In ten of the *HH*s, however, the Evocation is rather achieved by means of an Appeal to the Muses, as in "Sing of Hermes, Muse" (Ἑρμῆν ὕμνει, Μοῦσα, 4.1).[59] In either case, the theonym is typically dignified by a number of Honorific epithets or appositive phrases, as in "With ivy-haired Dionysus the mighty roarer I begin my song, Zeus' and glorious Semele's splendid son" (κισσοκόμην Διόνυσον ἐρίβρομον ἄρχομ᾽ ἀείδειν, | Ζηνὸς καὶ Σεμέλης ἐρικυδέος ἀγλαὸν υἱόν, 26.1–2).[60] This third-person manner of singing of the god is called "Er-Stil," which is typical of the first two sections of Rhapsodic Hymns. Three *HH*s, however, are irregularly cast entirely in the second person, addressed to the god in "Du-Stil" (21, 24, 29), which is more typical of Cultic Hymns.[61] Accordingly, these hymns begin exceptionally with the Subject's name in the vocative, which is not supplemented by epithets or

---

55 The following analysis is based on Janko 1981, with some slight modifications and additions to his terminology. For more on the structure of the *HH*s, see, e.g.: Lenz 1975: 9–13; Miller 1986: 2–4; Pavese 1991, 1993; Clay 1997: 493–494; Nünlist 2004: 35–37; Vamvouri Ruffy 2004: 27–32. Important earlier studies include Friedländer 1914 and Meyer 1933: 6–7, 19–24.
56 Miller 1986: 3.
57 Calame (2005: 22–24; 2011: 334 n. 2) thus distinguishes *evocatio* from *invocatio*.
58 The Evocatory Verbs used include ἄρχομ᾽ ἀείδειν (2.1, 11.1, 13.1, 16.1, 22.1, 26.1, 28.1), ἀείσομαι (10.1, 15.1, 23.1, 30.1), ᾄσομαι (6.2), ἀείδω (12.1, 18.1, 27.1), and μνήσομαι (7.2). More irregular constructions appear in 3.1 (μνήσομαι οὐδὲ λάθωμαι + gen.) and 25.1 (ἄρχωμαι + gen.).
59 *HH* 4.1, 5.1, 9.1, 14.2, 17.1, 19.1, 20.1, 31.1–2 (singling out Calliope), 32.1–2, 33.1. I prefer Janko's term "Appeal to the Muses" to distinguish Invocations of the Hymnic Subject from invocations of the Muse(s).
60 Vamvouri Ruffy (2004: 30–32) observes that these Honorific epithets often possess "une fonction proleptique," in that they anticipate the aspects of the god that will be praised in the *Laudatio*.
61 For Du-Stil vs. Er-Stil, see Norden 1956: 149–160, 163–166, and for its application to the *HH*s, see Miller 1986: 2–3. This narratological distinction appears already in ancient scholarship; see Nünlist 2009: 110–112.

other Honorifics. The transition out of the Exordium into the next section, the *Laudatio*, is accomplished by a "Hymnic Relative"—usually a relative pronoun, though the conjunctive adverb ὡς, "how," plays this role in *HH* 7.2.[62] Thus the Exordium of *HH* 10, for example, can be analyzed as follows:[63]

a. Evocation of Hymnic Subject with Honorific: "Of Cyprus-born Cytherea"[64]
b. Evocatory Verb: "I will sing"
c. Hymnic Relative: "**who** gives mortals kindly gifts ..."

I may pause at this point to note that the Exordial conventions surveyed so far should be familiar from the beginning of many epic poems, which, indeed, may have derived their introductory formulas precisely from the conventions of Rhapsodic Hymns.[65] For instance, both the *Iliad* (1.1–2) and the *Odyssey* (1.1) begin by naming their subject, or "theme,"[66] in the accusative (μῆνιν; ἄνδρα), with one epithet modifying it (οὐλομένην; πολύτροπον); this first word is the direct object of a verb of singing or telling (ἄειδε; ἔννεπε), in these instances combined with an Appeal to the Muses (θεά; Μοῦσα); and it is the antecedent of a relative pronoun that accomplishes the transition to a summary of the main narrative (ἥ; ὅς). Because the Iliadic "theme-word" is, unusually, an abstract concept ("wrath") rather than a concrete entity, it is further modified by Achilles' name (itself given a patronymic epithet) in the genitive case (Πηληϊάδεω Ἀχιλῆος); we find the same construction in the Exordium to the major *Homeric Hymn to Aphrodite* (ἔργα πολυχρύσου Ἀφροδίτης, 5.1), as well as the *Arg.* itself (παλαιγενέων κλέα φωτῶν, 1.1).[67] The fragmentary *Little Iliad* showcases an alternate epic introduction type, which dispenses with the Appeal to the Muses in favor of a first-person verb of singing:

---

62 On the Hymnic Relative, see Norden 1956: 168–176. The irregular *HH* 25 transitions into the *Laudatio* with γάρ; the second-person *Hymn* 21, with the pronoun σε; and the minor *Hymn* 13 lacks a midsection altogether.

63 Κυπρογενῆ Κυθέρειαν ἀείσομαι, ἥ τε βροτοῖσιν | μείλιχα δῶρα δίδωσιν ..., *HH* 10.1–2.

64 Note that Aphrodite's name cannot fit at the beginning of a hexameter, hence the use of the periphrasis "Cytherea" and the placement of the Honorific first in the line *metri causa*.

65 On the resemblances, see, e.g.: Meyer 1933: 19–20; Richardson 1974 ad *HH* 2.1–3; L. Lenz 1975: 9–10; A. Lenz 1980: 21–26; Evans 2001: 147–148. For the view that the epic convention is derived from hymnody, see, e.g.: Janko 1981: 23; Clay 2006: 5 (with earlier bibliography).

66 For the continuity in epic and hymnic use of such "theme-words," see, e.g., Kahane 1994b: 49–50.

67 The beginning of the *Odyssey* is also unusual because it does not reveal its subject immediately, but denotes him only mysteriously as "the man," who is slowly described in greater and greater detail over the course of the succeeding lines. Apollonius can be seen to imitate this device in designating his subject generically as "the people of old," whose identity then becomes clear in the appended relative clause (Händel 1954: 9).

"Ἴλιον ἀείδω καὶ Δαρδανίην εὔπωλον,
ἧς πέρι πόλλα πάθον Δαναοὶ θεράποντες Ἄρηος.

Of Ilios I sing, and Dardania land of fine colts, over which the Danaans, servants of Ares, suffered much.

The *Little Iliad*'s use of two theme-words in the accusative, only the latter of which serves as the antecedent for the relative pronoun, is paralleled by the *Homeric Hymn to Demeter* (2.1–3):

Δήμητρ' ἠΰκομον σεμνὴν θεὸν ἄρχομ' ἀείδειν,
αὐτὴν ἠδὲ θύγατρα τανίσφυρον, ἣν Ἀϊδωνεὺς
ἥρπαξεν ...

With **Demeter** the lovely-haired, the august goddess I begin my song, with her and her slender-ankled **daughter, whom** Aïdoneus seized ...

Within a small compass of divergences, this opening formula is remarkably stable across the Greek tradition, and it is consciously replicated by Vergil in *Aeneid* 1.1 (*arma virumque cano, Troiae qui* ...). As we will see in chapter 1, Apollonius exploits the identity of the Rhapsodic Hymnic and epic introductory formulas to fashion an introduction to the *Arg.* that could be appropriate to commence either an epic or a Homeric-style hymn.

But to return to the structure of the *HH*s: the second section, the *Laudatio*, is designed to praise the god so that she or he will be well-disposed toward granting the hymnist's ultimate request at the end of the hymn. In the *HH*s, the *Laudatio* takes one of two major forms, which are sometimes juxtaposed within one hymn: an Attributive Section, describing the god's "appearance, possessions, haunts and spheres of activity"[68] in the omnitemporal present tense,[69] or a Myth, recounting the deity's birth or deeds in the past tense.[70] In several cases, Myths end in a "Prolongation," which brings the mythic narrative into the omnitemporal present (e.g., at *HH* 4.576–578, we transition from the past

---

68   Janko 1981: 11.
69   This use of the present tense denotes activities that are "time-bound, but temporally unrestricted," for propositions to the effect that "something has been, is and always will be so" (Lyons 1977: 2.680), such as the habitual activities of the immortal gods. In narratological terms, this tense is characteristic of "simultaneous iterative narration," which is commonly employed in hymns (Nünlist 2007: 53–55).
70   For an analysis of each of the *HH*s in these terms, see Janko 1981: 16–20, 23–24.

narrative of the acquisition of Hermes' τιμαί to a description of his recurrent activities in the present).[71] Myths in particular are responsible for the variable length of the *HH*s. As Janko notes, Attributive Sections are never developed beyond about twenty-five lines, whereas Myths vary in length from 5 to 580 lines.[72]

I refer to the final section of an *HH* as the Envoi. In the *HH*s, it contains up to three elements, which almost always occur in a set sequence.[73] The first is the Salutation, which is introduced by a Salutatory Verb—usually χαῖρε or χαίρετε, but ἴληθ[ι] is used in three cases (1D.8, 20.8, 23.4)—followed by a vocative address to the god, often using a periphrasis instead of the theonym proper.[74] In most of the *HH*s, then, the Envoi is marked by a notable transition from Er-Stil in the Myth or Attributive Section to Du-Stil in the Salutation. In just over half of the *HH*s, a Prayer is included next, which is usually expressed by a second-person imperative verb.[75] In three hymns, however, we rather find indicative declarations of the type, "I supplicate you with my song" (λίτομαι δέ σ' ἀοιδῇ, 16.5; see further 19.48, 21.5). The Prayers are as a rule brief and relatively loosely coordinated with the content of the foregoing *Laudatio*, in contrast to the more personalized Prayers of Cultic Hymns.[76]

Third and finally, seventeen of the *HH*s conclude with a promise to transition to another song, an element that Janko terms the "Poet's Task." In twelve cases, it takes the stereotyped form, "And I will remember both you and another song" (αὐτὰρ ἐγὼ καὶ σεῖο [or, αὐτὰρ ἐγὼν ὑμέων τε] καὶ ἄλλης μνήσομ' ἀοιδῆς);[77] in three cases, a different formula is used: "After beginning from you, I will pass over to another song" (σέο δ' ἐγὼ ἀρξάμενος μεταβήσομαι ἄλλον ἐς ὕμνον,

---

71   The term "Prolongation" belongs to Janko 1981: 14, though the technique is recognized already by Richardson 1974 ad *HH* 2.483–489.

72   Janko 1981: 12, 14.

73   Note however, that in the unusual *HH* 29, the Prayer actually precedes the Salutation. *Hymn* 12 is unique in lacking an Envoi entirely.

74   Only three *HH*s lack a Salutation (2, 12, 24), though in 2.493–494 and 24.1–3 prominent vocative addresses may compensate for this omission (Janko 1981: 15–16).

75   Fifteen *HH*s lack a Prayer (1, 3, 4, 5, 7, 9, 12, 14, 17, 18, 23, 27, 28, 32, 33), though I argue in 1.2.1 that a request is implicit in *Hymn* 1D.8–10, 7.58–59. There is also a hint of entreaty in the epithet πρόφρον at *HH* 32.18 (Bernabé 2017: 400) and perhaps in the epithets emphasizing Hermes' generosity at 18.12 (χαριδῶτα ... δῶτορ ἐάων). See further Vamvouri Ruffy 2004: 84–92.

76   See, e.g.: Meyer 1933: 5–6, 22; Miller 1986: 4; Hall 2012: 113. For an analysis of the various "arguments" that link the *Laudatio* to the Prayer in the *HH*s, see Vamvouri Ruffy 2004: ch. 4.

77   This formula occurs at 2.495, 3.546, 4.580, 6.21, 10.6, 19.49, 25.7, 27.22, 28.18, 29.14, 30.19, 33.19.

5.293, 9.9, 18.11). And in two more cases, this formula is developed, with different wording in each case, into a promise to transition from the current hymn to a song whose genre is specified as heroic epic. These are *HH* 31.18–19:

ἐκ σέο δ' ἀρξάμενος κλήσω μερόπων γένος ἀνδρῶν
ἡμιθέων, ὧν ἔργα θεοὶ θνητοῖσιν ἔδειξαν.

After beginning from you, I will celebrate **the race of mortal men half-divine**, whose deeds the gods have disclosed to mortals.

and *HH* 32.18–20:

σέο δ' ἀρχόμενος **κλέα φωτῶν**
ᾄσομαι ἡμιθέων, ὧν κλείουσ' ἔργματ' ἀοιδοί
20   Μουσάων θεράποντες ἀπὸ στομάτων ἐροέντων.

Beginning from you, I will sing the **famous deeds of mortals half-divine**, whose deeds are celebrated by singers, the Muses' servants, from their lovely mouths.

Just seven of the *HH*s include all three of these closural elements—Salutation, Prayer, and Poet's Task—in their Envois.[78] A full example is provided by *HH* 6.19–21:

χαῖρ' ἑλικοβλέφαρε, γλυκυμείλιχε, δὸς δ' ἐν ἀγῶνι
20   νίκην τῷδε φέρεσθαι, ἐμὴν δ' ἔντυνον ἀοιδήν.
αὐτὰρ ἐγὼ καὶ σεῖο καὶ ἄλλης μνήσομ' ἀοιδῆς.

This Envoi may be analyzed as follows:
a.   Salutation: "Hail, quick-glancing, sweetly gentle goddess!"
b.   Prayer (twofold): "Grant me victory in this competition, and order my singing."
c.   Poet's Task: "And I will remember both you and another song."

---

78   These are *HH* 6.19–21, 10.4–6, 19.48–49, 25.6–7, 29.10–14, 30.17–19, 31.17–19. We could include in this category *Hymn* 2, if we consider the elaborate vocative address at 493–494 equivalent in function to a Salutation (Janko 1981: 15–16), as well as *Hymn* 18 and 32, if we understand the epithets in the Salutations as hinting at Prayer; see 14*n*75. The Envois of *Hymn* 1, 7, and 13 are analyzed in 1.2.1.

Although such jargon can be cumbersome, it will prove useful in facilitating the precise analysis of Apollonius' adaptation of these structural features of the *HH*s, especially in the examination of the *Arg.*'s "hymnic frame."[79]

2.3 Performance Context

Mention of the Poet's Task allows for a smooth transition from considerations of the formal features of the *HH*s to their original performance contexts. Aside from a few scattered hints as to the performance venue or occasion, such as the reference to "this competition" (ἀγῶνι ... τῷδε) that we just encountered at *HH* 6.19–20,[80] the Poet's Task formula provides our only internal evidence for the original context of these hymns.[81] The formula αὐτὰρ ἐγὼ καὶ σεῖο καὶ ἄλλης μνήσομ' ἀοιδῆς has been variously interpreted—is the poet promising to remember the god with another hymn to be delivered on a future occasion,[82] or is the "other song" to follow presently upon the completion of the hymn they are now concluding? The latter interpretation corresponds with the less ambiguous rendering of the Poet's Task that is found already in the oldest hymn in the collection, the major *Hymn to Aphrodite* (5.293): σέο δ' ἐγὼ ἀρξάμενος μεταβήσομαι ἄλλον ἐς ὕμνον. And as noted above, in *Hymns* 31–32, the Poet's Task is explicit in envisioning a transition from the hymn to a specifically epic composition.

The Poet's Task formula is an important piece of evidence supporting what we might call the "Proem theory" of the *HH*s' original performance context. First presented by Wolf in his 1795 *Prolegomena to Homer*, this view holds that the *HH*s served as preludes to epic lays in rhapsodic performances.[83] The internal evidence provided by the Poet's Task formula in the hymns themselves

---

79   See chapter 1.
80   Note also the reference to an annual Dionysiac festival at *HH* 26.12–13. See Vamvouri Ruffy 2004: 133–140 and Hall 2012: 135–139 for overviews of the evidence for festivals with musical contests featuring professional bards as the settings for the performance of Rhapsodic Hymns.
81   On this formula, see, e.g.: Richardson 1974: 324–325; De Martino 1980: 232–240; Fröhder 1994: 58–59; Calame 2005: 28–30; Nagy 2008: 232–246, 312. Petrovic (2012: 158–161) observes an important distinction between remembering the god (σεῖο) and remembering the other/rest of the song (ἄλλης ... ἀοιδῆς): the latter usage corresponds to the function of μνήσομαι as a technical term for the introduction of an epic tale (Moran 1975; see further Bakker 2005: ch. 8), whereas the former has a dedicatory function because of the nature of its divine object.
82   Theoc. *Id.* 17.135–136 evidently understood the formula (or at least adapted it such as) to refer to celebrating the god in question again on another occasion, presumably with another hymn (Fantuzzi 2001: 233 n. 1). See further Petrovic 2012: 156.
83   Wolf 1985: 112–113. Rather more recently, this thesis has been elaborated by Koller (1956) and Aloni (1980); more briefly, see also: Richardson 1974: 3–4; Càssola 1975a: xii–xvi.

can be supplemented by a range of external testimonies; the most decisive are those of Pindar, who refers to the rhapsodic practice of beginning with a προοίμιον ("proem, prelude") to Zeus (*Nem.* 2.1–3), and of Thucydides, who expressly refers to the major *Homeric Hymn to Apollo* (3) as a προοίμιον (3.104.4, 5).[84] The convention of prefacing an epic with a Hymnic Proem is well-attested across the Greco-Roman epic tradition,[85] and it is particularly revealing that both Hesiod's *Theogony* (1–115) and *Works and Days* (1–10) are prefaced by Hymnic Proems that follow the same structural conventions as the *HH*s.[86] Much remains uncertain about the exact connection between the *HH*s qua hymnic προοίμια and the epic performances that followed them,[87] and it is unclear whether the *HH*s that lack a Poet's Task also served a Proemial function.[88] Nevertheless, in its broad outlines, Wolf's hypothesis has achieved near consensus in contemporary scholarship,[89] and in chapter 1 I argue that Apollonius' opening allusion to *HH* 32.18–19 in his own epic introit positively alludes to the Proemial function of the *HH*s.[90]

---

84 For hymns as προοίμια, see also, e.g., Pl. *Phd.* 60d. For this designation for a *HH*, see: Costantini and Lallot 1987; Faulkner 2011b: 17–19; Clay 2011: 237–240; Nagy 2011: 324–329; Maslov 2012.

85 E.g., Aratus *Phaen.* and Theoc. *Id.* 17 begin with Proems to Zeus; Lucr. 1, with a Proem to Venus; and [Oppian] *Cyn.* 1, with a Proem to the divine Caracalla. On this practice, see, e.g.: West 1966 ad Hes. *Th.* 1–115; 1978 ad Hes. *Op.* 1–10.

86 See Janko 1981: 20–22, with earlier bibliography.

87 See Hall 2012: 140–148 for a good overview of this debate.

88 A few scholars have raised the possibility that these hymns without the Poet's Task formula might have served instead as postludes, that is, as epilogues to another performance (Càssola 1975a: xxi–xxii; Haubold 2001: 26; Hall 2012: 134–135). It may be, however, that the hymnist and their audience could simply take for granted the convention that another performance would follow the προοίμιον without an explicit declaration to this effect.

89 There is one notable exception: some scholars have thought that the major *HH*s are too long to have been recited as preludes to yet further song (e.g.: Wünsch in *RE* 9.1 s.v. "Hymnos," coll. 149, 151; AHS 1936: xcv; Nagy 1982: 53–54). Clay (2006: 7; 2011: 252–253) has speculated that they might have been performed for their own sake at festivals or symposia, along the lines of Demodocus' second lay in the *Odyssey* (8.268–367). Richardson (1974: 4) questions whether such doubts might underestimate the "powers of endurance" of the audiences for early epic; see further Lenz 1975: 278–286 and Hall 2012: 157.

90 In order to avoid confusion with hymns qua προοίμια, I use the term "introit" instead of the more usual "proem" to denote the opening section of an epic poem (cf., e.g., Gainsford 2003: 1; cf. also Wheeler 2002: 33, who uses "introit" for a similar purpose, but only of "the prayer for inspiration found at the beginning of Greek epic poems"). For instance, I consider *Arg.* 1.1–22 to be the "introit" of Book 1. For added clarity, I use the modifier "Hymnic" when referring to hymns that function as Proems, and I capitalize each word to indicate that I am using the term in a technical, hymnodic sense.

2.4 Attribution of Authorship

The true origins of each of the *HH*s is unknown, but I have already suggested that one of the most salient aspects of the *HH*s for Apollonius must have been their attribution to Homer, the very font of Greek ἔπος and the Alexandrian poet's chief literary model. Here, I would like to review some of the most important evidence for the belief in the hymns' Homeric authorship, which was not consistently credited in antiquity.[91] The earliest evidence for this claim appears in the *HH*s themselves. In a famous *sphragis* in the *Homeric Hymn to Apollo* (3.165–176), the narrator identifies himself as a blind man from Chios (τυφλὸς ἀνήρ, οἰκεῖ δὲ Χίῳ ἔνι παιπαλοέσσῃ, 172), in what is most likely a reference to the traditional image of Homer;[92] Thucydides (3.104.4–6), in any event, accepts Homeric authorship of this hymn in the course of a discussion that quotes these very lines, "in which [Homer] also mentions himself" (ἐν οἷς καὶ ἑαυτοῦ ἐπεμνήσθη, 3.104.5).[93] Less well known is the subtle claim to Homeric authorship made by the minor *Homeric Hymn to Artemis* (9), whose geography embraces the city of Smyrna and, significantly, its local river, the Meles (3–4). The banks of the Meles represent another of the traditional birthplaces of Homer (who is sometimes even made the son of the river god himself), but this stream is mentioned nowhere else in early Greek epic.[94]

In the introduction to their commentary on the hymns, Allen, Halliday, and Sikes (AHS) list some twenty-five testimonia affirming a belief in the *HH*s' Homeric authorship, ranging in time from Thucydides (loc. cit.) in the fifth century BCE to the twelfth-century Byzantine scholar Tzetzes (*praef.* ad Lycoph. *Alex.* p. 3.27–4.1 Scheer).[95] A few of these testimonia imply some measure of

---

91 For ancient testimonies regarding the authorship of the *HH*s, see AHS 1936: lxiv–lxxxii.
92 See Dyer 1975; Burkert 1987: 54–55; West 1999: 369–371. Even if the hymn did not originally mean to refer to Homer (cf. the cautious assessment of Graziosi 2002: 62–66), later Greeks like Apollonius would doubtless have taken it this way, as already Thucydides had done. The tradition of Homer's blindness, at any rate, is likely very old, because, as Beecroft 2011 shows, several later writers struggled with the idea that Homer could have both been blind and composed his poems, which, they assumed, would require literacy and hence sight. The tradition of blindness presupposes an oral poet.
93 For a possible Pindaric reference in *Paean* 7b to *HH* 3 as the work of Homer, see Bing 2008: 104–105.
94 Otherwise, a reference to the Meles may be intended in Asius' elegiac fragment (*ap.* Ath. 3.125b–e). For this interpretation of the hymn's reference to the Meles, see Graziosi 2002: 72–77.
95 AHS 1936: lxv–lxxviii. They comment on this testimony, "Compared to the vast mass of quotation from the *Iliad* and *Odyssey* it is slight" (lxxix), but as FVS (2016: 3) rejoin, "The attention ... paid to the *Iliad* and *Odyssey* is a disproportionate stick against which to measure the reception of any other ancient work." See further Faulkner 2011c: 176–178.

doubt about their Homeric authenticity by referring to "the hymns **ascribed to Homer**" (e.g., τοῖς εἰς "Ομηρον ἀναφερομένοις ὕμνοις, Σ ad Nic. *Alex.* 130).[96] A Pindaric scholiast (ad *Nem.* 2.1c Drachmann) actually asserts that one of the Homeridae, a Chian named Cynaethus, wrote the major *Homeric Hymn to Apollo* and passed it off as Homer's; Athenaeus 1.22b probably alludes to this same notion when he specifies the hymn's author as either "Homer or one of the Homeridae" ("Ομηρος ἢ τῶν Ὁμηριδῶν τις).[97] Most severely, one text expressly denies Homeric authorship of the *HH*s generally (*Vita Homeri* 9.3 West):

οὐδὲν δὲ αὐτοῦ θετέον ἔξω τῆς Ἰλιάδος καὶ τῆς Ὀδυσσείας, ἀλλὰ τοὺς Ὕμνους καὶ τὰ λοιπὰ τῶν εἰς αὐτὸν ἀναφερομένων ποιημάτων ἡγητέον ἀλλότρια καὶ τῆς φύσεως καὶ τῆς δυνάμεως ἕνεκα.

Nothing is to be acknowledged as his apart from the *Iliad* and *Odyssey*: the *Hymns* and the rest of the poems attributed to him are to be reckoned alien, in regard both to their nature and their effectiveness.

On the whole, many more sources credit the hymns to Homer than imply doubt, deny their authenticity, or attribute them to alternate authors.[98] Where the Alexandrians are concerned, however, AHS make an argument from silence that nevertheless carries real weight. No ancient commentary tradition survives for these works, and on multiple occasions when the Iliadic scholia might have elucidated Homeric usage by citing materials from the *HH*s, they fail to do so.[99] For instance, ΣA ad *Il.* 9.246 reports the opinion that Homer does not know the term "Peloponnesus," even though the word occurs at *HH* 3.250, 290. There is, in truth, but a single testimony implying the belief of an Alexandrian scholar in the hymns' Homeric authorship: Apollodorus, a pupil of the celebrated grammarian Aristarchus, is once cited in the scholia Genevese ad *Il.* 21.319 as making an argument from the appearance of the phrase γαῖα φερέσβιος "in Homer" (παρ' Ὁμήρῳ); the phrase does not occur in the HEs but only

---

96   See further Ar. fr. 590 fr. A col. 1.26–27 Henderson (= *POxy.* 2737), *Vita Homeri* 6.6 West, Suda s.v. Ὅμηρος.

97   For an overview of both the Homeridae and Cynaethus in particular, see Graziosi 2002: 208–217. For Cynaethus as the alleged author of the *Hymn to Apollo*, see, e.g.: Wade-Gery 1936; West 1975; Burkert 1979; Janko 1982: 112–115, 233–234; Aloni 1989; see further Bassino 2019: 188.

98   Cf. the situation of the epic cycle, whose claim to Homeric authorship was much weaker (see 2n5).

99   AHS 1936: lxxix–lxxii. They note similar tendencies in Strabo, Apollonius the Sophist, Lydus, Macrobius, and the Etymologica.

at *HH* 3.341.[100] For AHS, the Alexandrians did not take the usage of the *HH*s into account because they rejected their authenticity; Faulkner, Vergados, and Schwab (FVS) more generously use the term "deuterocanonical" to describe the view that Hellenistic scholars might have held regarding the *HH*s.[101] Regrettably, Apollonius' own judgment on the authorship of the *HH*s is unknown, if indeed he ever did pronounce upon the subject. From what little we know of Apollonius' scholarship, he does not seem either exceedingly skeptical or credulous: he defended the authenticity of the Hesiodic *Scutum* (fr. 21 Michaelis = arg. *Scuti* 1), but he athetized the work attached in antiquity to the end of the *Works and Days*, the Ὀρνιθομαντεία (fr. 20 Michaelis = Σ ad Hes. *Op.* 828a Pertusi).

But as FVS amply demonstrate, even if Homeric scholarship in the Hellenistic period left the *HH*s largely out of account, these poems were hardly neglected by Alexandrian poets—many of whom, like Apollonius, were themselves scholars of the highest caliber.[102] I would thus introduce an important distinction: his own professional opinion notwithstanding, Apollonius' sustained program of allusion to the *HH*s shows that, qua poet, he treats the *HH*s as on a par with the HEs and thus at least notionally ascribes them to Homer, his primary generic model.[103] Or to put the matter more precisely, regardless of the views of the historical Apollonius of Rhodes, the *Arg.*'s "implied author"— that is, "the author-image contained in a work and constituted by the stylistic, ideological, and aesthetic properties for which indexical signs can be found in the text"[104]—invests the *HH*s with the same authority as the HEs.

---

100 AHS 1936: lxxiii–lxxiv. See further Faulkner 2011c: 176 n. 7 on ΣT ad *Il.* 16.163 for evidence that this argument goes back to Aristarchus himself.
101 FVS 2016: 3.
102 Ibid.; see also Bernabé 2017: 10. For overviews of allusions to the *HH*s in Hellenistic poetry, see: Faulkner 2011c: 181–196; Petrovic 2012: 170–175; FVS 2016: 6–15.
103 Although Apollonius regularly alludes to many non-Homeric poets (e.g., Hesiod, as I discuss in the introduction, 4.1; 1.2.4; 2.2.3; and conclusion, 1), the natural inference from the prominence of allusions to the *HH*s in the *Arg.* is that Apollonius treats them alongside the *Iliad* and *Odyssey* as Homeric.
104 Schmid 2009: 161. Or as Chatman (1978: 148) puts it, perhaps more accessibly, the "implied author" is "'implied,' that is, reconstructed by the reader from the narrative. He is not the narrator, but rather the principle that invented the narrator, along with everything else in the narrative, that stacked the cards in this particular way, had these things happen to these characters, in these words or images." The term goes back to Booth (1983: 70–74). I assume in this study that the work of allusion to prior texts lies in the domain of the implied author (cf. Asper 2008: 181), though Morrison (2007: 279–280) raises the intriguing possibility that the scholarly narrator of the *Arg.* might be thought capable of making such allusions himself.

This contention gains support from the sheer volume of Apollonian allusion to the *HH*s, and particularly the prominence of such allusions in the poem's most programmatic passages. I discuss allusions to the *HH*s in the *Arg.*'s hymnic frame in chapter 1; here, I would like to point to one other programmatic passage in which Apollonius seems to set the *HH*s alongside the HEs among his most important poetic models. The passage in question is the Appeal to the Muse that opens Book 4 (1–5):

> Αὐτὴ νῦν κάματόν γε, θεά, καὶ δήνεα κούρης
> Κολχίδος ἔννεπε, Μοῦσα, Διὸς τέκος· ἦ γὰρ ἐμοί γε
> ἀμφασίη νόος ἔνδον ἑλίσσεται ὁρμαίνοντι,
> ἠέ μιν ἄτης πῆμα δυσίμερον ἢ τό γ' ἐνίσπω
> 5 φύζαν ἀεικελίην, ᾗ κάλλιπεν ἔθνεα Κόλχων.

Now, goddess, you yourself tell of the distress and thoughts of the Colchian girl, O Muse, daughter of Zeus, for truly the mind within me whirls in speechless stupor, as I ponder whether to call it the lovesick affliction of obsession or shameful panic, which made her leave the Colchian people.

Uniquely, in this Appeal, the Muse is dignified by three vocatives: "goddess," "Muse," and "daughter of Zeus." Since Rossi, these first two Honorifics have rightly been interpreted as allusions to the openings of the *Iliad* and the *Odyssey*: θεά recalls the Muse-invocation of *Il.* 1.1 (μῆνιν ἄειδε, θεά) while ἔννεπε, Μοῦσα recalls *Od.* 1.1 (where the phrase appears in the same *sedes*: ἄνδρα μοι ἔννεπε, Μοῦσα).[105] But as van den Eersten points out, while these allusions account for θεά and Μοῦσα, the third vocative, Διὸς τέκος, remains conspicuously unexplained.[106]

Muses are commonly called "daughters of Zeus" according to various formulas (e.g., Διὸς αἰγιόχοιο | θυγατέρες, *Il.* 2.491–492; θύγατερ Διός, *Od.* 1.10; τέκνα Διός, Hes. *Theog.* 104, *HH* 25.6),[107] and the phrase Διὸς τέκος is often applied in the HEs to gods such as Athena (e.g., *Il.* 1.202) or Apollo (e.g., *Il.* 21.229; like-

---

105 See, e.g.: Rossi 1968: 159–160; Livrea 1973 ad loc.; Feeney 1991: 91; Green 2007 ad loc.; Morrison 2007: 300; Hulse 2015 ad loc. Campbell's (1983b: 155) objection that this diction is not especially distinctive overlooks the fact that "the *Iliad* and the *Odyssey* have privileged status for later poets" (Hunter 1987: 134 n. 32).

106 Van den Eersten 2013: 53.

107 *Od.* 1.10 also addresses the Muse as θεά, and thus *Argon* 4.1–2 has also been viewed as a conflation of *Od.* 1.1, 10, in recognition of the Odyssean character of Book 4 (Livrea 1973 ad loc.; Albis 1996: 93; Acosta-Hughes 2010a: 43–44).

wise Thgn. 1). But before Apollonius, the only passage in which a Muse is so addressed is the Exordium of the *Homeric Hymn to Helius*: "And now, O Muse Calliope, **daughter of Zeus**, begin to sing of glowing Helius, whom ..." (ἥλιον ὑμνεῖν αὖτε Διὸς τέκος ἄρχεο Μοῦσα, | Καλλιόπη, φαέθοντα, τὸν ..., 31.1–2).[108] As with the phrase ἔννεπε, Μοῦσα, both passages set Διὸς τέκος in the same *sedes*, before the bucolic diaeresis.

An allusion to this *HH* would be especially appropriate here for two reasons. First, together with the *Homeric Hymn to Selene* (32), the *Homeric Hymn to Helius* forms a celestial diptych with a uniquely epic texture.[109] I have already noted that these are the only *Hymns* in the Homeric collection whose Poet's Tasks explicitly present the performances to follow as epic (31.18–19, 32.18–20). *HH* 31 invokes by name Calliope, the traditional Muse of epic poetry,[110] while *HH* 32 begins with a play on the opening words of the *Iliad*: "Sing of the Moon" (Μήνην ἀείδειν, 32.1) ludically echoes "Sing of the wrath" (μῆνιν ἄειδε, *Il*. 1.1).[111] These hymns with epic features likely attracted Apollonius' attention as he was writing his own hybridized "epic hymn," as I argue in chapter 2.[112]

Second, and relatedly, I have already mentioned that Apollonius prominently alludes to the Envoi of the *Selene* hymn in the introit of *Arg*. 1; that allusion turns out to be balanced by an echo of its companion piece's Exordium in the introit of *Arg*. 4.[113] I would thus propose that with the three vocatives in

---

108 Livrea 1973 ad loc.; Hunter 2015 ad loc. See further Hardie 2009: 19–20 for the ingenious suggestion that κάλλιπεν near the end of Apollonius' introit (4.5) points to Calliope (Καλλιόπη) as the Muse being invoked here. As Hardie notes, *HH* 31.1–2 provides the only Homeric instance of an invocation of a Muse by name (Καλλιόπη, 2) as well for the Muse-epithet Διὸς τέκος.

109 For these hymns as a diptych and for their date, see section 4.6.1 below.

110 So Walde in *DNP* s.v. "Kalliope [1]." The association of Calliope with epic poetry may not yet have been fully developed when *HH* 31 was written, though we can see its rudiments already in Hesiod, for whom she is the foremost of the Muses and patron of kings (*Th*. 79–80); see further Hardie 2009: 14–17. In any case, for Apollonius reading the hymn in the Hellenistic period, the connection likely would have been obvious (see Koster 1970: 156–157); cf. his similar association of Erato with love poetry in the introit of *Arg*. 3.

111 Editors who would emend away ἀείδειν at *HH* 32.1 and thus destroy this allusion fail to appreciate the affiliations with epic that this pair of hymns is at pains to cultivate. Moreover, ἀείδειν is defended by the longstanding hymnic affectation of employing the Evocatory Verb ἀείδω with a long alpha (Katz 2013: 93–96).

112 Cf. Hunter 1993: 129 n. 110: "The transmitted opening of the Hymn to Selene ... transfers an epic opening to a hymnic situation; the opening of *Arg*. reverses the process."

113 Apollonius is evidently playing with beginnings and endings: he alludes to the end of the diptych's second hymn in the introit of his first book and the beginning of its first hymn in the introit of his last book. For similar literary games in Apollonius and Callimachus,

Arg. 4.1–2, Apollonius programmatically alludes, perhaps in the conventional order,[114] to Muse-invocations from all three of his major Homeric models: the *Iliad* (θεά), the *Odyssey* (Μοῦσα), and the *HH*s (Διὸς τέκος)—this last as represented by a hymn with epic affiliations eminently suitable for the *Arg.*'s own experiments with genre.[115]

A final word on the purported Homeric authorship of the *HH*s. One reason for the scholarly neglect of ancient receptions of the *HH*s until quite recently has to do, I suspect, with our superior knowledge vis-à-vis antiquity with regard to certain aspects of Homeric poetry. We know today that "Homer" was not a historical individual but a name assigned to many works with diverse origins, ranging from the crystallization of centuries of oral tradition to Hellenistic pseudepigraphy. Insofar as the terms "Homer" and "Homeric" are retained, they tend to be reserved only for the *Iliad* and the *Odyssey*.[116] Thus, for instance, in the excellent *Studies in Ancient Greek Narrative* series published by Brill, the first chapter is invariably titled "Homer," though really, it is a study of the HEs, as is clear even from the Table of Contents: "The Homeric Hymns" are sequestered

---

see 100n73. For internal evidence from *HH* 31–32 that they were intended to be arranged in this order, see 62–63 below.

114 For modern scholars, it is natural to think of these poems in the order *Iliad*—*Odyssey*—*HH*s, but the opinion of antiquity on this matter is not entirely clear. In the narrative of the *Certamen Homeri et Hesiodi*, Homer writes the *Iliad* and the *Odyssey* first (16 West) and later performs the major *Homeric Hymn to Apollo* on Delos (18); this sequence may imply a belief that Homer wrote the hymns later in life (Pl. *Phd.* 60d may furnish a comparandum for such a conceit). By contrast, the pseudo-Herodotean *Vita Homeri* has Homer write his hymns first in this sequence (2.9 West); notably, there may be an allusion to this very tradition in the inclusion of the "Strangers" epigram in some manuscripts of the *HH*s, if its presence in the collection is not accidental (see n. 44 above). For the tradition that Homer wrote the *Iliad* before the *Odyssey*, see further [Longinus] *Subl.* 9.11–15 with Russel 1964 ad loc.; cf. Sen. *Dial.* 10.13.2, who indicates that this question was a common matter of contention in antiquity, and Lucian *True Story* 2.20, who claims that most people (οἱ πολλοί) held that the *Odyssey* was written first.

115 Many other resonances have been found in these lines, which I survey here. Paduano and Fusillo (1986 ad loc.) and Vian (2002: 3.147 ad *Arg.* 4.2) see an allusion to the *Aetia* in the question posed to a Muse; and with Vian, Valverde Sánchez (1996: 263 n. 570) also compares Callim. *Hymn* 1.4–5. Hunter (1987: 134) compares Pind. *Nem.* 11.22–25, in which the speaker poses another disjunctive question concerning a woman's motivation for a shameful action. Acosta-Hughes (2010a: 43) points to epic and lyric passages featuring hesitation between two options, particularly *Il.* 16.435–438. Uncertainty over a character's motive also has historiographic precedent; see: Fränkel 1968 ad loc.; Priestley 2014: 175–176; Hunter 2015 ad loc.; Morrison 2020: 75–76, 118.

116 There are, to be sure, some exceptions; among Apollonian studies, see, e.g., Giangrande 1971: 356.

off to their own chapter (notably, after Hesiod's). I certainly do not object to the practice of treating the hymns separately from the epics, but I do worry that this labeling practice tends to make us forget that for many ancients, "Homer" was a heading under which all of these works could be filed. In the realm of Apollonian scholarship, I would posit that a bias against the hymns as "Homerica" rather than "Homer" has disinclined scholars from paying them the level of attention that their rich reception history should warrant.

2.5   The Appeal of the Homeric Hymns in Third-Century Alexandria

I would like to conclude this overview of the *HH*s with a few remarks about what might have made the hymns attractive to third-century Hellenistic poets for emulation and engagement. For evidently they were attractive, and to all three of the major Alexandrian poets, not just Apollonius.[117] Callimachus seems to have revived the Rhapsodic Hymn as a genre with a collection of one elegiac and five hexameter hymns, which are deeply engaged with the *HH*s.[118] Theocritus, too, has several hymnic idylls that imitate the rhapsodic form (esp. 17, 22, 24).[119] This observation raises an important methodological point: the relative chronology of these poets and of their several works (and multiple editions thereof) has been endlessly debated. In this study, for heuristic purposes and convenience's sake, I will follow Köhnken's chronology of Theocritus—Callimachus—Apollonius.[120] Thus whenever Apollonius appears to be in dialogue with one of these two, I will assume that he is the alluding poet. Köhnken's arguments will not have convinced everyone, but luckily, most of the interpretations offered here that take Theocritean or Callimachean priority for granted are easily reversible if so desired. If there is truth to this assumption, then these contemporary Rhapsodic Hymns, and perhaps particularly Callimachus',[121] will have greatly influenced Apollonius, both in their own right and for the interest that they took in the *HH*s. Indeed, it will often be necessary to consider whether Apollonius' engagement with

---

117   See further the bibliography in n. 102 above (on the Hellenistic reception of the *HH*s in general).

118   See, e.g.: Vamvouri Ruffy 2004; Bing 2009: chs. 2–3; Acosta-Hughes and Cusset 2012; Werner 2013.

119   See, e.g.: Hunter 1996: 12, 46–57; 2003: 8–9, 142–145; Sens 1997: 13, 75–79. *Idyll* 26 is also hymnic, but with fewer Homeric features.

120   See Köhnken 1965, updated and defended in Köhnken 2008.

121   So, e.g., Sistakou 2001: 259: "Η αναβίωση του υμνικού είδους με νεοτερικούς όρους από τον Καλλίμαχο επηρεάζει και το έπος του Απολλωνίου."

the *HH*s is mediated through the precedent set by his illustrious predecessors; we will see several examples of such "two-tier allusions" in the investigation of Apollonius' hymnic narratological strategies in part 2 of this study.

Scholars have proposed both political and aesthetic explanations for the popularity of hymns, and particularly the *HH*s, in our period. Hunter points to the utility of hymnic poetry at a time when ruler cult and other divine honors for human beings precipitated renegotiations of the limits separating mortals and gods: "The 'Homeric hymn', which identified the areas of a god's power and placed him or her within the overall scheme of the divine, seems in retrospect an obvious vehicle for describing these shifting boundaries of power."[122] This thesis accounts well for a poem like Theocritus' *Idyll* 17, an "Encomium for Ptolemy Philadelphus" cast in the form of a Homeric-style hymn and constantly flirting with the idea that its subject might indeed deserve a hymn proper to a god rather than the encomium due to a mortal man;[123] or for those Callimachean hymns that compare the Ptolemaic king with a god, both explicitly (2.26–27, 4.160–190) and allusively—for instance, the *Hymn to Zeus* (1.87–88) praises Ptolemy in lines directly modeled on *HH* 4.17–18.[124] I shall have something to say about the possible connections between ruler cult and Apollonius' interest in the *HH*s in the conclusion to this study.

The *HH*s must also have been appreciated as "Homeric" poems that appeared more in tune with the stylistic and thematic preferences of the Hellenistic age than did the *HE*s.[125] Here it may suffice to quote a few scholars who have put the matter well. Bing has observed what Callimachus—and, we may add, Apollonius—might have seen in the *HH*s:

> They were pleasing in their limited size and lack of epic bombast, yet they could be viewed as genuinely "Homeric." Their use as a model would permit Callimachus to turn the Homeric tradition to productive use without trying to rival it, for here he would find those aspects that were less known, atypical, unfaded.[126]

---

122   Hunter 1996: 47. See also FVS 2016: 7: "The popularity of the *Hymns* in this period may be due in part to their suitability as a medium for encomiastic praise of patrons who themselves claimed divinity."
123   See the conclusion, section 2.1.
124   See Clauss 1986 and Petrovic 2012: 169. In general, on the gods in Callimachus' hymns as models for the Ptolemies, see Brumbaugh 2019.
125   Bornmann 1968: xxiv–xxvi; Hunter 2006a: 25; FVS 2016: 7.
126   Bing 2009: 34.

Indeed, with their "small-scale epic" narratives, the major *HH*s may be justly viewed as forerunners to the Hellenistic epyllion,[127] to which Apollonius' episodic narratives have often been compared.[128] Newman emphasizes some of the motifs and narrative devices that anticipate certain recurrent Hellenistic fixations:

> The *Homeric Hymns* too look as though they supplied valuable hints to a poet eager for fresh approaches. The *Hymn to Demeter*, for example, contains far more that is redolent of 'Hellenistic' epic than one might expect from compartmentalized histories of literature. The whole poem is a kind of *aetion*, and in its richness again calls Ovid to mind. The flowers, the golden chariot, the feeling for the child, the riot of proper names, the use of repetition are not so much "Hellenistic" as Ionian devices destined to enjoy a long history.[129]

FVS have also pointed to the playful tone of several of the *HH*s, especially of the major *Hymns to Hermes* and *Aphrodite*.[130] Finally, I would add here that for Apollonius, the *HH*s were particularly attractive in comparison to other potential hymnic models because of their close affinities with epic poetry: the *HH*s represent, in a way, a happy medium between the generic features of the HEs and Cultic Hymns.[131] They were thus ideal for allusive engagement and adaptation in an epic poem while simultaneously permitting certain narrative techniques, such as conspicuous intrusions by an "overt narrator," that were relatively foreign to the HEs, as we will see in detail in chapter 3.

---

127   See, e.g., Baumbach 2012 and Petrovic 2012. As Nünlist (2004: 38) observes: "Even the longest among the Homeric hymns are short (max. 580 lines) compared to other narrative texts."

128   Crump (1931: 247) once remarked, "The *Argonautica*, in fact, is little more than a collection of epyllia." See further Júnior (2021: 110), who interprets the echoes of the *HH*s in Apollonius' introit as "em provável alusão a uma espécie de poesia hexamétrica marcada pela concisão em relação à *Ilíada* e à *Odisseia*."

129   Newman 1986: 95. For the childhood motif, see esp. Pace 2004: 96–97, who points out that, with its depiction of the infant god, the major *Homeric Hymn to Hermes* provided Alexandrian poets with one of the only Archaic or Classical models of the child figure so beloved in the Hellenistic period; see further Ambühl 2005: 225–228.

130   FVS 2016: 7–8.

131   See on this score Hall 2012: ch. 3. For the *HH*s' self-reflection on their own status as a mixture of hymnody with epic, see: Haubold 2001: 24–25; Baumbach 2012: 136–144. See further Petrovic (2012: 167–168), who notes that some sections of the HEs have in fact been likened to extracts from Rhapsodic Hymns (most famously the second song of Demodocus: Wilamowitz 1895: 224–225; Evans 2001; Clay 2006: 4, 7; see further West 2011; Faraone 2016).

3 Method and Terminology

Intertextuality provides the major methodological framework for a study of this type, and here I would like to introduce some key theoretical issues and explain my use of certain terms that will recur throughout the book.[132] To begin with, I use the term "intertext" in this study to refer to any text that recollects, or "echoes," another;[133] the features of the text that facilitate this recollection shall be termed "parallels." I use the term "allusion" for instances of intertextuality that appear to be deliberate—that is, to me, the author seemingly **intends** to recollect an earlier text. With the idea of intention, I enter fraught theoretical territory, because for a variety of reasons, an author's intention is historically irrecoverable and thus unavailable to the literary critic.[134] But even if in theory, as Barthes declared, the author is dead,[135] nevertheless, in practice, its revenant survives, as readers deploy the Foucauldian "author function" to limit the proliferation of meaning in a given text.[136] In our discipline, Hinds has described this process well in his influential book on allusion and intertextuality:

> The axiom that meaning is constructed at the point of reception becomes a better tool for dealing with the kinds of case which interest students of philological allusion if it embraces the fact (i.e. rather than occluding it) that one of the most persistent ways in which both Roman and modern readers construct the meaning of a poetic text is by attempting to construct from (and for) it an intention-bearing authorial voice, a construction which they generally hope or believe (in a belief which must always be partly misguided) to be a reconstruction; and the author thus (re)constructed is one who writes towards an implied reader who will attempt such a (re)construction.[137]

---

132 For a good overview of our discipline's history in studying allusions, intertexts, etc., see van Tress 2004: 7–21. Some key works include: Thomas 1986; Conte 1986; Hinds 1998; Edmunds 2001. For contributions from the field of Hellenistic poetry, see below on Giangrande's articles.

133 Classical philology has departed considerably from the Kristevan use of the term, but for an attempt at recuperating some aspects of its original import, see Edmunds 2001: 8–16. For an overview of Kristeva's semiotics, see Eagleton 2008: 162–166.

134 With reference specifically to intertextuality in classical (Roman) poetry, Edmunds 2001: ch. 2 provides a good survey of the problems with divining an author's intention.

135 Barthes 1977: 142–148. In fact, the "intentional fallacy" goes back to New Criticism; see Wimsatt and Beardsley 1946.

136 Foucault 1984: 110, 118–119.

137 Hinds 1998: 49.

Yet as Hinds goes on to say, circumlocutions like "reader-constructed intention-bearing authorial voices" are both inefficient and unintuitive, epistemologically sound as they might be. Accordingly, in this study I use the language of "allusion" or "imitation" of "models," sometimes with cautious hedging ("Apollonius **appears** to allude to such-and-such text"), to mean that I am projecting my own construction of an intention-bearing Apollonius onto the text as a notional guarantor of the validity of my proposed reading, in hopes that my reading is indeed historically viable (i.e., Apollonius really could have intended it). When I do not (yet) feel comfortable doing so at a given stage of argument, I will speak in the intention-neutral language of "intertexts," "parallels," or "echoes" ("There is an intertextual relationship between these two passages"; "Such-and-such a parallel connects these passages"; etc.).

The limits on my readerly fantasy life—for I could in principle project onto the text any construction of Apollonius that I want[138]—are provided by the "interpretive community" in which I air my views: as a scholar, I aim to make my arguments as persuasive as possible to other scholars.[139] Fortunately, the rules of this game are fairly standardized. Thomas identifies two "absolute criteria" for recognizing allusions (or "references," in his terminology): "The model must be one with whom the poet is demonstrably familiar, and there must be a reason of some sort for the reference—that is, it must be susceptible of interpretation, or meaningful."[140] The first condition is easily met in the case of Apollonius, who must have had access to the *HH*s in the Library of Alexandria, though as I have already noted, it is unknown in what form he would have known the collection. The second criterion will be the real test: my intention is not to collect a list of parallels between the *Arg.* and the *HH*s, but to use these parallels to enrich our readings of Apollonius' poem by bringing to light features of the text that other analyses might miss.[141]

Beyond these two conditions, the strength of the argument is based on the strength of the parallels adduced to support it, and these gain in strength based on the correspondences in diction, theme, motif, and context that connect the two passages. The rarer and more detailed the correspondences, the

---

138   Cf. the pop culture concept of "headcanons"—idiosyncratic beliefs or interpretations held by fans that are not endorsed by the official "canon" of that fictional universe.
139   On interpretive communities, see Fish 1980, esp. 167–173. Consigny (2001: 17–21) provides a shrewd description of how scholarly discourses function as such interpretive communities.
140   Thomas 1986: 174.
141   So Knight 1995: 15: "Generally a reader can suggest there is an allusion if recollection of the Homeric context contributes (by similarity or difference) to a reading of the poem."

stronger the argument. For Hellenistic poetry, however, these criteria need to be adjusted somewhat to allow for *oppositio* or *variatio in imitando* (or *imitatio cum variatione*), that is, an allusion that involves a pointed departure from the source text. In a classic article on Apollonius' "arte allusiva," Giangrande catalogs many examples of such allusions to Homer in Alexandrian epic.[142] As he remarks in another article, "Plain echoing of the model was ... felt as far too rudimentary by the Alexandrian poet: therefore his reminiscence will, as a rule, imply a slight change in the wording of the model."[143] As Giangrande notes, Apollonius adopts this procedure when alluding to the *HH*s as well as the *HE*s. For instance, Matteo has shown that Apollonius follows Homer in using two synonymous nouns to denote "hunting," ἄγρη and θήρη, but that in his imitations of these usages he regularly reverses the Homeric choice in deploying one noun or the other. This policy applies equally to HE models (e.g., κύνε εἰδότε θήρης [*Il.* 10.360] ~ κύνες δεδαημένοι ἄγρης [*Arg.* 2.278], both line-final) and to one model from the *HH*s (ἄγρης ἐξανιών [*HH* 19.15] ~ θήρης ἐξανιών [*Arg.* 3.69; θήρη only here in the *Arg.*], both line-initial).[144] In addition to this lexical variety, Giangrande also recognizes a species of "conceptual *oppositio in imitando*,"[145] which involves pointed changes to a myth as given in a model text. We will encounter a good example of this in chapter 4 (4.2): in alluding to the Pythonomachy narrative of the major *Homeric Hymn to Apollo* (3.300–374), Apollonius also departs markedly from his model in a number of details (*Arg.* 2.705–714).

In addition to the terms surveyed so far, I make use of the whole panoply of analytical tools that have been formulated and developed in classical scholarship on intertextuality, such as multiple allusions,[146] "two-tier allusions,"[147]

---

142   Giangrande 1967; he traces this insight all the way back to Haacke 1842: 14–18, 29.
143   Giangrande 1970: 46.
144   Matteo 2002: 158–159; she shows that Apollonius makes the same sort of allusion to Callimachus as well (159–160).
145   Giangrande 1967: 90.
146   Thomas (1986: 193) defines "multiple reference" (or "conflation") as an allusion to "a number of antecedents" at once. This technique, once known under the older, pejorative-sounding name *contaminatio* (cf. Du Quesnay 1979: 44 with n. 86), is discussed already by Kroll 1924: 171–174.
147   The term "two-tier allusion" goes back to Hinds 1987: 151 n. 16, though the underlying concept of a poet alluding simultaneously to passages from predecessors that are themselves in dialogue is earlier (e.g., Du Quesnay 1977: 55 with n. 213 and addendum on p. 99; Cairns 1979: 121; see also the bibliography given in Nelis 2001: 5 n. 24). McKeown (1987: 37–45) uses the term "double allusion" for much the same thing, but I prefer the former to avoid confusion with "multiple allusion." The term "window reference," as originally defined by

"Alexandrian footnotes,"[148] "system references,"[149] and so forth. But in addition to these concepts that center around the perceived intention of an alluding author, in this study I also frequently invoke the construct of the "reader" or of "readers," as another way of thinking through the process by which I find meaning in Apollonius' text.[150] Sharrock has recently distilled well the practical function of "readers" in literary analysis: "'readers' in criticism are always heuristic tools, which we use to help us conceptualise the effects of a text, and in turn to help create larger interpretations, which in their own turn depend for their success on their acceptance, at least partial, by interpretative communities."[151]

Hypothetical readers are in many ways the mirror image of the modern critics' construction of an "intention-bearing authorial voice," but the category of "readers" is often particularly useful because of its essential plurality and mutability: we can imagine different sorts of readers who react to a given text in different ways, and in different circumstances. For instance, in chapter 1, I imagine several different interpretations that readers might apply to *Arg.* 1.1–2 on an initial encounter with the text; I then propose a new interpretation that those same readers could advance if they finish their first reading of the work and then *re*-read *Arg.* 1.1–2 in light of their memory of the poem's ending (*Arg.* 4.1773–1781).[152] We can also imagine readers with specific characteristics that might affect their response to a text, such as gender, ethnicity, or varying levels of access to the several contexts (cultural, historical, literary, etc.) in which Apollonius composed his work. In this study, I tend to use "readers" in a fairly broad, generic sense, but I would add two stipulations. First, there are

---

Thomas 1986: 188, has a more specific definition and is thus of more limited utility for my purposes: "It consists of the very close adaptation of a model, noticeably interrupted in order to allow reference back to the source of that model .... In the process the immediate, or chief, model is in some fashion 'corrected.'" For allusions as "corrections," see Thomas 1982: 146–154; cf. the concept of *aemulatio* (Conte 1986: 26, 36).

148 That is, expressions such as λέγεται, ὥς φασί, ὡς ἀκούομεν, and the like that serve to distance the narrator from a particular claim by appealing to some unspecified authority (such as earlier literary traditions). A classic article that broaches this subject is Stinton 1976, though the term was coined by Ross 1975: 77–78, building on the extensive notes in Norden 1956: 123–124. For the earlier history of the concept, see the bibliography in Horsfall 1988: 32 n. 13; 1990: 60–61 n. 3.

149 See 10n50.

150 I lay out my reasons for using the term "readers" rather than (listening) "audiences" in chapter 1 (94), though this distinction is not crucial to the arguments mounted in this book.

151 Sharrock 2018: 20–21.

152 I outline this "diachronic" method in the introductory section of chapter 1.

huge differences between the reading practices of antiquity and modern philological scholarship,[153] but as with my reconstruction of Apollonius' authorial intention, I would hope that the interpretations that I attribute to my readers are plausible reconstructions of readings that might actually have been made in antiquity by flesh-and-blood individuals with high degrees of access to Apollonius' context—for example, a contemporary Alexandrian reading public, Romans well-acquainted with the Greek literary tradition, etc.[154] Second, and relatedly, because of the intertextual nature of this study, I typically take the "learned reader" as my primary model—not because I subscribe to the dated view that most Alexandrian poetry was intended only for a select audience of *literati*, but because I am interested here in readers at least "learned" enough to catch Apollonius' allusions to the *HH*s or to other texts.

4 A Survey of Exemplary Intertexts from the *Homeric Hymns*

The foregoing discussion has established in abstract terms my approach to studying Apollonius' engagement with the *HH*s. Other methodological considerations and *termini technici* will be discussed elsewhere as they become relevant, especially as regards narratology in chapters 3 and 4. In this section, however, I would like to survey a limited number of intertexts from the *HH*s scattered throughout the *Arg.*, for two reasons. First, this survey shows in practice some of the criteria that allow us to recognize an intertext as the result of a more or less probable purposeful allusion by Apollonius, as in fact most of the examples considered below are. Second, this survey is organized around a series of concrete functions that intertexts from the *HH*s can serve in Apollonius' poem. In most of this study, I focus on allusions that speak to the generic affiliations of the *Arg.* as a whole, and this macroscopic orientation does not permit much consideration of the smaller-scale allusions to the *HH*s that are ubiquitous in the poem. This survey hardly compensates for that gap, but it should demonstrate that intertextuality with the hymns serves the same broad range of functions in the *Arg.* as that with the HEs.

---

153 See, e.g., Sharrock 2018: 21–22, 26–29.
154 In some cases, we have the testimony of actual ancient readers as to how they understood a text—for instance, some of the interpretations of *Arg.* 1.1 that I canvass in chapter 1 are recorded by the ancient scholiast ad loc. or seem to be presupposed by later poets' imitations of Apollonius' opening. Such testimony helps to confirm the plausibility of readings advanced in modern scholarship, but it is a luxury unavailable in most interpretative situations.

The six (often overlapping) types of *HH* intertext and allusion that I identify below include citations of the hymns as sources for mythology; borrowings from the *HH*s that contribute to Apollonius' construction of the "epic world" in which his heroic narrative unfolds; receptions of the Homeric gods filtered through the prism of the *HH*s; evocations of characters from the *HH*s as models against which to evaluate his own heroes; and recollections of *loci* from the *HH*s in order to offer diverse kinds of commentary upon the alluding passage in the *Arg*. Finally, I finish the survey with a more extended discussion of allusions with wider thematic purchase, focusing on the example of the programmatic allusion to the *Homeric Hymn to Selene* (32.18–19) with which the *Arg*. commences (1.1–2).

4.1 *The* Homeric Hymns *as Sources for Myth*

When Apollonius mentions a myth extraneous to his primary Argonautic narrative, he often cites one or more of his sources through a carefully crafted lexical allusion.[155] Partly it seems that he chooses to cite particular sources because he considers their treatments of the myth more or less "canonical," early versions thereof, but he does not simply reproduce the particulars of these sources robotically. Quite the opposite: he typically "updates" the source that he cites with mythological details that appear later in the tradition. For instance, when the Argonauts pass by the enchained Prometheus as they approach Colchis, Apollonius designates his "galling bonds" with the word ἀλυκτοπέδῃσι (*Arg*. 2.1249). As the commentators routinely note, before the time of Oppian (*Hal*. 2.385) and the lexicographers, this word occurs only here and in Hesiod—precisely in his account of the Titan's imprisonment at the hands of Zeus (*Th*. 521).[156] Apollonius is evidently citing Hesiod's account as a model for his own depiction of Prometheus, but rather than signaling a straightforward reliance on the *Theogony*, Apollonius' allusion actually underscores his divergences from the Boeotian poet in certain details.[157] In particular, Apollonius enhances Hesiod's rather hazy picture of the Titan's punishment with some borrowings from the Aeschylean *Prometheus* trilogy, such as his setting of the imprison-

---

155   For a Pindaric example of this practice (vis-à-vis Cronus' siring of Chiron), see n. 17 in the Appendix.

156   West (2001: 5, 6) conjectures that the word also occurred in the now-fragmentary major *Homeric Hymn to Dionysus* (1C.5) to refer to the bonds that Hephaestus crafted for Hera's throne. In our context, however, the allusion must be to Hesiod.

157   Notably, his Prometheus is not chained to a pillar, as in Hesiod (*Th*. 522), but to the Caucasian cliffs themselves (*Arg*. 2.1248–1249).

ment in the Caucasus.¹⁵⁸ The Archaic source is duly cited, but fleshed out with variants from another authority on the myth.

We find that Apollonius' procedure is much the same when he touches upon certain myths featured in the *HH*s, such as the story of Athena's prodigious birth in full armor from the head of Zeus. For instance, Apollonius describes the Libyan Herossae, "who once upon a time met Athena, after she leapt **gleaming from** her father's **head**, by lake Triton's waters and bathed her" (αἵ ποτ' Ἀθήνην, | ἦμος ὅτ' ἐκ πατρὸς **κεφαλῆς** θόρε **παμφαίνουσα**, | ἀντόμεναι Τρίτωνος ἐφ' ὕδασι χυτλώσαντο, 1309–1311). If we compare the longer *Homeric Hymn to Athena*'s description of the goddess's birth, "**out of** [Zeus'] august **head**, wearing battle armor of **shining** gold" (σεμνῆς **ἐκ κεφαλῆς**, πολεμήια τεύχε' ἔχουσαν, | χρύσεα, **παμφανόωντα**, 28.5–6), it emerges that Apollonius has condensed its description of the same event, with the single participle παμφαίνουσα (cognate to παμφανόωντα) serving by itself to conjure up Athena's flashing martial arms.¹⁵⁹

A few more parallels strengthen the link between these passages. Apollonius' brief reference is designed to explain the epithet Tritogenia by the name of the Libyan lake where Athena was bathed after being born; this very epithet appears at the end of the hymn's Exordium, immediately before the Myth of Athena's birth begins (Τριτογενή, τὴν αὐτὸς ἐγείνατο μητίετα Ζεύς | σεμνῆς ἐκ κεφαλῆς, 4–5).¹⁶⁰ Apollonius applies another of Athena's Honorifics from the hymn, the relatively rare epithet κυδρός, "glorious," paired with the substantive "goddess" (κυδρὴν θεόν, 1),¹⁶¹ to the Herossae themselves a few lines later

---

158 See, e.g.: Páskiewicz 1981: 266; Cusset 2001: 66–67; Vian 2002: 1.236 n. 1; Matteo 2007 ad *Arg.* 2.1246–1259, 1248–1249. This blending heightens the uncertainty that Byre (1996: 278) detects in the Titan's characterization: "We are not told enough to know whether the Apollonian Prometheus is the Hesiodic or the Aeschylean figure, whether he is the cunning trickster and hapless source of mankind's woes punished by Zeus, the supreme master of the universe, or the proud defier of a harsh and insecure tyrant and the benefactor, and indeed the savior and civilizer, of mankind." See also Williams 1991: 103.

159 Livrea 1973 ad *Arg.* 4.1310. Note that Apollonius uses παμφαίνω only once elsewhere, of Zeus' thunderbolt (1.732).

160 For Apollonius' play with the identity of the Tritonian body of water associated with Athena, see n. 10 in the Appendix. For Athena's connections to Libya, see Manakidou 2017: 194–196. The hymn's juxtaposition of Τριτογενή with the story of Athena's birth from Zeus' head may allude to a different etymology for the epithet that interpreted the τριτο- element as a dialect word for "head," thus yielding the meaning "head-born"; see Borthwick 1970: 21 n. 3.

161 The adjective is a *hapax* in the *Arg.* It is common in the HEs in its superlative form as a vocative (κύδιστε), but in its positive degree it occurs only at *Il.* 18.184 and *Od.* 11.580, 15.26; see also Hes. *Th.* 328, 442; *Op.* 257; *Cat.* 1.16. It is relatively commoner in the *HH*s (2.66, 179, 292; 4.461; 12.4; 28.1; forms of κυδίστη occur at 3.62, 5.42). Stürner (2022 ad loc.) adduces

(κυδραὶ θεαί, *Arg.* 4.1333), in the same *sedes* before the bucolic diaeresis. The allusion may suggest that the Herossae have derived a part of their own "glory" from the service they once rendered to the glorious Athena.[162] Notably, the motif of a goddess's attendance by three (4.1347) minor divinities at her birth is reminiscent of a scene from another *HH*, namely, the Horae's reception of the newborn Aphrodite on her arrival at Cyprus in *HH* 6.5–15.[163] As with Hesiod's Prometheus, Apollonius has departed from his hymnic model by incorporating variants from other traditions—notably, he alters the myth's localization to Libya, perhaps with a nod toward Callimachus,[164] and introduces the Herossae to the story.[165]

A further example of the citation of the *HH*s as sources for myth involves a simultaneous citation of one of the HEs, among other sources, and ably illustrates the sheer density of Apollonian "multiple allusion." When Aphrodite finds Ganymede playing knucklebones with her son Eros, Apollonius briefly narrates the boy's backstory in the space of a single relative clause (3.115–117):

115   ... μετὰ καὶ Γανυμήδεα, τόν ῥά ποτε Ζεὺς
      οὐρανῷ ἐγκατένασσεν ἐφέστιον ἀθανάτοισιν,
      κάλλεος ἱμερθείς.

... [Aphrodite found Eros not alone,] but with Ganymede, whom Zeus had once settled in heaven to live with the immortals, smitten with longing for his beauty.

The Homeric corpus relates the story of Ganymede's abduction twice. The first occurs in Aeneas' account of his own genealogy in the *Iliad* (20.232–235):

HH 28.1 as a model for the collocation κυδρός θεός, and suggests that it shows the influence of "hymnische Stilelemente" in Jason's address to the Herossae.

162   For this service to Athena as the source of the Herossae's fame, see Stürner 2022 ad 4.1305–1311.

163   Cf. Hes. *Th.* 201–202, where it is Eros and Pothus who attend to the newborn Aphrodite. Note a possible case of *oppositio in imitando*: in the hymn the Horae dress the goddess as she emerges from the sea; by contrast, the Herossae immediately bathe Athena, who is born in full armor. The Graces similarly bathe Aphrodite on Cyprus before her tryst with Anchises at *HH* 5.58–63.

164   The hymn seems to set the birth on Olympus (28.9–10); for the setting by Libyan Triton, Apollonius borrows from Callim. *Aet.* fr. 37 Pfeiffer, Harder (where n.b. Τρίτωνος ἐφ' ὕδασι in the same *sedes*) (Hunter 2015 ad *Arg.* 4.1309–1336).

165   These "heroines" appear also at Callim. fr. 602 Pfeiffer and Nicaenetus *AP* 6.225, though in neither instance are they associated with Athena.

... τε καὶ ἀντίθεος Γανυμήδης,
ὅς δὴ κάλλιστος γένετο θνητῶν ἀνθρώπων·
τὸν καὶ ἀνηρείψαντο θεοὶ Διὶ οἰνοχοεύειν
235 κάλλεος εἵνεκα οἷο, ἵν' ἀθανάτοισι μετείη.

> ... and godlike Ganymede, who was born the fairest of mortal men; and the gods caught him up on high to be cupbearer to Zeus because of his beauty, so that he might dwell with the immortals.

In the second instance, Ganymede occurs as an exemplum of the Trojans' godlike beauty in Aphrodite's long speech to Anchises (*HH* 5.202–206):

ἤτοι μὲν ξανθὸν Γανυμήδεα μητίετα Ζεύς
ἥρπασεν ὃν διὰ κάλλος, ἵν' ἀθανάτοισι μετείη
καί τε Διὸς κατὰ δῶμα θεοῖς ἐπιοινοχοεύοι,
205 θαῦμα ἰδεῖν, πάντεσσι τετιμένος ἀθανάτοισιν,
χρυσέου ἐκ κρητῆρος ἀφύσσων νέκταρ ἐρυθρόν.

> Resourceful Zeus seized flaxen-haired Ganymede because of his beauty, so that he should be among the immortals and serve drink to the gods in Zeus' house, a wonder to see, esteemed by all the immortals as he draws the red nectar from the golden bowl.

If we compare these three accounts, it emerges that Apollonius has drawn distinctive elements from both of his Homeric models at a fairly granular level. He has derived the general syntax of his brief aside from the Iliadic passage: καί + Ganymede's name + a relative clause (*Il.* 20.232–233). To provide the motive for the abduction, Apollonius also enjambs κάλλεος in *Arg.* 3.117 (κάλλεος ἱμερθείς) in imitation of *Il.* 20.235 (κάλλεος εἵνεκα οἷο; cf. the unenjambed ὃν διὰ κάλλος at *HH* 5.203). Apollonius agrees with the hymn, however, in making Zeus alone abduct Ganymede, not "the gods" generally, as at *Il.* 20.234 (θεοί). Indeed, his placement of Ganymede's and Zeus' names at the end of line 115 (Γανυμήδεα, τόν ῥά ποτε Ζεύς) replicates precisely the meter of *HH* 5.202 (Γανυμήδεα μητίετα Ζεύς).[166] Apollonius may also clarify a point in the hymn's presentation of

---

166 The nice color contrast of *HH* 5.206 also recurs in the Argonautic scene; cf. line-initial χρυσέου (of a golden bowl) with line-initial χρυσείοις (*Arg.* 3.118, of golden knucklebones) as well as ἐρυθρόν (of nectar) with ἔρευθος (*Arg.* 3.122, of Eros' blush). Note also the line-final ἀθανάτοισιν in both *Arg.* 3.116 and *HH* 5.205.

the Ganymede story by emphasizing Zeus' erotic interest in the boy (κάλλεος ἱμερθείς, 117). As the scholiast ad *Arg.* 3.114–117a notes, Zeus' relationship with Ganymede is not clearly sexual in the *Iliad*.[167] In context, however, the hymn implies that the nature of Zeus' relationship with Ganymede is analogous to that of Aphrodite's with Anchises, that is, erotic, as later versions, including Apollonius', make completely clear.[168]

Arg. 3.116, however, varies the formulations of both Homeric passages with a likely allusion to the early Hellenistic poet Moero, who had used a similar phrase to describe Zeus' immortalization of the eagle that fed him nectar as a child on Crete (Ζεὺς | ἀθάνατον ποίησε καὶ οὐρανῷ ἐγκατένασσεν, fr. 1.7–8 Powell).[169] Not only will Ganymede function in a similar cup-bearing capacity for the adult Zeus (cf. ἀφύσσων νέκταρ, *HH* 5.206),[170] but in the conventional form of the myth—though not in either of the Homeric passages[171]—Ganymede is himself abducted by Zeus' very eagle (or by Zeus turned into an eagle).[172] Apollonius' procedure in these intensely allusive two-and-a-half lines is complex, but revealing of his attitude toward the *HH*s. He carefully alludes to and harmonizes both the Iliadic and hymnic versions of the Ganymede story, appar-

---

167   Dover 1989: 196–197.
168   E.g., Thgn. 1345–1348, a passage that Apollonius may also have had in mind (Campbell 1994: 104); Soph. *Colchian Women* fr. 345 Radt may also have been important for Apollonius' choice to include Ganymede in his Argonautic narrative at all (cf. Hunter 1989 ad *Arg.* 3.115–118). Σ ad *Arg.* 3.114–117b may indicate that Apollonius has derived this erotic emphasis from Ibycus (fr. 289 Campbell), who could himself have drawn on the *Homeric Hymn to Aphrodite* (see Barron 1984: 18). The issue is vexed, however, because in the manuscripts this scholium is attached to *Arg.* 3.158; Wilamowitz's transposition of the scholium to its current location is accepted by Wendel 1935 and Lachenaud 2010 but rejected by, e.g., Campbell 1994 ad *Arg.* 3.158 f.
169   Gillies 1928 ad loc. The other half of Apollonius' expression in line 116 represents an intratextual echo of his own earlier description of Heracles' destined apotheosis (ναίειν δ' ἀθανάτοισι συνέστιον, *Arg.* 1.1319), which is itself curiously close to the beginning of Aesop 111 Perry (Ἡρακλῆς ἰσοθεωθεὶς καὶ παρὰ Διὶ ἑστιώμενος …). Perhaps this "hearth" language was traditional for describing a god's integration into the Olympian community.
170   Apollonius may allude to Ganymede's role as Zeus' cupbearer by setting his game of dice with Eros "in Zeus' fertile ἀλωή" (Διὸς θαλερῇ ἐν ἀλωῇ, 3.114), using a word which can denote a vineyard (or a "nectar-yard," where the gods are concerned?). At the same time, a "garden" would be a suitably erotic setting in which to find both Ganymede and Eros himself (Hunter 1989 and Campbell 1994 ad loc.; Daniel-Müller 2012: 109). For different interpretations of ἀλωή here, see: Gillies 1928 ad *Arg.* 3.158; Ardizzoni 1970: 40–41; Campbell 1983: 100 n. 48.
171   *HH* 5.208 has Ganymede abducted by means of a "miraculous whirlwind" (θέσπις ἄελλα); for possible interpretations of this phrase, see Faulkner 2008 ad loc.
172   See Campbell 1994 ad loc.

ently because he considered both to be authoritative, Homeric accounts of the myth. He "corrects" each account, however, on a number of points (Zeus as sole abductor; his erotic motivation; Ganymede's abduction via eagle), and notably, the last of these corrections is made subtextually, via an allusion to the earlier Hellenistic poet Moero. Apollonius' brief treatment of the Ganymede story represents in microcosm his approach to the *HH*s, which, like the HEs, he dutifully cites where relevant but is not above subverting, updating, and fleshing out, in typical Alexandrian fashion.[173]

An even more complex example of Apollonius' use of the *HH*s as sources of myth is afforded by the *Argonautica*'s scattered references to the fabulous locale of Nysa (2.905, 1214; 4.1134). In these remarkable passages, we can see the poet wielding evidence from multiple *HH*s to engage in a dizzying program of learned allusion and scholarly intervention in a number of ancient mythologico-geographic debates, including the localization not just of Nysa itself, but also of Dionysus' birth, Typhoeus' imprisonment, and Persephone's abduction by Hades.[174] At both 2.905 and 4.1134, Apollonius appears to allude to the common mythological tradition that Dionysus was either born or raised at Nysa via etymological wordplay, glossing his theonym (Διόνυσος) via the periphrasis "Zeus' Nysean son" (Διὸς Νυσήιον υἷα).[175] The association between Nysa and Dionysus' upbringing is already presupposed at *Il.* 6.133, which references the story of Lycurgus' persecution of the god and his nurses at this very site.[176] But the location of Nysa was itself a matter of controversy. Because Lycurgus is standardly a Thracian king, the *Iliad* would seem to set Nysa in that country (so *Etym. Magn.* s.v. Νυκτέλιος, quoted below), but the fragmentary *Homeric Hymn to Dionysus* memorably endorses a different view, in a passage that was also imitated prominently by Callimachus (*Hymn* 1.4–10).[177] After ten-

---

173 For a more extended example of Apollonius' approach, see Vergados (forthcoming), on the poet's revision of the Pythonomachy narrative in the *Homeric Hymn to Apollo*.
174 For the multifarious traditions surrounding Nysa and the competing localizations thereof, see, e.g.: Roscher 3.567–569; Preller 1894: 663–664, 702–703; *RE* 5.1.1035–1036, 17.2.1627–1628; Dodds 1960 ad Eur. *Bacch*. 556–559; *LIMC* Suppl. s.v. "Nysa I, Nysai."
175 See, e.g.: Páskiewicz 1981 ad loc.; O'Hara 2017: 28–29, 178. Massari (2017: 16) identifies a subtler example of this pun at 2.1214 (πεδίον Νυσήιον). Dionysus is also evoked as "the Nysean king" (ἄναξ ... Νυσήιος) at 4.431, which might just possibly allude to an alternate etymology for "Dionysus" from "Nysa" and a supposed Indian word δεῦνος meaning "king" (Juba *FGrH* 275 F 97). Cf. also the rationalization of Dionysius Scytobrachion (ap. D.S. 3.71.3, 72.1–2), in which a euhemerized Dionysus appears to be the literal king of Nysa.
176 For a possible Apollonian allusion to this passage at 4.1131–1134, see Campbell 1971: 421.
177 See, e.g.: McLennan 1977: 30, Hunter and Fuhrer 2002: 172–173; Depew 2004: 119; Vamvouri Ruffy 2004: 50; Stephens 2003: 82–84, 90; Faulkner 2011c: 179–180.

dentiously rejecting a number of other traditions for Dionysus' birthplace, the hymnist asserts that the god was born at "a certain Nysa, a mountain most high, burgeoning with forest, in a distant part of Phoenicia, almost at the waters of the Nile" (τις Νύση ὕπατον ὄρος ἀνθέον ὕλῃ, | τηλοῦ Φοινίκης, σχεδὸν Αἰγύπτοιο ῥοάων, *HH* 1A.9–10).[178]

Apollonius' references at 2.905 and 4.1134 do not make clear where he imagined Nysa, but another passage in Book 2 reveals that from the array of available options, the poet embraces the same setting near Egypt preferred in *HH* 1.[179] The Phrixid Argus, himself of Egyptian extraction and well-acquainted with that country's lore (cf. AR 4.259–281),[180] describes the flight of Typhaon following his fateful battle with Zeus: gravely wounded, the would-be usurper fled from Caucasus "to the mountains and plain of **Nysa**, where to this day he lies submerged beneath the waters of lake Serbonis" (οὔρεα καὶ πεδίον **Νυσήιον**, ἔνθ' ἔτι νῦν περ | κεῖται ὑποβρύχιος Σερβωνίδος ὕδασι λίμνης, 2.1214–1215).[181] In placing Typhoeus beneath Lake Serbonis, Apollonius follows Herodotus (3.5),[182] who describes the lake's situation on the northern coast of the Sinai Peninsula in similar terms to *HH* 1A.10, that is, as at the boundary between "Phoenicia" and Egypt proper.[183] Apollonius seems to have noticed the proximity of Herodotus' localization of the imprisoned Typhoeus and the placement of Nysa as described in *HH* 1, and thus he identifies and juxtaposes these originally

---

178 For rival claimants to Dionysus' birthplace, see *RE* 5.1.1034–1036.
179 Páskiewicz 1981 ad AR 2.1213–1214; cf. Delage 1930: 36. Both the scholia ad AR 2.1211c and Diodorus Siculus (1.15.7, 3.66.3, 4.2.4) actually cite *HH* 1 to support this localization of Nysa near Egyt. Cf. Antimachus fr. 162 Matthews with Matthews 1996 ad loc.; and on the Arabian Nysa, see further Chuvin 1991: 258–264.
180 Notably, Apollonius imitates *HH* 1A.9 (ἔστι δέ τις Νύση ὕπατον ὄρος [κέρας, v.l. Σ ad AR 2.1211], ἀνθέον ὕλῃ,) at AR 4.282* in Argus' Egyptian speech in Book 4 (ἔστι δέ τις ποταμός, ὕπατον κέρας Ὠκεανοῖο); the parallel is noted by Campbell 1981 ad loc. There may also be *oppositio in imitando* in Apollonius' next line (cf. νηὶ περῆσαι with West's reconstruction of *HH* 1A.11).
181 Apollonius' narrative hints at an etymology from καίω ("burn") for Caucasus (in this respect following Pherec. *FGrH* 3 F 54) and perhaps also for Casius, the mountain near Lake Serbonis that is here implicitly identified with the Mt. Nysa of legend. See further Massari 2017 on another implicit etymology in this narrative, viz. for the Ceraunian Mountains.
182 Other sources that place Typhoeus beneath Lake Serbonis include Herodorus (*FGrH* 31 F 61)—if this is not a mistake for "Herodotus" (Vian 2002: 1.284 ad AR 2.1215, Lachenaud 2010: 332 n. 315)—as well as Plut. *Vit. Ant.* 3.3, Eust. ad Dion. Per. 248.28–30, *Etym. Magn.* s.v. Τυφώς.
183 Cf. further the description of the lake in D.S. 1.30.4 with the account of Nysa in *HH* 1A.11–14.

unrelated mythological settings at the border of the Nile Delta.[184] Incidentally, it is striking that Apollonius, as an Alexandrian himself, prefers an Egyptian localization for both Nysa and Typhoeus' imprisonment,[185] much as he prefers a Libyan setting for Athena's birth. Indeed, by associating Typhoeus with Egypt, he is no doubt alluding to the *interpretatio graeca* by which this monster was identified with Set, the enemy of Horus.[186]

But returning to Nysa: we should take note of Apollonius' hybrid phrase, οὔρεα καὶ πεδίον Νυσήιον (2.1214), which reveals a conception of this locale that goes beyond what we find in *HH* 1. As we have seen, that hymn envisions Dionysus' birthplace as a forested mountain (ὕπατον ὄρος ἀνθέον ὕλῃ, A.9); in fact, the whole site is ringed by cliffs (13–14)—hence Apollonius' οὔρεα. This characterization is traditional,[187] but in fact, the *Homeric Hymn to Demeter* offers a strikingly different—and virtually unique—vision of Nysa's terrain. In that poem, the "soft meadow" (λειμῶν' ... μαλακόν, *HH* 2.7) where Persephone picks flowers prior to her abduction is revealed to be none other than "the **plain** of Nysa" (Νύσιον ... πεδίον, 17)—a phrase that finds a close echo in Apollonius' πεδίον Νυσήιον.[188] Now, Nysa is elsewhere almost always pictured as a mountain rather than a plain. In fact, beside *HH* 2 and Apollonius, only one other ancient

---

184   For this identification, see further Vian 2002: 1.284 ad AR 2.1215. The myths of Dionysus' birth and of Typhoeus' imprisonment are further connected by the shared motif of "hiding" (κρύπτων, *HH* 1A.8; κεκρύφθαι, Hdt. 3.5.3; see further Lloyd in Asheri et al. 2007 ad loc.).

185   Note that in the matter of Typhaon's localization, Apollonius is pointedly departing from Homer, insofar as AR 2.1211 must evoke *Il.* 2.783 (a rare example of φασί in HE narrator-text: de Jong 2004a: 48, 237–238; see Casali 2021: 179–182).

186   Fontenrose 1959: 133; Lane Fox 2008: 268–270. This identification is apparent already in Herodotus, Apollonius' probable source for this localization (see Hdt. 2.144.2 [= Hecataeus *FGrH* 1 F 300], 156.4; see further, e.g., Plut. *De Is. et Os.* 367d, 371b, 376b). Apollonius' narrative, in which the wounded Typhoeus flees toward Egypt, seems like a pointed reversal of another Greek myth (rather more discreditable to the gods: Ov. *Met.* 5.319–331), which accounted for the *interpretatio graeca* of the Egyptian pantheon by having the Greek gods assume animal disguises when they themselves fled into Egypt to escape Typhoeus; see [Apollod.] *Bib.* 1.6.3 with Frazer 1921: 1.49 n. 2. For Egyptian myth in Apollonius, see, e.g.: Stephens 2003: ch. 4 (who briefly touches upon Apollonius' Typhoeus on p. 216); Noegel 2004.

187   E.g., *HH* 26 similarly sets Dionysus' upbringing on a mountainous (Νύσης ἐν γυάλοις, 5) and forested (8–10) Nysa.

188   AHS 1936 ad loc.; Matteo 2007 ad loc. As Wilamowitz (1931: 2.50–51) notes, the presence of the Oceanids among Persephone's companions implies that *HH* 2 pictures Nysa by Ocean. If so, Apollonius has dispensed with this notion in favor of the localization proffered by *HH* 1.

source countenances this notion[189]—though notably, it suggests that the precise nature of Nysa's landscape could have become a mythological ζήτημα for ancient scholars and poets to puzzle over. *Etym. Magn.* s.v. Νυκτέλιος records the following opinions on Nysa (my trans.):

> Καλεῖται καὶ νυσήϊος, ἀπὸ Νύσης ὄρους Θράκης· οἷον,
>   "Ἤλυθον ἔνθ' ἐνέπουσι Διὸς Νυσήϊον υἷα [*Arg.* 2.905]
> Ἔστι δὲ καὶ νυσήϊον ὄνομα πεδίου. Ἡ τὴν λεγομένην νύσαν ὄρος Θράκης, Ἰλιάδος ζ' [*Il.* 6.133].

> [Dionysus] is also called "Nysean," from a Mt. Nysa in Thrace, as in:
>   They went, where they say that Zeus' Nysean son ... [*Arg.* 2.905]
> But "Nysean" is also the name of a plain. For the so-called Mt. "Nysa" in Thrace, see *Iliad* 6 [133].[190]

The etymologist shows that in addition to Nysa's geographic location, its topography (mountain or plain?) and its very identity (one site or two?) were up for debate.[191] But whereas the etymologist disaggregates the mountain and plain into two homonymous sites, Apollonius takes the opposite tack, harmonizing the competing traditions into a composite Nysa featuring both types of landscape (οὔρεα καὶ πεδίον Νυσήιον).[192]

On one level, then, Apollonius can be seen to harmonize the discordant data from *HH* 1A.9–10 and 2.17: the former passage especially contributes a relatively rare localization of Nysa near Egypt—even against the authority of the *Iliad*, with its probable Thracian setting—while the latter must provide Apollonius with the exceedingly rare detail of the Nysean plain. We might be tempted to

---

189   Though the Carian Nysa was apparently situated near a place called Λειμών ("meadow"): Strab. 14.1.45; see further 41*n*193. Cf. also the description of the Indian Nysa in Dion. Per. 625–626, with Lightfoot 2014: 405.

190   The etymologist is relying on HE authority for a mountainous Nysa, but their interpretation is not airtight. The citation of *Il.* 6.133 appears to be premised on the assumption that when Lycurgus chases Dionysus' nurses κατ' ἠγάθεον Νυσήϊον, the preposition will naturally mean "down" a sacred Mt. Nysa. In principle, however, κατά could equally refer to movement "over" a Nysean meadow, so that the phrasing is really equivocal.

191   Cf. Eust. *Il.* 2.260.16–261.3 van der Valk, who distinguishes between five mountains and two islands all called Nysa; Steph. Byz. s.v. Νῦσαι, who identifies ten different πόλεις of this name; and Hesychius s.v. Νῦσα καὶ Νυσήϊον, who lists fifteen different Nysas—all of them mountains.

192   Matteo 2007 ad AR 2.1214. Incidentally, the *Orphic Argonautica* also combines the *HH*s' two references to Nysa by reworking the description thereof at *HH* 1.9–14 in its own account of Persephone's abduction (see *Orph. Arg.* 1186–1202 with West 2011: 42–43).

see here an instance in which the *HH*s are privileged over the HEs, but in fact, if we probe further, we discover that other passages of the *Arg.* actually depart from both of these *HH*s on some major details in the Nysean orbit. To begin with the simpler case: the *Homeric Hymn to Demeter* was almost unique in proposing Nysa as the setting for the abduction of Persephone, as against the numerous other candidates put forward in other ancient sources.[193] Although he does not narrate the rape of Persephone itself, Apollonius nevertheless does hint at his preferred localization when he sets the Sirens, whom he casts as Core's guardians before her rape,[194] on an island off the coast of Campania in Italy (4.891–899).[195] Apollonius thus draws on *HH* 2.17 for one distinctive detail about Nysa (its πεδίον) while silently disagreeing with the hymn's equally distinctive choice of setting for its Myth.

In a similar way, another passage in Argonautica 4 reveals that despite his reliance on the *Homeric Hymn to Dionysus* as an authoritative source on Nysa's location, Apollonius actually differs from the hymnist's central contention, viz. that Dionysus was born there. The second instance of Apollonius' etymologizing gloss, Διὸς Νυσήιον υἷα, occurs in a digression concerning Macris, the infant Dionysus' first nurse (4.1134–1138):[196]

> κείνη δὴ πάμπρωτα Διὸς Νυσήιον υἷα
> 1135 Εὐβοίης ἔντοσθεν Ἀβαντίδος ᾧ ἐνὶ κόλπῳ
> δέξατο, καὶ μέλιτι ξηρὸν περὶ χεῖλος ἔδευσεν,

---

193 For discussion of this variant and a list of alternatives, see Richardson 1974 ad *HH* 2.17. As he notes, the city of Nysa ad Maeandrum in Caria would embrace the Nysean setting of Persephone's abduction as a local tradition. Notably, the Severan-era podium friezes from the city's Roman theater, now housed on the upper floor of the Aydın Archaeological Museum, interweave scenes of Dionysus' nursing by the Nysean nymphs with the cycle of Persephone's marriage to Hades; see, e.g.: Lindner 1994: 109–110; Price 2005: 119.

194 The connection between Persephone and the Sirens is visible already at Eur. *Hel.* 164–178. In the fuller version of the myth to which Apollonius gestures, the Sirens are transformed into avian hybrids either as a punishment for failing to protect Persephone from her abductor (Hyg. *Fab.* 141) or in order to facilitate their search for the missing girl (Ov. *Met.* 5.552–555).

195 See Chuvin 1991: 68–69. Apollonius' setting of the Sirens on a "Flowery" island (Ἀνθεμόεσσαν, *Arg.* 4.892; cf. *Od.* 12.159, Hes. fr. 27 MW; n.b. also *Arg.* 4.903) implies that it was there that Persephone was picking flowers when she was abducted (cf. *HH* 2.6–8, 417, 425–429; McPhee 2021a: 252 n. 48); cf. Strabo 6.1.5, who mentions a tradition that Persephone would come from Sicily to Vibo Valentina (on the Tyrrhenian coast) to pick flowers. For Apollonius' mapping of the Sirens, see further Delage 1930: 240–241; see also McPhee, forthcoming d.

196 For parallels with Callimachus' presentation of the infancy of Zeus (*Hymn* 1.32–54), see Zumbo 1978.

εὖτέ μιν Ἑρμείης φέρεν ἐκ πυρός· ἔδρακε δ᾽ Ἥρη,
καί ἑ χολωσαμένη πάσης ἐξήλασε νήσου.

She was the very first to take Zeus' Nysean son to her bosom in Abantian Euboea, and moistened his parched lips with honey, when Hermes brought him out of the fire. But Hera saw it and angrily drove her from the entire island.

Although it seems to have escaped the notice of commentators,[197] this remarkable passage in fact declares Apollonius' preference for the tradition that Dionysus was born in Thebes[198]—the very site that concludes the list of rejected birthplaces that comprise the foil to Nysa in the *Dionysus* hymnist's priamel (*HH* 1A.6).[199] The reference in line 1137 to Hermes' bringing Dionysus "out of the fire" relates to the myth of the death of the Theban princess Semele, annihilated by Zeus' lightning bolt while pregnant with the wine god.[200] Hermes apparently rescues the divine fetus from this fiery nativity, much as he saves Asclepius from the flames of Coronis' funeral pyre (Paus. 2.26.6), and conveys the god thus born directly from Thebes to Macris on Euobea for nursing.[201]

Notably, Apollonius' narrative completely dispenses with Dionysus' second birth from Zeus' thigh.[202] Moreover, he elides the tradition not just of Diony-

---

197 The one exception I have been able to find is Ville de Mirmont 1894: 167–168, who notes that Apollonius may be following Homer in suppressing the myth of Dionysus' double birth. Cf. Massari 2017: 17–18, who proposes to find an allusion to Dionysus' birth from Zeus' thigh at AR 2.1210, in my view on rather tenuous grounds.

198 *Pace* Zumbo (1978: 1040). The other passage that paraphrases Dionysus' name with Διὸς Νυσήιον υἷα (2.905) also happens to mention Thebes, in particular as Dionysus' destination following his Indian campaign. Indeed, if with Fränkel we read κατενίσσετο in line 906 (see Páskiewicz 1981 ad loc.), Dionysus will actually be "returning" to Thebes (as the site of his birth, or at least as his familial homeland). Matteo (2007 ad AR 2.906) is certainly wrong that Apollonius means the Egyptian Thebes there; cf., e.g., Eur. *Bacch.* 1–23.

199 As the city of Dionysus' mother Semele, Thebes is naturally the other major contender besides Nysa for the honor of Dionysus' birthplace (*RE* 5.1.1014–1015).

200 E.g., Hunter 2015 ad loc.

201 Note that Dionysus' lips are parched (ξηρόν ... χεῖλος, 1136), evidently due to the flames that attended his birth (Hopkinson 1994: 218 ad Nonnus *Dion.* 21.193b); cf. Eur. *Bacch.* 519–525 with Faraone 1997: 42.

202 As Stephens (2003: 82) notes, reference to this myth can be discerned in *HH* 1 even in its fragmentary state (see further: Gantz 1993: 473; Vamvouri Ruffy 2004: 145–146). Possibly some rationalistic motive impelled Apollonius to eliminate the story of the god's second birth from his mythic story-world; cf., e.g., Eur. *Bacch.* 286–297 with Hawes 2014: 14–15; for other rationalizations of the myth, see 246.

sus' birth at Nysa, but also of his nursing by the Nysean nymphs:²⁰³ the narrator emphasizes that Macris was the very first (πάμπρωτα) to nurse the god, and that she did so on Euboea.²⁰⁴ We may contrast the version of the short *Homeric Hymn to Dionysus*, whose Myth begins with the nymphs of Nysa receiving the baby Dionysus to nurse directly from Zeus (26.3–5), apparently right after his birth (as, e.g., at D.S. 4.2.3, Luc. *Dial. d.* 12.2).²⁰⁵ Probably the poet intends us to understand that Dionysus was ultimately relocated to Nysa to be reared there following Hera's persecution of Macris,²⁰⁶ but at all events he has left the precise nature of Dionysus' connection to Nysa mysterious, even as he insists upon it via the epithet Νυσήιον (4.1134).

In sum, the complex web of allusions that inform Apollonius' engagement with the varied lore surrounding Nysa proves instructive for his use of the *HH*s as mythological sources. As in our previous examples, Apollonius is citing the *Hymns* as authoritative, early accounts of some of the myths that he references; but more than that, here we find Apollonius the *doctus poeta* actually mining the *HH*s for recherche data to fuel his scholarly interventions regarding a num-

---

203   The substitution of Macris for Dionysus' Nysean nurses is also pointed up at *Arg.* 4.540, where Apollonius' designation of the Euboean heroine as "the nurse of Dionysus" (Διωνύσοιο τιθήνην) closely replicates the *Iliad*'s sole reference to the god's Nysean nurses (Διωνύσοιο τιθήνας, 6.132; Campbell 1981 ad loc.). Both phrases occur at line-end with "nurse(s)" in the accusative case, but of course, Apollonius exchanges Homer's plural for the singular to reflect his substitution with Macris (Zumbo 1978: 1041).

204   For Dionysus' veritable legion of nurses, at Nysa and elsewhere, see, e.g.: Roscher 1.1048–1049, 3.567–569; Preller 1894: 662–664; *RE* 17.2.1628–1630. In preferring Macris as Dionysus' first nurse, Apollonius is following a much rarer variant (Preller 1894: 676; cf. D.S. 3.70.1, Opp. *Cyn.* 4.265–276, Nonnus *Dion.* 21.193–195). Incidentally, there was a Nysa on Euboea (Valverde Sánchez 1996: 189 n. 335; Vian 2002: 3.30 n. 2), but even if Apollonius is alluding to a tradition of Dionysus' rearing at this Nysa, his narrative is still at odds with that of *HH* 1.

205   In fact, Apollonius draws our attention to *HH* 26 through some verbal echoes in order to underline his departures therefrom. As Zumbo (1978) notes, line-initial δεξάμεναι κόλποισι (*HH* 26.4) ~ κόλπῳ | δέξατο (AR 4.1135–1136), and line-initial ἄντρῳ ἐν εὐώδει (*HH* 26.6) ~ ἄντρῳ ἐν ἠγαθέῳ (v.l. ζαθέῳ) (AR 4.1131).

206   This would give point to πάμπρωτα: Dionysus had other nurses after Macris. Such relocations to new nurseries are common in Dionysiac myth, which accommodates an impressive number of τιθῆναι for the young god (see n. 204 above); for examples, see Pherecydes *FGrH* 3 F 90 with Fowler 2013: 371–372; [Apollod.] *Bib.* 3.4.3 with Preller 1894: 602, Gantz 1993: 112. Nonnus develops a particularly convoluted schema, passing Dionysus from the daughters of Lamus to Ino and finally to Rhea (*Dion.* 9), but elsewhere making learned allusions to yet other of the god's traditional nurses, including Macris (21.193–195; see Hopkinson 1994: 218 and Tissoni in Del Corno 1999 ad loc.) and perhaps also the Nysiades (21.109; cf. 29.272, 35.362).

ber of mythological ζητήματα.²⁰⁷ Much as we saw in Apollonius' allusion to the rape of Ganymede, the poet harmonizes details from different texts, in this case drawing on both the *Homeric Hymns to Dionysus* and *Demeter* in order to sketch a topographically composite Nysa. And notably, in the matter of localizing this fabulous site, Apollonius actually follows *HH* 1 in preference to the *Iliad*. Even so, our poet hardly feels obliged to follow the *HH*s in every detail; in fact, he pointedly "corrects" these hymns (as well as *HH* 26) in the matters of localizing the sites both of Dionysus' birth and infancy and of Persephone's abduction. Ironically, the only mythological event that Apollonius does positively associate with the site is the imprisonment of Typhoeus, which is nowhere else set at Nysa per se.²⁰⁸ Ultimately, Apollonius approaches the *HH*s with the same close interest, critical acumen, and independent spirit that he brings to bear vis-à-vis the HEs.

Before moving on, I would like to speculate briefly about one other passage, in one of Apollonius' lost works, in which the poet may also have alluded to the *HH*s in the same complex fashion. According to the manchette to Antoninus Liberalis' *Metamorphoses* 23,²⁰⁹ Apollonius treated the story of Battus, the old man turned to stone by Hermes, in his epigrams (fr. 50 *SH*).²¹⁰ We know from Antoninus himself and from Ovid (*Met.* 2.687–707) that this story is set during the same sequence of events treated in the *Homeric Hymn to Hermes* (4.87–94, 187–212)—Battus is the name supplied by later tradition for the old man who sees the infant Hermes in the act of stealing Apollo's cattle and who later reports what he has seen to Apollo.²¹¹ It is not difficult to imagine how such a subject would lend itself to epigrammatic treatment—perhaps the petrified Battus tells the story of his fate as a speaking object—and Apollonius may have used the opportunity to update or perhaps even "correct" the story in the hymn, which does not mention any punishment for Battus' divulgence of Her-

---

207   The attitude that Apollonius evinces here stands in stark contrast to the apparent neglect of the *HH*s by Alexandrian philologists (see 19*n*99).

208   Though note that Typhoeus is linked to Nysa in a different connection at [Apollod.] *Bib.* 1.6.3.

209   For these manchettes (brief notes appended to the narratives in Antoninus Liberalis and Parthenius indicating other works in which their stories can be found), see Lightfoot 1999: 246–256.

210   On Apollonius' epigrams, see Bowie 2000: 4–5. For the improbable theory that Apollonius used this epigram to advance his polemic against Callimachus, the "son of Battus" (*ep.* 35.1 Pfeiffer = *AP* 7.415.1), see Papathomopoulos 1968: xii.

211   The old man is unnamed in the hymn, but his stated occupation in the text could allude to (or may have been the source for) the name "Battus": Apollo addresses him as a culler of brambles (βατοδρόπε, 190) (Celoria 1992: 168 n. 277; Clay 2006: 114).

mes' secret.²¹² Unfortunately, in the absence of a new papyrological discovery, the foregoing must remain speculation.

4.2 Epic World-Building

Another use that Apollonius made of the *HH*s is perhaps easy to overlook, but it represents a notable type of system reference that is related to what I call epic "world-building": Apollonius' consistent representation of the norms, practices, and other *Realien* associated with the mythical Age of Heroes.²¹³ World-building represents an important part of Apollonius' evocation of the "Homeric code,"²¹⁴ in Contean terms, but the mythical world in which the heroic sagas were set was in fact the common property of all ancient mythological poetry, including the *HH*s.²¹⁵ Thus Apollonius seems to draw on Homer's hymns as a supplement to the epics as sources of phraseology and "scene-setting" details that conjure a suitably "heroic" atmosphere in his poem.²¹⁶

A few examples will clarify what I have in mind. For one, Apollonius consistently depicts the Argo in the archaizing manner of a Homeric ship rather than a contemporary vessel.²¹⁷ For the most part, Apollonius' depiction of seafaring is indebted to the HEs, but the contribution made by the *HH*s is shown, for instance, by Apollonius' use (1.379, 389) of the nautical term σκαλμός (the

---

212 Apollonius may have combined the hymnic narrative with a version of the story in one or more of the other authors mentioned in the manchette to Ant. Lib. *Met.* 23, such as Hesiod or Antigonus (of Carystus?). Didymarchus' date is unknown, while Nicander and Pamphilus postdate Apollonius. For an attempt to explain the old man's lack of punishment in the hymn, see Tzifopoulos 2000: 153–158.

213 Distinctive elements of heroic society as projected by the HEs were already commented upon by Plato (*Resp.* 4.404b–c) and figured into a great deal of ancient scholarship; see, e.g., Schmidt 1976 for such discussions in the bT scholia to the *Iliad*, or Heath 2000 on ancient debates over the Homeric diet. For Apollonius' "ethnographic" approach to the Heroic Age, see Morrison 2020: 84–94.

214 Conte's idea of "Model as Code" bears certain resemblances to what Edmunds calls a "system reference" (see n. 48) vis-à-vis genre. As Segal summarizes it, a literary "code" consists of "the objective narrative structure, conventions, expectations defined by … a literary genre"; for instance, "heroic combat, divine interventions, [and] extended similes" all represent parts of the "epic code" (in Conte 1986: 13; see further 31, 142–143). This useful concept could be invoked often in this study; e.g., passages that scholars often label "(quasi-)hymnic" may be analyzed as invoking elements of the "(Homeric) hymnic code."

215 Cf. Johnston's (2015) concept of the "Greek mythic story world."

216 Cf. Agosti 2016 on the use of "tags," or distinctive phraseology, from the *HH*s as system references for HE and hymnody among Late Antique poets. For the term "tag," see Hunter 2014: 15–16.

217 As was demonstrated at length by Ville de Mirmont 1895; see also Naber 1906: 1–2; Peschties 1912: 34–44.

'*pin* or *thole* to which the Greek oar was fastened by the τροπωτήρ," per LSJ), which is unexampled in all of early Greek epic except for *HH* 7.42.[218] Or, for another quick example: it has been observed that the poet's description of the Argonauts' preparation of a fire at Mysia (1.1182–1184) draws on the description of Hermes' quasi-sacrificial feast in his major *HH* (4.111–113, 136),[219] but to what end? There is perhaps some purposeful connection between these passages,[220] but the primary effect of Apollonius' borrowing, in my view, is to imbue this section of his narrative with a properly archaizing character suggestive of the world of Homeric ἔπος. The *Iliad* and *Odyssey* both feature descriptions of kindling fires, but the fullest account in early hexameter poetry belongs to the *Hymn to Hermes*, and so Apollonius has chosen it as a source for this practice.[221]

Notably, Apollonius draws on another distinctive detail from this same scene elsewhere in the *Arg.*: when the Argonauts build an "altar to the twelve blessed gods" (μακάρεσσι δυώδεκα ... βωμόν, *Arg.* 2.531–532) at Thynia,[222] Apollonius avails himself of a cultic concept, the grouping of the "Twelve Olympians," whose earliest attestation may in fact occur in this very passage of the major *Homeric Hymn to Hermes* (4.128–129). The infant god's twelvefold division of the portions of meat he prepares by the banks of the Alpheus constitutes a transparent reference to, and perhaps implicit αἴτιον for, the famous cult of the Twelve Gods at Olympia.[223] The *HH*s were thus a source for details in matters of ritual praxis, too, that were otherwise absent from the Homeric corpus. Another example of this type occurs in the Libyan episode: Jason's unusual procedure of slaughtering a sheep over the *Argo*'s stern while the crew searches for

---

218 Peschties 1912: 41.
219 Vergados 2013: 115.
220 E.g., we could say that Apollonius is making a learned allusion to the πρῶτος εὑρετής of fire-sticks, as the *Hymn* presents Hermes (111). For another Apollonian intertext with the *Hermes* passage, see Clauss 1993: 69–74, 2016: 62–65 (cf. Vergados 2013: 113 with n. 75).
221 Notably, πυρεῖον and related forms do not occur in the HEs, but in the form πυρήια it does occur as a *hapax* in both the *HH*s (3.111) and the *Arg.* (1.1184). Theocritus' Argonauts also use fire-sticks once (*Id.* 22.33), in what is yet another piece of the chronological puzzle surrounding these two poets (e.g., Gow 1942: 11 n. 3).
222 The Argonauts' sacrifice to the Twelve Gods is traditional (e.g., Polyb. 4.39.6, relying on an independent tradition: Fränkel 1968: 195 n. 107; see further Vian 2002: 1.273 ad 2.532; Matteo 2007 ad 2.532), but note that some sources rather mention sacrifices to Poseidon at this juncture (Pind. *Pyth.* 204–206, Timosth. fr. 28 Wagner). Apollonius thus had some leeway in whether or not to incorporate this reference to the δωδεκάθεον, which was alien to the HEs.
223 For discussion of this challenging scene, see esp. Vergados 2013: 324–329; see further the comments ad loc. in Richardson 2010 and Schenck zu Schweinsberg 2017.

an outlet from Lake Triton (*Arg.* 4.1593–1602) replicates the procedure of the distraught sailors of *HH* 33.10–11, who make similar maritime sacrifices to the Dioscuri.[224]

A less straightforward example concerns nothing less than the *Arg.*'s representation of one of the mythological "races" that populate his story world, namely, the nymphs.[225] The internal narrative of Paraebius' father (2.468–489), probably invented by Apollonius in answer to Callimachus' Erysichthon Myth in his sixth hymn,[226] treats the tale of a Hamadryad nymph (ἀμαδρυάδος νύμφης, 477) who curses a mortal man for cutting down "an oak tree that was as old as she, in which she had continually lived her long life" (δρυὸς ἥλικος, ᾗ ἔπι πουλὺν | αἰῶνα τρίβεσκε διηνεκές, 479–480).[227] Nymphs receive frequent mention in the HEs, but their precise nature—especially their lifespans and connection with trees—is clarified in a digressive passage in the *Homeric Hymn to Aphrodite* (256–273):[228]

> τὸν μὲν ἐπὴν δὴ πρῶτον ἴδῃ φάος ἠελίοιο,
> νύμφαί μιν θρέψουσιν ὀρεσκῷοι βαθύκολποι,
> αἳ τόδε ναιετάουσιν ὄρος μέγα τε ζάθεόν τε·
> αἵ ῥ' οὔτε θνητοῖς οὔτ' ἀθανάτοισιν ἕπονται.
> 260 δηρὸν μὲν ζώουσι καὶ ἄμβροτον εἶδαρ ἔδουσιν,
> καί τε μετ' ἀθανάτοισι καλὸν χορὸν ἐρρώσαντο,
> τῇσι δὲ Σειληνοί τε καὶ εὔσκοπος Ἀργειφόντης
> μίσγοντ' ἐν φιλότητι μυχῷ σπείων ἐροέντων.
> τῇσι δ' ἅμ' ἠ' ἐλάται ἠὲ δρύες ὑψικάρηνοι
> 265 γεινομένῃσιν ἔφυσαν ἐπὶ χθονὶ βωτιανείρῃ·
> καλαὶ τηλεθάουσαι ἐν οὔρεσιν ὑψηλοῖσιν
> ἑστᾶσ' ἠλίβατοι, τεμένη δέ ἑ κικλήσκουσιν

---

224 See 175n152.
225 Larson (2001: 53) comments, "Apollonius' epic poem, the *Argonautica*, is a virtual encyclopedia of mythopoetic and genealogical themes pertaining to nymphs." For a study of nymphs in the poem, see Richey 2008.
226 See, e.g., Murray 2004.
227 With the phrase πουλὺν | αἰῶνα cf. *Arg.* 2.508–509, where Apollo makes his consort Cyrene a "long-lived nymph" (νύμφην | ... μακραίωνα).
228 Larson (2001: 20–34) collects the evidence for the conception of nymphs in the HEs, *HH*s, and Hesiod, noting that the *Hymn to Aphrodite* passage is "the most detailed and lengthy description of nymphs in all of early Greek literature" (31), though it is paralleled in some particulars in the Hesiodic corpus. This passage likely stands in the background of Callim. *Hymn* 4.79–85 as well (Mineur 1984 ad 81; Vamvouri Ruffy 2004: 239; Hunter 2006b: 162).

ἀθανάτων· τὰς δ' οὔ τι βροτοὶ κείρουσι σιδήρῳ.
ἀλλ' ὅτε κεν δὴ μοῖρα παρεστήκῃ θανάτοιο,
270 ἀζάνεται μὲν πρῶτον ἐπὶ χθονὶ δένδρεα καλά,
φλοιὸς δ' ἀμφιπεριφθινύθει, πίπτουσι δ' ἄπ' ὄζοι,
τῶν δέ θ' ὁμοῦ ψυχὴ λείπει φάος ἠελίοιο.
αἳ μὲν ἐμὸν θρέψουσι παρὰ σφίσιν υἱὸν ἔχουσαι.

As for the child [Aeneas], as soon as he sees the light of the sun, the deep-breasted mountain Nymphs who inhabit this great and holy mountain shall bring him up. They rank neither with mortals nor with immortals: long indeed do they live, eating heavenly food and treading the lovely dance among the immortals, and with them the Sileni and the sharp-eyed Slayer of Argus mate in the depths of pleasant caves; but at their birth pines or high-topped **oaks spring up with them** upon the fruitful earth, beautiful, flourishing trees, towering high upon the lofty mountains (and men call them holy places of the immortals, and **never mortal lops them with the axe**); but when the fate of death is near at hand, first those lovely trees wither where they stand, and the bark shrivels away about them, and the twigs fall down, and at last the life of the Nymph and of the tree leave the light of the sun together. These Nymphs shall keep my son with them and rear him.

This passage lays out the same information regarding nymphs that is presupposed by Apollonius' account. Moreover, certain details suggest that Apollonius had it particularly in mind when composing the Paraebius narrative. For one, line 264 suggests an etymology for "Hamadryrad" (τῇσι δ' ἄμ' ἠ' ἐλάται ἠὲ δρύες) that Apollonius' own diction points up (2.477, 479).[229] But most important is the hymn's interdiction against cutting down trees sacred to the nymphs (268)—the very crime committed by Paraebius' father. Lexical parallels are lacking, so that we cannot be sure that Apollonius has used this model directly. Nevertheless, the *Homeric Hymn to Aphrodite* fills out some important details of the epic world that Apollonius has inherited from early Greek ἔπος, and this passage may well have inspired Apollonius' substitution of Callimachus' Demeter with a Hamadryad nymph.

---

229 Murray 2004: 211 with n. 12; see also Michalopoulos 2003: 166–169; Vamvouri Ruffy 2004: 239. Note that Apollonius' δρυὸς ἥλικος (2.479) marks a likely allusion to Callim. *Hymn* 4.81 (ἥλικος ... δρυός; Hunter 2006b: 162), which has its own connections to the *Aphrodite* passage; see previous note.

4.3 The Reception of the Homeric Gods

Another key concept for this study is reception—a term that, in its disciplinary sense within Classics, was once largely limited to periods that postdate "Late Antiquity," but which can also embrace "receptions in antiquity."[230] In its Iserian sense, the word "reception" can be used broadly to refer to "how any reader reads any text."[231] Here, I would like to use the word in its narrower Jaussian sense as it has developed in the interdisciplinary field of "reception studies." In this context, the mantra that "meaning is always realized at the point of reception" takes on specifically historical dimensions, locating the "point of reception" in particular social and cultural contexts that determine the "horizon of expectations" with which readers come to the text—contexts that, importantly, include earlier receptions of that text.[232] For my study, the reader in question is Apollonius himself, insofar as allusions in the *Arg.* reveal him as a reader of the *HH*s; but what distinguishes the study of reception from that of intertextuality is that the former approach seeks to understand Apollonius' intertextual engagement with the hymns in the context of his position as part of a reading public in a particular milieu—namely, that of third-century Ptolemaic Alexandria.[233]

I examine some of the potential political dimensions of Apollonius' reception of the *HH*s in the Conclusion to this study. Here, I would like to highlight just one example from the domain of more purely "literary" history. Barchiesi, in a seminal article highlighting the need for further research into the hymns' literary influence, emphasizes that for later authors, the hymns offered attractive character sketches of several of the major gods in the Olympian pantheon, distilling and, in some measure, fixing their "orthodox" personalities and attributes. In this capacity, the hymns provided "a panorama of divine operations, an indispensable complement to Hesiod and to the epic Homer."[234] Barchiesi's points were made in reference to Ovid's *Metamorphoses*, but they

---

230 See, e.g., Hardwick 2003: ch. 2; Porter 2008: 471–473. In recent years, many companions on the reception of classical authors have begun to appear, and typically, these begin with chapters on receptions in antiquity.
231 Hardie 2013: 191, in a discussion of the two senses of the term.
232 The "mantra" (so Murnaghan 2007) quoted here is adapted from Martindale 1993: 3, a book that introduced "reception studies" as such to Classics and whose methodology I attempt to outline here. For the "horizon of expectations," see Holub 1995: 322–324. A good, succinct description of the methodology of reception studies can be found in Hardwick 2003: 5; see also her list of key terms (9–10).
233 Thus Hardie (2013: 193–194) responds to Goldhill's (2010) critique of reception studies that focus on individual authors' reception of earlier works.
234 Barchiesi 1999: 123–126 (quotation from 123).

apply just as well to the humanizing portrayals of the gods in the *Arg*. Especially in the finer details, Apollonius' characterization of the gods often derives from post-HE representations of the divine as found in the *HH*s.

For instance, when Hera proposes that Aphrodite be recruited to bewitch Medea with love for Jason, Athena responds diffidently (3.32–35):

> Ἥρη, νήιδα μέν με πατὴρ τέκε τοῖο βολάων,
> οὐδέ τινα χρειὼ θελκτήριον οἶδα πόθοιο·
> εἰ δέ σοι αὐτῇ μῦθος ἐφανδάνει, ἦ τ' ἂν ἐγώ γε
> 35 ἑσποίμην, σὺ δέ κεν φαίης ἔπος ἀντιόωσα.

> Hera, my father bore me without knowledge of [Eros'] arrows, nor do I know of any enchantment to induce desire. But if you yourself approve of the plan, truly I would follow along, but please do the speaking when making the request.

In this humorous passage, Apollonius innovatively connects Athena's quasi-parthenogenic birth narrative (Hes. *Th*. 924–929t; *HH* 3.308–325, 28) with her own status as a perpetual virgin.[235] Athena's virginity is not stressed in the HEs; rather, the *locus classicus* for this motif is *HH* 5.8–15,[236] a passage to which Callimachus and other poets expressly allude in reference to Athena's celibacy.[237] As lexical parallels between the passages are lacking, it is difficult to argue that this specific passage from *HH* 5 has informed Apollonius' characterization of Athena—although it is worth noting that such an allusion would continue a sequence of references to the *Homeric Hymn to Aphrodite* here[238] and thereby reintroduce the theme of love vs. war, so prominent in the third book of the

---

[235] The humor is enhanced by the fact that Athena's reference clumsily reminds Hera of a reality that, traditionally, inspires tremendous fury in her: Zeus had given birth to Athena without her help (Hes. *Th*. 928, 929a; *HH* 3.308–325).

[236] So Hunter 1989 ad loc. Campbell (1994: 43) notes that Aeschylus had connected Athena's birth narrative with a different character trait, namely, her pro-male bias (*Eum*. 736–738). Cf. AR fr. 11 Powell, probably from Apollonius' lost *Foundation of Rhodes*, in which the poet is supposed to have connected Athena's fireless sacrifices on Rhodes to her disdain for Hephaestus, the fire god, because of his attempted rape in the Erichthonius myth. This brand of divine characterization, assigning motives and (dis)inclinations to the gods in light of episodes from their mythological *vitae*, would become commonplace in later poets like Ovid and Nonnus.

[237] See, e.g., on Callim. *Hymn* 5: Hunter 1992: 12; Hadjittofi 2008: 26–27; Faulkner 2010a; and on Ovid *Met*. 5: Malten 1910: 520; cf. Hinds 1987: 154 n. 12.

[238] See, e.g., Campbell 1994: 43.

poem. Be that as it may, what we can say with certainty is that the portrait of the goddess in Apollonius' epic sits in a tradition that has been shaped by literary depictions stretching back to the *HH*s. Excepting Lucan, the gods were an indispensable part of the machinery of the epic plot from the *Iliad* on, and the literary portrayal of the gods of post-Homeric epic had to be filtered through the *HH*s, too. Or, put in terms of reception theory: the reception of the gods in the *HH*s had become a part of all subsequent receptions of the HEs.[239]

4.4 *Allusive Characterization*

Apollonius often uses allusion as a technique for characterization by evoking Homeric models against which his own characters can be measured; it is my contention that Apollonius deploys this same technique using models drawn from the *HH*s as well as the HEs. Apollonius' characterizing allusions can be comparative, but just as frequently contrastive: surface similarities with a Homeric predecessor often serve to emphasize the deeper differences that set Apollonius' characters apart.[240] For example, one of the most sustained and best-recognized character-analogies in the poem serves to liken Medea to Nausicaa, the Phaeacian princess of *Odyssey* 6–8, but as Campbell observes, "Medea is anything but a normal girl .... Indeed, the Nausicaa-Medea equation is not an equation at all. It is carefully set up only to be swept aside."[241] Clauss has even called Medea "the Mephistophelean Nausicaa," a young girl who turns out to be "the helper-maiden from Hell." To achieve success, Jason must make a deal, not quite with the devil, but at any rate with a "Hecatean power."[242] By invoking the standard of the Homeric Nausicaa, Apollonius sets Medea's otherness in relief.[243]

---

239 It is also the case that some gods who are absent from the HEs make their "Homeric" debuts in the *HH*s—most prominently, the Phrygian mother goddess Cybele (Subject of *HH* 14), who appears in the *Arg.* syncretized with Rhea. The episode of her propitiation on Mt. Dindymum, which is itself "structured as a hymn transposed to narrative" (Hunter 1993: 83), actually provides an Argonautic αἴτιον for the frenzied style of worship described in the Attributive Section of her *HH*; in this connection note that τύπανον (*HH* 14.3, *Arg.* 1.1139) is a *hapax* both in the *Arg.* and all of early Greek epic.
240 So Pavlock 1990: 67–68: "[Apollonius] revealed the potential for creative imitation by inverting the ethical implications of the Homeric originals and offered a model for creating a context in which characters could be fully played out against their originals." See further Newman 1986: 81 n. 23, 85; Klooster 2018: 82–83.
241 Campbell 1983: 60.
242 Clauss 1997; quotations are from the title of his chapter and 175, 176, respectively.
243 Clauss 1997: 177. For more on the Medea-Nausicaa analogy, see esp. Pavlock 1990: 51–63; Knight 1995: 224–244.

Here, I will briefly present a single parallel example from the *HH*s, staying with Medea but turning from Nausicaa to another maiden from the Homeric corpus, the Persephone of the major *Homeric Hymn to Demeter*.[244] The analogy between Medea and the goddess is most obviously intimated in the scenes that preface Medea's meeting with Jason at the temple of Hecate in Book 3. As she awaits his arrival, she proposes to pass the time first by playing (μολπῇ, 897) with her group of attendant handmaidens, like Nausicaa before meeting Odysseus (*Od.* 6.100–101);[245] but she also suggests gathering flowers (τὰ δὲ καλὰ τερείνης ἄνθεα ποίης | λεξάμεναι, *Arg.* 3.898–899)—a suggestion laden with allusive significance. In Greek literature, the motif of a girl's flower-gathering, especially with playmates of like age, serves as a common prelude to rape or abduction.[246]

The *locus classicus* for this motif is *HH* 2.5–6 (see also 425), where Persephone picks flowers with a group of Oceanids prior to her abduction by Hades. Substantial verbal parallels are lacking, but we can be confident that Apollonius wanted to evoke the *Homeric Hymn to Demeter* because of the "collective security" afforded by other marked allusions to the hymn in the lead-up to this scene.[247] For instance, Medea's riding out to the temple of Hecate for this meeting with Jason is likened to Artemis' driving her chariot to receive a sacrifice (*Arg.* 3.876–886). In this simile, Artemis' "golden chariot" (χρυσείοις ... ἅρμασιν, *Arg.* 3.878) finds direct Homeric precedent in the "golden chariot" (ἅρμασι χρυσείοισι, *HH* 2.431) in which Hades abducts Persephone.[248] Suffice it to say, Medea's meeting with Jason is anticipated by a series of allusions that have the effect of suggesting an analogy between the relationship of Medea and Jason and that of Persephone and Hades. The difference is that, while Persephone is abducted against her will but in accordance with her father's wishes, Medea's

---

244   For more on Apollonius' use of models from the *HH*s for the purpose of characterization, see McPhee 2021a, parts of which are summarized in this subsection. See further Pace 2004 and Clayton 2017.

245   Note that Apollonius also characterizes Persephone's activities before her abduction as play (or singing and dancing: see Rengakos 1994: 115–116) using the cognate word μελπόμεναι (4.898) in his own reference to this myth.

246   See, e.g.: Richardson 1974 ad *HH* 2.6 ff.; Campbell 1983: 61; Rosenmeyer 2004: 176 n. 29 (who notes the Apollonian passage).

247   "Collective security" refers to the idea that one clear allusion to a work increases the likelihood that another less clear allusion to the same work is also intentional (Hinds 1998: 28).

248   Note that ἅρμασι(ν) in the same *sedes* in each passage. The motif of the golden chariot also resonates with Callim. *Hymn* 3.111, though the wording there is different (χρύσεον ... δίφρον). Cf. Sappho fr. 1.8–9 LP, where χρύσιον may go with ἅρμ'.

flight aboard the Argo is the direct result of her own love for Jason and the aid that she surreptitiously lends him in opposition to her father.[249] As with Nausicaa, Apollonius does not set up a simple equivalence between Medea and Persephone; rather, the analogy that he draws between the two throws into relief the question of Medea's agency in departing from Colchis with Jason.

4.5   Allusions to the Hymns as Metacommentary

Frequently Apollonius deploys allusions to earlier models, including the *HH*s, in order to suggest various kinds of commentary upon his own text. This technique works by inviting the reader to relate the content of the target text to the immediate context within the *Arg*. Depending on the interrelation between these passages that are thus put into dialogue, the poet may generate any number of effects to condition our interpretation (e.g., by producing irony, offering an explanation, foreshadowing later events, etc.). In this subsection, I offer four examples in which intertexts from the *HH*s conjure authorial comments of this type. Each of the following "echoes and imitations" is noted by Campbell,[250] but to my knowledge none of them has been interpreted as a potentially meaningful allusion that enriches our understanding of the relevant *loci* in the *Arg*.

4.5.1

When Polyxo is introduced to the narrative of the Lemnian episode, she is immediately described as "tottering on **feet shriveled** with age" (γήραϊ δὴ ῥικνοῖσιν ἐπισκάζουσα πόδεσσιν, *Arg*. 1.669). The adjective ῥικνός, "wrinkled," is a Homeric *hapax* that occurs only at *HH* 3.317: Hera explains that she bore "Hephaestus, **with his withered feet**" (Ἥφαιστος ῥικνὸς πόδας), and consequently hurled him from Olympus into the sea.[251] Apollonius uses this same phrase once elsewhere to describe Phineus' **"withered feet"** (ῥικνοῖς ποσίν, *Arg*. 2.198). That parallel is formally stronger because the phrases occur in the same metrical *sedes*, but there are contextual parallels with the Polyxo passage that better satisfy Thomas' second criterion for the identification of an allusion, namely, that it "be susceptible of interpretation."[252] In the Iliadic version of the myth, it is the fall from heaven itself that seems to leave Hephaestus disabled, and

---

249 It is thus significant, for instance, that in the hymn, it is the rapist Hades who drives the chariot that bears off Persephone (2.431), whereas at *Arg*. 3.878, Apollonius likens Medea, who should be the maiden Persephone's counterpart, to a goddess driving her own chariot of her own volition.
250 See Campbell 1981 ad loc.
251 The adjective occurs once in Callim. *Hec*. fr. 74.10 Hollis, of the aged Hecale's skin.
252 See 28*n*140.

he lands not in the sea, but on the island of Lemnos, where "the Sintian men" nursed him back to health (Σίντιες ἄνδρες, *Il.* 1.594).²⁵³ Apollonius alludes to this myth at the very beginning of the Lemnian episode when he introduces the island as "Sintian Lemnos" (Σιντηίδα Λῆμνον, *Arg.* 1.608), and he recalls the smith god's connection with the island again when he records that Aphrodite inspires love between the Argonauts and the Lemnian women "as a favor to Hephaestus" (Ἡφαίστοιο χάριν, 851), that his island might be repopulated.²⁵⁴ In this context, Polyxo's resemblance to Hephaestus is striking, for it is she who plays the plot-critical role of advising the Lemnian women to welcome the heroes into the city and reminding them of their need to procreate (675–696). The allusion hints that, fittingly, Hephaestus' will is being accomplished through an agent who resembles him.²⁵⁵

4.5.2

At *Arg.* 3.535–536, Argus suggests that the heroes solicit Medea's aid in Aeetes' ordeal through the intermediary of his mother, and Medea's sister, Chalciope, in hopes that she "**might be able to persuade** her to help in the contest" (εἴ κε δύναιτο ... πεπιθεῖν ἐπαρῆξαι ἀέθλῳ). In the event, Chalciope plays an important role in the plot insofar as her sisterly appeal on behalf of her sons gives Medea "plausible deniability" for helping Jason,²⁵⁶ though her true motive lies more in her newfound love for the handsome stranger than in concern for her family's welfare. There is thus a good deal of dramatic irony in the fact that, unbeknownst to Argus or the Argonauts, the words he has chosen echo a phrase repeated twice in the major *Homeric Hymn to Aphrodite*, specifying of the goddess that there are only three persons "whose minds she **cannot persuade** or outwit" (οὐ δύναται πεπιθεῖν φρένας οὐδ' ἀπατῆσαι, 5.7, 33).²⁵⁷ Almost in the manner of cledonomancy, the allusion ominously corrects Argus—the real source of Medea's motivation will be Aphrodite, not Chalciope—and anticipates the bird-sign that follows immediately after his speech (*Arg.* 3.540–543), which, indeed, reminds the Argonauts of Phineus' oracle (2.423–424) that their "return

---

253   The term Σίντιες recurs, again in connection with Hephaestus, at *Od.* 8.293.
254   See, e.g., Cusset 2015: 138.
255   Further connections between Polyxo and Hephaestus will be explored by Alastair Daly in his forthcoming Trinity College Dublin dissertation, of which I heard a preview in his talk at the 2023 meeting of the Classical Association in Cambridge.
256   See, e.g., Byre 2002: 81–84.
257   The collocation of a form of δύναμαι with πείθω occurs also at *HH* 2.328, but Apollonius' use of the reduplicated aorist infinitive πεπιθεῖν in the same *sedes* makes the parallel to *HH* 5.7, 33 much stronger.

would lie with the goddess Cypris" (θεῇ ἐνὶ Κύπριδι νόστον ... ἔσσεσθαι, 549–550). This allusion is a good example of *oppositio in imitando*, for while Aphrodite may not be able to persuade the minds of Athena, Artemis, or Hestia, she can certainly persuade Medea's.

4.5.3

In her effort to convince Thetis to help the Argonauts through the Wandering Rocks, Hera claims, among her past services to the Nereid, to have arranged for her to marry Peleus, "the best of the mortals" (τὸν ἄριστον ἐπιχθονίων, *Arg.* 4.805)—a striking assertion, given the contestation of the status of "the best of the Argonauts" that is so prominent in the poem's first book.[258] But as with Argus in the previous example, Hera's words are ironically undermined by an echo of an earlier work: the only other place in all of Greek literature in which this phrase occurs is *HH* 15.1–2, where it is Heracles who is "**far** the finest of men on earth" (μέγ' ἄριστον ... ἐπιχθονίων).[259] It serves Hera's rhetorical interests to present Thetis' mortal husband in the best possible light (cf., e.g., *Il.* 18.429–441), but the allusion to the *Homeric Hymn to Heracles* exposes Hera's appraisal of Peleus as self-interested and biased: Heracles, whom she detests (*Arg.* 1.996–997), is inarguably the true best of mortals.[260]

4.5.4

When Aphrodite saves the Athenian Argonaut Butes from the Sirens and resettles him on Cape Lilybaeum in Sicily, she is identified by the periphrasis "**Cypris, the goddess who rules** over Eryx" (θεὰ Ἔρυκος μεδέουσα | Κύπρις, *Arg.* 4.917–918). The reference to Eryx constitutes an allusion to the son that Butes and Aphrodite will have together, the eponym of Mt. Eryx and founder of the temple there dedicated to Aphrodite Erycina.[261] But Apollonius' formulation also alludes to the Salutation of the minor *Homeric Hymn to Aphrodite*: "Hail,

---

258 See on this subject above all Clauss 1993. Note that the best of the Argonauts is *a fortiori* likely to be the best of all mortals as well (see *Arg.* 1.548).

259 The collocation of forms of ἄριστος and ἐπιχθόνιος otherwise occurs only in a proverb (Thgn. 425 = *Certamen* 7) and quotations thereof, in a very different context: "It is best of all for mortals not to be born" (πάντων μὲν μὴ φῦναι ἐπιχθονίοισιν ἄριστον).

260 Notably, Cuypers (1997: 47 n. 18) makes the same objection to Hera's assessment without recourse to the *HH*. Note *Arg.* 1.1285–1286, where Heracles is regarded by all as "the best man of their comrades" (τὸν ἄριστον ... | σφωιτέρων ἑτάρων). On another level, however, the declaration that Peleus is the "best" foreshadows the greatness of his son Achilles, who really will be the undisputed "best of the Achaeans" at Troy (cf. Harder 2019a: 11–13 with n. 35).

261 See 165*n*108.

goddess, ruler of well-built Salamis and sea-girt **Cyprus**" (χαῖρε, θεά, Σαλαμῖνος ἐυκτιμένης μεδέουσα | εἰναλίης τε Κύπρου, *HH* 10.4–5). There is a less precise parallel (from, however, a much more prominent hymn) in the Salutation of the major *Homeric Hymn to Aphrodite* (χαῖρε, θεά, Κύπροιο ἐυκτιμένης μεδέουσα, 5.292). All three passages feature line-final μεδέουσα in apposition to θεά, but I consider 10.4–5 the closer parallel because of the reference to two of Aphrodite's cult sites (Salamis/Eryx and Cyprus) and the enjambment of the phrase εἰναλίης τε Κύπρου, which corresponds to the enjambed Κύπρις of *Arg.* 4.918. The allusion does honor to Eryx by adding it subtextually to the number of Aphrodite's oldest cult sites.[262] I would also draw attention to the fact that in his adaptation, Apollonius has left the epithet "well-built" (ἐυκτιμένης) unaccounted for. This omission may serve to acknowledge the fact that, in the "narrative present" of the Argonautic narrative, Eryx has not yet been born and thus his eponymous city, proleptically mentioned at *Arg.* 4.917, has not yet been built (let alone *well* built).

4.6 Thematic Allusions: Apollonius' Programmatic Allusion to the Homeric Hymn to Selene

I would like to conclude this survey by considering the category of allusion of greatest moment for the interpretation of the *Arg.*, namely, those allusions that resonate with the thematic economy of the poem as a discursive whole. As a signal example, I will be considering at relatively greater length Apollonius' programmatic allusion to the Envoi of the *Homeric Hymn to Selene* in his poem's opening words. I have already had occasion to mention this allusion earlier in this introduction (4, 17, 22), and I will have even more to say about it hereafter. But as I hope my arguments will demonstrate, the richness of Apollonius' allusion fully justifies such ample treatment; in fact, I would go so far as to say that, given its programmatic position and carefully crafted ambiguity (explored in further detail in chapter 1), Apollonius' reworking of the *Selene* Envoi may well be the most underinterpreted allusion in all of Hellenistic poetry.[263] To be sure, this intertext is regularly acknowledged in Apollonian scholarship, but it is often dismissed, especially on the grounds of the hymn's uncertain date;[264] and

---

262   For the identity of the Salamis mentioned at *HH* 10.4, see 7n36. For allusions that league "new" cults established by the Argonauts with a god's more established cult sites, see 313n148.

263   Tsakiris (2022: 22 n. 59) also notes the scholarly reticence actually to unpack the potential significance of this allusion.

264   See, e.g.: Campbell 1983: 128 n. 2; Clauss 1993: 16; Albis 1996: 7 n. 25; Guinee 1999: 16 n. 13;

INTRODUCTION

even those scholars who do offer interpretations of the allusion generally consider it only in generic terms, as one constituent in the "hymnic frame" with which the *Arg.* commences and concludes.[265] This generico-structural function is indubitably a vital aspect of Apollonius' allusion, to which I myself will be returning at some length in chapter 1.[266] Nevertheless, it is unfortunate that scholarly analysis has largely stopped here, content with the notion that Apollonius is making a generic system reference to the *HH*s rather than a more pointed allusion to the specific context within the *Homeric Hymn to Selene*. In what follows, I seek to probe the thematic nuances of this allusion and thereby demonstrate the potential rewards of taking the *HH*s seriously as sophisticated models—each with individual poetic agendas and aesthetic profiles—with which Apollonius can engage in meaningful allusive dialogue.

The first sentence of the *Arg.* reads (1.1–4):

Ἀρχόμενος σέο, Φοῖβε, παλαιγενέων κλέα φωτῶν
μνήσομαι, οἳ Πόντοιο κατὰ στόμα καὶ διὰ πέτρας
Κυανέας βασιλῆος ἐφημοσύνῃ Πελίαο
χρύσειον μετὰ κῶας ἐΰζυγον ἤλασαν Ἀργώ.

Beginning with you, Phoebus, I shall recall the famous deeds of mortals born long ago, who, at the command of King Pelias, sailed the well-benched Argo through the mouth of the Black Sea and between the Cyanean rocks to fetch the golden fleece.

With this introit we may compare the conclusion of the *Selene* hymn (*HH* 32.17–20):

Χαῖρε ἄνασσα θεὰ λευκώλενε δῖα Σελήνη
πρόφρον ἐϋπλόκαμος· σέο δ' ἀρχόμενος κλέα φωτῶν
ᾄσομαι ἡμιθέων ὧν κλείουσ' ἔργματ' ἀοιδοί
20 Μουσάων θεράποντες ἀπὸ στομάτων ἐροέντων.

Vox 1999: 163–165; Vian 2002: 1.50 n. 1; Llanos 2017b: 7 n. 9. But for the hymn's (in my view) pre-Apollonian date, see below.

265 A clear-cut articulation of this approach is provided by Carspecken (1952: 111 n. 26): "Apollonius is consciously imitating, in the proemion to his poem, this particular example of a formula common to the hymns (e.g., 31.18–19; 5.293; 9.9; 17.11)." On the poem's "hymnic frame," see the full discussion in chapter 1.

266 See in particular section 1.2 of that chapter, on the "Hymnic Proem" interpretation of Apollonius' introit.

Farewell, Lady, white-armed goddess, divine Selene, gracious, fair-haired. **Beginning with you, I shall sing the famous deeds of mortals half-divine, whose** deeds are acclaimed by singers, servants of the Muses, from their lovely mouths.

The parallels between the bolded portions of these texts are beyond dispute; indeed, they would make for one of the clearest cases of lexical borrowing in all of the *Arg.* if the direction of influence were not in doubt. Assuming that Apollonius is the alluding poet, he has transposed the hymn's σέο δ' ἀρχόμενος (eliminating the particle) and shifted it to the head of the verse;[267] reproduced the exceedingly rare clausula κλέα φωτῶν verbatim and in the same *sedes*;[268] attached an epithet to φωτῶν that effectively identifies the subjects of the forthcoming song as heroes (παλαιγενέων; cf. ἡμιθέων); varied the enjambed ᾄσομαι with another, semantically equivalent verb of narration in the same grammatical form and metrical position (μνήσομαι);[269] and capped this allusive sequence with a relative pronoun (his οἵ answering the hymn's ὧν).[270] But before the work of interpretation can get underway, we must first contend with the objections critics have raised against the probability that Apollonius is in fact alluding to our hymn, in the following subsection.

4.6.1 The Date and Design of *HH* 32

The main objection to an Apollonian allusion to our hymn is temporal: the *Homeric Hymn to Selene* has nigh universally been thought Hellenistic or even Roman in date, primarily on the grounds that its diction and recondite mythology smack of Alexandrianism.[271] If this is right, then *Selene* could postdate Apollonius and its hymnist might be the one adapting the beginning of the *Arg.* rather than vice versa. But in point of fact, Càssola has long since exposed the

---

[267] This transposition owes at least in part to the demands of meter, but Romeo (1985: 22) sees a potentially meaningful difference of emphasis as well: by beginning with a participle with a first-person speaker as its antecedent (ἀρχόμενος), the Apollonian narrator gives himself pride of place before the god (σέο)—the source of his inspiration, as Romeo would have it (see 102*n*79).

[268] Beyond quotations of Apollonius' introit in grammatical texts, this phrase occurs elsewhere only in an epigram of Christodorus (*AP* 2.378); see 146*n*8.

[269] For the equivalence of these verbs in this context, 88*n*18.

[270] Note that Romeo (1985: 27) has detected further echoes of *HH* 32 later in the introit as well, comparing 1.18 (κλείουσιν ἀοιδοί) to 32.19 (κλείουσ' ... ἀοιδοί) and 1.22 (ὑποφήτορες ... ἀοιδῆς) to 32.2 (ἵστορες ᾠδῆς, also compared by De Martino 1984–1985: 105).

[271] For details, see Hall 2013: 15–17.

subjective basis for these late datings,²⁷² and more recently Hall has argued for the likelihood of allusions to the hymn already in Aristophanes and especially Empedocles in the fifth century.²⁷³

To these arguments for an early dating of *Selene*, I would add the following confirmatory evidence: if the hymnist is adapting the *Arg.*, then *Selene*'s alteration of μνήσομαι ("I shall recall," *Arg.* 1.2) to ᾄσομαι ("I shall sing," *HH* 32.19) appears entirely unmotivated. In the converse scenario, however, Apollonius' replacement of ᾄσομαι with μνήσομαι would constitute a transparent example of what Faber has called "memory as trope for literary allusion."²⁷⁴ Faber argues that the practice of using references to memory as signposts for literary allusions, familiar from Latin poetry (*memini, memor*, etc.), is actually derived from their Hellenistic predecessors. For example, the verb ἐμνήσθην in Callimachus' Heraclitus epigram (*ep.* 2.2 Pfeiffer = *AP* 7.80.2) serves on the metapoetic level to mark a *literary* reminiscence, in this case of *Iliad* 1.605–608.²⁷⁵ The same trope is in evidence in Apollonius; for instance, when Medea asks Jason always to remember her (μνώεο, *Arg.* 3.1069; cf. 1110–1111, 4.383), she recalls both the intratextual model of Hypsipyle (μνώεο, 1.896) and the intertextual model of Nausicaa (μνήσῃ, *Od.* 8.462). This example is particularly witty because Apollonius uses forms of μνάομαι to serve both as the vehicle and signal for the allusion taking place.²⁷⁶ *Arg.* 1.2 is clever in a different way, as the poet's substitution of μνήσομαι for *Selene*'s ᾄσομαι manages to bolster the introit's evocation of the

---

272 Càssola 1975a: 440, 447, cited approvingly by Fantuzzi 1988: 23 n. 35; Tsakiris 2022: 23 n. 61. Faulkner (2011b: 16) cites Càssola's arguments with the comment, "A fifth-century date seems reasonable, but an earlier date cannot be ruled out entirely." In this connection it may be relevant that the earliest evidence for Selene's lunar chariot occurs precisely in the first quarter of the fifth century: in iconography, it appears first on an Attic red-figure kylix from Vulci attributed to the Brygos Painter and dated to 490–480 BCE (Berlin F2293 = *LIMC* Selene, Luna 47); in securely dated literature, we find it first in Pind. *Ol.* 3.19–20, which celebrates a victory dated to 476 BCE. On the other hand, Eos has a chariot already in the *Odyssey* (23.244–246), as does Helius in several other *HH*s (2.63, 88–89; 4.69; 28.14); it would require no great leap of imagination for an Archaic poet to equip their sibling Selene with a chariot as well.

273 Hall 2013. See further Phillips 2018: 201 n. 42, who contemplates a possible allusion to the hymn in Pindar.

274 Faber 2017, who discusses this example at 85. It is possible that Apollonius' replacement of ἡμιθέων ("half-divine," *HH* 32.19) with παλαιγενέων ("born long ago," *Arg.* 1.1) functions similarly, given the potential for indications of "chronological perspective" to mark allusions in classical poetry (Nelson 2023: 244).

275 Faber 2017: 81–82.

276 Ibid. 83. Cf. Faber's analysis of an allusion to Ovid in Rutilius Namatianus, in which case *meminisse* similarly "functions as an allusion, and as the signal of an allusion" (86).

diction of the *HHs*[277] while simultaneously acknowledging his allusive "recollection" of the model text in *HH* 32. In sum, there is good internal as well as external evidence to favor the priority of the hymn, to which Apollonius alludes in a characteristically self-conscious way.

There is, however, another objection besides relative dating that might preclude an Apollonian allusion to *HH* 32.18–19: Fantuzzi and Hunter have cautioned that the phrase in the hymn that Apollonius apparently adapts "may have been much more widespread in hymnic poetry than we can now establish."[278] In other words, Apollonius might not have *Selene* specifically in mind, but could just be making a system reference after all, echoing a generic closural formula once common in a now-lost tradition of Rhapsodic Hymnody. This is certainly a valid methodological concern in the abstract, but I consider it unlikely to apply to the specific case of *HH* 32.18–19 because of the manifest individuality of this particular *Homeric Hymn*. We have already seen something of the singularity of this hymn earlier in this introduction (2.2), when I noted that the *HH*s to *Helius* (31) and *Selene* (32) are unique within the collection in that their Envois explicitly frame them as Hymnic Proems preceding the recitation of an epic lay.[279] In fact, this pair of consecutively ordered hymns share many more distinctions beyond this exceptional twist on the "Poet's Task" formula. As I will delineate, *HH* 31–32 constitute nothing less than a consciously-designed celestial diptych distinguished by singularly epic affiliations and a drive toward careful lexical *variatio*.[280]

On a structural level, the *Hymns* exhibit marked similarities and complementary differences. The poems are nearly equivalent in length,[281] and indeed,

---

277 See 88*n*15.
278 Fantuzzi and Hunter 2004: 91 n. 10. In context, they are referring especially to the phrase κλέα φωτῶν, but I take them to mean that this clausula could have been part of a stereotyped formulation of the Poet's Task matching what we find in *HH* 32.18–19 (as otherwise there would be little reason to imagine that κλέα φωτῶν might have been typical of hymnic poetry particularly).
279 And note that these two Envois use different wording in each instance.
280 The complementarity of these hymns is such that I think we must regard them as the work of a single author (so, e.g.: Baumeister 1860: 368; Gemoll 1886: 355–356; West 2003a: 19; Hall 2013: 24–25; Bernabé 2017: 393), rather than merely the product of the same "scuola rapsodica" (Càssola 1975a: 440). Ludwich (1908: 283–297) believed that one poet was responsible for the entire sequence of *HH* 27–33, and that together with *HH* 31–32, *H* 30 (to Gaia) and *H* 33 (to the Dioscuri, identified with St. Elmo's fire) formed a celestial (or perhaps better, cosmic) subgroup within this cycle. I agree that *HH* 30–33 may have been grouped together by the arranger of our collection because of their similar cosmico-celestial themes (see West 2003a: 21; Hall 2021: 24), but the internal correspondences across this quartet (or, indeed, this septet) are less convincing than those within just the dyad of *HH* 31–32.
281 Gemoll 1886: 355.

might be exactly so depending on whether we posit one or more lacunae in *HH* 31.[282] Both hymns open with relatively grandiloquent (by the standards of the *HH*s) Appeals to the Muses, include a genealogical Myth as well as an Attributive Section that describes the deity's luminous chariot ride through heaven, and end with Envois that, as we have seen, uniquely specify their function as preludes to an epic performance to follow. The particularly epic texture of these poems is affirmed also in their Exordia: *HH* 31.1–2 requests inspiration specifically from Calliope, the Muse of epic poetry, while *HH* 32 begins with a delightful play on the *incipit* of the *Iliad* (Μήνην ἀείδειν [*HH* 32.1] ~ μῆνιν ἄειδε [*Il.* 1.1]).[283]

The complementarity of these pieces is especially apparent in light of the structural quirks exhibited by their middle sections. *HH* 31 launches upon its Myth (2–7) immediately following its Exordium (1–2); the hymnist traces the sun god's genealogy from his parents (Hyperion and Euryphaessa) back to his grandparents (Gaia and Uranus), and also notices the birth of his sisters, Eos and Selene herself. A relative clause in line 8 (ὅς) then accomplishes the transition to an Attributive Section, which describes the sun's daily circuit through the sky (8–16). In *Selene*, by contrast, an Attributive Section detailing her nightly course through the heavens (3–13) follows directly from the Exordium (1–2), and only then do we get a (highly unusual) Myth relating the birth of Pandia,

---

282   Hermann plausibly identified a lacuna after *HH* 31.14; probably one line has fallen out, to the effect of the supplement proposed by AHS 1936. I disagree, however, with Allen and Sikes (1904) that a lacuna is discernible after line 15 (and notably, they retracted this suggestion in AHS 1936; cf. West 2003a). This latter lacuna would be especially unnecessary if we adopt Ruhnken's emendation of ἑσπέριος for θεσπέσιος at line 16 (cf. AR 3.1191–1192). This change finds support from the correspondence that would thus result with ἑσπερίη at the beginning of *HH* 32.11. Thus reconstructed, the passage would read:

    ὑπὸ δ' ἄρσενες ἵπποι
14a ⟨ἀΐσσουσ', ὄφρ' ἂν μέσον οὐρανὸν αὐτὸν ἵκωνται·⟩
15   ἔνθ' ἄρ' ὅ γε στήσας χρυσόζυγον ἅρμα καὶ ἵππους
     ἑσπέριος πέμπῃσι δι' οὐρανοῦ Ὠκεανόνδε.

Below him his stallions ⟨speed on till they reach the very mid-point of heaven⟩; there he halts his horses and gold-yoked car, and at evening he guides them through the sky towards Ocean's stream.

The resulting description mildly truncates the course of the day, but not intolerably; cf., e.g., *HH* 4.17–18. But it may be worth considering an emendation to ἑσπέριον, which would eliminate these temporal problems altogether: "and he guides them through the sky towards the **western** Ocean" (cf., e.g., Aratus *Phaen.* 407, 431, 858; AR 3.311; Ov. *Met.* 11.257–258). In any case, adopting either of the reconstructions endorsed here would result in a hymn of twenty lines, matching *Helius* and *Selene* perfectly.

283   See above, 22.

Selene's daughter by Zeus (14–16), introduced via the relative pronoun τῇ.²⁸⁴ The abrupt intrusion of this Myth after the Attributive Section is an untraditional structural phenomenon within the collection,²⁸⁵ and it is particularly odd that the genealogy thus introduced focuses on Selene's daughter rather than on Selene herself, as the piece's Hymnic Subject. The explanation, as many critics have perceived, is that the poet has already provided Selene's γένος in *HH* 31, thus freeing *HH* 32 to extend the genealogical chain one generation forward with the birth of one of their progeny.²⁸⁶ The chiastic arrangement of the Mythic and Attributive Sections in these hymns underlines their interlocking structures, in much the same way that in their respective ecphrases, the sun god's course ends (31.16) precisely when and where Selene's begins (32.7, 11), at evening in Ocean; thus *Selene* picks up where *Helius* had left off.²⁸⁷

The features considered thus far could be explained by a later poet writing one of the hymns, probably the more atypical *Selene*, in light of the other,²⁸⁸ but this hypothesis would not explain the way that the opening lines of both hymns encode their cyclicality through unique continuity markers. Scholars have been troubled by the transmitted opening of *Hymn* 32 (Μήνην ἀείδειν τανυσίπτερον ἔσπετε Μοῦσαι), as ἔσπετε, if it means "tell of" (as, e.g., at *HH* 33.1), seems redundant after the Evocatory Verb ἀείδειν, "to sing." The typical remedy has been to emend away ἀείδειν,²⁸⁹ but I believe that AHS struck upon a preferable solution when they compared the line to the *incipit* of *HH* 31 ("Ἥλιον ὑμνεῖν αὖτε Διὸς τέκος ἄρχεο Μοῦσα). The identical articulation of the transmitted phrases suggests that Μήνην ἀείδειν ... ἔσπετε Μοῦσαι answers Ἥλιον ὑμνεῖν ... ἄρχεο Μοῦσα,²⁹⁰ with the hymnist apparently treating ἔσπετε as a form of ἔπο-

---

284 The obscure Pandia seems to tie the hymn to an Attic context; see: AHS 1936 ad loc.; Càssola 1975a ad loc.; West 2003a: 19. Ní Mheallaigh (2020: 16) interprets her as a personification of the full moon.

285 Janko 1981: 20.

286 E.g.: Gemoll 1886: 358; Zanetto 1996: 312; Poli 2010: 449; Bernabé 2017: 399.

287 The Myths in these hymns also exhibit a complementary taste for relatively obscure mythological variants (or, perhaps, innovations): as the commentators uniformly note, the pair's mother Euryphaessa and Selene's daughter Pandia are otherwise virtually unattested. Euryphaessa's epithet "very famous" (ἀγακλειτήν, 31.4) ironically draws attention to (or is meant to disguise) the poet's novelty; for a similar device in Euripides' *Ion*, cf.: Mastronarde 2003: 303 n. 33; Cole 2008: 315.

288 An idea floated by AHS (1936: 431); cf.: Zanetto 1996: 312; Poli 2010: 449.

289 Cf. 22*n*11.

290 Both lines follow a pattern of accusative direct object + complementary infinitive ... imperative + vocative address to the Muse(s). The middle of the verse is in each case occupied by an Honorific epithet for the Hymnic Subject or the Muse (plus, in the case of *HH* 31.1, the adverb αὖτε).

μαι, "to follow."²⁹¹ Thus the Muses are asked to "begin to hymn" Helius in *HH* 31 and to "go on to sing" of Selene in that poem's "sequel," *HH* 32.²⁹² To these insights I would add only the role played by αὖτε in *HH* 31.1. This adverb, which properly means "again," has also bothered commentators, since it could imply (despite ἄρχεο in the same line) that the Muse has already been asked to sing one or more hymns prior to launching upon *Helius*. This interpretation is not inevitable,²⁹³ but I would suggest that αὖτε allows *HH* 31 to be repeated after the recitation of *HH* 32. That is, after finishing the "sequel" *Selene*, the Muse may return to "begin again" with *Helius*, thus inaugurating an endless cycle alternating between these hymns just like the real-life procession of the sun and the moon that they depict.²⁹⁴ This dynamic interaction points to a common intention animating both hymns, which were jointly designed to accommodate an infinitely iterable sequence of hymnody.²⁹⁵

HH 31–32 also dovetail closely on a verbal level through an extended series of lexical and semantic correspondences, though the poet has striven to achieve a high degree of *variatio* throughout.²⁹⁶ For example, just in the opening lines, we have already seen how Μήνην ἀείδειν varies Ἥλιον ὑμνεῖν and how ἔσπετε caps ἄρχεο; we may also observe the fluctuation in the number of the Muses (Μοῦσα ~ Μοῦσαι), which is matched by synonymous but distinct expressions of their Jovian paternity (Διὸς τέκος [31.1] ~ κοῦραι Κρονίδεω Διός [32.2]). One aspect of these responsions that critics seem to have missed is their gendered dimension: the hymnist is at pains to register the masculinity of the god and the femininity of the goddess in corresponding fashion.²⁹⁷ For instance, there seems little point in specifying that the horses that pull Helius' chariot are stallions (ἄρσενες ἵπποι, 31.14), except to create a contrast with the colts (πώλους, 32.9) that

291 For this interpretation of ἔσπετε, see further Ludwich 1908: 286–287.
292 AHS 1936 ad *HH* 32.1 ("Hymn xxxii would then be a 'sequel' to xxxi"); see also Allen and Sikes 1904 ad loc. As examples of ἕπομαι + inf., they cite Arist. *Eth. Nic.* 3.1.2 (ἕπεται διελθεῖν) and (in their addenda) Porph. *De antr. nymph.* 21 (ἕπεται … ζητεῖν τὸ βούλημα).
293 Cf. AHS 1936 ad loc.
294 This function of αὖτε finds a nice parallel in the opening of the *Epigoni* (fr. 1 Bernabé), whose introit was probably created to bind it together with the other poems of the epic cycle (Wheeler 2002: 42).
295 Cf. Petrovic 2013 on the hymnic aspiration toward endlessness.
296 Of course, a certain degree of overlap in content would be unavoidable in any two poems describing these radiant deities (Càssola 1975a: 440), but the correspondences between our hymns are in fact closer and more systematic than previous scholarship has recognized.
297 For Helius and Selene as a typical masculine-feminine dyad, see, e.g., Pind. fr. 104 Maehler (= Σ Theoc. *Id.* 2.10b), according to which men in love would swear by Helius, women, by Selene.

serve Selene. Or to take another example: both hymns detail their Subject's brilliant appearance, beginning with the deity's head and working their way down (31.9–13, 32.2–6). Although both gods wear resplendent robes (λάμπεται ἔσθος | λεπτουργές [31.12–13], εἵματα ... τηλαυγέα [32.8]), Helius' head bears a "golden helm" from which "his eye gaze fearsomely" (σμερδνὸν δ' ὅ γε δέρκεται ὄσσοις | χρυσέης ἐκ κόρυθος, 31.9–10); Selene, by contrast, is equipped with a "golden circlet" (χρυσέου ἀπὸ στεφάνου, 32.6 [also line-initial]), and "a rich beauty emerges" (πολὺς δ' ὑπὸ κόσμος ὄρωρεν, 4) as the brightness "from her immortal head" (κρατὸς ἀπ' ἀθανάτοιο, 4) shines forth. These different types of headgear are matched by different affective responses associated with the gods: while an atmosphere of feminine eroticism suffuses *Selene*,[298] *Helius* emphasizes its Subject's awe-inspiring brilliance.[299]

But the best example of the hymnist's painstaking *variatio* comes in the Envois of these twin compositions. The poet has done practically everything he can to express the same ideas in different language, from varying tenses and constructions (e.g., ἐκ ... ἀρξάμενος vs. ἀρχόμενος) to employing cognate

---

[298] For Selene's attractions, note κόσμος (4), χρόα καλόν (7), λευκώλενε (17), ἐυπλόκαμος (18); note also the emendation εὐειδῆ (1), with which, however, I disagree (see 22n111). Notably, Selene is given a miniature bathing and dressing scene before she quits the stream of Ocean (32.7–8), much like Aphrodite in two of her *HH*s (5.58–67, 6.5–15). Selene's horses are also beautifully maned (καλλίτριχας, 10) and her daughter Pandia possesses outstanding beauty among the immortal gods (ἐκπρεπὲς εἶδος ἔχουσαν ἐν ἀθανάτοισι θεοῖσι, 16). In *HH* 31, Selene also figures among the κάλλιμα τέκνα (5) of Hyperion and Euryphaessa and again receives the epithet ἐυπλόκαμον (6).

[299] To be sure, *HH* 31 is much concerned with Helius' appearance and does ascribe to him the good looks proper to any deity (note χαρίεν ... πρόσωπον [31.12], καλόν ... ἔσθος [13]); there is, however, less emphasis thereupon than we find in its companion piece *Selene*. *Helius*' Myth is revealing in this regard: in the list of "lovely children" (κάλλιμα τέκνα, 5) whom "ox-eyed Euryphaessa" (Εὐρυφάεσσα βοῶπις, 2) bears to Hyperion, Eos is given the epithet "rosy-armed" (ῥοδόπηχυν, 6) and Selene, "with fine hair" (ἐυπλόκαμόν, 6), but Helius is described as "tireless, like the immortals" (ἀκάμαντ', ἐπιείκελον ἀθανάτοισιν, 7). That is, Helius' female kin are dignified with epithets relating to their beauty, but the sun god himself is described in terms of his activity (ἀκάμαντ') and with an epithet better suited to a Homeric warrior than an actual god (ἐπιείκελον ἀθανάτοισιν). In fact, Càssola (1975a ad loc.) has shown that this rather clumsy hexameter is the result of a sonic merger of the hemistich Ἥέλιον δ' [or: τ'] ἀκάμαντα (*Il*. 18.239, 484) with a description of the Trojan hero Acamas at *Il*. 11.60 (ἠΐθεόν τ' Ἀκάμαντ' ἐπιείκελον ἀθανάτοισιν; see earlier Ludwich 1908: 284). But this logical lapse is in any case revealing: the hymnist is evidently intent on investing Helius, unlike his lovely sister, with something of a martial air. Incidentally, this sort of error could point to an oral compositional context (Cantilena 1982: 319), and thus probably to an earlier dating for *HH* 31 (and, by extension, its companion piece *HH* 32).

INTRODUCTION

synonyms (e.g., ἔργα vs. ἔργματα). For convenience of presentation, I will now quote both Envois and present their correspondences in tabular form. First, *HH* 31.17–19:

> Χαῖρε, ἄναξ, πρόφρων δὲ βίον θυμήρε᾽ ὄπαζε.
> ἐκ σέο δ᾽ ἀρξάμενος κλήσω μερόπων γένος ἀνδρῶν
> ἡμιθέων, ὧν ἔργα θεαὶ θνητοῖσιν ἔδειξαν.

> Farewell, Lord! Graciously bestow heart-cheering livelihood. After beginning from you, I will celebrate the race of mortal men half-divine, whose deeds the gods have disclosed to mortals.

Here is *HH* 32.17–20 again:

> Χαῖρε ἄνασσα θεὰ λευκώλενε δῖα Σελήνη
> πρόφρον ἐϋπλόκαμος· σέο δ᾽ ἀρχόμενος κλέα φωτῶν
> ᾄσομαι ἡμιθέων ὧν κλείουσ᾽ ἔργματ᾽ ἀοιδοί
> 20   Μουσάων θεράποντες ἀπὸ στομάτων ἐροέντων.

> Farewell, Lady, white-armed goddess, divine Selene, gracious, fair-haired. Beginning with you, I shall sing the famous deeds of mortals half-divine, whose deeds are acclaimed by singers, servants of the Muses, from their lovely mouths.

Note the studied variations of expression across these texts:

31.18–19	32.17–20
Χαῖρε ἄναξ	Χαῖρε ἄνασσα
πρόφρων δὲ βίον θυμήρε᾽ ὄπαζε	πρόφρον
ἐκ σέο δ᾽ ἀρξάμενος	σέο δ᾽ ἀρχόμενος
κλήσω	κλέα ... ᾄσομαι (cf. κλείουσ᾽ ... ἀοιδοί)
μερόπων γένος ἀνδρῶν | ἡμιθέων	φωτῶν | ... ἡμιθέων
ὧν ἔργα	ὧν ... ἔργματ᾽
θεοὶ θνητοῖσιν ἔδειξαν.	ἀοιδοί | Μουσάων θεράποντες ἀπὸ στομάτων ἐροέντων.

Two points deserve special comment here. The first is *Selene*'s substitution of φωτῶν for ἀνδρῶν. The latter term ("men") is unequivocally masculine, but the former is more ambiguous. While in some passages φώς does seem to denote a "man" specifically, in others it appears gender neutral, much like ἄνθρωπος.[300] We thus might translate φωτῶν more inclusively as "people" or "mortals," in contrast to *Helius*' decidedly male designation of the subject of the forthcoming epic performance. Second, the way that each hymn characterizes the origins of epic poetry varies in ways that are equally significant. *HH* 32 conceptualizes epic in a strikingly feminine mode, with songs proceedings from the "lovely" (ἐροέντων) mouths of bards, who are subservient to the (feminine) Muses (Μουσάων θεράποντες).[301] *Helius*, by contrast, emphasizes the status of epic as revelation from the (masculine) gods (θεοί)[302]—appropriately so, given the hymn's emphasis on the sun god's function in providing light for mortals.[303] Indeed, Hall has used these examples to argue for the potentially important role of aesthetics in determining the content of the *HH*s qua Hymnic Proems: by choosing to describe a particular deity in a particular way before beginning their epic lays, bards could prime their audience to receive their performances with a certain set of evaluative criteria in mind.[304]

One could continue to plumb the depths of the correspondences between *HH* 31–32, but the foregoing analysis should be enough to settle the concerns raised by Fantuzzi and Hunter that Apollonius could be alluding to a generic closural formula at *Arg.* 1.1–2, rather than to the Envoi of *Selene* specifically. In fact, *HH* 32 shows every sign of being a singular composition indeed, with an Envoi uniquely tailored to a specific poetic program. This excursus on the date and design of this celestial diptych has also revealed major features of the poem that serves as Apollonius' model for *Arg.* 1.1–2, and this background will prove indispensable in drawing out the potential meanings of the *Argonautica*'s inaugural allusion.

---

300   See LSJ s.v. II, III. Ancient scholiasts gloss the word with both ἀνήρ and ἄνθρωπος (e.g., Σ *Od*. 1.355b, c Pontani).

301   As Hall (2013: 26) notes, ἐροέντων is surely a transferred epithet; it is the bards' songs that are lovely.

302   Matthiae proposed emending to θεαί ("goddesses," i.e., the Muses), but in this context θεοί is preferable as the *lectio difficilior*.

303   Per Hall (2013: 27): "It is only natural to touch on the divine revelation of poetry just after hymning that ultimate divine revealer, Helios."

304   Hall 2013: 25–30. His approach is especially convincing in the case of *HH* 31–32, since cults of Helius and especially Selene were rare in ancient Greece. Accordingly, instead of a festival context (cf. 16n80), aesthetic considerations might have provided a more plausible motive for composing Hymnic Proems to these particular deities.

4.6.2 Interpretation: Three Major Approaches

Allusions are a slippery thing, and the present case is no exception. Apollonius has expressly invited us to read his epic's opening words in light of the passage he has so decisively evoked, but of course, the task of construing the hermeneutic ramifications of the connection he has drawn between *Arg.* 1.1–2 and *HH* 32.18–19 inevitably falls to us, his readers; the interpretation is not provided readymade.[305] To my mind, there are at least three major interpretive routes a critic could pursue, depending on which features of this intertextual connection one chooses to privilege. First, because *HH* 31–32 is a celestial diptych, we could understand Apollonius to be evoking both of these hymns via his allusion to just one of them; the one poem naturally conjures the other. Second, and conversely, we could view the poet's allusion to *Selene* as preferential: he has chosen to invoke the moon goddess's hymn over its companion piece, for presumably the former better suits his poetic agenda in the introit. But third and finally, we might regard the intrusion of an altogether new deity as decisive for deciphering Apollonius' adaptation: the poet has effectively written Selene herself out of the text he reworks, since σέο now refers to Phoebus (Φοῖβε) rather than to the goddess (or, indeed, to her brother Helius). In what follows, I will limit myself only to outlining some of the directions that our interpretations could take depending on which of these approaches we favor.

4.6.2.1 *Selene and Helius*

Among the handful of critics who have forwarded interpretations of Apollonius' allusion, it is this first approach that has generally prevailed. Whether emphasizing the status of *HH* 31–32 as a diptych or simply recognizing the patent similarities between their Envois, these scholars find that an allusion to *Selene* naturally evokes *Helius* as well.[306] But the Sun and Moon enjoyed rich symbolic associations in antiquity, especially in view of the increasing Greek tendency to syncretize these gods with other deities. Unsurprisingly, then, scholars pursuing these connections have reached different conclusions. Vox, for instance, has noted the contemporary identifications of this celestial pair with Isis and Osiris (Manetho *FGrH* 609 F 17, Hecataeus *FGrH* 264 F 1, Diod. Sic. 1.11) and of Apollo (cf. Φοῖβε, *Arg.* 1.1) with their son Horus (attested already in Hdt. 2.156). As the Ptolemies were themselves identified with each member

---

[305] Fowler 1997: 24: "Meaning is realised at the point of reception, and what counts as an intertext and what one does with it depends on the reader."

[306] For the likelihood that Apollonius makes a lexical allusion to *Helius*' Exordium in the introit of *Arg.* 4, see 21–23 above.

of the Egyptian divine family, Vox suggests that we might read the opening allusion of the *Arg.* as a kind of tribute to the sovereigns of Ptolemaic Egypt.[307]

Tsakiris, conversely, adopts a different tack, relying on yet another set of associations possessed by the sun and moon in Greek thought.[308] As he notes, by Apollonius' day, Helius had increasingly become identified with Apollo,[309] and Selene could likewise be identified with Artemis.[310] Since the Apollonian (hereafter, AR) narrator later compares Jason (1.307–311) and Medea (3.876–886) precisely to Apollo and Artemis, respectively,[311] Tsakiris sees the allusion to *HH* 31–32 in *Arg.* 1.1–2 as a kind of foreshadowing of the primary protagonists of the epic, several lines before the first mention of Jason at 1.8 and well before Medea's first explicit appearance at 3.3.[312] Now, strictly speaking, Apollonius keeps all of these deities distinct throughout his narrative,[313] but in the case of Apollo, at least, there is good reason to think that the poet gestures toward his syncretism with Helius. As Hunter observes, "A hymn to the sun has an obvious connection with Apollo whose solar identity is exploited by Apollonius when the Argonauts see him in the Black Sea and again in his epiphany at Anaphe."[314]

In this connection it should also be noted that *Arg.* 1.1 invokes Apollo specifically in his radiant aspect as the "Bright" god, Phoebus (Φοῖβε),[315] even though

---

307   See Vox 1999: 164–165, with bibliography. A striking example of the close association that could obtain between these celestial divinities and the Ptolemies occurs in Dionysus Scytobrachion's euhemerizing account of the origin of the gods (ap. Diod. Sic. 3.57.5), in which Selene is termed φιλάδελφον (= the royal epithet of Arsinoe II) because of her affection for her brother Helius (see Constantakopoulou on *BNJ* 32 F 7).

308   See also Clauss 1993: 16 n. 8; Kronenberg 2018b: 30 n. 52.

309   This identification is attested first in Euripides, if not Aeschylus (see Diggle 1970 ad Eur. *Phaethon* 225–226 [p. 147]), and might even be implicit already in *HH* 3.363–369 (Rusten 1982: 33 n. 18). For Helius' assimilation with Apollo in the Hellenistic period, see further, e.g.: Williams 1978 ad Callim. *Hymn* 2.9; Domaradzki 2012: 127–128, 136.

310   The earliest text to make this identification is Aesch. fr. 170 Radt, although before the Roman period, the equation Selene-Artemis seems to be attested much less frequently than that of Helius and Apollo (see *RE* 2nd ser., 2.1.1142.50–58).

311   On these similes, see 3.2.1.

312   Tsakiris 2022: 23. Jason is briefly compared to Apollo again at 3.1283. For Medea's connections to the moon, see further below in this section. Tsakiris' interpretation is in fact compatible with Vox's, insofar as the romance of Jason and Medea, if analogized with the sibling relationship of Apollo and Artemis, would gain an incestuous connotation that may evoke the dynastic marriages of Ptolemaic Egypt (cf. Hardie 2006: 28).

313   Cf., e.g., his more overt identification of Hecate with Persephone at 3.862 (McPhee 2021a: 257).

314   Hunter 1993: 129 n. 110. For Apollo's solar aspect in the *Arg.*, see further Hunter 1986: 52–53; for possible Egyptian connections, see Stephens 2003: 232–235; Noegel 2004: 130–131.

315   Collins 1967: 10. Apollonius could also be punning on Φοίβη as an epithet for Artemis-

an oracular epithet (e.g., Loxias) might have more obviously suited the context (cf. 1.5, 8).[316] Indeed, the epithet's evocation of the god's luminous aspect may be picked up (and further activated) by φωτῶν at the end of the line,[317] given the well-known ancient wordplay connecting φώς, "person," with φῶς, "light."[318] In fact, the earliest exemplar of this pun, Parmenides' transformation of the Homeric expression "foreign **man**" (ἀλλότριος φώς; e.g., *Od.* 16.101) into "another's **light**" (ἀλλότριον φῶς, fr. 14.3 DK), has to do precisely with the fact that the moon does not emit its own light, but reflects that of the sun.[319] By a similar principle, perhaps, Apollonius' narration has its source in the brilliant god Apollo (ἀρχόμενος σέο, Φοῖβε), whence the narrator transitions to the lesser lights, as it were, constituted by the glorious deeds of his heroes (κλέα φωτῶν).[320]

4.6.2.2   *Selene, not Helius*
We have seen that it is fully possible to integrate both *Helius* and *Selene* into an interpretation of the *Arg.*'s opening allusion,[321] but here I would like to

---

Selene, if, in fact, this usage (so familiar from Latin poetry: Bömer 1958 ad Ov. *Fast.* 2.163) was already extant in his period.

316   Cusset 2018: 82; cf. Klooster 2011: 220.
317   Fränkel (1968: 35) notes the assonance connecting σέο, Φοῖβε and κλέα φωτῶν; note also the consonance of φ.
318   In fact, ancient etymologists derived φώς from φῶς (as do some modern etymologists, though Beekes 2010 s.v. φώς doubts the connection), either because of the "light" of life by which mortals live (e.g., Σ *Od.* 1.44 Dindorf [p. 20.2–4]) or the "light" of reason in the human mind (e.g., Apollonius Soph. *Lexicon Homericum* s.v. φῶτες). See further Orion Gramm. s.v. φώς, who hedges his bets by connecting the lemma either with the "illumination of reason" (φωτίζων τῷ λόγῳ) or τὸ φῶ, glossed as τὸ λέγω, "to speak," both activities characteristically human and naturally interrelated. Note that Murray (2018: 202, 206) seems to activate the potential pun between φώς and φῶς by translating κλέα φωτῶν as "the song-worthy glories of **splendid** mortals."
319   See Cosgrove 2011: 29 n. 5 with bibliography. Cf. Hall 2013: 21–22, who argues that Empedocles fr. 45 DK similarly alludes to both *HH* 32 and Parmenides. Parmenides' ἀλλότριος tropes his adaptation as a kind of theft from Homer; I wonder if we could interpret Apollonius as taking φώς/φῶς for himself in turn, with an eye to both the Homeric and Parmenidean usages. Further passages in which a play on φώς/φῶς could be present include *IG* 14.2012A38–39, Opp. *Hal.* 1.652–654, Quint. Smyrn. 7.39–41, Nonnus *Paraphrase* 4.4–5; see also Tralau 2008: 244 on Soph. *Ant.* 102, 107. More cautiously, I would adduce the prologue of the Gospel of John, in which Jesus appears as "the light of human beings" (τὸ φῶς τῶν ἀνθρώπων, 1:4) who also incarnates as a human being—in other words, as a φῶς who becomes a φώς.
320   Of course, it is ironic that Apollonius' allusion itself derives from the *Homeric Hymn to Selene*—in this sense, the "moon" actually provides the source for "Phoebus."
321   Schematically, the interpretations considered above boil down to: 1) Helius/Selene

point out that the status of *HH* 31–32 as a diptych is in fact dual-edged. More specifically, while it is certainly true that Apollonius' allusion has the potential to evoke both members of this pair of hymns, the fact that the poet quotes only from *Selene*, retaining none of the distinctive verbiage of the *Helius* Envoi, might equally point us toward a more antagonistic reading: Apollonius is choosing to allude to *HH* 32 over 31, presumably because *Selene* is in one way or another more congenial to his poetic agenda than its companion piece would be.[322]

The question is, what could have made Apollonius prefer to evoke *HH* 32 in favor of 31? I believe that the key to answering this question is the realization that, in selecting which of these twin compositions to evoke, Apollonius did not face a choice between arbitrary variants of a standard closural formula from an undifferentiated pair of minor *Homeric Hymns*. Rather, he had to choose between the two halves of a skillfully crafted celestial diptych, one coded male and foregrounding the status of epic poetry as divinely revealed, the other coded female and highlighting the loveliness of epic song. Given these options, it is little wonder that Apollonius chooses *Selene* over *Helius*. As is well known, Apollonius' introit de-emphasizes the traditional theme of the narrator's dependence on the Muses, who are first evoked only at 1.22, and in terms that may even invert the normal hierarchy between poet and inspiring goddesses (Μοῦσαι δ' ὑποφήτορες εἶεν ἀοιδῆς).[323] In these circumstances, *Helius*' insistence on the supernatural authorization of epic by the Muses may have seemed unappealing. But perhaps more importantly, *Selene*'s distinctive aesthetic program could have proved a positive attraction for our avant-garde Alexandrian poet. Given its notorious downplaying of martial modes of heroism in favor of the "love theme,"[324] by all accounts the *Arg.* cleaves much closer to the feminine and erotic mood of *Selene* than the fearsome and masculine aspect of *Helius*.

In this vein, we may make three further observations. First, an allusion to *Selene* is particularly apt because of the moon's popularity as a symbol of erotic love throughout Greek literature. Apollonius himself exploits this resonance

---

—Osiris/Isis—the Ptolemaic king/queen; 2) Helius/Selene—Apollo/Artemis—Jason/Medea.

322 It should be noted that interpretations #1 and 2 are not mutually exclusive. We could imagine, for instance, that Apollonius did want to evoke both *Helius* and *Selene* as a diptych, but that he preferred to use the latter hymn for this purpose because some of its distinctive qualities were particularly amenable to his artistic aims in their own right.

323 For the (controversial) interpretation of this line, see further 232*n*8, 234*n*15.

324 The bibliography on this subject is immense, but the following provide a good starting place: Beye 1969, 1982, 2006: ch. 6; Heiserman 1977: ch. 2; Zanker 1979.

repeatedly in the *Arg.*,³²⁵ and in one passage, in which the Moon herself posits a direct analogy between her passion for Endymion and Medea's love for Jason (4.54–65), he uses language that recalls the allusion to *Selene* in the poem's introit.³²⁶ Second, in the Hellenistic context specifically, the moon may have possessed particular aesthetic significance in light of Aratus' famous ΛΕΠΤΗ acrostic,³²⁷ which is set in a passage of the *Phaenomena* that describes the meteorological import of different phases of the moon (783–787) to which Apollonius alludes elsewhere.³²⁸ *Selene* would thus serve as a vehicle both to foreshadow the erotic themes of Apollonius' innovative epic and to symbolize the avant-garde λεπτότης that characterizes his poetics.

Third and finally, we should note the gender dynamics of the Homeric-hymnic diptych, which shed particular light on the interpretation of κλέα φωτῶν in *Arg.* 1.1. Apollonius' phrase is typically interpreted as a programmatic *imitatio cum variatione* of the epic tag κλέα ἀνδρῶν familiar from the HEs (*Il.* 9.189, 524; *Od.* 8.73).³²⁹ But several critics have also seen the potential for a meaningful semantic difference in Apollonius' choice of κλέα φωτῶν over κλέα ἀνδρῶν, especially as regards gender.³³⁰ Apollonius' formulation has been regarded as typical of the male bias inherent in the epic tradition,³³¹ but this

---

325 See particularly Bremer 1987.
326 In particular, cf. σεῖο … | μνησαμένη (4.59–60) with σέο … | μνήσομαι (1.1–2). For memory as a trope for allusion, see 59*n*274.
327 I owe this observation to Max Leventhal. The subject of "lunar poetics" in the Hellenistic period would be worth exploring further, and in this connection *AP* 9.24 seems highly relevant. In that epigram, Leonidas of Tarentum likens Homer to the sun, which makes the moon seem faint in comparison—but of course, we should remember that the moon's light is none other than the sun's, reflected back more softly. The background provided by the metaphor of Homer as "sun poet" and Aratus as "moon poet" (Kronenberg 2018b: 13) would invest Apollonius' allusion to *Selene* rather than *Helius* with rich metapoetic significance relating to innovation and epigonality; e.g., we could say that Apollonius thus aligns himself with Aratean λεπτότης even while acknowledging Homer as the inimitable ultimate source of his poetic σοφία—and fittingly, Apollonius would be alluding to Homer's own hymns to make this point.
328 See Kronenberg 2018a: 2; 2018b: 3–4, 9, 12–13, 17–18.
329 See 146. Scholars have also observed that Apollonius' variation might be meant to make a philological point: κλέα φωτῶν shows that he interprets the alpha in κλέα as naturally short (as also at *Arg.* 4.361), whereas in κλέα ἀνδρῶν it could be understood as a long vowel shortened via epic correption (e.g., Hunter 1993: 129 n. 110; see further West 2001: 125). The allusion to *HH* 32.18 may serve as a "Homeric" prooftext for this scansion and programmatically flag our poet's marked interest in Homeric scholarship (see 3*n*8).
330 Cf. Carspecken 1952: 111, who would understand κλέα φωτῶν as the "glorious deeds of mortals," i.e., of ordinary folk as opposed to the superhuman heroes of the HEs.
331 E.g., Keith 1999: 214 with n. 1; Ziogas 2013: 186.

assessment relies on the assumption that φωτῶν must mean "men," whereas we have seen that φώς can also be translated in gender-neutral fashion as "mortal" or "person."[332] Given the allusive background of Apollonius' use of κλέα φωτῶν, which he has drawn precisely from the feminine half of a gendered diptych (*HH* 32.18; cf. κλήσω μερόπων γένος ἀνδρῶν, *HH* 31.18), the conclusion that Apollonius is here evoking a more gender-inclusive conception of epic seems to me inescapable.[333] In the context of the *Arg.* itself, the upshot of this reading is that φωτῶν ("people") leaves room for the "glorious deeds" of Medea as well as those of her male crewmates to be celebrated as the subject of the *Arg.*[334] In this way, the allusion to *Selene* at the beginning of the poem paves the way for Medea's formal introduction in the introit of Book 3.

4.6.2.3 *Phoebus, not Selene (or Helius)*

The foregoing analysis has yielded several plausible motives for Apollonius' introit to recollect *HH* 31–32 as a diptych as well as *Selene* in contradistinction to *Helius*. And yet it must be admitted that, even as Apollonius allusively evokes the gods of moon and sun, in another sense, he puts them under erasure by changing the referent of the second-person pronoun σέο: with the insertion of a new vocative, it turns out that the narrator begins neither with Helius nor even Selene, but with Phoebus Apollo (Φοῖβε, 1.1). This reading might prove especially attractive because, while in some scenes the *Arg.* could be raising the pos-

---

332 See above, 66n300. In this context it is notable that Apollonius' expression simultaneously varies the gender-neutral *iunctura* παλαιγενέων ἀνθρώπων from *HH* 2.113, though with a significant semantic twist. As Giangrande (1977: 273) notes, παλαιγενής in Homer means "born long ago" in the sense of "superannuated, senior" (*Il.* 3.386, 17.561; *Od.* 22.395; *HH* 2.101, 113; 4.199); Apollonius' use of the adjective in the sense of "antique, belonging to the remote past" thus constitutes another programmatic example of *imitatio cum variatione* (cf. 146).

333 See further McPhee 2017: 115 (from which I have drawn for this paragraph), where I stage a different argument that reaches the same conclusion. Other scholars who admit both men and women into their interpretation of κλέα φωτῶν include: Goldhill 1991: 288; DeForest 1994: 39; Albis 1996: 41; Vox 2002: 158 with n. 28; Nishimura-Jensen 2009: 17 n. 56. For more gender-inclusive encapsulations of the subject matter of epic, cf. esp. *HH* 3.160 (μνησάμεναι ἀνδρῶν τε παλαιῶν ἠδὲ γυναικῶν, compared by: Albis 1996: 41; Schaaf 2014: 37; Tsakiris 2022: 83 n. 213); and Hes. *Th.* 100 (κλέεα προτέρων ἀνθρώπων, compared by: Hunter 1993: 125–126; Ransom 2014: 640 n. 8; Llanos 2017a: 4). See further Corinna fr. 664b *PMG*.

334 Medea's aid is instrumental for the Argonauts' success, and the sorceress even enjoys her very own ἀριστεία when she dispatches Talos on Crete, in parallel to Polydeuces in Bebrycia, the Boreads in Thynia, Orpheus at Anthemoessa, etc. (see 188). For Medea as an Argonaut and heroine, see, e.g.: Dyck 1989: 455, 468; Richey 2008: 159–170; Álvarez Espinoza 2018; cf. Daniel-Müller 2012.

sibility of identifying Apollo with Helius, there is arguably even more evidence for a subtle rivalry between these two (distinct) deities running throughout the poem. Thus, for instance, Hunter offers an interpretation of Apollo's epiphany at Thynias that reads the scene not as an announcement of the brilliant god's conflation with Helius, but rather as

> part of a contrast, devised by Apollonius to inform much of the epic, between Apollo, a sun god of beneficent power, and the older god Helios and his descendants whose light, whether it be the radiance of Aietes' helmet (3.1228–1230) or the sinister gleam in Medea's eye (3.886, 4.726–729, 1669–1672), is threatening and destructive.[335]

It is easy to see how much of the data considered above could be reshuffled to accommodate this oppositional framing of the relationship between Apollo and Helius (and, I would add, between Apollo and Selene). Jason's close ties with Apollo can now be connected to his enmity with Aeetes, Helius' son and virtually his living icon on earth.[336] For her part, Medea inherits these same solar connotations from her father, as Hunter notes, but she is also associated multiple times with the moon: her sorcery empowers her to control its courses (3.533, 4.59–61),[337] and as noted above, Mene directly compares herself to Medea in her soliloquy in Book 4 (54–65).[338] On this reckoning of the evidence, Apollo, the second-generation Olympian sun god, is associated with our Greek protagonist, while the older sun and moon deities, children of the Titan Hyperion, are connected to his Colchian antagonist and love interest (whose relationship with Jason is, needless to say, frequently ambivalent and ultimately tragic).[339]

This contrast, in turn, can be integrated into a larger network of oppositions between Greeks and "barbarians" in the *Arg.*, the chief among which is

---

[335] Hunter 1995: 18.

[336] See 3.245–246, 307–313; 4.220–221, and especially 3.1228–1230, a description of Aeetes' golden helm that draws directly on the ecphrasis of Helius in his *Homeric Hymn* (31.10–12; Campbell 1981 ad loc.).

[337] Note that like Artemis, Medea's patron goddess Hecate could also be assimilated to Selene (first in Soph. fr. 535 Radt).

[338] It must be admitted, however, that Mene frames her relationship to Medea in decidedly antagonistic terms. Żybert (2009: 86) notes that the literal kinship between Medea and Selene (her great-aunt) adds piquancy to this scene. Given Aeetes' solar connections, note also the alternative tradition that makes Selene Helius' daughter (see Roscher 2.3170–3171).

[339] For the associations of Colchis with Helius and Selene, see Braund 1994: 21; Schaaf 2014: 149–151.

temporal. For all the stress that Apollonius lays on the Argonauts' venerable antiquity, from their very first epithet (παλαιγενέων, 1.1.)[340] to the scores of αἴτια that they inaugurate in the course of their adventure, the roots of Colchian civilization simply dwarf those of the Greeks in historical remoteness. Colchis is, as Vian calls it, a pre-Olympian land,[341] which the narrator himself dubs "Titanian" (Τιτηνίδος Αἴης, 4.131).[342] It is a realm in which Prometheus is still bound (2.1246–1259, 3.865–866)[343] and where the strongest oaths are sworn by Gaia and Uranus (3.699, 714–716),[344] the most archaic generation in the pantheon.[345] As per the excursus on Colchian history related by Argus in Book 4, Colchis is a primordial civilization, founded as a colony of Egypt at a time when, significantly, the only people in Greece were the Arcadians, who existed even before the moon did (4.264).[346] The use of the moon as a temporal marker implies that it, too, is of extraordinary antiquity, and this impression is confirmed elsewhere in the poem. In Orpheus' cosmogony, the generation of the sun, moon, and stars are preceded only by the earth, sea, and sky (1.496–500); and just like Aea, the narrator applies the epithet "Titanian" to the moon goddess, too (Τιτηνὶς ... θεὰ ... Μήνη, 4.54–55).[347]

340   For παλαιγενέων as a metageneric tag for epic poetry, underscoring the fact that the genre's heroes belong to the mythical past, see 256n110. In fact, Apollonius' usage finds a good precedent outside of epic poetry that is also contextually apropos in Pindar's mention of the "ancient Minyae" (παλαιγόνων Μινυᾶν, Ol. 14.4). The Theban poet is referencing the great antiquity of Orchomenus, which is directly connected to Jason's own heritage (cf. Arg. 3.1085–1095); moreover, Apollonius may be playing on the fact that the Argonauts too are called "Minyae" (cf. Pyth. 4.69, Arg. 1.229–233).
341   Vian 2002: 1.174.
342   On this epithet, see Hunter 2015 ad loc.
343   See further Hunter 1991: 87.
344   Colchian burial customs reflect the same religious mentality: at death, men are hung in trees and women are buried in the earth, so that Uranus and Gaia each have a share of the dead (3.200–209; Schaaf 2014: 149).
345   Caneva 2007: 90 (= 2010a: 173). Caneva also notes the Colchians' predilection toward Hecate, who is repeatedly identified as the daughter of the Titan Perses (3.467, 478, 1035; 4.1020).
346   Notably, Egypt is described as "the mother of earlier-born, vigorous people" (μήτηρ Αἰγυπτος προτερηγενέων αἰζηῶν, 4.268). It is tempting to read the rare comparative adjective προτερηγενής (found only here and at Callim. Hymn 1.58 in extant Greek literature) as responding to παλαιγενέων in the proem (1.1): the Egyptians are even more ancient than the heroes of Greek legend. For other hints in this speech of Egyptian primacy over Greek civilization, see further McPhee 2021b: 182–184. Argus' speech implicitly shows up Jason's Hellenocentric claim that his ancestor Deucalion founded the first cities (Arg. 3.1087–1088), since Sesostris' foundations long predate his (Caneva 2007: 94; 2010b: 51 n. 4; see further 58; Hunter 1991: 97).
347   Elsewhere Apollonius applies the epithet Τιτηνίς only to the root of the flower generated from Prometheus' ichor (3.865).

There is, moreover, a particular ethnic dimension to the opposition of Apollo against Helius and Selene. In associating the sun and the moon with the Colchians, Apollonius exploits the popular Greek perception that these are primal gods especially venerated by "barbarians." For instance, the ethnographic tradition commonly attributed lunar and solar worship with varying degrees of exclusivity to non-Greek peoples;[348] Plato speculated that because of their observable circuits through the heavens, the sun and moon were among the earliest gods and were worshipped by all people everywhere;[349] and Aristophanes can even imagine a comic scenario in which Helius and Selene wish to deliver Greece into the hands of their barbarian worshippers (*Pax* 406–411). Apollo, conversely, is the preeminent "god of the Greeks," as Herodotus' Croesus calls him (τὸν θεὸν τῶν Ἑλλήνων, 1.90.2); indeed, when the Aeschylean Atossa sees an omen presaging the outcome of Xerxes' invasion of Greece, it is Apollo's bird, the hawk, which symbolizes the Greek armies in their struggle against the Persians (*Pers.* 205–210).[350] Apollo's role as the god who directed Greek colonization efforts is especially germane in the context of the Argonautic myth;[351] in fact, from at least the fifth century BCE, the historical Colchis boasted a cult of Apollo Hegemon, which may have been associated with the site's Greek colonization.[352]

To draw all these threads together: it should now be clear how Apollonius' substitution of Apollo in place of Helius and especially Selene could be incorporated into a particularly triumphalist reading of the *Argonautica*. In particular, the replacement of a barbarian-coded Titanic goddess connected with the Colchians by a Greek Olympian god associated with the Argonauts could adumbrate many of the most chauvinistic features of the myth boiled down

---

348 E.g., according to Herodotus, the Persians worship only the sun (cf. 7.54), moon (cf. 7.37.4), and other natural elements (1.131.2); the Massagetae worship only the sun (1.216.4; cf. 1.212.3); the Egyptians sacrifice swine only to the moon and Dionysus (2.47.2), and they also worship the sun (2.59.3, 73, 111.4); and the Libyan nomads only sacrifice to the moon and the sun (4.188). This trope would continue among the Romans; e.g., Caesar (*BG* 6.21) reports that the Germans worship only the gods they can see for themselves, like the sun, Vulcan, and the moon (see Rose 1937: 173–174).
349 Pl. *Cra.* 397c–d; see further *Ap.* 26d, *Leg.* 10.887d–e. See also Prodicus fr. D16 Laks-Most.
350 See Garvie 2009: 102–103 (referring in this context to Apollo as "that most Greek of all gods").
351 For colonial themes in the Argonautic myth and in Apollonius' treatment thereof, see, e.g.: Moreau 2000; Stephens 2003: 173–196, 2011; Karanika 2010; Thalmann 2011: ch. 4. For Apollo's role in colonization narratives, see, e.g., Dougherty 1993: 18–21.
352 See Braund 1996: 17–18.

to its structuralist essentials: new over old, Greek over barbarian, man over woman. This movement would correspond with the expansion of Greek civilization into new portions of the οἰκουμένη, which in turn mirrors the poem's Hesiodic conception of cosmic history as a story of transition from a state of originary chaos to the order guaranteed by the reign of Zeus.[353] And, finally, this argument could draw support from many other passages in which these polarities are in evidence—perhaps the starkest example is the Amycus episode (2.1–163), which stages the Greek victory over lawless, even monstrous barbarity in stridently black-and-white terms.[354]

4.6.3 Conclusion: Apollonius' Multivalent Allusion to *HH* 32.18–19

Having sketched out these three major approaches to reading the *Arg.*'s very first allusion, I would now like to take a step back and reflect holistically on the result. To begin with, I have not advocated for the rightness of just one of these approaches, and that is for two reasons. First, the matter of how any given reader might react to Apollonius' allusion strikes me as highly subjective; the evidence from modern scholarship alone testifies that different readers will naturally configure the relationships obtaining between Helius, Selene, and Apollo in this intertextual network into diverse arrangements. Second, I find that while each of the interpretations presented above genuinely keys into important aspects of the *Arg.*'s thematic economy or of Apollonius' historical context, none of them is hermeneutically airtight, as it were. The *Arg.* is a rich text that frequently invites us to draw internal and external connections, but it is also sufficiently complex to make overly schematic interpretations difficult to sustain over the entire course of the poem. For instance, if we insist on the syncretism of Apollo and Helius, we must then find a way to account for Jason's association with the former deity and his enemy Aeetes' simultaneous association with the latter. But if we instead choose to read Apollo and Helius as oppositional figures, we will then have to contend with the challenge posed by Medea, who occupies a much more ambiguous position both in terms of the plot (her aid to Jason is indispensable, and yet she will ultimately prove to be a dangerous ally) and on a symbolic level (e.g., she is a Heliad, but she is also likened to Apollo's beloved twin sister Artemis). Similarly, while I find that many of the themes of the "triumphalist" reading presented above are

---

353 For such a reading of the *Arg.*, see Clauss 2000, who demonstrates that throughout the poem, the old is relentlessly replaced by the new as time marches ever onward toward the Hesiodic Iron Age.

354 See, e.g.: Hunter 1991: 87–90; Durbec 2008: 69.

implicit in the Argonautic myth, Apollonius' own rendition thereof in the *Arg.* often works to complicate such superficial appraisals—we need think only of his sympathetic portrait of the lovestruck Medea or of his problematic presentation of Jason's heroism, to name just two of the most obvious counter-indicators. But that is a subject for another occasion.

For the purposes of this book, my primary aim has been to demonstrate the enormous potential of taking Apollonius' allusions to the *HH*s seriously. It should be clear that, however we choose to interpret the *Arg.*'s inaugural allusion, the decision to interrogate in depth the original context of the model text—even in the case of a "minor hymn" like *HH* 32—can uncover layers of nuance and sophistication that resonate profoundly with the alluding text, and on a variety of levels. We can thus greatly enrich our reading of the *Arg.* if we follow Apollonius' lead and treat the *HH*s as poetic models of the first order—on a par, in fact, with the *Iliad* and *Odyssey*.

Indeed, the survey of exemplary *HH* intertexts and allusions undertaken in this section of the introduction should indicate both the depth and range of Apollonius' engagement with this corpus. Naturally, given the subject matter of the hymns, a great number of Apollonius' allusions relate to his portrayal of the gods and of divine influence on human affairs, but our poet is also capable of mining the collection for more human details with which to flesh out his epic world and of putting contexts from the hymns in dialogue with the *Arg.* to achieve a variety of other ends (e.g., to serve a commentarial function or to offer a lens through which to view his multifaceted characters). In fact, this survey has not even touched on other potential categories of intertexts that a more comprehensive classifactory scheme might encompass. For instance, "philological allusions," which would evoke prooftexts in the *HH*s to marshal evidence on debated grammatical points,[355] and allusions to particular hymnic contexts made by reusing *hapax legomena* from the *HH*s—a phenomenon that will surface several times in this book—are both subjects deserving of systematic investigations in their own right. But at this point, now that this survey has suggested the rich returns in store for those who would study Apollonius' localized engagements with the *HH*s, I may now begin to transition to the core of this book's argument, which will seek to erect a framework on which future studies can situate themselves by elucidating the contours of Apollonius' engagement with these models at the macroscopic level.

---

355 E.g., see 71n329 on the scansion of κλέα.

5 Outline of Chapters

By reviewing the essential facts surrounding the *HH*s, especially their formal features, and by establishing Apollonius' thoroughgoing interest in initiating an allusive dialogue with Homer's corpus of hymns, this introduction has prepared the way for the analysis to come. In the chapters that follow, I detail the *Arg.*'s formal affinity with the genre of hymnic as well as heroic ἔπος and reveal Apollonius' overarching poetic strategy of uniting the two streams of the Homeric hexameter tradition—Homer's epics and his hymns—into one innovative package, an "epic hymn" in honor of the Argonauts. This generic hybridity is encoded above all by the poem's hymnic frame, but is also reflected in certain metapoetic passages scattered throughout the work. Furthermore, the poem's affiliation with hymnody conditions the presentation of the epic narrative itself through a variety of narrative devices that can be associated with the AR narrator's "hymnic voice." Demonstrating these theses will be the burden of the next four chapters, whose contents I will now preview.

The body of the book is divided into two parts of two chapters each. The first is dedicated to establishing the *Arg.*'s generic hybridity on formal grounds; the second, to a narratological study of the narrator's hymnic voice. Chapter 1 scrutinizes the *Arg.*'s beginning and ending, those places in a poem where generic signals tend to cluster most densely. I argue that these passages (esp. *Arg.* 1.1–2, 4.1773–1775) frame the poem as a Homeric-style hymn dedicated to the Argonauts themselves in their capacity as the divinized objects of hero cult; the hymn's Myth in this case is blown up to the proportions of a four-book epic narrative. My analysis relies on a diachronic method of reading and rereading: on a first-time, linear reading of the *Arg.*, its introit can be understood in a variety of ways, including as the evocation of a Hymnic Proem dedicated to Apollo. The hymnic Envoi at the end of the *Arg.* is, however, unambiguously addressed to the Argonauts and thus retrospectively reveals the poem as a hymn dedicated to its own epic protagonists. With this insight, the re-reader is equipped to reinterpret the epic conventions of the *Arg.*'s introit as their nigh-identical brethren, the formal features of the Exordium to a *HH*. My analysis of the *Arg.*'s hymnic frame also includes a survey of its numerous intertexts, especially from the *HH*s.

The second chapter builds on the first by examining Apollonius' depiction of hero cult within his epic narrative. In a marked departure from Homer, Apollonius portrays the practices of hero cult repeatedly and explicitly. In a series of close readings, I interpret several of these passages as metapoetic commentaries on the dual generic significance of the *Arg.* as both epic and hymn; this generic hybridity is facilitated by the ambivalence at the heart of the Greek cultural concept of the "hero," who is at once the subject of epic memorializing and the object of religious veneration in cult that includes, inter alia, worship in hymns. These metapoetic passages also suggest a possible motive for Apollonius' decision to render the introit so ambiguous and to reveal the hymnic status of the *Arg.* in full clarity only at the end of the poem: the great heroes of myth conventionally win heroization through their commission of great labors (ἄεθλοι), and it is only when the Argonauts' trials have finally come to an end (*Arg.* 4.1775–1777) that the narrator openly acknowledges their present status as divinized heroes. Apollonius' experiment in uniting the two great Homeric hexametric genres into a singular "epic hymn" finds smaller-scale parallels in the work of his contemporaries, Callimachus and Theocritus, as well as intriguing precedents in Simonides' Platea elegy and in one of the *HH*s themselves, the *Hymn to Heracles the Lionhearted*. I suggest that this last piece might even have served as a model for certain aspects of the structure of the *Arg.* qua epic hymn.

The second half of the book constitutes a study of the hymnic dimension of the Apollonian narrator's multitextured voice. As such, chapters 3 and 4 treat narratological issues, although intertextuality with the *HH*s remains an ever-present tool of analysis. Chapter 3 begins by examining features of Apollonius' epic narrative that find precedent not in the HEs, but in the *HH*s. Many of these narrative devices are associated with broader trends in Hellenistic poetry, and especially with Callimachus, such as the narrator's conspicuous interventions in the narrative in his own voice or etiological "external prolepses" (i.e., "flash-forwards" past the time of the Argonautic narrative) that declare that "to this day" (ἔτι νῦν) some trace of the mythical expedition still persists in the places touched by the Argo. My thesis is that Apollonius might have looked to the *HH*s for Homeric authorization of these "Alexandrian" literary devices; indeed, in some cases, I show that Apollonius uses "two-tier" allusions to signal his debt to the *HH*s as well as his contemporaries as models for a given device.

Chapter 4 turns to the clearest manifestations of the Apollonian narrator's hymnic voice: the numerous passages within the *Arg.* in which the narrator or his characters engage in hymnody themselves. The narrator adopts a hymnic tone in his apostrophes to Eros (4.445–449) or to the Argonauts in the Libyan episode (4.1383–1387), but what is especially noteworthy is how often Apollonius blurs the boundary between his characters' hymnic speech and that of his narrator (in narratological terms, this device is a species of "metalepsis"). In some passages, the narrator seems to get swept up in his characters' religious enthusiasm and joins in their praise of a god *in propria persona*, in a device that I call "contagious hymnody"; in others, the voices of the narrator and the character invoking a god can hardly be distinguished, in a device that I have dubbed "hymnic narratization." Many of the narrative techniques surveyed in both chapters 3 and 4 come together in the Argonauts' worship of Apollo in the Thynias episode (*Arg.* 2.669–719), which, from a narratological point of view, is perhaps the most complex passage in the poem. Here, more than anywhere else, the Apollonian narrator's hymnic voice is on full display, and Apollonius' hymnic narrative techniques are integrated with a sophisticated program of allusions to other Rhapsodic Hymns to Apollo, namely, the Homeric (3) and Callimachean (2).

In this study's conclusion, I first summarize the results of the investigation, and I then leave off with final meditations on two issues raised obliquely by the analysis of the body chapters but which are of central importance in any interpretation of the *Arg*. First, I build on the body of recent scholarship that has sought to contextualize Apollonius' epic within third-century BCE Alexandria by pointing to the political overtones of the poet's transfiguration of the "secular" genre of Homeric epic into an "epic hymn" dedicated to its own divinized heroes. I argue that this generic innovation may correlate to the contemporary divinization of the Ptolemies, whose relatively innovative ruler cult resonated with the centuries-old Greek worship of heroes in a number of ways. The second issue I ponder is the relationship between the Argonauts' heroization and their often-problematic heroism, especially with regards to their leader Jason. I show that Apollonius, far from shying away from this problem, actually throws it into relief on more than one occasion by juxtaposing some of the heroes' shabbiest behavior with foreshadowing of their destined heroization. These two issues are interrelated, insofar as Jason especially has increasingly been read as a model of leadership aligned with the Ptolemaic dynasty. What are the political implications of a nuanced portrayal of the Argonauts' heroism if their heroization is analogous to the Ptolemaic ruler cult? It is my hope that this line of inquiry may productively reframe from a new perspective a long-standing debate in Apollonian studies on the status of heroism in the *Arg*.

PART 1

The Argonautica *as Epic Hymn*

∴

CHAPTER 1

A Diachronic Reading of the *Argonautica*'s Hymnic Frame

This chapter is devoted to hardly more than thirty verses, and the real focus falls on only about five of them. Despite their brevity, however, they are critically placed at the beginning and end of the *Arg.* and have major ramifications for our construal of the poem's hybrid genre.[1] Consequently, they are some of the most widely discussed passages in the poem, though it is my hope that a new approach may add something new to the conversation. I refer to the poem's "hymnic frame,"[2] consisting of the opening Invocation of Apollo in the introit[3] (1.1–22, esp. 1–2) and the Salutation and Prayer to the Argonauts themselves at the conclusion of the narrative (4.1773–1781). Despite a sizable bibliography on these passages, some basic questions still remain. For example, if the *Arg.* does indeed bear a "hymnic frame," then what *sort* of hymn does this frame presuppose? I argue that the poem possesses not merely a "hymnic" frame, but more specifically, a "Homeric-hymnic" frame. Other critical questions include: where does the "hymn" end and the "epic" begin? What (fictional) performative or discursive context(s) does the poet's hymnic frame conjure up? And if we are right to speak of one coherent "hymnic frame," then who, precisely, is being hymned—Apollo, invoked at the beginning, or the Argonauts, hailed at the end?

In this chapter, I hope to lay out sound answers to all of these questions through a close reading of the hymnic frame and its intertexts. More particularly, I aim to shed new light on these problems through a diachronic approach to the text, which distinguishes first-time readers, who do not possess knowledge of later parts of the poem as they read through it in linear fashion, from re-readers, whose memory of the entire poem can enable them to make con-

---

1 Genre markers tend to cluster especially around the beginning of a work (Fowler 1982: ch. 6; see further Conte 1986: 70; Harrison 2007: 30–31), but in Apollonius' case, the beginning of the *Arg.* is highly ambiguous, as we will see, and it is the work's ending that clarifies the poem's generic affiliations.
2 A term used by, e.g.: Goldhill 1991: 287; Hunter 1996: 46; Vox 2002 ("cornici innodiche"); similar "framing" terminology is used by Belloni 1996: 148 ("incorniciare") and Hitch 2012: 156 ("a sort of pious frame around the whole poem").
3 For my use of the term "introit," see 17n90.

nections with later portions of the poem as they reread earlier ones.⁴ In my view, most scholars have missed the true complexity of the hymnic frame either because they read one passage in isolation from the other or, on the contrary, because they read synoptically, viewing both passages at once from the lofty vantage point of the critic well-acquainted with the whole poem. This analysis misses the dynamic quality of Apollonius' introit, whose potential meanings fluctuate over time as readers are presented with new data about the poem's genre at its conclusion.⁵

Notably, this diachronic approach is not only truer to the way that most readers actually experience a given text, but it is almost explicitly endorsed by Apollonius himself at the end of the *Arg.*, where the narrator effectively prays that first-time readers will become re-readers: "May these songs year after year be sweeter for men to sing" (αἵδε δ' ἀοιδαὶ | εἰς ἔτος ἐξ ἔτεος γλυκερώτεραι εἶεν ἀείδειν | ἀνθρώποις, 4.1773–1775).⁶ How would the *Arg.* become "sweeter" and sweeter with each passing year? One answer, I would posit, is that the poem becomes hermeneutically richer each time it is reread; and indeed, if our putative first-time readers answer the narrator's Prayer and return to the beginning

---

4 The classic example of this "diachronic" method within the discipline of Classics is Winkler's groundbreaking narratological study of Apuleius' *Golden Ass* (1985); see esp. the exposition of his method at 10–11. A more recent example of this method, applied to Xenophon's *Cyropedia*, is provided by Altman 2022. See further Sharrock 2018 for valuable insights on the importance of memory and rereading in forming literary interpretations. Among Apollonian studies, Byre 2002 adopts a linear style of reading the poem as if for the first time, though he does not explore the ramifications of rereading.

5 In this chapter, I assume for simplicity's sake a hypothetical reader who reads and rereads the entire *Arg.* essentially as we know it today, but the poem's actual publication history during Apollonius' lifetime was probably much more complicated than this model assumes. For instance, Apollonius may well have given readings or otherwise circulated excerpts of the poem while composition was still underway (see, e.g.: Hutchinson 1988: 89; Harder 2012: 1.33; Clauss 2019b), and in a few places, the scholia even offer quotations of an earlier edition (προ-έκδοσις) of the *Arg.* (see Pfeiffer 1968: 141–142). But as important as these considerations are for a variety of issues (such as establishing the relative date[s] of the *Arg.*'s "publication[s]"), I sidestep these vexed questions here by basing my analysis on the *Arg.* in the "finalized" form in which it has come down to us.

6 Although Apollonius' text here speaks of "singing," it is conventionally understood to refer to reading—whether for the reason that Fränkel (1968: 621 n. 356) provides ("'Lesen' heißt hier ἀείδειν [*sic*]: im Altertum las man in der Regel laut, und Hexameter wurden nicht gesprochen sondern im Singsang vorgetragen"; for reading aloud in antiquity, see, e.g., Knox 1968 and Svenbro 1993), or because ἀοιδαί and cognates in Apollonius can be interpreted as a literary "conceit," according to the stylized manner in which epic refers to itself, even after it had ceased to be sung (González 2000: 283 n. 37). But on the question of written-ness vs. performance see further below.

of the *Arg.*, their readings really will become enriched as the introit begins to take on new meanings.[7] I propose that such a dynamic reading and rereading of the hymnic frame does justice to its carefully crafted complexity.

I will proceed as a real first-time reader would, beginning in section 1 with an analysis of the introit without presupposing knowledge of the Envoi at the other end of the poem. I show that several elements of the introit do indeed resonate with the rhetoric of Greek hymnody, and specifically with the subcategory of the *HH*s, but I also show that the introit itself is engineered to achieve a high degree of ambiguity for a first-time reader. The hymnic elements in the introit could be taken to support the widespread view that the *Arg.* begins with a Hymnic Proem dedicated to Apollo, but the introit can equally be understood in other ways with no connections to hymnody; two of the most prominent views hold that Apollo is invoked as the god who inspires the *Arg.*'s composition or as the god whose oracle to Pelias catalyzes the poem's plot. Nevertheless, the "Hymnic Proem" interpretation is powerfully supported by an allusion to the *Homeric Hymn to Selene* (32.18–19), among a number of other intertexts, including Aratus' Hymnic Proem to Zeus and several other Hymnic Proems in honor of Apollo. I round off this reading of the introit with an excursus considering the (in my opinion) mistaken view that the Invocation of Apollo functions not as a Hymnic Proem to Apollo, but as an Exordium to the entire *Arg.* qua hymn dedicated to that god.

Section 2 turns to the *Arg.*'s Envoi. Through a careful consideration of the structure and rhetoric of this passage, read in light of a number of important intertexts, I locate Apollonius' Envoi, just like his introit, firmly within the tradition of the *HH*s. I then make note of the significance of Apollonius' Envoi, which cannot be overstated: the narrator's Salutation and Prayer to the Argonauts presupposes their postmortem divinization as cult heroes—a key piece of information that had been unavailable to the reader experiencing the introit for the first time. Accordingly, section 3 returns to the introit to reevaluate it in light of the new interpretative data presented in the Envoi. I argue that the Envoi retrospectively recasts the entire *Arg.* as a hymn to its own heroized protagonists, and to confirm this hypothesis, I show that the introit can indeed be reread as the Exordium to a hymn to the Argonauts on the model of the *HH*s. Such a reading would hardly occur to a first-time reader, still ignorant of the

---

[7] See further Clare 2002: 284–285; Schaaf 2014: 330–331. Hunter (2000) has quite fittingly used the phrase εἰς ἔτος ἐξ ἔτεος γλυκερώτεραι as the title for his survey of scholarship on the poem since Fränkel's 1961 OCT edition, for the passage of time has certainly enriched our reading of the *Arg.*

cult status that will ultimately be claimed for the Argonauts, but it is available to the re-reader in light of the poem's Envoi. To the extent that the *Arg.* is now recognized as a hymn to the Argonauts, the Apolline "Hymnic Proem" interpretation of the introit will, for most readers, turn out to have been a red herring. I conclude by drawing some preliminary inferences about Apollonius' approach to using the *HH*s as poetic models.

1 The Introit

1.1 *What Kind of Hymn?*

The *Arg.* begins with a relatively long introit of twenty-two lines,[8] whose structure is conventionally divided into three parts of unequal length: a statement of the general theme (1.1–4), a summary of the "prehistory" of the Argonautic narrative (5–17), and the announcement of the poem's narrative program (18–22):[9]

> Ἀρχόμενος σέο, Φοῖβε, παλαιγενέων κλέα φωτῶν
> μνήσομαι, οἳ Πόντοιο κατὰ στόμα καὶ διὰ πέτρας
> Κυανέας βασιλῆος ἐφημοσύνῃ Πελίαο
> χρύσειον μετὰ κῶας ἐύζυγον ἤλασαν Ἀργώ.
> 5 τοίην γὰρ Πελίης φάτιν ἔκλυεν, ὥς μιν ὀπίσσω
> μοῖρα μένει στυγερή, τοῦδ᾽ ἀνέρος, ὅν τιν᾽ ἴδοιτο
> δημόθεν οἰοπέδιλον, ὑπ᾽ ἐννεσίῃσι δαμῆναι.
> δηρὸν δ᾽ οὐ μετέπειτα τεὴν κατὰ βάξιν Ἰήσων
> χειμερίοιο ῥέεθρα κιὼν διὰ ποσσὶν Ἀναύρου
> 10 ἄλλο μὲν ἐξεσάωσεν ὑπ᾽ ἰλύος, ἄλλο δ᾽ ἔνερθεν
> κάλλιπεν αὖθι πέδιλον ἐνισχόμενον προχοῇσιν.
> ἵκετο δ᾽ ἐς Πελίην αὐτοσχεδὸν ἀντιβολήσων
> εἰλαπίνης, ἣν πατρὶ Ποσειδάωνι καὶ ἄλλοις
> ῥέζε θεοῖς, Ἥρης δὲ Πελασγίδος οὐκ ἀλέγιζεν.
> 15 αἶψα δὲ τόν γ᾽ ἐσιδὼν ἐφράσσατο, καί οἱ ἄεθλον
> ἔντυε ναυτιλίης πολυκηδέος, ὄφρ᾽ ἐνὶ πόντῳ
> ἠὲ καὶ ἀλλοδαποῖσι μετ᾽ ἀνδράσι νόστον ὀλέσσῃ.

---

8 In this respect Apollonius imitates (and outdoes) the *Odyssey*, with its twenty-one-line introit (see Gainsford 2003), rather than the *Iliad*, whose introit is only seven lines long.

9 For a structural analysis of the introit, see, e.g.: Hurst 1967: 39–44; Fusillo 1985: 365; Clauss 1993: 22–23.

νῆα μὲν οὖν οἱ πρόσθεν ἔτι κλείουσιν ἀοιδοὶ
Ἄργον Ἀθηναίης καμέειν ὑποθημοσύνῃσιν.
20 νῦν δ' ἂν ἐγὼ γενεήν τε καὶ οὔνομα μυθησαίμην
ἡρώων, δολιχῆς τε πόρους ἁλός, ὅσσα τ' ἔρεξαν
πλαζόμενοι· Μοῦσαι δ' ὑποφήτορες εἶεν ἀοιδῆς.

> Beginning with you, Phoebus, I shall recall the famous deeds of people born long ago, who, at the command of King Pelias, sailed the well-benched Argo through the mouth of the Black Sea and between the Cyanean rocks to fetch the golden fleece.
> For such was the oracle that Pelias heard, that a horrible fate awaited him in the future: to perish through the designs of that man whom he would see coming from the people with only one sandal. And not long afterwards, in accordance with your prophecy, as Jason was crossing the streams of the wintry Anaurus on foot, he rescued one sandal from the mud, but left the other there in the depths, held back by the current. He came right away to Pelias to share in the banquet that the king was offering to his father Poseidon and the rest of the gods, but to Pelasgian Hera he paid no regard. As soon as he saw Jason, he took note, and arranged for him the ordeal of a very arduous voyage, so that either on the sea or else among foreign people he would lose any chance of returning home.
> As for the ship, the songs of former bards still tell how Argus built it according to Athena's instructions. But now I wish to relate the lineage and names of the heroes, their journeys on the vast sea, and all they did as they wandered; and may the Muses be inspirers of my song.

As we will see, Apollonian scholarship is nearly unanimous in deeming this introit, and particularly its first line and a half, "hymnic."[10] More specifically, these lines contain several elements that collectively constitute a "system reference" to the Greek genre of hymns broadly conceived.[11] Signals to this effect include, for instance, the sustained address to a god (σέο, Φοῖβε, 1; τεήν, 8)[12] or the use of οἵ in line 2, which in this context could be interpreted as a Hymnic

---

10   Cf. Köhnken 2000: 56 n. 5 for a firm exception.
11   For "system references," see 10n50.
12   Emphasized particularly by Collins 1967: 7. Interestingly, several critics have objected to the transmitted τεήν in line 8 on the grounds that "it is not in accordance with epic convention that, after the invocation, reference should be made to it" (Seaton 1914: 17), over-

Relative that facilitates the transition from the initial Evocation to the Attributive Section or Myth.[13]

In this subsection, however, I argue that a well-read ancient audience would have interpreted the system reference even more specifically as a reference to a particular subset of Greek hymns, namely, the *HH*s—not least because, as is well known, the epic begins with an allusion to the Envoi of the *Homeric Hymn to Selene*: "Beginning with you [Selene], I will sing the famous deeds of mortals half-divine" (σέο δ' ἀρχόμενος κλέα φωτῶν | ᾄσομαι ἡμιθέων, 32.18–19). I will return to this allusion later in this chapter, but for now, suffice it to say that it signals the importance of the *HH*s for Apollonius' project.[14]

But for the reader who does not recognize the specific allusion to *Selene*, there is another distinctive reference to the diction of the *HH*s in the second line's μνήσομαι, the verb with which Apollonius replaces the *Selene* hymn's ᾄσομαι.[15] This verb in this form is characteristic of the "Poet's Task"[16] formula with which many of the *HH*s conclude: "And I will remember both you and another song" (αὐτὰρ ἐγὼ καὶ σεῖο καὶ ἄλλης μνήσομ' ἀοιδῆς).[17] Significantly, the verb is also used in two exceptional cases to introduce the Subject of the hymn.[18] The first instance occurs in the major *Hymn to Apollo* (3); the second, in the midlength *Hymn to Dionysus* (7):[19]

Μνήσομαι οὐδὲ λάθωμαι Ἀπόλλωνος ἑκάτοιο ...

Let me call to mind and not forget Apollo the far-shooter ...
HH 3.1

looking the fact that Apollonius here mixes epic with hymnic conventions; cf. Campbell 1971: 402.
13 See the discussion of the structure of the *HH*s in introduction, section 2.2.
14 See further the discussions of this allusion in the introduction, sections 2.4 and 4.6.
15 Morrison 2020: 129.
16 For the term, see Janko 1981: 15.
17 The Poet's Task formula is adduced as a parallel to *Arg.* 1.1–2 by: De Marco 1963: 351; Collins 1967: 3; Romeo 1985: 21; Goldhill 1991: 287 n. 7; Belloni 1996: 140 n. 19; DeForest 1994: 38; Sistakou 2001: 259 n. 69; Wheeler 2002: 45–46; Scherer 2006: 116 n. 391; Faulkner 2011c: 193; Murray 2018: 205–206; Júnior 2021: 110 n. 7.
18 Cf. Evans 2001: 63. The equivalence of μνήσομαι and forms of ἀείδω in this context may reflect the Homeric usage of μιμνήσκομαι as "a kind of technical term" within "the vocabulary of epic verse-making" that denotes the bard's use of his recollective faculties in oral composition; see Moran 1975 (quotations at 198).
19 These hymns that use μνήσομαι as their Evocatory Verb are adduced as parallels by: Stenzel 1908: 14; Romeo 1985: 21; Fantuzzi 1988: 22 n. 35; Goldhill 1991: 287 n. 7; Sistakou 2001: 259 n. 69; Berkowitz 2004: 60 n. 27; Scherer 2006: 116 n. 391; Faulkner 2011c: 193 with n. 80; Hall 2013: 24; Júnior 2021: 110 n. 7; Tsakiris 2022: 20.

Ἀμφὶ Διώνυσον Σεμέλης ἐρικυδέος υἱόν
μνήσομαι, ὡς ἐφάνη παρὰ θῖν' ἁλὸς ἀτρυγέτοιο ...

Concerning Dionysus, glorious Semele's son, I will remember how he appeared by the shore of the barren sea ...
HH 7.1–2

The *Dionysus* hymn matches the *Arg.* introit in its placement of the enjambed verb and thus provides an exact precedent for Apollonius' usage. The parallel with the *Apollo* hymn is perhaps less precise on formal grounds,[20] but its use of μνήσομαι as the first word of one of the major hymns grants it special prominence; moreover, the verb's object is Apollo, the addressee of *Arg.* 1.1, in the genitive case (cf. Apollonius' σέο).

The *Arg.*'s first word, ἀρχόμενος, similarly resonates with the *HHs*. This present-tense participle is drawn directly from the Envoi of the *Selene* hymn (σέο δ' ἀρχόμενος, 32.18), but it has further parallels in the Envois of several other *HHs* that use its aorist form in their "Poet's Task" (σεῦ δ' ἐγὼ ἀρξάμενος: 5.293, 9.9, 18.11; ἐκ σέο δ' ἀρξάμενος, 31.18).[21] It is also true that many hymns in the collection begin with a form of ἄρχομαι, though here the parallel is less exact: the hymns typically employ the introductory formula ἄρχομ' ἀείδειν with the name of the god to be celebrated in the accusative, as in "With Demeter the lovely-haired, the august goddess I begin my song" (Δήμητρ' ἠΰκομον, σεμνὴν θεόν, ἄρχομ' ἀείδειν, 2.1).[22] Apollonius' construction, with the name of the god in the genitive, is almost unparalleled in the collection of *HHs*.[23] It does, however, find precedent in the irregular *HH* 25, which, perhaps notably, features Apollo among its Hymnic Subjects: "With the Muses let me begin, and Apollo and Zeus" (Μουσάων ἄρχωμαι Ἀπόλλωνός τε Διός τε, 1).

---

20 In this case, μνήσομαι is line-initial but not enjambed, and because it is paired with λάθωμαι, it should be construed as a short-vowel subjunctive rather than a future indicative (hence West's translation, "Let me call to mind"). Campbell (1983: 128) notes that Apollonius' μνήσομαι could be taken as subjunctive as well, though it is usually regarded as a performative future.

21 These Envois that use the phrase σεῦ/σέο ἀρξάμενος are adduced as parallels by, e.g.: Carspecken 1952: 111 n. 26; DeForest 1994: 38; Belloni 1996: 140 n. 18; Pietsch 1999: 69 n. 163; Llanos 2017: 6–7; Murray 2018: 205–206. See also Morrison 2020: 129.

22 *HH* 2.1, 11.1, 13.1, 16.1, 22.1, 26.1, 28.1; cf. 9.8, 31.1 (ὑμνεῖν ... ἄρχεο Μοῦσα). Outside of the *HHs*, the ἄρχομ' ἀείδειν construction appears once in an epic-style introit written on an Attic red-figure kylix painted by Douris (Berlin, Antikensammlung, Staatliche Museen 2285), on which see Sider 2010.

23 So Clay 2011: 238: "The use of the genitive of the god to be celebrated with ἄρχομαι does not seem hymnic." See further ibid. n. 25; Rijksbaron 2009: 242 n. 4.

But despite these formal differences, in this context, and especially in light of the Homeric-hymnic μνήσομαι, Apollonius' use of ἀρχόμενος is still reminiscent of the ἄρχομ' ἀείδειν formula found in so many *HH*s. Not only have many modern scholars felt this connection;[24] so did another ancient Greek poet who imitated Apollonius, namely, Dionysius the Periegete.[25] His introit affords an excellent illustration of a critical principle once articulated by Martindale, and to which we will have recourse more than once in this chapter: "Numerous unexplored insights into ancient literature are locked up in imitations, translations and so forth."[26] Dionysius' poem begins (1–3):

Ἀρχόμενος γαῖάν τε καὶ εὐρέα πόντον ἀείδειν
καὶ ποταμοὺς πόλιάς τε καὶ ἀνδρῶν ἄκριτα φῦλα,
μνήσομαι Ὠκεανοῖο βαθυρρόου.

Beginning to sing of the earth and the broad sea, and of the rivers and the cities and the countless tribes of men, I shall recall deep-flowing Ocean.[27]

In the manner of a "two-tier allusion," Dionysius' adaptation of the opening of the *Arg.* also clarifies its background in the *HH*s by melding together their distinctive styles.[28] Dionysius keeps Apollonius' opening with the participle ἀρχόμενος, but instead of providing it with a genitive object as Apollonius does (σέο),[29] he folds it into a version of the Homeric-hymnic ἄρχομ' ἀείδειν formula, to which a series of accusative objects (his geographical subjects) are attached. He thus frames the first line with an allusion first to Apollonius with line-initial ἀρχόμενος and then to the *HH*s with ἀείδειν at line-end. In light of Dionysius' adaptation, it is safe to say that in addition to recalling the Envoi of the hymns to *Selene* and others, Apollonius' ἀρχόμενος also evokes in a more general way the most common introductory formula in the *HH*s, ἄρχομ' ἀείδειν.

---

24   The ἄρχομ' ἀείδειν formula is adduced as a parallel to Apollonius' ἀρχόμενος by, e.g.: De Marco 1963: 351; Collins 1967: 3; Goldhill 1991: 287; DeForest 1994: 38; Albis 1996: 6–7; Wheeler 2002: 45; Petrovic 2012: 153; Júnior 2021: 110 n. 7; Tsakiris 2022: 19–20.
25   Dionysius' imitation is adduced by Stenzel 1908: 14 and Vox 1999: 163, and it is discussed at length by Vox 2002: 154–159.
26   Martindale 1993: 7.
27   The text of Dionysius is from Lightfoot 2014; the workmanlike translation is my own.
28   For this term, see 29*n*147.
29   Dionysius recoups the genitive, however, with the object of μνήσομαι (Ὠκεανοῖο βαθυρρόου). In essence, Dionysius has artfully reversed the Apollonian syntax, incorporating ἀρχόμενος into a formula that takes accusative objects and using μνήσομαι, as is in fact more usual, with the genitive (Lightfoot 2014 ad loc.).

Accordingly, whether or not Apollonius' introit activates memories of any specific passages (e.g., *HH* 32.18–19, 3.1, or 7.1–2), his readers will likely have caught its particularly "Homeric-hymnic" tone. I stress this point because it should serve as a guide to "hymnic" interpretations of the introit and indeed, of the epic as a whole: the programmatic allusions to the *HH*s at the beginning of the *Arg*. suggest that Apollonius privileges them specifically among many potential hymnic models, just as the *Iliad* and *Odyssey* are particularly privileged among the *Arg*.'s epic precursors. Critics should not be discouraged from pursuing possible allusions to non-Homeric hymnody (e.g., Thgn. 1–4, considered below), but the allusions at the beginning of the *Arg*. do add some argumentative weight to interpretations that adduce the *HH*s.

1.2 The *"Hymnic Proem"* Interpretation

Having established the Homeric-hymnic tone of *Arg*. 1.1–2, I now turn to the question of the interpretation of these lines, particularly for a reader encountering them for the first time. Critical opinion on this question is divided into several camps, with many idiosyncratic variants as well as areas of overlap among them. The key phrase on which the debate turns is the poem's first three words, "Beginning with you, Phoebus" (ἀρχόμενος σέο, Φοῖβε). In context, this phrase has inspired at least three major interpretations, each of which has found supporters both in antiquity and in modern scholarship. I will examine each in detail, but for orientation, I first summarize them as follows:

1) The *"Hymnic Proem"* interpretation: Apollo is the addressee of a Hymnic Proem (προοίμιον) that prefaces the epic.
2) The *"inspiration"* interpretation: Apollo inspires the composition of the poem.
3) The *"narrative catalyst"* interpretation: Through his oracle to Pelias, Apollo sets off the chain of events that launches the poem's plot.

I begin with the first, hymnic interpretation of these lines, which comes naturally given the pointed evocations of the *HH*s that we have already encountered. Indeed, the oldest explicit interpretation of the passage on record belongs to the ancient scholiast's comment on the lemma ἀρχόμενος (ad 1.1–4a Wendel),[30] and its analysis has been influential in modern scholarship:

---

30 I say "explicit" interpretation to distinguish "implicit" readings of *Arg*. 1.1–2 that may be reflected in imitations of the passage by other poets, such as we saw with Dionysius' adaptation in the previous section. Scholia are always difficult to date, but the notice at the end of the Book 4 scholia claims that they are collated from commentaries by Theon of Alexandria (first century BCE), Lucillus of Tarrha (mid-first century CE), and a grammarian named Sophocleus (second century CE); see Dickey 2007: 62–63.

Ἀρχόμενος: ἀπὸ περιεκτικοῦ ῥήματος ἡ μετοχὴ ἐσχημάτισται. περιεκτικὰ δέ εἰσιν, ὅσα ⟨καὶ⟩ δρᾶσιν καὶ πάθος ἐμφαίνουσιν, οἷον βιάζομαι, δωροῦμαι, σφαγιάζομαι. οὕτω καὶ τὸ ἄρχομαι τὸ μέν τι σημαίνει 'ἀπὸ σοῦ τὴν ἀρχὴν ποιοῦμαι'— ἔθος γὰρ ἀπὸ θεῶν προοιμιάζεσθαι· 'ἐκ Διὸς ἀρχώμεσθα' (Arat. *Phaen.* i; Theoc. XVII i)—, τὸ δέ τι σημαίνει 'ἀρχαιρεσιαζόμενος ὑπὸ σοῦ' οἷον ἐνθουσιῶν. παραπλησίως γὰρ τοὺς ποιητὰς τοῖς μαινομένοις ἐνθουσιᾶν ⟨λέγεται⟩. κέχρηται δὲ ἐπὶ τοῦ **ἀρχόμενος** παρατατικοῦ μετοχῇ, ἀντὶ τοῦ ἀρξάμενος.

"**Beginning**": the participle is conjugated from a "comprehensive" verb. "Comprehensive" verbs are those that exhibit ⟨both⟩ active and passive meanings, such as βιάζομαι, δωροῦμαι, and σφαγιάζομαι. So, too, in one respect, "**I begin**" means something like "I make a beginning from you"— for it is customary to make a prelude from the gods; e.g., "Let us begin with Zeus" (Arat. *Phaen.* 1; Theoc. *Id.* 17.1)—but in another respect, it means "elected by you," i.e., "inspired." For ⟨it is said⟩ that poets are inspired almost like madmen. With "beginning" rather than "having begun," he uses an imperfective form of the participle.[31]

The scholiast in fact offers two interpretations of Apollonius' ἀρχόμενος (i.e., ἀπὸ σοῦ τὴν ἀρχὴν ποιοῦμαι vs. ἀρχαιρεσιαζόμενος ὑπὸ σοῦ), but for now I will focus only on the first. With the phrase "**make a prelude** from the gods" (ἀπὸ θεῶν **προοιμιάζεσθαι**), the scholiast refers to the practice of prefacing a poem or collection of poetry with a Hymnic **Proem** (προοίμιον) dedicated to a god.[32] There are many examples of such hymnic προοίμια in ancient Greek literature of all periods, with or without the particular verb ἄρχομαι.[33] For instance, Hesiod's *Works and Days* begins with a short Hymnic Proem to Zeus (1–10), and by the same token, the scholiast suggests, Apollonius begins his epic with a brief Hymnic Proem dedicated to Apollo.[34] But Apollonius' introit bears particular comparison with the Hymnic Proem to Zeus that begins Aratus' *Phaenomena*, which may be the source of the scholiast's quotation (ἐκ Διὸς ἀρχώμεσθα), if he does not have in mind Theoc. *Id.* 17.1. Aratus' Proem has long been recognized

---

31 Text of the *Arg.* scholia is taken from Wendel 1935; the translation is my own. For both text and translation, I have also consulted Lachenaud 2010.

32 It is in this restricted, hymnic sense that I use the term "Proem" in this book; see 17n90.

33 Kidd (1997 ad Arat. *Phaen.* 1) collects several examples that specifically use the verb ἄρχομαι.

34 The scholiast's gloss of ἀρχόμενος as 'ἀπὸ σοῦ τὴν ἀρχὴν ποιοῦμαι' makes it clear that he considers Apollo, as the narrator's addressee and the object of the participle, to be the recipient of the Hymnic Proem.

as the likely inspiration for a peculiar structural feature of Apollonius' introit, which delays the traditional wish for inspiration from the Muses until the end (*Arg.* 1.22),[35] reserving its first line instead for "beginning with" a god (ἀρχόμενος σέο, Φοῖβε, 1). Aratus likewise begins his introit with Zeus (using a form of ἄρχομαι) and ends it with a prayer to the Muses to guide his song (*Phaen.* 16–18).[36]

I refer to the view outlined by the scholiast as the "'Hymnic Proem' interpretation," and in addition to the ancient scholiast, it has numerous modern supporters to its credit. There is some disagreement, however, as to what parts of the introit constitute the Hymnic Proem: the first few words, the first few lines, or the entire prelude. Phinney, for instance, takes the first approach, considering the opening phrase ἀρχόμενος σέο, Φοῖβε alone to execute the Proemial function.[37] Others appear to view the entire first sentence (1.1–4) as the Proem,[38] whereas for Collins, the whole of the introit is a hymn: lines 1–4 comprise its Exordium, lines 5–17 (the "prehistory") function as the equivalent of its central Mythic narrative, and the Appeal to the Muses in line 22 takes the place of the hymnic Envoi.[39] Most critics, however, do not explicitly delimit the boundaries of the Hymnic Proem to Apollo so precisely.[40] Of these views, I find Phinney's the most plausible, since after the word Φοῖβε the Argonauts become the narrator's primary focus—though admittedly the second-person address to Apollo is maintained until line 8.[41] In fact, I will argue below (1.1.4) in

---

35   For the manner of Apollonius' Appeal to the Muses (a Prayer using an optative verb) as another "elemento hímnico" in his introit, see Llanos 2017b: 10–12.

36   For Aratus' Hymnic Proem as a model for Apollonius' introit, see: De Marco 1963: 351–352; Hurst 1967: 40 n. 3; Tarditi 1989: 41; Clauss 1993: 18–20; Solomon 1998: 24–25; Vox 2002: 156; Llanos 2017b: 8–10.

37   The Hymnic Proem = ἀρχόμενος σέο, Φοῖβε: see Phinney 1963: 1–3. He is followed by DeForest (1994: 38–40), who views the compression of an entire Proemial Hymn into three words as a programmatic example of "Callimachean brevity" (38). See further: Kahane 1994a: 125–126; Nishimura-Jensen 1996: 11; Llanos 2017a: 4–5, 6–7. Cf. Murray 2018: 205, with 105*n*90 below.

38   The Hymnic Proem = 1.1–4: see, e.g.: Mooney 1912: 67; Levin 1971: ch. 1; Sistakou 2001: 259.

39   The Hymnic Proem = 1.1–22: see: Collins 1967: 3–10; cf. Fusillo 1985: 33; Murray 2005b: 91. For the correspondence of Apollo and the Muses at either end of the introit, see further: Collins 1967: 30; Hurst 1967: 40; De Martino 1984–1985: 104; Clauss 1993: 22–23; Vian 2002: 1.3.

40   See, e.g.: Blumberg 1931: 7; Faerber 1932: 89; Händel 1954: 9; De Marco 1963: 351–352; Goldhill 1991: 287; Albis 1996: 7; Green 2007 ad *Arg.* 1.1; Faulkner 2011c: 193–194; cf. also Morrison 2007: 287.

41   See 87*n*12.

favor of a modified version of Phinney's view: the analogy raised by Apollonius' allusion to *HH* 32.18–19 encourages us to view ἀρχόμενος σέο, Φοῖβε as announcing the transition to the epic song after a *notional* full-scale Hymnic Proem to Apollo, which we are to imagine preceding the beginning of our (textual) experience of the *Arg*.

As this anticipation of a later stage in my argument suggests, the "Hymnic Proem" interpretation figures well into what may be termed "performative" readings of the *Arg*. As a matter of historical fact, we do not know how or even whether the *Arg*. might have been performed. Scholars have often assumed that Apollonius intended his bookish epic strictly for a reading, not listening, public, and indeed, the presence in his poem of such "purely visual phenomena" as acrostics do show that he did positively expect at least some segment of his audience to experience his poetry in written form.[42] Accordingly, I refer throughout this study to Apollonius' "readers," assuming a textual engagement with the poem. Nevertheless, scholarship in recent decades has emphasized the persistence of poetic performance in the Hellenistic period,[43] and for Apollonius we do possess ancient references, in the poet's *vitae*, to his recitation of the *Arg*. in public ἐπιδείξεις.[44] Most importantly, it must be stressed that regardless of the medium in which the poem was consumed, its own references to itself in the traditional epic language of "song"[45] would evoke the conceit of an oral performance even for someone reading the text.[46] Apollonius' procedure is an example of the common Hellenistic poetic technique of encoding the once-integral performance contexts of Archaic "song culture" into the fictive world projected by the text.[47]

---

42 Cf. Bing 2008: 15 (whence the quotation); for acrostics in the *Arg*., see, e.g.: Danielewicz 2005: 330–332; Stewart 2010; Cusset 2013; McPhee 2017: 115–119; Adkin 2019.

43 The two poles of the debate over Hellenistic "book culture" vs. poetic performance are conveniently represented by Bing 2008 (originally published in 1988) and Cameron 1995, respectively. For orality and literacy as a spectrum in Alexandrian poetry, see Bruss 2004.

44 On this testimony, see Belloni 1995: 183; 1996: 136–138.

45 ἀοιδῆς (1.22, 1220; 4.451), ἀείδειν (1.921, 4.249), ἀείδω (4.1381), αἵδε δ' ἀοιδαί ... ἀείδειν (4.1773–1774). The narrator also refers frequently to other poets as singers; see Caneva 2007: 105 n. 1.

46 Belloni 1996; Cuypers 2004: 51 (cf. 57, 62); Caneva 2007: ch. 8; see also Morrison 2007: 275. Klooster (2022: 105) speaks of "the fiction of an oral community in which the narrator operates"; cf. Bruss's notion of "the illusion of [an] oralist fiction" in Callimachus (2004: 62).

47 The term is from Herington 1985: ch. 1; see also Kurke 2000 for an introduction to Greek "song culture." Callimachus' "mimetic" *Hymns* (2, 5, 6) offer a splendid example of the Hellenistic practice mentioned here, for whether they were performed or not, they at least textually recreate the cultic atmosphere appropriate to a hymnic performance; see,

In the last few decades, many scholars have recognized that the specific performance context conjured up by Apollonius' text is that of the archaic bard or rhapsode.[48] The introit provides much evidence for this idea. For example, the μέν-δέ contrast in 1.18-20 between "former bards" who still acclaim the Argo's construction (νῆα μὲν οὖν οἱ πρόσθεν ἔτι κλείουσιν ἀοιδοί, 18; cf. 59) and the narrator himself, with his own poetic agenda (νῦν δ᾽ ἂν ἐγὼ ... μυθησαίμην, 20), implicitly identifies him as a present-day ἀοιδός in the same tradition.[49] The well-established allusions in the introit to the performances of Demodocus and Phemius, the two professional bards depicted in Homer's *Odyssey*, add further support to this interpretation.[50]

Of particular interest for the present argument is the introit's echo of *Od.* 8.499, which describes how Demodocus began his song on the sack of Troy (ὁρμηθεὶς θεοῦ ἤρχετο). Ancient scholars evidently debated how the phrase in question should be taken. According to the T scholiast ad loc., either Demodocus "having been moved by the god, began," or "having been moved, began with the god."[51] That is, he either received divine inspiration and then began his song, or he offered a hymn to "the god" before his primary composition, in the rhapsodic manner.[52] Notably, the other scholiasts ad loc. discover the same ambiguity in the word ἤρχετο alone, irrespective of ὁρμηθείς, just as the Apollonian scholiast believes that Apollonius' ἀρχόμενος in *Arg.* 1.1 might serve both to commence a Hymnic Proem to Apollo and to announce the poet's inspiration from that god.[53] Indeed, Apollonius might have meant to tap into precisely this

---

e.g.: Bulloch 1985: 6–8, 44–45; Harder 1992; Depew 1993, 2000: 78–79; Cameron 1995: 63–67; Bing 2009: ch. 2; Acosta-Hughes and Stephens 2012: 145–147; Stephens 2015: 11–12.

48   Cf., however, Duncan 2001, esp. 49–51, who argues that through the figure of Medea, Apollonius likens his poetry to a witch's spellcasting and conjures up the pretense of a magic ritual as his performance context. Cf. also Murray 2005a: chs. 1, 4, who argues that by means of metapoetic imagery, Apollonius establishes his fictional performance context as that of a paean.

49   See also Hunter 1989 ad *Arg.* 3.1 for evidence from the introit of Book 3.

50   For Demodocus, see: Nuttall 1992: 12–13; Hunter 1993: 121; Albis 1996: 17–19; Schaaf 2014: 41; Llanos 2017a: 7; Harder 2019b: 20 n. 39; for Phemius: Clauss 1993: 20–21; Vox 2002: 157–158; Hunter 2008: 116 n. 6; Llanos 2017b: 5–7. Additional evidence from beyond the introit would include the well-known sympathy between the Argonauts' own bard, Orpheus, and the narrator (see 327n217).

51   My own translations are provided for the sake of illustration.

52   See Hainsworth's comment ad loc. in Heubeck, West, and Hainsworth 1988.

53   Nuttall 1992: 13–14. See further Koller 1956: 190 n. 1, comparing θεοῦ ἤρχετο to formulas that employ ἄρχομαι in the *HH*s. On the "inspiration" interpretation of Apollonius' introit, see the next subsection.

ancient debate with his ambiguous use of a form of ἄρχομαι + the name of a god in the genitive.[54] In any event, according to the "Hymnic Proem" interpretation of the introit, the *Arg.* itself structurally replicates the rhapsodic practice of prefacing an epic performance with a hymnic προοίμιον. In the words of Albis, the chief exponent of this interpretation:

> The *Argonautica* presents itself not just as a text of an epic poem but as the equivalent of an epic poem as performed in its appropriate context. Apollonius' hymnic proem can be viewed as compensation for the loss of the social context in which epic had once been performed.[55]

The allusions to the *HH*s in the poem's opening lines would strengthen this interpretation, given the evidence (discussed in the introduction, 2.3) for the rhapsodic practice of reciting the *Hymns* as προοίμια for epic song.

1.3 *The Ambiguity of "Beginning with You, Phoebus"*

The first interpretation of ἀρχόμενος σέο, Φοῖβε proferred by the ancient scholiast quoted above is the "Hymnic Proem" interpretation, but what is so interesting about this scholium is that its author does not commit to just a single reading of this *incipit*. Instead, ambiguity predominates from the very beginning of the phrase's history of explication. The scholiast actually presents two interpretations: a hymnic interpretation on the one hand (τὸ μέν), but also what I will term an "'inspiration' interpretation" on the other (τὸ δέ).[56] According to this second view, Apollo is invoked for inspiration as the god of poetry, much as the Muses are standardly invoked at the beginning of epic.[57] Other

---

54 I wonder as well if the debate recorded in the Pindaric scholia over the meaning of ἐξ Ἀπόλλωνος (*Pyth.* 4.176) could be relevant: does Orpheus join the Argonauts as the "son of Apollo," or with musical skills "imparted by Apollo"? See the scholia ad Pind. *Pyth.* 4.313a, b Drachmann; for Orpheus as a figure of the Apollonian narrator, see 327n217. See Murray 2018: 216 for an argument that Apollonius engages tendentiously with Orpheus' Pindaric genealogy in the hero's Catalogue entry.

55 Albis 1996: 8. For the introit's replication of the structure of a rhapsodic performance as a textual recuperation thereof, see 1–8 and his expansion on the idea in ch. 2 (esp. 19–20). Albis' basic insight is anticipated in a passing observation by Goldhill (1991: 287), and Belloni (1996, esp. 148) comes close to it contemporaneously. See further: Cuypers 2004: 44; Schaaf 2014: 36–38; Llanos 2017a; Murray 2018: 202–207.

56 Notably, the scholiast does not even say that ἀρχόμενος could mean one thing or the other; apparently they think that both meanings are "there" in the word (τὸ μέν τι σημαίνει … τὸ δέ τι σημαίνει). Many modern scholars, too, are willing to see in the phrase multiple meanings that are not mutually exclusive; see 100n74.

57 The extension of the apostrophe to Apollo all the way to line 8 via the second-person pos-

scholia to the *Arg.* assume this understanding elsewhere as well,[58] and many modern scholars stand in agreement.[59] Epic-generic expectations could easily lead our putative first-time readers to this understanding of the phrase, especially since the god's name in the vocative appears in more or less the same place occupied by the address to the Muse in the first lines of the *Iliad* and *Odyssey*.[60]

Indeed, allusions in later poets show that the "inspiration" interpretation of ἀρχόμενος σέο, Φοῖβε must have arisen quite naturally for ancient readers. This sense of the phrase is plainly the one imitated by Valerius Flaccus in his Flavian-era Latin *Argonautica*. After announcing his Argonautic theme in the first four lines, the Valerian narrator asks Phoebus for inspiration (1.5–7):[61]

5   Phoebe, mone, si Cymaeae mihi conscia vatis
     stat casta cortina domo, si laurea digna
     fronte viret.

---

sessive pronoun τεήν is no obstacle to this interpretation; cf. the opening of the *Odyssey*, where the address to the Muse is maintained for ten lines. Cf. Morrison (2007: 287–288), who objects to this interpretation on the grounds that epic normally requests inspiration from the Muses using an imperative.

58 See the scholia ad 1.1–4b, 3.1–5c.

59 Advocates of the "inspiration" interpretation include: Blumberg 1931: 7; Faerber 1932: 49 with n. 4; Händel 1954: 11; Drögemüller 1956: 128, 232; Collins 1967: 5–6; Livrea 1973 ad *Arg.* 4.1–2; Preininger 1976: 118; Heiserman 1977: 14; Nuttall 1992: 10–14; Caneva 2007: 106 with n. 7; Wolff 2020: 56; Stürner 2022: 60; see further 100n74. This understanding is also presupposed by an increasingly popular interpretation of *Arg.* 1.22, according to which it is Apollo who inspires the narrator through the intermediary of the Muses; see 234n15.

60 Note the identical rhythmical articulation of the Appeal to the Muse in *Od.* 1.1 (Ἄνδρα μοι ἔννεπε, Μοῦσα) and the address to Apollo in *Arg.* 1.1 (Ἀρχόμενος σέο, Φοῖβε). Likewise, in *Il.* 1.1, the word "goddess" (= "Muse") appears, like Φοῖβε, in the vocative case as the third word in the line (Μῆνιν ἄειδε, θεά). Cf. Grillo 1988: 42.

61 See, e.g., Kleywegt 2005: 11–12. The address to Phoebus in this vatic mode also recalls the role of Apollo's oracle at the beginning of Apollonius' narrative; see below on the "narrative catalyst" interpretation. Lines 5–6 have been taken to mean that the historical Valerius was numbered among the *quindecimviri sacris faciundis*, a college of Roman priests charged with preserving and consulting the Sybilline Books (see Boyancé 1964; cf. Spaltenstein 2002: 12 and ad VF *Arg.* 1.5); if so, he would have special reason to invoke Apollo toward the beginning of his epic, beyond Apollonius' precedent. Barchiesi (2001: 327) intriguingly suggests that the Valerian narrator's self-presentation as a priest of Apollo responds to one of the Apollonian scholiast's glosses of ἀρχόμενος (*Arg.* 1.1), ἀρχαιρεσιαζό-μενος ὑπὸ σοῦ ("elected by you"). Cf. Apollonius' own status as a priest of the Muses and Apollo in the Museum (Klooster 2011: 91).

Phoebus, be my guide, if there stands in a pure home the tripod that shares the secrets of the Cymaean prophetess, if the green laurel lies on a worthy brow.

The "inspiration" interpretation is also presupposed by the likely allusion at the beginning of the late Hellenistic Homeric parody, the *Batrachomyomachia* (1–8):[62]

> Ἀρχόμενος πρώτης σελίδος χορὸν ἐξ Ἑλικῶνος
> ἐλθεῖν εἰς ἐμὸν ἦτορ ἐπεύχομαι εἵνεκ' ἀοιδῆς,
> ἣν νέον ἐν δέλτοισιν ἐμοῖς ἐπὶ γούνασι θῆκα,
> δῆριν ἀπειρεσίην, πολεμόκλονον ἔργον Ἄρηος,
> 5 εὐχόμενος μερόπεσσιν ἐς οὔατα πᾶσι βαλέσθαι,
> πῶς μύες ἐν βατράχοισιν ἀριστεύσαντες ἔβησαν,
> γηγενέων ἀνδρῶν μιμούμενοι ἔργα Γιγάντων,
> ὡς λόγος ἐν θνητοῖσιν ἔην· τοίην δ' ἔχεν ἀρχήν.

As I begin on my first column, I pray for the chorus from Helicon to come into my heart for the song that I have just set down in tablets on my knees, bidding to bring that boundless conflict, the war-rousing work of Ares, to the ears of all mortals: how the mice went triumphant among the frogs, emulating the deeds of those earthborn men, the Giants, as the tale was told among men. And this is how it began.[63]

Through his Appeal to the Muses for inspiration and his references to the physical act of writing, the poet of the mock-epic firmly connects ἀρχόμενος to the process of poetic composition. Indeed, the allusion to the prologue of Callimachus' *Aetia* in the third line even evokes the image of Apolline inspiration,[64] in addition to the inspiration from the Muses that is explicitly mentioned in the text (χορὸν ἐξ Ἑλικῶνος, 1).[65] Notably, however, the word ἀρχήν (8), with which

---

62 I consider the decision to commence an epic poem with the participle ἀρχόμενος and a genitive object to be sufficiently striking to constitute an allusion to Apollonius, especially given how densely allusive such introits are. The use of τοίην to introduce the narrative (8) is perhaps reminiscent of *Arg.* 1.5 (τοίην γὰρ Πελίης φάτιν ἔκλυεν). For the influence of the *Arg.* on other parts of the *Batrachomyomachia*, see, e.g.: Hosty 2013: 8; Kelly 2014.
63 Text and translation are from West 2003a.
64 The Callimachean narrator records how Apollo advised him in matters of poetics "when I put a writing-tablet on my knees for the first time" (ὅτ᾿$_1$ε πρώτιστον ἐμοῖς ἐπὶ δέλτον ἔθηκα | γούνασι$_1$ν, fr. 1.21–22).
65 Text and translation of the *Aetia* are taken from Harder 2012. Conceivably Apollo is com-

the poet neatly brackets the introit in ring-composition, refers rather to *narrative* beginning—the events that catalyze the conflict between the frogs and mice that constitutes the poem's plot ("And this is how it began"). This observation leads my discussion into a third possible understanding of Apollonius' ἀρχόμενος: one that the scholiast does not consider, but which is perhaps the most popular understanding of the term in modern scholarship.

This third sense is that of selecting a starting point (ἀρχή) for a narrative or other sort of utterance.[66] According to this "narrative catalyst" interpretation, Apollo provides the narrative's ἀρχή,[67] because (note γάρ, 5) it is his oracle to Pelias that sets the plot in motion.[68] Choosing a suitable beginning for the narrative is one of the burdens commonly discharged by the epic introit (e.g., *Il.* 1.8, *Od.* 1.10). Considered from the point of view of his Argonautic precursors in particular, Apollonius' opening effectively answers the question that launches the main thread of Pindar's version of the myth: "**What beginning took them on their voyage, and what danger bound them with strong nails of adamant?**" (τίς γὰρ ἀρχὰ δέξατο ναυτιλίας, | τίς δὲ κίνδυνος κρατεροῖς ἀδάμαντος δῆσεν ἅλοις; *Pyth.* 4.70–71).[69] Pindar, too, had begun his narrative with Apollo's oracle to Pelias (71–78), and Apollonius self-consciously replicates this beginning, even as his elliptical account (*Arg.* 1.5–17) avoids too much overlap with the lengthy treatment of Pelias' imposition of the labor on Jason in *Pythian* 4 (78–168).[70] Apollonius' ἀρχόμενος also bears comparison with the ἄ⌊ρχ⌋μενος ὡς that launches the narrative of the second episode in Callimachus' *Aetia* (fr. 7c.7

---

prehended in the phrase "chorus from Helicon," since he is often represented as the "chorus-leader" (χορηγός) of the Muses as Apollo Μουσαγέτης; see, e.g., Nagy 1990a: 360–361, and the various parallels assembled by Stenzel 1908: 15 n. 1.

66 See Race 1982a: 6 n. 3. A non-narrative example of this usage of ἀρχή is Aesch. *Choeph.* 85.
67 So Zissos 2008 ad VF *Arg.* 1.1–4: "In accordance with Aristotelian prescriptions, [Apollonius] provides an indication of the narrative beginning or ἀρχή."
68 Advocates of the "narrative catalyst" interpretation include: Mooney 1912 ad *Arg.* 1.1; Wilamowitz 1924: 2.217; Eichgrün 1961: 104–105; De Marco 1963: 352–353; Ardizzoni 1967 ad *Arg.* 1.5; Hurst 1967: 39 with n. 2; Zyroff 1971: 46, 76–77; Kühlmann 1973: 158–159; Fusillo 1985: 364, 366 (but cf. 33 with n. 42); Paduano and Fusillo 1986 ad *Arg.* 1.1; Grillo 1988: 16, 42; Gummert 1992: 119; Belloni 1996: 140; Valverde Sánchez 1996: 93 n. 1; Theodorakopoulos 1998: 193–194; Vian 2002: 1.3–4; Berkowitz 2004: 59, 61; Morrison 2007: 287, 2020: 130; see further 100n74.
69 Scholars who connect the two passages include: Campbell 1983: 128; Gummert 1992: 119; Hunter 1993: 124; Manuello 2011: 111–112; Kampakoglou 2019: 357–358.
70 For Apollonius' desire to avoid duplicating too much of the Pindaric backstory, see, e.g.: Händel 1954: 14; De Marco 1963: 353; Collins 1967: 26; Cuypers 2004: 44. For a comparison of Apollonius' "prehistory" with Pindar's account, see Köhnken 2000: 57–58; Manuello 2011: 111–129.

Harder = fr. 7.25 Pfeiffer), on how the Argonauts founded aeschrological rites at Anaphe for none other than Apollo.[71] Callimachus' tremendous emphasis on "beginning" as this episode gets underway draws attention to the fact that the story he includes near the start of the *Aetia* in fact takes place near the very end of the Argonauts' homeward voyage (cf. *Arg.* 4.1694–1730);[72] as Harder has detailed, this play with beginnings and endings is part of a larger series of tantalizing structural correspondences between the *Arg.* and the *Aetia*.[73]

These are, in sum, the three major explanations scholars have offered for why Apollo represents a suitable beginning for the poem: he is either honored with a Hymnic Proem, invoked for inspiration, or selected as a starting point for the narrative. I would make two further points about these interpretative possibilities. First, they need not be mutually exclusive. For instance, a great number of scholars endorse, with varying emphases, both the "inspiration" and "narrative catalyst" interpretations: Apollo represents the starting point of the poem both from a narratival and compositional perspective.[74] Or to take another combination: the Late Antique *Orphic Argonautica* begins with a hymnic Invocation to Apollo followed by a request for the god's inspiration. "Orpheus" begins his song (1–6):

Ὤναξ Πυθῶνος μεδέων, ἑκατηβόλε, μάντι,
ὃς λάχες ἠλιβάτου κορυφῆς Παρνασσίδα πέτρην,
σὴν ἀρετὴν ὑμνῶ· σὺ δέ μοι κλέος ἐσθλὸν ὀπάσσαις·

---

71   Albis 1996: 128–129; Harder 2019b: 13, 20. Jason's invocation of Apollo later in this episode (σήν, Φοῖβε, κατ' αἰσιμίην, *Aetia* fr. 18.9) also resonates with the narrator's twin addresses to the god in the *Arg.* introit (Φοῖβε, 1.1; τεὴν κατὰ βάξιν, 8); see Vox 2002: 158 n. 25; Hunter 1993: 123.

72   In addition to ἄ[ρ]χμενος ὡς, n.b. ἤρχετο Καλλιόπη (7c.4; cf. the "inspiration" interpretation of *Arg.* 1.1), π]ρῶτ[ον ἐνὶ μ]νήμῃ κάτθεο (7c.6; cf. Apollonius' μνήσομαι), and ἐς ἀρχαίην﹐ ἔπλεον Αἱμονίην (7c.8; Haemonia is "ancient," but also the **starting-point** of any Argonautic itinerary related in linear fashion, as in Apollonius).

73   See Harder 1993: 106–107, 109; 2002: 217–223; 2019b: 19–22.

74   Scholars who endorse both the "inspiration" and "narrative catalyst" interpretations include: Herter 1944–1955: 336; Collins 1967: 5–10; Fränkel 1968: 35; Goldhill 1991: 288; Williams 1991: 297–299; Nyberg 1992: 61; Clauss 1993: 19; Harder 1993: 106; DeForest 1994: 37; Albis 1996: 20–26; Glei and Natzel-Glei 1996: 1.147 n. 1; Belloni 1999: 232; Pietsch 1999: 69–70; Sansone 2000: 158; Wray 2000: 250–251; Dräger 2002 ad *Arg.* 1.1; Vox 2002: 157; Cuypers 2004: 44; Cerri 2007: 163; Corradi 2007: 71; Klooster 2007: 64, 2011: 221, 2013a: 163; Green 2007 ad *Arg.* 1.1; Lye 2012: 233–234; Schaaf 2014: 39–41; Llanos 2017a: 8, 2017b: 9; cf. Cusset 2018: 81–82.

πέμπε δ' ἐπὶ πραπίδεσσιν ἐμαῖς ἐτυμηγόρον αὐδήν,
5 ὄφρα πολυσπερέεσσι βρότοις λιγύφωνον ἀοιδὴν
ἠπύσω Μούσης ἐφετμαῖς καὶ πηκτίδι πυκνῇ.[75]

> O Lord who rules over Pytho, Far-shooter, Seer, whose lot is Parnassus' rock with its lofty peak, your excellence do I hymn! May you grant me goodly fame, and send truth-proclaiming speech into my heart, that I may utter a clear-voiced song to far-flung mortals at the commands of the Muse and to the accompaniment of my close-built harp.

Fittingly for such an "Orphic" poem, the first two lines invoke Apollo in the fulsome manner of an Orphic rather than a Homeric hymn;[76] in the third line, the three words σὴν ἀρετὴν ὑμνῶ succinctly accomplish the praise of the god while underscoring the "hymnic" mode of this introit;[77] and this miniature hymn would seem to conclude with a Prayer for the poet's fame in the latter half of line 3. Appended to this Prayer, however, is another directive to the god, namely, a request for inspiration (4–6). Quite plausibly, this complex opening gesture could reflect its author's understanding of lines 1–2 of Apollonius' introit (possibly filtered through the Argonautic scholia), which she or he unpacks according to a combination of the "Hymnic Proem" and "inspiration" interpretations (cf. Σ ad Ap. Rhod. Arg. 1.1–4a).[78]

The second point I would make about Apollonius' ambiguous introit is that it is also easy to imagine the interpretations of first-time readers evolving as they progress through the passage. The first words might give rise to one impression, but readers may enrich or revise their first impressions as new data are presented in the subsequent lines, especially lines 5–8, where Apollo's priority in the narrative is made clear. Beye offers a nice illustration of this process in action, combining the "inspiration" and "narrative catalyst" interpretations:

---

75 Text of the *Orphic Argonautica* is taken from Vian 1987; the translation is my own.
76 For the Hymnic Proem of the *Orphic Argonautica*, see Wünsch in *RE* 9.1 s.v. "Hymnos," col. 172, and esp. Schelske 2011: 26, 190, and his comments ad loc.
77 These words constitute "eine *praedicatio* bzw. Aretalogie *in nuce*" (Schelske 2011: 26).
78 For the poet's interaction with Apollonius in these opening lines, see Schelske 2011 ad *Orph. Arg.* 1–2. Ziegler (*RE* 18.1.1318) suggests that the *Orphic Argonautica* begins with Apollo in order to allude to an Orphic theogony that began with an elaborate apostrophe to Apollo-Helius, who is the source of the poet's mystical knowledge (fr. 102.1 in Bernabé 2004). I would not doubt it, but the precedent of Apollonius' *Arg.* must loom large as well. In general on the *Orphic Argonautica*'s debt to Apollonius, see Venzke 1941 and Vian 1987: 18–21; interesting comments as well in Hunter 2005 and Nelis 2005b.

The initial phrase sets up the conventional combination of poet and divine inspiration. After four lines of general introduction, the poet tells of the oracle which motivates Pelias to send Jason after the fleece. The oracle, which of course comes from Apollo's shrine at Delphi, suddenly offers additional meaning to *Archomenos seo Phoibe*, that is, the poet shall begin the narrative with its original motivator, the prophetic god, Apollo.[79]

Still, we cannot say that lines 5–8 make the "narrative catalyst" interpretation inevitable, as Beye's account might imply. One reading of line 5 ("**For** such was the oracle that Pelias heard" [τοίην γὰρ Πελίης φάτιν ἔκλυεν]) holds that the poet had begun from Apollo (ἀρχόμενος σέο, Φοῖβε, 1) **because** his oracle catalyzes the narrative. This reading is supported by the second reference to "your [*sc*. Apollo's] prophecy" (τεὴν ... βάξιν) in line 8, which keeps Apollo's role in inaugurating the narrative in the reader's mind.[80] But another reading would take the γάρ of line 5 to imply a different logical connection between lines 1–4 and what follows: King Pelias ordered the Argonautic expedition (βασιλῆος ἐφημοσύνῃ Πελίαο, 3) **because** he had heard an oracle from Apollo to the effect that Jason would prove to be his doom. This reading is supported by the larger purpose of the "prehistory" narrative (5–17), which serves to explain Pelias' motivation for ordering the mission.[81] Apollonius' introit turns out to be stubbornly ambiguous: the text offers support to all three of the major interpretations I have outlined, allowing the first-time reader to adopt any or all of them, but it does not compel the reader to adopt any one of them in particular; they all "work"—at least on a first reading.

In addition to these three major interpretations, scholars have advanced several other explanations for Apollonius' decision to "begin with Apollo."[82] Of

---

79 Beye 1982: 13; see further Romeo 1985: 21; Clare 2002: 24–25.
80 Cusset 2018: 81 with n. 7.
81 For this second interpretation of γάρ in line 5, see, e.g.: Blumberg 1931: 7; Levin 1971: 9, 13. The twofold function of γάρ here is recognized by: Gummert 1992: 119; Köhnken 2000: 57; and particularly Berkowitz 2004: 57–61, who offers a full discussion.
82 For example, Apollo may be highlighted because:
    1) he is a model for Jason's characterization (Collins 1967: 6; Williams 1991: 300–301; Cuypers 2004: 44);
    2) the opening is meant to establish a parallel between the narrator and Jason, who also claims to begin his voyage with Apollo (οὗ ἔθεν ἐξάρχωμαι) at 1.362 (Vox 2002: 157; Llanos 2017a: 8; the parallel is commonly noted and is part of Apollonius' larger strategy of presenting his narrative as coterminous with the Argonauts' voyage [see 196n247]);

these, I will mention one that can claim ancient authority, being presupposed by an allusion in Ovid: through use of the epithet "Phoebus," Apollonius "suppresses" the form of the theonym (Ἀπόλλων) after which he himself is named (Ἀπολλώνιος).[83] In this way, Apollonius obliquely embeds the derivation of his own name in the opening of his poem as a sort of *sphragis*, rather as Aratus (Ἄρατος) paradoxically puns on his own name with ἄρρητον, "unspoken," in the second line of the *Phaenomena*.[84] Ovid bears witness to this interpretation in his own tribute to Apollonius in *Metamorphoses* 7.365, when he has Medea fly over the toponymous island of one of his major sources for this section of his narrative, "Phoebean Rhodes" (*Phoebeamque Rhodon*).[85] This phrase conceals the name of "Apollonius of Rhodes" in much the same way that ἀρχόμενος σέο, Φοῖβε could be taken to signal the derivation of Apollonius' name: the poet himself has taken his first beginnings from Apollo in his own personal biography. Read thus, "beginning with Apollo" becomes a way of incorporating a poetic signature of sorts into the introit of the new poem.[86]

What this survey of different interpretations of the introit shows is that despite the allusions to the *HH*s in *Arg.* 1.1–2 surveyed earlier in this chapter, first-time readers can reasonably understand the introit in any of several ways, most of which are not "hymnic." This is an important point to which I will be returning later in this chapter. Nevertheless, as I argue in the next subsection,

---

3) Apollo symbolizes Callimachean poetics, as in the *Aetia* prologue and the Envoi of the *Hymn to Apollo* (Goldhill 1991: 288; Williams 1991: 299–300; DeForest 1994: 37; Albis 1996: ch. 6; Belloni 1996: 141; Wheeler 2002: 45; Mori 2008: 40–41; cf.: Preininger 1976: 118; Kahane 1994a: 125); or

4) Apollo is chosen for his role in the Hellenized Pharaonic ideology of the Ptolemies (Vox 1999: 165; Stephens 2003: 236).

83 For Apollo as Apollonius' eponym, see, e.g.: Collins 1967: 10; Cuypers 2004: 43, 44; Cusset 2018: 82; Klooster 2011: 91, who also notes the relevance of Apollonius' "function as a 'priest of the Muses and Apollo' in the Museum of Alexandria." For the concept of "suppression" in etymological wordplay, see O'Hara 2017: 79–82. Albis (1996: 22) effectively explains how this technique works here: "Apollonius invokes Phoebus, whose other name, Apollo, forms the base of the poet's own name. In his proem, he addresses his divine patron as Phoebus rather than Apollo, perhaps to avoid making the play on names too obvious." See further Tsakiris 2022: 23, who suggests that the intertext with the *Homeric Hymn to Helius* at *Arg.* 1.1–2 might also encode Apollonius' connection to Rhodes, given that the island was the sun god's most prominent domain.

84 A common comparison; see, e.g.: Williams 1991: 304 n. 29; Albis 1996: 22; Vox 2002: 157. On Aratus' pun, see Bing 1990.

85 See McPhee 2018: 56 n. 6, with bibliography.

86 See also Albis 1996: 22–23, who connects the name pun to Apollo's role in inspiring the poet, just as, e.g., Musaeus is a legendary poet named for his relationship to the Muses; similarly Murray 2018: 203.

a number of allusions to other Hymnic Proems in these lines constitute strong prima facie evidence that Apollonius positively wants his first-time readers to embrace this particular understanding of his poem's opening lines. Ultimately, I argue that this interpretation is essentially a red herring, for as we will see, it is incompatible with certain data that will be presented in the poem's hymnic Envoi—but the first-time reader cannot know that yet. Accordingly, I devote the remainder of section I of this chapter to fleshing out the evidence for reading *Arg.* 1.1–2 as a Hymnic Proem to Apollo. I first examine a number of the introit's intertexts that would seem to point in this direction, and I then embark upon a brief excursus to consider a related but, in my opinion, erroneous view that sees *Arg.* 1.1–2 not as a Hymnic Proem to Apollo, but as an Exordium to the *Arg.* itself, understood as a large-scale hymn to the same god.

1.4 The Case for the "Hymnic Proem" Interpretation

The evidence in favor of the "Hymnic Proem" interpretation of *Arg.* 1.1–2 is considerable, and indeed, some of it has already emerged earlier in this chapter. The likelihood that Apollonius structured his introit after Aratus' Hymnic Proem to Zeus is highly suggestive, for if Apollonius designed his own introit on the model of a Hymnic Proem, it stands to reason that he meant for it to be construed as a Hymnic Proem as well. Moreover, the system references to the *HH*s in these lines (examined in 1.1 above) make this reading even more attractive, as the *HH*s functioned as Hymnic Proems for epic performances and were thus called προοίμια (note the Apollonian scholiast's verb, προοιμιάζεσθαι).[87] The most important piece of evidence in this regard is Apollonius' allusion to the Envoi of the *Homeric Hymn to Selene*, for along with the *Homeric Hymn to Helius* (31), *Selene* is the only hymn in the Homeric collection that makes its function as a Hymnic Proem for an epic performance totally explicit[88]—in fact, it does so in precisely the passage to which Apollonius alludes.

This point deserves careful exposition. Apollonius not only *begins* his poem with a precise allusion to the *ending* of the *Homeric Hymn to Selene*; he alludes to a very specific section within the traditional structure of a Rhapsodic Envoi, namely, *Selene*'s distinctive rendition of the Poet's Task formula: "Beginning with you [Selene], I will sing the famous deeds of mortals half-divine" (σέο δ' ἀρχόμενος κλέα φωτῶν | ᾄσομαι ἡμιθέων, *HH* 32.18–19). By alluding to one of the two passages that most clearly explicate the proemial function of the *HH*s, Apollonius raises a suggestive structural analogy between his own epic poem

---

87   See introduction, 2.3.
88   See introduction, 2.2.

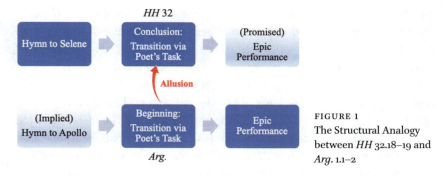

FIGURE 1
The Structural Analogy between *HH* 32.18–19 and *Arg.* 1.1–2

and a traditional rhapsodic performance: just as the singer of the *HH* "begins" by celebrating Selene before promising to transition to an epic recitation to come, Apollonius begins *as though* he has just finished a hymn in honor of Apollo; and having thus begun with this deity, he announces a transition to the Argonauts as the subject of his epic song. That is, if we pursue the logic of Apollonius' allusion, Selene would correspond to Apollo as the addressee of σέο, that is, the god who is currently receiving a Hymnic Proem (cf. ἀρχόμενος); the κλέα φωτῶν promised in *Selene* will then correspond to the κλέα φωτῶν of *Arg.* 1.1, that is, the primary epic narrative about the Argonauts that follows Apollonius' introit.[89] The parallel thus established between the structures of the *Selene* hymnist's performance and that of Apollonius' own epic poem encourages us to imagine that a hymnic προοίμιον dedicated to Apollo, precisely on the model provided by the *Homeric Hymn to Selene*, has just preceded what for us marks the first line of our (textual) *Arg.*[90] The chart above (Figure 1) visualizes how this structural analogy works. It is as if the *Arg.* as we have it is merely the textual record of the epic portion of an original rhapsodic performance, which we must imaginatively reconstruct on the basis of the traces it has left therein— much as scholars like Apollonius himself would have done when reading the editions of Archaic and Classical poetry in the Library of Alexandria.[91] The integration of the conclusion of a Hymnic Proem to Apollo into the opening of the textualized *Arg.* is just such a trace, serving to evoke a rhapsodic performance context at the level of mimesis.

89   Phinney 1963: 2; see also: Levin 1971: 11 with n. 1; Vox 2002: 157; cf. Tsakiris 2022: 26.
90   See further Murray 2018: 202–209, who reaches a similar conclusion by comparing Apollonius' introit to the Envois of several different *HH*s, including 32. I am unsure, however, how some elements of her discussion cohere with this thesis, especially the idea that "the *Argonautica* is in some way a hymn to Apollo" (202–203).
91   For this conceit, see Llanos 2017a, esp. 8. For "performative" readings of the *Arg.*'s introit, see above (1.1.2).

For the first-time reader savvy to it, then, this opening allusion to *HH* 32.18–19 incontrovertibly affirms the "Hymnic Proem" interpretation of *Arg.* 1.1–2. In fact, even if the reader does not recall *HH* 32 precisely, they may still arrive at this interpretation if they can recognize the metabatic character of Apollonius' introit (i.e., the fact that it begins as if in mid-transition between a Hymnic Proem to Apollo and an epic song about the Argonauts) based on its echoes of the "Poet's Task" formula characteristic of the Envois of the *HH*s (surveyed above, 1.1). There is, moreover, a sizable pool of further intertexts for Apollonius' introit from which the "Hymnic Proem" interpretation stands to gain even further support: other Hymnic Proems addressed to Apollo in earlier Greek literature. Ipso facto, all of these passages lie in the intertextual background of *Arg.* 1.1–2. If, however, any of them rise to the level of a probable deliberate allusion on Apollonius' part,[92] they have great potential to clarify his poetic intention for the first-time reader by placing Apollonius' introit within the long Greek tradition of Hymnic Proems dedicated to Apollo. Certain gods commonly receive the honor of being invoked at the "beginning" (and often, the end), such as Zeus or Hestia,[93] but Apollo, too, gets his fair share of Hymnic Proems in extant literature. Those with points of contact with Apollonius' introit will be reviewed here.

One of the standardly cited parallels for Apollonius' introit is the opening of the Theognidean corpus (1–4), which thematizes the practice of "beginning with Apollo":[94]

ὦ ἄνα, Λητοῦς υἱέ, Διὸς τέκος, οὔποτε σεῖο
 λήσομαι ἀρχόμενος οὐδ' ἀποπαυόμενος,
ἀλλ' αἰεὶ πρῶτόν τε καὶ ὕστατον ἔν τε μέσοισιν
 ἀείσω· σὺ δέ μοι κλῦθι καὶ ἐσθλὰ δίδου.

O lord, son of Leto, child of Zeus, I will never forget you at the beginning or at the end, but I will ever sing of you first, last, and in between; and do you give ear to me and grant me success.

---

92 For my use of the terms "intertext" and "allusion," see introduction, section 3.
93 For "beginning with" Zeus, see: Gow 1952 ad Theoc. *Id.* 17.1; Kidd 1997 ad Arat. *Phaen.* 1; cf. Apollonius' ecphrasis of Jason's cloak, which in a sense begins with Zeus as well (1.730–734; cf. Lawall 1966: 155 n. 8). For Hestia, see Diggle 1970 ad Eur. *Phaethon* 249–250. In the *HH*s, Dionysus also receives this honor (1D.8–9).
94 Scholars who adduce this parallel include: De Marco 1963: 351; Phinney 1963: 3; Collins 1967: 3 n. 8; Cuypers 1997: 238.

The vocative address to the god[95] paired with the participle ἀρχόμενος makes this passage a good comparandum for the *Arg.* introit,[96] especially because Apollonius directly quotes Theognis' opening words elsewhere in the poem, in Phineus' apostrophe to Apollo (ὦ ἄνα Λητοῦς | υἱέ, *Arg.* 2.213–214).[97] Moreover, the phrase οὔποτε σεῖο | λήσομαι ("I will never forget you") corresponds semantically with Apollonius' μνήσομαι (literally something like "I will bring to memory"),[98] while the verbs rhyme and match in position (enjambed in the second verse), although the object of each verb differs. If Apollonius intends to allude to Theognis, perhaps the substitution of μνήσομαι for οὐ ... λήσομαι was suggested by the synonymous use of different forms of these expressions in another of his intertexts, namely, the beginning of the major *Homeric Hymn to Apollo*, quoted above (μνήσομαι οὐδὲ λάθωμαι Ἀπόλλωνος ἑκάτοιο, 3.1).

This Theognis passage exemplifies the practice of beginning a poetry collection with a Proemial Hymn, and in this connection, I would note that the Alexandrian edition of Alcaeus evidently began with a hymn to Apollo as well. Because, however, Aristophanes of Byzantium's editorial work most likely postdates the composition of the *Arg.*, we do not know in what form Apollonius would have known Alcaeus' poetry.[99] In any case, although Apollonius may have drawn on Alcaeus' hymn for his Thynias episode,[100] the poem's preserved opening line ("Lord Apollo, son of great Zeus" [ὦναξ Ἄπολλον, παῖ μεγάλω Δίος, fr. 307a Campbell]) has nothing in common with *Arg.* 1.1 beyond the second-person address to the god.

More tantalizing is an alternate first line of the *Iliad* apparently preserved in an old copy of the poem owned by the early first-century BCE book collector Apellicon of Teos:[101]

---

95 The second poem of the collection (5–11) is also hymnic and similarly begins with a vocative address to Apollo, this time as Φοῖβε, as in *Arg.* 1.1.
96 In these respects, cf. also Alcman fr. 48 Campbell: "Son of Leto, (beginning with?) you (I ...?) the choir" (Λατοΐδα, τέο δ' ἀρχ⟨όμεν⟩ος χορόν).
97 This allusion is noted by Giangrande 1968: 54 and Cuypers 1997 ad loc., who connects the phrase to *Arg.* 1.1 as well.
98 De Marco 1963: 351.
99 On the Alexandrian editions of Alcaeus' works, see Liberman 2002: 1.xl–lxi, esp. lv–lvi on the hymns. Horace, at least, seems to have alluded to the ordering of Alcaeus' opening poems in the Alexandrian edition in *Odes* 1.9–11; see Lyne 2005: 547–552.
100 See 309n128; cf. Acosta-Hughes (2010: 105), who finds "no discernible traces of Alcaeus in Apollonius's *Argonautica*."
101 This alternate Iliadic opening is adduced by: Campbell 1983: 128 n. 1; Wheeler 2002: 45; Faulkner 2011c: 193–194; cf. also Murray 2018: 208. Other scholars simply note that Apollonius begins his narrative with Apollo, just as the *Iliad* does: Hunter 1993: 119; Vox 2002: 158; Nelis 2005a: 356; Ransom 2014: 641.

Ἡ δοκοῦσα ἀρχαία Ἰλιάς, λεγομένη δὲ Ἀπελλικῶντος, προοίμιον ἔχει τοῦτο· 'Μούσας ἀείδω καὶ Ἀπόλλωνα κλυτότοξον,' ὡς καὶ Νικάνωρ μέμνηται καὶ Κράτης ἐν τοῖς Διορθωτικοῖς.

What is considered the old *Iliad*, the one known as Apellicon's, has this proem: "Of the Muses I sing, and Apollo famed for his bow," as recorded both by Nicanor [a grammarian of the second century CE] and by Crates [the Pergamene grammarian, second century BCE] in his *Text-critical Notes*.[102]

The quoted line serves as a brief Hymnic Proem for the *Iliad*, and it is suggestive for hymnic interpretations of *Arg.* 1.1 for several reasons. First and foremost, if Apollonius was aware of it, this alternate opening line would provide direct HE precedent for heroic poetry that begins with a Hymnic Proem addressed to Apollo (as well as the Muses, whom Apollonius evokes at the end of his introit). Second, it is striking just how succinct the quoted Proem is. Evidently even so short a Proem as this—or, indeed, ἀρχόμενος σέο, Φοῖβε, on Phinney's reading—might be adequate to introduce so grand an epic as the *Iliad*. Last, it should be noted that the gods invoked are those with whom the epic begins: the Muse(s),[103] from whom the bard claims inspiration in the first line of the vulgate *Iliad* (*Il.* 1.1),[104] and Apollo, the god whose anger against Agamemnon sets the plot in motion.[105] This alternate beginning to the *Iliad* thus combines all three of the functions that we have seen dispersed in the major interpretations of Apollonius' introit surveyed above: the line is a Hymnic Proem that begins both with the poem's inspiring deities and with the god who catalyzes its plot.[106]

---

102 I quote the text and translation of West 2003a: 454–455. On this Hymnic Proem and its relationship to the mainstream Iliadic introit, see, e.g.: Nagy 2010: 109–119; Katz 2013.

103 The fluctuation between the singular Muse (the "goddess" of *Il.* 1.1) and the plural "Muses" is quite common; cf. Rhianus' dictum that an Appeal to one Muse is an Appeal to them all (fr. 19 Powell = Σ ad Apoll. Rhod. *Arg.* 3.1–5c). There would be no fluctuation, however, if this Hymnic Proem preceded the alternate "Cyclic" introit for the *Iliad* (printed in Bernabé 1987: 64).

104 Cf. Faraone 2015: 399–400.

105 So much is clear from Apollo's epithet κλυτότοξον, "famed for his bow," which reflects his use of arrows in sending the plague against the Achaean camp at the beginning of the Iliadic narrative (1.44–53; cf. lines 21, 37, 42). Apollo's plot-catalyzing function is foregrounded by the Iliadic narrator's question and its subsequent answer in lines 8–9: "Who then of the gods was it that brought these two [Achilles and Agamemnon] together to contend? The son of Leto and Zeus ..." (Τίς τ' ἄρ σφωε θεῶν ἔριδι ξυνέηκε μάχεσθαι; | Λητοῦς καὶ Διὸς υἱός ...).

106 In this connection, I might add that the phrase σέο, Φοῖβε (*Arg.* 1.1) echoes two other

Additionally, there are several intertexts from the *HH*s themselves, which, as noted earlier, were called προοίμια (cf. the Apollonian scholiast's verb, προοιμιά-ζεσθαι) and were recited as preludes to epic performances. I have already cited the beginning of the major *Homeric Hymn to Apollo* (3.1), to which Apollonius' use of the verb μνήσομαι may allude. In this context at least three further passages from the *HH*s deserve to be mentioned. The first is not itself a Hymnic Proem, but rather a description of the marvelous performance of the Delian maidens in the *Homeric Hymn to Apollo* (3.156–161):

> πρὸς δὲ τόδε μέγα θαῦμα, ὅου κλέος οὔ ποτ' ὀλεῖται,
> κοῦραι Δηλιάδες Ἑκατηβελέταο θεράπναι·
> αἵ τ' ἐπεὶ ἄρ πρῶτον μὲν Ἀπόλλων' ὑμνήσωσιν,
> αὖτις δ' αὖ Λητώ τε καὶ Ἄρτεμιν ἰοχέαιραν,
> 160 μνησάμεναι ἀνδρῶν τε παλαιῶν ἠδὲ γυναικῶν
> ὕμνον ἀείδουσιν, θέλγουσι δὲ φῦλ' ἀνθρώπων.

And besides, this great wonder, the fame of which will never perish: the maidens of Delos, the servants of the Far-shooter, who, after first hymning Apollo, and then in turn Leto and Artemis profuse of arrows, turn their thoughts to the men and women of old and sing a song that charms the peoples.

The connections between this passage and the *Arg.* introit are remarkable.[107] Both passages emphasize the priority of Apollo (cf. πρῶτον μὲν Ἀπόλλων' ὑμνήσωσιν, 158) and strikingly use a line-initial form of the verb μνάομαι with reference to "the men and women of old" in the genitive case (cf. μνησάμεναι ἀνδρῶν τε παλαιῶν ἠδὲ γυναικῶν, 160, with παλαιγενέων κλέα φωτῶν | μνήσομαι, *Arg.* 1.1–2).[108] Moreover, while the Delian maidens' performance is choral and not rhapsodic,[109] the hymn's reference to a song for Apollo and his family that

---

Iliadic passages that Apollonius' learned readers might have recalled. Among the characters apostrophized in the HEs (Patroclus, Menelaus, Eumaeus, etc.), Apollo is the only god so addressed, both times as "you, archer Phoebus" (σύ/σέ, ἤιε Φοῖβε, *Il.* 15.365, 20.152; the phrase recurs in a hymnic context at *HH* 3.120; on this Apolline apostrophe, see Klooster 2013a: 154–156). These passages provide good epic precedent for a narratorial apostrophe to Apollo, particularly under the title of "Phoebus." See De Martino 1984–1985: 105, with his appendix (116–117) for a list of apostrophized characters in the epics; see further: Grillo 1988: 43–44 with n. 107; Vox 2002: 158 n. 25; Klooster 2013a: 165–166.

107   The passage is adduced as a parallel by: Albis 1996: 41; Vox 2002: 158; Schaaf 2014: 36–38.
108   For φωτῶν as inclusive of both genders in *Arg.* 1.1, see 66n300.
109   As emphasized by Clay 2006: 48; cf. her comment on the next page: "The order of their [sc.

precedes a song about the ancient heroes is reminiscent of the rhapsodic tradition of using Hymnic Proems as preludes for epic performances—precisely the tradition evoked by the "Hymnic Proem" interpretation of *Arg*. 1.1–2.

The strength of this intertext is such that I would deem it a conscious allusion on Apollonius' part, especially given the ongoing interest that he evinces in the *Apollo* hymn's "Delian maidens" passage elsewhere in the *Arg.*, as I discuss later in this chapter (1.2.3). At least two significant conclusions follow from this finding. First, this allusion joins the poet's allusion to the *Selene* Envoi in lending firm support to the "Hymnic Proem" interpretation, for here again we have Apollonius alluding to a passage that makes explicit the rhetorical structure underlying that reading: a song for gods precedes a song about the ancient heroes. Second, it is striking that by means of this allusion, Apollonius connects his own narratorial persona to the model of the Delian maidens. I would add this chorus of young women to the ranks of Phemius and Demodocus as "Homeric" performers whom Apollonius programmatically invokes in his allusive introit.[110] As performers, the maidens' chief distinction—the μέγα θαῦμα mentioned in line 156 of the *Hymn*—is the way in which they imitate the speech of all peoples (162–164),[111] and there are potentially many ways in which we could relate this amazing mimetic ability to Apollonius' poetics. Albis relates it to the Apollonian narrator's characteristic "empathy" for his characters, whose experiences he often mirrors in the manner of his own narration; for instance, the narrator metaphorically "wanders off" on a digression (ἀποπλάγξειεν, 1.1220) just as Heracles et al. literally wander off from Jason's crew in the Mysian episode (ἀποπλαγχθέντες, 1.1325).[112] We might also think of the many different voices that the Apollonian narrator adopts as he frequently imitates different predecessors at different points in his multitextured narrative.[113] The enchanting quality of the Delian maidens' song (θέλγουσι, *HH* 3.161) also finds ready parallels in Apollonius' own description of the effects of his charac-

---

the Delian maidens'] song—first gods, then men—appears to be canonical and is common to both epic/rhapsodic and choral poetry." For the content of the Delian maidens' song, see, e.g., the intriguing suggestion of Furley and Bremer 2001: 1.151.

110 For Phemius and Demodocus as models for the Apollonian narrator, 95*n*50.

111 The meaning of this skill is much debated; for different interpretations, see Bing 2009: 47–48.

112 Albis 1996: 41. One of Albis' chief contributions to Apollonian studies is to delineate precisely this narratorial "empathy," which he describes as an "assimilation of poet and character that is ubiquitous in the *Argonautica* and is one of the poet's essential narrative devices" (95). Albis discusses the Heracles example at 61–62; see further "empathy between poet and characters" in his index.

113 On this point, see 231–232.

ters' songs (1.26–31, 515, 740–741; 4.894; cf. 1.570–579, 2.162, 4.150, 1665 [if θέλγε is read]) and narratives (2.772). As several of these passages are regularly regarded as cases of mise-en-abyme, reflecting Apollonius' own desire to bewitch his audience with his poetry,[114] the captivating performance of the Delian maidens provides him with an apt model explicitly praised by "Homer" himself in *propria persona*.[115]

Two more *HH*s furnish further parallels of *Arg.* 1.1–2 that might support the "Hymnic Proem" interpretation. *HH* 21 is a short hymn to Apollo, only five lines in length:[116]

Φοῖβε, σὲ μὲν καὶ κύκνος ὑπὸ πτερύγων λίγ' ἀείδει
ὄχθῃ ἐπιθρῴσκων ποταμὸν πάρα δινήεντα
Πηνειόν· σὲ δ' ἀοιδὸς ἔχων φόρμιγγα λίγειαν
ἡδυεπὴς πρῶτόν τε καὶ ὕστατον αἰὲν ἀείδει.
5 καὶ σὺ μὲν οὕτω χαῖρε, ἄναξ· ἵλαμαι δέ σ' ἀοιδῇ.

> Phoebus, of you the swan too sings in clear tones to the accompaniment of its wings[117] as it alights on the bank beside the eddying river Peneus; and of you the bard with his clear-toned lyre and sweet verse ever sings in first place and last. So hail to you, lord; I seek your favor with my singing.

Two features make this passage stand out in the field of potential precursors to Apollonius' introit. First, there is the hymn's unusual opening with a vocative address to Apollo as "Phoebus" (Φοῖβε). Cultic Hymns regularly begin in "Du-Stil" by announcing their Subject in the vocative,[118] but such a beginning is in fact atypical of Rhapsodic Hymns like the *HH*s: the only other ones to do so within the Homeric corpus are the two short hymns to Hestia (24, 29).[119] Begin-

---

114 For this metapoetic interpretation of θέλξις in the *Arg.*, see, e.g.: Albis 1996: ch. 4; Spentzou 2002: 109. Fränkel (1968: 623) offers an exemplary reading of the end of the *Arg.* as replicating the enchanting effect of Orpheus' cosmogony. See further Duncan 2001 for Medea qua enchantress as an analogue to the AR narrator.

115 In this same passage of the hymn, the narrator identifies himself as a blind bard from Chios, i.e., as Homer; see introduction, 2.4, and 1.2.3 below.

116 Adduced as a parallel by: Romeo 1985: 21 n. 11; Tsakiris 2022: 20 n. 54.

117 According to AHS (1936 ad loc.), ὑπὸ πτερύγων refers to the ancient belief that a swan's music is at least partly produced by the movement of its wings. In context, these musical wings correspond to the lyre of line 3 as part of the analogy that the hymn is drawing between the Apolline bird and bard (Vamvouri Ruffy 2004: 152–154).

118 See Race 1982a: 5–6.

119 See Janko 1981: 10; Calame 2005: 22. To this list could be added the *Homeric Hymn to Ares* (8), were it not a late intruder in the collection (see 7n35).

ning with Φοῖβε is thus noteworthy within the collection, and it is suggestive that Apollonius uses the same theonym in the vocative in his introit. Second, it is notable that, like the Theognis passage discussed above (1–4), this hymn thematizes "beginning with Apollo" in line 4. Indeed, the first-time reader will not know so yet, but Apollonius, too, might be said to sing of Apollo "in first place and last" (πρῶτόν τε καὶ ὕστατον, 4): he explicitly begins with Apollo, but he also gives the god a place of prominence near the very end of the poem, when he has him rescue the Argonauts from the eerie "shroud" of darkness on the sea near Anaphe (4.1694–1730).[120] As Phinney notes, by making Apollo the first and the last god to appear in the poem, "Apollonius shapes his plot in accordance with a hymnal formula."[121] Indeed, by giving pride of place to the god in this way, the Apollonian narrator fulfills the criteria that this brief hymn sets out for an ἀοιδὸς ἡδυεπής.

The last intertext from the *HH* collection is *Homeric Hymn* 25, a pastiche of Hesiodic quotations adapted from the Hymnic Proem of the *Theogony*:[122]

    Μουσάων ἄρχωμαι Ἀπόλλωνός τε Διός τε·
    ἐκ γὰρ Μουσάων καὶ ἑκηβόλου Ἀπόλλωνος
    ἄνδρες ἀοιδοὶ ἔασιν ἐπὶ χθονὶ καὶ κιθαρισταί,
    ἐκ δὲ Διὸς βασιλῆες· ὃ δ᾽ ὄλβιος, ὅν τινα Μοῦσαι
5   φίλωνται· γλυκερή οἱ ἀπὸ στόματος ῥέει αὐδή.
    χαίρετε, τέκνα Διός, καὶ ἐμὴν τιμήσατ᾽ ἀοιδήν·
    αὐτὰρ ἐγὼν ὑμέων τε καὶ ἄλλης μνήσομ᾽ ἀοιδῆς.

With the Muses let me begin, and Apollo and Zeus. For from the Muses and far-shooting Apollo men are singers and lyre-players on earth, and from Zeus they are kings. He is fortunate whom the Muses love: sweet is

---

120 For the climactic status of this episode, cf.: Clauss 1993: 77; Chuvin 2003; Sistakou 2012: 60. Note, Apollo's oracle to Jason is mentioned in the next episode (4.1747) and the Hydrophoria, whose establishment serves as the poem's final *aition*, was a festival dedicated to Apollo, although the narrator does not mention this fact.

121 Phinney 1963: 3; cf. Hunter 1993: 85. Phinney specifically has Theognis 1–4 in mind, but it is unclear to me whether Apollonius does what Theognis promises to do, viz. to sing of Apollo first, last, **and in the middle** (πρῶτόν τε καὶ ὕστατον ἔν τε μέσοισιν, 3), given Apollo's absence from the plot from 2.714 all the way to 4.1702. But cf. Grillo (1988: 45 n. 113), who supposes that the poet does sing of Apollo "in the middle" by means of Orpheus' internal hymn to the god in Book 2.

122 Adduced by: Händel 1954: 9; Campbell 1983: 128 n. 1; Williams 1991: 298; Belloni 1996: 140 n. 18; Pietsch 1999: 69 n. 162; Berkowitz 2004: 59–60 n. 26. For the possibility that the *Theogony*'s Proem is in fact an expanded version of this hymn, see Nagy 1990b: 55–56.

the voice that flows from his mouth. Hail, children of Zeus! And honor my singing. And I will remember both you and another song.

The main point of contact between this hymn and the *Arg.* introit is the use of a form of ἄρχομαι with Apollo's name in the genitive (cf. ἀρχόμενος σέο, Φοῖβε)—a unique mode of Evocation within the *HH*s that is adapted from the *Theogony*.¹²³ If Apollonius' construction using ἄρχομαι + gen. is enough to remind his readers of this peculiar hymn, it would add an interesting Hesiodic resonance to the opening line, in keeping with a clearer allusion to the introit of the *Works and Days* (10) at *Arg.* 1.20.¹²⁴

The various intertexts considered so far vary in strength, but several of them offer quite persuasive parallels for Apollonius' introit. To me, the most convincing cases for a deliberate allusion are *HH* 32.18–19 (n.b. σέο δ᾿ ἀρχόμενος κλέα φωτῶν | ᾄσομαι) and 3.156–161 (n.b. esp. μνησάμεναι ἀνδρῶν τε παλαιῶν ἠδὲ γυναικῶν, 160), both on lexical grounds and because they thematize beginning with the gods before singing of heroes, in accordance with Apollonius' procedure at the beginning of the *Arg.*¹²⁵ Aratus' Hymnic Proem (1–18) offers a clear structural precedent for Apollonius' introit, which begins (using a form of ἄρχομαι) with a god and ends with a wish for inspiration from the Muses. Finally, because of the *Iliad*'s privileged status as a model for Apollonius' epic, its alternate opening with a Hymnic Proem to the Muses and Apollo would constitute an undeniable paradigm for Apollonius' decision to begin with Apollo, if we could be sure that he knew of it.¹²⁶ The case for conscious allusions to the other passages surveyed here are less decisive, but—at the risk of overdetermining the potential sources of *Arg.* 1.1–2—it may be that some of these texts nuanced certain of Apollonius' usages—for instance, *HH* 21.1 and 25.1 offer

---

123   Clay 2011: 238 n. 25. *Theog.* 1 ("Let us begin our song with the Heliconian Muses," Μουσάων Ἑλικωνιάδων ἀρχώμεθ᾿ ἀείδειν; adduced by Corradi 2007: 71 n. 4) combines the name of the gods to be hymned in the genitive with a version of the ἄρχομ᾿ ἀείδειν formula common in the *HH*s, but a likelier model for *HH* 25.1 is *Theog.* 36 ("Let us begin with the Muses," Μουσάων ἀρχώμεθα), where the hymn to the Muses essentially restarts. On the complex structure of the *Theogony* Proem, see, e.g.: Minton 1970; Verdenius 1972; Nünlist 2004; Rijksbaron 2009 (with bibliography).
124   On this last allusion, see: Livrea 1966: 462–463; Ardizzoni 1967 ad loc.; Rossi 1968: 161; Campbell 1981: 1; Grillo 1988: 18 n. 25; Belloni 1996: 143–144; Clare 2002: 263; Vox 2002: 156.
125   Cf. Thgn. 1–4, which thematizes beginning with Apollo, but with weaker lexical parallels and a different generic affiliation.
126   Similarly, Pind. *Pyth.* 4.70–78 and Callim. *Aet.* fr. 7c.4–8 Harder (= fr. 7.22–26 Pfeiffer) very probably stand behind Apollonius' introit as well because of the importance of these poems among our poet's chief models for the *Arg.*

unique precedents from within the corpus of Homer's hymns for Apollonius' use of the vocative Φοῖβε and the ἄρχομαι + gen. construction, respectively. In any event, *Arg.* 1.1–2 evokes a strong intertextual background of earlier Hymnic Proems to Apollo, and the conclusion that Apollonius meant to deploy allusions to at least some of them in order to style ἀρχόμενος σέο, Φοῖβε as part of a Hymnic Proem to Apollo seems unavoidable.

1.5   *Excursus: A Hymnic Proem or a Hymn to Apollo?*

Before moving on from the introit to examine the *Arg.*'s hymnic Envoi, I would like to pause to examine another reading of the introit that seems to be gaining support in more recent scholarship. I have reserved consideration of it until now because, unlike the three major interpretations outlined above, I consider it a critical misreading. This interpretation draws on much of the same evidence for the hymnic subtext of Apollonius' introit adduced so far in this chapter, but it takes this evidence in a different direction: rather than reading the introit as a Hymnic Proem in honor of Apollo, this view regards the entire *Arg.* as a hymn dedicated to the god, which the introit serves to introduce in the manner of an Exordium.

It was, to my knowledge, Williams who introduced the idea that the *Arg.* constitutes "a quasi-hymn in honor of the god Apollo."[127] It would seem odd that so much of the *Arg.* is not about Apollo if the poem is a hymn in his honor, but for Williams, because of the god's role in catalyzing the expedition, he delights in hearing of the Argonautic Myth. She argues that there is an "*aretalogia* of the god himself ... embedded sporadically in the poem" in the form of episodes or digressions (e.g., 1.759–762, 4.611–618) that feature him. Moreover, various Honorific epithets used of the god throughout the poem redound to his honor, and he is the subject of several prayers and celebrations both in the narrative proper and within similes.[128] In this way, it is as though an originally autonomous hymn to Apollo has been diced up and sprinkled throughout a narrative intended for the god's delectation (though admittedly related to him somewhat tangentially). This thesis connects to the subject of Williams' book, *Landscape in the Argonautica of Apollonius Rhodius*, insofar as Apollo is a god particularly appreciative of natural beauty, and the *Arg.*'s loving descriptions thereof are meant especially for him as addressee.[129] Nine years later, González articulated the same basic view, apparently independently, adding more evi-

---

127   Williams 1991: ch. 13 (at 302).
128   Ibid. 303–304.
129   Ibid. 305–316.

dence of Apollo's "pervasive influence" throughout the poem, such as the high profile of seers in the epic.[130] Murray develops another form of this argument, proposing that "the poem defines itself as a paean" according to a metapoetic interpretation of what she takes to be the programmatic simile of 1.536–541, which compares the Argonauts to a chorus of young men worshipping Apollo as they row out from Pagasae to Orpheus' accompaniment.[131] Most recently, Tsakiris has developed a new version of this argument, contending that Apollonius' "hidden Hymn to Apollo" is limited just to Books 1–2, which embed a series of hymnic moments dedicated to the god.[132] Several other scholars have also advanced the claim that the *Arg.* is a hymn to Apollo, though without in-depth arguments.[133]

These scholars have made the strongest case possible for construing the *Arg.* as a hymn to Apollo, but many of these arguments are tenuous. For instance, I suspect that if one were so inclined, similar arguments could be mounted for the subtle-but-pervasive influence of gods like Hera, Athena, or Aphrodite and Eros—but the *Arg.* is not a hymn to any of these deities.[134] As to Apollo, his role

---

130 González 2000: 278–280 (at 279).
131 See Murray 2005a, esp. 6–7, 26–27, 42, 82 (at 6). Tsakiris (2022: 42–48) elaborates a comparable interpretation of this simile. See further Bauer 2017, who likewise views the epic as adopting the "Form eines Apollonhymnos/Paians" (70) based on his reading of the Thynias episode.
132 Tsakiris 2022: ch. 1 (whose subtitle provides the quotation). In particular, Tsakiris views *Arg.* 1.1 as inaugurating a kind of Hymnic Proem to Apollo that occurs *during* the narrative of Books 1–2 (cf. my own view, 189 below) in the form of "fragmental hymnic material accommodated in the underlying epic narrative" about the Argonauts (41); this hidden hymn ultimately attains closure in the direct address to the god at 2.708–710. Tsakiris' latent hymn is modeled especially on the *Homeric Hymn to Apollo* and culminates in the Argonauts' establishment of a new cult for the god on Thynias, in parallel to the inauguration of Apollo's Delphinian cult in *HH* 3. Tsakiris manages to avoid some of the chief problems that beset the "hymn to Apollo" interpretations of the *Arg.* (discussed below) by limiting his version of the Apollo-hymn from *Arg.* 1.1–2.713. But how does this view square with the presence of similar Apolline material with seemingly equal "hymnic" potential later in the poem? Tsakiris' answer is that hymns naturally resist closure, so that "some hymning to Apollo still occurs ... at the background" (79); but this allowance can make his decision to isolate the hymnic segments just to the first two books feel arbitrary.
133 In addition to those already named, scholars who regard the *Arg.* as a hymn to Apollo include: Pietsch 1999: 70; Cuypers 2004: 43–44, 59 (but cf. 45); Nagy 2010: 117; cf. Klooster 2011: 87–91, 2013a: 163. This view also seems implicit in Theodorakopoulos 1998: 199; Clauss 2016a: 69; and Morrison 2007: 287 could be taken to support it. Cf. Stürner 2022 ad 4.1702: "Die *Arg.* sind in mancherlei Hinsicht ein Apoll-**Epos**" (my emphasis).
134 E.g., if it is true that, because of a pair of early similes connecting the two (1.307–311, 536–541), Apollo is "subtly called to mind" whenever Jason appears in the text (González 2000: 279), we might equally say that Athena maintains a background presence throughout the

in the poem should be kept in the proper perspective, which the spotlight of the poem's opening verse tends to distort.[135] Although he is firmly connected to the beginning of the narrative and plays an important role in the poem's backstory (as revealed in several external analepses),[136] Apollo actually figures in the plot much less often than his initial prominence might suggest.[137] Even the Argonauts themselves seem to have been misled: they sacrifice to no god more than Apollo, but, largely unbeknownst to them, Hera (who never receives sacrifices of her own from them) is actually their greatest benefactor (cf. 2.216–217, 3.383).[138] Apollo decisively saves the Argonauts once, when he makes Anaphe appear to them;[139] otherwise, the Far-worker helps them only indirectly, through a pair of talismanic tripods he had given to Jason, which the Argonauts give away to secure guidance (4.526–536, 1547–1550), and arguably through the prophecies he inspires in Phineus.[140] It is unclear whether Apollo's mysterious appearance to the Argonauts at Thynias, which the crew celebrates with hymns and the institution of new cults (2.669–719), is even intentional on his part: they catch sight of him seemingly at random, and he takes no notice

poem by virtue of the Argo, since it is her handiwork. In fact, I think that most real-life readers would need other cues to recall the absent Apollo during Jason's scenes.

135   Phinney 1963: 2: "The invocation does not imply that Apollo will often appear again or that he will have a central place in the action. His role throughout the poem is, in fact, nebular."

136   References to Jason's consultation of the Delphic oracle prior to the voyage are scattered throughout the poem; see Fontenrose 1978: 389–390 for a reconstruction of the incident. Cf. *Od.* 8.79–81 for a similar reference to Agamemnon's inquiry at Delphi in the backstory of the HEs.

137   See: Vian 2002: 1.3; Heiserman 1977: 36 (who, however, is prone to confuse Apollo and Helius); and the comment of Albis 1996: 40 n. 62: "This [sc. Williams' argument] is an attractive idea but for the fact that the god is conspicuously absent throughout all of Book 3." Theodorakopoulos (1998: 193) offers a much stronger formulation of my argument: "Apollo is, deceptively, set up at the opening as a form of guide and protector, but he fails spectacularly to fulfil this role." See also Byre 1997: 111; Cusset 2018: 80–88. Williams herself acknowledges Apollo's absence from most of the latter half of the poem (1991: 201).

138   The crew makes offerings specifically to Apollo on eight separate occasions (Mori 2007: 463 with n. 21); Hera receives her portion only amidst general sacrifices to the Olympians (2.531–532). On the Argonauts' comparative neglect of Hera (and, to a lesser extent, Athena), see: Phinney 1963: 43; Knight 1995: 269; Vian 2002.: 1.4; Clare 2002: 161; see also Pavlock 1990: 32–33. It is especially ironic given that Pelias alienates Hera precisely by forgetting to sacrifice to her (*Arg.* 1.14, 3.64–65).

139   Even the reality of this intervention has been doubted by some skeptical critics (Theodorakopoulos 1998: 195–196; Clauss 2016b: 147); cf. Hunter (1986: 52–53; 2009: 145) for the idea that Apollo's epiphany at Thynias could be understood in rationalizing terms as the weary Argonauts' misinterpretation of the sunrise (see further Rieu 1959: 23–24).

140   See: Albis 1996: 111; Pietsch 1999: 224–225; Clare 2002: 75; McPhee 2017: 117 n. 34.

of his mortal onlookers,[141] who themselves receive no tangible benefit from the experience.[142] Apollo is mentioned in numerous digressions and similes and is given many epithets over the course of the poem, but then so are other gods (e.g., the conspicuously absent Zeus), in keeping with the poet's learned style.[143] Apollo is undoubtedly an important character in the *Arg.*, but for all these reasons, it strains credulity to think of him as the true recipient of the poem qua hymn. Indeed, I can think of no other hymn, quasi- or otherwise, in which the Subject is so submerged as Apollo would be according to this interpretation.[144]

To be sure, first-time readers will not know any of the things I have just said as they encounter the introit, and perhaps they might initially interpret ἀρχόμενος σέο, Φοῖβε as the poem's declaration of its genre as a (quasi-)hymn, sung in honor of Apollo—certainly this reading has seemed sensible to a number of modern scholars. Even so, I would argue that the text itself works against this reading. Grammatically speaking, the use of the participle ἀρχόμενος, whose action is subordinated to the main verb μνήσομαι, suggests that Apollo is pre-

---

141 See: Feeney 1991: 75–77; Theodorakopoulos 1998: 194–195; Belloni 1999: 233–234; Clauss 2016b: 147; Vergados, forthcoming; see also Danek 2009: 281. For the idea that Apollo is uninterested in the Argonauts, see: Blumberg 1931: 43; Beye 1982: 118; DeForest 1994: 82; Knight 1995: 273. Cf. Albis 1996: 111–112 for the argument that "Apollo's epiphany here is a sign of his benevolence" (111) before his temporary withdrawal from the poem; see further along these lines, e.g.: Ville de Mirmont 1894: 485; Lawall 1966: 160–161; Fusillo 1985: 59; Hunter 1986: 50; Belloni 1999: 238; Vian 2002: 1.124–125; Clare 2002: 238.

142 It must be admitted, however, that even if the epiphany does not directly aid the Argonauts, there are nonetheless subsidiary social benefits from the crew's joint religious worship, which includes inaugurating an altar to Concord ('Ομόνοια); see Hunter 1986: 53–54; Fernández Contreras 1996: 28; Brioso Sánchez 2003: 41–42; Lye 2012: 234.

143 It is true, per Williams 1991: 304, that in at least one episode Apollonius substitutes Apollo for a god who plays the homologous role in earlier treatments of the myth: she adduces Jason's prayer at Pagasae, which is directed to Zeus in Pindar's version (*Pyth.* 4.194–200) but to Apollo in Apollonius'. But elsewhere such substitutions promote other gods, as when Athena intervenes at the Clashing Rocks (2.598–603) instead of the Pindaric Poseidon (cf. *Pyth.* 4.204–211). And in one case, Apollonius actually eliminates Apollo where Pindar has him, as the father of Orpheus (*Pyth.* 4.176–177 with scholia; *Arg.* 1.25); see further Murray 2018: 212, 216–218. All of these changes could instead reflect Apollonius' well-known reluctance to involve the major gods (with the prominent exception of Hera) in his narrative—in each case, major deities are replaced by figures who rank lower on the great chain of being. For the distanced representation of the high gods and the relative prominence of lesser divinities, see 142n249.

144 Cf. the concession of González 2000: 279: "Apollo's hymnic function in the *Argonautica* may indeed be regarded as non-traditional, insofar as the poem does not focus on him or his exploits." In these circumstances, "non-traditional" is something of an understatement.

cisely *not* the focus of the poet's song:[145] the god is a starting point, but the object of the poet's recollection is "the famous deeds of people born long ago," which, the reader will soon discover, is indeed the poem's theme.[146] Moreover, we have seen that the allusion to *Selene* here implies that Apollo is the recipient of a Hymnic Proem, not of the entire epic qua hymn. But the most decisive evidence against the idea that the whole *Arg.* in an Apolline hymn is presented in the poem's hymnic Envoi, and it is to this passage that I now turn.

2 The Envoi

2.1 *The Rhetorical Structure of the Envois of the* Argonautica *and the* Homeric Hymns

Now that the hymnic elements in the *Arg.*'s introit have been examined, the other end of the poem's hymnic frame may be analyzed. At 4.1770–1772, an etiology marks off the end of the brief episode of the Argonauts' stopover on Aegina (4.1765–1772), deep into the narrative of the crew's return journey that has occupied the bulk of Book 4. Then, rather abruptly,[147] the narrator ends the poem by addressing the Argonautic crew collectively (4.1773–1781):[148]

ἵλατ' ἀριστήων[149] μακάρων γένος· αἵδε δ' ἀοιδαὶ
εἰς ἔτος ἐξ ἔτεος γλυκερώτεραι εἶεν ἀείδειν

---

145 Cf. Grillo 1988: 17 n. 33, who refers to Phoebus as "invocato *en passant* al v. 1 mediante un sintetico costrutto participiale." See further Cusset 2018: 82.
146 See further De Marco 1963: 352, who notes that it is not in the hymnic style for the objects of μνήσομαι and forms of ἄρχεσθαι to refer to different entities.
147 Regarding the sudden ending of the *Arg.*, it is customary to quote Hadas (1932: 53), who labels our passage "the most abrupt stop in literature." I sympathize with this (hyperbolic) reaction, though I think that once the Argonauts reach Aegina, we can sense that the end must be in sight; could the poet really "just as easily have continued riffing aetiologies," as Wray (2000: 242) supposes, so close to the Argo's destination? Note, with Paduano and Fusillo 1986 ad *Arg.* 4.1773–1781, that the narrator ends precisely where he had promised (1.20–22), with the completion of the Argonauts' there-and-back-again voyage.
148 See Vox 2002: 162 n. 44, 164–165 for interesting comments on the effect that this transition might have on a first-time reader: Book 4 is so full of apostrophes and prayers with forms of ἱλατ[ε] that this passage might not be recognized initially as a hymnic Envoi—indeed, the Salutation to the Argonauts in line 1773 might, for a second, be taken as an Aeginetan ritual Invocation of the Argonauts as mythic founders of the Hydrophoria.
149 I here follow the manuscript reading of ἀριστήων in line 1773, though many scholars follow Fränkel's emendation to ἀριστῆες. For a defense of the transmitted text, see the discussion at the end of this section.

1775 ἀνθρώποις. ἤδη γὰρ ἐπὶ κλυτὰ πείραθ' ἱκάνω
     ὑμετέρων καμάτων, ἐπεὶ οὔ νύ τις ὔμμιν ἄεθλος
     αὖτις ἀπ' Αἰγίνηθεν ἀνερχομένοισιν ἐτύχθη,
     οὔτ' ἀνέμων ἐριῶλαι ἐνέσταθεν, ἀλλὰ ἕκηλοι
     γαῖαν Κεκροπίην παρά τ' Αὐλίδα μετρήσαντες
1780 Εὐβοίης ἔντοσθεν Ὀπούντιά τ' ἄστεα Λοκρῶν,
     ἀσπασίως ἀκτὰς Παγασηίδας εἰσαπέβητε.

Be gracious, you race of blessed heroes, and may these songs year after year be sweeter for men to sing. For now I have come to the glorious conclusion of your toils, since no further trial befell you as you returned home from Aegina, nor did any storm winds block your way, but after calmly passing by the Cecropian land and Aulis within Euboea and the Opuntian towns of the Locrians, you gladly set foot on the shores of Pagasae.

Structurally, this passage begins with a Salutation (1773), followed by a Prayer (1773–1775), which is identifiable as such by its volitive optative verb (εἶεν, 1774).[150] This combination represents a standard closural device in Greek hymns, and so in the following γάρ clause (1775–1776), the poet acknowledges that he is indeed concluding the narrative and explains his decision to do so with an appended ἐπεί clause (1776–1778). From there, the poem ends with a brief catalog of the final phases of the Argonauts' νόστος (1778–1781).[151] Throughout this passage, the narrator maintains an extended apostrophe to the Argonauts through the use of the vocative case (γένος) and a series of second-person plural verbs (ἴλατ', εἰσαπέβητε) and pronouns (ὑμετέρων, ὔμμιν), just as the poem had begun with a sustained address to Apollo (1.1–8).[152]

The *Arg.* ends, in other words, with a recognizably hymnic conclusion, complete with a formal Salutation and Prayer.[153] More specifically, I argue that

---

150 On the use of the optative in executing this Prayer, see below.
151 ἀσπασίως in line 1781 effectively signals closure; see Hunter 1993: 120 n. 77. In the same place, Hunter also provides an even-handed overview of the argument of Rossi 1968 that the line alludes to *Od.* 23.296, the verse considered to be the original ending of the epic by Aristophanes and Aristarchus.
152 As Fränkel (1968: 625) notes, at nine verses, Apollonius' closing apostrophe to the Argonauts is the longest in the poem, exceeding even apostrophes to the gods. Grillo (1988: 53 n. 142) argues that the apostrophe to Canthus should be reckoned just as long, but even by his count, it is only 8.5 lines long (from 4.1485 to the first half of 1493).
153 See further Gummert 1992: 129 with n. 41, commenting on the "hymnische Ton" of the sound patterns in 4.1773–1774. Cf. Belloni (1999: 241), who refers to 4.1773–1781 as the poem's "inno finale"; I would rather analyze it as the final section (i.e., the Envoi) of a hymn.

in the Envoi, Apollonius follows the structuring conventions governing the conclusions of the *HH*s. Probably his Envoi's most striking Homeric-hymnic feature is its (sudden) transition from a mythic narrative in Er-Stil to a conclusion in Du-Stil.[154] Such a transition is atypical of Cultic Hymns, which often maintain Du-Stil throughout, but is one of the most prominent characteristics of Rhapsodic Hymns, including those attributed to Homer.[155] Notably, the resumption of the narrative of the Argonauts' voyage in lines 4.1775–1781 is not in the usual hymnic style, since ordinarily the poet's Salutation marks the definitive end of the Mythic narrative. Nevertheless, by casting these lines in Du-Stil, Apollonius has managed to subsume the conclusion of his epic narrative within the hymnic style of his Envoi, thus achieving a remarkable generic fusion in the last lines of the poem.[156]

One element in this Envoi actually represents a mild innovation vis-à-vis the rhetoric of the *HH*s, though intriguingly, Apollonius may be availing himself of the precedent set in some contemporary Rhapsodic Hymns. In the *HH*s, the Prayer is always expressed by a second-person imperative verb, whereas Apollonius uses a verb in the optative mood (εἶεν, 1774). This more deferential usage[157] finds parallels in the (similarly metapoetic) Prayers at the conclusion of Theocritus' *Hymn to the Dioscuri* and Callimachus' *Hymn to Apollo*.[158] It is instructive to compare Apollonius' Appeal to the Muses at the end of the introit: there, too, the poet opts for an optative verb—in fact, the very same one (εἶεν, *Arg.* 1.22)—in favor of the imperative that is traditional in the HEs (ἄειδε, *Il.* 1.1; ἔννεπε, *Od.* 1.1).[159] Apollonius' optative Prayer may signal that his imita-

---

154 Belloni 1995: 181.
155 See introduction, 2.2.
156 Cf. Vox 2002: 162 on the persistence of the first and second persons past the hymnic conclusion proper (4.1773–1775). For a formally similar travel catalog rendered in Du-Stil in the major *Homeric Hymn to Apollo* (3.216–246, 277–282), see 236*n*31.
157 Cf. the similar affectation of casting the Salutatory Verb in "a deferential optative" that "suggests the tone of a suppliant" (Kidd 1997 ad Arat. *Phaen.* 16); see further Theoc. *Id.* 26.33, 35; Herod. 4.1–9 (with Wünsch 1904: 97); and esp. Callim. *Hymn* 4.326, which is likely based precisely on the precedent set by the third-person optative in the quasi-Salutation at *HH* 3.165 (see Mineur 1984 ad loc.; on this passage, see 1.2.3); cf. also AR 1.920. In general on the literary and intellectual background behind Apollonius' optative Prayer, see the illuminating discussion in Corradi 2007.
158 "Farewell, children of Leda; **may you** **confer** fair fame on my hymns" (χαίρετε, Λήδας τέκνα, καὶ ἡμετέροις κλέος ὕμνοις | ἐσθλὸν ἀεὶ πέμποιτε, *Id.* 22.214–215); "Hail, King! And Blame, **may he go** there, where Envy dwells" (χαῖρε, ἄναξ· ὁ δὲ Μῶμος, ἵν' ὁ Φθόνος, ἔνθα νέοιτο, Callim. *Hymn* 2.113). Note that as in Apollonius' Prayer, Callimachus' is also cast in the third person.
159 See Corradi 2007: 73–74; and Llanos 2017b: 10–12 (both of whom note other precedents for optative Prayers of this sort in Pindar and Bacchylides).

tion of the *HH*s has been filtered through changes in the Rhapsodic Hymnic tradition spearheaded by his experimental contemporaries.

Apollonius' Salutation and Prayer recognizably reproduce the rhetorical patterns of Rhapsodic Hymnody, but another such element in the passage lies somewhat concealed, and hence requires further explanation. Apollonius' Envoi apparently lacks one element that is distinctive of the Envois of the *HH*s (though hardly present in all of them), that is, the "Poet's Task," or promise to remember the god as the rhapsodic speaker moves from Proemial Hymn to epic performance.[160] It would have been odd (if humorous) for Apollonius to speak explicitly of transitioning to another song in the style of the *HH*s,[161] as if his 6,000-line poem had really been a προοίμιον for another epic all along.[162] Perhaps for this reason a complete statement of the Poet's Task is absent from his hymnic conclusion.[163]

Nevertheless, I posit that Apollonius' Prayer for continual reperformances of his songs effectively combines the aspect of the Poet's Task still applicable to his own agenda, that is, the promise of remembrance, with another, ordinarily discrete element of an Envoi, the Prayer to the deity.[164] Apollonius' Prayer is hermeneutically rich, because it can be interpreted from the perspective of

---

160 Once again, see introduction, 2.2.
161 Cf., however, the announcement of a transition to Callimachus' *Iambi* at the end of *Aetia* 4 (fr. 112 Pfeiffer, Harder), which itself draws on the *HH*s' "Poet's Task" formula (Harder 2012 ad fr. 112.9).
162 In fact, some scholars have read the Envoi in this way, such as Goldhill 1991: 287: "It is as if the complete *Argonautica* has been a (hymnic) prelude; as if the pretext to end is—playfully—an epic to come"; see also Wheeler 2002: 46. In a related vein, Joseph Bringman has suggested to me that Apollonius' poem might function as a προοίμιον for Euripides' *Medea*. My own view is different: if the *Arg.* poses as a prelude to any "epic to come," it would be itself, in reperformance (4.1773–1775); cf. McNelis (2003: 160), who makes a similar argument about Callimachus' *Hecale*. In this sense I approve of Belloni's (1996: 141–142) paradoxical reading: the poem's hymnic frame seems to constitute "un proemio alle *Argonautiche* che però includa le *Argonautiche* medesime." See further Petrovic 2013 on the tendency of Greek hymns to "attempt to create an illusion of endlessness" (208).
163 Cf. Murray 2018: 207. Perhaps owing to Apollonius' example, both the imitations of Dionysius the Periegete (1181–1186) and Pseudo-Manetho (*Apotelesmatica* 6.751–754) also omit the "Poet's Task" formula from their Envois, but do include a Salutation and Prayer to the subjects of the poem. For Dionysius' allusion to the Apollonian Envoi, see: Vox 2002: 159–168; Lightfoot 2014: 507–508; for Pseudo-Manetho's, see: Stenzel 1908: 14; Vox 2002: 164, 165 n. 56.
164 So Lightfoot 2014: 508 n. 11: "Given that the prayer is for a reiteration of the poem, it could also be seen as an allusion to the third traditional element [sc. in the Envois of *HH*s] …, namely the transition to another song." See also Wheeler 2002: 46.

the interests of both the poet and his divine addressees.¹⁶⁵ On the one hand, in making this Prayer, Apollonius wishes for his own literary immortality as the author of a perennial classic; on the other, this request will also benefit the Argonauts (and thus they will be inclined to grant it), because every reperformance of the *Arg.* bolsters their own κλέος as the poem's heroic subjects.¹⁶⁶ This Prayer thus neatly combines "the hymnic terminology of closure with a sense of epic memorializing among men," as Goldhill puts it, reflecting the *Arg.*'s generic hybridity as both epic and hymn;¹⁶⁷ and in so doing, it exemplifies the sort of χάρις-relationship of mutual benefit that Greek hymns strive to establish between mortal and divinity. In praying for the enduring success of a song that glorifies the Argonauts, Apollonius incorporates into his Envoi the most important part of the Poet's Task, namely, the promise that the deity will not be forgotten even though the hymn is ending.¹⁶⁸

There is some precedent in the *HH*s for this "subliminal" execution of the Poet's Task. The one-line Envoi of the minor *Homeric Hymn to Demeter* lacks a Poet's Task, but its second Prayer, because it is concerned with the continuation of the hymnist's performance, seems to discharge that function: "Hail, goddess! Keep this city safe, **and give my song its beginning**" (χαῖρε, θεά, καὶ τήνδε σάου πόλιν, ἄρχε δ' ἀοιδῆς, 13.3).¹⁶⁹ Moreover, two of the *Hymns to Diony-*

---

165   For the Prayer's dual aspect, see: Fränkel 1968: 620–621; Hunter 1991: 90, 2008: 122, 2015 ad loc.; Stürner 2022 ad 4.1775.
166   Cf. **κλυτὰ πείραθ**, 1775, harkening back to the **κλέα φωτῶν** of 1.1 (see further 195–196 below). This dual reading would, I suspect, have been intuitive for Apollonius' ancient readers, since the reciprocity between the κλέος of poets and their subjects is a traditional topos in Greek poetry. For comparisons of such passages to Apollonius' Prayer, see: Fränkel 1968: 621 n. 354 (citing Bacchyl. 13.228–231, Pind. *Nem.* 9.53–55); Belloni 1995: 175–176 (citing Bacchyl. 3.96–98); 1996: 147 n. 43 (citing Ibyc. fr. 282.47–48); cf. Valverde Sánchez 1996: 337 n. 824 (citing Pind. *Pyth.* 6.10–17). Cf. further the elaborate working-out of this motif in the Envoi of Theocritus' Homeric-style *Hymn to the Dioscuri* (22.214–223).
167   Goldhill 1991: 295. For the *Arg.*'s generic hybridity, see chapter 2.
168   Hunter 2015 ad *Arg.* 4.1773: "ἵλατ᾽ both bids farewell to the Argonauts and begs them to be understanding if he is now going to stop his poetic celebration of them"; the Prayer for the epic's continual reperformance then offers the Argonauts further consolation (Fränkel 1968: 619–621). The apologetic nuance of the *HH*s' Poet's Task formula is noted by Bundy 1972: 52–54; see further Calame 2011. The conciliatory note struck by ἵλατ[ε] in connection with the cessation of praise is nicely illustrated further by Pseudo-Manetho's imitation of our passage (see 121n163): that poet uses the same Salutatory Verb (ἵλατε, *Apotelesmatica* 6.754) after explicitly announcing the end of his "hymn" (εὐξάμενος λιγὺν ὕμνον ἐμὴν καταπαύσω ἀοιδήν, 752; text from Köchly 1858; note that εὐξάμενος here has the unusual meaning *consecrans*, per the 1698 translation of Gronovius, and the "sweet-sounding hymn" in question here is the entire foregoing poem).
169   See Calame 2005: 29–30.

sus end without a formal Prayer or Poet's Task, instead substituting a maxim about the impossibility of singing for those who would forget the god. Thus the fragmentary *Hymn to Dionysus* concludes (1D.8–10):

> ἴληθ', Εἰραφιῶτα γυναιμανές· οἱ δέ σ' ἀοιδοί
> ᾄδομεν ἀρχόμενοι λήγοντές τ'· οὐδέ πῃ ἔστιν
> 10   σεῖ' ἐπιληθόμενον ἱερῆς μεμνῆσθαι ἀοιδῆς.

> Be propitious, bull god, women-frenzier! We singers sing of you as we begin and as we end; there is no way to remember holy song while heedless of you.

The Envoi to the seventh *HH* is similar (58–59):

> χαῖρε, τέκος Σεμέλης εὐώπιδος· οὐδέ πῃ ἔστι
> σεῖό γε ληθόμενον γλυκερὴν κοσμῆσαι ἀοιδήν.

> Hail, child of fair Semele; there is no way to adorn sweet song while heedless of you.

Janko hesitates whether to call the statements with which these Envois close a Prayer or a version of the Poet's Task.[170] Especially in the latter passage, we might understand the point of the maxim in lines 58–59 to be an indirect expression of the hymnist's desire for the god, now duly honored, to "adorn" his "sweet song."[171] That this is the rhetorical purpose of these lines is suggested by parallel Prayers in other *HH*s that concern the aesthetic success of the hymnist's song: "order my song" (ἐμὴν δ' ἔντυνον ἀοιδήν, 6.20);[172] "grant me beautiful song" (δὸς δ' ἱμερόεσσαν ἀοιδήν, 10.5); and "bestow beauty on my song" (χάριν δ' ἅμ' ὄπασσον ἀοιδῇ, 24.5).[173] At the same time, the emphasis on not forgetting

---

170   Janko 1981: 15.
171   Hall 2013: 28, who notes that *HH* 7 begins precisely with the hymnist's remembrance (μνήσομαι, 2) of Dionysus (cf. ληθόμενον, 59).
172   Adduced as a parallel for Apollonius' Prayer by Fränkel 1968: 620; Harder 1993: 105 n. 29.
173   Cf. also "honor my song" (ἐμὴν τιμήσατ' ἀοιδήν, *HH* 25.6). On these metapoetic Prayers in the *HH*s, see Vamvouri Ruffy 2004: 81–83. Petrovic (2012: 174–175) adduces all four of these Homeric-hymnic Prayers as parallels for Apollonius' Prayer. Each of these Homeric Prayers is followed by a full enunciation of the Poet's Task (cf. *HH* 13.3). As per Harder (1993: 105 n. 30), Theocritus' *Herakliskos* ended with a similar Prayer to the hymned hero (Heracles) for the success of the poet's song; see: Gow 1952 ad *Id*. 24.141 ff.; Gutzwiller 1981: 12–16; Fantuzzi and Hunter 2004: 201.

Dionysus and, at 1D.10, **remembering song** (μεμνῆσθαι ἀοιδῆς), evokes the most typical Poet's Task formula: "And I will **remember** both you and another **song**" (αὐτὰρ ἐγὼ καὶ σεῖο καὶ ἄλλης μνήσομ' ἀοιδῆς). Effectively, these maxims meld together by implication the functions of both the Prayer and the Poet's Task, in a way that bears comparison to Apollonius' procedure at *Arg.* 4.1773–1775. Moreover, as we will see in the next subsection, there is independent reason to think that Apollonius might have had his eye on both of these passages in composing his Envoi.

To bolster this interpretation further, I here present two parallel passages from Theocritus and Catullus that adapt the traditional formulas of Homeric-hymnic Envois in ways that illuminate certain aspects of Apollonius' rhetoric. The first passage is the Envoi of Theocritus' encomium to Ptolemy Philadelphus, which is itself styled after a *HH* (*Id.* 17.135–137):

Χαῖρε, ἄναξ Πτολεμαῖε· σέθεν δ' ἐγὼ ἶσα καὶ ἄλλων
μνάσομαι ἡμιθέων, δοκέω δ' ἔπος οὐκ ἀπόβλητον
φθέγξομαι ἐσσομένοις· ἀρετήν γε μὲν ἐκ Διὸς αἰτεῦ.

Farewell, lord Ptolemy! **I shall make mention of you just as much as of the other demigods, and I think my account will not be rejected by future generations.** As for virtue, you should request that from Zeus.[174]

The bolded portion represents Theocritus' version of the "Poet's Task," promising Ptolemy future remembrance. Notably, Theocritus has joined a straightforward enunciation of the "Poet's Task" motif ("I shall make mention of you ...") with a non-standard element, a prediction of his song's enduring legacy ("and I think my account will not be rejected by future generations"). The addition of this prediction demonstrates, I argue, the close logical connection between the Poet's Task and the hope for the hymn's future survival. They are, really, two sides of the same coin. The Poet's Task focuses on the poet's own remembrance of the addressee while the hope for survival highlights the addressee's remembrance by the human audience, but both function to assure the addressee that she or he will indeed enjoy remembrance in song.[175] The-

---

[174] For the adaptation of the closural formulas from the *HHs* here, see Perrotta 1978: 182. Notably, lines 135–136 may allude to the Envois of the *Homeric Hymns to Helius* and *Selene* (see Hunter 2003: 196), the latter being the same passage that Apollonius adapts at the beginning of his hymnic introit.

[175] For the idea that hymns presuppose a threeway discursive situation—the hymnist and the Hymnic Subject, but also the hymn's mortal audience—see, e.g., Miller 1986: 2.

ocritus' unusually explicit, bipartite version of the Poet's Task shows that Apollonius' Prayer for his song's continual reperformance can be readily comprehended as the functional equivalent of the traditional Poet's Task, even if it represents an innovation upon the rhetoric of the HHs.

Catullus' adaptation of Apollonius' Envoi sheds further light on how it could have been interpreted in antiquity.[176] The bulk of Catullus' celebrated epyllion (c. 64) is taken up with a description of the wedding of Peleus and Thetis (25–46, 267–383) and the lengthy ecphrasis that punctuates it (47–266). The poem begins, however, in a rather misleading fashion, as though launching upon an Argonautic narrative (1–24),[177] and it is closely engaged with Apollonius' *Arg.* throughout.[178] Fittingly, Catullus ends the poem's Argonautic prologue with an elaboration of Apollonius' concluding address to the Argonauts (c. 64.22–24):

> o nimis optato saeclorum tempore nati
> heroes, salvete, deum genus! o bona matrum
> 23b progenies, salvete! iter⟨um, salvete, bonarum!⟩
> vos ego saepe, meo vos carmine compellabo.

> O, hail, heroes, offspring of gods, born in the happiest time of the ages! O noble children of ⟨noble⟩ mothers, hail ⟨and hail ag⟩ain! You, yes, you I will often invoke in my song.[179]

Catullus' adaptation produces a more enthusiastic effect by modulating some of the proportions of the Apollonian original: the vocative address is lengthened to encompass all of line 22 and half of 23; the Salutation is expanded to include an impressive double- or, if the restoration of 23b is correct, even triple-*salvete*;[180] and Anaphora of *vos* in 24 ratchets up the emotional inten-

---

176 For the principle that allusions to a text by other poets can unlock new interpretations thereof, see 90n26.
177 For this misleading beginning, see especially Clare 1996: 60–65, who works out the complexities of Catullus' "manipulation of reader expectation" (63) with particular nuance.
178 Studies devoted to Catullus' adaptation of the *Arg.* in c. 64 include: Avallone 1953; Clare 1996; DeBrohun 2007; and now a full monograph, Calzascia 2015. Thomas 1982, which does not focus solely on Apollonian allusion, represents another major contribution.
179 The restorations are those printed in Thomson 1997; the translation is my own.
180 In defending this supplement, Thomson 1997 ad loc. compares the triple-χαῖρε at the end of Callimachus' *Hymn to Zeus* (91, 94). I have wondered if Callimachus' triple Salutation could have been inspired in turn by the presence of "Rhapsodenvarianten" in his text of the *HH*s (Lenz 1975: 10 n. 2), which would have led to the doubling of the Salutation in a

sity and effectively achieves two Ich-Du juxtapositions, arranged chiastically almost back-to-back (*vos ego ... meo vos*).[181] Additionally, whereas Apollonius' Envoi lacks a proper Poet's Task, Catullus' lacks a Prayer. Nevertheless, despite these differences, the core allusion to the *Arg.* is unmistakable in the phrase *heroes, salvete, deum genus* (23), an adaptation of Apollonius' Salutation (ἵλατ' ἀριστήων μακάρων γένος, 4.1773).[182] Line 24 evidently reworks the Apollonian Prayer for continued reperformances of the poet's songs in the future, but, as many Catullan commentators have noted (if not in these terms), the Roman poet's promise to invoke the Argonauts often in his song is also plainly a version of the Poet's Task, modeled on those in the *HH*s.[183] Catullus' adaptation may thus function as a two-tier allusion, clarifying the Homeric-hymnic background of Apollonius' Prayer to the Argonauts.[184]

2.2 *Further Parallels for the Envoi from the* Homeric Hymns

In sum, both internal evidence and comparison with parallel passages show that Apollonius' Envoi replicates the structure of those of the *HH*s, though our poet has followed the less common precedent of only a few hymns that meld together the Poet's Task and the Prayer, and his use of the optative rather than an imperative in the Prayer may reflect influence from contemporary Rhapsodic Hymnody. In the next few pages, I continue to pursue the relationship between Apollonius' Envoi and those of the *HH*s by examining Apollonius' diction, in order to clarify the traditional background of his rhetoric. I discuss four key words and phrases: 1) ἵλατ[ε], 2) μακάρων, 3) ἀοιδαὶ | ... γλυκερώτεραι, and 4) εἰς ἔτος ἐξ ἔτεος.[185]

---

couple of hymns (1D.8–12, 18.10–12). Vox (2002: 162 n. 41) notes that Catullus' use of *salvete* in this adaptation shows that he recognized χαίρετε and ἵλατ[ε] as interchangeable; see 127*n*186.

181 Catullus may be drawing out the much less prominent Ich-Du juxtaposition in his model, namely, Apollonius' phrase ἱκάνω | ὑμετέρων (4.1775–1776), a first-person verb with enjambed second-person possessive pronoun (noted by Clare 2002: 284).

182 West 1965. See further 1.2.4.

183 In addition to the commentaries ad loc., see: Perrotta 1931: 187; Klinger 1964: 167–168; Petrovic 2012: 175–176.

184 On two-tier allusions, see 29*n*147.

185 To be sure, Apollonius' Envoi does have important intertexts beyond the *HH*s. Worthy of mention here is Callim. *Aetia* fr. 7.13–14, which uses the same Salutatory Verb (in a different dialect form: ἔλλατε) and prays to another group of divinities (the Charites) for a long afterlife for the poet's work (Gercke 1889: 249 with nn. 4–5; Fränkel 1968: 620; Massimilla 1994: 325; Vox 2002: 163; Hunter 2008: 122; Harder 2012: 2.134, 2019: 14; Petrovic 2012: 175). This passage occurs at the end of the first *aition*; tellingly, the poem's second *aition* con-

1. Apollonius' Salutatory Verb, ἵλατ[ε], is not restricted in its usage to the *HH*s; many Cultic Hymns use ἱλάομαι and its cognate verbs (ἱλάσκομαι, ἱλήκω) and adjective (ἵλαος) in their Salutations. Indeed, this Salutatory Verb is relatively rare in the *HH*s, the great majority of which introduce the Salutation with either χαῖρε or χαίρετε. A few *HH*s do, however, use ἱλάομαι or ἱλήκω as the functional equivalent of χαίρω.[186] One example, which we have just encountered in a different connection above, is even aurally reminiscent of Apollonius' Envoi. The first *Homeric Hymn to Dionysus* concludes: "Be propitious, bull god, women-frenzier! We singers sing of you as we begin and as we end" (ἴληθ', Εἰραφιῶτα γυναιμανές· οἱ δέ σ' ἀοιδοί | ᾄδομεν ἀρχόμενοι λήγοντές τ', 1D.8–9). Line 8 ends after the bucolic diaeresis with a clausula (οἱ δέ σ' ἀοιδοί) remarkably like that of *Arg.* 1773 (αἵδε δ' ἀοιδαί),[187] and the *figura etymologica* in ἀοιδοί | ᾄδομεν may be picked up by Apollonius' ἀοιδαί ... ἀείδειν (*Arg.* 4.1774–1775). In the next subsection of this chapter, I canvass Giangrande's view that Apollonius' Salutatory Verb may be influenced by *HH* 3.165.

2. The Salutation hails the Argonauts as "**blessed** heroes" (ἀριστήων μακάρων), using an Honorific for which there is precedent in the Envois of some *HH*s, such as in the Prayer to Poseidon at *HH* 22.7.[188] A slightly more precise parallel is to be found, yet again, in the *Homeric Hymn to Apollo*—this time in the Salutation that rounds off its prelude, which is itself structured as a minia-

---

cerns the Argonauts, and we can be confident that Apollonius does allude to this passage elsewhere (see 99–100 above and the discussion of etiology in chapter 3).

186   *HH* 1D.8, 3.165, 20.8, 23.4, passages variously adduced as Apollonian parallels by: Stenzel 1908: 13–14; Phinney 1963: 158 n. 3; Fränkel 1968: 620; Albis 1996: 39 n. 61; Haubold 2001: 26 n. 20; Tsakiris 2022: 21 n. 55; see also Vox 2002: 163 n. 46, 164 for these and other parallels. Additionally, two Envois include the formula "I seek your favor with my song" (ἵλαμαι δέ σ' ἀοιδῇ, 19.48, 21.5; adduced by Fränkel 1968: 620). For the equivalence between forms of χαίρω and ἱλάομαι in this context, see Bundy 1972: 51; Janko 1981: 16.

187   The echo is duly cited by Campbell 1981: 90.

188   Stenzel 1908: 13 n. 1. *HH* 22.7 is a weak parallel for *Arg.* 4.1773, but the context, a Prayer for sailors, is at least suggestive for the *Arg.* Note that the Argonauts erect an altar to Poseidon just some 150 lines before the Envoi (at 4.1620–1622). Note that μάκαιρα also appears in one manuscript (M) in a variant reading of the Salutation to Aphrodite at *HH* 10.4. Beyond the *HH*s, Vox (2002: 163) adduces as a parallel fr. ep. adesp. 10 Davies (= the "hymn fragment" printed in West 2003a: 220–221), which the lexicographer Aelius Dionysius (*Attic Lexicon* α 76 Erbse) quotes as a typical example of how a rhapsode begins an Envoi: "But now, **blessed** gods, be unstinting of blessings" (νῦν δὲ θεοὶ **μάκαρες** τῶν ἐσθλῶν ἄφθονοι ἔστε). This fragment provides an interesting glimpse of Rhapsodic Hymns that were not included in the Homeric collection—if, that is, Aelius has not made it up himself *exempli gratia*. If this line really is the very beginning of an Envoi, the lack of a separate Salutation is surprising, and the generic address to the "blessed gods" rather than an individual addressee is strikingly un-Homeric.

ture hymn: "Hail, O **blessed** Leto" (χαῖρε **μάκαιρ**' ὦ Λητοῖ, 3.14). Here the form of μάκαρ occurs in the Salutation itself, as in *Arg.* 4.1773. There is another reason to think that Apollonius might have had his eye on this verse of *Apollo*. In the HEs, humans never use the emotive particle ὦ when addressing deities,[189] but a handful of exceptions can be found in two of the *HH*s (3.14, 179, 526; 26.11), on whose authority Apollonius seems to have allowed himself three such usages, which are limited to just two passages (2.213; 4.1411, 1414).[190] Of these, the Salutation to Leto, together with the Salutation to Dionysus at *HH* 26.11 (another intertext for the Envoi, quoted below), is significant for Apollonius because it features a postponed ὦ (χαῖρε μάκαιρ' ὦ Λητοῖ). The HEs have some "secular" examples of this anastrophe in addresses to mortals,[191] but in an address to deities, postponed ὦ is a decidedly "hymnic" affectation suggestive of religious enthusiasm.[192] It is thus telling, given Apollonius' fastidious use of the particle, that he permits postponed ὦ in only one passage, namely, Orpheus' Invocation of the Hesperides at *Arg.* 4.1411 (δαίμονες ὦ καλαὶ καὶ εὔφρονες);[193] he may well have done so under the auspices of *HH* 3.14 and 26.11.

3. The motif of the "sweetness" of song (ἀοιδαὶ | ... γλυκερώτεραι, *Arg.* 4.1773–1774) is not very striking in itself, finding numerous parallels in lyric poetry.[194] In early hexameter poetry, however, this noun-adjective pairing particularly recalls the Envoi of another hymn I have already had occasion to quote above, the midlength *Hymn to Dionysus*: "There is no way to adorn **sweet song** while heedless of you [*sc.* Dionysus]" (οὐδέ πη ἔστι | σεῖό γε ληθόμενον **γλυκερὴν** κοσμῆσαι **ἀοιδήν**, 7.58–59).[195] I argued above that this statement can be interpreted at least partly as a Prayer for Dionysus to adorn the speaker's song,

---

189   See Gildersleeve and Miller 1903: 197.
190   See Giangrande 1968: 52 on the (major) *HH*s and 53–54 on the *Arg*.
191   See *Il.* 4.189 and *Od.* 8.408 (= 18.121, 20.199), and Harder 2012: 2.775 for further examples and references.
192   See the parallels collected by AHS 1936 ad *HH* 3.14, Livrea 1973 ad 4.1411.
193   See Gildersleeve and Miller 1903: 199; Giangrande 1968: 57, who notes in the same place that Callimachus admits this usage once in his *Hymns* as well, in his Salutation to Delos (4.325). This passage, it should be pointed out, concludes by mentioning Leto in the next line (326). Is Callimachus pointing up the source of his usage (*HH* 3.14)? Note that, in fact, another postponed ὦ occurs in an apostrophe to Pelion in line 118—in a speech spoken by Leto herself.
194   E.g., see Livrea 1973 ad loc.
195   Campbell 1981: 90; Gummert 1992: 130; Belloni 1995: 174–175. The lattermost scholar finds programmatic significance in Apollonius' use of this adjective to describe his songs. See further Phinney 1963: 159 n. 4, who cites some Prayers from the *HH*s and further parallels from lyric poetry.

given the other *HH*s that offer Prayer for the aesthetic success of the hymnist's performance.¹⁹⁶ If Apollonius did not have *HH* 7.58–59 itself in mind when composing his Envoi, he could at least draw on this category of Prayer in the *HH*s as precedent for his Prayer for the increasing sweetness of his songs.

4. One final element that may derive from the *HH*s is Apollonius' reference to the reperformance of his songs "year after year" (εἰς ἔτος ἐξ ἔτεος, 4.1774). This temporal expression could represent a studied variation on a pair of comparable phrases in the Envoi of yet another of the *Dionysus* hymns (26.11–13):¹⁹⁷

> καὶ σὺ μὲν οὕτω χαῖρε, πολυστάφυλ᾽ ὦ Διόνυσε·
> δὸς δ᾽ ἡμᾶς χαίροντας ἐς ὥρας αὖτις ἱκέσθαι,
> ἐκ δ᾽ αὖθ᾽ ὡράων εἰς τοὺς πολλοὺς ἐνιαυτούς.

And so hail to you, Dionysus of the abundant grape clusters! Grant that we may come again in happiness at the due time, and **time after time for many a year**.

The parallel is semantic rather than lexical: where the hymn has ἐς ὥρας ... | ἐκ ... ὡράων, Apollonius has the tighter expression εἰς ἔτος ἐξ ἔτεος, using a different noun that is synonymous, however, with the hymn's other temporal item, ἐνιαυτούς. But the real value of this parallel lies in the hymn's reference to an annual religious festival as the context for its performance,¹⁹⁸ because the hymnic style of Apollonius' Envoi combined with a wish for yearly reperformance may evoke just such a fictive performance context as the setting of his narration. Indeed, annual reperformances would be particularly appropriate to the worship of heroes like the Argonauts, as Hunter suggests: "It is tempting to associate the hoped-for annual repetition of the epic (4.1774) by men (ἀνθρώποις), as distinguished from the μακάρων γένος, with the annual performances which characterised hero-cult."¹⁹⁹

---

196 See 123.
197 Adduced by Fränkel 1968: 620; De Martino 1984–1985: 104. The phrase appears also in seemingly unrelated contexts in Theocritus (*Id*. 18.15, 25.124); see the comment of Gow 1952 on the former passage. Apollonius' allusion to *HH* 26 in his Envoi would be especially fitting if, as Hall (2021: 22–23) theorizes, this hymn marked the conclusion of the original "proto-collection" of *Homeric Hymns*.
198 See introduction, 2.3.
199 Hunter 1993: 128. Vamvouri Ruffy (2004: 64 n. 57) cites the Envoi of *HH* 26 as a comparandum for the expectation of annual reperformance implied by Callim. *Hymn* 6.121–127; cf. also 3.266. Vox (2002: 166 n. 59) notes the reference to a religious festival, the Hydrophoria,

2.3 *Apollonius' Envoi and* HH *3.165–176*

Another *HH* intertext for Apollonius's Envoi deserves its own discussion. Giangrande has advanced as Apollonius' primary model in the Envoi the famous *sphragis* from the major *Homeric Hymn to Apollo*.[200] We have already noted an intertext with Apollonius' introit in the section of the hymn that describes the marvelous performance of the Delian maidens (3.156–161).[201] A few lines after that passage, the hymnist modifies and "secularizes" the typical Envoi formulas employed by the *HH*s, applying them not to gods but to the Delian maidens themselves, in order to dismiss them as subjects of praise (165–176):[202]

165 ἀλλ᾽ ἄγεθ᾽ ἱλήκοι μὲν Ἀπόλλων Ἀρτέμιδι ξύν,
χαίρετε δ᾽ ὑμεῖς πᾶσαι· ἐμεῖο δὲ καὶ μετόπισθε
μνήσασθ᾽, ὁππότε κέν τις ἐπιχθονίων ἀνθρώπων
ἐνθάδ᾽ ἀνείρηται ξεῖνος ταλαπείριος ἐλθών·
"ὦ κοῦραι, τίς δ᾽ ὕμμιν ἀνὴρ ἥδιστος ἀοιδῶν
170 ἐνθάδε πωλεῖται, καὶ τέῳ τέρπεσθε μάλιστα;"
ὑμεῖς δ᾽ εὖ μάλα πᾶσαι ὑποκρίνασθαι ἀφήμως·
"τυφλὸς ἀνήρ, οἰκεῖ δὲ Χίῳ ἔνι παιπαλοέσσῃ·
τοῦ πᾶσαι μετόπισθεν ἀριστεύουσιν ἀοιδαί."
ἡμεῖς δ᾽ ὑμέτερον κλέος οἴσομεν, ὅσσον ἐπ᾽ αἶαν
175 ἀνθρώπων στρεφόμεσθα πόλεις εὖ ναιεταώσας·
οἳ δ᾽ ἐπὶ δὴ πείσονται, ἐπεὶ καὶ ἐτήτυμόν ἐστιν.

But now, may Apollo be favorable, together with Artemis, and hail, all you [Delian maidens]! Think of me in future, if ever some long-suffering stranger comes here and asks, "O maidens, which of the singers who visit here do you consider sweetest, and whom do you enjoy most?" Then you must all answer with one voice, "It is a blind man, and he lives in rocky Chios; all of his songs remain supreme afterwards." And we will carry your

---

in the αἴτιον immediately preceding Apollonius' Envoi. I would emphasize that Apollonius here conjures a probably fictive performance context, since no cults for the Argonauts as a collective are known; cf. McNelis 2003: 159: "Recollection of hero-cult in Alexandrian literature need not be tied to actual religious practice." For the Envoi's presupposition of the Argonauts' cultic status, see 1.2.4.

200 Giangrande 1968: 56 n. 1; followed by: James 1981: 83; De Martino 1984–1985: 104; Grillo 1988: 58 n. 157; Albis 1996: 40–42; Vox 2002: 166; Green 2007 ad *Arg.* 4.1773.
201 See 109–111.
202 On the rhetoric of this passage, see the careful analysis of Miller 1979 (summarized in Miller 1986: 60–62).

reputation wherever we go as we roam the well-ordered cities of men, and they will believe it, because it is true.

That Apollonius took an active interest in this passage is proved by his allusion to it in Orpheus' hymn to Apollo in Book 2, which uses a very similar form of the *hapax legomenon* ἱλήκοι with reference to the same god (ἱλήκοις, "be gracious," 2.708).[203] Giangrande even suggests that the hymn's ἱλήκοι influenced Apollonius' cognate Salutatory Verb ἵλατ[ε] (4.1773). In any case, this passage is well known for its identification of the narrator as a blind man from Chios, that is, as Homer himself,[204] and for that reason it might be expected to have caught the interest of a Homeric scholar like Apollonius.

Giangrande proffers a few specific parallels between our passages: "the motifs of sweetness of epic" (γλυκερώτεραι, *Arg.* 4.1774; ἥδιστος ἀοιδῶν, *HH* 3.169)[205] "and of survival of such epic" (ἀοιδαὶ | εἰς ἔτος ἐξ ἔτεος, *Arg.* 4.1774; τοῦ πᾶσαι μετόπισθεν ἀριστεύουσιν ἀοιδαί, *HH* 3.173). He notes that the nominative plural form ἀοιδαί occurs only here in both the *Arg.* (4.1773) and all of Homeric ἔπος (*HH* 3.173); indeed, I would add that ἀοιδαί occupies the same metrical *sedes* in both passages,[206] and in each case a line-initial ἀνθρώποις/ἀνθρώπων follows two lines later.[207] More generally, it is notable that here the *Apollo* hymnist apostrophizes a group—a relative rarity in both the HEs and the *HH*s, which are generally addressed to only one or sometimes two divinities;[208] moreover, both

---

203   Vox 1999: 166, who further notes a pair of two-tier allusions in later texts (Dion. Per. 447, Andromachus the Elder *GDRK* 62.169–174) that connect *Arg.* 2.708 to its hymnic model. The verb ἱλήκω is quite rare, a *hapax* in Apollonius as well as both the *Odyssey* and the collection of *HH*s. Remarkably, in all three cases Apollo is the grammatical subject, but the *Odyssey* passage, in which the suitors revile Eumaeus (21.363–365), seems to have little in common with Apollonius' usage. Note that before Apollonius, Arat. *Phaen.* 637 uses the verb ἱλήκοι, evidently also with an eye to *HH* 3.165. Kidd (1997 ad loc.) suggests that Apollonius imitates Aratus' usage in a different passage (*Arg.* 4.984–985), as do Livrea (1973 ad *Arg.* 4.984) and Vian (2002: 3.112 n. 4).
204   See introduction, 18n92.
205   Cf. Belloni 1995: 175.
206   The same could be said of ἀοιδαί in Theoc. *Id.* 22.223, also adduced by Giangrande; this passage in fact explicitly refers to Homer as "the Chian bard" (Χῖος ἀοιδός, 218).
207   The hymnist's ἀριστεύουσιν ἀοιδαί (173) may also find an echo in Apollonius' ἀριστήων ... ἀοιδαί (4.1773).
208   In fact, the HE narrator never apostrophizes any plurality other than the Muses (Grillo 1988: 52 n. 139). A few *HH*s are dedicated to pairs of divinities: both hymns to the Dioscuri (17, 33), to be sure (Gummert 1992: 129–130 n. 43), but also the *Homeric Hymn to Demeter*, which is really also "to Persephone" (n.b. 2.1–2, 490–495; Suter 2002: 11); cf. the *Homeric Hymn to Hestia* (29), which introduces Hermes as a second Hymnic Subject in its latter

groups consist of mortals (whether heroized or not) who are addressed with formulas otherwise reserved for the gods in the *HH*s. It is furthermore striking that the hymnist envisions a reciprocal χάρις-relationship between himself and his plural addressees of the very sort that Apollonius' Prayer does: the hymnist and his (current) subjects, the Delian maidens, are to spread each other's κλέος, much as Apollonius hopes that the Argonauts will grant his poem, written in their honor, an enduring afterlife.

Before we leave this passage, I would like to venture a tentative suggestion. The referent of the pronoun ἡμεῖς in line 174 may be regarded as the hymnist ("Homer"), using the first-person plural for singular;[209] but this passage has also been interpreted as a reference to the Homeridae, the group of Chian rhapsodes who took their name from the original bard whose poetry they supposedly inherited and performed.[210] This possibility is striking because Apollonius' Prayer to the Argonauts can be interpreted in an analogous way. The wording of his wish (αἵδε δ᾽ ἀοιδαὶ | εἰς ἔτος ἐξ ἔτεος γλυκερώτεραι εἶεν ἀείδειν | ἀνθρώποις, *Arg.* 4.1773–1775) is ambiguous: it could mean "May these songs year after year be sweeter **for men to sing**" or "May these songs year after year be sweeter **to sing to men**."[211] Moreover, both of these possibilities can be imagined in different ways: we might think of a reader "singing" or reciting the text aloud, as the ancients often did, either alone or with others listening along;[212] or we could picture a performer singing Apollonius' material before an audience, in a number of different contexts, such as an ἐπίδειξις or a rhapsodic performance.[213] This last option is especially intriguing given Albis' argument that Apollonius' introit evokes a rhapsodic performance context. Thus interpreted, Apollonius' hope that other singers will perform his songs into the indefinite future finds a good parallel in the Homeridae's claim to pass down and reperform the songs of Homer, which "remain supreme afterwards (μετόπισθεν)."[214]

---

half. The one *HH* to address more than two deities is the irregular twenty-fifth, which is dedicated to Zeus, Apollo, and the Muses.

209 For the interchangeability of the first-person plural and singular in certain contexts in Homer, see Floyd 1969.

210 For this reading, see: Dyer 1975; Graziosi 2002: 65; cf. Vamvouri Ruffy 2004: 134, 147 n. 61. This interpretation may be further related to the view, attested in a scholium to Pindar (ad *Nem.* 2.1c Drachmann), that the "Homeric" *Hymn to Apollo* was forged in Homer's name by one Cynaethus, a prominent Homerid; see introduction, 19n97.

211 Race 2008: 471 with n. 204.

212 See 84n6.

213 See 94n44.

214 Cf. Pindar's description of the preservation of Ajax's fame through rhapsodic reperformances of Homeric poetry for future generations (*Isthm.* 4.37–39, with Currie 2005: 76).

Could Apollonius' conclusion (boldly? facetiously?) suggest his desire to inaugurate his own rhapsodic *tradition*—a clan of "Apolloniadae," as it were, singing his songs forevermore?[215] The parallel with the *sphragis* of the *Homeric Hymn to Apollo* raises this possibility.

2.4 The Text and Significance of Arg. 4.1773

In the foregoing subsections, I hope to have shown that several major structural and rhetorical parallels with the Envois of the *HH*s recognizably establish Apollonius' own Envoi within the Rhapsodic Hymnic tradition. Now, I wish to address a major point of interpretation that I have so far left to the side: how can the Argonauts be saluted and prayed to in the style of the *HH*s if they are mortals? The answer, as a number of critics have seen, lies in the distinctive Greek institution of "hero cult."[216] I take up this point at length in chapter 2, but for now suffice it to say that the Greeks worshipped the powerful dead as "heroes," who were thought capable of exercising their supernatural influence from beyond the grave and who were sometimes actually envisioned as living out an immortal afterlife in a paradise like Elysium or the Islands of the Blessed. By saluting the Argonauts in hymnic style and even praying to them, the narrator makes clear that in these lines he regards his protagonists precisely in their present-day capacity as "cult heroes" who have been divinized after death.[217]

This insight has direct relevance to a vexed textual problem in the Salutation at *Arg.* 4.1773. The reading I have adopted here and throughout this study is the one that the manuscripts uniformly transmit: ἵλατ' ἀριστήων μακάρων γένος ("Be gracious, you race of blessed **heroes**").[218] But in his 1961 OCT, Fränkel emended ἀριστήων from a genitive modifying γένος to an independent vocative in apposition to it: ἵλατ' ἀριστῆες, μακάρων γένος ("Be gracious, **heroes**, offspring of the blessed ones").[219] Fränkel explains the emendation in his app. crit.:

---

215 Cf. Albis 1996: 42: "Apollonius envisions for his *Argonautica* a future of performance, such as he knew had been granted Homer since the distant past."
216 See, e.g.: George 1977: 363 n. 5; Hunter 1993: 8, 128; Tsakiris 2022: 220; and the studies cited below in connection with the text of *Arg.* 4.1773.
217 The Apollonian narrator has just emphasized the temporal distance between the Argonauts' mortal careers and his own time with the Hydrophoria etiology that immediately precedes the Envoi (at 4.1770–1772). We might interpret this passage as a "Prolongation," a section at the end of some Mythic narratives in the *HH*s that bridges the Myth and the Envoi by transitioning from the past tense into the omnitemporal present. See 14*n*71.
218 I quote Race's translation here, as elsewhere, but note that ἀριστήων does not literally mean "heroes" but something like "best men" or "excellent men"; it is one of several terms by which Apollonius regularly denotes the Argonauts.
219 Fränkel's emendation has been adopted in the editions and translations of Vian, Paduano

μάκαρες apud Apollonium (17ies) dei sunt, at Argonautae non dei erant sed deorum proles (e.gr. iii. 402 θεῶν γένος [i.e., "descendants of gods"], ii. 1223 μακάρων σχεδὸν αἵματος ἐκγεγαῶτας [i.e, "closely related by blood to the blessed gods"]), neque aliter turba illa poterat vocari γένος (v. ad i. 548). [bracketed translations added]

Fränkel's first point, that it would be inappropriate to apply the adjective μάκαρες ("blessed") to the Argonauts when Apollonius uses it elsewhere only of gods,[220] precisely misses the hymnic context of *Arg.* 4.1773, where the Argonauts are no longer regarded as mortal heroes of the age of myth but as divinized heroes capable of worship in the narrator's present.[221] Indeed, Livrea points out that Apollonius' Salutatory Verb ἵλατε, in this form, is associated exclusively with deities elsewhere in the *Arg.* (4.984, 1333, 1411),[222] so that Fränkel's emendation would not even remove the perceived problem of diction appropriate only to divinities in this passage—to say nothing of the Prayer made to the Argonauts in the following sentence, which presupposes their divinization.

Fränkel's second point, that the Argonauts cannot be called a γένος except in the sense of "offspring,"[223] is contradicted by one of the passages that he himself cites: at *Arg.* 1.548–549, at the launch of the Argo, the gods look down upon

---

and Fusillo, Glei and Natzel-Glei, Green, and Hunter, whereas Livrea, Valverde Sánchez, Dräger, and Race retain the traditional reading. Stürner is inconsistent in printing ἀριστήων (2022: 413) or ἀριστῆες (62, 63), but her translation assumes a vocative ("ihr Helden," 107).

220 This argument is reproduced by Vian 2002: 3.222; Hunter 2015 ad loc.
221 Phinney 1963: 158 n. 1; Giangrande 1968: 56 n. 1; James 1981: 83–84. Curiously, Beye (1982: 14) does not consider the Argonauts to have been divinized, but he is nevertheless untroubled by the application of the epithet μάκαρ to them in light of the "hymnlike" quality of the poem's ending. Cuypers (2004: 45) likewise denies the full weight of "race of blessed ones" by interpreting it metaphorically: "The Argonauts, it is suggested, have become immortal; not because, as their one-time companion and all-time *exemplum*, Heracles, they have gained a seat on Olympus, but because Apollonius has immortalized them with his epic, which he prays will be 'sung' forever"; see further Klooster 2013a: 160–161. Kampakoglou (2019: 102 n. 10) sketches a similar interpretation before dismissing the Salutation to the divinized Argonauts as an "ambiguous afterthought"—despite directly acknowledging "the cult honors that they have received in the time after the expedition." In general, one gets the impression that scholarship on the *Arg.* has not taken sufficiently seriously the reality of hero cult as an integral facet of Greek religion.
222 Note however, the use of the singular ἵλαθι at *Arg.* 4.1014, in Medea's supplication of Arete, and of the infinitive ἱλάεσθαι at 4.479 for the expiation of bloodguilt. See further: George 1977: 363 n. 5; Hitch 2012: 141 n. 32, 157.
223 Vian (2002: 3.222 ad loc.) repeats this argument.

"the **race** of demigods, the best of men who then were sailing over the sea" (ἡμιθέων ἀνδρῶν γένος, οἳ τότ' ἄριστοι | πόντον ἐπιπλώεσκον).²²⁴ The key to interpreting Apollonius' use of γένος in this passage is his close adaptation therein of the phrase that denotes the heroes in Hesiod's myth of the Five Ages: "the godly **race** of men-heroes, who are called demigods" (ἀνδρῶν ἡρώων θεῖον γένος, οἳ καλέονται | ἡμίθεοι, *Op.* 159–160).²²⁵ Thus at the beginning of their voyage (*Arg.* 1.548), Apollonius portrays the Argonauts as representatives of Hesiod's entire Age of Heroes;²²⁶ it is eminently fitting that Apollonius would evoke this macroscopic conception again at the end of their voyage, and of his narrative.²²⁷ Notably, Catullus brings out this dimension of Apollonius' Salutation in his imitation of *Arg.* 4.1773 at c. 64.22–23, quoted already above: "O, hail, heroes, offspring of gods, born **in the happiest time of the ages!**" (*o nimis optato saeclorum tempore nati* | *heroes, salvete deum genus!*). The "happiest time of the ages" is the Hesiodic Age of Heroes, for which the Catullan narrator feels a strong nostalgia amid the present degeneracy of the Iron Age.²²⁸ The internal echo of *Arg.* 1.548 at 4.1773 can also be appreciated as reflective of the change in status that the Argonauts have undergone after death: whereas in life they were a "race of demigods" (ἡμιθέων ἀνδρῶν γένος), in death they have become a "race **of blessed** heroes" (ἀριστήων μακάρων γένος).²²⁹ The adjective μάκαρες signals their transformation into cult heroes and suggests their present exis-

---

224 Fränkel's note in the app. crit ad 1.548 glosses the phrase in context as "[dei] suam prolem ... spectabant," which can hardly work with the genitive phrase ἡμιθέων ἀνδρῶν attached to γένος. See further: James 1981: 84; Hitch 2012: 157 n. 71.
225 Fränkel himself used the Hesiodic allusion here to argue for the reading γένος in 1.548 over the variant μένος (1964: 134–137). For more on this allusion, see 2.2.3.
226 Apollonius may have felt entitled to take such license in light of *Il.* 12.23, where those who died at Troy cannot constitute literally the entire ἡμιθέων γένος ἀνδρῶν. On this passage, see 2.2.3.
227 For *Arg.* 4.1773 as evoking Hes. *Op.* 159, see: Händel 1954: 48; Livrea 1983: 426; Grillo 1988: 58 n. 154; Belloni 1995: 178; Vox 2002: 162–163; Martin *ap.* Vian 2002: 3.145–146 n. 5; Green 2007 ad loc. Theocritus' hymn to the Dioscuri (*Id.* 22) similarly broadens out in its Envoi to embrace the heroes (ἡρώεσσιν, 216) of the Trojan War era generally (214–223). The Salutation of Aratus' Hymnic Proem to Zeus might likewise end by pairing its proper Hymnic Subject with the heroes, at least on one ancient interpretation of the phrase προτέρη γενεή (see Σ and Kidd 1997 ad Arat. *Phaen.* 16). Note further those *HH*s whose Salutations are extended from the Hymnic Subject announced in the Exordium to include "all goddesses as well" (θεαί θ' ἅμα πᾶσαι, 9.7, 14.6; see also 27.21).
228 See on this theme, e.g., Harmon 1973.
229 Hitch 2012: 146, 156–157; Belloni 2017: 94–96. Note as well the argument that ἀριστήων μακάρων represents a pointed reversal, or *oppositio in imitando*, of the Homeric phrase ἄνδρες ἀριστῆες (Giangrande 1968: 56 n. 1; Livrea 1973 ad *Arg.* 4.1773). Campbell (1976: 338) dismisses this view as "bizarre" without argument.

tence on the Islands **of the Blessed**, which Hesiod specifies as the fate of the heroes immortalized by Zeus in his myth of the Five Ages (ἐν **μακάρων** νήσοισι, *Op.* 171).[230]

In sum, Fränkel's arguments for emending ἀριστήων are not persuasive. Fränkel's procedure is also vulnerable to criticism in its own right. As Livrea argues, the emendation can be rejected on text-critical grounds according to the principle of *utrum in alterum abiturum erat?* (also formulated as *lectio difficilior potior*): ἀριστήων μακάρων γένος is a more difficult and unusual phrase and thus, if it were not the accurate reading, would have likelier been altered to the easier (and, as Livrea says, "banalizzante") ἀριστῆες, μακάρων γένος than vice versa.[231]

Nevertheless, Fränkel's emendation has found a strong ally in West, who first adduced Catullus' adaptation at c. 64.23 (*heroes, salvete, deum genus!* ["Hail, heroes, offspring of gods"]) to support Fränkel's correction (ἵλατ' ἀριστῆες, μακάρων γένος, *Arg.* 4.1773).[232] The correspondence is indeed striking; Catullus seems virtually to have translated Apollonius' text precisely as Fränkel has corrected it. In this case I am not convinced, however, of the methodological validity of using an allusion in a later text to alter its model, especially when the reasons brought against the validity of the original, much richer reading have turned out to be dubious. Can Catullus' imitation "confirm" an emendation that has nothing else to recommend it? As students of intertextuality well know, allusions regularly involve transformations or even "corrections" of their models, and Catullus might have had any number of reasons to make the slight tweak from "race of blessed heroes" to "heroes, offspring of the blessed ones." For instance, he could be "contaminating" *Arg.* 4.1773 with another Apollonian *locus*, such as 3.402 (θεῶν γένος, "descendants of gods").[233] Such an alteration would be of a piece with his strong thematic interest in the **birth** of his heroes

---

230 Dräger 2002 ad loc.; Hitch 2012: 157. See further the discussion of Hesiodic heroism in 2.2.3. The name "Islands of the Blessed" likens the immortalized heroes' postmortem existence to that of the "blessed" gods (Roloff 1970: 98). See further, e.g., Pind. *Pyth.* 5.94–95, of Battus, the founder of Cyrene: "He was **blessed** while he dwelt among men, and afterwards a **hero** worshiped by his people" (μάκαρ μὲν ἀνδρῶν μέτα | ἔναιεν, ἥρως δ' ἔπειτα λαοσεβής).

231 Livrea 1983: 426.

232 West 1965. Vian (2002: 3.145 n. 5) seems to view this argument as particularly decisive in favor of Fränkel's emendation. Köhnken (2010: 143) asserts that Apollonius modeled ἀριστῆες, μακάρων γένος on Medea's address to the heroes at the beginning of Pindar's Argonautic narrative (παῖδες ὑπερθύμων τε φωτῶν καὶ θεῶν ["sons of great-hearted men and gods"], *Pyth.* 4.13), but the parallel is not especially compelling. Cf. Acosta-Hughes 2010a: 180 n. 33 for this line as a possible precursor for φωτῶν in *Arg.* 1.1.

233 Adduced by, e.g.: Perrotta 1931: 188; Thomson 1997 ad Catull. c. 64.23.

in c. 64 (n.b. *nati*, 21), for their very existence testifies to the unions of gods (*deum*, 22) and mortals (*matrum*, 22) that used to transpire in former times (cf. 382–396), and of which the marriage of Peleus and Thetis is a banner example. Catullus' transformation would also serve to de-emphasize the motif of hero cult, which was an essentially Greek, not Roman, phenomenon.[234]

Ultimately, this debate is not the most consequential, because, even in the reading ἀριστῆες μακάρων γένος, both the meanings "heroes, offspring of the blessed ones" and "heroes, race of blessed ones" are possible.[235] Thus Hunter opines, "Fränkel is correct that the basic meaning is 'offspring of the gods,' but the Hesiodic background adds the resonance 'race of blessed heroes.'"[236] My preference is for the arresting expression "blessed heroes" of the manuscript tradition, but the major point I would emphasize here is that the Envoi presents the Argonauts as heroes divinized after death.

3   Rereading the Introit in Light of the Envoi

The previous section has fleshed out the traditional background provided by the *HH*s for the structure, diction, and substance of Apollonius' Envoi. Much more could be said about this fascinating passage, but at this point, I would like to underline two essential points that have emerged from the foregoing analysis:

1) The *Arg.* ends with a hymnic conclusion on the model of the *HH*s.
2) This Envoi unambiguously salutes and prays to the Argonauts, who now must be regarded in their capacity as divinized heroes.

These data have important ramifications for the reader's reinterpretation of the introit and, indeed, the poem as a whole. Both the introit and the Envoi of the *Arg.* have "hymnic" elements and thus jointly make up the poem's "hymnic frame," but the introit is, as we have seen, highly ambiguous: it is capable of multiple interpretations, some of which are not "hymnic" at all. The Envoi,

---

234 See, e.g., *ThesCRA* 2.151, 186–187.
235 Cuypers 2004: 45. As she notes (45 n. 7), the latter interpretation gives point to the enjambed ἀνθρώποις (1775), "for *humans*" (as opposed to μάκαρες); see further Hunter 1993: 128. Tsakiris (2022: 220) notes that μακάρων γένος, in the sense "race of blessed (gods)," occurs in the same *sedes* at Hes. *Th.* 33 (the subject Hesiod is commissioned to sing by the Muses); see further Manuello 2012: 140 n. 62.
236 Hunter 1993: 128 n. 108. Thus Belloni (2017: 95), for instance, follows Fränkel's text but apparently understands μακάρων γένος at 4.1773 as "race of blessed ones," in a purposeful variation on the similar phrase at 1.548. See further Green 2007 with his note ad loc.

however, clarifies the import of the "hymnic frame" considerably. If the *Arg.* ends with a hymnic conclusion, then the reader may safely assume that the entire poem has been a hymn "all along," for the simple reason that this highly distinctive closural device is characteristic of this type of discourse (the *HH*) and thus marks the poem as such.[237] And as the recipients of the poet's Salutation and Prayer, the Subject of that hymn must be the Argonauts. In light of the Envoi, Williams et al. are not wrong to consider the entire *Arg.* to be a sort of hymn, but the poem cannot be construed as a hymn to Apollo, since if it were, the god would have been named in the hymn's Salutation.[238] The Envoi rather presents the *Arg.* as a Homeric-style hymn to the Argonauts themselves, who have, indeed, been the poem's Subject throughout.[239]

---

237 Haubold (2001: 24, 39) emphasizes that within the body of early Greek hexameter poetry, the *HH*s alone possess a fixed ending, which is thus the most distinctive characteristic of their structure; see further Ford 2011: 107, and cf. the open-endedness of early epics (Valverde Sánchez 1996: 33–34). An interesting parallel that shows the difference an ending can make is presented by the transmission history of Theocritus' incomplete twenty-fourth *Idyll*. The *Herakliskos* was long considered purely an epyllion until a papyrus find turned up its hymnic Envoi and retrospectively revealed that the poem had been a hymn all along (Barber 1968: 269; Kampakoglou 2021: 24).

238 Williams (1991: 304) actually cites the hymnic conclusion of the *Arg.* as evidence for her interpretation of the poem as a quasi-hymn to Apollo, but with a revealing concession: "The epic closes with an invocation (ἵλατ' IV.1773) which is standard at the end of hymns, *although here it is addressed to the heroes, not to Apollo*" (emphasis added). Cf. also the intermediate position of Cuypers 2004: 45: "The epilogue resumes the genre of the proem: hymn. However, what started out as a hymn to Apollo now ends as a hymn to the Argonauts." Petrovic (2012: 153) and Klooster (2013a: 163) express similar views, and Schaaf (2014: 329) explains this switch as "eine Strategie pindarischer Dichtung," since Pindar praises both "human exploits and the gods" (Cuypers 2004: 44). I myself have argued (1.1.5) that whereas the introit can be regarded as a Hymnic Proem, there are serious problems with reading it as an Exordium to the poem *in toto* as a hymn to Apollo. Moreover, this "mixed hymn" view misses the *flexibility* of the introit, which can be read without hymnic overtones or, indeed, as the Exordium of a hymn to the Argonauts, as I argue below. Finally, whereas *HH* 29 shows that a second Hymnic Subject can be introduced and hailed in the Salutation, the original Subject is never left out of the Envoi (Janko 1981: 17), as Apollo would be at *Arg.* 4.1773.

239 Scholars have been surprisingly reluctant to declare outright that the *Arg.* is a hymn to the Argonauts, but for this view, see: Phinney 1963: 158; Sistakou 2001: 260 with n. 71; and especially Hunter 1996: 46, who also notes the "Homeric" inflection of the poem qua hymn. Cf. Tsakiris 2022: 206–221, who identifies only the last third of Book 4 (from Libya onwards) as a Homeric-style hymn to the heroes. Cf. further Murray 2018: 202–209, who recognizes several Rhapsodic elements in the hymnic frame that point to the Argonauts as the Hymnic Subject, though she seems unwilling to countenance the possibility of anyone other than Apollo fulfilling this function. Klooster (2011: 88) asserts that "surely it goes too far to claim, as some have done, that the whole *Argonautica* is

This interpretation seems to me demanded by the Envoi, but its real "test" is its compatibility with the hymnic elements in the introit. After all, it is easy to imagine our first-time readers thoroughly surprised and perhaps confused by the poem's sudden hymnic ending. If they now decide to become re-readers of Apollonius' epic, will it be possible for them to fit the introit into a coherent understanding of the whole *Arg.* as a unified, Homeric-style hymn to the Argonauts? No less than their Envois, the Exordia of *HH*s abide by a more or less fixed set of conventions that we should expect the *Arg.* introit to follow if it really does possess a Homeric-hymnic frame as I claim.

Accordingly, I now revisit the introit in order to demonstrate that it can indeed be read as an Exordium to an Argonautic hymn. The focus will be the critical portion of the introit in which most of its "hymnic" elements are concentrated, 1.1–2:[240]

Ἀρχόμενος σέο, Φοῖβε, παλαιγενέων κλέα φωτῶν
μνήσομαι, οἵ ...

Beginning with you, Phoebus, I shall recall the famous deeds of people born long ago, who ...

As discussed in the introduction (2.2), both Archaic epics and Rhapsodic Hymns begin according to the same conventions, and so on a first reading it would be easy to regard Apollonius' introit as more or less standardly epic.[241] In light of the poem's hymnic Envoi, however, this line and a half can be appreciated anew. In proper Homeric-hymnic style, the Argonauts are named as the Hymnic Subject in Er-Stil using an oblique case (παλαιγενέων ... φωτῶν, to be identified further in the relative clause). μνήσομαι serves as the Evocatory Verb—an unusual usage in the *HH*s, to be sure, but one that is paralleled by *HH* 3.1 (**Μνήσομαι** οὐδὲ λάθωμαι Ἀπόλλωνος ἑκάτοιο) and 7.1–2 (Ἀμφὶ Διώνυσον

---

intended as one long hymnic proem"—I would prefer "one long hymn"—but she offers no argument as to how or why "it goes too far." Klooster's own view is that the hymnic frame is designed to link Apollonius' poetry to the songs of Orpheus, which are frequently hymnic (87–91). I agree that Orpheus is important as an internal "alter ego" of the hymnic narrator (see 327n217), but I see no reason why this parallel should prevent us from interpreting the hymnic frame as, precisely, a framing device that structures the *Arg.* as a hymn.

240 The only potentially "hymnic" element not found in these lines is the second-person pronoun τεήν in line 8, though as noted above in the discussion of *HH* 21, most of the *HH*s restrict the use of Du-Stil to their Envois.

241 As, e.g., Händel (1954: 9–10) does.

Σεμέλης ἐρικυδέος υἱόν | μνήσομαι), as we saw at the beginning of the chapter. Likewise, the *HH*s normally name their Subjects as the first word of the poem (if metrically feasible) and in the accusative case, as the object of the Evocatory Verb; but in fact, there is a solid precedent for Apollonius' alternative construction in the major *Homeric Hymn to Aphrodite* (5.1–2):

Μοῦσά μοι ἔννεπε ἔργα πολυχρύσου Ἀφροδίτης
Κύπριδος, ἥ ...

Muse, tell me of the deeds of Aphrodite rich in gold, the Cyprian, who ...[242]

Apollonius may have been attracted to this construction by his desire to include an adapted form of the phrase κλέα ἀνδρῶν in his opening line.[243] The Hymnic Subject is modified, as usual, with an epithet, παλαιγενέων. The relative pronoun οἵ in *Arg.* 1.2 can now be understood as a standard example of the "Hymnic Relative," effecting the transition from the Exordium to the middle section, or *Laudatio*, of the hymn—much like the ἥ in the second line of the *Aphrodite* hymn quoted above.[244] We are now equipped to recognize that in this instance, the *Laudatio* takes the form of an unusually lengthy Myth about the Hymnic Subjects, namely, the entire epic narrative stretching from οἵ in 1.2 all the way to the outbreak of the Envoi at 4.1773.

The integration of what is effectively a full Argonautic epic into this hymnic framework leads me to describe the *Arg.* specifically as a kind of generically hybrid "epic hymn"—but a full explication of this concept must wait until chapter 2. For present purposes, we may conclude that *Arg.* 1.1–2 can indeed be satisfactorily understood as the Exordium to a hymn about the Argonauts, even if it does not positively demand such an interpretation on a first reading. But what of the very first words, ἀρχόμενος σέο, Φοῖβε? How do they fit into this revised understanding of the introit? To begin with, I think it is still possible to regard these three words, with Phinney and others, as (evoking) a Hymnic Proem in their own right. Other versions of the "Hymnic Proem" interpretation, which posit a Proem consisting of lines 1.1–4 or even the entire introit (1.1–22), are effectively ruled out by the view that *Arg.* 1.1–2 introduces the poem as an

---

242 On this peculiar announcement of the Hymnic Subject, see Clay 2006: 155–157 (with earlier bibliography); Vamvouri Ruffy 2004: 31.
243 See the discussion of genre in the next chapter.
244 *Pace* Llanos (2017a: 5, 2017b: 4), who considers such relative clauses as an affectation only of epic, not hymnic, introits.

Argonautic hymn; for how can the same lines function simultaneously as part of a Hymnic Proem to Apollo that precedes an epic composition about the Argonauts and as the Exordial section of a hymn to the Argonauts? But Phinney's view can survive such a rethinking of the *Arg.* introit: the Hymnic Proem is cordoned off to the poem's first phrase (Ἀρχόμενος σέο, Φοῖβε), while the next phrase serves to introduce the poem qua hymn (παλαιγενέων κλέα φωτῶν | μνήσομαι, οἵ …). It is admittedly awkward to imagine a hymn, even an "epic" one, endowed with its own hymnic prelude, but Phinney himself seems to have subscribed to this view, to judge from his separate comments on the introit and the Envoi;[245] such a conceit might even be understandable as a sort of Alexandrian jeu d'esprit.

Nevertheless, I suspect that most readers who had subscribed to the "Hymnic Proem" interpretation will now wish to discard it, acknowledging that μνήσομαι (1.2), one of the principal "hymnic" markers in the introit, really "goes with" the Argonauts as the poem's Hymnic Subject, not with the apostrophized Apollo.[246] More important, perhaps, is the reader's sense that the very genre of the poem has shifted. On a first reading, it was possible to think that the *Arg.* was an ordinary epic that happened to be prefaced by a Hymnic Proem, like Hesiod's *Theogony*. Now that the poem has turned out to be a hymn to the Argonauts, the "hymnic" interpretation that makes the most sense regards the introit not as a Proem, but as the Exordium of a hymn. Does this reading leave room for a Hymnic Proem to Apollo?[247] For many readers, to the extent that ἀρχόμενος σέο, Φοῖβε at first seemed hymnic, the phrase will now appear to have been a characteristic case of Apollonian misdirection.[248] The elements of the phrase that at first appeared very obviously hymnic—the use of a form of ἄρχομαι and especially the vocative address to a deity, which is extended to line 8 by

---

245   See Phinney 1963: 1–2 (on the introit's Hymnic Proem to Apollo) and 158 (on the poem as a hymn to the Argonauts).

246   It is thus not fully accurate to say, as Williams (1991: 302) does, that the poem "begins with an invocation to Apollo which includes μνήσομαι (1.2) and ἀρχόμενος (1.1)," just as a hymn might, because μνήσομαι is not connected to the Invocation of Apollo.

247   Goldhill (1991: 287) appears to dramatize this change of heart over the space of a few sentences.

248   Apollonius' use of such "red herrings" is well-documented; see, e.g. Fränkel 1968 ad 4.646–648, and Knight 1995: 114–117 on the multiple instances in which an epic battle seems to loom on the horizon and yet never materializes (on such "atti mancati," see further Fusillo 1985: 160–161), or Byre 1997, 2002: *passim* on the misleading character of the beginning of the poem, which seems to promise high heroic epic filled with divine intervention and feats of valor. For another red herring in the introit itself, which seems to suggest that Poseidon may reprise his Odyssean role as the poem's divine antagonist, see Wray 2000: 255–256.

means of the second-person possessive pronoun τεήν—now feel incompatible with the true Hymnic Subject of the poem.[249]

The genius of Apollonius' introit, however, is that the phrase ἀρχόμενος σέο, Φοῖβε need not be understood according to the "Hymnic Proem" interpretation. As we saw in section I of this chapter, a great deal of ambiguity is built into the introit, such that this phrase can be understood from a number of angles; the two major alternatives to the "Hymnic Proem" construal are the "inspiration" and "narrative catalyst" interpretations. Thus, on realizing that the *Arg.* is "actually" a hymn to the Argonauts, re-readers are free to revise their understanding of this phrase and adopt either or both of these alternatives. The "inspiration" interpretation may be especially attractive on a rereading, for about a third of the *HH*s open with second-person Appeals to the Muses, just as in epic introits.[250] The introit's ambiguity thus facilitates both the first-time reader's potential "misreading" and the re-reader's revised reading.

4 Conclusion

To summarize, these are the main points I have attempted to demonstrate in this chapter:
- The *Arg.*'s hymnic frame is modeled specifically on the formulas that characterize the Exordia and Envois of the *HH*s, which are thus marked as the poet's privileged generic models within the wider category of ὕμνος.
- Apollonius' introit is highly ambiguous, especially on a first reading. "Beginning with you, Phoebus" may initially suggest a Hymnic Proem to Apollo, and this reading is supported by a number of intertexts with other Hymnic Proems. But there are other interpretative options as well.
  - The two major alternatives: Apollo could be invoked for inspiration, or as a starting point in the narrative; these possibilities are not mutually exclusive.
- The poem's Envoi, however, unambiguously marks the whole poem out as a hymn to the Argonauts.

---

249 The refocusing of the Argonauts as the Hymnic Subject of the entire *Arg.*, in preference to Apollo as the Subject of a Hymnic Proem, is in keeping with Apollonius' tendency to set his major gods in the background in favor of minor and new divinities. On this phenomenon, see, e.g.: Herter in *RE* Suppl. 13 s.v. "Apollonios," col. 34; Feeney 1991: ch. 2; Hunter 1993: 78–79; Knight 1995: ch. 5; Brioso Sánchez 2003: 32; Clauss 2016b: 142–149.
250 See 11*n*59.

- Thus in hindsight, the introit can be reread as the Exordium of a hymn, invoking the Argonauts in Er-Stil as the Subject of an "epic hymn": a Homeric-style Rhapsodic Hymn whose *Laudatio* consists of a Myth extended to epic proportions.
  - The suggestion of a Hymnic Proem in the words ἀρχόμενος σέο, Φοῖβε thus turns out to have been misdirection (unless the reader is prepared to view the *Arg.* as a hymn to the Argonauts endowed with its own Hymnic Proem to Apollo).

The *Arg.*'s hymnic frame is complex and densely textured, and this chapter has hardly exhausted its hermeneutic riches, to which I will be returning in the next. But before proceeding, I would like to pause to reflect on what we can learn so far about Apollonius' poetic technique from his adaptation of the formulas and other precedents provided by the *HH*s to his own hymnic Exordium and Envoi. My overwhelming impression is that Apollonius was keenly interested in exceptional constructions and irregular variants on common formulas. Furthermore, I think that it must be by design that in every case, Apollonius' practice is not unprecedented, and is indeed recognizable as deriving from the *HH*s, but nevertheless consistently combines a series of rare usages to create completely unique formulations. To wit: Apollonius eschews the common Evocatory Verbs in favor of the unusual μνήσομαι (as in *HH*s 3.1, 7.1–2); the object of that verb is not the name of the Hymnic Subject in the accusative but a neuter plural noun to which the honorand is attached in the genitive (as in 5.1); his Salutatory Verb is a form of ἱλάομαι instead of the much commoner χαῖρε (as in 1D.8, 3.165, 20.8, 23.4);[251] he omits a formal Poet's Task, but executes the same essential function in his Prayer to the heroes (as in 1D.8–10, 7.58–59);[252] and his Exordium confusingly invokes Apollo even as it evokes the Argonauts—perhaps in the same way that many *HH*s appeal to the Muses in their Exordia (4.1, 5.1, 9.1, 14.2, 17.1, 19.1, 20.1, 31.1–2, 32.1–2, 33.1). In apostrophizing Apollo, moreover, Apollonius uses two singular constructions applied specifically to this deity in the hymns: ἄρχομαι + gen. (as in 25.1) combined with a vocative address to Phoebus (as in 21.1).[253]

---

251 Indeed, Apollonius uses a form of the verb that never appears in the hymns as such, the plural imperative ἵλατ(ε).

252 Note as well that Apollonius' use of the optative instead of imperative in the Prayer could be based on the precedent of Callimachean or Theocritean Rhapsodic Hymns.

253 We also saw that Apollonius could also have found precedent in the *HH*s for his decision to hymn a large collectivity, i.e., the entire crew of the Argo. The *HH*s provide a few examples of hymns dedicated to pairs of divinities (2, 17, 29, 33), and exactly one to a larger group (25: Zeus, Apollo, and the Muses).

This allusive method is characteristically Alexandrian, and is also consonant with Apollonius' approach to the HEs—he is everywhere drawn to rare usages and revels in modifying Homeric formulas, avoiding overly-close borrowings.[254] Whether he adapts the HEs or *HHs*, the result is a recognizably Homeric texture that is nevertheless fresh and striking. We have also seen another example of a *hapax legomenon* that Apollonius draws from the *HHs* (ἰλήκοις, 2.708, from *HH* 3.165). The results of this chapter support the hypothesis that Apollonius treats the *HHs* just as he does the *Iliad* and *Odyssey*: as authoritative models to be invoked and creatively transformed.

---

254 See on this point esp. Giangrande 1967, 1970.

CHAPTER 2

Heroization and Generic Hybridity

The diachronic reading advanced in the previous chapter highlights the ambiguous generic affiliations of Apollonius' poem, which shifts from epic to hymn as it is read and reread. As we have seen, on a first reading, the introit may be regarded as conforming to purely epic standards of composition, like the beginning of the *Iliad* or *Odyssey*. Even reading the introit as a Hymnic Proem will not change this fact, as Goldhill observes:

> This hymnic invocation at the beginning of the epic is often taken as a wilful "mixing of genres"—an effect which turns the familiar recognition of a generic sign to a defamiliarized recognition of difference. Yet the performance of Greek epic poetry was normally preceded by a short hymn, and the *Theogony* of Hesiod—an author to whom the Hellenistic poets indicated an especial affiliation—offers a fine example of the hymnic proem as an integral part of a hexameter poem.[1]

Thus, on a first reading, the introit's "hymnic" qualities can be entirely incorporated within and subordinated to an epic macrostructure: no "mixing of genres" need be involved.[2] With the Envoi, however, Apollonius wryly flips this hierarchy on its head. The entire poem will now be seen as a hymn to the Argonauts, and the epic narrative—from the Hymnic Relative οἵ in 1.2 all the way up to the hymnic Salutation at 4.1773—turns out to have been the "Mythic" section of that hymn. As Hunter puts it, the *Arg.* becomes "a 'Hymn to the Argonauts,' that is a hymn on the traditional 'Homeric' model in which the central mythic narrative has been greatly extended, but in which the hymnic frame remains."[3]

---

1 Goldhill 1991: 287. See further Llanos 2017a: 8.
2 By this phrase Goldhill alludes to the "Kreuzung der Gattungen," a term coined by Kroll (1924: ch. 9) to describe the experiments with generic hybridity so characteristic of Hellenistic poetry. More recent discussions of this phenomenon include Fantuzzi 1980 and Rossi 2000.
3 Hunter 1996: 46, quoted approvingly by Schaaf 2014: 329. Cf. Janko (1982: 14) on the length of the *HH*s: "The development of the Myth may proceed unhindered by any forces of genre to whatever length the poet wishes or his audience might require." Note that there is precedent for epic subject matter in the Myth of a *HH* in the *Homeric Hymn to Heracles* (15.4–6); see 2.4.4–2.5.

But even if, formally speaking, the *Arg.* is structured as a hymn, it would be difficult to deny the poem's strong de facto affiliation with the genre of epic. The length of the poem alone would suggest as much,[4] not to mention the fact that its protagonists are, for the most part, mortal heroes whose eventual divinization comes firmly into focus only in the poem's final lines (4.1773–1781). Most tellingly, perhaps, Apollonius insists upon his poem's status as epic when he declares his theme to be κλέα φωτῶν (1.1),[5] an artful variation[6] on a generic term for the subject of epic poetry already in use in Homer, κλέα ἀνδρῶν (*Il.* 9.189, 524;[7] *Od.* 8.73).[8] Indeed, the nesting of this epic tag in between two markers of pointedly hymnic terminology (ἀρχόμενος σέο, Φοῖβε ... μνήσομαι) reproduces the structure of the entire poem in miniature: epic deeds enclosed by a hymnic frame. Thus I would argue that the introit does announce a genuine mixing

---

4   For length as a generic marker, see Fowler 1982: 62–64. Apollonius' poem, it is true, is much shorter than either of the Homeric epics (so Klein 1975: 22: the *Arg.* "must ... be given the credit for being one of the shortest ancient epics"), but it is several times longer than even the longest of the *HH*s; we might view it as a happy medium between the two forms. For the idea that the *Arg.* satisfies Aristotelian prescriptions for the proper length of an epic poem, see, e.g.: Pfeiffer 1968: 143; Heiserman 1977: 36; Beye 1982: 7, 2006: 192; Green 1988: 2; Cusset 2001: 74–75; Nelis 2005a: 355; Caneva 2007: 71; Hunter 2008: 133; cf. Fusillo 1985: 156 n. 94. It must be noted, however, that Archaic epics could be equally short; for instance, the Argonautic epic attributed to Epimenides was reportedly 6,500 lines long (Diog. Laert. 1.111), which does not exceed the *Arg.* by much at all; see further Hunter 2008: 144–145.

5   This point is made, e.g., by: Zanker 1979: 53; Schwinge 1986: 93–94; Albis 1996: 17; Pietsch 1999: 66; Nelis 2005a: 356; Hunter 2008: 115; Ransom 2014: 639–640; see also the studies mentioned in the following notes. Cf. Guinee 1999: 16 for the interesting idea that Apollonius could be framing his own *Arg.* as the κλέα ἀνδρῶν that Achilles "will" sing, so to speak, at *Il.* 9.189. The Argonautic quest is indeed one of the major cycles of earlier heroic myth of which Achilles might have sung: see Stat. *Achil.* 190–191.

6   For κλέα φωτῶν as a programmatic example of Apollonian *imitatio cum variatione* in adapting Homeric diction, see Beye 1969: 35; Giangrande 1977: 273.

7   At *Il.* 9.524, Phoenix in fact uses the phrase "the glorious deeds of men of old" (τῶν πρόσθεν ... κλέα ἀνδρῶν) to preface his Meleager *exemplum*, which is explicitly cast in parallel with the plot of the *Iliad* itself (Llanos 2017a: 3–4). As Llanos notes, the phrase itself is very close semantically to Apollonius' παλαιγενέων κλέα φωτῶν, and Phoenix actually uses the adverb πάλαι to set his story in time at line 527. Levin (1971: 10) notes the appearance of the phrase σέο δ' ἄρξομαι earlier in Book 9, too, at line 97.

8   For κλέα ἀνδρῶν as a generic term for epic, see, e.g.: Conte 1986: 70–72; Fantuzzi and Hunter 2004: 90–91; O'Hara 2007: 45; for some caveats, cf. Ford 1992: 57–67; and for the term κλέος in general, see Nagy 1974: 244–255. Notably, the variant ἀνδρῶν can be found in place of φωτῶν in codex E—to be sure, an inferior reading (likely derived from a gloss), but one that reflects the inevitability with which Apollonius' phrase recalls Homer's. Cf. also *AP* 2.378: Christodorus' highly epicizing description of Herodotus' work casts the historian's subject as ὠγυγίων κλέα φωτῶν ("the glorious deeds of ancient people"), an epic tag modeled closely on Apollonius' παλαιγενέων κλέα φωτῶν (Tissoni 2000a: 241; 2000b: 217).

of genres. The *Arg.* is, in a word, an "epic hymn," an innovative fusion of the two branches of Homeric poetry, both the epics and the hymns, into a unique generic hybrid, a hymn that celebrates its divinized addressees by recounting their deeds in a self-consciously epic register.[9]

In the realm of extant Greek literature, Apollonius' bold generic experiment is almost unparalleled:[10] no poem before the *Arg.* could be considered an epic hymn in the same fashion, and perhaps only one after it could be so regarded, namely, Dionysius' *Periegesis*, a product of the Hadrianic era that frames itself as a sort of "didactic epic hymn" in imitation of Apollonius.[11] Nevertheless, this blending of epic and hymnody hardly arose in a sociocultural or literary-historical vacuum. In this chapter, I seek the conceptual underpinning of this conceit in the duality of the Greek concept of the hero, whose double valence as both a secular figure of myth and poetry and as the object of cultic veneration corresponds to the *Arg.*'s own generic hybridity as both epic and hymn.[12]

I proceed, first, with an overview of the concept of the hero in Greek literature and culture generally, in section 1. Section 2 then offers a survey of the evidence for hero cult and related phenomena within the *Arg.* This survey demonstrates the thematic importance of heroization in the poem, in stark

[9] See further Romeo 1985: 22–23. I consider the *Argonautica* generically hybrid in that it combines the formal features of epic and Rhapsodic Hymnody at the macro level, but I would, of course, additionally acknowledge the influence of a wide range of genres on Apollonius' narrative, including, *inter alia*, lyric (see, e.g.: Rosenmeyer 1992; Acosta-Hughes 2010a: *passim*; Kampakoglou 2019: chs. 3, 9), historiography and ethnography (e.g.: Clauss 2012; Priestley 2014: chs. 3–4; Morrison 2020), and tragedy (e.g., Cusset 2001; Schmakeit 2003; Sistakou 2016: ch. 6; Stoessl 1941 shows its age, but is still suggestive for the abundance of tragic material in the *Arg.*). Apollonius' other, lost poems may have revealed a similar penchant for generic experimentation; see, e.g., Sistakou 2008b: 336–340.

[10] Cf. Grillo 1988: 56–59 on Apollonius' unprecedented Envoi to his epic heroes. From the *Arg.*, this device enters the repertoire of closural gestures used in later epic (though see already Hes. *Th.* 963–964 for a χαῖρε-formula used to dismiss one subject and transition to the next, as at *Arg.* 1.920). Silius Italicus' *Punica* furnishes a good example: this historical epic ends with a hymnic address to its protagonist, Scipio Africanus, and affirms his divine lineage (17.651–654). Notably, the poem's first word, *ordior*, "I begin," may reflect Apollonius' ἀρχόμενος (Stenzel 1908: 15). Rather surprisingly for an epic about a god, Nonnus' *Dionysiaca* concludes without a Salutation or Prayer; the poet maintains epic Er-Stil throughout the ending.

[11] For allusions to the *Arg.*'s hymnic frame in Dionysius, as well as in Pseudo-Manetho's *Apotelesmatica*, see 121n163.

[12] I use the thoroughly modern religious/secular dichotomy as a convenient shorthand for "with/without a view to cult honors." This distinction may be anachronistic, but it is useful given the fact that HEs tend to suppress references to hero cult and in this sense "secularize" the concept of the hero, whereas other sources, including Apollonius, openly acknowledge the cultic dimension of heroism; see 2.2.

contrast to the HEs, and identifies several passages in which the Argonauts' own divinization is foreshadowed. Section 3 turns squarely to the topic of generic hybridity with a series of close readings of passages in which, I argue, Apollonius self-consciously conflates secular-Homeric and religious heroism as a way of expressing metapoetically his poem's hybrid generic affiliations: as an epic, the *Arg.* commemorates its protagonists' glorious deeds in the style of the HEs, but as a hymn, it acknowledges their cultic status as heroes divinized and worshipped after death. Section 4 then seeks to contextualize Apollonius' generic experiment in light of contemporary and earlier examples of poets who were similarly drawn to the language of the *HH*s when acknowledging both the epic and religious dimensions of their subjects' heroism. Finally, section 5 homes in on one of these precursors, the *Homeric Hymn to Heracles* (15), as a model "epic hymn" from the Homeric collection itself that sheds light on important aspects of the *Arg.*'s hymnic structure.

1   The Duality of the Concept of the Hero in Greek Culture

The *Arg.*'s dual status as epic and hymn is made possible by, and, indeed, capitalizes on, the duality of the concept of the "hero" (ἥρως) in Greek culture. *In nuce*, this term can be used in a secular, literary way or with reference to immortalized human beings worshipped in what modern scholars have labeled hero cult.[13] My argument is that Apollonius combines these two ways of understanding heroes in the *Arg.* because each resonates with one of his hybrid poem's generic affiliations: as an epic, the *Arg.* commemorates the Argonauts in traditional Homeric terms, while as a hymn, it celebrates them in their capacity as the divinized objects of cult. In order to contextualize this claim and to inform the analysis that follows, in this section I offer a brief sketch of these two ways of being a hero in Greek culture.

---

13   West 1978: 370–373 and Nagy 1999: 114–117 are fundamental on the distinction between epic and cultic heroes. For these two types as located on a continuum, see Whitley 1995: 52. A notable dissenting view is that of van Wees 2006: 366–370, who argues that ἥρως never possesses a secular sense in early Greek epic (cf. Hadzisteliou Price 1973: 130). His arguments have been challenged (e.g.: Bravo 2009: 26–27, nn. 21, 32; see also Currie 2005: 62–70), but even if correct, we could still speak of a "mythic" vs. a "cultic" way of representing heroes that would approximately correspond with the epic/cultic distinction, especially given Homer's reticence to acknowledge the worship of his heroes in cult (see below in this section). Van Wees also acknowledges that Hellenistic scholarship struggled with Homer's use of the term (2006: 369; see also Rohde 1925: 142 n. 26; Jones 2010: 3 with n. 3), and Apollonius' own usage seems pointedly to contrast the cultic with the Homeric usage, as I argue below.

I begin with the earlier-attested usage. In a great deal of Greek poetry, and especially in the HEs, the word ἥρως is used generally of freeborn men who lived in the age of myth—that is, of the generations born roughly before the fall of Troy.¹⁴ More specifically, to quote West's formulation, ἥρως is, in the *Iliad*, "used for warriors generally, and later, in the *Odyssey*, for almost anyone respectable who played a part in the narrative"—for example, elites like Laertes (e.g., *Od.* 1.189) or Telemachus (4.21), but also working professionals like the bard Demodocus (8.483) or the herald Mulius (18.423). In every case, the word is used without "any hint of a religious significance, [or] a connection with cult after death."¹⁵ Heroes of this sort were especially prominent in epic, whose very meter, the dactylic hexameter, could be identified as "heroic" as early as Plato (*Leg.* 12.958e).

In the HEs, heroes are almost uniformly mortal, a fact that distinguishes the *Iliad* and, to a lesser extent, the *Odyssey* from the poems of the epic cycle, in which several heroes are granted immortality.¹⁶ There are, to be sure, a few exceptions to this generalization.¹⁷ For instance, the Catalog of Ships already mentions annual sacrifice in Athens to Erechtheus (*Il.* 2.550–551), evidently conceived of as a hero who lives on to receive cult.¹⁸ In the *Odyssey*, Menelaus

---

14 In Homer, heroes are exclusively male; the category of heroine (ἡρωίς, ἡρωίνη, ἡρῷσσα) is first attested only with Pindar (*Pyth.* 11.7). Curiously, this term has a wider semantic range in Greek than its male counterpart, embracing both (onetime) mortal women as well as minor female divinities who were never human (see, e.g.: Kearns 1989: 22–23, 126–127). Apollonius' own Libyan "heroines" (ἡρῷσσαι, 4.1309, 1323, 1358) are a case in point (Nock 1944: 165 n. 81 = 1972: 2.596 n. 81): they are identified both as daughters of the eponymous nymph Libya (4.1323, 1358; cf. 2.504–505) and as local goddesses (χθόνιαι θεαί, *Arg.* 4.1322; cf. 1316, 1333, 1347); cf. Callim. fr. 602 Pfeiffer, Nicaenetus 3 Powell = *AP* 6.225. On Greek heroines generally, see: Larson 1995; Lyons 1997; Kearns 1998.
15 West 1978: 373, 370. See further: Barrigón 2000: 2; Bravo 2009: 13–15; and, for extensive citations from Homeric epic, van Wees 2006: 367–369.
16 See Griffin 1977: 42; Burgess 2001: 167. Phillips (1953: 55) suspects that the hero cult of Odysseus himself may have figured into the *Telegony*. Nagy (2005: 81) notes that the motif of heroic immortalization appears in the Hesiodic and Orphic corpora as well.
17 The extent to which the Homeric epics refer to or presuppose the existence of hero cult is controversial. For proposed acknowledgments of the practice, see, e.g.: Hack 1929; Hadzisteliou Price 1973; Dué 2001: 44–45; Currie 2005: 50–57; Nagy 2012. All of these scholars argue that while for one reason or another Homer mostly avoids explicit references to hero cult, its implicit presence can be detected in many passages. See also van Wees 2006: 372–375.
18 See on this passage Kirk 1985 ad *Il.* 2.547–551, 549–551. Earlier scholars intent on denying any trace of hero cult in Homer often explained this passage as interpolated or late, or claimed that Erechtheus was originally regarded as a god, not a hero; see Hadzisteliou Price 1973: 130–132, 135–137, 140. Apollonius, in any event, would most likely have seen a reference to hero cult in this passage, whose authenticity does not appear to have been questioned in antiquity.

is destined to enjoy an immortal life of ease in the Elysian Field at the ends of the earth, simply because he is the son-in-law of Zeus (4.561–569), and different forms of deification have been granted to Heracles (11.601–604) and the Dioscuri (11.300–304). I might add in this connection that the *HH*s contain one sure reference to hero cult, in Demeter's prophecy of the Eleusinians' annual worship of her nursling Demophon (2.263–267).[19] Many more debatable examples could be marshaled,[20] but nevertheless, a Homeric critic as sensitive as Apollonius must have been struck by the rarity of these passages, and by their exceptional status within the HEs. Indeed, as a Homeric scholar, Apollonius was probably aware of certain ancient philological debates that went to the heart of the "authentic" Homeric view of life after death—for instance, the question of the authenticity of *Od.* 11.602–604.[21] In the main, Homer lays an unusual amount of stress on his heroes' mortality, which supplies the major moral and emotional stakes in his narratives.[22] A classic statement of this aspect of the Homeric worldview is Griffin's:

> In the *Iliad* no rule is more ineluctable than that expounded by Patroclus' ghost, xxiii 69ff.: the dead do not return. Even Heracles could not evade

---

19 On Demophon's cult, see Richardson 1974 ad *HH* 2.265–267. Apollonius prominently alludes to the Demophon episode at *Arg.* 4.867–879; see 177*n*159. The hymns also mention other well-known cult heroes without, however, making note of their heroized status; e.g., Triptolemus (2.153, 474, 477) or Trophonius and Agamedes (3.296).

20 See 149*n*17. I note one further example of the "evidence" for hero cult in Homer that Apollonius may have recognized, even if scholars today hardly would. On at least one ancient interpretation, Homer alludes to Achilles' immortal afterlife on the White Island subtextually, by means of the ΛΕΥΚΗ ("White") acrostic at *Il.* 24.1–5. For this tradition, see: Burgess 2001: 163–166; West 2013: 156; for this interpretation of the acrostic, see Korenjak 2009. But this acrostic was interpreted in different ways and often through an Aratean lens, including by Apollonius himself; see Kronenberg 2018a; 2018b: 3–4, 9, 12–13, 17–18. "Homer" seems to reject the White Island tradition at the beginning of the final book of his other epic: at *Od.* 24.11, the narrator mentions the White Rock (Λευκάδα πέτρην) among the landmarks passed en route to the underworld, where he will actually locate Achilles and the other heroes (Lye 2016: 57; cf. Edwards 1985).

21 For a number of reasons many ancient critics considered this passage describing Heracles' apotheosis to be an interpolation, including the fact that Homer elsewhere has Achilles affirm that not even Heracles could escape death (*Il.* 18.117–119). See Petzl 1969: 28–37, esp. 28–31. Apollonius actually alludes to *Il.* 18.117 in the very words that introduce Heracles to the *Arg.* (1.122), perhaps to foreground the question of heroic (im)mortality, which he will approach very differently from Homer (Feeney 1987: 53).

22 On the centrality of death in the *Iliad* especially, see, e.g.: Reinhardt 1960: 5–15; Marg 1976; Schein 1984: ch. 3. On the HE view of death generally, see, e.g.: Rohde 1925: ch. 1; Sourvinou-Inwood 1995: ch. 2; Clarke 1999: ch. 6; Johnston 1999: 7–16; Albinus 2000: 21–97.

death: *Il.* xviii 117 οὐδὲ γὰρ οὐδὲ βίη Ἡρακλῆος φύγε κῆρα, | ὅς περ φίλτατος ἔσκε Διὶ Κρονίωνι ἄνακτι. Hector the favourite of Zeus and Sarpedon his son must die; they can receive no more than the honours of burial. Achilles himself is under the shadow of death, and that fact is vital for the *Iliad*, especially its latter books … This is what makes the *Iliad* both true and tragic, and the very different procedure of the Cycle indicates profoundly different attitudes to the fundamental nature of human life and death, and consequently to human heroism and the relation of men to the gods.[23]

This emphasis on the finality of death goes a long way toward explaining the crucial place of glory in the Homeric economy of values. Denied the literal immortality enjoyed by the happy few like Menelaus, most Homeric heroes can only hope for the metaphorical immortality of "imperishable renown" (κλέος ἄφθιτον, *Il.* 9.413) as their consolation for death.[24] In this respect, the Homeric heroes are as human as Theognis' beloved Cyrnus, whose only recourse against death is the same figurative immortality granted by poetic memory (Thgn. 243–252). Homer thus typifies what Currie calls the "'exclusive' conception of immortality": the only sort of "life" after death vouchsafed his heroes is that furnished by κλέος.[25]

Whatever the reasons behind it, Homer's conception of the hero as stubbornly mortal is in fact highly idiosyncratic from the perspective of later Greek culture.[26] In other sources, the term ἥρως regularly denotes an intermediate ontological category between gods and mortals, as in the question that commences Pindar's second *Olympian* ode: "What god, what hero, and what man shall we celebrate" (τίνα θεόν, τίν' ἥρωα, τίνα δ' ἄνδρα κελαδήσομεν; *Ol.* 2.2).[27] In

---

23 Griffin 1977: 42–43. In a section of the quotation I have excised, Griffin observes of the other HE: "Even in the less austere *Odyssey*, where by his own account Menelaus is exempted from death 'because he has Helen and is son-in-law of Zeus', iv 561, Achilles is really dead, and bitterly does he deplore his lot, xi 488 ff."
24 For this aspect of the Homeric worldview, see, e.g.: Fränkel 1975: 84; King 1987: 32–37; Edwards 1987: 150–152; Nagy 1999: 118–119. Griffin (1980: 95–102) offers a nuanced reading of this theme in Homer, concluding that ultimately "the consolation of glory is a chilly one" (102).
25 Currie 2005: 72–74.
26 The traditional explanation of Homer's difference in this regard is that the Homeric bardic tradition was simply ignorant of hero cult, for chronological or geographical reasons, but many other scholars have proposed that particular literary aims precluded acknowledgments of hero cult in the *Iliad* and *Odyssey* (see 149n17).
27 An example quoted by Kearns 1989: 1, who also cites Lucian *Dial. mort.* 340; for further par-

the realm of Greek religion, heroes were a type of divinity generally less powerful than the Olympian gods[28] and more firmly tied to a given locality.[29] Perhaps the clearest line of demarcation separating them from gods was the experience of death: heroes were held to have been mortals who had died.[30] They were also, however, believed to live on somehow after death in a state of immortality.[31] As a result, both death and immortalization are key themes in the ideology of hero cult.[32] Although firmly located in their graves, cult heroes could possess a certain degree of mobility, appearing, for example, in epiphany to aid their people in battle,[33] and they were often thought to live on simultaneously in paradisiacal realms such as the Islands of the Blessed or Elysium, located at the ends of the earth or in the underworld.[34]

Cities and other groups propitiated these numinous powers, often annually,[35] with a distinctive type of "hero cult."[36] The origins of this practice have

allels, see: Rohde 1925: 141 n. 25; Currie 2005: 60 n. 7, 176 n. 94. Cf. Ekroth's schema, which places cult heroes on a spectrum between the gods and the ordinary dead (2002: 330–334; 2007: 113–114; cf. Pl. *Resp.* 427b, *Leg.* 717a–b). For the intermediate position of the hero in the ontological hierarchies of Greek philosophy, see Rodríguez Moreno 2000.

28 Artemidorus (*On Dreams* 2.40, 4.78) makes this power differential explicit; see also Paus. 10.31.11 (Rohde 1925: 150 n. 91).
29 As Larson (2007: 197) puts it: "In many cases, heroes and heroines were simply 'little gods,' concerned for the most part with the daily comings and goings in their own neighborhoods." For the cult hero's strong sense of locality, see, e.g.: Nilsson 1967: 187–188; Ekroth 2009: 138–139; Parker 2011: 104; cf. Hall 1999.
30 See, e.g.: Brelich 1958: 80–90; Seaford 1994: 114–120; Ekroth 2002: 20; 2007: 100; 2015. For the much rarer (and in many cases, controversial) instances of heroic honors for the still-living, see: Currie 2005, esp. ch. 9; Jones 2010: 93–95; cf. Widzisz 2007: 275.
31 Kearns 1989: 128–129, who notes that heroes may even be said to have escaped death by virtue of their immortalization. Other heroes do not strictly "die" but are translated to the Islands of the Blessed, are swallowed by the earth, or simply disappear (Brelich 1958: 87–88; Johnston 1999: 13).
32 So Nagy 2005: 84, 86: "To say that the *hêmitheoi* are mortal is not to say that heroes do not become immortal: they do, but only after they have experienced death. After death, heroes are eligible for a life of immortality ... The hero was considered *dead*—from the standpoint of the place where the hero's *sôma* (body) was situated; at the same time, the hero was considered simultaneously *immortalized*—from the standpoint of the paradisiacal place that awaited all heroes after death" (italics original). See further Rohde 1925: 117; Nagy 1999: 174–175.
33 See, e.g., Brelich 1958: 90–92; Pritchett 1979: ch. 2.
34 Farnell 1921: 371–372. As postmortem paradises for cult heroes, Elysium and the Islands of the Blessed are functionally interchangeable and possess similar characteristics; see, e.g.: Roloff 1970: 93–101; Heubeck, West, and Hainsworth 1988 ad *Od.* 4.563 ff.; West 1978 ad Hes. *Op.* 171.
35 See Eitrem in *RE* 8.1 s.v. "Heros," col. 1125.47–50.
36 One of the best overviews of this phenomenon, with extensive catalogs of ancient evi-

long been controversial.[37] On surviving evidence, the term ἥρως itself is first used in a clearly religious sense in the late sixth century BCE (Heraclitus B 5 DK),[38] but in the archaeological record, the practice can be traced back at least to the eighth century.[39] Its emergence, crystallization, and/or spread at this juncture has been connected to various historical factors, including the influence of Homeric and other epic poetry,[40] the rise of the *polis*,[41] tensions over land ownership,[42] and the desires of various communities, including colonies, to reinforce group identity or to stake territorial claims.[43] Hero cult is a diverse phenomenon, however, and none of these theories individually can explain every sort of hero cult,[44] nor are these explanations necessarily mutually exclusive.[45]

Hero cult could include various rites, including processions, games, and especially sacrifice.[46] Insofar as heroes were dead and buried, it was once thought that chthonic elements predominated in hero cult; and indeed, in some limited cases contact with the dead hero was thought to render worshippers ritually impure.[47] Nevertheless, Ekroth's study of the sacrificial rituals of

---

dence, is to be found in *ThesCRA* 2.125–214, esp. 125–159. For accessible introductions, see further: Ekroth 2007; Jones 2010; Parker 2011.

37 Useful overviews of the scholarly debate surrounding the origins of hero cult can be found in, e.g.: Kearns 1989: 129–137; Parker 1996: 36–39; Ekroth 2002: 335–431; Bravo 2009.

38 Bremmer 2006: 18. This date can be pushed back earlier if certain later testimonies can be relied upon; e.g., Porph. *Abst.* 4.22 attributes legislation concerning the worship of gods and heroes to the seventh-century Athenian lawgiver Draco (Rohde 1925: 115; Burkert 1985: 205; Antonaccio 1994: 390). *Pace* Bremmer, there is no reason to think that the associated beliefs and practices of hero cult could not have preexisted the religious usage of the term ἥρως itself (Snodgrass 1988: 20–22).

39 See Antonaccio 1993, 1994, 1995, who emphasizes the difference between the recurrent practice of hero cult and the earlier, more provisional phenomenon of tomb cult.

40 The idea that epic poetry was crucial in promoting the rise of the hero cult is especially associated with: Farnell 1921: ch. 11 (with conclusions at 340–342); Cook 1953; Coldstream 1976. Against this opinion, see, e.g.: Hadzisteliou Price 1979; Snodgrass 1988; Antonaccio 1994, 1995.

41 See particularly Bérard 1982; de Polignac 1995: ch. 4.

42 See esp. Snodgrass 1977: 30–31; 1980: 38–40; 1982.

43 See, e.g., Whitley 1988 and Malkin 1993, both of whom offer insightful critiques of Snodgrass's theory.

44 For attempts to taxonomize the different categories of hero (e.g., culture heroes, epic heroes, eponymous heroes, etc.), see, e.g., Farnell 1921: 19.

45 A point emphasized in the surveys cited above, n. 37. See also, e.g., Whitley 1988, who notes the need to take regional factors into consideration, and Morris 1988, who argues for a range of meanings that hero cults could have possessed for different communities.

46 Ekroth 2002: 13.

47 Parker 1983: 39.

hero cult has shown that in most cases, heroes and the Olympian gods were worshipped in analogous fashion: "Ritually speaking, the heroes belonged with the gods."[48] Indeed, heroes are sometimes said to be worshipped like gods (e.g., Pind. *Ol.* 7.79, Diod. Sic. 29.18, Paus. 3.16.6);[49] "gods and heroes" is a common pairing in Greek prose to denote the divine generally (e.g., Hdt. 2.45.3, Thuc. 2.74.2, Pl. *Ion* 531c–d, Dem. *De cor.* 184, Polyb. 3.48.9); and many earlier sources casually refer to heroes as gods.[50] This evidence suggests that the Greeks could imagine heroes and gods in broadly analogous terms as divine, superhuman entities.

As with the gods, the cult of heroes could also include the singing of hymns—a crucial fact for the *Arg.*'s construal as an epic hymn. One ancient definition of the hymnic genre actually specifies that heroes as well as gods were celebrated in hymns: "the 'hymn' is a poem comprising praises of the gods **and heroes** with thanksgiving" ("Ύμνος ἐστὶ ποίημα περιέχον θεῶν ἐγκώμια **καὶ ἡρώων** μετ' εὐχαριστίας).[51] Unfortunately, although we possess several ancient references to the role of hymns within hero cult,[52] few examples of such heroic hymns have survived.[53] Pindar may furnish an early example with his fifteenth *Paean*, which is entitled "for the Aeginetans, to Aeacus" (Α[ἰ]γινήταις εἰ[ς] Αἴα-κον). The title evidently indicates that the poem honors the hero Aeacus in hymnic fashion; indeed, the *HH*s follow a similar titling convention, with the formula εἰς + the name of the god to be celebrated in the accusative.[54]

---

48   Ekroth 2002: 341. Ekroth's study builds on the classic work of Nock (1944, reprinted in Nock 1972: 2.575–602), who also emphasizes the continuity between sacrifices to heroes and gods.

49   On such phrases, see, e.g.: Ekroth 2002: 206–212; Pirenne-Delforge 2008: 150; cf. Currie 2005: 184–189.

50   For the slippage between the terms "hero" and "god," see the examples collected by, e.g.: Rohde 1925: 150 n. 90; Nock 1944: 163–164 (= 1972: 2.594); Kearns 1989: 125; Ekroth 2002: 21 n. 28; Harrison 2002: 159–162; Parker 2011: 110.

51   Σ Dion. Thrax p. 451.6–7 Hilgard (translation from Furley and Bremer 2001: 1.9). Much is uncertain about the date of the Τέχνη γραμματική ascribed to Dionysius (2nd c. BCE), and consequently, of its commentary tradition; see Dickey 2007: 77–78. See also Aelius Theon Rhet. *Prog.* p. 109.20–26 Spengel (1st c. CE).

52   See Deneken 1884–1890: 2503.30–50; Lozynsky 2014: 58, 261–262; add to their citations Hdt. 4.35.3.

53   E.g., Heliod. *Aeth.* 3.2 (= *AP* 9.485) is a literary representation of a processional hymn sung at Delphi: it begins with an Evocation of Thetis as its Hymnic Subject but embraces in its praises Peleus, Achilles, and finally Neoptolemus, to whom the Prayer is addressed as local cult hero.

54   Cf. *Paean* 18, which has the name "Electryon" in the title, though probably without εἰς preceding (Rutherford 2001: 427). On these and other possible instances of hymning heroes in Pindar's *Paeans*, see Lozynsky 2014: 58.

Cultic heroes could be historical figures, like the Spartan general Brasidas at Amphipolis (Thuc. 5.11.1) or the Athenian tyrannicides Harmodius and Aristogeiton,[55] and city-founders (οἰκισταί) in particular enjoyed regular hero cult in their settlements.[56] But they could also be the great men and women of the mythic age—an Achilles, Hector, or Alcestis, or indeed, a Jason or Medea.[57] And it is with this category that the two types of heroism outlined so far converge:[58] the same heroes whose mortality the Homer epics are at pains to stress were thought to be living a second life as immortalized objects of cult throughout the Greek world. The worship of Homeric heroes has occasioned much debate in modern scholarship about the relationship between early epic and the rise of hero cult,[59] but the conflation of epic and religious heroism seems not to have posed a problem for Greeks of a later age. Pindar, for instance, often presents mythic heroes in recognizably "Homeric" terms, but also acknowledges their receipt of cultic honors.[60] The same may be said of Attic tragedy, which in some cases even restages Homeric episodes with the added promise of hero cult for the slain, as in the *Rhesus* (962–973). Especially striking examples of this sort of conflation occur in narratives in which Homer himself interacts with the divinized versions of the heroes of whom he sang, as in the story of Helen's blinding him for maligning her virtue in his poems.[61]

---

55   On this duo, see, e.g., Kearns 1989: 55, 150. For surveys of heroized historical personages, see: Farnell 1921: 420–426; Connolly 1998: 21; Currie 2005: 85–200.
56   For the cult of founders, see above all Malkin 1987: chs. 5–8.
57   Farnell 1921: 408–413 provides a convenient list of "heroes of epic and saga" who received cult worship.
58   Snodgrass 1988: 24; Whitley 1994: 220.
59   See 153n40.
60   Cf., e.g., the presentation of Pelops in *Ol.* 1 (Currie 2005: 74–75): in life he is an exponent of a basic tenet of Homer's heroic ideology ("But since men must die, why would anyone sit in darkness and coddle a nameless old age to no use, deprived of all noble deeds?" 82–84); in death, however, he is a recipient of hero cult at Olympia (90–93).
61   The story first appears for us in Pl. *Phdr.* 243a–b, in his account of Stesichorus' famous *Palinode*. Plato does not explicitly identify the divine agency at work here, but most other sources cite the wrath of the divine Helen herself; see also his contemporary Isocrates on Stesichorus' parallel punishment (*Hel.* 64–65). For an overview of these blinding stories, see Graziosi 2002: 147–150. Owing to his encomiastic agenda, Isocrates speaks of Helen as if she were fully a goddess, not a heroine (see Edmunds 2011), but note that a couple of sources explicitly refer to Helen in this story as a "heroine" (ἡρωΐνης, Homeric *Vita* 7.5 in West 2003a; Hermias ad Pl. *Phdr.* 243a [p. 75.9 Couvreur]); cf. Helen's appearance on the White Island with other Homeric heroes in another version of the story (Conon *Narr.* 18, Paus. 3.19.11–13, Hermias ad Pl. *Phdr.* 243a [p. 75.10–26 Couvreur]; see also Lucian *Ver. hist.* 2.15).

In sum, Greek ἥρωες possessed a literary existence as the protagonists of epic and other genres of mythological storytelling, but the HEs are unique in stressing their mortality almost without exception. In the realm of Greek religion, heroes quite literally had a second life as an intermediate grade of divinity constituted by the powerful dead, who were thought to live on in some capacity and to influence events in the mortal plane from beyond the grave. Crucially, these heroes consisted of women and men from all periods, including the mythic Age of Heroes, and they received cult that included the singing of hymns. The generic duality of the *Arg.* as both epic and hymn maps neatly onto these two significations borne by the term ἥρως.

2 Hero Cult and Immortalization in the *Argonautica*

For Apollonius, the worship of Homeric heroes was a centuries-old practice that, indeed, was taking on increasing prominence in the Hellenistic period.[62] It is thus no surprise that, in addition to depicting his heroes—however problematically—in an epic mold,[63] Apollonius also freely acknowledges the practice of hero cult, in a significant departure from Homeric precedent.[64] The Argonauts themselves are made to participate in hero cult;[65] the learned narrator mentions other hero cults both contemporaneous with the Argonauts and belonging to the historical period; and the poem foreshadows the Argonauts' own heroization, both as a group and, in some cases, individually, in several places and in multiple ways. These frequent, often casual references to hero cult partly reflect Apollonius' typically Alexandrian interest in etiology and in religious rites,[66] but they also have the effect of normalizing the practice within the

---

62 For the surge of interest in epic hero cult in the Hellenistic period, reflected particularly in the veneration of epic heroes at Mycenean tombs, see Alcock 1997. The Hellenistic age witnessed several other developments in hero cult that were not directly related to the epic heroes; these included the establishment of private cults by family members, the use of the term "hero(ine)" on the gravestones of the ordinary dead, and an increase in the frequency of public heroizations. For overviews, see, e.g.: Rohde 1925: 527–533; Hughes 1999. I discuss the related phenomenon of Ptolemaic ruler cult in the conclusion, 2.1.

63 I consider the question of how the Argonauts' heroization bears on the (often-problematic) portrayal of their heroism in the conclusion, 2.2.

64 A point made by, e.g.: Händel 1954: 47–48; Goldhill 1991: 318; Saïd 1998: 18–19; Hitch 2012: 131.

65 Cf. the situation in the HEs: "While both the Greeks and the Trojans in the *Iliad* on several occasions make sacrifices to the gods, pray to them, and vow future sacrifices and offerings to them, not once do they perform any ritual for a dead mortal" (Bravo 2009: 16).

66 Cf. Hitch 2012: 133.

epic world that the poem constructs. I have argued in the previous chapter that the hymnic Salutation and Prayer to the Argonauts in the poem's Envoi (4.1773–1775) presuppose their heroization. The Argonauts' sudden transformation into divinized heroes in the Envoi may be abrupt, but it comes only after the groundwork has been carefully laid.[67] Hero cult is an ordinary part of the Argonauts' religious world, and thus something that the readers can confidently expect to be accorded to heroes of their caliber.

In the following subsections, I survey the passages in the poem that touch on hero cult and related phenomena. I proceed first with the most explicit references to hero cult in the poem; second, with some more ambiguous cases that seem to envision hero cult without explicit signals to that effect; third, with Hesiodic allusions that implicitly present the Argonauts as heroes destined for an immortal afterlife; and finally, with the poem's references to the related phenomenon of apotheosis, which sheds some oblique light on the hero cult theme.

2.1 Explicit References to Hero Cult

The poem's clearest references to hero cult are here presented in list format with key religious terminology given in the Greek:[68]

---

67 Cf. Hitch 2012. By tracking a set of motifs that she connects to divinity, including adoration by admiring crowds and astral imagery, she argues that the Argonauts are increasingly presented as godlike figures over the course of the poem. This ongoing process of heroization culminates, Hitch argues, with the Salutation to the heroes in the poem's Envoi (154).

68 This list is largely derived from Hitch 2012 (cf. the briefer list in Currie 2005: 55 n. 56), though I include only the most unambiguous examples of hero cult in the poem, excluding more subtle hints of heroization for which Hitch argues, such as "the god-like effect the heroes have upon other people" (134). In a few cases I also disagree that the hero in question has in fact been heroized. For example, Hitch (2012: 135 n. 14) claims that "being swallowed by the earth signifies heroization" in the cases of Caeneus (1.59–64) and Theseus (1.101–104), but these heroes are hardly "swallowed by the earth" in the manner of, say, an Amphiaraus. Ustinova (2002: 277) advances a similar interpretation of the Caeneus myth and points to the hero's supposed appearance on the coins of his native Gyrton (per Rossbach 1901: 410–411) as indicative of local cult worship. But the identification of these images, which show an unlabeled pair of male and female heads, has rightly been questioned by Delcourt (1953: 146–147), who points out that Caeneus' interment—really, his being forcibly hammered into the earth like a nail—is nowhere connected to hero cult in any of our evidence. As for Theseus, he is actually destined to *escape* the underworld with the help of Heracles (as noted, e.g., by Palombi 1985: 133). The peculiar postmortem fate of Aethalides (1.644–648) is of a different order still: as Hitch herself recognizes (2012: 136 with n. 19), the digression on the migrations of his soul relates to the Pythagorean doctrine of metempsychosis—not to hero cult.

1) As the Argonauts pass the tomb (τύμβος, 585) of a certain Dolops on the Magnesian coast, adverse winds cause them to put in at evening.[69] At nightfall,[70] they honor Dolops (κυδαίνοντες, 1.587) with burnt offerings of sheep (ἔντομα μήλων | κεῖαν, 587–588).[71] These details suggest a stereotypically "chthonic" sacrifice, thus emphasizing Dolops' status as a dead hero and lending this episode an uncanny air.[72] The Argonauts' motive for making this sacrifice is not stated, but they presumably want to avert the bad weather.[73] Two days later, the weather evidently clears up and they set sail again, perhaps because of their propitiation of Dolops.[74] The port where they had been detained is now called Ἀφέται Ἀργοῦς ("launching of the Argo") because of their visit (1.583–591).

[69] The identity of this Dolops is debated, but the scholiast ad *Arg*. 1.587 claims that he is a Magnesian son of Hermes whom Apollonius took over from Cleon's *Argonautica* (fr. 339 *SH*). For other possible identifications, see: Delage 1930: 78–79; and Brelich 1958: 144 (eponym of the Dolopians); Livrea 1979: 151–152 (brother of Chiron). Fränkel (1968: 88) suspects that this episode serves as an etiology for a local cult to Dolops.

[70] For sacrifices to heroes "towards evening or at night," see Rohde 1925: 140 n. 9.

[71] Ekroth (2002: 270) glosses this procedure as "a killing and bleeding of sheep and then burning them." ἔντομα is a neuter plural substantive related to the verb ἐντέμνειν, a technical term for the slitting of a victim's throat so as to make a blood offering; see Casabona 1966: 225–229; Rudhardt 1992: 285–286.

[72] Cf. the sacrifices to Sthenelus cited below. It is doubtful whether nighttime sacrifices were in fact normative in the early centuries of hero cult, as later sources assert (Parker 2005: 41 with n. 22). Likewise, wholly-burnt offerings were typical for the dead, though not necessarily typical of hero cult, as was once thought (Ekroth 2002: 307–310). But regardless of real-world praxis, these details constitute a literary evocation of the chthonic type of ritual; cf. esp. Jason's sacrifices to Hecate at *Arg*. 3.1029–1041, 1194–1223, which are closely modeled on the Homeric *Nekyia* (*Od*. 10.516–534, 11.15–47; Schaaf 2014: 196–206).

[73] Allusions to the Aulis myth (Clauss 1989: 196–198) and to Herodotus (see next note) suggest this motive, as does Apollonius' description of the sacrifice itself (see Fränkel 1968: 87; cf. Livrea 1979: 152 n. 2; Vian 2002: 1.77 n. 4).

[74] The Dolops episode is modeled on an incident in Hdt. 7.188–191, in which a storm wrecks much of the Persian fleet when it, too, is moored at Magnesia. The Magi cast spells and make sacrifices (the same rare word, ἔντομα, is used [191.2]) to the wind as well as to Thetis and the Nereids, and on the fourth day the wind dies down. Herodotus explicitly raises the possibility, however, that the wind had abated of its own accord (ἢ ἄλλως κως αὐτὸς [*sc*. ὁ ἄνεμος] ἐθέλων ἐκόπασε, ibid.), not for any supernatural reason. Apollonius quietly reproduces the Herodotean uncertainty as to what causes the change in weather by inserting a two-day delay between the Argonauts' sacrifice and the resumption of sailing. Cf. in this regard 1.1151–1152: when the Argonauts propitiate Cybele in the night, the winds detaining them at Cyzicus have already died down by dawn. For the Herodotean background of the Dolops episode, see esp. Priestley 2014: 149–155, Morrison 2020: 174–177.

2) Apollo directs the Ionian colonists of Cyzicus to "dedicate" the Argo's original anchor stone "as a holy offering, as was proper, in the temple of Athena Jasonia" (ἱδρύσαντο | ἱερόν, ᾗ θέμις ἦεν, Ἰησονίης ἐν Ἀθήνης, 1.959–960).[75] Relics of this sort often figure into hero cult,[76] and the cult title "Jasonia" may imply that Jason was worshipped in conjunction with Athena at Cyzicus.[77]

3) The rock to which the Argonauts attached their ship cables on their second landing at Cyzicus is still called "Sacred Rock" (Ἱερὴ ... πέτρη, 1.1019), evidently because it has come into contact with the heroes, who are thus conceived of as holy themselves.[78]

4) To this day, the people of Cyzicus "glorify with heroes' honors" (τιμαῖς ἡρωίσι κυδαίνουσιν, 1.1048) those Doliones slain by the Argonauts.[79] The inhabitants "pour annual libations" (ἐτήσια χύτλα χέωνται, 1075)[80] and ritually abstain from grinding meal at home in remembrance of the commu-

---

75 On this temple, cf. Ehrhardt 1995: 29–30. Jason also lends his name to a path (Ἰησονίη ... ὁδός, 1.988) and to a fountain (Ἰησονίην ... κρήνην, 1148–1149) in the etiology-rich Cyzicus episode. Note 1.966: the Argonauts dedicate an altar to Apollo Ecbasius; according to the scholiast ad loc., however, the local historian Deiochus of Cyzicus (*FGrH* 471 F 5) spoke of a ἱερόν dedicated to Apollo Jasonius in the same place. Cf. Pliny *HN* 36.99 with Fränkel 1968: 124 n. 257.

76 See Pfister 1909: 331–339, who notes this anchor stone at 335.

77 Farnell 1921: 410 n. 77; Paduano and Fusillo 1986 ad loc.; Hitch 2012: 138. For this sort of cult title, note, e.g., Zeus Ἑκάλειος, worshipped in tandem with the heroine Hecale (Plut. *Vit. Thes.* 14.2–3 = Philochorus *FGrH* 328 F 109); further examples in Farnell 1921: 17; Currie 2005: 138 n. 112. For the worship of heroes in the shrines of goddesses in particular, see Price 1973: 136. See further on god-hero pairings in cult, e.g.: Kearns 1992: 77–93; Lyons 1997: 71–77. Given this background in Greek religion, Kampakoglou (2019: 102 n. 10) dismisses the possibility that this cult title implies hero cult for Jason much too lightly.

78 Cf. Σ ad loc., discussed in the conclusion, 345*n*70. See further *Arg.* 4.1153–1154, where the narrator observes of the cave in which Medea and Jason are wed: "To this day that holy cave is called Medea's cave" (καὶ εἰσέτι νῦν ἱερὸν κληίζεται ἄντρον | Μηδείης). We could also translate, "That cave is to this day called the **sacred cave of Medea**" (Seaton), which rendering would imply that the cave's sacredness stems from its connection with Medea, who must therefore be conceived of as a holy heroine. The cave had already been ἱερόν, however, because of its association with Macris; see below in this section. Hitch (2012: 155) thinks that Medea replaces Macris as the heroine associated with the cave; see further Walter 2020: 127–128.

79 For the religious sense of τιμή as "worship," see Nagy 1999: 118–119 and esp. Mikalson 1991: 183–202. Ekroth (2002: 200) argues that in the context of hero cult, τιμαί will refer to "some kind of cult with sacrifices taking place," whether of animal victims or bloodless offerings.

80 For libations of various sorts in hero cult (wine, water, milk, honey, oil, blood, and other liquids), see Henrichs 1983: 93–100, esp. 99 n. 58.

nity's grief (1071–1076).⁸¹ Elements of King Cyzicus' funeral rites (1058–1062) may be meant to suggest features of his cult.⁸²

5) After navigating the Clashing Rocks, the Argonauts sail past the "shrine" (ἱερόν, 2.658) of one Dipsacus, the son of a meadow nymph and the river Phyllis.⁸³

---

81   The heroized Dolionians presumably include King Cyzicus himself, whose death is treated more expansively (1.1030–1039) before the catalog of the other slain warriors (1040–1047) to which this etiology is appended. At 1075–1076, the narrator mentions the annual offerings given to these dead, who now seem to include as well Cyzicus' wife Cleite, whose suicide has just been described (1063–1069) (so Hasluck 1910: 240 with n. 1; Paduano and Fusillo 1986 ad *Arg.* 1.1070–1077). In addition to the royal couple, Apollonius identifies the twelve other slain Dolionians by name, and several of these appear to represent eponyms for authentic Cyzicene places and institutions; see Hasluck 1910: 240; Cuypers in *BNJ* 471 F 8b. The scholiast ad 1039 asserts that Apollonius took these names over from Deiochus (*FGrH* 471 F 8b), while the scholiast ad 1040–1041 claims that Apollonius invented at least two of them. On this problem, see Wendel 1932: 106; Fränkel 1968: 129; Vian 2002: 1.99 n. 1; Goldhill 1991: 316–319, 328–329; Clauss 1993: 166 n. 38; Cuypers in *BNJ* 471 F 8b.

82   Cyzicus is mourned by the whole community (Hitch 2012: 139; cf. 166*n*112 below), though we could expect as much of a king. Perhaps more saliently, Cyzicus' funeral rites generally follow Homeric precedent, with one important exception (Saïd 1998: 17–19): his funeral games are held at the site of his tomb (*Arg.* 1.1060–1062). Funeral games for important personages are a typical part of the epic world that Apollonius has inherited from Homer, and they are presented as standard practice within the *Arg.* Thus Cyzicus' games are held "as is fitting" (ἣ θέμις, 1.1061), and elsewhere the narrator mentions funeral contests for Pelias (1.1304), Priolas (2.780–783; on this figure, see the next subsection), and a generic king in a simile (3.1273); of these, Pelias' funeral games are a traditional part of the Argonautic saga (see Davies and Finglass 2014: 213–218). But in Homer, these games occur away from the honorand's tomb (Saïd 1998: 18). Apollonius' setting of the games by Cyzicus' barrow is an innovation possibly consistent with his un-Homeric presentation of the hero's tomb as the focus of cult activity (18–19). In this context, Apollonius may be alluding to the (both mythic and historical) practice of institutionalizing a hero's funeral games as a recurrent contest to be held in perpetuity (cf. Callim. fr. 384.30 Pfeiffer, Harder); see, e.g.: Rohde 1925: 116–117; Roller 1981: 6–10, 12; Seaford 1994: 120–123. Cf. Hasluck 1910: 159, who assumes that Apollonius refers to just such an institution of games in Cyzicus' honor.

83   Fränkel 1968: 223 emends ἱερόν to ἠρίον, on analogy with the "tomb" of Aegaeon, similarly passed by the Argonauts at 1.1165, but Campbell (1973: 78) is right to point out that we do not know enough about the obscure Dipsacus to justify changing the text. The term ἱερόν itself does not reveal much about Dipsacus' ontological status. In some contexts, ἱερόν can be contrasted with ἡρῷον to denote the shrines proper to gods and to heroes, respectively (e.g., Thuc. 2.17.1, Conon *Narr.* 45 *fin.*; cf. *Arg.* 2.807). But ἱερόν is also the more general term of the two (cf., e.g., schol. ad Ar. *Vesp.* 819: θηρῷον· τὸ ἱερὸν τοῦ ἥρωος Λύκου) and can be used with reference to heroes' shrines (e.g., Strabo 9.2.10: τὸ ἱερὸν τοῦ Ἀμφιαράου), especially those lacking tombs; see further: Kearns 1992: 65–68;

6) Apollo directs the colonists of Heraclea Pontica to found their city around the tomb (τύμβος, 2.842) of the Argonautic seer Idmon and to worship (ἱλάεσθαι, 847) him as their "city guardian" (πολισσοῦχον, 846),[84] but to this day the city honors (κυδαίνουσιν, 850) a certain Agamestor instead.[85]

Pirenne-Delforge 2008: 150–151, 168–170. Dipsacus, who has apparently lived and died (note the imperfect verbs in 2.655–657), seems more like a hero than a god. Perhaps he was immortalized for hosting Phrixus; cf. the category of "hospitality heroes" identified by Larson (1995: 36). Note as well that the prosaic ἡρῷον is never used in Greek epic; ἱερόν may therefore provide a poetic equivalent. Apollonius also follows the poetic practice of using σηκός for sanctuaries generally (4.1285), not precincts for heroes specifically (Casevitz 1984: 94).

84 On this title, common in the cult of city-founders, see Malkin 1987: 75–76; 1993: 231–232. Heroes commonly "possess" (with ἔχω and other verbs) the city or land that worships them: see Rohde 1925: 155 n. 137. Elsewhere, another Argonaut, Polyphemus, founds the city of Cius (1.1322, 1346; 4.1472), though he is not said to be worshipped there. In fact, his grave is located elsewhere (1.1323, 4.1474–1477), and the city takes its name not from him, but a local river (Foster 2007: 259–260). The tradition of his founding of the city seems to have been rather tenuous; see Ehrhardt 1995: 30–35.

85 Who is this Agamestor? The scholiast ad 2.844–847a, citing Apollonius' probable source Promathidas (FGrH 430 F 3), interprets the passage to mean that the Boeotian and Megarian colonists did not know the identity of the hero whom Apollo directed them to worship; consequently, they wrongly assumed that Agamestor, a certain local hero, was the one buried under Idmon's funeral mound (see also Σ ad Arg. 2.848–850b, Cuypers in BNJ 430 F 3). Quint. Smyrn. 6.464 seems to make Agamestor a local hero as well (Cuypers in BNJ 430 F 3; cf. Wilamowitz 1924: 2.237 n. 4). Fontenrose (1978: 300) speculates that the legend of Idmon's confusion with Agamestor arose to account for the existence of two competing traditions about the occupant of the tomb; one of these traditions was authentically local (Agamestor), while the other was an attempt to anchor the Argonautic legend in the real-world topography of the Euxine coast (Idmon); cf. Händel 1954: 73. Other proposed identifications of Agamestor include:

– Either a preexisting local hero who was syncretized with Idmon or an individuation of one of Idmon's epithets, since the name Agamestor ("Excellent Counselor") is synonymous with Idmon's ("The Knowing One"): Robert 1921: 775; Rohrbach 1960: 58; Giangiulio 1981: 21–22 with n. 102, Malkin 1987: 76.
– A reflex of a local Bithynian god: Fontenrose 1959: 480–481.
– A son of the Theban king Laius, honored as an ancestor of the Boeotian colonists: Fraser 1972: 631; Jackson 1995: 64 n. 22 (but see Ehrhardt 1995: 38–39 on this supposed Boeotian contingent of colonists).
– An Athenian king: Roux 1949: 69.
– One of the colony founders, perhaps particularly the Boeotian leader: Jacoby in his commentary with n. 15 on FGrH 430 F 2–3; Saïd 1998: 19; Vian 2002: 1.162 n. 1; Lachenaud 2010: 304 n. 250. Burstein (1976: 103 n. 103) objects, however, that "the cult of a founder would have preserved his identity" (see further Ehrhardt 1995: 40).
– A generic name ("Excellent Counselor") conjured up for a hero whose name the colonists did not know: Thalmann 2011: 108–109.

7) The Argonauts witness the epiphany of the "soul" (ψυχήν, 2.916) of Sthenelus,[86] a warrior who died during Heracles' quest for Hippolyta's belt,[87] and the seer Mopsus directs them to propitiate him with libation offerings (λοιβῇσί τε μειλίξασθαι, 923). In the event, the Argonauts "paid homage to Sthenelus' tomb" (Σθενέλου τάφον ἀμφεπένοντο, 925)[88] both with drink offerings (χύτλα τέ οἱ χεύαντο, 926)[89] and with the sacrifice of sheep (ἥγνισαν ἔντομα μήλων, 926).[90] "Then, apart from the libations" (ἄνδιχα δ' αὖ χύτλων, 927), the Argonauts erect an altar to Apollo, and Orpheus dedicates his lyre, whence the place is now called Lyra (2.911–929).[91]

86 Sthenelus must in some sense remain under the power of Persephone like any ordinary spirit of the dead, for it is this goddess who mercifully sends forth his soul (2.915–916), "begging to behold even for a moment men of his own kind" (λισσομένην τυτθόν περ ὁμήθεας ἄνδρας ἰδέσθαι, 917). There is something numinous about the idea that Sthenelus could tell that "men of his own kind" were about to pass by his tomb, as if he could somehow sense their presence from within his grave. Cf. Fränkel 1968: 247 n. 255 as well as the treatment of Valerius, who evidently felt the need to explain Sthenelus' knowledge of the Argonauts' imminent approach via the "κλέος-reaching-even-unto-Hades" topos (5.82–89). Durbec (2008: 65) suggests that we are to imagine Sthenelus' soul being identified "with an imaginary heroic statue of the deceased which would have decorated his tomb."

87 The scholiast ad 2.911–914 claims that Apollonius adopted the figure of Sthenelus from the local historian Promathidas of Heraclea (FGrH 430 F 4), but that he invented his epiphany to the Argonauts. Fränkel (1968: 246) and Vian (2002: 1.163 n. 6) compare Achilles' apparition over his own tomb in the Nostoi and in the Polyxena myth; for further parallels, see Hitch 2012: 142 n. 34. As Cuypers (ad BNJ 430 F 5) points out, the Sthenelus apparition rounds out the quasi-κατάβασις represented by the Argonauts' stay in Acherusia (cf. esp. 2.735, 743) and is immediately preceded by a reference to Dionysus' "'unsmiling orgies' (ὀργιάσαι, 907; ἀμειδήτους, 908), that is to say, mystic rites concerning death and the afterlife." The whole sequence from Idmon's heroization to Sthenelus' epiphany hints at the possibility of life after death for the Argonauts themselves.

88 Páskiewicz (1981 ad loc.) notes that the phrase echoes the last line of the Iliad (ἀμφίεπον τάφον, 24.804), concerning Hector's burial. Characteristically, Apollonius has transferred the phrase from a heroic funeral to hero cult.

89 These offerings are denoted by the same figura etymologica used earlier for the annual offerings made to the Dolionian heroes in Cyzicus (χύτλα χέωνται, 1.1075). This intratext, along with several marked parallels with the Dolops episode (see Clauss 1989: 198), suggests that Sthenelus is the recipient of hero cult, not merely a restless ghost who must be propitiated. Indeed, the fact that Sthenelus has been buried would seem to rule out his being a restless ghost; he must rather receive special permission from Persephone to view the passing heroes.

90 Cf. the Argonauts' earlier sacrifices to Dolops (ἔντομα μήλων | κεῖαν, 1.587–588). In this sacrificial context, ἁγνίζω will likewise mean "burn" (Páskiewicz 1981 and Matteo 2007 ad loc.; cf. Rudhardt 1992: 171). Again, Apollonius presumably intends to represent this sacrifice as chthonic; when the Argonauts proceed to sacrifice to Apollo, they burn only the thigh pieces (μῆρ' ἔφλεγον, 2.928), as per the normal mode of Greek sacrifice.

91 Valverde Sánchez (1989: 93) pairs this episode with that of Dolops as examples of etiolo-

8) On arriving in Colchis, Jason makes a libation (χέε λοιβάς, 2.1272) of honey[92] and neat wine to Gaia, the local gods, and "the souls of the dead heroes" (ψυχαῖς τε καμόντων | ἡρώων, 1273–1274) native to the land,[93] beseeching (γουνοῦτο, 1274) their aid before the next major leg of his adventure.

9) Hera predicts to Thetis the future marriage of her son Achilles to Medea in the "Elysian Field" (Ἠλύσιον πεδίον, 4.811), a paradise reserved for immortal heroes.[94]

10) Dogged by Hera, Dionysus' nurse Macris, daughter of Aristaeus, settled in a "sacred cave" (ἄντρῳ ἐν ἠγαθέῳ, 4.1131; ἱερῷ ἐνί ... ἄντρῳ, 1139; ἱερόν ... ἄντρον, 1153) on Phaeacia and "bestowed immense prosperity on the inhabitants" (πόρεν ὄλβον ἀθέσφατον ἐνναέτῃσιν, 1140). This latter detail suggests the benefaction of a local heroine,[95] perhaps with a cult centered around her holy cave.[96]

These ten unambiguous references to hero cult or heroization follow an interesting pattern of distribution. At least five are connected to αἴτια (1, 2, 3, 4, 6),[97]

---

gies connected to hero cult. It is unclear, however, to whom Orpheus dedicates his lyre: Apollo, Sthenelus (cf. VF 5.98–100), or both? The sacrifices to Apollo are conceived of as separate from those to Sthenelus (cf. ἄνδιχα δ᾽ αὖ χύτλων, 2.927), and Orpheus' dedication, which follows Apollo's sacrifices, may therefore be made only to the god (Händel 1954: 49, Fränkel 1968 ad *Arg.* 2.911–935, Cuypers ad *BNJ* 430 F 5, Schaaf 2014: 62). The lyre is, in any case, one of Apollo's commonest attributes.

92 The libations are qualified with the adjective μελισταγέας (1272), which may simply mean "sweet as dropped honey" (LSJ s.v. A.2) but might also refer to an offering of honey mixed with wine.

93 In this ritual context and in light of parallel passages (e.g., Xen. *Cyr.* 3.22; see further Guthrie 1950: 29), the heroes in question must be local Colchian ones (so Dräger 2002 ad loc.), not the Argonauts who have died along the way, as Vian assumes (2002: 1.175).

94 This passage alludes to *Od.* 4.561–569, where another god, Proteus, similarly prophesies Menelaus' fated afterlife in paradise; note the occurrence of the phrase ἐς Ἠλύσιον πεδίον in the same *sedes* at *Od.* 4.563 and *Arg.* 4.811; νημερτέα at *Arg.* 4.810 may allude to Proteus' stock epithet νημερτής (*Od.* 4.349, 384, 401, 542; 17.140; cf. Hes. *Th.* 235). But whereas Menelaus himself is the recipient of this prophecy in the *Odyssey*, Apollonius has, characteristically, kept Medea ignorant of her fate.

95 A similar phrase is used of Aeetes' enriching of Phrixus at *Arg.* 2.1181, but for a nurse to enrich the population of an entire island she would presumably need to be a divinity of some kind (Weinberg 1986: 67; Hitch 2012: 155; Hunter 2015 ad loc.). Cf. Hes. *Op.* 379 (πόροι Ζεὺς ἄσπετον ὄλβον, noted by Campbell 1981: 40 ad *Arg.* 2.1181) and, though verbal parallels are lacking, Zeus' enriching of the island of Rhodes at *Il.* 2.670 (καί σφιν θεσπέσιον πλοῦτον κατέχευε Κρονίων). Hera's hostility toward Macris is reminiscent of the myth of Ino, another of Dionysus' nurses, who is herself transformed into the goddess Leucothea.

96 For sacred caves, see: Weinberg 1986: ch. 4; Roux 1999: ch. 15; Ustinova 2009: ch. 2.

97 For the ambiguity of the connection of the etiology for the name Lyra in example 7, see

and the frequent citations of local historians in the scholia to these passages show that these references are the product of Apollonius' diligent researches. Almost more interesting, however, are the seemingly unmotivated references to hero cult, especially in the casual mention of Dipsacus' shrine in example 5. This passage shows what a natural part of the epic world hero cult has become in Apollonius' hands.[98] Absent from this survey is the ever-exceptional Book 3; its tight plotting, setting in a single land (Colchis), and paucity of αἴτια perhaps explain this disparity.[99] It is also suggestive that only two examples occur in Book 4. The exotic and sometimes fantastical geography of the return journey may not have accommodated hero cult, with its strong local aspect, quite as easily as the outward itinerary.[100] The relevance of hero cult to the Argonauts' own futures is suggested by the fact that both of the instances in Book 4 (examples 9, 10) relate directly or obliquely to the future of Jason and Medea's marriage. In example 9, Hera reveals that Medea will marry Achilles in Elysium—following the failure of her marriage to Jason, we may infer.[101] Likewise, Macris' sacred cave in passage 10 provides the setting for Jason and Medea's wedding, but an earlier narratorial digression (4.539–541) had revealed that Heracles had once come to this same Macris in order to be purified for the murder of his own children. By means of this almost subliminal association, Apollonius contrives for Jason and Medea's marriage to take place under the sign of child-murder, a grisly portent of the destined fruit of their newfound union.[102]

It is also significant that the Argonauts participate in hero cult themselves on three occasions (1, 7, 8), including in their first stop following the departure from Pagasae (1). Valerius and "Orpheus" evidently saw little point in Apollonius' Dolops episode and thus have the heroes of their *Argonauticas* sail past Dolops' tomb without stopping (VF *Arg.* 2.10, *Orph. Arg.* 461). Apollonius is no doubt partly attracted to this setting by the possibility for etiology, allusion, and mythological harmonization,[103] but arguably more is at stake here, too: the Argonauts' participation in hero cult here serves to foreshadow their own hero-

---

162*n*91. Hunter (1993: 128) comments, "The pervasive aetiological interests of the *Argonautica*, which present us with tangible, continuing evidence for past lives, make heroes (in the 'religious' sense) and their cult an obvious source of interest."

98   For an interpretation of Dipsacus' pastoral vignette, see, e.g., Fusillo 1985: 171–172.
99   Though note that Colchian heroes are worshiped at the very end of Book 2, in example 8 above.
100 On these differences between the outward and return journeys, cf. Harder 1994: 20–21, 26–29.
101 Feeney 1991: 63.
102 Ibid.; Hunter 1993: 74.
103 See Händel 1954: 29 and 158*n*73.

ization, which, in the manner of ring-composition, Apollonius finally acknowledges at the very end of their journey (4.1773–1775).[104] This, I believe, is the programmatic significance with which Apollonius invests this minor episode by making it the first incident of the outward journey.

2.2 Ambiguous Cases of Hero Cult

In addition to these relatively clear-cut examples, there are several more ambiguous passages in which hero cult is not as explicit, but could be implied by some combination of allusion and the reader's potential knowledge of the local traditions that inform Apollonius' narrative.[105] For instance, when the Argonaut Butes is about to succumb to the Sirens' alluring song, Aphrodite "who rules over Eryx" ("Έρυκος μεδέουσα, 4.917) snatches him up (ἀνερέψατο, 918) from the sea to dwell at Cape Lilybaeum in Sicily (4.912–919); there, tradition holds, he is to become by Aphrodite the father of Eryx, eponym of the Sicilian city and mountain and the founder of the goddess's famous temple there.[106] Hunter has pointed out a probable allusion in this passage to Hes. *Th.* 988–991, where Aphrodite similarly snatches up (ἀνερειψαμένη, *Th.* 990) the young Phaethon, whom she makes "her innermost temple-keeper in her holy temples, a divine spirit" (ζαθέοις ἐνὶ νηοῖς | νηοπόλον μύχιον ποιήσατο, δαίμονα δῖον, 990–991).[107] For Hunter, the same fate has "plainly" befallen Butes,[108] and the intertext does encourage us to think so; perhaps we are to imagine Butes being buried in or near the temple that Eryx will found for his mother.[109]

---

104 See further Hitch 2012: 136–137.
105 In addition to the passages discussed below, see 4.2.1 for the possibility that *Arg.* 4.1763–1764 alludes to hero cult for Theras, the eponymous founder of Thera. See also McPhee (forthcoming d) for Apollonius' etymologizing allusion to Parthenope, the Siren who received hero cult in Naples.
106 For ancient sources, see Wernicke in *RE* 3.1 s.v. "Butes," col. 1082. The myth is examined from the perspective of Greek colonization by D'Aleo 2012.
107 On this passage's relation to hero cult, see West 1966: 428–429.
108 Hunter 2015 ad *Arg.* 4.918. In light of this intertext, I would add a parallel passage in Theocritus: *Id.* 17.46–50 describes Aphrodite's snatching (ἁρπάξασα, 48) Queen Berenice I out of Hades before she could cross the Acheron; the goddess then immortalizes her and installs her in her own temple to share cult honors. Berenice's fate resembles a mixture of those of Apollonius' Butes and Hesiod's Phaethon. If Apollonius does imitate Theocritus here, it would strengthen the argument for a cultic subtext in Butes' translation to Lilybaeum.
109 In the case of the other Argonauts who are separated from the crew (Hylas, Polyphemus, and Heracles), Apollonius is careful to relate their fates in some detail (1.1317–1325, 1345–1357; 4.1472–1477). The poet only hints at Butes' fate, however, by mentioning Eryx in line 917 and, perhaps, by alluding to the parallel fate of Phaethon in the *Theogony*.

Another passage redolent of hero cult occurs when the Mariandynian king Lycus recollects Heracles' earlier adventures in his realm. In the course of his reminiscences, he mentions two local champions, Priolas and Titias, who were the eponyms for a pair of towns in the area (2.780–785):[110]

780 ἔνθα δ' ἐπὶ Πριόλαο κασιγνήτοιο θανόντος
ἡμετέρου Μυσοῖσιν ὑπ' ἀνδράσιν, ὅν τινα λαὸς
οἰκτίστοις ἐλέγοισιν ὀδύρεται ἐξέτι κείνου,
ἀθλεύων Τιτίην ἀπεκαίνυτο πυγμαχέοντα
καρτερόν, ὃς πάντεσσι μετέπρεπεν ἰθέοισιν
785 εἶδός τ' ἠδὲ βίην, χαμάδις δέ οἱ ἤλασ' ὀδόντας.

Then he [sc. Heracles], competing in the games held when my brother Priolas was killed by the Mysians, whom the people have mourned ever since with most sorrowful dirges, defeated in boxing mighty Titias, who surpassed all the young men in beauty and strength, and knocked his teeth to the ground.

In this passage, Lycus' brother Priolas is remembered with public mourning (λαὸς ... ὀδύρεται, 781–782; note the present tense, indicative of habitual action) accompanied by threnodies (οἰκτίστοις ἐλέγοισιν, 782). The phrase ἐξέτι κείνου ("ever since," 782) sounds an etiological note[111] that reinforces the impression that Lycus is describing the origin of a cultic ritual. Hitch does not discuss this particular passage, but her comment on the cult afforded the slain Dolionians is equally apt here: "Acts of mourning performed by communities, rather than families, and repetitive ritual are some of the characteristic features which distinguish hero cult from tendence [sic] of the dead."[112]

Notably, the scholiast ad 780–783b claims that Apollonius is unique (ἰδίως) in making Priolas, not Titias' son Borimus (or "Bormus"), the subject of the Mariandynians' lament.[113] Indeed, Apollonius is our only source for the hon-

---

110   Their eponymous status is noted by Σ ad *Arg.* 2.780–783a.
111   See Páskiewicz 1981 ad loc.
112   Hitch 2012: 139; see 140, 143–144 for similar points vis-à-vis Idmon and Jason. Cf. 160n82 for possible parallels with King Cyzicus (similarly mourned with funeral games, which may have been institutionalized). For ritual mourning in hero cult, see: Brelich 1958: 82–86; Nilsson 1967: 187; Seaford 1994: 139 nn. 151–152.
113   See van der Kolf in *RE* 22.2 s.v. "Priolas," col. 2317, for an important discussion of this scholium. She argues that the scholiast does not equate Priolas and Borimus (e.g., as comparable vegetation deities) but rather shows himself familiar with the Mariandynians' ritual lament for the one figure (Borimus) but not the other (Priolas) based on his knowl-

ors afforded to Priolas, but several ancient testimonies mention comparable rituals for Borimus, whose very name denoted a Mariandynian style of θρῆνος (Poll. *Onom.* 4.54–55, Hesych. s.v. Βῶρμον).[114] This Borimus was a Hylas-like figure with agricultural associations; the Mariandynians began to hold a ritual search and lament for him every summer following his disappearance while he was out either looking for water or hunting. Apollonius will likely have known the Borimus story from reading Nymphis (*FGrH* 432 F 5), a local Heracleote historian who was probably his older contemporary.[115] At the very least, we may be confident that the poet's reference to οἰκτίστοις ἐλέγοισιν (note the superlative) reflects his awareness of the Mariandynians' reputation for threnody, attested already in Aeschylus (*Pers.* 938) and closely associated with the figure of Borimus.[116] If Apollonius did know the Borimus myth, it is curious that he dispensed with it in favor of the story that he tells about Priolas.[117] Certainly the latter figure is more traditionally "epic" and better accommodates Lycus' Heracles narrative.[118] Priolas' death in battle provides a venue for Heracles' boxing match with Titias via his funeral games, but, more importantly, it also furnishes a reason for Heracles to avenge the Mariandynians by subduing the Mysians and several other neighboring peoples on their behalf (2.786–791).[119]

---

edge of the local historians Nymphis and Callistratus. Burstein (1976: 104 n. 110) assumes from this scholium that Apollonius invented these rites for Priolas, but as van der Kolf notes, he might equally have borrowed them from a source unknown to the scholiast.

114   For the confused traditions surrounding Priolas, Titias, and Borimus, see, e.g.: Robert 1921: 836 n. 5; Vian 2002: 1.277–278.
115   The *Arg.* scholia mention Nymphis repeatedly and once observe that the poet seems to have taken material directly from him (παρ᾽ οὗ Ἀπολλώνιος ἔοικε ταῦτα μεταφέρειν, Σ ad 2.729–735a = Nymphis fr. 3). For Apollonius' probable use of Nymphis, see Desideri 1967: 380–387, with earlier bibliography. Possibly Apollonius has used Nymphis' Borimus as a partial model for his version of both Priolas and Titias. With Apollonius' description of Titias (2.784–785), cf. Nymphis' description of Borimus: "They say that … in his beauty and his comeliness at its height he far surpassed the rest" (τοῦτον δὲ λέγουσιν … τῷ δὲ κάλλει καὶ τῇ κατὰ τὴν ἀκμὴν ὥρᾳ πολὺ τῶν ἄλλων διενεγκεῖν, *FGrH* 432 F 9b; translation my own). In transferring some of Borimus' well-known characteristics to his more shadowy father Titias, Apollonius engages in "reverse-genealogical characterization" (Hunter 1993: 99); for further examples of this technique, see: Harder 2019a: *passim*; McPhee 2023c: 173 with n. 2.
116   In fact, the Aeschylean scholiast ad loc. is one of our sources for Borimus' story. For the role of the superlative in ethnography, see Bloomer 1993.
117   Apollonius' "creative selectivity" in his choice and combination of mythic variants has been stressed by Jackson, particularly in his 1993 monograph.
118   Cf. Páskiewicz 1988: 60, who suggests that Apollonius has invented some details in his Priolas narrative in order to justify Heracles' war against the Mysians.
119   As Lycus makes clear, the Argonauts continue Heracles' work by killing the Bebrycian king

But regardless of his precise relationship to Borimus, Apollonius does appear to present Priolas as a local cult hero, and he has been interpreted as such by modern scholars.[120]

Interestingly, however, it is Heracles' boxing opponent Titias whom we actually know to have been a local hero, though Apollonius makes no reference to this fact. In discussing the homonymous Cretan Dactyl named Titias, the scholiast ad *Arg.* 1.1126–1131a quotes a fragment of Domitius Callistratus (= *FGrH* 433 F 2), another local historian of Heraclea Pontica, as follows:

> Καλλίστρατος δὲ ἐν τῇ β' τῶν Καθ' Ἡράκλειαν περὶ Τιτίου φησίν· 'ὁ δὲ Τιτίας ἥρως ἐγχώριος, ὃν οἱ μὲν μυθεύουσι παῖδα Διός, οἱ δὲ τὸν πρεσβύτατον τῶν Μαριανδυνοῦ τοῦ Κιμμερίου παίδων, δι' ὃν μάλιστα τὸ ἔθνος ηὔξηται καὶ προάγεται ἔτι εἰς εὐδαιμονίαν· ἀπεθεώθη δὲ ὑπὸ Μαριανδυνῶν.' Καὶ Προμαθίδας δὲ ἐν τοῖς Περὶ Ἡρακλείας [*FGrH* 430 F 1] λέγει περὶ Τιτίου ὅστις ἦν, καὶ Θεοφάνης [188 F 2].

> Callistratus, in Book 2 of *On Heraclea*, says of Titias: "Titias is a local hero, whom some say is the son of Zeus, others, the eldest of the children of Mariandynus the Cimmerian. It was chiefly because of him that his people have grown in power and continue to increase in prosperity, and he was deified by the Mariandynians." Promathidas also discusses who Titias was in his *About Heraclea* [*FGrH* 430 F 1], as does Theophanes [188 F 2].[121]

Apollonius has evidently cast a local cult hero (or god? n.b. ἀπεθεώθη) for a minor role in Lycus' Heracles narrative, though nothing in his text would suggest this destiny for Titias. The same phenomenon may be observed at *Arg.* 2.955–961, when the Argonauts pick up the three sons of Deimachus, who had been left behind at Sinope during the course of Heracles' Amazonian labor (cf. 2.912–913).[122] Apollonius names all three of these brothers (956) without

---

Amycus, who had been a thorn in the Mariandynians' side since Heracles' departure (792–798). For a good overview of Heracles' various conquests in this region, see Páskiewicz 1981 ad *Arg.* 2.786. For the political subtext of this narrative, see: Wilamowitz 1924: 2.237 n. 2; Fränkel 1968: 232 n. 218; Palombi 1993: 162–163; Vian 2002: 1.159–161.

120 E.g.: van der Kolf in *RE* 22.2 s.v. "Priolas," coll. 2316.26–28, 2317.62–67; Páskiewicz 1988: 59; Matteo 2007: 519.

121 Text is taken from Wendel 1935; the translation is my own. The phrase ἀπεθεώθη δὲ ὑπὸ Μαριανδυνῶν has been transposed from its original place at the end of this quotation, where it seems inorganic; see Wendel's apparatus.

122 The foregoing digression (946–954) on the city's eponymous nymph, the abducted Asopid Sinope (see Jackson 1999), serves to identify the site by name and put the reader in mind of

letting on that at least one of them, Autolycus, was in fact worshipped as the founder (οἰκιστής) of Sinope and had an oracle attributed to him there.[123] In the notes to the list of definite references to hero cult above, I recorded several cases in which the scholia claim that Apollonius has incorporated an obscure cult hero (Dolops, the slain Dolionians, Agamestor, Sthenelus) from a poetic predecessor (Cleon of Curium) or local historian (Deiochus, Promathidas); probably other obscure cult heroes (Dipsacus?) derive from similar sources. It is a testament to Apollonius' enthusiasm for hero cult that he has filled out the population of his epic world with several cult heroes drawn from his extensive reading.

2.3 Hesiodic Heroization

Another important means by which Apollonius hints at the Argonauts' destined immortalization is through allusion to Hesiod, and particularly to an influential passage from the *Works and Days*. In his account of the fourth of the Five Ages, the Ages of Heroes, Hesiod explains how many of the mythic heroes came to be immortalized after death; I quote his account in full (*Op.* 156–173):[124]

    αὐτὰρ ἐπεὶ καὶ τοῦτο γένος κατὰ γαῖα κάλυψεν,
    αὖτις ἔτ' ἄλλο τέταρτον ἐπὶ χθονὶ πουλυβοτείρῃ
    Ζεὺς Κρονίδης ποίησε, δικαιότερον καὶ ἄρειον,
    ἀνδρῶν ἡρώων θεῖον γένος, οἳ καλέονται
160 ἡμίθεοι, προτέρη γενεὴ κατ' ἀπείρονα γαῖαν.
    καὶ τοὺς μὲν πόλεμός τε κακὸς καὶ φύλοπις αἰνὴ
    τοὺς μὲν ὑφ' ἑπταπύλῳ Θήβῃ, Καδμηίδι γαίῃ,

---

foundation narratives (n.b. καθίσσατο, 947). Sinope thus emerges as doubly Greek through the Deimachids and its transplanted nymph. If he knew the story, Apollonius may have been consciously suppressing an alternate version that connected Sinope to an eponymous Amazon (see Ehrhardt 1995: 44); indeed, the fact that the Deimachids had been part of Heracles' expedition against the Amazons seems pointed in this regard.

123 See: Páskiewicz 1981 ad *Arg*. 2.955; Malkin 1987: 207–208; Vian 2002: 1.280–281 ad *Arg*. 2.961. Besides Autolycus, another of the Deimachids, Phlogius, is apparently mentioned in a dedicatory inscription from Sinope (*CIG* 4162 = Robinson 1905: 306), which suggests that he received cult there too. On the basis of this evidence, Ehrhardt 1995: 43 infers that all three of the brothers named by Apollonius were likely worshipped as κτίσται in Sinope.

124 With this passage cf. also Hes. *Cat*. fr. 155.64–65 Most (= fr. 204.102–103 MW). The question of the authenticity of line 166, and more generally whether Hesiod limited translation to the Islands of the Blessed to only some of the fourth generation, is much debated; see, e.g.: West 1978 ad loc.; Solmsen 1982: 21–24; Koenen 1994: 5 n. 12.

ὤλεσε μαρναμένους μήλων ἕνεκ᾽ Οἰδιπόδαο,
τοὺς δὲ καὶ ἐν νήεσσιν ὑπὲρ μέγα λαῖτμα θαλάσσης
165 ἐς Τροίην ἀγαγὼν Ἑλένης ἕνεκ᾽ ἠυκόμοιο.
ἔνθ᾽ ἤ τοι τοὺς μὲν θανάτου τέλος ἀμφεκάλυψεν,
τοῖς δὲ δίχ᾽ ἀνθρώπων βίοτον καὶ ἤθε᾽ ὀπάσσας
168 Ζεὺς Κρονίδης κατένασσε πατὴρ ἐς πείρατα γαίης,
170 καὶ τοὶ μὲν ναίουσιν ἀκηδέα θυμὸν ἔχοντες
ἐν μακάρων νήσοισι παρ᾽ Ὠκεανὸν βαθυδίνην·
ὄλβιοι ἥρωες, τοῖσιν μελιηδέα καρπὸν
τρὶς ἔτεος θάλλοντα φέρει ζείδωρος ἄρουρα.

When the earth covered up this [bronze] race too, Zeus, Cronus' son, made another one in turn upon the bounteous earth, a fourth one, more just and superior, the godly race of men-heroes, who are called demigods, the generation before our own upon the boundless earth. Evil war and dread battle destroyed these, some under seven-gated Thebes in the land of Cadmus while they fought for the sake of Oedipus' sheep, others brought in boats over the great gulf of the sea to Troy for the sake of fair-haired Helen. There the end of death shrouded some of them, but upon others Zeus the father, Cronus' son, bestowed life and habitations far from human beings and settled them at the limits of the earth; and these dwell with a spirit free of care on the Islands of the Blessed beside deep-eddying Ocean—happy heroes, for whom the grain-giving field bears honey-sweet fruit flourishing three times a year.

Hesiod's account may presuppose, but is not explicit about, the cult worship of these heroes.[125] Hesiod's switch from aorist to present-tense verbs in lines 170–174 indicates his belief in the heroes' eternal life (cf. βίοτον ... ὀπάσσας, 167): even now they enjoy their carefree existence at the ends of the earth.[126] In one instance, Homer appears to presuppose a comparable conception of a mythic Age of Heroes, retrospectively referring to the warriors who died at Troy as "the race of men half-divine" (ἡμιθέων γένος ἀνδρῶν, Il. 12.23).[127] Tellingly,

---

125 See Bravo 2009: 15–16, with earlier references. Apollonius would have been familiar with later Greek literature that does testify to cultic honors for those who dwell on the Islands of the Blessed (e.g., Pl. Resp. 540b–c).

126 Later accounts certify that the inhabitants of the Islands of the Blessed are indeed immortal (e.g., Hellanicus FGrH 4 F 19b, scolion 894 Campbell).

127 De Jong 2004a: 88–89. Homer's view of his protagonists as part of a distinct race of yore emerges also from the unfavorable comparisons he sometimes draws between the

though, the context of this reference is the elimination of any lasting trace of the Achaean army in the Troad by a godsent flood—a far cry from Hesiod's notion of the demigods' continued vitality as immortalized heroes.[128] In any case, Hesiod's account of the race of heroes is the *locus classicus*, and was imitated at length in the Hellenistic period by Apollonius' predecessor Aratus (*Phaen.* 96–136).

Hesiod's importance to the mythological chronology that undergirds the *Arg.* has increasingly been recognized in recent years, particularly in light of a series of important studies by Clauss.[129] Apollonius explicitly adopts the Hesiodic framework near the end of the epic, when Talos is referred to as "the last of the bronze race of men born from ash trees still living in the time of the demigods" (τὸν μὲν χαλκείης μελιηγενέων ἀνθρώπων | ῥίζης λοιπὸν ἐόντα μετ' ἀνδράσιν ἡμιθέοισιν, 4.1641–1642).[130] Long before this point in the text, however, Apollonius allusively locates the Argonauts in the Heroic Age by referring to them with variations of Hesiod's identifying phrase, "the godly race of men-heroes, who are called demigods" (ἀνδρῶν ἡρώων θεῖον γένος, οἳ καλέονται | ἡμίθεοι, *Op.* 159–160). Most prominent is the scene of the Argo's launch, where the narrator describes the gods as looking down at "the race of demigods, the best of men who then were sailing over the sea" (ἡμιθέων ἀνδρῶν γένος, οἳ τότ' ἄριστοι | πόντον ἐπιπλώεσκον, *Arg.* 1.548–549).[131] Apollonius' wording carefully combines the HEs' single reference to "demigods," quoted above (ἡμιθέων γένος ἀνδρῶν, *Il.* 12.23),[132] with the syntax of Hesiod's phrase, with its expansion by means of a relative clause (γένος, οἵ ...).[133] This combination may be taken as emblematic of Apollonius' synthesis of two types of heroism: Homeric and Hesiodic, epic and cultic.[134] Twice elsewhere as well, Apollonius transparently reworks Hesiod's phrase, referring to the Argonauts as "a god-like expedition of

---

strength of his heroes and "men as they are now" (*Il.* 5.302–304; 12.381–383, 447–449; 20.285–287) (Hack 1929: 68–69; van Wees 1992: 8).

128 On this passage, see, e.g.: Reinhardt 1961: 267–269; Scodel 1982; Saïd 1998: 17; Nagy 2005: 83.
129 See especially Clauss 2000, 2016b, the latter of which builds on Clauss 1990.
130 Vox 2002: 158 n. 30; Hitch 2012: 146.
131 The Hesiodic echo is noted by, e.g., Hunter 1993: 128; Hitch 2012: 146.
132 For other Homeric echoes in Apollonius' phrase, see Campbell 1981: 10.
133 Cf. also *HH* 31.18–19, 32.18–19 (cited by Hitch 2012: 146 n. 46).
134 Cf. Hitch 2012: 145, speaking of Apollonius' terminology for his protagonists in general: "Apollonius combines Homeric and Hesiodic epic diction to demonstrate that the Argonauts are both Homeric heroes (*herôes* [sic], *aristoi*) and members of Hesiod's fourth race (*hêmitheoi*) in anticipation of their future blessed afterlife." Vílchez (1986: 84) rather suggests that Apollonius' use of the term ἡμιθεῶν may evoke Pindar, who uses this word only with reference to the Argonauts (*Pyth.* 4.12, 184, 211).

heroic men" (ἀνδρῶν ἡρώων θεῖος στόλος, *Arg.* 1.970; ἀνδρῶν ἡρώων θεῖον στόλον, 2.1091).[135] Finally, several scholars have heard an echo of Hesiod in the Salutation to the Argonauts in the poem's Envoi, "race of blessed heroes" (ἀριστήων μακάρων γένος, 4.1773). As we saw in chapter 1, the very conceptual underpinning of the Envoi (and in turn the *Arg.*'s self-presentation as a hymn) lies in the Argonauts' status as divinized heroes, who are thus capable of receiving the narrator's Salutation and Prayer. In this context, the epithet "blessed" may allude to Hesiod's description of the Islands of the Blessed (μακάρων νήσοισι, *Op.* 171) as the home of the heroes rendered immortal by Zeus.[136] These sustained allusions to Hesiod's Age of Heroes encourage the reader to understand the Argonauts in Hesiodic as well as Homeric terms: they are mortal heroes destined for an immortal afterlife.

2.4 Apotheosis

I round out this survey of hero cult and related phenomena in the *Arg.* by examining a final category that is strictly distinct from heroization but closely related to it, namely, the deification enjoyed by a few select mortals.[137] Like their heroized counterparts, these figures have surpassed the limits of their mortality, but they have attained a higher ontological status that assimilates them to gods rather than cult heroes. In the *Arg.*, they serve an important function as models for the Argonauts' own destined transcendence of their human stations, even if most of the crew cannot follow them all the way to full deification. The inimitable Heracles is the most important paradigm for the Argonauts in this regard. The sea god Glaucus explicitly prophesies Heracles' apotheosis upon his separation from the rest of the crew in Mysia,[138] making clear that the hero will actually join the Olympian gods (1.1317–1320)—the highest possible form of immortalization.[139] As Feeney has shown, in the wake of Heracles' departure

---

135 Hunter 1993: 128; Hitch 2012: 145 n. 45.
136 Hitch 2012: 146. See further the discussion in 136*n*230.
137 "Beiden Phänomenen [*sc.* heroization and apotheosis] lag also ein bestimmter Glaube an die Möglichkeit einer Veränderung zugrunde, die dem Menschen unter bestimmten Voraussetzungen von Leistung und Anerkennung (menschlicher- und göttlicherseits) den Zugang zu höheren Stellungen der spirituellen Weltordnung offen hielt" (Buraselis et al. in *ThesCRA* 2.126). For a survey of deified mortals in Greek myth, see Sourvinou-Inwood 2005: 332–345.
138 Walter (2020: 125–126) perceptively notes that the fact that the Mysians fear Heracles' wrath to this very day, as the αἴτιον connected with Hylas' disappearance implies (1.1348–1357), presupposes the hero's apotheosis.
139 In fact, there is evidence that Heracles sometimes received cult as a hero instead of, or concurrently with, his worship as an Olympian (Burkert 1985: 208 with n. 3), though Lévêque

from the crew at the end of Book 1, the Argonauts often replicate collectively and in a minor key the feats that Heracles had accomplished without them.[140] This pattern climaxes in the Libyan episode with Heracles' final intervention in the plot, as the Argonauts literally follow in his footsteps and are saved by him as by a god,[141] even in his absence.[142] As in Pindar, Heracles represents a heroic standard that the other Argonauts cannot hope to match.[143] Nevertheless, the Argonauts' partial emulation of their onetime crewmate culminates in their heroization, which represents a more muted form of his singular destiny.[144]

The other major paradigms of immortalization in the epic are the Dioscuri, Polydeuces and Castor. More than Heracles, the divine twins occupy a gray area between hero and god.[145] Already in the *Odyssey*, they are said to live and die on alternate days below the earth, an honor they have received from Zeus (11.301–304; cf. *Il.* 3.243–244). Pindar takes a similar view, though his Dioscuri alternate between their tombs at Therapna and the company of Zeus on Olympus (*Nem.* 10.55–59, 83–90). Still other sources, following the tradition that only

---

and Verbanck-Piérard (1992) argue that the Greeks mainly worshipped Heracles as a god; see further Larson 2007: 183–184 and Stafford 2010, both with earlier bibliography. *Arg.* 1.1317–1320 makes it clear that Apollonius, at least, envisions deification, not heroization, as Heracles' fate.

140   Feeney 1987: 56–66. See further Köhnken 2003b: 19–22, 27.
141   Feeney (1987: 59) notes that the Argonauts also partly "[follow] the trail Heracles has blazed" in his Amazonian labor as they proceed along the Black Sea littoral in Book 2.
142   By uncovering a spring in Libya, Heracles indirectly "saves his companions, even though he is far away" (ἢ καὶ νόσφιν ἐὼν ἐσάωσεν ἑταίρους, 4.1458), when the Argonauts are dying of thirst. This formulation suggests that, like a god, he is already saving mortals from afar (Feeney 1987: 63). Rostropowicz (1990: 34) notes that the verb ἐσάωσεν could constitute a nod to Heracles' cult epithet Σωτήρ, "Savior," though cf. Hunter 1993: 29 n. 79. Feeney (1987: 63) influentially read Heracles' final appearance in this episode—Lynceus' hazy vision of Heracles marching off into the distance after he has retrieved the Golden Apples—as a premonition of his apotheosis: "He is passing out of the world of men, and into the world of gods." For the (rather slim) evidence that these apples symbolized immortality, see, e.g.: Gantz 1993: 413; Stafford 2005: 78 with n. 27; 2010: 238; 2012: 47.
143   See, e.g.: Pike 1984: 16; Kampakoglou 2019: 114–115, 130. We might also compare Heracles' (mostly implicit) status as a heroic foil already in the *Iliad*: his earlier sack of Troy makes him a forerunner for the present campaign, but one that stands head and shoulders above the Achaean army, who struggle to accomplish with 1,186 ships what Heracles had managed with just six (*Il.* 5.638–642). See further *Il.* 18.117, *Od.* 8.223–225, Galinsky 1972: 15.
144   Hitch 2012: 135; Tsakiris 2022: 211–212. Feeney (1987: 49–50, 58–59) focuses on Heracles' immortalization as a paradigm for that of the Dioscuri, but he does not connect either of these apotheoses to the general heroization of the Argonauts.
145   The ambiguous status of the Dioscuri is documented well by Farnell 1921: ch. 8. In general on this duo, see further Nilsson 1967: 406–411; Burkert 1985: 212–213.

Polydeuces is Zeus' son, Castor being the son of the mortal Tyndareus, assert that Castor is buried beneath the earth but that Polydeuces has become an Olympian god (e.g., Plut. *Quaest. Graec.* 23).[146] Cult practice presents a similar range of opinion. The twins were sometimes worshipped as heroes, especially at the site of their grave in Therapna, but at other times as gods. They had a special connection to their Spartan homeland, where they served a number of typically heroic functions,[147] but their powers were also universal in scope, as befits the gods. As "Saviors" (Σωτῆρες), the twins were thought to appear in epiphany to help mortals in acute distress, especially at sea.[148] Notably, the *HH*s include two hymns for the Dioscuri (17, 33), who, alongside Heracles (15) and Asclepius (16), are thus conceived of as Panhellenic gods despite their erstwhile mortality.

For his part, Apollonius emphasizes the Panhellenic aspects of the Dioscuri and thus seems to regard them as destined for apotheosis rather than heroization.[149] Unlike Heracles, the Dioscuri remain for the entirety of the Argonautic adventure, which Apollonius actually presents as the αἴτιον for their deification and for their special connection to mariners.[150] After the murder of Apsyrtus, the divine beam of the Argo warns the Argonauts to seek purification from Circe in order to appease the anger of Zeus (4.557–561, 580–588); and to reach Circe in the Ausonian (Tyrrhenian) Sea, the beam further instructs Polydeuces and Castor to pray to the gods for safe passage through the Eridanus (Po) and Rhodanus (Rhone) Rivers (588–591). The brothers do so immediately (592–594), and when the Argo successfully emerges into the Tyrrhenian Sea, the

---

146 On the different paternities assigned to the Dioscuri, see, e.g., Gantz 1993: 318–319.
147 The Dioscuri were closely associated with Sparta's dual monarchy and were thought to accompany the army into battle alongside Menelaus (Hdt. 5.75.2; cf. Simon. fr. 11 W², in which the Dioscuri as well as Menelaus lead the Spartan forces at Platea and are explicitly dubbed "heroes," ἥρωσι, 31).
148 On this epithet, which attaches to a great range of Greek divinities and rulers, see, e.g., Nock 1972: 1.78, 2.720–735.
149 *Pace* Hitch 2012: 148–149, who speaks of the "heroization" of the Dioscuri; cf. also Kampakoglou 2019: 101.
150 See also 2.806–810, a passage I discuss in greater detail below. I disagree with the interpretation of Natzel (1992: 109) that at 4.649–653 Apollonius is referring to altars to the Dioscuri set up on the Stoechades specifically (by the Argonauts themselves? So Moreau 1994: 148, Kampakoglou 2019: 155). The contrast at 4.652–653 between "**not only … that** voyage" (οὐδ᾽ οἶον κείνης … ναυτιλίης) and "future sailors **as well**" (καὶ ὀψιγόνων) suggests a more universally-applicable αἴτιον, namely, of the worship that all sailors everywhere render to the Dioscuri (Williams 1991: 191–192). As Hunter (2015 ad loc.) comments, line 653 envisions Zeus in his Hesiodic role as the supreme god distributing τιμαί (in this case, guardianship over mariners) to a pair of new divinites.

narrator credits their prayer and reveals their destined role as divine saviors of sailors (649–653):

μεσσότατον δ' ἄρα τοί γε διὰ στόμα νηὶ βαλόντες,
650   Στοιχάδας εἰσαπέβαν νήσους σόοι εἵνεκα κούρων
Ζηνός· ὃ δὴ βωμοί τε καὶ ἱερὰ τοῖσι τέτυκται
ἔμπεδον· οὐδ' οἶον κείνης ἐπίουροι ἔποντο
ναυτιλίης, Ζεὺς δέ σφι καὶ ὀψιγόνων πόρε νῆας.

And then, by sailing their ship through the centermost mouth of the river, they disembarked on the Stoechades islands, safe and sound, thanks to the sons of Zeus. For that reason altars and rites were established forever in their honor, for not only did they accompany that voyage as guardians, but Zeus entrusted them with ships of future sailors as well.

The reference to the Tyndarids as "the sons of Zeus" (κούρων | Ζηνός) faintly conceals the gods' most common designation, "the Dioscuri" (Διόσκο[υ]ροι), while σόοι looks forward to the cult title Σωτῆρες, "Saviors," by which they will be hailed after their apotheosis. Indeed, given that the earliest attestation of their theonymic appellation as "sons of Zeus" (Dioscuri) occurs in the opening Evocation of the longer *Homeric Hymn* dedicated to the twins (ἀμφὶ Διὸς κούρους, 33.1),[151] Apollonius appears to be name-checking *the* Homeric model for Castor and Polydeuces' role as "saviors ... of swift-faring ships" (σωτῆρας ... ὠκυπόρων τε νεῶν, 5–6).[152] Apollonius has effectively penned the αἴτιον for the recurrent situation of nautical salvation celebrated in this hymn (cf. also Theoc. *Id.* 22.6–22). Notably, the AR narrator here casts the Dioscuri as "guardians" of "that voyage"—evidently in its entirety, not only for this stretch of the journey in Book 4;[153] the Argonautic voyage in toto thus becomes the basis of their

---

151   Διὸς κούρους is also repeated at line 9. The echo is noted by Campbell 1981 ad loc.
152   For allusions to *HH*s via the name of their Hymnic Subjects, cf. Jackson 1990. This hymn is also among the earliest texts to dub the Dioscuri Σωτῆρες; see Roscher 4.1254. The HEs are silent regarding the Dioscuri's connection with sailing (cf. Hall 2021: 28). Apollonius appears to have had recourse to this *HH* in other scenes of nautical trouble as well. The hymn's account of desperate sailors praying to the Dioscuri before their salvific epiphany (5–17) bears comparison to the plotting of his Anaphe episode, while its apparent reference to sacrificing lambs over the ship's stern (10–11 with AHS 1936 and Càssola 1975a ad loc.) is borrowed for Jason's sacrifice to Triton prior to that god's maritime epiphany (*Arg.* 4.1593–1602).
153   ἕποντο (652) shows that κείνης ... ναυτιλίης refers to the whole Argonautic voyage, not just a particular leg of it. This verb is frequently used to denote a hero's participation in the

deification and their special patronage of sailors. At the same time, the Dioscuri become a promising paradigm for the other Argonauts, who have participated in the same labors aboard the Argo and will win a lesser grade of immortality for themselves, namely, heroization.

Besides Heracles and the Dioscuri, a few other figures appear sporadically who seem to have become gods, or at least to have been immortalized in a non-heroic manner:

- The nymph who seizes Hylas presumably immortalizes him when she makes him her husband (1.1324–1325), as Calypso had wanted to do for Odysseus (*Od.* 5.206–224, 7.256–258, 23.335–337).[154] In response to Hylas' disappearance, Heracles establishes a ritualized search for his erstwhile page among the Cians that continues to this day (1.1348–1357).[155]
- Apollonius mentions several aspects of the cult of Aristaeus, including his titles Ἀγρεύς ("Hunter") and Νόμιος ("Shepherd"; 2.506–507).[156] He also attributes to him skill in healing and prophecy (512), which may reflect elements of the god's cult.[157]

---

expedition (1.71, 163, 470, 771; 2.802; 3.58; cf. 4.349, 369), which the Dioscuri did indeed "accompany" in its entirety.

154 This parallel is proposed by Clayton 2017: 154 n. 34. Indeed, echoes of the Homeric Calypso in these lines do imply that Hylas has succumbed to the fate refused by Odysseus and become the nymph's immortal consort. Apollonius identifies Hylas' nymph, like Calypso (e.g., *Od.* 1.14), as both a nymph and a goddess (θεά ... νύμφη, *Arg.* 1.1324), and the phrase φιλότητι ... ποιήσατο ... ὃν πόσιν (1324–1325) recalls Calypso's phrase, φίλον ποιήσετ᾽ ἀκοίτην (*Od.* 5.120, noted by Campbell 1981 ad loc.). For the immortalization of a νυμφόληπτος, see further Callim. *Epigr.* 24.1–2. Kampakoglou (2019: 134) relates Hylas' fate to the mytheme of apotheosis via drowning.

155 For a reconstruction of this Cian ritual, see Sourvinou-Inwood 2005: 74–79. Sourvinou-Inwood argues that Hylas is deified rather than heroized (330–331, 343–345), as, e.g., Larson (2001: 68) assumes. Still other scholars speak only of Hylas' death (e.g., Beye 1982: 30).

156 These lines (καλέουσιν | Ἀγρέα καὶ Νόμιον) allude to Pindar's account of Aristaeus' immortalization in *Pyth.* 9.59–65 (Ἀγρέα καὶ Νόμιον ... καλεῖν, 65; Levin 1969: 499). The rustic god's deification occurs also in the euhemerizing account of Diod. Sic. 4.81.2–3; 82.5, 6 (cf. Hes. *Cat.* fr. 159–160 Most, Serv. ad Verg. *G.* 1.14), and Paus. 8.2.4 explicitly refers to Aristaeus as a mortal who became a god. Elsewhere in Apollonius, the Phaeacian "precinct of Apollo Nomius" (Νομίοιο ... ἱερὸν Ἀπόλλωνος, 4.1218) may in fact belong to Aristaeus, given his daughter Macris' connection to the area; see Green 2007 ad *Arg.* 4.1217–1222.

157 There is some evidence for Aristaeus' association with healing beyond this passage (*RE* 2.1, col. 857.39–48), but I am not aware of other attestations of his prophetic powers. Apollonius may have derived both of these traits from Aristaeus' father Apollo (*RE* 2.1, col. 857.39–48, Matteo 2007 ad *Arg.* 2.498–530). In light of Aristaeus' beekeeping (*Arg.* 4.1132–1133), cf. also the association of bees with prophecy in Greek thought (Scheinberg 1979: 16–26).

- Apollo makes his consort Cyrene "a long-lived nymph" (ποιήσατο νύμφην | ... μακραίωνα, 2.508–509). Poets can call gods "long-lived" (e.g., δαροβίοισι θεοῖσιν, Aesch. *Sept.* 524), but in this case Cyrene's epithet probably implies that she is not immortal, in keeping with Apollonius' portrayal of nymphs elsewhere in the poem.[158]
- The narrator mentions "Ganymede, whom Zeus had once settled in heaven to live with the immortals" (Γανυμήδεα, τόν ῥά ποτε Ζεὺς | οὐρανῷ ἐγκατένασσεν ἐφέστιον ἀθανάτοισιν, 3.115–116).
- The Moon's reference to her consort Endymion (4.57–58) may presuppose the myth of his immortalization.
- Ariadne's relationship with Dionysus comes into view at 4.430–434 (cf. 3.1001–1002); in the traditional myth, Zeus renders her "immortal and ageless" (ἀθάνατον καὶ ἀγήρων, Hes. *Th.* 949) as part of her marriage to his son.
- Though Apollonius' Achilles is destined for heroization (*Arg.* 4.811), I should note here that the poet mentions Thetis' failed attempt to immortalize him as a baby (4.869–879), in a section of the narrative based on Demeter's aborted immortalization of the infant Demophon in the *HH*s (2.233–291).[159]

Like Heracles and the Dioscuri, all of these figures help to normalize the theme of the hero's passage from mortality to a higher grade of being within the epic world that Apollonius creates. They thus serve as oblique reminders of the Argonauts' own destined heroization, if not actual deification.

3 The Duality of the Hero and Generic Hybridity

In light of the foregoing survey, it is clear that Apollonius, unlike Homer, felt no compunction about alluding to the immortalization of his epic heroes. This observation prompts Hitch, author of the only study of hero cult in the *Arg.* to date, to make the following claim near the beginning of her article:

> There is no distinction between heroes of epic and heroes of cult for an epic poet in the third century BC, even if such a distinction can be argued

---

158 Matteo 2007 ad loc.; cf. Páskiewicz 1981 ad loc., and see the discussion of the story of Paraebius' father in the introduction, 4.2. The same epithet is applied to nymphs generally at Soph. *OT* 1099 (τᾶν μακραιώνων), where Jebb (1883 ad loc.) sees a reference to the notion of nymphs' mortality.

159 This passage's debt to the *HH*s is among the best-known in the scholarly literature. See, e.g.: Livrea 1973 ad *Arg.* 4.868; Bulloch 1977: 119–120; Jackson 1990; Mackie 1998: 330–331; Vian 2002: 3.178; Mirto 2011; Manuello 2012: 137–138.

for the presentation of heroes in the Homeric poems. For Apollonius, the Argonauts were well-established heroes of both epic and cult.¹⁶⁰

Hitch is right to recognize that Apollonius' heroes are both "heroes of epic and heroes of cult," but I would not therefore conclude that for Apollonius, "there is no distinction" between the two categories. It is a priori probable that Apollonius was conscious of the extent to which his own usages departed from those of his chief generic exemplars, the HEs. But more importantly, Apollonius must have been conscious of the duality of the hero within Greek culture because it is this crucial distinction that informs his generic innovation. That is, the generic hybridity of the *Arg.* as an epic hymn is directly tied to the duality of the Greek category of hero. In their mortal aspect, heroes can be the subject of epic poetry; in their immortal aspect, heroes can be hymned like the gods. This double nature serves as the basis for Apollonius' merger of epic and hymn within the framework of a single poem that honors the Argonauts in both of these capacities. Apollonius' un-Homeric acknowledgment of the cultic aspect of his epic heroes should thus be regarded not as a kind of automatic or unthinking effect of the state of Greek religion in his day but as a meaningful artistic choice reflective of the *Arg.*'s generic hybridity.

Indeed, I would argue that Apollonius' very use of the term ἥρως points to his awareness of the difference between epic and cultic heroism even as he sometimes seems to conflate the two. On the one hand, Apollonius frequently imitates the Homeric usage of ἥρως, which he regularly employs without overt religious significance to denote Jason,¹⁶¹ the Argonauts as a body,¹⁶² and various other men of the mythic age.¹⁶³ On the other hand, Apollonius also uses ἥρως and the related adjective ἡρωΐς at least twice in an incontrovertibly religious sense,¹⁶⁴ and both times in ways that signal his self-conscious departure from

---

160 Hitch 2012: 131.
161 Jason: 1.781; 2.410; 3.509; 4.477, 750, 784, 1162, 1528. A few other individual Argonauts are also dubbed ἥρως in the singular: Polyphemus (1.1240), Heracles (2.766, 967), and Clytius (2.1042).
162 The Argonauts (in whole or in part): 1.21, 100, 124, 196, 243, 397, 552, 970, 1000, 1012, 1023, 1055, 1329; 2.97, 144, 241, 270, 429, 592, 668, 852, 1091; 3.167, 348, 638, 993–994, 1166, 1194, 1233, 1255, 1293; 4.69, 77, 251, 254, 485, 515, 522, 594, 682, 733, 831, 998, 1099, 1127, 1192, 1226, 1619, 1690, 1725, 1728. At least once, the plural "heroes" is used generally to denote the race of demigods (3.921); see also Medea's wish at 3.464–466: "Whether he [Jason] goes to his death as the best of all the heroes or the worst, let him go" (εἴθ' ὅ γε πάντων | φθίσεται ἡρώων προφερέστατος εἴτε χερείων, | ἐρρέτω).
163 Cyzicus: 1.948; Apsyrtus: 4.471; Nausithous: 4.550; and Triton disguised as Eurypylus: 4.1564. On this last example, see the discussion in the conclusion, 2.1.
164 Valverde Sánchez 1989: 93.

Homeric usage. First, when the Argonauts arrive at the Phasis River, Jason pours libations "in honor of Earth, the indigenous gods, and the souls of the dead heroes" (Γαίῃ τ' ἐνναέταις τε θεοῖς ψυχαῖς τε καμόντων | ἡρώων, 2.1273–1274). The phrase "souls of heroes," with enjambed ἡρώων, echoes the introit of the *Iliad*: Achilles' wrath "sent down to Hades many valiant souls of heroes" (πολλὰς δ' ἰφθίμους ψυχὰς Ἄϊδι προΐαψεν | ἡρώων, 1.3–4).[165] These lines from the very opening of the *Iliad* exemplify the Homeric view of his heroes' postmortem fate: their "souls flitter down to a meaningless existence in Hades."[166] Apollonius' radical transformation of the Iliadic context underlines the *Arg*.'s difference from the Homeric worldview here: the Iliadic heroes doomed to oblivion in the model text have instead become local divinities to be propitiated in adaptation.[167] Second, after a barebones, Iliadic-style catalog of the Dolionian warriors slain by the Argonauts at Cyzicus (1.1040–1047), the narrator observes that these victims still receive "heroes' honors" (τιμαῖς ἡρωΐσι, 1.1048) from the inhabitants to this day. As Goldhill observes, the juxtaposition of this cultic αἴτιον with such a perfunctory version of a Homeric kill catalog (ἀνδροκτασία) "sets in tension two sets of heroes, two sorts of heroization."[168]

Because the *Arg*.'s twin generic affiliations each exert their own pressures on Apollonius' representation of his heroes, the Argonauts appear sometimes in an epic, sometimes in a hymnic guise. Accordingly, on a metaliterary level, we can associate markers of Homeric heroism like the catalog of slain Dolionian warriors with the poem's status as epic, whereas Apollonius' acknowledgments of hero cult correspond to his poem's hymnic intentions; and passages that juxtapose these competing drives can be read metapoetically as illustrations of the poem's status as an epic hymn that unites them together. For instance, the heroization motif traced in the previous section stems from the "hymnic" dimension of the poem, but it stands in tension with the κλέος motif that the *Arg*. has inherited from the HEs. As a strictly metaphorical remedy against death, κλέος

---

165   A TLG search reveals no examples of this collocation anywhere else before Apollonius. Interestingly, we happen to know from the bT scholia ad loc. that Apollonius qua philologist read κεφαλάς in place of ψυχάς in *Il*. 1.3, a reading which implies that he probably followed Zenodotus in athetizing lines 4–5 as well; see: Rengakos 1993: 50; Cusset 2017: 145–146. Nevertheless, Apollonius arguably alludes to the vulgate text of *Il*. 1.3–5 elsewhere, too (see, e.g.: Romeo 1985: 25; Hunter 1993: 119 n. 76; Cuypers 1997: 201 and ad A.R. 2.264 s.v. ἐλώριον; cf. also Abbamonte 2008), in keeping with the Alexandrian penchant for alluding to variant readings of the Homeric text (see, e.g., Giangrande 1970: 47–56).
166   Bravo 2009: 15.
167   Notably, the Apollonian scholiast ad 2.1273 compares Jason's offerings to Alexander's propitiation of the local divinities and heroes on his visit to Troy.
168   Goldhill 1991: 318. See further Levin 1971: 102–103; Hunter 1993: 43.

in Homer is conceptually opposed to the sort of literal immortalization presupposed by hero cult.[169] And yet despite the prevalence of hero cult in his poem, Apollonius' heroes are as eager to win κλέος as any of their Homeric forebears; indeed, the pursuit of glory provides the motive for most of them to join the expedition.[170] Apollonius thus subscribes to what Currie calls "an 'inclusive' model of immortality": he imagines that his heroes will live on both metaphorically through poetic memory and literally in cult.[171] The complementarity of the drives to celebrate the Argonauts in poetry and to worship them as eternal divinities is directly tied to the *Arg.*'s dual status as both epic and hymn. Below, I explore four particularly instructive examples of this sort of juxtaposition in light of the poem's generic hybridity: in the description of Idmon's tomb, in the celebration of Polydeuces' victory over Amycus, in the nadir of despair in the Syrtes episode, and finally, in the *Arg.*'s hymnic Envoi.

3.1   Idmon and Agamestor

As the poet underlines twice before the voyage gets underway, the Argonautic seer Idmon leaves Argos to embark on the Argonautic expedition knowing full well that he is destined to die in Asia, but he nonetheless accepts his fate with a typically epic motive: "so that his people would not begrudge him glorious fame" (μή οἱ δῆμος ἐυκλείης ἀγάσαιτο, 1.141; cf. 443–447). The motif of the seer who knowingly goes to his death is a mythic archetype—Amphiaraus is an obvious parallel[172]—but Idmon's decision finds a close Homeric precedent in Achilles, whose foreknowledge comes from his divine mother Thetis and who submits to an early death with the promised consolation of undying fame (*Il.* 9.410–416).[173]

---

169   See in this regard esp. Sarpedon's famous speech to Glaucus at *Il.* 12.322–328; see also on this opposition van Wees 2006: 373–375.

170   For references, see Pietsch 1999: 90–93. For other motivations for joining the crew, see the summary in Carspecken 1952: 54. Pindar's Argonauts, too, are motivated by the pursuit of glory like typical Homeric heroes (*Pyth.* 4.184–187, with the interpretation of Race 1985).

171   See Currie 2005: 72–78.

172   Indeed, there are other connections between the *vitae* of these seers, who were both sometimes Argonauts and may have been rivals of sorts; see Fowler 2013: 214; Cuypers in *BNJ* 471 F 2; see also Jackson 1993: 9 n. 26. Amphiaraus' foreknowledge of his own death also figures into Euripides' *Hypsipyle* (fr. 752k.17–21), a tragedy closely connected to the Argonautic saga. For Apollonius' debt to this play, see Giaquinta 2021.

173   The proximate cause of Achilles' decision is his desire to avenge Patroclus (Finkelberg 1995: 1 with n. 3), but later Greek literature shows that Achilles could still be said to have chosen to die for the sake of κλέος (e.g., Pl. *Symp.* 208c–e). For Idmon as an Achilles or Amphiaraus figure, see Hensel 1908: 9–13. Klooster (2007: 73 n. 39) further compares the Iliadic seer Merops, whose story features the motif of foreknowledge of (his sons') death,

But whereas Homer's Achilles is destined for Hades like any other mortal, Idmon's postmortem fate turns out to be different, as Apollonius reveals in a fascinating passage following his account of the seer's death at the future site of Heraclea Pontica. After a burial scene reminiscent of the funerals of the HEs (2.835–840), the poet adds the following, thoroughly un-Homeric details about the future of Idmon's tomb (841–850):[174]

καὶ δή τοι κέχυται τοῦδ' ἀνέρος ἐν χθονὶ κείνῃ
τύμβος· σῆμα δ' ἔπεστι καὶ ὀψιγόνοισιν ἰδέσθαι,
νηίου ἐκ κοτίνοιο φάλαγξ· θαλέθει δέ τε φύλλοις
ἄκρης τυτθὸν ἔνερθ' Ἀχερουσίδος. εἰ δέ με καὶ τὸ
845 χρειὼ ἀπηλεγέως Μουσέων ὕπο γηρύσασθαι,
τόνδε πολισσοῦχον διεπέφραδε Βοιωτοῖσιν
Νισαίοισί τε Φοῖβος ἐπιρρήδην ἰλάεσθαι,
ἀμφὶ δὲ τήν γε φάλαγγα παλαιγενέος κοτίνοιο
ἄστυ βαλεῖν, οἱ δ' ἀντὶ θεουδέος Αἰολίδαο
850 Ἴδμονος εἰσέτι νῦν Ἀγαμήστορα κυδαίνουσιν.

And so this man's burial mound was raised in that land, and upon it stands a marker for future generations to see, a trunk of wild olive used for shipbuilding. It flourishes with leaves, a little below the Acherusian headland. And if I must, at the Muses' insistence, forthrightly declare this fact as well, Phoebus explicitly[175] directed the Boeotians and Nisaeans to worship this man as "city guardian" and to establish a town around the trunk of ancient wild olive, but instead of the god-fearing Aeolid Idmon, to this day they honor Agamestor.

---

though not the motif of a self-chosen death (*Il.* 2.830–834, 11.328–335). See further Lawall 1966: 140 for interesting comments on Idmon's motivation.

174 For the Homeric-epic reminiscences in Idmon's burial, see: Páskiewicz 1981 ad *Arg.* 2.836 ff.; Hunter 1993: 44: Saïd 1998: 17–18; for the scene's departures from the standard Homeric funeral—principally in the acknowledgment of hero cult centered around the tomb—see Saïd 1998: 18–19.

175 Race's translation takes ἐπιρρήδην ("explicitly," "by name"; 847) with διεπέφραδε in the previous line, in which case Apollo may have revealed Idmon's name directly to the colonists; such is also the interpretation of, e.g., Mooney 1912 ad loc.; Händel 1954: 73. Others, however, take the adverb with ἰλάεσθαι, in which case Apollo may have instructed the colonists to propitiate Idmon "by name" without actually revealing it to them—a typical case of oracular obscurity (Fränkel 1968: 237 with n. 231; Matteo 2007 ad loc.; Thalmann 2011: 108 n. 83). The latter scenario seems to be presupposed in Promathidas, Apollonius' probable source for the story of the Idmon-Agamestor mixup; see 161n85.

The word ἥρως is not used,[176] but Idmon is here conceived of as an immortalized hero and the rightful recipient of cult, though one Agamestor appears to have appropriated his honors. The fact that the wild olive trunk is made of wood used for shipbuilding (νηίου, 843) should have served as proof of the buried hero's connection to sailing, and thus of his identity as the Argonaut Idmon rather than Agamestor.[177] But the trunk is also significant because, just like Idmon himself and the rest of the mythic Argonauts (cf. παλαιγενέων ... φωτῶν, 1.1),[178] it is "ancient" (παλαιγενέος, 2.848) and yet continues to flourish down to the present (note present-tense θαλέθει, 843), thus symbolizing Idmon's continuing life after death as an immortal hero.[179]

The juxtaposition of a typically Homeric heroic burial with such an extended and complex notice of hero cult already suggests a type of generic synthesis: the conventions of epic have been enriched with a "hymnic" recognition of Idmon's status as a cult hero. But the reverse is true as well: the episode's hymnic dimension is complemented by the traditional Homeric conception of the hero that is revealed in the way that the narrator speaks of this cult. To wit: Apollo directs the colonists to "worship" Idmon (ἱλάεσθαι, 2.847), but instead they "honor" Agamestor (κυδαίνουσιν, 850). These line-final verbs are cast in parallel as if equivalent in meaning, but in this context, a difference in their semantic ranges may be significant. ἱλάεσθαι is properly religious,[180] and κυδαίνω, likewise, can be used of the worship of cult heroes, as Apollonius' own usage twice elsewhere attests (1.587, 1048).[181] But this denominative verb

---

176   The Argonauts, however, are so identified two lines later (ἥρωες, 852), in a description of their burial of a second comrade who dies in Heraclea, the helmsman Tiphys. This juxtaposition may call to mind the destined heroization of the rest of the Argonauts as well as Idmon.
177   Fränkel 1968 ad *Arg.* 2.841–848.
178   Cuypers 2004: 55; Hitch 2012: 141.
179   For this vegetal motif, cf. Cohen 1998: 135 with n. 53. The religious dimension of this grave marker is further suggested by the scholiast's report ad 2.843: the φάλαγξ was in fact one of the Argo's rollers (denoted by the same word at 1.375–376, 388; cf. the oar marking Elpenor's grave at *Od.* 11.77, 12.15), which the Argonauts erected at the direction of Orpheus—their regular guide in spiritual matters. The roller sprouted (miraculously, apparently; cf. *Il.* 1.234–237) and is still shown today. See also Malkin 1987: 75; Robert 2013: 214–215 with n. 61. Cf. the white poplar by Polyphemus' tomb (*Arg.* 4.1476) with the analysis of Foster 2007: 261, and cf. also the Boreads' grave markers (1.1305–1308), one of whose continued motion (note present-tense κίνυται, 1308) in the wind might similarly signify ongoing life after death.
180   Notably, Apollonius uses the cognate verb form ἵλατε to introduce his hymnic Envoi to the Argonauts (4.1773).
181   This usage with reference to cult honors is not, however, altogether common; I have been able to trace no example before our passage and Lycoph. *Alex.* 721, 929, 1213. Apollonius'

derived from κῦδος belongs first and foremost to the semantic field of "glory," much like the "glorious fame" (εὐκλείης, 1.141; cf. 447) for which Idmon gives his life.[182] A good illustration of this resonance of κυδαίνω can be found in a passage from Lycophron's *Alexandra* that describes cult honors for another epic hero, in this case Hector. Cassandra prophesies that Zeus will oversee the transfer of Hector's remains from the Troad to Thebes (1189–1211), and she concludes her apostrophe to her brother: "And the chiefs of the Ectenes [i.e., Boeotians] shall with libations **celebrate** your **glory** in the highest, even as the immortals" (**κλέος** δὲ σὸν μέγιστον Ἐκτήνων πρόμοι | λοιβαῖσι **κυδανοῦσιν** ἀφθίτοις ἴσον, 1212–1213). Lycophron makes the close connection between cult honors and epic glory quite obvious here by setting up κλέος as the direct object of κυδανοῦσιν, which is itself juxtaposed with λοιβαῖσι.[183] I argue that Apollonius establishes the same connection, if more subtly, by setting the clearly cultic verb ἱλάεσθαι in parallel with the epic-tinged κυδαίνουσιν.

This observation may help to explain why the Muses, the daughters of Memory (Μνημοσύνη) and the guarantors of poetic remembrance, insist that the Apollonian narrator relate this embarrassing history of cultic confusion, which in fact could be taken to damage his narrative's credibility.[184] It is not just that Idmon has been deprived of the rites denoted by ἱλάεσθαι. In Homer, the hero's tomb is supposed to function as the physical instantiation and medium of his

---

use of the verb in this relatively unusual way at 1.587 and 1048 may similarly serve to link hero cult with epic celebration.

182 κλέος and κῦδος originally represented distinct concepts, namely, "glory" and a kind of talismanic charisma, respectively (Benveniste 1969: 2.57–69; Scodel 2008: 25–26). In Apollonius' usage, however, κῦδος has the meanings "Ehre, Ansehen, Würde" (Reich and Maehler 1991: 522) or *gloria* (Pompella 2002: 392). Note esp. 1.287, where κῦδος is set in parallel with ἀγλαΐην ("splendor"; cf. 4.1027–1028) and ἀγητή ("admired," 1.285); 1.1292, where Heracles' κῦδος would have obscured (καλύψῃ) Jason's; 4.205, where we have a contrast between κῦδος and κατηφείη, "dejection"; and 4.1749, where κῦδος is qualified as ἀγλαόν, "glorious."

183 The epic resonance of κλέος (1212) at the beginning of this sentence is enhanced by the poet's use of ἀφθίτοις at its end. The final lines of Cassandra's address to Hector are thus framed in such a way as to recall the "imperishable renown" (κλέος ἄφθιτον, *Il*. 9.413) that lay in store for his killer, Achilles (McNelis and Sens 2011: 63–64). Cassandra, however, makes her brother the beneficiary of such renown, in a polemical correction of Homer. On the complementarity of glory and cult worship in the *Alexandra*, see Biffis 2021.

184 The Muses' insistence is quite ironic given that, as Llanos (2017b: 8) notes, Apollonius typically uses etiologies to authenticate his narrative, whereas in this case, the Muses—the avatars of poetic truth themselves—force him to acknowledge that the facts on the ground in contemporary Heraclea Pontica actually contradict his narrative. But see above for the argumentative function of the "trunk of wild olive" (2.843) that marks the grave and which should prove that it is Idmon, not Agamestor, who is buried there.

κλέος;[185] and indeed, Apollonius describes the φάλαγξ atop Idmon's barrow as "a marker for future generations to see" (σῆμα ... καὶ ὀψιγόνοισιν ἰδέσθαι, 2.842). This detail serves to draw our attention to the dual function of Idmon's tomb, which should rightfully constitute both an epic memorial for him and the center of his cult. The worship of Agamestor in Idmon's stead thus also entails that the seer has been forgotten at the very site of the death that he willingly embraced for the sake of renown.[186] The "Muses' insistence" (χρειώ ... Μουσέων, 845) that the record be set right can thus be reevaluated as a recuperative intervention on behalf of Idmon's κλέος,[187] which Apollonius represents as bundled together with his cult. That is, through the medium of the *Arg.*, the Muses apparently hope to restore both Idmon's fame and his cultic honors in Heraclea, because the two are inextricably linked.[188] Both are the rightful rewards of the mythic hero, and indeed, both cult and poetry have the effect of perpetuating a hero's remembrance. This passage can thus be read as a paradigmatic example of the complementarity of epic κλέος and religious worship, the very conceit on which the *Arg.*'s generic hybridity is founded.[189]

3.2   *Polydeuces in Bebrycia*

We may derive additional insight into Apollonius' self-conscious mixture of the epic and hymnic modes of praising his heroes by examining his lone use of the word ὕμνος, in a context charged with metapoetic potential.[190] The term ὕμνος

---

185   Saïd 1998: 12–15. In fact, Homer already shows epic song to be a more reliable vehicle than such physical monuments for preserving κλέος (see, e.g., Grethlein 2008: 28–32), and Apollonius reinforces this point by showing the ambiguity that can attach to such σήματα in the confusion over the true occupant of Idmon's tomb (Durbec 2008: 63–64).

186   Fusillo (1985: 369–370) notes that this passage represents the only Apollonian etiology that marks discontinuity between the mythic past and the present time of the audience, and he interprets the Muses here as "portatrici della storia argonautica, ma soprattutto ... ipostasi delle norme e delle convenzioni epiche" (370). See also Llanos 2017b: 8. Perhaps fancifully, I would suggest that Idmon's loss of glory may be reflected in Agamestor's very name, which seems to recall the phrase μή ... ἀγάσαιτο from Idmon's Catalogue entry (1.141) in the manner of an anagram. Note that ἄγαμαι is a hapax in the poem.

187   Goldhill 1991: 324; Barnes 2003: 93–94.

188   Cf. Ehrhardt 1995: 24, 45, who raises the possibility that the *Arg.* could have had an actual effect in the cities whose local traditions it mentions. In point of fact, however, the *Arg.*'s impact was probably minimal in this case, as both Idmon and Agamestor were later eclipsed by Heracles qua mythical founder of Heraclea Pontica (46).

189   Hitch (2012: 154–155) makes a similar argument vis-à-vis the wedding of Jason and Medea, which, she argues, is described in both cultic and epic language (4.1142–1143).

190   Hunter (1996: 46 with n. 2) describes the "hymn to Polydeuces" as one of "many hymnic elements within the main body of the narrative ... that recall the hymnic status of the whole [*Arg.*]."

evinces an increased range of nuance in Hellenistic poetry that make it, like ἥρως, capable of straddling the secular/religious divide.[191] In Archaic and early Classical Greek, ὕμνος could refer to any "song," perhaps with connotations of praise or celebration, whether the subject of that song was divine or not. For example, in the HHs, ὕμνος occurs thrice in a Poet's Task formula to denote the next "song" to which the speaker promises to transition, which, according to Wolf's Proem theory, will have been an epic lay (HH 5.293, 9.9, 18.11). The only other usage of ὕμνος in the corpus, in the major Hymn to Apollo, denotes a song explicitly concerned with mortals (3.161).[192] In the HEs, ὕμνος is a *hapax* used to denote Demodocus' singing (Od. 8.429), which mixes mortal and divine subjects.[193] As early as the fourth century, however, the word had become a generic term for songs in praise **of gods**, as is apparent from the distinction Plato draws in Resp. 10.607a (ὕμνους θεοῖς καὶ ἐγκώμια τοῖς ἀγαθοῖς).[194]

By the Hellenistic period, poets could avail themselves of both the Archaic meaning of ὕμνος that they had inherited as part of the poetic *Kunstsprache* as well as the more technical generic term that even then was being elaborated and formalized in Alexandrian scholarship.[195] They could also exploit the resultant ambiguity for their own purposes. Thus, for instance, Theocritus uses the word in an unmarked way to refer to Thyrsis' bucolic song (Id. 1.61; cf. Ep. 2.2 = AP 6.177.2),[196] whereas his use of the same noun and the related verb form throughout his hymn to the Dioscuri has a marked religious inflection (Id. 22.1,

---

[191] Regarding the term ὕμνος, I have benefited from the discussions of, *inter alia*, Bremer 1981: 193–194, Fowler 1987: 94–95, Pulleyn 1997: 43–55, Furley and Bremer 2001: 1.10–11, Calame 2005: 20–21, Carey 2009: 26, Hall 2012: 81–85, Lozynsky 2014: 259–263. See further the studies cited in the following notes.

[192] The verb form ὑμνέω, however, occurs seven times, always with a god as its object (3.19, 4.1, 9.1, 14.2, 19.27, 27.19, 31.1); cf. the adjectives εὔυμνος (3.19) and πολύυμνος (26.7), applied to Apollo and Dionysus, respectively.

[193] To be specific, Queen Arete uses this word in a prospective reference to Demodocus' third lay, which will turn out to concern the sack of Troy, a thoroughly epic topic. For the idea, however, that Demodocus' second lay is a modified version of a Homeric-style hymn, see 26n131 in the Introduction.

[194] For Plato's use of ὕμνος here and in the *Laws*, see Ford 2002: 12, 259–260.

[195] The Alexandrian use of ὕμνος as a generic term is illustrated by the classification of subsets of the old lyric poetry under this heading; for instance, one book of Pindar's collected poetry was devoted to his ὕμνοι, but specific subsets of this genus each received their own books: paeans, dithyrambs, prosodia, and perhaps also the (quasi-hymnic?) partheneia and hyporchemata (Pfeiffer 1968: 184; Willcock 1995: 3); thus ὕμνοι must have indicated a sort of "miscellaneous hymns" category (Furley and Bremer 2001: 1.11). For ὕμνος as an umbrella term, see further: Harvey 1955: 165–168; Furley 1995: 31–32; Rutherford 2001: 92; Cairns 2007: 91–92; Nagy 2011: 332–333; Hall 2012: 161–162.

[196] See Hunter 1999 ad Id. 1.61, and cf. his comment ad 143–145.

4, 26, 135, 214).[197] And when he uses the same vocabulary in characterizing his encomium for Ptolemy II Philadelphus (17.8), he "exploits, indeed plays with, the semantic breadth of ὑμνεῖν to bring Ptolemy closer to the gods."[198]

Apollonius plays with the ambiguity of ὕμνος in much the same way as Theocritus does in *Idyll* 17. Like the HEs, the *Arg.* employs this noun just once: in the aftermath of the Bebrycian episode, the Argonauts sing a "ὕμνος to the accompaniment of Orpheus' lyre in beautiful harmony" (Ὀρφείῃ φόρμιγγι συνοίμιον ὕμνον ἄειδον | ἐμμελέως, 2.161–162) in order to "celebrate Zeus' son from Therapna" (κλεῖον δὲ Θεραπναῖον Διὸς υἷα, 2.163). Here, ὕμνος is being used in its more general sense and in context must refer to a kind of epinician "song" praising Polydeuces' success in his boxing match with Amycus.[199] Indeed, Fränkel suggests that this episode might be meant to function as an etiology for the epinician genre.[200]

Nevertheless, many scholars have detected the presence of this term's modern resonance ("religious hymn") hiding behind its literal signification here, especially given the persistent link that Apollonius establishes between the Bebrycian episode and the Dioscuri's destined apotheosis.[201] To summarize the hints that point toward Polydeuces' deification: first, during the boxing match, the narrator compares Amycus to a child of Typhoeus or Gaia, brought forth in her anger at Zeus (2.38–40). This comparison likens the boxing match to a Giganto- or Typhonomachy and implies that Amycus' opponent is, accordingly, playing the role of Heracles, or even of Zeus himself. Second, and in contrast,

---

197   As Dover 1971 ad Theoc. *Id.* 22.4 observes, "In line 1, ὑμνέομεν amounts to, 'This poem is a hymn to the Dioskouroi.'" In line 219, however, the verb is used with the subject matter of the *Iliad* as its object.
198   Hunter 2003 ad loc.; see further his introductory comments ad *Id.* 17.1–12. I discuss this passage in greater detail in the conclusion, 2.1. Similar examples occur in *Id.* 16, which begins with an ostentatious juxtaposition of two uses of the verb ὑμνέω, first with gods, then with the deeds of men as object (ὑμνεῖν ἀθανάτους, ὑμνεῖν ἀγαθῶν κλέα ἀνδρῶν, 2). Line 50 repeats the verb with reference to epic poetry, and 103 with reference to the praise of the poem's dedicatee, Hiero II.
199   Cf. the Argonauts' celebration of Jason's victory in Aeetes' contest (Köhnken 2000: 67 n. 45).
200   Fränkel 1968 ad *Arg.* 2.161–163; see further Bauer 2017: 72–73; Murray 2018: 201; cf. Kampakoglou 2019: 124–125 for a similar interpretation of *Arg.* 4.68–69. Cf. Pindar's projection of the singing of epinician odes into mythical times (*Ol.* 10.76–79, *Nem.* 8.50–51).
201   See: Rose 1984: 125–126; Hunter 1991: 89; Cuypers 1997 ad *Arg.* 2.163; Vian 2002: 1.268 ad *Arg.* 2.163. Nishimura-Jensen (2009: 5–6 with n. 14) suggests that the Argonauts' hymn may put us in mind specifically of the *Homeric Hymn to the Dioscuri* (33), if not Theocritus' *Hymn to the Dioscuri* (*Id.* 22), which, of course, itself narrated a version of Polydeuces' boxing match with Amycus. See further Tsakiris 2022: 75–76.

the narrator likens Polydeuces to a star (2.40–43), in a transparent anticipation of his future catasterism. Third, later in Book 2, Apollonius has King Lycus and the Mariandynians bestow godlike honors on the Dioscuri in gratitude for Polydeuces' slaying of the Bebrycian king, their longtime enemy (2.752–758, 806–810). These favors include both a temple (ἱερόν, 807) situated on a headland, so that sailors may see it from the sea and beseech (ἱλάξονται, 808) the twins, and also fields set apart for them "as for gods" (οἷα θεοῖσιν, 809).[202] Fourth, in the victory celebration itself, Orpheus' lyre-playing (2.161) is suggestive in light of his usual function among the Argonauts as the crew's religious adviser.[203] Finally, the exalted title "Zeus' son from Therapna" is also suitably "hymnic."[204] Indeed, out of context, the phrase could denote Polydeuces or, equally, Apollo himself, whom the scholiast ad loc. implausibly understands as the referent.[205]

As a part of this consistent program of foreshadowing Polydeuces' deification, Apollonius' use of the *hapax* ὕμνος has strong "hymnic" undertones in addition to what must be its contextual denotation, namely, "song." But the poet also characterizes this celebration with κλεῖον (263), a verb evocative of epic κλέος, and one that, indeed, Apollonius uses elsewhere in the *Arg.* to denote epic song (cf. *Od.* 1.338; *HH* 31.18, 32.19). For instance, the introit contains a *recusatio* on the construction of the Argo, which "earlier bards still celebrate" (οἱ πρόσθεν ἔτι κλείουσιν ἀοιδοί, 1.18);[206] the poet pointedly contrasts these old songs with his own epic agenda (20–22), in lines that allude to the introits of both the *Iliad* and the *Odyssey*.[207] The Bebrycian episode thus ends with a musical performance characterized in quick succession by a pair of words (ὕμνον, 261;

---

202 On these first three points, see Cuypers 1997 ad *Arg.* 2.38–45, section A and under B. 1d.
203 Cf. esp. 2.704, where Orpheus hymns Apollo on the lyre. See 306*n*116 for more on Orpheus' character in the *Arg.*
204 Cf. the discussion of "hymnic narratization" in 4.3. Hitch (2012: 149) notes in this connection that as the site of their burial, Therapna was one of the Dioscuri's principal cult sites.
205 The scholiast may have been misled by the mention of the laurel crowns the Argonauts are wearing in this celebration (2.159)—an Apolline plant, to be sure, but one that is also appropriate to this epinician context (see Kampakoglou 2019: 146–147). Notably, ὕμνον ἄειδον at 2.161 echoes ὕμνον ἀείδουσιν in the major *Homeric Hymn to Apollo* (3.161), a rare passage in early Greek epic in which ὕμνος is applied to songs about human beings (Vian 2002: 1.268 ad 2.163).
206 An exactly parallel usage occurs at 1.59, if the text is in fact sound (see Fränkel 1968 ad loc.). This verb (or its cognate κλήζω) also appears in the sense of "make famous" (3.993, 4.1202) and "tell (a story)" (4.618, 987). These same verbs are often used in the more mundane sense of "to call (by a certain name)": 1.217, 238; 2.687, 977; 3.277, 357, 1003; 4.267, 829, 990, 1153; cf. 2.296, 1156; 3.246.
207 See Romeo 1985: 25; Hunter 1993: 119 n. 76.

κλεῖον, 263) each related to one of the *Arg.*'s primary generic affiliations: hymn and epic, respectively.[208]

The resultant effect of mise-en-abyme encourages the (re-)reader to understand the foregoing episode as generically hybrid, just like the *Arg.* itself. Polydeuces' boxing match can be appreciated both as one of the many "famous deeds of people born long ago" (παλαιγενέων κλέα φωτῶν, 1.1) promised in the introit—that is, as an epic ἀριστεία for the mortal hero Polydeuces[209]—and as a miniature hymnic narrative, or "Myth," celebrating one of the many exploits of Zeus' now-deified son.[210] As I argued above, Polydeuces and his brother are, like Heracles, destined for a more exalted form of divinity than are the other Argonauts, but their example also sets a precedent suggestive of the honors that the rest of the crew will receive upon heroization.[211] Likewise, this episode starring Polydeuces suggests a way of reading every other episode in the poem in which the talents of just one or two Argonauts are allowed to shine. For example, in the very next episodes, the helmsman Tiphys skillfully steers the Argo out of harm's way when a monumental wave threatens to overwhelm her (2.164–176), and soon thereafter the winged Boreads rescue Phineus from harassment by the Harpies (262–300). These episodes, too, can be understood both as epic ἀριστεῖαι and as chances for individual heroes to receive special hymnic praise within the Mythic section of the poem's collective hymn to the Argonauts.[212]

A final word on the Bebrycian episode. Modifying ὕμνον in line 161 is the adjective συνοίμιον, which occurs nowhere else in Greek literature. Based on the context and etymological analysis it should mean something like "harmonious," relating to a "strain of song" (οἶμος) that is "together with" (συν-) something else—in this case, Orpheus' lyre (Ὀρφείῃ φόρμιγγι, 161); the term is effectively glossed by the adverb ἐμμελέως ("in beautiful harmony") in the next

---

208   That this interplay of epic and religious language is deliberate is suggested by its recurrence in the scene of the Argonauts' reception in the court of King Lycus. The Mariandynians have heard the report (κλέος, 2.754) of their enemy Amycus' death and thus honor Polydeuces like a god (ὥς τε θεόν, 756); soon, as noted above, Lycus even promises to build a temple and dedicate certain crop fields to the Dioscuri (806–810) (Hitch 2012: 147–148).
209   I borrow the language of ἀριστεῖαι for those episodes that spotlight the talents of individual Argonauts from Kyriakou 1995: 191 (cf. Lawall 1966: 134).
210   Kampakoglou 2019: 148. Cf. Theoc. *Id.* 22, in which the very same episode does feature as a hymnic narrative.
211   See 2.2.4.
212   I thank Suzanne Lye for the suggestion that the *Arg.* can be read as a sort of "anthology" of hymns, with many individual Argonauts receiving the hymnist's attention at different points.

line.²¹³ Yet the word also evokes—and is even glossed by the *Suda* as—προοίμιον, the technical term for a hymn of the Homeric type that precedes an epic performance.²¹⁴ Apollonius' use of συνοίμιον is thus a further pointer to the hymnic, and particularly the Homeric-hymnic, dimension of the Argonauts' praise of Polydeuces.²¹⁵ If I may speculate somewhat, I wonder if in this context, the prefix συν- might also point to the generic hybridity of the episode and, indeed, of the poem as a whole as hymn *cum* epic. To go even further: if a προοίμιον precedes an epic performance, could συνοίμιον indicate a performance that is both hymnic and epic at once? As an epic hymn, the *Arg.* could be construed as simultaneously a Homeric-hymnic προοίμιον and the epic performance that such hymns typically promise.²¹⁶ Perhaps Apollonius invented this term, if it is indeed his coinage, to reflect the synthetic nature of his inventive experiment with the epic and hymnic genres.

3.3 The Syrtis and the Envoi

My final two examples of passages that reflect the poem's generic hybridity may be considered together, for both passages conceptualize the relationship between epic deeds and heroic hymnody in the same revealing way. I begin with the earlier passage. Near the end of their adventure, the Argonauts find themselves stranded in the Syrtis, a vast, barren sandbar off the coast of Libya. With no way to return to the sea, it seems that they will waste away and perish—a possibility that prompts the following counterfactual statement from the narrator (4.1305–1307):

> καί νύ κεν αὐτοῦ πάντες ἀπὸ ζωῆς ἐλίασθεν
> νώνυμνοι καὶ ἄφαντοι ἐπιχθονίοισι δαῆναι
> ἡρώων οἱ ἄριστοι ἀνηνύστῳ ἐπ᾽ ἀέθλῳ.

> And so in that place all the best of the heroes would have departed from life, **leaving no names and no traces for humans to know of them**, with their mission unfulfilled.

Ultimately, the Argonauts do survive to complete their task, but this counterfactual nevertheless effectively establishes the stakes of the Argonauts' mission:

---

213 Hunter (1996: 143 n. 14) wonders if συνοίμιον adds a "quasi-technical flavour" to the description.
214 See the discussion of Wolf's "Proem theory" in the introduction (2.3).
215 Kampakoglou 2019: 149.
216 See 121*n*162.

if they die, they will leave no trace to be remembered by. The fear of being forgotten is deep-rooted in epic poetry, in whose value system such a fate is tantamount to a second death.[217] In fact, Jason elsewhere expresses a similar fear when the Argonauts are stranded not in Libya, but in Acherusia in Book 2: "An evil fate will bury us here **without fame** as we grow old in vain" (καταυτόθι δ' ἄμμε καλύψει | ἀκλειῶς κακὸς οἶτος ἐτώσια γηράσκοντας, 2.892–893).[218] Both of these passages, in Libya and Acherusia, are essentially tied up with the memorializing function of epic and are markedly metatextual: if the Argonauts really had failed in their quest, they would have won no κλέος for themselves and thus the *Arg.* itself, as well as other epics about them (cf. 1.18–19), would never have been written.[219] The narrator's counterfactual in the Libya passage thus jolts the reader out of the preceding mythological narrative to consider her place in the ongoing "reception history" of the poem: each new generation of readers (cf. 4.1773–1775) takes their place among the ἐπιχθόνιοι who learn (δαῆναι) of the Argonauts through the medium of this very poem.[220]

In this sense, this counterfactual statement dramatizes the function of epic in preserving the memory of great achievements from the past. But in addition to commenting on the role of epic poetry, I would argue that this passage also comments on the nature of heroic hymns through its use of the very rare adjective νώνυμνοι in line 1306. The translation I quote renders this word as "leaving no names," interpreting the adjective as a form of the privative prefix νη- combined with the word for "name," ὄνομα.[221] But in fact, the meaning of this word was debated in antiquity, and some grammarians preferred to parse it instead as a combination of the privative prefix with the word ὕμνος, "song, hymn."[222]

---

217 Glei and Natzel-Glei 1996: 2.201 n. 127.
218 Hutchinson 1988: 135. For the comparable situations in Acherusia and Libya, see further, e.g., Fantuzzi and Hunter 2004: 123; Morrison 2007: 307.
219 See, e.g., Morrison 2007: 304. Wray (2000: 254) puts the matter well: "The *fact* that contradicts the epithets νώνυμνοι and ἄφαντοι, we could say, is precisely the bookroll in the reader's hands, proving not only that the Argonauts made it safely home (for otherwise there could be no κλέος and no poem) but also that the safe end is in sight (there are no more rolls in the case, and this one is very near its spool)."
220 Cf. the metapoetic interpretation of the speech of the Libyan heroines, who are soon to save the Argonauts, advanced by Feeney (1991: 92) and Hunter (1993: 126): it is the Argonauts' epic κλέος that motivates the goddesses to rescue them. As Hunter comments, "It is poetry which secures the real 'success' of the voyage by saving the Argonauts and retelling the story for each generation."
221 Apollonius uses the adjective with this sense indisputably at 2.982.
222 See: Merkel and Keil 1854: clxxxiii–clxxxiv; Livrea 1973 ad loc.; Rengakos 1994: 118. The relevant ancient sources include Apoll. Soph. 117.20 Bekker, Σb ad *Il.* 12.70, ΣT ad *Il.* 13.227.

In order to explain the adjective's use in the context of *Il.* 12.70 = 13.227 = 14.70, they interpreted the ὕμνος element that they discovered in the word as a reference specifically to a θρῆνος ("dirge"), and thus they construed νώνυμνος to mean "unlamented." Apollonius plainly alludes to this interpretation by pairing νώνυμνοι with ἄφαντοι, which at *Il.* 6.60 is similarly paired with ἀκήδεστοι, "unmourned."²²³ Be that as it may, I propose that beyond entering into a learned glossographical debate, in this metapoetic context Apollonius' allusion to an etymology from ὕμνος may be particularly salient, resonating as it does with the "hymnic" form of the *Arg.* itself.²²⁴ If we try to read νώνυμνοι in its more radical sense of "leaving no ὕμνοι," then this passage establishes a parallelism between the conditions under which heroes are honored in epic and hymnody. Just as a premature death would have robbed the Argonauts of epic κλέος, this passage suggests that failure to accomplish their task, their ἄεθλος, would have also made the heroes unworthy of worship in cult—and consequently, for celebration in Apollonius' epic hymn to the Argonauts.

I want to focus on the connection forged here between the receipt of hymns and the completion of ἄεθλοι, for I would argue that this nexus of ideas taps into the widespread ancient belief, which was only gaining more currency in the Hellenistic period, that regarded the attainment of cultic honors as a reward for personal merits.²²⁵ As noted above, in the *Odyssey*, Menelaus' destined heroization is premised on nothing more than the fact that he is Zeus'

---

223 Vian (2002: 3.218 ad *Arg.* 4.1306) objects that "leaving no names" is more salient in this context than being "unlamented," and he cites the imitation at *Orph. Arg.* 1161–1162 in support of his interpretation. I believe that Apollonius is showing his awareness of both of the adjective's possible meanings. The recollection of *Il.* 6.60 suggests the sense "unlamented," but note that the phrase immediately following νώνυμνοι (ἄφαντοι ἐπιχθονίοισι δαῆναι) effectively glosses its other proposed meaning, "leaving no names" (i.e., "obscure"). There is no need to decide between these two options but only to recognize the connotative richness of Apollonius' diction. I will say, for what it is worth, that "leaving no names and no traces for humans to know of them" is essentially redundant, whereas Apollonius' model in *Il.* 6.60 offers the semantically differentiated pairing ἀκήδεστοι καὶ ἄφαντοι, "unmourned and unseen," in Agamemnon's wish that the Trojans be utterly annihilated (cf. Apollonius' simile of the doomed city just earlier, 4.1280–1289); note also the pair of non-synonymous adjectives with privative prefixes in another of Apollonius' models, Emped. 31 B 12.2 D.-K. (ἀνήνυστον καὶ ἄπυστον).

224 Cf. Hunter 2015 ad loc., who argues that the meaning "unmourned" does not fit in this context, but that the adjective's radical sense of "without ὕμνοι" works well; he further points out that, like the *Arg.*, these ὕμνοι may be understood both as epic "songs" and as proper "hymns," in accordance with the multiple meanings of the term ὕμνος (see the discussion of this term in the previous subsection of this chapter).

225 For explicitly articulated logical justifications for divinization on the basis of εὐεργεσία, especially in the Hellenistic period, see *ThesCRA* 2.161–162.

son-in-law (4.561–569); nepotism is all the justification needed for his receipt of a blessed afterlife.[226] In later Greek literature, however, different explanations for the heroization and apotheosis of select mortals begin to be put forward. These blessed few have somehow earned their immortalization, either because of their moral worth or because of their tremendous accomplishments on earth.[227] For example, Pindar mixes the doctrine of metempsychosis with a belief that those who have lived righteous lives win heroization as their (final?) reward (*Ol.* 2.68–80, fr. 133), while Isocrates speaks generally of the people of prior ages who won immortalization because of their virtue (δι' ἀρετήν, 9.70).[228] Apollonius' own contemporary Istrus, another reputed pupil of Callimachus (*FGrH* 334 T 1–2, 6), applies the same language to a historical figure, claiming that the Athenians honored the poet Sophocles with hero cult (under the name Dexion) "because of the man's virtue" (διὰ τὴν τοῦ ἀνδρὸς ἀρετήν, *FGrH* 334 F 38 [51]).[229] The same discourse of divinization as a type of reward is reflected in Euhemerist speculations about the origins of religion in the postmortem apotheosis or heroization of great rulers and inventors of the past in recognition of their achievements and benefactions to humanity.[230]

But the hero who best exemplifies this logic of apotheosis is Heracles. Beginning potentially as early as Hesiod,[231] the tradition is increasingly explicit in

---

226   Roloff 1970: 100; Heubeck, West, and Hainsworth 1988 ad *Od.* 4.563 ff.; see further Scodel 1982: 37 n. 10.

227   These two reasons are not mutually exclusive in light of the typical Greek belief that "virtue" (ἀρετή) manifests itself in "deeds of excellence" (ἀρεταί).

228   For such sentiments, see further Currie 2005: 177–178. Euripidean tragedy furnishes a few etiologies for hero cults in which heroization is justified by the recipient's virtue; e.g., in Eur. fr. 446 Collard and Cropp, from *Hippolytus Veiled*, the chorus explicitly proclaims that the titular character's heroization is a reward (χάρις) for his piety (εὐσεβίας) and virtue (ἀρετῆς), in particular his chastity (σωφροσύνην). For self-sacrificing, patriotic heroines (and occasionally heroes) like Macaera in the *Heracleidae*, see Larson 1995: 101–109.

229   Connolly (1998) doubts the authenticity of this tradition, but that matters little for my purposes here.

230   Note Diod. Sic. 1.2.4, a euhemerist passage that mentions men becoming gods and heroes for their inventions or other benefactions to humanity. Notably, Hecataeus of Abdera (*ap.* Diod. Sic. 1.13) expresses similar opinions about the deification of the early Pharaohs; see further conclusion, 2.1.

231   Hes. *Th.* 954–955 speaks of Heracles' attainment of divinity after accomplishing an unspecified great deed among the immortals (μέγα ἔργον ἐν ἀθανάτοισιν ἀνύσσας, 954); the implication seems to be that the former is the reward for the latter. West (1966 ad loc.) suggests a reference to Heracles' participation in the Gigantomachy, which is elsewhere associated with his deification, including in the Pindaric passage cited below; perhaps Apollonius, too, has this episode chiefly in mind among the "few more" labors that Heracles must complete to win Olympus at *Arg.* 1.1319–1320 (quoted below). Cf. Apollonius'

regarding his deification as, in Pindar's words, "the choicest recompense for his great labors" (καμάτων μεγάλων | ποινάν ... ἐξαίρετον, *Nem.* 1.70).[232] Notably, Apollonius himself has the sea god Glaucus foretell Heracles' apotheosis in the following terms upon his separation from the crew at Mysia (*Arg.* 1.1317–1320):

Ἄργεῖ οἱ μοῖρ' ἐστὶν ἀτασθάλῳ Εὐρυσθῆι
ἐκπλῆσαι μογέοντα δυώδεκα πάντας ἀέθλους,
ναίειν δ' ἀθανάτοισι συνέστιον, εἴ κ' ἔτι παύρους
1320 ἐξανύσῃ.

At Argos it is his [Heracles'] destiny to toil for arrogant Eurystheus and accomplish twelve labors in all, and to dwell in the home of the immortals **if he completes a few more.**

As Feeney observes, the conditionality of Glaucus' prophecy serves to present Heracles' deification as "a reward for what the labours signified—a reward, that is, for endurance, and for the beneficent cleansing of evils from the world."[233]

I have already had occasion to note the Argonauts' emulation of the inimitable Heracles following his departure at the end of Book 1.[234] Here we may extend this analysis by observing that Jason's quest, too, is frequently framed in Heraclean terms as an ἄεθλος or a series of ἄεθλοι,[235] and that these Argonautic labors frequently effect the same sort of "beneficent cleansing of evils from the

---

reference to the hero's battle with the Giant-like earthborn men at Cyzicus as another "labor" (ἀέθλιον, 1.997) Hera might have devised for him.

232   For Heracles' winning immortality through his labors, see further Soph. *Phil.* 1418–1422, Isoc. 1.50, Apoll. Rhod. *Arg.* 1.1317–1320 (quoted below); cf. Theoc. *Id.* 24.79–85 (where the participle τελέσαντι may be conditional); and for later citations, see, e.g.: Pease 1958 ad Cic. *Nat. D.* 2.62 s.v. *hinc* (p. 700); Nisbet and Rudd 2004 ad Hor. *Carm.* 3.2.21–22, 3.3.9.

233   Feeney 1987: 58. Similarly, Páskiewicz (1981 ad *Arg.* 2.849) argues that Apollonius presents Idmon's piety and ancestry as the grounds for his receipt of cult honors; cf. Händel 1954: 72–73.

234   See 2.2.4 above.

235   For the Argonautic expedition generally as an ἄεθλος or a series of ἄεθλοι, see 1.15, 32, 255, 362, 414, 442, 841, 903; 2.411, 424, 617, 869, 877, 1217; 4.1031, 1307; cf. 1.469; see further Hutchinson 2008: 77–80. Most commonly, this terminology is applied specifically to the ordeal imposed by Aeetes (3.407, 428, 480, 502, 522, 536, 561, 580, 619, 624, 720, 778, 788, 906, 942, 989, 1050, 1177, 1189, 1211, 1255, 1268, 1279, 1407; 4.8, 68, 342, 365, 733; cf. 3.1082). It also refers once to the battle with the earthborn men of Cyzicus in connection with both Heracles and all the other Argonauts (1.1012). For the Heraclean resonance of these terms, see 1.997, 1318, 1347; Galinsky 1972: 112; DeForest 1994: 66–67, 113–114; Finkelberg 1995: 4. At *Arg.* 3.997 the term is applied to Theseus' labors.

world" as do Heracles'; in Greek terms, the Argonauts frequently function, like Heracles, as ἀλεξίκακοι, "averters of evil."[236] The principal benefit conferred by the Argonautic expedition on humankind is the pacification of the Clashing Rocks, whose neutralization opens routes for trade and colonization between the Black Sea and the Mediterranean.[237] A number of other collateral benefits also accrue to various localities through which the crew passes. For instance, Crete becomes accessible to future travelers through the elimination of Talos (4.1636–1693),[238] and the Boreads drive the Harpies who had been harassing Phineus back into their cave (2.298–300).[239] In several cases, the Argonauts' εὐεργεσία is directly linked to Heracles' own. The Argonauts join Heracles in what begins, essentially, as his individual labor (ἀέθλιον Ἡρακλῆι, 1.997)[240] against the earthborn men of Cyzicus, which thus becomes in the end a collective labor for all of the heroes (cf. ἥρωες δ', ὅτε δή σφιν ἀταρβὴς ἔπλετ' ἄεθλος, 1012).[241] King Lycus casts the Argonauts' killing of the tyrannical Amycus and their defeat of his forces as a sequel to Heracles' own services to the Marian-

---

236 For heroization as a reward for the completion of ἄεθλοι, see Finkelberg 1995: 5–12. For the Argonauts as ἀλεξίκακοι, see, e.g.: Clauss 2000: 26; Klooster 2014: 531–532 (though these scholars do not use this term).

237 *Arg.* 2.604–606; see further 258n120 . It is traditional that the successful navigation of the Symplegades represents the Argonautic achievement *par excellence*; see Fantuzzi 1989. Ironically, however, in Apollonius' account, the first beneficiaries of the decommissioning of the Clashing Rocks turn out to be the Colchian fleet that pursues the Argonauts through the Bosporus, on a route that their quarry had themselves only recently opened up (4.303–304, 1001–1003; Natzel 1992: 113; Nishimura-Jensen 2000: 307); this Colchian contingent later settles in Phaeacia before a series of further migrations (4.1206–1216). Thus the first wave of colonization to follow from the Argonautic expedition is not in fact Greek, but "barbarian" (cf. also 4.507–521): the Bosporus is, as it were, a two-way street.

238 There may be a chronological contradiction in the fact that Theseus had already sailed to and from Crete before the Argonauts had dispatched Talos (3.1000–1001, 4.434). He was presumably freely allowed onto Crete in order to be served up as prey to the Minotaur, and perhaps he was allowed to leave the island unharried because he had Princess Ariadne in tow—or because Minos really did consent to her marriage with Theseus, as Jason claims (3.1000–1001, 1100–1101).

239 I here focus on the Argonauts as ἀλεξίκακοι, but their mission also has other important world-historical ramifications, such as repopulating Lemnos and setting in motion the future Greek colonization of Cyrene.

240 The narrator does not specify whether or not the younger men with whom Heracles had been guarding the ship join the battle with him (1.992).

241 I thus disagree with DeForest (1994: 60–61) that Apollonius' object in having the Argonauts join this battle is to criticize their assistance as "unnecessary [and] unwanted" (61); see further Stoessl 1941: 16–17. Of course, the almighty Heracles may not have strictly needed his comrades' help, but I would rather view the Argonauts' participation in what begins as a

dynians some decades earlier (2.774–798).[242] Most explicitly, the Argonauts' strategy for driving the birds of Ares from their island is modeled directly on Heracles' method of routing the Stymphalian birds (2.1047–1067);[243] the Argonauts thus render Aretias safe for further human exploitation just as Heracles had liberated Stymphalus from its avian pests.[244]

The persistent modeling of the Argonauts' beneficent ἄεθλοι on those of Heracles, combined with Glaucus' conditioning of Heracles' apotheosis on his completion of such ἄεθλοι, suggests the operation of a simple syllogism: the Argonauts, too, can expect to be rewarded for their heroic labors. To be sure, theirs will be a lesser grade of divinity, in proportion to the magnitude of their (collective) achievements relative to Heracles' (primarily individual) ones; they will be heroized, not deified.[245] Nevertheless, we are now equipped to understand why the Argonauts would have been "unhymned" (νώνυμνοι, 4.1306) had their labor remained unaccomplished (ἀνηνύστῳ ἐπ' ἀέθλῳ, 1307): their heroization is predicated precisely on their commission of heroic deeds.

This insight, in turn, sheds new light on the poem's Envoi. For convenience, I quote once more its opening lines (4.1773–1777):

ἵλατ' ἀριστήων μακάρων γένος· αἵδε δ' ἀοιδαὶ
εἰς ἔτος ἐξ ἔτεος γλυκερώτεραι εἶεν ἀείδειν
1775 ἀνθρώποις. ἤδη γὰρ ἐπὶ **κλυτὰ** πείραθ' ἱκάνω
ὑμετέρων καμάτων, ἐπεὶ οὔ νύ τις ὔμμιν **ἄεθλος**
αὖτις ἀπ' Αἰγίνηθεν ἀνερχομένοισιν ἐτύχθη ...

Be gracious, you race of blessed heroes, and may these songs year after year be sweeter for men to sing. For now I have come to the **glorious** con-

---

solo fight as a way of leaguing them alongside Heracles as allies and continuators of his cosmic project of rendering the world safe for human exploration and habitation.

242 Feeney 1987: 49–50, 58. See 167n119 above.
243 Indeed, if we identify the Stymphalian birds with the birds of Ares, as several other sources do (Timagetus fr. 4 Müller; Hyg. *Fab.* 20, 30.6; Serv. ad Verg. *Aen.* 8.299; Tzetz. *Chil.* 2.292), we can see the Argonauts as directly continuing Heracles' salvational work in the wider world beyond Greece.
244 The first beneficiaries of the Argonauts' cleansing of Aretias are the sons of Phrixus, who can thus safely meet and join the heroes following their shipwreck (3.320–326). But it is ironic that the other beneficiaries of the Argonauts' action are, once again, their would-be enemies (cf. 2.985–995) the Amazons, whose discontinued use of this island (note 2.1172–1173) is presumably linked to the arrival of the monstrous birds (which I take to be the same birds that Heracles drove away from Stymphalus).
245 With the exception of the Dioscuri, discussed above (2.2.4).

clusion of your toils, since no further **trial** befell you as you returned home from Aegina ...

It would be tautological to observe that the Envoi activates the poem's affiliations with hymnody; indeed, the preceding chapter demonstrated how crucial these lines are for the poem's construal precisely as a hymn addressed to the Argonauts. In this chapter, however, a couple of further points should be stressed. First, I bold the adjective κλυτά because with this word Apollonius again injects an epic sensibility into a markedly hymnic context.[246] It is the "conclusion" of the Argonauts' labors that is particularly "glorious" because it marks the successful completion of their undertaking. The sentiment here is the positive corollary to the counterfactual from the Libyan episode, that the Argonauts would have become **unknown** (ἄφαντοι ἐπιχθονίοισι δαῆναι, 4.1306) had their labor been left **unfulfilled** (ἀνηνύστῳ ἐπ' ἀέθλῳ, 1307). As we saw in chapter 1, the narrator's Prayer for the continual reperformance of his songs would further propagate the epic glory that the Argonauts have won. Moreover, by ending his poem here, at the conclusion of his subjects' toils, Apollonius shows epic to be coterminous with heroic labor; he reminds us that glorious deeds, the κλέα φωτῶν promised in 1.1, are the proper subject of epic.[247]

The passage evokes the idea that glorification in epic song is the hero's just reward for great achievements. The second point I would like to make, though, once again concerns the relationship between ἄεθλοι, heroization, and hymnody. The Envoi's Salutation hails the Argonauts as a "**race of blessed heroes**" (ἀριστήων μακάρων γένος, 4.1773).[248] As Belloni has argued, this phrase recalls the Argonauts' identification as "the **race** of demigods, the **best** of men who then were sailing over the sea" (ἡμιθέων ἀνδρῶν γένος, οἳ τότ' ἄριστοι | πόντον ἐπιπλώεσκον, 1.548–549) at the outset of their journey, in the scene of the Argo's first departure from Pagasae.[249] The intratextual echo of this phrase at

---

246 Goldhill 1991: 295, already quoted in an earlier discussion of the Envoi in chapter 1 (122n167). The metapoetic implications of κλυτά are further analyzed by, e.g.: Hunter 1993: 122; Clare 2002: 284; Schaaf 2014: 329.

247 Fränkel 1968: 621; Klooster 2007: 78; see also the poet's program at 1.20–22. That the poet's "journey" and "labors" align with those of his subjects is frequently observed in Apollonian scholarship. See, e.g.: Hurst 1967: 137–139; Beye 1982: 14; Fusillo 1985: 101–102, 385; Goldhill 1991: 295; Hunter 1993: 84, 120–121; DeForest 1994: 42; Albis 1996, esp. chh. 3–4; Wray 2000: 240–247; Vian 2002: 3.67; Clare 2002: 283–284; Vox 2002: 167; Cuypers 2004: 45; Morrison 2007: 305–306; Asper 2008: 173–174; Tsakiris 2022: 36–39.

248 For the text and meaning of *Arg.* 4.1773, see 1.2.4.

249 Belloni 2017, esp. 94–96. Formally, such careful variations reflect Apollonius' flexible,

4.1773 marks, via ring-composition, the very end of the Argo's voyage as the crew returns to their starting point, but with a crucial difference: the Argonauts who began their adventure as "demigod men" return home transformed into "blessed heroes." What has made the difference in the interim? It is the journey itself, and all the trials (cf. ἄεθλος, 1776) they have overcome along the way. The Argonauts' labors have, in other words, elevated them to a new ontological status, from the secular heroes of epic to the divinized heroes of Greek religion.[250] The mixture of hymnic and epic elements in the Envoi tells us that to complete a heroic labor means both to win epic fame and to receive worship after death in hero cult, and as an epic hymn, the *Arg.* instantiates both of these rewards for "the best of the heroes" (ἡρώων οἱ ἄριστοι, 4.1307).

In light of the foregoing analysis, perhaps we can now understand why Apollonius decided to play a sort of trick on his first-time readers in the way that he frames his poem as a hymn. As was argued in chapter 1, the introit is susceptible to many different interpretations on an initial reading, and it is only when the reader reaches the very end of the poem, with its Salutation and Prayer to its own protagonists, that the design of the poem as a hymn to the Argonauts is finally and fully clarified. Apollonius might have engineered this effect for any number of reasons—for instance, to treat his readers to one last surprising twist or to enrich his poem's capacity for rereading (cf. 4.1773–1775). But his motives might also have been geared toward more thematic considerations. Since it is only by virtue of accomplishing their ἄεθλος that the Argonauts win for themselves heroization and the right to be worshipped in hymns, it is in a sense only fitting that Apollonius would wait for the final passage of the *Arg.*, when, he says, "no further trial (ἄεθλος) befell" his protagonists, to reveal in unequivocal terms, first, their transformation into cult heroes and, consequently, the hymnic status of his epic. Thus the "hymnicization" of the poem on a generic level appears in tandem with the heroization of its protagonists on a narrative level—after the successful completion, and narration, of their labors.

"quasi-formulaic" style in adapting the conventions of early Greek epic (Fantuzzi and Hunter 2004: 266–267; Fantuzzi 2008a: 232).

250   Belloni 2017: 95. For the Argonauts' winning heroization through their deeds, see further: Green 2007 ad *Arg.* 4.1773; Hunter 2015 ad *Arg.* 4.1773–1781. Note particularly Hitch 2012: 150 on ἄεθλος as "the programmatic term for the labors of heroes which lead to their immortalization"; she mostly has in mind Jason's ordeal, but she notes that the term is repeated in the Envoi.

4 Literary Precedents for Apollonius' Generic Experiment

In sum, the evidence explored thus far in this chapter suggests that in crafting the *Arg.*, Apollonius has self-consciously united a series of elements that could otherwise be opposed according to a secular-religious binary (table 1).

Apollonius recognized that heroes could be both mortal figures restricted to the age of myth, as in the HEs, and cult figures with enduring vitality down to the present. Accordingly, they might equally be the subject of epics and hymns. Apollonius was also aware that Homer had written both epics and hymns, and thus, it seems, an innovative synthesis suggested itself. The *Arg.* represents a conflation of all of these categories—an epic hymn that incorporates both the secular and religious dimensions of Greek heroism and of Homeric poetry into its very generic fabric.

Perhaps the boldest aspect of this fusion is the resultant association of the *Homeric Hymns* with hero cult, since the *HH*s are actually addressed entirely to gods, not to heroized human beings. It is understandable that in trying to extend the secular heroes of Homeric epic into the cultic realm, Apollonius would be drawn to Homer's "religious" poetry. Additionally, as we saw in the Introduction, the *HH*s are, relative to other varieties of Greek hymn, replete with "epic" elements, including their "heroic" meter, the dactylic hexameter; they were thus ideally suited to an experimental merger with epic poetry proper. In effect, Apollonius can be seen to channel Homer's authority as the fountainhead of Greek literature and as an author of both epic and hymnic poetry to justify what is in fact a daring generic innovation: at once a neo-Homeric epic framed as a Rhapsodic Hymn and a neo-*Homeric Hymn* blown up to epic proportions.

In this section, I seek to support my reconstruction of the associative logic that informs the *Arg.*'s generic hybridity by examining parallel passages from contemporary and earlier poets in which the same set of associations are operative. Apollonius' poem is virtually unprecedented as a full-length poem in several thousands of lines that experiments with the dual generic affiliations of both "epic" and "hymn." Nevertheless, there are revealing moments in other Greek poetry in which heroes are praised using the conventions of the *HH*s even as the epic dimension of their heroism is held firmly in view. These passages show how natural it was for poets to unite Homer's epics and *Hymns* when celebrating the mythic heroes, who straddled the categories of epic and religion no less than Homer's own poetic output did.

I begin with two of Apollonius' Hellenistic contemporaries, Callimachus and Theocritus. The poems to be discussed do not certainly predate the *Argonautica*, so the question of their potential influence on Apollonius must remain

TABLE 1 Opposed elements synthesized in Apollonius' generic experiment

	Heroes	Heroic poetry	Homeric ἔπος
Secular	Figures of myth	Epics about heroes	*Iliad* & *Odyssey*
Religious	Figures of cult	Hymns to heroes	*Homeric Hymns*

speculative. Nevertheless, they at least testify to an interest in blending the two branches of Homeric hexameter poetry current in Apollonius' Alexandrian milieu. Indeed, the fact that similar examples of heroic praise that fuses the language of Homer's epics and *Hymns* can be found in all three of the major third-century Alexandrian poets suggests that there was something intuitive and attractive about this sort of merger for these *literati* steeped in Homeric poetry and philology. The third passage I examine, from Simonides, certainly predates Apollonius, as does my final example, which comes from one of the *Homeric Hymns* themselves—the short *Hymn to Heracles* (15).

4.1 Callimachus' Hecale

My first and briefest example concerns a fragment of Callimachus' *Hecale*, an epyllion[251] that takes as its setting Theseus' capture of the Marathonian bull, one of his six canonical labors. As the poem's title suggests, however, Callimachus boldly elects to focus not on Theseus but on Hecale, an old widow who offers what humble hospitality she can to the Athenian hero during the commission of his quest.[252] Hecale passes away during the course of Theseus' adventure, but ultimately, she can take solace in a promise that must have come near the end of the work:[253] "Often, good mother … will we remember your hospitable hut" (πολλάκι σεῖο, | μαῖα, ⟨ ⟩ φιλοξείνοιο καλιῆς | μνησόμεθα, fr. 80.3–5 Hollis). This promise of remembrance, delivered in an apostrophe to the protagonist near the end of the work, already suggests a striking parallel with Apollonius' Salutation and Prayer to the Argonauts in his Envoi (*Arg.* 4.1773–1775).[254]

In the fuller context of the *Hecale*, this parallel becomes even more intriguing. We do not know the identity of the speaker in this fragment; we might

---

251 On this term, and for a defense of its use in modern scholarship, see Most 1981: 111.
252 On this innovative subject, see, e.g., Zanker 1977.
253 For the location of the fragment, see Lehnus 1997; Hollis 2009: 264.
254 A comparison made by, e.g.: McNelis 2003: 159; Hunter 2015 ad *Arg.* 4.1773–1781.

imagine it is one of the characters (e.g., Theseus), but it might equally have been the narrator (as in Apollonius). These twin possibilities suggest different ways of taking μνησόμεθα, though in a poet as self-conscious as Callimachus, it is probable that each of these interpretations would have inevitably suggested the other anyway. On the one hand, Callimachus' epyllion makes clear that Hecale will be remembered in her community through the concrete honors afforded by hero cult, for which the poem provides an etiology: in return for her hospitality, Theseus made Hecale the eponymous heroine of an Attic deme, instituted an annual festival in her honor, and established a cult of Zeus Ἑκά-λειος (fr. 81–83, *Dieg.* 11.5–7). But as McNelis argues, it is also possible to read this fragment on a metaliterary level:

> The presence of the verb meaning "remember" raises the possibility that another way for contemporary audiences to celebrate and to honor Hecale will be through poetry, and specifically through Callimachus' poem. After all, memory and poetry are closely related even before the Hellenistic period. Read self-referentially, the phrase "we will often remember your kind hospitality" suggests that Hecale's cult will be recalled through repeated (πολλάκι) readings or performances of the *Hecale*.[255]

On this reading, Callimachus envisions the same combination of literary and literal immortality for Hecale that Apollonius would ascribe to the Argonauts.[256] But what is especially revealing for my argument is that, as has long been noted, Callimachus' σεῖο ... μνησόμεθα irresistibly recalls the Poet's Task formula with which so many *HH*s end: "And I will take heed both for you and for other singing" (αὐτὰρ ἐγὼ καὶ σεῖο καὶ ἄλλης μνήσομ᾽ ἀοιδῆς).[257] It seems that both Callimachus and Apollonius were drawn to the *HH*s as natural vehicles for wedding the prerogatives of epic memorialization and hero cult.

---

255 McNelis 2003: 159–160. McNelis' argument that the Callimachean Hecale receives the dual "heroic" honors of localized cult and epic memorialization anticipates my own argument vis-à-vis Apollonius' Argonauts.

256 See particularly my discussion of the Envoi in 1.2.1.

257 Naeke 1845: 281; D'Alessio 1996: 1.328 n. 107; cf. Faber 2017: 84 with n. 26. For this formula, see introduction, 2.2–3. With Callimachus' πολλάκι cf. also *saepe* in Catullus' rendition of the Poet's Task formula (c. 64.24; this passage discussed in 1.2.1).

4.2 Theocritus' Idyll 22

My second example of the mixture of Homeric epic and hymnody is from Theocritus.[258] The Syracusan poet draws on the HHs in several of his Idylls,[259] but his "most explicit imitation of a rhapsodic Homeric hymn" must be Id. 22.[260] This Hymn to the Dioscuri is structured after the pattern of the HHs and also alludes directly to the Dioscuri's own longer Homeric Hymn (33) in its introductory vignette (1–22).[261] In the Envoi, however, Theocritus seems to present another model for his poem (Id. 22.214–223):

> χαίρετε, Λήδας τέκνα, καὶ ἡμετέροις κλέος ὕμνοις
> 215 ἐσθλὸν ἀεὶ πέμποιτε. φίλοι δέ τε πάντες ἀοιδοί
> Τυνδαρίδαις Ἑλένῃ τε καὶ ἄλλοις ἡρώεσσιν,
> Ἴλιον οἳ διέπερσαν ἀρήγοντες Μενελάῳ.
> ὑμῖν κῦδος, ἄνακτες, ἐμήσατο Χῖος ἀοιδός,
> ὑμνήσας Πριάμοιο πόλιν καὶ νῆας Ἀχαιῶν
> 220 Ἰλιάδας τε μάχας Ἀχιλῆά τε πύργον αὐτῆς·
> ὑμῖν αὖ καὶ ἐγὼ λιγεῶν μειλίγματα Μουσέων,
> οἷ' αὐταὶ παρέχουσι καὶ ὡς ἐμὸς οἶκος ὑπάρχει,
> τοῖα φέρω. γεράων δὲ θεοῖς κάλλιστον ἀοιδαί.

> Farewell, children of Leda; may you always confer fair fame on my hymns. All bards are dear to the Tyndaridae, to Helen and to the rest of the heroes who helped Menelaus to sack Troy. The Chian bard devised fame for you, lords, when he hymned the city of Priam, the ships of the Greeks, the fighting at Troy, and Achilles, that tower of strength in battle. I too bring you such pleasant offerings as my resources can provide: for the gods, songs are the best gift of honor.[262]

---

258 I here focus on Id. 22 as a particularly crisp example, but similar arguments could be made for Theocritus' other hymns with Rhapsodic affiliations—e.g., Theocritus' epyllion-like Herakliskos (24) begins with an allusion to HH 15 (Hunter 1996: 11) and concludes with a hymnic Envoi (see 123n173, 138n237). For Id. 17, see conclusion, 2.1.
259 For an overview, see Hunter 1996: 46–52.
260 Sens 1997: 13.
261 On the recursive rhapsodic structure both of the Idyll overall and in each of its component "hymns" to the individual twins, see, e.g., Sens 1997: 13–15. For its allusions to HH 33, see further, e.g., ibid. ad Theoc. 22.1–26; Hunter 1996: 52–57; cf. also Sens 1994.
262 For the Envoi's adaptation of Homeric-hymnic elements, see, e.g., Kowerski 2008: 570–571. For parallels with Apollonius' Envoi, see, e.g., Griffiths 1976: 367; Hunter 1996: 54–55.

With αὖ καὶ ἐγώ in line 221, Theocritus draws a direct parallel between his own poetic activity and that of Homer, the Χῖος ἀοιδός of line 218. And yet lines 218–220 frame Homer's poetry in highly Iliadic terms (cf. esp. Ἰλιάδας [!], 220), so that Theocritus effectively compares his poem not to a *Homeric Hymn*—the primary generic model he has, in fact, been imitating up to now—but to a Homeric epic.

The interpretation of these lines is controversial, especially because the Dioscuri do not really feature in the *Iliad*, from which they are conspicuously and explicitly absent: as the HE narrator makes clear in a famous section of the Teichoscopia, the twins had died before the outbreak of the Trojan War (*Il.* 3.236–244). The implication that this passage should be Theocritus' prooftext for Homer's supposed celebration of Castor and Polydeuces is particularly troubling because it fails even to mention their deification—the theological basis for Theocritus' own hymn. It is not my purpose to solve this notorious crux here,[263] but I would like to underline one relevant phenomenon, namely, this Envoi's insistent blurring of the generic categories of epic and hymn. αὖ καὶ ἐγώ (221) serves to liken Theocritus' Homeric-style hymn to the *Iliad* as described in lines 218–220, but the poet simultaneously characterizes Homer's epic with a markedly hymnic term (ὑμνήσας, 219) that he has used several times so far to denote his own composition (1, 4, 26, 135, 214).[264] Moreover, after comparing himself to Homer, the hymnist continues to describe Homer's poetry in religious terms: he, too (καὶ ἐγώ), brings μειλίγματα (221, a word with the connotation "propitiatory offering": LSJ s.v. A2) as gifts of honor for the gods (γεράων ... θεοῖς, 223).[265] These terms are appropriate to *Idyll* 22 qua hymn, but they fail to substantiate the parallel that the speaker proposes with the *Iliad*, which is not a "gift of honor for the gods" in any obvious sense.

Whatever Theocritus is doing here, his insistent conflation of his own hymn with Homeric epic and of the *Iliad* with hymnody does accurately reflect the duality of the Dioscuri themselves as erstwhile mortal heroes who have undergone apotheosis.[266] Indeed, Theocritus underlines the mixed status of

---

263 The terms of the problem were first laid out by Gow (1942: 16; 1952 ad Theoc. *Id.* 22.218–220). For some possible solutions, see the overview in Sens 1992; 1997: 22–23, 218–219.

264 See 2.3.2, on the dual valence of ὕμνος in Hellenistic poetry. Hunter (1996: 75) notes that Theocritus' use of ὑμνήσας "paradoxically accommodates Homer to his own poetic project, rather than vice versa."

265 Hunter (1996: 54) notes the "special connections with hero cult and the cult of the dead" that make μειλίγματα particularly apt with reference to the Dioscuri. For the twins' ambiguous ontological status, between heroes and gods, see 173n145 above.

266 Griffiths 1976: 367.

his Hymnic Subjects by celebrating the deified Dioscuri with two "epic" narratives drawn from their mortal lives (27–135, 135–213)[267]—a decision, as we shall see, with only a single precedent in the Homeric-hymnic collection.[268] Theocritus' hymn concerns deified, not heroized mortals, but these two categories are broadly analogous,[269] and in any event, Theocritus closely matches Apollonius in correlating his poem's play with genre (an "epicizing" *Homeric Hymn*)[270] with the Dioscuri's dual identities as both mythic heroes and figures of cult.

4.3   Simonides' Platea Elegy

The Platea elegy brought to light among the "new Simonides" features a passage that sets a striking precedent for Apollonius' epic hymn: a remarkable transitionary moment in which Homeric-hymnic formulas are deployed with reference to a cult hero precisely in the course of a discussion of epic memorialization. The first fourteen lines of the major fragment (Simon. fr. 11 W²) appear to describe Achilles' death and the Achaeans' subsequent sack of Troy.[271] The poet then begins his careful transition to the subject of Platea by shifting his temporal focus to the present (cf. perfect-tense κέχυται, 15);[272] I quote this critical turning-point in the poem with full context (14–28):

---

267   Sens 1997: 20; Sistakou 2007: 83–84; the hymn has even been read as "commenting on both the style and subject matter of traditional epic" (Moulton 1973: 46; cf. Sens 1997: 22). The Castor narrative ultimately descends from the *Cypria*, while the Polydeuces narrative could have been modeled on—or served as a model for—Apollonius' own Bebrycian episode.
268   We may contrast these mythic episodes narrated in the past tense with the hymn's opening vignette—drawn directly from *HH* 33—which uses the present tense to describe the Dioscuri's rescuing sailors at sea. This difference in tense underlies a difference in status: formerly men, they are now gods. In another sense, however, the Dioscuri are already quite godlike in Theocritus' dual narratives; see Sens 1997: 16–20.
269   See 2.2.4. It is notable that Theocritus directly leagues the Dioscuri with the other heroes of the Trojan War, and that bards are said to be dear to all of them (215–217). That these other heroes have been immortalized is implied by the notion that bards can still be their φίλοι, in a timeless gnomic statement, but Menelaus and the rest will have been heroized, not deified like the Dioscuri themselves.
270   See Griffiths 1976: 367 and further Sistakou 2008a: 47, who describes the *Idyll* as "on the cusp between the epic and the hymn" and as engaged in a "dialectic" between the HEs and *HH*s, among other models.
271   Probably the Platea elegy itself began with this section, which amounts to a hymnic προοίμιον for Achilles; see Rawles 2018: 279–280.
272   This switch to present time is a common closural device in the Mythic narratives of the *HH*s, dubbed the "Prolongation" by Janko (1981: 14–15); see 14n71. Although Homer's "pouring" of glory on the Achaean heroes predates the speaker's present, the Greek perfect tense denotes a state that exists at the moment of utterance (Rijksbaron 2002:

```
        ]ώων ἀγέμαχοι Δαναοί[
15   οἷσιν ἐπ' ἀθά]νατον κέχυται κλέος ἀν[δρὸς] ἕκητι
     ὃς παρ' ἰοπ]λοκάμων δέξατο Πιερίδ[ων
     ]θείην καὶ ἐπώνυμον ὁπ[λοτέρ]οισιν
     ἡμ]ιθέων ὠκύμορον γενεή[ν.
     ἀλλὰ σὺ μὲ]ν νῦν χαῖρε, θεᾶς ἐρικυ[δέος υἱέ
20   κούρης εἰν]αλίου Νηρέος· αὐτὰρ ἐγώ[
     κικλῄσκω] σ' ἐπίκουρον ἐμοί, π[     ]ε Μοῦσα,
     εἴ πέρ γ' ἀν]θρώπων εὐχομένω[ν μέλεαι·
     ἔντυνο]ν καὶ τόνδ[ε μελ]ίφρονα κ[όσμον ἀο]ιδῆς
     ἡμετ]έρης, ἵνα τις [μνή]σεται ὑ[
25   ἀνδρῶ]ν, οἳ Σπάρτ[ῃ        δούλιον ἦμ]αρ
     ....] ἀμυν[]..[              ]ω[
     οὐδ' ἀρε]τῆς ἐλάθ[οντο       ]ν οὐρανομ[ήκ]ης,
     καὶ κλέος ἀ]νθρώπων [ἔσσετ]αι ἀθάνατο⟨ν⟩.
```

... Danaan battle chiefs ... (on whom imm)ortal glory has been poured thanks to a m(an who) received (from the violet-wr)eathed Muses of Pieria ... truth/divine(?) and ... the short-lived rac(e) of (dem)igods a famous name for l(at)er men. (But you) now rejoice, O (son) of the glori(ous) daughter of Nereus of the sea. But I (invoke) you, Muse, as my ally, (if you care for) the prayer(s) of humans, (arrang)e thi(s sw)eet or(nament) of o(ur so)ng, too, so that someone ... may (re)call (the me)n who for Spart(a) ... d(ay of servitude) ... war(d off) ... (Nor did they for)get their (vir)tue ... reaching the heavens (and glory) of men (will) be immortal ...[273]

The link that facilitates the transition from the Trojan section of the elegy to the Platean is the role played by Muse-inspired poets in conferring "immortal glory" (ἀθάνατον κλέος, a phrase restored in both lines 15 and 28) upon their martial subjects.[274] Much as with Theocritus' αὖ καὶ ἐγώ (*Id.* 22.221),[275] with καὶ τόνδ[ε in line 23, the speaker draws an explicit analogy between himself and the unnamed poet (presumably Homer) who glorified the Achaeans (15–18): he

---

4); that is, κέχυται tells us that the heroes *are* famous because of Homer's singing of their exploits.

273   Text and translation are based on Sider 2001.
274   For the logic of this passage, which sets Homer and Achilles in parallel with Simonides and the Greeks at Platea, see further Boedeker 2001: 153–163.
275   On this parallel, see Kowerski 2008.

asks the Muse to inspire "this" song, "too," so that he may memorialize Sparta's soldiers (24–28) just as Homer has done for the Achaeans at Troy. Notably, the passage goes on to describe the Dioscuri and Menelaus as the leaders (ἡγεμόνες, 32) of the Spartan army, evidently in their capacity as divinized heroes.[276] As one of the primary leaders of the Trojan expedition as well, Menelaus in particular forges another connection between the glorious Greek triumphs over the Trojans in the past and the Persians in the present.

Simonides develops the idea of "immortal glory" along markedly Homeric lines. The epithet "immortal" (ἀθά]νατον, 15) stands in pointed contrast to his description of the Achaean heroes as "the short-lived rac(e) of (dem)igods" (ἡμ]ιθέων ὠκύμορον γενεή[ν, 18). The adjective ὠκύμορον is especially apt here because four of its five uses in the *Iliad* describe Achilles, the hero who knowingly embraced an all-too-short life in exchange for "imperishable renown" (κλέος ἄφθιτον, *Il.* 9.413).[277] And yet Simonides couches the adjective ὠκύμορον in a phrase evocative of Hesiod's concept of the Five Ages (ἀνδρῶν ἡρώων θεῖον γένος, οἳ καλέονται | ἡμίθεοι, *Op.* 159–160), according to which select heroes live on after death in the paradisiacal Islands of the Blessed. As it happens, we know from another of his fragments (558 *PMG*) that Simonides did indeed subscribe to the tradition of Achilles' immortal afterlife in Elysium. And in fact, in the very next lines the poet addresses Achilles himself in strikingly hymnic fashion (ἀλλὰ σὺ μὲ]ν νῦν χαῖρε, 19)[278] before adapting the opening words of the Poet's Task formula from the *HH*s (αὐτὰρ ἐγώ, 20) to announce the transition to the Battle of Platea.[279] Simonides' use of these formulas implies an analogy between the bipartite structure of his own song and that of a rhapsodic performance: a Hymnic Proem to Achilles precedes the primary, Platean section of the elegy, which the poet explicitly compares to heroic epic in its memorializing function.

Several scholars have already drawn parallels between Simonides' hymnic address to Achilles and the Envoi of the *Argonautica* (4.1773–1781), which sim-

---

276 These are the Spartan army's leaders on the divine level, as it were; the poet next mentions Pausanias as their mortal leader (33–34). For the ontological status of the Dioscuri, see 173n145.

277 Achilles is ὠκύμορος at *Il.* 1.417, 505 (ὠκυμορώτατος); 18.95, 458.

278 Cf. the formula καὶ σὺ μὲν οὕτω χαῖρε, commonly employed in the Salutations of the *HH*s (1D.11, 3.545, 4.579, 9.7, 14.6, 16.5, 18.10, 19.48, 21.5, 26.11, 28.17). Another fragment of Simonides contains a similar hymnic Salutation to an evidently heroized Hecuba: "and you, mother of twenty children, be gracious" (καὶ σὺ μὲν εἴκοσι παίδων | μᾶτερ Ἔλλαθι, fr. 559 *PMG*).

279 On this transition formula, see, e.g.: Obbink 2001: 69–70; Aloni 2001: 93–94. For the "Poet's Task," see introduction, 2.2.

ilarly bids the Argonauts farewell in a hymnic mode.[280] Verbal parallels are sparse, but the conceptual overlap between the two passages is remarkable, and much deeper than has heretofore been appreciated. In the lead-up to the elegiac speaker's apostrophe, Achilles and the other Achaean chieftains are presented as explicitly literary heroes (fr. 11.15–18), and with the adjective ὠκύμορον (18) Simonides evokes the Homeric conceit of immortal κλέος as a consolation for death. Such a presentation presupposes a mortal hero of the Homeric type, and yet by means of this Hymnic Proem Simonides acknowledges Achilles' status as an immortalized cult hero fully capable of being hymned like a god.[281] Apollonius similarly juxtaposes the epic and cultic status of his protagonists, throughout the poem but especially in the Envoi: as we saw in chapter 1 (2.1), this passage is addressed to the Argonauts as divinized heroes by means of formulas adapted from the *HH*s, but simultaneously, the narrator acknowledges the κλέος that the Argonauts have achieved (cf. κλυτά, 4.1775) and hopes to renew it yearly with repeat performances of the epic (1773–1775). What is especially striking about this parallel is that in order to acknowledge their subjects' dual status as heroes of cult as well as epic, both poets have recourse to the *HH*s in addition to the HEs. Thus in this brief passage Simonides maps the generic duality of Homeric hexameter poetry (epic/hymn) onto the conceptual duality of the hero in Greek culture (epic/cultic). The Cean poet makes, in other words, the very same moves that will inform the generic hybridity of the entire *Arg.* some two centuries later.

4.4   *The* Homeric Hymn to Heracles *(15)*

My final example takes us all the way back to the *Homeric Hymns* themselves, where, I argue, Apollonius could have found a model for the sort of "epic hymn" he was writing in *HH* 15, dedicated to *Heracles the Lionhearted* (15).[282] At only

---

280   Vox 2002: 164; Klooster 2011: 88 n. 44. Vox compares several other "saluti ad eroi," including the famous epigram also attributed to Simonides that begins χαίρετ' ἀριστῆες (*AP* 7.254).
281   Similarly Fantuzzi 2001: 233 n. 3: "This cultic worship of the traditional mortal epic hero Achilles … may have allowed Simonides to apostrophize him through the hymnodic form which would appear to have been reserved to gods." See further West 1993: 5; Boedeker 2001; cf. Capra and Curti 1995: 30; Aloni 2001: 94 n. 30.
282   Note also the epic texture of *HH* 31–32, which might have contributed to Apollonius' decision to allude to them at *Arg.* 1.1–2 (see 22). The provenance of *HH* 15 is unknown, because despite the mention of Thebes in its second line, "so Panhellenic was the worship of Herakles that there is no good reason to ascribe the hymn to a Theban rhapsode" (Athanassakis 2004: 87). West (2003a: 17–18) suggests a quadrennial festival celebrating Heracles at Marathon as a possible performance context. The hymn is often dated to the sixth century or later for its conception of Heracles as a god and its clear relationship

nine lines long, this minor hymn would seem an unlikely precursor for a full-scale epic in four books like the *Arg.*, if, that is, it did not share a very distinctive trait with it. What is provocative about the conceit of the "epic hymn," besides the fact of generic hybridity itself, is the necessarily dual ontological status of its honorands. For instance, I have argued that the *Arg.* is framed as a "Hymn to the Argonauts," and yet its very first line announces the Subject of this hymn as φῶτες, "mortals." As we have seen, there are many hints of their destined heroization throughout the poem, but it is only at its very end, in the narrator's hymnic petition to the heroized Argonauts (4.1773–1775), that their divinity finally comes firmly into focus.[283]

Such a maneuver is almost without precedent in the collection of *HH*s, which focuses exclusively on gods. Four of its hymns do address deified mortals—Heracles (15), Asclepius (16), and the Dioscuri twice over (17, 33)[284]—but of these, the last three do not acknowledge their Subjects' mortal existences, treating them almost as if they were gods from birth.[285] The *Hymn to Heracles* alone concerns itself not just with Heracles' birth from a mortal mother (1–3) and with his present divinity (7–9), but also with his pre-Olympian life as a hero (4–6):

Ἡρακλέα Διὸς υἱὸν ἀείσομαι, ὃν μέγ' ἄριστον
γείνατ' ἐπιχθονίων Θήβης ἔνι καλλιχόροισιν

---

with certain other passages in early Greek epic that have been suspected of being interpolated (*Od.* 11.602–604, Hes. *Cat.* fr. 22.26–33 Most); see AHS 1936: 396. Càssola (1975a: 336–337) objects, however, that neither of the assumptions underlying this inference is certain. For other opinions on the hymn's date, see van der Valk 1976: 445 ("archaic"); Hall 2012: 39–40 ("an archaic or classical date"). For present purposes, it only matters that the hymn predates Apollonius, and as Hunter (1996: 11 n. 39) says, "The date of the hymn is uncertain, but there is no compelling reason to think it post-classical."

283   Cf. Theocritus' *Hymn to the Dioscuri* (*Id.* 22), discussed above: there the twins appear first in their divine aspect as "rescuers of mortals" (θνητοῖσι βοηθόοι, 23), but the Mythic narratives that follow both relate exploits from their mortal lives.

284   Van der Valk (1976: 420) notes that the arranger of the collection evidently saw fit to group *HH*s 15–17 for their shared subject of deified humans; this fact suggests that some readers would have been conscious of the special status of these gods as they read their hymns. *Hymn* 33, however, rather treats the Dioscuri in their "meteorological aspect" (i.e., as St. Elmo's fire) and is thus grouped with the celestial hymns to Helius (31) and Selene (32) (West 2003a: 21). See further Torres-Guerra 2003: 9; Hall 2021: 17–18, 24.

285   *HH*s 16 and 33 pass directly from their Subject's birth Myths (16.2–3; 33.4–5) to Attributive Sections celebrating the benefits that they provide humankind in the present (16.4; 33.6–17), without demarcating their mortal from their immortal careers. *HH* 17, a shorter version of 33, makes room only for the birth Myth (17.2–4) before its Envoi begins.

Ἀλκμήνη μιχθεῖσα κελαινεφέϊ Κρονίωνι·
ὃς πρὶν μὲν κατὰ γαῖαν ἀθέσφατον ἠδὲ θάλασσαν
5 πλαζόμενος πομπῇσιν ὕπ' Εὐρυσθῆος ἄνακτος
πολλὰ μὲν αὐτὸς ἔρεξεν ἀτάσθαλα, πολλὰ δ' ἀνέτλη·
νῦν δ' ἤδη κατὰ καλὸν ἕδος νιφόεντος Ὀλύμπου
ναίει τερπόμενος καὶ ἔχει καλλίσφυρον Ἥβην.
χαῖρε, ἄναξ Διὸς υἱέ· δίδου δ' ἀρετήν τε καὶ ὄλβον.

Of Heracles the son of Zeus I will sing, far the finest of men on earth, born in Thebes of the beautiful dances to Alcmena in union with the dark-cloud son of Kronos. Formerly he roamed the vastness of land and sea at the behest of King Eurystheus, causing much suffering himself and enduring much; but now in the fair abode of snowy Olympus he lives in pleasure and has fair-ankled Hebe as his wife.

I salute you, lord, son of Zeus: grant me excellence and fortune.

As Haubold observes, there is a palpable tension already in the first two lines between the hymnic form of the introduction (Ἡρακλέα Διὸς υἱὸν ἀείσομαι, 1) and the characterization of Heracles at his birth as "far the finest of **men on earth**" (μέγ' ἄριστον | ... ἐπιχθονίων, 1–2)—that is, as a mortal. "This beginning cries out for resolution ... How, then, does Heracles become our hymnic god?"[286]

In fact, Heracles' duality as the man who became a god is, I would argue, the central thread around which the entire hymn is woven, as its thematic structure reveals.[287] The hymn is artfully composed in three sections of three lines each that together sketch the Heracles myth in full,[288] from his birth (1–3) to his heroic career (4–6) to his life as a god on Olympus (7–9).[289] Heracles' duality emerges already from his parentage: he is born to a mortal mother as one of the ἐπιχθόνιοι,[290] and yet he is distinguished from them by his surpassing superiority (μέγ' ἄριστον, 1), a mark of his heavenly paternity (Διὸς υἱόν, 1;

---

286 Haubold 2001: 28; see also Hall 2012: 112.
287 By "thematic structure," I mean to distinguish the hymn's transitions from one topic to another (birth, heroic career, divinity) from the poem's rhetorical structure, which this hymn shares with so many of its counterparts in the *HH* collection: Exordium (1), Myth (1–8), Envoi (9).
288 Cf. Stafford 2012: 19, who quotes the hymn as a "neat summary" of Heracles' story.
289 The hymnist's petition is cleverly incorporated into this last section as part and parcel of Heracles' new role as one of the θεοί, δωτῆρες ἐάων, as it were.
290 Alcmene's mortality is further emphasized through her association with a worshipful (καλλιχόροισιν) Thebes.

κελαινεφέϊ Κρονίωνι, 3).[291] This tension prepares for the next two sections, which are carefully designed to correspond with each other almost line-for-line in a series of significant contrasts between Heracles' earthly life as a mortal hero and his present existence as an immortal god. The most clearly marked contrast is temporal, before vs. now (πρὶν μέν, 4; νῦν δ᾽ ἤδη, 7),[292] but several other oppositions build up starkly contrasting pictures of humanity and divinity: wandering (πλαζόμενος, 5) the earth and sea vs. possession of a fixed dwelling on Olympus (ἕδος ... ναίει, 7–8);[293] great suffering vs. supreme luxury;[294] reciprocal violence (πολλὰ μὲν αὐτὸς ἔρεξεν ἀτάσθαλα, πολλὰ δ᾽ ἀνέτλη, 6) vs. reciprocal benefit (χαῖρε ... δίδου);[295] and serving an ἄναξ (ὕπ᾽ Εὐρυσθῆος ἄνακτος, 5) vs. being one (χαῖρε, ἄναξ, 9).[296] The boons requested in the closing petition once again nicely encapsulate Heracles' dual nature: the hero's valor (ἀρετήν) and the god's Olympian prosperity (ὄλβον).[297] Thus the hymn's structure articulates Heracles' life according to a well-defined teleological arc: his birth as a demigod, his adventures as a hero, and his ultimate happiness as an Olympian.[298]

---

291 The four-word third line, Ἀλκμήνη μιχθεῖσα κελαινεφέϊ Κρονίωνι, skillfully captures Heracles' duality as a demigod while hinting at the trajectory of his life (and the poem), from mortality to divinity.
292 See Richardson 1974 ad *HH* 2.483–489, and for "Prolongation" to the present in hymnic Myths, see 14n71.
293 Haubold 2001: 28; Montiglio 2005: 45. Note the repetition of κατά in the same *sedes* in lines 4 and 7 (Haubold 2001: 29).
294 Cf. in particular the contrast between Eurystheus and Hebe, whose name-epithet clusters end the corresponding lines in each of their sections (ὕπ᾽ Εὐρυσθῆος ἄνακτος, 5; ἔχει καλλίσφυρον Ἥβην, 8). Heracles' mortal life is defined in terms of passivity in subjection to his older cousin, traditionally an inferior, despicable man, while his immortal lot is defined in terms of his active possession of the beautiful goddess of youth.
295 On the χάρις motif implied by χαῖρε followed by the imperative δίδου in this line, see Race 1982: 10–11; cf. Calame 2005: 26–28.
296 Haubold 2001: 29–30. These correspondences further confirm the readings of lines 5–6 given above (and by most recent editors) over the variant readings offered in the *Codex Mosquensis*; see van der Valk 1964: 613–614.
297 For the divine Heracles' association with ὄλβος, see Hes. *Th.* 954–955, Pind. *Isthm.* 4.57–58. The petition itself may be formulaic; at least, it is also applied to Hephaestus at *HH* 20.8 (see Hall 2021: 18). But if so, the formula is well-chosen for this context (Athanassakis 2004 ad loc.; cf. AHS 1936 ad loc.; Galinsky 1972: 15; Haubold 2001: 30–31; Vamvouri Ruffy 2004: 83–84). As per Race 1982: 10: "When there is a petition at the end of a hymn, it must of course be consonant with the god's powers as established in the body of the hymn." Callimachus actually brings such considerations to the surface in his expansive imitation of the same prayer-type at *Hymn* 1.94–96; see Vamvouri Ruffy 2004: 56.
298 Haubold (2001: 30) also speaks of the hymn's "teleology," referring specifically to the way that the first eight lines of the poem "lead up to and make possible the final address" to the deified Heracles.

This hymn is exceptional for its acknowledgment of its divine honorand's erstwhile mortality, but it is also notable that the hymnist chooses to cast Heracles' mortal life in decidedly epic terms, as Nagy has noted.[299] Heracles is ἄριστος (1), like Achilles and Odysseus in their respective HEs; he is associated with ἀτάσθαλα (6), like the Iliadic Achilles; and a set of unmistakable allusions to the introit of the *Odyssey* associate Heracles' mortal wanderings with those of the homecoming Odysseus. The *Odyssey* begins (*Od.* 1.1–5):

> Ἄνδρα μοι ἔννεπε, Μοῦσα, **πολύτροπον**, ὃς μάλα **πολλὰ**
> **πλάγχθη**, ἐπεὶ Τροίης ἱερὸν πτολίεθρον ἔπερσεν·
> **πολλῶν** δ' ἀνθρώπων ἴδεν **ἄστεα** καὶ νόον ἔγνω,
> **πολλὰ** δ' ὅ γ' ἐν **πόντῳ** πάθεν ἄλγεα ὃν κατὰ θυμόν,
> ἀρνύμενος ἥν τε ψυχὴν καὶ νόστον ἑταίρων.

Tell me, Muse, of the man of **many** devices, **driven far astray** after he had sacked the sacred citadel of Troy. **Many** were the men whose **cities** he saw and whose minds he learned, and **many** the **woes he suffered** in his heart upon the **sea**, seeking to win his own life and the return of his comrades.

The parallels with lines 4–6 of the hymn, outlining Heracles' heroic career, come fast and thick:[300]
1) anaphora of forms of πολύς;
2) consonance of π (cf. particularly πλαζόμενος πομπῇσιν ὕπ' in the hymn);
3) enjambed forms of πλάζω (πλάγχθη; πλαζόμενος);
4) a universalizing land-sea doublet (ἄστεα/πόντῳ; γαῖαν/θάλασσαν);[301]

---

299 Nagy 1990b: 13–14, upon which this paragraph is based. Haubold (2001: 28) refers to lines 4–6 especially as the hymn's "'epic' section," and on 29 he argues that the verb ἔρεξεν in line 5 has specifically epic connotations.

300 Outside of the *Odyssey* introit, Montiglio (2005: 40 n. 51) further compares *Od.* 4.271, which applies the phrase ἔρεξε καὶ ἔτλη to Odysseus; cf. *Od.* 23.306–307. For the meaning of Odysseus' name as "to inflict and suffer pain," see, e.g., Dimock 1956. The introit suggests something of this duality in Odysseus' character in the disjunction between his sacking Troy on the one hand and suffering on his homeward journey on the other.

301 For such expressions, see Lloyd 1966: 91. A land-sea doublet is not unexpected in a summary of Heracles' extensive travels; e.g., the Pindaric Tiresias begins his prophecy of Heracles' fortunes with "all the lawless beasts he would slay on land, and all those in the sea" (ὅσσους μὲν ἐν χέρσῳ κτανών, | ὅσσους δὲ πόντῳ θῆρας ἀϊδροδίκας, *Nem.* 1.62–63); cf. Pind. *Isthm.* 4.55–56. In an environment so full of other Odyssean echoes, however, this instance is particularly Odyssean.

5) the idea of great heroic suffering (πολλὰ ... πάθεν ἄλγεα; πολλὰ ... ἀνέ-
τλη).[302]

Nagy concludes from these features that the hymn "is not only a functional prayer to a hero in his capacity as a cult figure but also a glorification of his epic attributes—the very same epic attributes that seem to be divided up between Achilles and Odysseus in the overall epic diction of the *Iliad* and *Odyssey*."[303]

To judge from the hymn's transmitted title, "to Heracles the Lionhearted" (εἰς Ἡρακλέα Λεοντόθυμον), Nagy was far from the first to notice the epic quality of this hymn. Although the formation of the compound is not unparalleled,[304] λεοντόθυμος is a *hapax* in surviving Greek, no doubt in part because of its incompatibility with the dactylic hexameter. Nevertheless, the closely related θυμο- λέων does occur in Archaic poetry and has strong epic connotations. In the *Iliad*, the epithet is applied only to Heracles (5.639) and Achilles (7.228); in the *Odyssey*, only to Heracles (11.267) and Odysseus (4.724, 814). Thus, as Wilson observes, Homer restricts his usage of the epithet to connect the hero of each of his epics to Heracles, the Greek hero par excellence.[305] The title of the hymn apparently takes the opposite tack, deploying a cognate epithet to reinforce Heracles' connections to the Homeric Achilles and Odysseus. The provenance of the title is unknown, but whoever affixed it must have recognized the hymn's epic texture. Indeed, some scholars have suspected that the hymn may have functioned as a προοίμιον for an epic celebrating Heracles as its central hero;[306] the allusions to the introit of the *Odyssey* certainly bolster this impression. For our purposes, it is enough to note that the *HH*s already contain a miniature sort of "epic hymn" that shares marked affinities with the *Arg.*, celebrating a hero under both his "epic" and "cultic" identities.[307]

---

302 πολύτλας, "much-enduring," is Odysseus' regular epithet in the *Odyssey* (e.g., 5.171, 354, 486, etc.).

303 Nagy 1990b: 14. In this context it may be notable that Heracles' name itself contains the key epic term κλέος and is even inflected such as to end in -κλέα (Ἡρακλέα, *HH* 15.1), as if to evoke the hero's "glorious deeds" (cf. the κλέα φωτῶν of *Arg.* 1.1). On the traditional etymology of Heracles' name as "glory of Hera," see, e.g., Gantz 1993: 378; for his part, Apollonius may allude to this etymology at *Arg.* 1.997 (O'Hara 2017: 28, 205–206).

304 AHS 1936: 396 adduce several other compounds beginning in λεοντο-.

305 Wilson 2002: 253.

306 A suggestion reaching back to Groddeck (1786: 48) and Ilgen (1796: 590); West (2003a: 18) is non-commital.

307 Albeit Heracles' cult is Olympian, not heroic like that of the Argonauts. Nonetheless, I have argued above (2.2.4) that within the *Arg.*, Heracles' apotheosis functions as a paradigm for the Argonauts' heroization.

In sum, all four of the poets surveyed in this section—Callimachus, Theocritus, Simonides, and the *Heracles* hymnist—bear comparison with Apollonius by virtue of their common decision to blend together generic markers associated with the HEs and the *HH*s in order to capture both the epic and the cultic aspects of their protagonists' heroism. Within this quartet, however, it is instructive to distinguish two divergent approaches to negotiating this merger of epic and hymnody. On the one hand, Theocritus' *Id.* 22 and the *Homeric Hymn to Heracles* might seem the closer parallels to the *Arg.* Both compositions represent hymns to deified heroes that, with a high degree of self-consciousness, still find room to celebrate their Subjects' "epic" exploits, set in the days before they achieved godhood. Thus, like the *Arg.* itself, we could label these poems "epic hymns." On the other hand, Callimachus' *Hecale* and Simonides' Platea elegy furnish closer parallels in other respects; in particular, these intertexts are notable for applying the formulary of the *HH*s to divinized cult heroes (Hecale, Achilles) rather than to fully deified ones (the Dioscuri, Heracles). Apollonius' choice to compose an "epic hymn" that presses the Rhapsodic Hymnic tradition into the service of hero cult represents a happy medium between these alternative approaches.

5   In the Footsteps of *Heracles*

In the final section of this chapter, I would like to expand on the preceding analysis of *HH* 15 in order to explore a possibility that, on the face of it, might seem to border on the absurd: could Apollonius have reckoned this minor hymn, only nine lines in length, among the chief models for his four-book epic? Despite their incongruous lengths, these poems are united, after all, by a very distinctive trait, in that both poems amount to "epic hymns" whose Myths recount the mortal labors of their divinized honorands. In fact, there is even some evidence that Apollonius programmatically signals his debt to this unassuming hymn through some potential allusions in his introit. But whether or not we are completely convinced that Apollonius positively encourages us to scrutinize the *Arg.* in light of *Heracles the Lionhearted*, I hope to demonstrate that a comparison of these epic hymns has, in any event, a good deal to teach us about the structure of the *Arg.*'s Mythic narrative.

5.1   *Correspondences between* Arg. *1.1–22 and* HH *15.4–6*
We have already encountered a likely Apollonian allusion to *HH* 15 in the introduction (4.5.3), and in fact there exists another close verbal correspondence between *HH* 15.7 (ἕδος νιφόεντος Ὀλύμπου) and *Arg.* 1.1099 (νιφόεν θ' ἕδος

Οὐλύμποιο).³⁰⁸ But proving that Apollonius' introit actively alludes to *HH* 15 is a trickier matter, as in this case the intertextual signals are subject to a great deal of interference from the opening of the *Odyssey*. As we saw in the previous section, *Heracles* borrows markedly from *Od.* 1.1–5 in order to characterize its hero's globetrotting labors according to a recognizably epic paradigm. Apollonius himself, of course, alludes to these same lines in his own epic introit. For example, when Pelias contrives the quest for the Golden Fleece "so that either on the sea or else among foreign people [Jason] would lose any chance of returning home" (ὄφρ' ἐνὶ πόντῳ | ἠὲ καὶ ἀλλοδαποῖσι μετ' ἀνδράσι νόστον ὀλέσσῃ, *Arg.* 1.16–17), the poet deploys a universalizing land-sea doublet in the context of losing one's νόστος, features that strongly recall *Od.* 1.3–5 (cf. also 9).³⁰⁹ Odyssean diction recurs just a few lines later, when the narrator announces his poetic program (1.20–22):

νῦν δ' ἂν ἐγὼ γενεήν τε καὶ οὔνομα μυθησαίμην
ἡρώων, δολιχῆς τε πόρους ἁλός, ὅσσα τ' ἔρεξαν
πλαζόμενοι.

But now I wish to relate the lineage and names of the heroes, their journeys on the vast sea, and all they did as they **wandered**.

The enjambed πλαζόμενοι naturally recalls πλάγχθη at the beginning of *Od.* 1.2.³¹⁰

Because the fifteenth *HH* is relatively obscure—granted, almost any poem is obscure in comparison with the opening of one of the HEs—one might be tempted to dismiss whatever intertextual connections it might have with the *Arg.* introit as a reflex of their common allusions to the *Odyssey*. On closer inspection, however, it turns out that the *Arg.* introit has discrete intertextual links with both the hymn and the *Odyssey* introit; moreover, when an element is shared by all three passages, the echo between the *Arg.* and *HH* 15 is sometimes more direct than that between the two epic introits.³¹¹ The elements linking the passages in question may be tabulated (table 2).

---

308 Noted by Campbell 1981 ad loc.
309 See, e.g.: Clare 2000: 8; 2002: 25; Klooster 2012: 64. Other land-sea doublets that occur in summary references to the Argonauts' adventures include 2.628–630 and 3.348–349; cf. 4.231–232.
310 De Martino 1984–1985: 106; Hunter 1993: 119; Clare 2000: 8; Vox 2002: 158; Nelis 2005a: 356. Cf. the enjambment of ἡρώων in line 21, recalling *Il.* 1.4 (Romeo 1985: 25; Hunter 1993: 119 n. 76; Phillips 2020: 34).
311 The *Arg.* introit also has intertextual connections with other parts of the *Odyssey* beyond

TABLE 2   Parallels between the introits of the *Arg.* and *Od.* and the Myth of *HH* 15

	Arg. 1.1–22	*Od.* 1.1–5	*HH* 15.4–6
a universalizing **land-sea doublet**	ἐνὶ πόντῳ | ἠὲ καὶ ἀλλο-δαποῖσι μετ' ἀνδράσι	ἀνθρώπων ... ἄστεα ... ἐν πόντῳ	κατὰ γαῖαν ... ἠδὲ θάλασσαν
emphasis on **extent** of travels	δολιχῆς τε πόρους ἁλός	ὃς μάλα πολλὰ | πλάγχθη	κατὰ γαῖαν ἀθέσφατον ἠδὲ θάλασσαν | πλαζόμενος
enjambed forms of πλάζω	ὅσσα τ' ἔρεξαν | πλαζόμενοι	ὃς μάλα πολλὰ | πλάγχθη	κατὰ ... θάλασσαν | πλαζόμενος
the idea of **great suffering**	ναυτιλίης πολυκηδέος	πολλὰ ... πάθεν ἄλγεα	πολλὰ δ' ἀνέτλη
the importance of νόστος	ὄφρ' ... νόστον ὀλέσσῃ	ἀρνύμενος ... νόστον ἑταίρων	–
the motif of **deeds** performed during travels	ὅσσα τ' ἔρεξαν | πλαζόμενοι	–	πλαζόμενος ... πολλὰ μὲν αὐτὸς ἔρεξεν
the **taskmaster** motif	βασιλῆος ἐφημοσύνῃ Πελίαο	–	πομπῇσιν ὕπ' Εὐρυσθῆος ἄνακτος

In sum, the hymn is missing two elements that are shared by the *Odyssey* and *Arg.* introits: the importance of the concept of νόστος and the mention of foreign peoples in the land-sea doublet (ἀλλοδαποῖσι μετ' ἀνδράσι vs. ἀνθρώπων ... ἄστεα).[312] Moreover, the *Arg.*'s ἐνὶ πόντῳ is a far closer match to the *Odyssey*'s ἐν πόντῳ than the hymn's κατὰ ... θάλασσαν. Yet the hymn's emphasis on the vastness of the land and sea traveled by Heracles (κατὰ γαῖαν ἀθέσφατον ἠδὲ θάλασσαν) corresponds to Apollonius' δολιχῆς ... πόρους ἁλός better than the *Odyssey*'s vaguer μάλα πολλὰ \| πλάγχθη.[313] Likewise, Apollonius' enjambed πλαζόμενοι echoes the hymn's enjambed πλαζόμενος with far greater sonic fidelity than the *Odyssey*'s πλάγχθη. In addition, the theme of the Argonauts' deeds as

its introit, as a perusal of, e.g., the first page of Campbell 1981 will reveal. The most important is the singling out of the Cyanean Rocks (1.2–4) for a preview among the Argonauts' many trials—Circe's reference to this particular episode (*Od.* 12.69–72) is the only explicit mention of the Argonautic myth in Homer. For allusions to Phemius and Demodocus, see 95n50.

312   Odysseus' goal is to gain his comrades' νόστος; Pelias', to destroy Jason's.
313   πόρους ἁλός, however, alludes to *Od.* 12.259, where we also find Odysseus using the phrase ὅσσ' ἐμόγησα (cf. ὅσσα τ' ἔρεξαν): Fantuzzi and Hunter 2004: 269–270.

they wandered using the verb ἔρεξαν echoes the hymn's ἔρεξεν almost exactly, but the *Odyssey* introit has no parallel. These correspondences raise the possibility that Apollonius' introit is making a "two-tier allusion" to *Odyssey* 1.1–5 through the lens of one of that passage's own intertexts, *HH* 15.4–6.

The likelihood of such an allusion is in my view increased by two additional pieces of evidence. The first is a correspondence with *Heracles* on a detail that is missing from the *Odyssey*, but which is crucial to the opening lines of Apollonius' epic. I refer to Pelias' role as the Argonauts' taskmaster in the *Arg.*'s very first sentence (1.1–4):

Ἀρχόμενος σέο, Φοῖβε, παλαιγενέων κλέα φωτῶν
μνήσομαι, οἳ Πόντοιο κατὰ στόμα καὶ διὰ πέτρας
Κυανέας βασιλῆος ἐφημοσύνῃ Πελίαο
χρύσειον μετὰ κῶας ἐΰζυγον ἤλασαν Ἀργώ.

Beginning with you, Phoebus, I shall recall the famous deeds of men born long ago, who, **at the command of King Pelias**, sailed the well-benched Argo through the mouth of the Black Sea and between the Cyanean rocks to fetch the golden fleece.

There are a few reasons to believe that the phrase "at the command of King Pelias" should be given unusual weight. In the first place, it is key to the narrator's train of thought, as the next thirteen lines of the introit (the "prehistory" portion: 1.5–17) proceed to explain (τοίην γὰρ Πελίης φάτιν ἔκλυεν [1.5], etc.) Pelias' motivation for giving the command.[314] Moreover, the motif of the taskmaster who commands a heroic journey is of remarkably regular interest to Apollonius, occurring some twenty times in the poem, with reference both to the Argonauts' quest[315] and the quests of other heroes and sailors:[316]
1) Jason and the Argonauts: 1.3, 242–243, 279, 362, 981; 2.210, 615, 624, 763; 3.333–336,[317] 390, 431;

---

314 For this interpretation of γάρ in line 5, see 102n81.
315 Sistakou 2012: 59: "Although Pelias hovers in the background of the story and never becomes an organic part of it, he is omnipresent in the role of the commanding lord, a role articulated through a series of formulaic expressions." See also Levin 1971: 20.
316 Cuypers (1997 ad 2.210) cites a good many of these examples. On the divine level, cf. Iris (4.757) and the Nereids (4.753, 845–846, 858, 967), who similarly go on missions at the behest of Hera.
317 In this passage, Argus describes Pelias as sending (πέμπει, 3.336) the Argonauts; cf. Eurystheus' πομπῆσιν (*HH* 15.5).

2) Heracles: 1.1317, 1347;
3) Aristaeus: 2.518;
4) The Phrixides: 2.1096, 1152; 3.263–264;
5) The Colchian fleet: 4.230;
6) Perseus: 4.1515.

In fact, a couple instances of the taskmaster motif take on added significance because they occur in passages directly modeled on the introit, such as Phineus' opening address to the Argonauts (2.209–211):[318]

κλῦτε, Πανελλήνων προφερέστατοι, εἰ ἐτεὸν δὴ
οἵδ' ὑμεῖς, οὓς δὴ **κρυερῇ βασιλῆος ἐφετμῇ**
Ἀργῴης ἐπὶ νηὸς ἄγει μετὰ κῶας Ἰήσων.

Hear me, greatest of all the Hellenes, if truly you are the ones whom Jason, **at the dire command of his king**, is leading on the ship Argo to fetch the fleece.

Pelias' command thus appears almost as an indispensable element in the introit.[319] Most tellingly, when the narrator uses indirect speech to convey Jason's summary of the contents of the poem thus far to King Lycus, the information given in the introit is condensed entirely to the phrase "Pelias' commands" (Πελίαό τ' ἐφετμάς, 2.763).[320] The implication is that the narrator conceives of Pelias' command as the introit's defining detail, at least for the purposes of his plot. It therefore seems to me significant that the identical motif appears in *HH* 15.5 (πομπῇσιν ὑπ' Εὐρυσθῆος ἄνακτος), with Eurystheus playing the same role in a summary of Heracles' labors as Pelias does vis-à-vis the Argonautic quest. Admittedly, Pelias' role as taskmaster is a traditional element in such outlines of the Argonautic myth.[321] Nevertheless, these common motifs do increase the general structural resemblances between our passages; and it should also be noted that Pelias and Eurystheus are further analogized within the *Arg.* itself by their common epithet ἀτάσθαλος (1.1317;[322] 3.390) and especially by their respective opposition to an Argonaut's participation

---

318 Hunter (1993: 91) notes the allusion to the introit here. The introduction of the Phrixides to the narrative (2.1093–1096) provides a similar example; see Clare 2002: 106.
319 Though cf. 4.1319–1321, quoted below.
320 As noted by Byre (2002: 43), who further compares the phrase's appearance in Jason's introductory words to Cyzicus (Πελίαό τ' ἐφετμάς, 1.981).
321 See, e.g., Hes. *Th.* 995–996, Mimnermus fr. 11.3 West, Eur. *Med.* 6 (Levin 1971: 9–10).
322 Cf. the ἀτάσθαλα that Heracles himself suffered on Eurystheus' missions (*HH* 15.5–6).

in the quest: Acastus participates Πελίαο παρὲκ νόον (1.323); Heracles, παρὲκ νόον Εὐρυσθῆος (1.130).

The second datapoint that supports an allusion to *HH* 15.4–6 in the *Arg.* introit is an intratextual echo of the latter passage that more clearly reworks our hymn, namely, the résumé of the Argonautic journey so far in the Libyan Herossae's address to Jason (4.1319–1321):

> ἴδμεν ἕκαστα
> 1320 ὑμετέρων καμάτων, ὅσ' ἐπὶ χθονός, ὅσσα τ' ἐφ' ὑγρὴν
> πλαζόμενοι κατὰ πόντον ὑπέρβια ἔργα κάμεσθε.

> We know every one of your trials—all the extraordinary deeds you accomplished on land and all those on water as you wandered over the sea.

Notably, when Jason reports this message to his comrades, he slightly alters the heroines' original wording (1359–1360):

> καὶ δ' ὁπόσ' αὐτοὶ πρόσθεν ἐπὶ χθονὸς ἠδ' ὅσ' ἐφ' ὑγρὴν
> ἔτλημεν, τὰ ἕκαστα διίδμεναι εὐχετόωντο.

> … and moreover they claimed to know full well everything that we ourselves had endured up to now on land and on water.

These passages summarizing the voyage thus far look back to the preview thereof found in the introit (particularly 1.16–17, 20–22),[323] and they share with that passage several points in common with *HH* 15.4–6,[324] including a land-sea doublet,[325] the enjambed πλαζόμενοι, and the generalizing mention of deeds performed during these wanderings. It is particularly notable that Jason alters the heroine's original reference to what the crew has **done** (κάμεσθε, 4.1321) to substitute what they have **suffered** instead (ὁπόσ' αὐτοὶ … | ἔτλημεν, 1359–1360). Apollonius thus manages to split the two halves of *HH* 15.6 (πολλὰ μὲν αὐτὸς ἔρεξεν ἀτάσθαλα, πολλὰ δ' ἀνέτλη) across these twinned passages.

---

323 Hunter 2015 ad loc.; Phillips 2020: 32–34.
324 An allusive evocation of Heracles is appropriate at this point, as the Argonauts are literally following in the hero's footsteps in Libya, where he has just completed one of his final labors. The Heraclean diction in καμάτων (4.1320: "labors") may also help to conjure the son of Zeus in our passage.
325 Compared to *Od.* 1.3–4 by Hunter 2015 and Stürner 2022 ad loc.

The notion of the Argonauts' endurance (ἔτλημεν) represents a parallel with *HH* 15 that is missing from the *Arg.* introit itself. Similarly, *Arg.* 4.1320–1321 reveals a marked difference from 1.21–22 in its characterization of the deeds that the Argonauts have performed. Whereas the narrator had simply promised to relate "**all** [that they] did as they wandered" (ὅσσα τ' ἔρεξαν | πλαζόμενοι), the heroines refer more specifically to "**all the extraordinary deeds** you accomplished ... as you wandered" (ὅσσα τ' ... | πλαζόμενοι ... ὑπέρβια ἔργα κάμεσθε). In fact, the word here rendered "extraordinary," ὑπέρβια, makes for a highly ambiguous qualifier for the Argonauts' ἔργα, given how frequently this term carries negative undertones of arrogance or lawlessness—and not least in the *Arg.* itself.[326] At this point in the poem, readers are now in a position to know, as they had not been when first encountering the introit, that in addition to positively evaluated "extraordinary deeds," the Argonauts have also committed some rather more "wanton deeds" during their adventure, the most clearcut example being the treacherous and impious murder of Apsyrtus earlier in Book 4.[327] This negative valence finds a ready correlate in *Heracles*, whose hymnist frankly admits that the hero committed many "reckless deeds" (πολλὰ μὲν αὐτὸς ἔρεξεν ἀτάσθαλα, 6) in the course of his labors. Here we can discern an important parallel between the *Arg.* and *HH* 15, in that neither of these epic hymns hesitates to acknowledge the less seemly incidents in their honorands' heroic careers.[328] But for now, suffice it to say that the clearer evocation of *HH* 15.4–6 in the Herossae's variation on the *Arg.* introit helps us to detect its presence there, too.

5.2 The Teleology of Heroism

If we review the intertextual correspondences between the *Arg.* introit and *HH* 15, the most distinctive parallel must be that between the AR narrator's overview of the epic plot to come (*Arg.* 1.20–22) and the hymnist's synopsis of the mortal Heracles' heroic career (*HH* 15.4–6). To re-present the correspondences:

20 νῦν δ' ἂν ἐγὼ γενεήν τε καὶ οὔνομα μυθησαίμην
    ἡρώων, δολιχῆς τε πόρους ἁλός, ὅσσα τ' ἔρεξαν
    πλαζόμενοι· Μοῦσαι δ' ὑποφήτορες εἶεν ἀοιδῆς.

---

326 Phillips 2020: 33. For citations, see Stürner 2022 ad loc.
327 On this moral nadir, see conclusion, 2.2.
328 Haubold (2001: 29–30) warns against the modern scholarly impulse to downplay the problematic effect of ἀτάσθαλα at *HH* 15.6, which he connects to the "transgressive potential" of epic (30); see also Galinsky 1972: 15.

But now I wish to relate the lineage and names of the heroes, their journeys on the vast sea, and **all they did as they wandered**; and may the Muses be inspirers of my song.

ὃς πρὶν μὲν κατὰ γαῖαν ἀθέσφατον ἠδὲ θάλασσαν
5 πλαζόμενος πομπῇσιν ὕπ' Εὐρυσθῆος ἄνακτος
πολλὰ μὲν αὐτὸς ἔρεξεν ἀτάσθαλα, πολλὰ δ' ἀνέτλη.

Formerly **he roamed** the vastness of land and sea at the behest of King Eurystheus, **causing much** suffering himself and enduring much.

The verbal echoes bolded above take on added significance given the comparability of these contexts: both passages speak in summary fashion (ὅσσα; πολλά) of the various deeds that their heroes perform (ἔρεξαν; ἔρεξεν) as they wander (πλαζόμενοι; πλαζόμενος) over vast stretches of the world (cf. ἀθέσφατον with δολιχῆς). As noted above, Apollonius' πλαζόμενοι is formally closer to the hymn's πλαζόμενος than the *Odyssey*'s πλάγχθη (1.2), and the mirroring of ἔρεξεν with ἔρεξαν does not have a parallel in the *Odyssey* introit.

If we allow that Apollonius could be alluding to *HH* 15 in these programmatic lines, then at least one interpretation immediately suggests itself. We have seen above (2.2.4) that the superheroic Heracles serves as a foil to Jason and his crew throughout the *Arg.*, often accomplishing singularly what the Argonauts only manage to do collectively.[329] An allusion to the hero-god's *Homeric Hymn* at this point would mean that this program of *aemulatio Herculis* begins right from the very start. But to my mind, the programmatic role of *Arg.* 1.20–22 in outlining the contents of the poem raises a further possibility. In this passage, the AR narrator is announcing the overall structure of the coming narrative: he promises to relate (μυθησαίμην) first "the lineage and names of the heroes" (γενεήν τε καὶ οὔνομα ... | ἡρώων) and then "their journeys on the vast sea, and all they did as they wandered" (δολιχῆς τε πόρους ἁλός, ὅσσα τ' ἔρεξαν | πλαζόμενοι).[330] These two subsections correspond to the Catalog of Argo-

---

[329] In this respect, Apollonius' modulation of the hymn's singular forms (πλαζόμενος ... ἔρεξεν) into plurals (ἔρεξαν ... πλαζόμενοι) is highly significant. Cf. Phillips 2020: 34 nn. 22–23.

[330] Clare (2000: 8–9, 2002: 29–30) argues that πλαζόμενοι in 1.22 refers specifically to the Argonauts' detours in Book 4 to atone for the murder of Apsyrtus (cf. 1.81; 4.1041, 1395), since the Argonauts do not generally "wander" but have a clear goal in mind (Colchis) in the first two books. It is certainly true that, in keeping with a common pattern in Greek myth, the Argonauts' voyage home is much more difficult than the outward journey and takes the crew off-course (see Montiglio 2005: 229–231). Nevertheless, at various points, in fact, all

nauts (1.23–233) and the epic narrative proper (1.234–4.1772), respectively. In this context, I would propose that the allusion to *HH* 15 at *Arg.* 1.20–22 could be serving to point up an analogy between the overall structure of the two works in question—and of the destiny in store for their respective honorands.

The *Homeric Hymn to Heracles* is possessed of a tight, teleological structure that might well have appealed to Apollonius as he crafted his own epic hymn. As was outlined above, Heracles' birth narrative emphasizes his status midway between mortal and god (15.1–3); the middle section summarizes his heroic career in epic fashion (4–6); and the piece concludes with a description of Heracles' eternal life on Olympus and the hymnist's prayer to the deified hero (7–9). Translated into Apollonian terms, we could say that the first section of the hymn relates Heracles' "lineage and name" (γενεήν τε καὶ οὔνομα, *Arg.* 1.20), while the second summarizes his heroic career in terms similar to those of *Arg.* 1.21–22. If the first two sections of the hymn correspond so well to the two sections of the *Arg.* promised in its introit, can we expect that the third section of the hymn (15.7–9) will also find its counterpart in Apollonius' poem? I believe so: in the Envoi at 4.1773–1781, the narrator's Salutation and Prayer to the Argonauts finally and decisively confirms their collective heroization. Apollonius' allusion to *Heracles the Lionhearted* thus foreshadows the Argonauts' own Heraclean ascension to a higher plane of being on the other side of their labors, even though this fate is not explicitly promised in the program at *Arg.* 1.20–22.[331]

Let us examine the structural analogy that I am proposing between the *Arg.* and *HH* 15 in greater detail.[332] As I have said, the opening of the *Hymn to Heracles* (15.1–3) corresponds to Apollonius' Catalog of Argonauts, whose

---

the Argonauts' travels, both to and from Colchis, are spoken of in the language of "wandering" (2.11, 774; 3.348, 1066; 4.1321, 1395; cf. 4.1473); cf. further the "wandering" of the Phrixides (πλάγξασθαι, 3.261), whose journey Clare calls "the westward counterpart of the *Argo* voyage" (2002: 106). The Argonauts' travels can be called "wandering" in toto because they are conceived of as a movement outward into parts unknown, without firm control over their itinerary (cf. Montiglio 2005: 223 apropos of "wandering" in the Greek novel). Thus I maintain that the words δολιχῆς τε πόρους ἁλός, ὅσσα τ' ἔρεξαν | πλαζόμενοι refer jointly to the total epic narrative of Books 1–4, though the two halves of the phrase emphasize different aspects thereof (the Argonauts' route and deeds, respectively). There is a comparable tension in the diction of the *Homeric Hymn to Heracles*, in which the hero is said to "wander" even as he undertakes specific "missions" set for him by Eurystheus (πλαζόμενος πομπῇσιν, 15.5; Haubold 2001: 29).

331   For the analogy between heroization and deification, see 2.2.4.
332   Cf. Gutzwiller 1981: 12–13, who similarly argues that Theocritus might have structured the narrative of *Id.* 24 after the model provided by *HH* 15.

entries each provide (in varying measure) the same sorts of information typically found in the Exordia of the *HHs*.³³³ Besides their "lineage and names," the narrator often supplies his heroes' standard epithets, local connections, special abilities (if applicable), and other distinguishing qualities; and in some cases, these entries also receive minor narrative expansions.³³⁴ The entry for the Dioscuri offers a straightforward example (1.146–150):³³⁵

> καὶ μὴν Αἰτωλὶς κρατερὸν Πολυδεύκεα Λήδη
> Κάστορά τ' ὠκυπόδων ὦρσεν δεδαημένον ἵππων
> Σπάρτηθεν· τοὺς δ' ἥ γε δόμοις ἔνι Τυνδαρέοιο
> τηλυγέτους ὠδῖνι μιῇ τέκεν· οὐδ' ἀπίθησεν
> 150 λισσομένοις· Ζηνὸς γὰρ ἐπάξια μήδετο λέκτρων.

Moreover, Aetolian Leda sent mighty Polydeuces and Castor, skilled with swift-footed horses, from Sparta. These much-beloved sons she bore in one birth in Tyndareus' palace, and she did not oppose their pleas to go, for she had aspirations worthy of Zeus' bed.

This passage, which may allude to the Dioscuri's own *HHs*,³³⁶ skillfully weaves into its dramatic vignette of Leda's sending off her sons all the same introduc-

---

333   This observation leads both Sistakou (2001: 259) and Scherer (2006: 116) to compare Apollonius' Catalog to the introductory sections of the *HHs*, independent of the analogy with *HH* 15 I am proposing here.
334   Sistakou (2001: 259–260 with n. 70) likens the various micro-narratives found in Apollonius' Catalog to miniaturized versions of the Mythic narratives of the *HHs*, which often deal with similar themes: the god's birth, erotic liaisons, and exploits and achievements that reflect the god's special characteristics. For an overview of these narrative themes in the *HHs*, see 6*n*30.
335   Tsakiris (2022: 32) makes the same comparison and further notes similarities between Heracles' Catalog entry (1.122–131) and his *HH* (15).
336   Apollonius' κρατερὸν Πολυδεύκεα is traditional (Hes. fr. 154b.3; Theoc. *Id.* 22.92, 173) and avoids too heavy-handed a reference to Polydeuces' skill as a boxer (πὺξ ἀγαθός: *Il.* 3.237, *Od.* 11.300), which will feature in the Amycus episode; cf. also the Dioscuri's designation as κρατερόφρονε παῖδε in their mother's entry in the *Nekyia*'s "Catalog of Heroines" (*Od.* 11.299; on resemblances between this catalog and Apollonius', see Sistakou 2001: 251 n. 43). *Arg.* 1.147 probably draws on Castor's traditional designation as "Castor the tamer of horses" (Κάστορά θ' ἱππόδαμον; *Il.* 3.237, *Od.* 11.300, *HH* 33.3, Hes. fr. 154c.8, d.1, *Cypria* fr. 16.6 West; restored at Ibyc. 282a.17 Campbell), but Apollonius appears to have blended this formula with the Dioscuri's joint epithet from the Salutations of their *HHs*, "riders of swift steeds" (ταχέων ἐπιβήτορες ἵππων*, 17.5, 33.18); cf. also Alcm. fr. 2 Campbell (Κά[στωρ τε πώλων ὠκέων] δματῆ[ρε]ς [ἱ]ππόταl[ι σοφοὶ καὶ Πωλυδεύκης] κυδρός).

TABLE 3 A comparison between an entry from Apollonius' Catalogue of Argonauts and the Exordium of *HH* 15

	Arg. 1.146–150	*HH* 15.1–3
Name	Πολυδεύκεα ... Κάστορά	Ἡρακλέα
Epithet/Distinction	κρατερὸν; ὠκυπόδων ... δεδαημένον ἵππων	μέγ' ἄριστον ... ἐπιχθονίων
Parentage	Λήδη; δόμοις ἔνι Τυνδαρέοιο; Ζηνὸς ... λέκτρων	Διὸς υἱὸν; γείνατ' ... Ἀλκμήνη μιχθεῖσα ... Κρονίωνι
Locality	Αἰτωλὶς ... Λήδη; Σπάρτηθεν	Θήβης ἔνι καλλιχόροισιν

tory elements present at the beginning of many *HH*s,[337] including Heracles' (15.1–3) (table 3).[338]

The analogy between the *HH*s and Apollonius' Catalog may not seem especially distinctive, since Apollonius' most important model here, Homer's Catalog of Ships,[339] often provides the same "basic information" about the Achaean leaders.[340] Two factors, however, speak to the importance of the Homeric-hymnic model. First is Apollonius' placement of the Catalog immediately after the introit—a departure from the practice of Homer,[341] whose Catalog in the latter half of *Iliad* 2 occurs after the plot has already gotten well underway.[342]

---

337   Leda is the lone mother to play this role in the Catalog, which more commonly focuses on the Argonauts' fathers (Sistakou 2001: 255). Although "Aetolian" (Αἰτωλίς, 146) in origin, here she lives up to the ideals of Spartan motherhood in urging her sons on to a dangerous expedition.

338   Indeed, genealogical material in particular is standard in all Greek hymnody, as Menander Rhetor observes (1.2.5).

339   For Apollonius' imitation of (and innovation upon) the Iliadic Catalog of Ships and the briefer Trojan Catalog, see, e.g.: Kaibel 1887: 511 with n. 1; Walther 1894: 4–9; Delage 1930: ch. 2, esp. pp. 38–39; Carspecken 1952: 38–58; Levin 1971: 24–28; Kühlmann 1973: 158–167; Beye 1982: 22–23, 80–81; Clauss 1991, 1993: ch. 2; Sistakou 2001, esp. 240–252.

340   Beye (1964: 346) distinguishes between three sorts of details included in the Homeric Catalog entries: "basic information," "anecdote" (including birth narratives), and "contextual information" (that is, information relevant to the specific purpose of the catalog, such as the number of ships in a contingent).

341   Indeed, Klein (1975: 24–25) views Apollonius' decision to "[*begin*] his epic with a long catalogue of heroes" (emphasis original) as a subversion of Homeric epic in favor of "Hesiodic 'cataloguing.'" Asper (2008: 184) and Hunter (2008: 135) view this subversion as an implicit critique of the Homeric model: such catalogs rather belong at the beginning.

342   Cf. Valerius' incorporation of his Catalog of Argonauts more directly into the narrative midway through his first book (352–483), in what is often seen as a conscious improvement on Apollonius' technique (Zissos 2008: 240).

Indeed, Apollonius' decision to postpone his epic narrative proper with over 200 lines of catalog has been criticized for placing excessive demands on his readers' patience.[343] Apollonius' placement of the Catalog makes sense, however, if we take seriously the notion that the *Arg.* is cast as a kind of *Homeric Hymn to the Argonauts*, in which case the narrator qua hymnist follows standard convention in establishing his honorands' introductory details straightaway. The Catalog format is necessitated by the fact that this hymn, uniquely, is dedicated to fifty-five individual Subjects.[344] Second, we should note the distinctive way in which Apollonius' Catalog begins: "First then **let us mention** Orpheus" (πρῶτά νυν Ὀρφῆος μνησώμεθα, 1.23). I have argued in the first chapter that in *Arg.* 1.2, Apollonius uses the same verb (μνήσομαι) as an Evocatory Verb that serves to identify the Argonauts as his Hymnic Subject. The verb's recurrence here, this time with a particular Argonaut as its object, suggests that the Catalog is designed to reintroduce the Hymnic Subject now on an individual rather than a collective basis.[345] Orpheus is particularly well-chosen for this function because he himself often plays the role of hymnist elsewhere in the poem.[346]

To turn now from the Catalog: the second major correspondence between the structure of *HH* 15 and the *Arg.* concerns the properly "epic" narrative of each poem. The brief précis of Heracles' heroic career in the former (15.4–6) finds its structural correlate in the *Arg.*'s primary narrative, which, as we have seen, Apollonius himself summarizes (1.20–22) in language that recalls the Myth in *Heracles* (cf. further 4.1319–1321, 1359–1360). We have already had occasion to note that both of these Mythic narratives strikingly impute moral faults to their Hymnic Subjects (ἀτάσθαλα, *HH* 15.6; cf. ὑπέρβια ἔργα, 4.1321), despite the genre's typically laudatory agenda.[347] A broader parallel between the two poems concerns the strict limits of their narratives. Notoriously, the AR narrator stays true to his stated intention of recounting the Argonauts' "journeys on the vast sea, and all they did as they wandered" (*Arg.* 1.21–22)—no more

---

343   See, e.g.: Herter 1944–1955: 338; Toohey 1992: 71, 89; Knight 1995: 25; Scherer 2006: 3.
344   Not including the eight additional Argonauts who will join the journey later on and are thus introduced to the poem separately (McPhee 2017: 112–113).
345   The hymnic resonance of μνησώμεθα (1.23) is noted by Sistakou 2001: 259 and Scherer 2006: 78, 116, the latter of whom notes the parallel with the hymnic μνήσομαι at 1.2. Sistakou also considers the use of ἀοιδή and its derivates in the Catalog to be hymnic. For the cataloguing of the individual members of a group Hymnic Subject, cf. the roll call of the Muses in the Hymnic Proem of Hesiod's *Theogony* (77–79).
346   See particularly 4.4.
347   On the moral dimension of heroization in the *Arg.*, see conclusion, 2.2.

and no less.³⁴⁸ He begins the narrative with the heroes' preparations to depart from Iolcus and ends it the very moment they have returned to Pagasae, which marks "the glorious conclusion" both "of [their] labors" (κλυτὰ πείραθ' ... | ὑμετέρων καμάτων, 4.1775–1776) and of the poem itself.³⁴⁹ Most of the backstory for this quest must be reconstructed from stray references scattered throughout the poem, and several fundamental plot points remain in doubt.³⁵⁰ Even more pressingly, Apollonius' reticence on some of the most interesting parts of the Argonautic saga, and particularly the future of Jason and Medea's marriage, has prompted some critics to interpret the ending as arbitrary and open: "the end of the poem is no real end."³⁵¹ Scholars have detected allusions to the couple's grim future at many points in the poem, but the matter is ultimately shrouded in silence.³⁵² Instead of resolving these storylines, Apollonius' Envoi (4.1773–1781) represents a radical and sudden temporal shift: the narrator regards his protagonists no longer as belonging to the mythical past but addresses and prays to them as beings whose interests extend to the present and, indeed, the indefinite future.³⁵³ He skips, in other words, from the Argonauts' νόστος in Pagasae straight to their enduring status as immortalized heroes in his own day.

It is revealing to discover similar dynamics in the Mythic narrative of *Heracles the Lionhearted*. The hymn's summary of Heracles' heroic career focuses exclusively on the labors he undertakes at Eurystheus' behest (15.4–6). The grisly motive that traditionally impels these labors—namely, Heracles' need to expiate the murder of his children and first wife Megara (cf. *Arg.* 4.539–541)—remains unspoken. By a similar token, Heracles' fiery death—a necessary precondition to his deification—is skipped over entirely in the transition from the past tense in line 6 to the present in 7.³⁵⁴ Nevertheless, certain details, such as the hero's propensity both to commit and suffer ἀτάσθαλα and par-

---

348 See, e.g., Júnior 2021: 111–112.
349 For the labors of heroes and poet as coextensive, see 196n247.
350 E.g., must the Golden Fleece be recovered to satisfy Zeus' wrath, or is this a pretextual lie concocted by Pelias? See Berkowitz 2004: 27–42 for a thorough analysis of this problem.
351 Hunter 1993: 119; see further, e.g., Goldhill 1991: 295–297. Understandably, Jason and Medea receive the lion's share of the critics' attention, but Apollonius also forecloses on, while often hinting at, the future that lies in store for other of the Argonauts; see, e.g., McPhee, forthcoming c.
352 See 347n81.
353 Belloni 1995: 181.
354 *HH* 15 is often cited as an example of the "introduction of a new deity to Olympus" motif (e.g., Richardson 2015: 27), but in fact the narrative shifts from Heracles' mortal condition to his present-day existence in heaven without depicting the circumstances of his arrival there.

ticularly his marriage to Hebe, may bring to mind the tragic chain of events by which his (second) earthly marriage to Deianeira came to such a violent end.³⁵⁵

What motivates these pregnant silences? They do not appear to stem from a concern to avoid mentioning the ugliest incidents in their addressee's *vitae*, or at least not primarily: we have seen that both of these epic hymns are content to record their Hymnic Subjects' moral transgressions quite candidly. Instead, I would suggest that these matters are passed over because they are marginal to the logic of divinization on which these poems (qua hymns dedicated to erstwhile mortals) depend. Neither the *Arg*. nor *HH* 15 offers an explicit rationale for why their honorands have suddenly transitioned from their heroic careers to a higher ontological status, but as we have seen (2.3.3), such fates were typically regarded as rewards for the completion of heroic labors. If the focus of the Myths in these epic hymns falls squarely on their heroes' ἄεθλοι, it is because the commission of these labors is precisely what wins them the divinity that entitles them to worship in hymnody in the first place.

In the case of *Heracles*, the hymn's dualistic structure raises this very idea by juxtaposing its summary of Heracles' labors with an account of his life on Olympus, which are diametrically opposed in their details:³⁵⁶ by undergoing and overcoming the trials that typify the human condition (4–6),³⁵⁷ Heracles wins for himself the divine ease that is their opposite (7–9).³⁵⁸ In spatial terms, the superhuman scope of Heracles' wandering over the humanly accessible parts of the cosmos, which the hymnist terms ἀθέσφατον (*HH* 15.4), "beyond even a god's power to express,"³⁵⁹ qualifies him for Olympus: manifestly, he has transcended mortal limitations.³⁶⁰ The structural analogy between *HH* 15 and

---

355 Cook (1999: 149) points out that Heracles' ἀτάσθαλα may evoke such incidents as the hero's murder of his family in Thebes and the sack of Oechalia (which formed part of the preliminaries for his own death). With the mention of Hebe, cf. Hera's foreknowledge that Medea will marry Achilles in Elysium (*Arg*. 4.811–815), which implies the end of her current marriage to Jason without spelling out the circumstances of its dissolution (Byre 2002: 136).
356 See the analysis in 2.4.4.
357 For the longstanding Greek association of wandering with the human condition, affirmed by the AR narrator himself at *Arg*. 2.541–542, see Montiglio 2005, esp. ch. 3.
358 Galinsky (1972: 15) has a similar intuition: "In the hymn, Herakles' endurance leads to his acceptance into heaven."
359 LSJ s.v. Of course, the adjective also covertly excuses the hymnist from presenting a fuller account of Heracles' interminable wanderings.
360 Cf. especially Pind. *Isthm*. 4.55–60, where a description of Heracles' travels to the edges of the world on land and sea gives way to a description of his joyous life on Olympus. Elsewhere Pindar famously employs the proleptic phrase ἥρως θεός (*Nem*. 3.22) in the context

the *Arg.* suggests that, by collectively replicating Heracles' wanderings across the length of the known world, the Argonauts, too, have by their ἄεθλοι won for themselves a lower rank of divinity. It is only logical that an epic hymn dedicated to heroized mortals would take as the theme for its Myth the very glorious deeds by which its Hymnic Subjects had attained to such immortal honors as hymnody.

6 Conclusion

This chapter has sought to clarify the cultural, religious, and literary backgrounds that inform Apollonius' novel experiment in marrying together epic and hymnody within the generic framework of his singular "epic hymn." As figures of myth, Greek heroes were commemorated in epic song, à la the *Iliad* and *Odyssey*, but as divinized cult objects, they were also entitled to worship in the form of hymnody. In a substantial departure from the HEs, Apollonius recognizes both sides of this duality and self-consciously integrates the cultic dimension of Greek heroism into his epic narrative, with explicit references sprinkled throughout the *Arg.* to the postmortem worship enjoyed by a number of its characters, including, above all, its own protagonists. This divinization provides the theological basis for the *Arg.*'s "hymnic frame," which, as we saw in chapter 1, reveals the poem to be a hymn dedicated to the Argonauts themselves. The survey in section 3 identified several passages in which Apollonius appears to acknowledge this foundation for his poem's generic hybridity by commingling elements that resonate in a metapoetic key with each of the *Arg.*'s twin generic affiliations. The traditional concerns of Homeric heroism reflect the poem's "epic" character, while its hymnic identity finds expression in juxtaposed pointers toward hero cult and reverential praise.

In some ways, the merger of epic and hymnody tracked in this chapter did not actually require any great stretch of the imagination, given the close interconnections between epic poetry and Rhapsodic Hymns in terms of meter, diction, narrative style, and even certain structural features, in the case of their common introductory formulas.[361] Moreover, we have seen more than once in this chapter how Apollonius strives to demonstrate the complementarity of the

---

of the establishment of the pillars of Heracles as markers of the utmost limits of human travel by sea. Horace captures Heracles' arc succinctly in the *Odes* (*vagus Hercules* | *enisus arcis attigit igneas*, 3.3.9–10).

361 See introduction, 2.2.

traditional themes and motifs he has inherited from the HEs with those introduced by the hymnic dimension of his poem. Thus Idmon's grave is the rightful focal point both of his remembrance (an epic motif) and cult worship (a hymnic one); Polydeuces' victory over Amycus simultaneously makes for a proper epic ἀριστεία and suggests itself as a suitable Myth for the *Laudatio* of a hymn; the Argonauts' ἄεθλοι are natural subjects for epic song, but these achievements also justify the crew's heroization and subsequent worship via hymnody; and the Catalog of Argonauts belongs in the traditions of both the Iliadic Catalog of Ships and of the Exordial sections of hymns. Such insights may not have been unique to Apollonius—the survey in section 4 showed that they can be paralleled in some measure in the work of his contemporaries Callimachus and Theocritus and even traced back further to Simonides and ultimately to the *HH*s themselves. But Apollonius was unique in seizing upon this conceit as the premise for an entire four-book "epic hymn" on a truly epic scale.

The hymnic aspect of the *Arg.* largely complements rather than conflicts with its status as epic, but it also does introduce some elements and emphases that represent real departures from the models of the *Iliad* and the *Odyssey*. For instance, the *Arg.*'s extensive theme of hero cult and apotheosis, surveyed in section 2, is essentially alien to the tone and tenor of the HEs, and of the *Iliad* especially. In view of the prospect of literal immortality, both the specter of death and the promise of κλέος as compensation for death arguably lose some of their thematic purchase in the *Arg.* In this respect, Apollonius, so notorious for his "pessimism,"[362] in fact holds out a much cheerier vision of the eschatological fate of his protagonists than the severe outlook of the HEs provides.[363] But the *Arg.*'s frequent and prominent references to hero cult represent just one example of the encroachment of the poem's hymnic perspective into the epic texture of the narrative. It is to these moments of difference, in which the poem's hymnic side asserts itself in ways foreign to the HEs, that I now turn in Part 2 of this study, on the hymnic voice of the Apollonian narrator.

---

362 See, e.g.: Lawall 1966: 167–169; Paduano 1971: 67; Opelt 1978: 187–188; Clack 1982: 405; Newman 1986: 94; Grillo 1988: 39; Cuypers 2004: 53; Nelis 2005a: 361; Manuello 2012: 126–128, 134–137.

363 Cf. Griffin 1977, an influential article (referenced above, 151*n*23) that made the triviality of death one of its major critiques of the epic cycle in comparison with the HEs.

PART 2

The Apollonian Narrator's Hymnic Voice

∴

CHAPTER 3

Narratological Features with Precedent in the *Homeric Hymns*

Part 1 of this study was devoted to establishing the overarching generic affiliations of the *Arg*. I argued that the poem is framed as an "epic hymn" dedicated to the Argonauts, a conceit that exploits the duality of the Greek concept of the "hero" in order to bring together the two genres of Homeric hexameter poetry, epic and hymn, into one hybridized composition. Part 2 moves away from the poem's structural features in order to concentrate on some aspects of its content. This chapter and the next examine the poem from a narratological perspective: I consider how the hymnic dimension of the poem conditions the narrator's voice and affects his presentation of the narrative—his stylistic choices, his interests and emphases, and especially his exploitation of such devices as apostrophe and the "metaleptic" blending of the voices of narrator and character.[1] As we shall see, besides the introit and Envoi, sundry passages in the poem have been labeled "hymnic" in character in the scholarly literature, and one scholar has even claimed that "into every part of the poem [Apollonius] breathes a unity of mood …, until the whole assumes … almost the quality of a hymn."[2] The goal of these chapters is to substantiate these widespread impressions and to integrate them into a more holistic understanding of Apollonius' narratological techniques.

Happily, I am aided in this endeavor by a number of high-quality narratological studies both of the *HH*s[3] and of the *Argonautica*, which was in fact one of the first texts to receive extended narratological analysis within the discipline of Classics, in a trailblazing monograph by Fusillo.[4] The endeavor is com-

---

1   For the term "metalepsis," see 4.1.
2   Carspecken 1952: 138.
3   The chief studies are: Nünlist 2004, 2007; de Jong 2012, 2018, 2022b; Hunzinger 2012; Richardson 2015; Faulkner 2015.
4   Fusillo 1985; for its place in the history of our discipline, see de Jong 2014: 9. Studies of narrative time in the *Arg*. include Fusillo's monograph as well as: Rengakos 2004; Caneva 2007; Klooster 2007; studies of space in the poem include Thalmann 2011; Klooster 2012, 2013b. Danek 2009 and Klooster 2014 straddle both of these categories. Studies focusing on the Apollonian narrator include, *inter alia*: Grillo 1998; Albis 1996; Byre 2002; Berkowitz 2004; Cuypers 2004; Morrison 2007; Manuello 2012. See further Klooster 2018 and 2022 for narratological studies of Apollonius' methods of characterization and of representing character-speech, respectively.

plicated, conversely, by the sheer complexity of Apollonius' narratorial voice, which blends together an astonishing number of influences from the whole gamut of earlier Greek literature. Cuypers, for instance, parses Apollonius' "Protean narrative *persona*" as "an amalgam of (at least) the Homeric singer of epic, the hymnic and Pindaric singers of praise, the Herodotean historian, and the Callimachean scholar."[5] This complexity stems partly from Apollonius' well-known penchant for generic experimentation, an innovatory drive that we have already seen on full display in part I of this study. Another important factor is Apollonius' evident desire to "update" the traditional mythological epic by incorporating an enormous range of "learned" materials, drawn from the domains of science, philosophy, ethnography, geography, and beyond.[6] Even cutting-edge Alexandrian medical and physiological theories find their place in Apollonius' work.[7] Study of the Apollonian narrator is further complicated by the fact that he is in many respects a moving target, developing dynamically over the course of the poem's four books. Thus Morrison has identified a narratorial arc of increasing reliance on the authority of the Muses over the course of the poem, a phenomenon that he has called the narrator's "crisis of confidence."[8]

For all of these reasons, generalizations about the AR narrator frequently hold good only for select portions of the poem. I have argued that the *Arg.* is, from a formal point of view, an epic hymn, and thus the hymnic mode is necessarily an important ingredient in this mélange. Nevertheless, in a work so multifaceted and experimental, no single generic affiliation—not even a hybrid one—can be said to determine all of the poem's contents. Given these intricacies, in this study I do not pretend to do full justice to Apollonius' rich store of narrative modes and personas. Instead, I wish to examine only the dimension of the AR narrator that Cuypers calls "the hymnic singer of praise," in isolation from his other personalities so far as is practicable.

---

5 Cuypers 2004: 43.
6 I draw this "updating" language from Fusillo 1994: 100 ("actualiza el mito").
7 See, e.g., Solmsen 1961: 195–197.
8 Morrison 2007 (quotation at 35). Morrison provides the most thorough exposition of this idea (see esp. 286–310), but it has many antecedents in prior scholarship. Earlier scholars sensed oscillations (or, more harshly, contradictions, or even recantations) in the narrator's attitude to the Muses throughout the poem (Gercke 1889: 135–136; Eichgrün 1961: 104–107; Paduano Faedo 1970: 380 n. 9; Livrea 1971: 47–48; 1973 ad 4.1381), but it remained for later scholars to realize that these different attitudes rather reflected a diachronic development as the poem progressed (Beye 1982: 15–17; Hunter 1987: 134; Feeney 1991: 90–91; Goldhill 1991: 294; Brioso Sánchez 1995; Albis 1996: 119–120; Clare 2002: 268; Powers 2002: 99–100; Nelis 2005a: 356).

The present chapter is devoted to narrative techniques that find "Homeric" precedents not in the HEs, but in the *HH*s, including the AR narrator's conspicuous intrusions in the narrative (section 1), his loud displays of piety (section 2), his interest in etiology (section 3), and his use of assorted other devices with antecedents in the hymns (section 4). It is not always certain that the *HH*s represent the proximate influence on Apollonius' narratorial technique in each case, and some specific devices that I analyze in this chapter, like the pious apology to the gods, find only limited exemplification in the hymnic collection. By a similar token, in several cases, the various strands of Apollonius' multitextured persona appear tangled together, and one cannot be considered apart from the others. For instance, we will see that scholars have connected Apollonius' "pious silences" not only to the *Homeric Hymn to Demeter*, but also to Pindar, Herodotus, and Callimachus. I will try to make note of such cases to avoid oversimplifications. Nevertheless, the perceived Homeric authority of the hymns could have made them especially attractive models for an epic poet seeking sanction for practices that departed markedly from those of the HEs.[9] Moreover, in some cases, as in his pointing of αἴτια, Apollonius alludes to the *HH*s in such a way as to show his awareness of the precedent that they furnished for what have otherwise been regarded as his most typically "Alexandrian" affectations. Apollonius' procedure has the effect of constructing a literary genealogy: many apparently "Callimachean" elements in his narration can in fact be traced back to the influence of Homer's hymnic voice.

1   The Overt Narrator

To begin with, one of the most remarked-upon differences between the HE and AR narrators has to do with their relative prominence in their own narratives.[10] The HE narratorial persona is famously submerged. Only rarely does

---

9   To some degree, by invoking the unified category of the "HEs," my analysis flattens some of the real differences in narrative technique that separate the *Iliad* and the *Odyssey* (cf., e.g., Rengakos 2004 for considerations on how the *Arg*.'s linear storytelling strategies relate differently to each of these models). Nevertheless, it is my hope that this chapter's focus on precisely those narrative devices that find no firm precedent in *either* of these poems reduces some of the risk of unduly homogenizing Homer's epics.

10 Indeed, Fusillo (1985: 383) views the greater prominence of the AR narrator as Apollonius' most radical innovation vis-à-vis the HEs, which he sums up as a transformation of an "onniscienza neutra" into an "onniscienza dell'autore-editore." On this difference between the HE and AR narrators, see further, e.g.: Beye 1982: 18; Grillo 1988: 13 and ch. 1 *passim*;

he draw attention to himself as narrator or focalizer; when he does, it is primarily through such devices as Appeals to the Muses, apostrophes, or the occasional use of editorializing language such as νήπιος ("fool"), which he otherwise restricts to character-text.[11] To be sure, no story tells itself, and the HE narrator can always be seen behind the scenes, masterfully manipulating his audience's responses to the narrative. For the most part, however, he does so in an indirect way, by implication, rather than asserting his own point of view as a character might.[12]

If the HE narrator is thus "covert," the AR narrator is decidedly "overt"—one of those narrators who "refer to themselves and their narrating activity, tell us about themselves, and openly comment upon their story."[13] For instance, the Alexandrian poem ostentatiously commences in the first person (ἀρχόμενος ... μνήσομαι, 1.1–2),[14] and the narrator's personal control over the enunciation is further reinforced by first-person references in line 20 (νῦν δ' ἂν ἐγώ ... μυθησαίμην) and by the deferral of the (third-person) Appeal to the Muses until line 22 (Μοῦσαι δ' ὑποφήτορες εἶεν ἀοιδῆς).[15] The AR narrator continues to assert his

---

Hunter 1993: 101–119; Cuypers 2004: 43; Rutherford 2005: 32–33; Morrison 2007: 271–272; Stürner 2022: 56–59.

11 See on this score the useful overviews in Richardson 1990: chs. 6 and esp. 7; de Jong 2004b: 13–18.

12 So de Jong 2004b: 17–18. See further Minchin 1999: 60–62 on the distinction between explicit "external evaluation," which the HE narrator generally avoids, and the indirect mode of "internal evaluation," which he favors.

13 De Jong, Nünlist, and Bowie 2004: xvii.

14 See, e.g., Goldhill 1991: 287: "It is ... significant that the beginning word of the epic is 'beginning'. It focuses attention on the act of narration; and this self-reflexiveness is without doubt programmatic." Petrovic (2012: 164, 170) considers this first-person manner of beginning a poem another feature of the *HHs* that influenced the Hellenistic poets; see further Morrison 2007: 287.

15 See, e.g.: Zyroff 1971: 46–47; Clare 2002: 261–268; Fantuzzi and Hunter 2004: 119; Morrison 2007: 287; Júnior 2021: 110. Of course, on some interpretations of the wish in 1.22, Apollonius might even envision a startlingly untraditional "inversione del rapporto poeta-Musa" (Paduano Faedo 1970) that would make the goddesses positively subordinate to the AR narrator. For a reading along these lines that regards Apollonius' phrase as an instance of *oppositio in imitando* subverting the Muses' epithet ἵστορες ᾠδῆς at *HH* 32.2, see Romeo 1985: 105. It is beyond the scope of the present analysis to intervene in the longstanding debate over the significance of Apollonius' controversial prayer. For a careful overview of the problem, see Morrison 2007: 286–293. To briefly lay out my own sympathies: I find myself increasingly convinced by the view that the Muses serve as the "interpreters" (ὑποφήτορες) not of the narrator, but of the oracular-poetic god Apollo as invoked at *Arg.* 1.1 (Albis 1996: 20–22; González 2000; Köhnken 2000: 56–57; Cerri 2007; Klooster 2011: 217–222; Schaaf 2014: 39–41; Bauer 2017: 69 n. 71)—but I would register two caveats. First, this reading typically assumes an "inspiration" interpretation of Apollo's

control over the narrative with first-person verbs in the Catalog (μνησώμεθα, 23; πευθόμεθ', 123; ἴδμεν, 135) and beyond,[16] and, in sum, throughout the poem he frequently breaks the "epic illusion"[17] and draws attention to himself qua narrator in the act of narrating through such multifarious devices as Appeals to the Muses, apostrophe,[18] second-person addresses to the narratee,[19] his citation of sources (especially via the so-called Alexandrian footnote),[20] the use of interactional particles such as που in his own voice,[21] instances of mise-en-abyme,[22] and even explicit metapoetic commentary on his own song.[23] Most of these devices find some precedent in the HEs, but their relative frequency and conspicuousness in the *Arg.* are in each case considerably higher. For instance, the AR narrator occasionally pronounces his characters νήπιοι (2.66, 137; 4.875) or σχέτλιοι (1.1302; 3.1133; 4.916, 1524; cf. 4.445) in the HE manner, but he also uses a wide range of other affective terms that the HEs would restrict to character-text.[24] Likewise, the AR narrator's apostrophes are not only proportionally more common, but they can be maintained for many more lines than the HE narrator would allow.[25]

---

invocation at *Arg.* 1.1, which, as we have seen in chapter 1, is not inevitable (cf. Morrison 2007: 291). Second, the immediate context of 1.18–22 emphatically foregrounds the narratorial *ego*, whereas Apollo has not been in view since line 8; it is understandable, then, that many readers have assumed that subordination (ὑπο-) to the narrator is at issue (Borgogno 2002: 13). Ultimately, because ὑποφήτορες is modified by an abstract genitive (ἀοιδῆς) rather than a personal one (cf. Giangrande 1968: 55 n. 9) and because no dative of advantage is present, the (network of) relationship(s) with the Muses presupposed by this wish remains unclear—perhaps provocatively so (cf. Morrison 2007: 291–292).

16 The narrator's use of the first person is catalogued by De Martino 1984–1985: 113–114.
17 I borrow the terminology of Bassett 1938.
18 The AR narrator's Appeals to the Muses and apostrophes are catalogued and discussed in Grillo 1988: ch. 1.
19 For second-person addresses to the narratee, see Byre 1991.
20 See, e.g., Cuypers 2004: 49–51.
21 See: Hunter 1993: 108–109; Cuypers 2004: 51, 56; 2005: 41–45; Morrison 2007: 275–278.
22 See Fusillo 1985: 361–363.
23 Beyond the introits and the end of the poem (where metapoetic commentary is expected), see *Arg.* 1.648–649, 1220; 4.451.
24 See, e.g., Zyroff 1971: 309–313; Hunter 1993: 107–113, 118; Morrison 2007: 271 n. 4, 284–286. See also Hunter 1993: 104–106 and Morrison 2007: 281–282 on the AR narrator's γνῶμαι cast in the first person, in contrast to HE practice.
25 Grillo (1988: 41) considers Apollonius' long apostrophes perhaps his most important narratorial innovation, and he points to the *HH*s as well as Callimachus' hymns as potential models (46 n. 115). See further Klooster 2013a: 159: "Apollonius' use of apostrophe … is markedly different from that of Homer, and in fact more aligned with hymnic practice."

The AR narrator's conspicuous interventions in the narrative have been well studied, so I hardly need to catalog them all here.[26] Rather, I would like to underline the overtness of another "Homeric" narrator who exhibits much greater affinities with his counterpart in the *Arg.*, namely, the narrator (or, more rightly, narrators) of the *HH*s. As Bing observes apropos of Callimachus, the *HH*s "provided the only 'Homeric' model that permitted the unmediated involvement of the poet's persona apart from the formulaic first person of the opening and closing of the poem."[27] The *HH*s collectively foreshadow the overtness of the AR narrator in several respects, such as an increased tendency vis-à-vis the HEs to use evaluative language,[28] but the hymn that Bing has particularly in mind is the long *Homeric Hymn to Apollo*. As he observes, after their Exordia and before their Envois, most of the *HH*s resemble the HEs in their general lack of first- or second-person references.[29] The *Hymn to Apollo*, however, exhibits a number of narratological usages that are more or less unique within the collection:[30]

– Frequent narratorial deployment of the first person (19, 166, 174, 177, 207, 208), even outside the bounds of the Exordium (1) and Envoi (546).
– Regular and in some cases extensive apostrophes to Apollo (19–29, 120, 127–129, 140–149, 179–181, 207–215), Leto (14), and the Delian maidens (166–167, 171, 174), even before the Envoi (545–546). Furthermore, the narrative of Apollo's search for a suitable location for his temple is almost entirely cast in Du-Stil (216–246, 277–282).[31]

---

26   In addition to the studies cited in the previous notes, many of these phenomena are surveyed as well in Beye 1982: ch. 1; Fusillo 1985: ch. III.B.
27   Bing 2009: 34–35; this observation's applicability to Apollonius as well is noted by Petrovic (2012: 155 n. 29). Likewise for Redondo (2000: 131 n. 8), "The Homeric Hymns provide a clear model" for the greater prominence of Apollonius' narratorial persona. See further: Bornmann 1968: xxiv–xxvi; Grillo 1988: 58 n. 156; Hunter 1993: 116. De Hoz (1998: 50) considers the increased prominence of the first person a "lyric" feature that the *Homeric Hymns* share in common with Cultic Hymnody.
28   Hunter 1993: 110, drawing on Kraup 1948.
29   See also Nünlist 2004: 36.
30   For the anomalous narrative strategies of this hymn, see Nünlist 2004, esp. 40–42. The same author comments in another article, "The *Hymn to Apollo* really is a narrative text *sui generis*" (2007: 54). For its influence on Callimachus' hymnic voice, see Vamvouri Ruffy 2004: 53.
31   This second-person travel catalog is reminiscent of the final lines of the *Arg.* (4.1775–1781); see also 4.1706. Nünlist (2004: 36) notes that the fragmentary *Homeric Hymn to Dionysus* seems to have employed Du-Stil much as the *Hymn to Apollo* does, as one of the fragments includes a stretch of six lines in this mode (1A.2–7). See further on these features Hunzinger 2012: 41–43, 54–58. In addition, the non-narrative *HH*s 21, 24, and 29 are cast entirely in Du-Stil, and 30.4–16 features a lengthy apostrophe to Gaia before the Envoi.

- The address of two rhetorical questions to Apollo himself (not the Muses) about the direction that the narrative should take (19, 207–208).[32]
- The inclusion of a remarkable *sphragis* that identifies the author as a blind man from Chios, that is, as Homer (166–178).

These narrative strategies may be anomalous within the collection, but there is good reason to think that Apollonius would have paid special regard to the major *Hymn to Apollo*, as indeed his older contemporary Callimachus had certainly done.[33] The hymn's *sphragis* amounts to a claim to Homeric authorship (credited by Thuc. 3.104.5) that would certainly have attracted the attention of a Homeric scholar like Apollonius. Moreover, we have seen in chapter 1 that there is strong evidence that Apollonius alludes to this passage in the context of Orpheus' own hymn to Apollo (*HH* 3.165 ~ *Arg.* 2.708) as well as in his own introit (*HH* 3.160 ~ *Arg.* 1.1–2). We also saw that a case can be made for reworkings of other elements in the passage in the final Envoi to the Argonauts (esp. 4.1773–1775), not to mention other more or less probable allusions to other parts of the hymn (*HH* 3.1 ~ *Arg.* 1.1–2, and perhaps *HH* 3.14 ~ *Arg.* 4.1411, both featuring postponed ὦ).[34] There are, to be sure, overt narrators in a great deal of Greek poetry,[35] but the *Homeric Hymn to Apollo* provides a flamboyant example in Archaic hexameter poetry with a claim to Homeric authorship.[36] In the following section, we will see that some of the specific devices by which the AR narrator inserts himself into his narrative can indeed be traced back to the *HH*s.

2   The Narrator's Piety

Among the clearest manifestations of the AR narrator's hymnic voice are the assorted passages that seem to advertise his piety or his expertise in matters

---

32   Both questions are examples of the ἀπορία topos: the hymnist struggles to isolate just one of the innumerable themes with which he could praise the god. See Race 1982a: 6–8; Miller 1986: 20–21, 70–71.

33   As Hunter (2006a: 25) remarks, "Callimachus himself reworked the *Homeric Hymn to Apollo* no less than three times in his hymns to Apollo, Artemis, and Delos."

34   For potential Apollonian allusions to this passage in Orpheus' hymn, see 131; in the introit, see 109, 113; in the Envoi, see 1.2.3. For potential allusions to *HH* 3.1 and 14, see 88–89 and 127–128, respectively.

35   Morrison (2007: 271–272, 280) associates the overtness of the AR narrator with Theocritus and especially Callimachus, particularly where his scholarly persona is concerned. The allusion to Hes. *Op.* 10 at *Arg.* 1.20 (see 113) might also programmatically flag Hesiod as an important model for the overt AR narrator.

36   Notably, Cuypers (2004: 43) also connects the overtness of the AR narrator to the *Homeric Hymn to Apollo*.

of cult and theology. This aspect of the AR narrator's persona may not seem especially striking given that the HE narrator is hardly impious himself. For instance, the HE narrator constantly shows the reverence due to the gods through his abundant use of divine epithets, which (like his use of epithets in general) is much more extensive than Apollonius'.[37] From time to time, the HE narrator voices pious sentiments *in propria persona* (e.g., "But ever is the mind of Zeus stronger than that of men" [ἀλλ' αἰεί τε Διὸς κρείσσων νόος ἠέ περ ἀνδρῶν, *Il.* 16.688]),[38] and he is intimately acquainted with the particulars of Greek sacrificial ritual (e.g., *Il.* 1.458–474). Nevertheless, in several respects, the AR narrator goes beyond Homeric practice in his pious self-fashioning. For instance, in his numerous etiological digressions, the AR narrator exhibits an interest in cultic practice per se unlike anything in HE narrator-text; he is not afraid to offer vocal criticisms of his characters for their impiety;[39] his use of expressions like ἧ θέμις (ἐστί), which the HE narrator limits to character-text,[40] positions him as a competent arbiter of correct ritual usages; and he chooses the (reformed) seer Phineus to serve as one of his most prominent narratorial "alter egos," in addition to more traditional avatars like the bardic Orpheus (in the manner of Homer's Demodocus).[41]

Once again, Apollonius is far from alone in constructing a pious persona for his narrator. For instance, with regard to the AR narrator's proclivity to voice his moral and emotional reactions to his own narrative, Morrison observes that Apollonius' "moralising persona recalls those we find in Hesiod, Archaic mon-

---

37 See the Appendix.
38 For narratorial γνῶμαι in the HEs, see, e.g., Lardinois 1997: 230–232.
39 E.g., the narrator repeatedly underlines the ὕβρις of Amycus and the Bebrycians in *Arg.* 2.1–129. As Cuypers (2004: 61) observes, "Congruous with his aim of 'hymning' the Argonauts ..., the narrator shows a strong awe for the gods and for the heroes of the past about whom he narrates, and an outspoken disapproval of those who oppose either."
40 Morrison 2007: 271 n. 3. The AR narrator uses such expressions twice each to describe libation offerings (1.517, 4.1129), funerary rites (1.1061, 2.840), and foreign customs (2.1174, 3.205; for these usages, see Morrison 2020: 89–90). See also 1.921 (where θέμις is used of maintaining mystic secrecy), 960 (of a dedication), 1035 (in a gnome about the ineluctability of destiny); 2.1019 (of thing proper to do in public); 4.479 (of the μασχαλισμός ritual), 700 (of purification for bloodguilt), 1511 (of uttering an irreverent hyperbole). It is debatable who speaks line 2.709 (of Apollo's unshorn hair); see 4.4.3.
41 For Phineus as a surrogate for the narrator, see McPhee 2018: 62–63, with earlier bibliography. Note that Orpheus, too, is a spiritual guide to the Argonauts; for his status as a narratorial alter ego, see 327n217. Vergados (2013: 13–14) identifies interesting precedents for narratorial alter egos in the major *Homeric Hymns*; on Hermes in *HH* 4 in particular, see further the bibliography at Walter 2020: 73 n. 134.

ody, elegy, *iambos*, and in Pindar."[42] In the analysis that follows, I try to keep this rich literary background in mind in assessing some of the passages in which the AR narrator's piety is most to the fore. My primary purpose, however, is to establish that an important place in this background is occupied by the *HH*s, which establish Homeric precedent for each of the narratorial experiments surveyed here.

2.1   Pious Similes

Apollonius often introduces alternatives into the vehicle of his similes to suggest the arbitrariness of any given comparison, as in his famous likening of Medea's fluttering heart to a shifting sunbeam "as it leaps from water freshly poured into a cauldron **or perhaps** into a bucket" (ὕδατος ἐξανιοῦσα, τὸ δὴ νέον ἠὲ λέβητι | ἠέ που ἐν γαυλῷ κέχυται, *Arg.* 3.757–758).[43] In certain passages with a divine vehicle, however, Apollonius takes this mannerism to the extreme by listing two, three, four, or even seven alternate cult places or other typical haunts, to or from any of which the god might be traveling. Each of the poem's major characters (including the Argonauts as a collective) receives their own such simile:[44]

---

42   Morrison 2007: 273. At 280–284 he particularly emphasizes Pindar as a model for the AR narrator's projection of moral authority.
43   There is HE precedent for this device (Schellert 1885: 15 n. 2); see, e.g., *Il.* 2.460 or 4.142.
44   Studies of epic similes often classify them according to type of vehicle, so that most of the similes listed here are grouped with passages such as *Arg.* 1.636, 2.38–40, or 3.1282–1283 (all with "mythological" vehicles), whereas my passage 2 might be grouped separately because of its strictly "human" vehicle (e.g.: Goodwin 1891: 2–3; Kerekes 1913; Wilkins 1920). This approach obscures the connections among these four "pious similes," which are only rarely recognized as a distinctive subtype of simile based on their geographic content and style (Bulloch 1985 ad Callim. *Hymn* 5.60–65; Hunter 1989 ad *Arg.* 3.1240–1245; see also: Schellert 1885: 15 with n. 2; Broeniman 1989: 69 n. 160, 73–74, 83–84). Nevertheless, interconnections between individual similes within this group, especially passages 1 and 4, are commonly noted: see, e.g.: Kofler 1890: 24–25 with n. 51, 51–52; Walther 1894: 103; Kerekes 1913: 405; Faerber 1932: 49; Drögemüller 1956: 127–128; James 1981: 76; Stanzel 1999: 267 n. 64; Niedergang-Janon 2002: 212. More particularly, passages 1 and 2 are often connected as matching Apolline similes; see, e.g.: Clausing 1913: 43–44; Carspecken 1952: 96–97; Fusillo 1985: 344 n. 14. Similarly, passages 1 and 3 are frequently read as a thematic pairing as well (Jason: Medea: Apollo: Artemis); see, e.g.: Newman 1986: 85; Broeniman 1989: 80–81; Nelis 1991: 102; Natzel 1992: 71 n. 139; Nyberg 1992: 119–120; Pietsch 1999: 236 n. 253; Stanzel 1999: 267; 68n312. Adaptations in the *Aeneid* suggest that Vergil already perceived the complementarity of passages 1 and 2 as well as 1 and 3; see, e.g., Nelis 2001: 133, 135.

1) Jason departs from his home for Pagasae (*Arg.* 1.307–311):

οἷος δ' ἐκ νηοῖο θυώδεος εἶσιν Ἀπόλλων
Δῆλον ἀν' ἠγαθέην ἠὲ Κλάρον, ἢ ὅ γε Πυθὼ
ἢ Λυκίην εὐρεῖαν ἐπὶ Ξάνθοιο ῥοῇσιν·
310 τοῖος ἀνὰ πληθὺν δήμου κίεν, ὦρτο δ' ἀυτὴ
κεκλομένων ἄμυδις.

And as Apollo goes from his fragrant temple **through holy Delos or Claros, or through Pytho or broad Lycia by the streams of Xanthus**, so [Jason] went through the crowd of people, and a shout went up as they cheered with one voice.[45]

2) The Argonauts depart from Pagasae (*Arg.* 1.536–541):

οἱ δ', ὥς τ' ἠίθεοι Φοίβῳ χορὸν ἢ ἐνὶ Πυθοῖ
ἤ που ἐν Ὀρτυγίῃ ἢ ἐφ' ὕδασιν Ἰσμηνοῖο
στησάμενοι, φόρμιγγος ὑπαὶ περὶ βωμὸν ὁμαρτῇ
ἐμμελέως κραιπνοῖσι πέδον ῥήσσωσι πόδεσσιν·
540 ὣς οἱ ὑπ' Ὀρφῆος κιθάρῃ πέπληγον ἐρετμοῖς
πόντου λάβρον ὕδωρ, ἐπὶ δὲ ῥόθια κλύζοντο.

And they, as when young men form a chorus to honor Phoebus **either in Pytho, or perhaps in Ortygia, or by the waters of Ismenus**, and around the altar to the lyre's accompaniment with swift feet they beat the ground all together in rhythm—thus to the accompaniment of Orpheus' lyre did they smite the rushing water of the sea with their oars, and the surge washed over the blades.[46]

---

45 Clarus is not mentioned in the HEs, but appears as Apollo's cult site at *HH* 9.5 (see also *HH* 3.40, Callim. *Hymn* 2.70). Lycia and Delos occur in a list of Apollo's sanctuaries at *HH* 3.179–181 (adduced ad loc. by: Wellauer 1828; Mooney 1912; Campbell 1981; and Vasilaros 2004; see also Vian 2002: 1.64 n. 2). The "fragrant temple" of line 307 finds a direct model in *HH* 2.385 (νηοῖο ... θυώδεος, of Demeter's temple at Eleusis). κεκλομένων reinforces the religious coloring of the passage, as this verb can be used to denote divine Invocation (as at *Arg.* 3.1211). Beyond the *HH*s, our passage also likely alludes to Ananius fr. 1, a parodic prayer to Apollo summoning him from various of his cult sites, including Delos, Pytho, and Clarus; see McPhee 2022.

46 The hymnic resonance of these lines is enhanced by Apollonius' allusive recombination of *Il.* 18.567, 569–572 (the description of the Linus-song on the shield of Achilles) with *HH* 3.510, 516–517 (Apollo's priests process to his temple, singing the paean). The phrase ἐν

3) Medea drives to meet Jason at Hecate's temple (*Arg.* 3.876–886):

οἵη δὲ λιαροῖσιν ἐφ' ὕδασι Παρθενίοιο,
ἠὲ καὶ Ἀμνισοῖο λοεσσαμένη ποταμοῖο
χρυσείοις Λητωὶς ἐφ' ἅρμασιν ἑστηυῖα
ὠκείαις κεμάδεσσι διεξελάῃσι κολώνας,
880 τηλόθεν ἀντιόωσα πολυκνίσου ἑκατόμβης·
τῇ δ' ἅμα νύμφαι ἕπονται ἀμορβάδες, αἱ μὲν ἀπ' αὐτῆς
ἀγρόμεναι πηγῆς Ἀμνισίδος, αἱ δὲ λιποῦσαι
ἄλσεα καὶ σκοπιὰς πολυπίδακας· ἀμφὶ δὲ θῆρες
κνυζηθμῷ σαίνουσιν ὑποτρομέοντες ἰοῦσαν·
885 ὣς αἵ γ' ἐσσεύοντο δι' ἄστεος, ἀμφὶ δὲ λαοὶ
εἶκον ἀλευάμενοι βασιληΐδος ὄμματα κούρης.

And as when **by the warm waters of Parthenius, or after bathing in the Amnisus river**, Leto's daughter stands in her golden chariot drawn by swift deer and drives through the hills, coming from afar to partake of a savory hecatomb, and with her follow nymphs in attendance—some gathering **from the very source of the Amnisus, others having left groves and peaks with many springs**—and all around wild animals fawn on her, cowering with whimpers as she makes her way; thus did they hasten through the city, and all around them the people gave way as they avoided the eyes of the royal maiden.[47]

4) Aeetes rides to the field of Ares to watch Jason's ordeal (*Arg.* 3.1240–1244):

Ὀρτυγίη (537) occurs in the same *sedes* at *HH* 3.16, which contrasts Ortygia as Artemis' birthplace with Delos as Apollo's. Apollonius' adaptation (if that is what it is) may be meant to affirm his view, shared by Callimachus and others (see Williams 1978 ad Callim. *Hymn* 2.59), that these were alternate names for the same island; see also *Arg.* 1.419, 4.1705.

47 This simile alludes to *HH* 5.68–74, and line 878 alludes to *HH* 2.431 as well as Callim. *Hymn* 3.110–112; see McPhee 2021a: 253, 261–263. In addition, line 884 likely adapts *HH* 3.2 (a description of the trembling that Artemis' brother Apollo inspires at his coming). The categorization of the nymphs by typical haunt in *Arg.* 3.881–883 recurs in a non-simile context in 1.1226–1229. Similar passages occur at *Il.* 20.9–10, *Od.* 6.123–124, *HH* 5.97–99 (n.b. σκοπιῇ in line 100). The fact that the simile begins without choosing between the Parthenius or the Amnnisus (*Arg.* 3.876–877) but goes on to take the Amnisus for granted (882) is a good illustration of the "continuity of thought" principle (Nünlist 2004: 41 n. 20), according to which the poet embraces the most recently mentioned alternative.

1240 οἷος δ' Ἴσθμιον εἶσι Ποσειδάων ἐς ἀγῶνα
     ἅρμασιν ἐμβεβαώς, ἢ Ταίναρον ἢ ὅ γε Λέρνης
     ὕδωρ ἠὲ καὶ ἄλσος Ὑαντίου Ὀγχηστοῖο,
     καί τε Καλαύρειαν μετὰ δὴ θαμὰ νίσσεται ἵπποις,
     Πέτρην θ' Αἱμονίην ἢ δενδρήεντα Γεραιστόν·
1245 τοῖος ἄρ' Αἰήτης Κόλχων ἀγὸς ἦεν ἰδέσθαι.

Like Poseidon, when he goes **to the Isthmian games** mounted in his chariot, **or to Taenarus or Lerna's waters or to his precinct at Hyantian Onchestus**, and often travels with his horses **to Calaurea and Haemonian Petra or forested Geraestus**—such was Aeetes, leader of the Colchians, to behold.[48]

Apollonius found some precedent for this device in the HEs: one of the models for passage 3 is the famous simile comparing Nausicaa to Artemis, in which the goddess is imagined hunting "along the ridges **of lofty Taygetus or Erymanthus**" (κατ' οὔρεα ... ἢ κατὰ Τηΰγετον περιμήκετον ἢ Ἐρύμανθον, *Od.* 6.102–103).[49] But Apollonius' adaptations differ quantitatively[50] and, more importantly, qualitatively from this HE model because of their religious content,[51] and especially the listing of a god's various sanctuaries, which "gives the simile[s] a tone of prayer."[52] Indeed, it is common to invoke a god by their several

---

48   ἅρμασιν ἐμβεβαώς (1241) echoes *Il.* 5.199 almost exactly (ἅρμασιν ἐμβεβαῶτα), but the synonymous ἵπποις ἐμβεβαώς occurs in the same *sedes* at *HH* 31.9 (Helius rides in his chariot) and is a much richer parallel in context, because Aeetes' resemblance to his father Helius has been pointed up just a few lines earlier (*Arg.* 3.1228–1230). ἄλσος ... Ὀγχηστοῖο in line 1242 echoes two nearly identical lines, *Il.* 2.506 and *HH* 3.230, but the latter may connect more significantly to the Apollonian context because: 1) it describes the travel of a god (Apollo) to Onchestus; and 2) this passage introduces a digression on a religious ritual in which chariots are dedicated to Poseidon.

49   See, e.g., Hunter 1989 ad *Arg.* 3.876–877, 1993: 78 n. 14. Another probable model is Callim. *Hymn* 5.60–65, which features the motif of a goddess riding to cult places that are listed disjunctively, just as in passages 3 and 4; see Bulloch 1985 ad loc. See also Callim. *Hymn* 3.170–176 (a disjunctive list of cult sites where nymphs dance for Artemis), which is closer to passage 2 (DeForest 1994: 43 n. 16).

50   Händel (1954: 59 n. 1) notes that the HEs never list more than two or three alternatives in a simile.

51   Even in passage 3, which naturally is closest to the HE model, Artemis is no longer hunting but is participating in her cult, traveling to one of her temples to partake of a sacrifice. Moreover, passage 3 gains in religious solemnity from its intratextual correspondence to these other "pious similes," especially passage 1; see 239n44.

52   DeForest 1994: 49. See further 43 as well as, e.g.: Drögemüller 1956: 128, 232; Broeniman 1989: 69 n. 159; Hunter 1989 ad *Arg.* 3.3.876–877, 1240–1245. Gillies (1928 ad *Arg.* 3.1244)

domains, as in the prayer to Pan in Thyrsis' Daphnis song in Theocritus' first *Idyll*: "O Pan, Pan, **whether** you are on the high mountains of Lycaeus **or** are ranging over great Maenalus, come to the island of Sicily."[53] This device pleases and flatters the deity by mentioning their favorite domains, and it may also emphasize the devotee's personal connection to the god in one of their local aspects, as in Chryses' prayer to Apollo as ruler of Chryse, Cilla, and Tenedos at the beginning of the *Iliad* (1.37–38).[54] Often, as in the Theocritean example, this device serves the practical function of summoning the god to come or to hearken to the prayer from wherever they may be.[55]

Apollonius' similes differ from these passages, however, in that these latter occur in character-text, not in primary narration. For this reason, Apollonius' similes bear more direct comparison to the Attributive Sections of a hymn, in Janko's terminology—those sections that describe the god in terms of "appearance, possessions, haunts and spheres of activity," generally using the same omnitemporal present tense characteristic of the epic simile.[56] In addition to the verbal parallels recorded in the footnotes on the previous pages, the general motif of a god's regular travel to or from their cult sites recurs several times in the *HH* corpus. Here, I would point to just one example that may have caught Apollonius' eye, the shorter *Homeric Hymn to Artemis* (9):

Ἄρτεμιν ὕμνει, Μοῦσα, κασιγνήτην Ἑκάτοιο,
παρθένον ἰοχέαιραν, ὁμότροφον Ἀπόλλωνος,
ἥ θ' ἵππους ἄρσασα βαθυσχοίνοιο Μέλητος
ῥίμφα διὰ Σμύρνης παγχρύσεον ἅρμα διώκει
5   ἐς Κλάρον ἀμπελόεσσαν, ὅθ' ἀργυρότοξος Ἀπόλλων
ἧσται μιμνάζων ἑκατηβόλον Ἰοχέαιραν.
καὶ σὺ μὲν οὕτω χαῖρε θεαί θ' ἅμα πᾶσαι ἀοιδῇ·
αὐτὰρ ἐγὼ σέ τε πρῶτα καὶ ἐκ σέθεν ἄρχομ' ἀείδειν.

Sing, Muse, of Artemis, sister of the Far-shooter, the virgin profuse of arrows, fellow nursling of Apollo; who after watering her horses at the

---

particularly compares Apollonius' tendency to pile up cult epithets in certain passages; see the discussion of "hymnic narratization" in the next chapter.
53   Theoc. *Id.* 1.123–125 (ὦ Πὰν Πάν, εἴτ' ἐσσὶ κατ' ὤρεα μακρὰ Λυκαίω, | εἴτε τύγ' ἀμφιπολεῖς μέγα Μαίναλον, ἔνθ' ἐπὶ νᾶσον | τὰν Σικελάν ...).
54   Race 1982a: 10 n. 18.
55   See, e.g.: Bulloch 1985 ad Callim. *Hymn* 5.60–65; Furley and Bremer 2001: 1.54–55.
56   Janko 1981: 11. For this feature of the *HHs*, see de Jong 2012: 41. For the "omnitemporal present tense," see 13*n*69.

reedy Meles drives her chariot all of gold swiftly through Smyrna to vine-terraced Claros, where silverbow Apollo sits awaiting the far-shooting one, the profuse of arrows. And so hail to you in my song and to all goddesses as well! With you and from you I begin my song.

From a literary-historical perspective, this hymn's significance lies in the subtle claim to Homeric authorship constituted by the mention of the Smyrnean Meles River (3–4)—one of the traditional birthplaces of Homer, but mentioned nowhere else in early Greek epic.[57] For this reason alone, it might have drawn Apollonius' critical attention. As noted in the footnote to passage 1 above, Clarus is never mentioned in the HEs, but it appears in this hymn as one of Apollo's cult sites (5), thus justifying, perhaps, its inclusion in the list of Apollo's cult sites at *Arg.* 1.308.[58] But I would particularly connect this hymn with passage 3: both passages envision Artemis' riding in a golden chariot from a river to a cult site.[59] Especially intriguing is the notion that Artemis is riding to meet Apollo. In the context of *Arg.* 3, Medea is in fact on her way to meet Jason, who had himself been likened to none other than Apollo in the first of these "pious similes" (passage 1); and as we have seen, that passage has in common with our hymn a rare mention of the Apolline cult site of Clarus.[60] If I am right to see connections between this unassuming hymn and passages 1 and 3, it may be that Apollonius is signaling that such Attributive Sections in the *HH*s constitute one of his models for this unique subgroup of similes.

2.2   *Pious Silences*

In two passages, the AR narrator describes the Argonauts' participation in religious rites whose particulars he refuses to divulge:

---

57   See 18n94.
58   As I demonstrate in detail in McPhee 2022, Clarus was not commonly included in lists of Apollo's major cult places before the oracle's heyday in the Imperial period. Most likely its appearance at *Arg.* 1.308 owes to Ananius' mention of it in his first fragment (ibid.), but its Homeric attestation in *HH* 9 could have proved serendipitous as Apollonius sought to forge subtextual connections between passages 1 and 3; see below.
59   But note that Apollonius has replaced the rather masculine motif of Artemis' watering her horses (*HH* 9.3) with the more erotically charged (and potentially dangerous) motif of Artemis' bathing (*Arg.* 3.877; Knight 1995: 237 with n. 353). He has also replaced Artemis' horses with (more specifically Dianic) deer, with a probable nod toward Callim. *Hymn* 3.110–112. Artemis also rides to Delphi, another of Apollo's cult sites, in *HH* 27, where she leads a dance among the Muses and Graces.
60   There is a reversal, however, in that whereas Apollo waits for Artemis at his own temple in the hymn (6), it will be Medea who waits for Jason at her own temple in the *Arg.* (3.948–956).

1) The Argonauts are initated into the Samothracian Mysteries (*Arg.* 1.915–921):

915 ἑσπέριοι δ᾿ Ὀρφῆος ἐφημοσύνῃσιν ἔκελσαν
νῆσον ἐς Ἠλέκτρης Ἀτλαντίδος, ὄφρα δαέντες
ἀρρήτους ἀγανῇσι τελεσφορίῃσι θέμιστας
σωότεροι κρυόεσσαν ὑπεὶρ ἅλα ναυτίλλοιντο.
τῶν μὲν ἔτ᾿ οὐ προτέρω μυθήσομαι, ἀλλὰ καὶ αὐτὴ
920 νῆσος ὁμῶς κεχάροιτο καὶ οἳ λάχον ὄργια κεῖνα
δαίμονες ἐνναέται, τὰ μὲν οὐ θέμις ἄμμιν ἀείδειν.

At evening, on Orpheus' instructions, they put in at the island of Electra, Atlas' daughter, so that by learning secret rites through gentle initiations they might sail more safely over the chilling sea. Of these things, however, I shall speak no further, but bid farewell to the island itself and to the local divinities, to whom belong those mysteries of which I am forbidden to sing.

2) The Argonauts propitiate Hecate beside the Halys (4.244–252):

ἠοῖ ἐνὶ τριτάτῃ πρυμνήσια νηὸς ἔδησαν
245 Παφλαγόνων ἀκτῇσι πάροιθ᾿ Ἅλυος ποταμοῖο·
ἡ γάρ σφ᾿ ἐξαποβάντας ἀρέσσασθαι θυέεσσιν
ἠνώγει Ἑκάτην. καὶ δὴ τὰ μέν, ὅσσα θυηλὴν
κούρη πορσανέουσα τιτύσκετο—μήτε τις ἴστωρ
εἴη μήτ᾿ ἐμὲ θυμὸς ἐποτρύνειεν ἀείδειν—
250 ἅζομαι αὐδῆσαι· τό γε μὴν ἔδος ἐξέτι κείνου,
ὅ ῥα θεᾷ ἥρωες ἐπὶ ῥηγμῖσιν ἔδειμαν,
ἀνδράσιν ὀψιγόνοισι μένει καὶ τῆμος ἰδέσθαι.

On the third morning they secured their ship's cables to the shore of the Paphlagonians at the mouth of the Halys river, because Medea ordered them to disembark and propitiate Hecate with sacrifices. Now all the things that the girl prepared in order to carry out the sacrifice—may no one know them, nor may my heart urge me to sing of them—I dread to tell, and yet from that time the sanctuary which the heroes built on the shore for the goddess remains even to this day for later generations to see.

In both of these passages, the Argonauts stop at the urging of a religious expert to participate in some cultic practice,[61] but the narrator declines to describe the rites in detail, citing a general religious prohibition.[62] In passage 1, the narrator's statement that it would not be θέμις for "us" to sing of these matters alludes to the mystery cult's injunction to secrecy; the first-person plural pronoun ἄμμιν adds the suggestion that he is obeying a sanction of general applicability.[63] Likewise, in passage 2 the narrator wishes that "no one [may] know of" Hecate's rites and presents himself as obliged by religious compunctions not to reveal them (ἄζομαι | αὐδῆσαι, 250). In point of historical fact, it is unclear if Hecate's rites in Paphlagonia actually were mystic,[64] but there are ancient references to mystery cults for this goddess,[65] including, notably, one cult centered around the cave of Zerynthus on Samothrace.[66] Hecate does not seem to have been identified with one of the Μεγάλοι Θεοί, but her Samothracian cult is associated with theirs in some literary sources.[67] This link would further enhance the parallelism between these two (quasi-)mystic initiations near the outset of both the Argonauts' outward and return journeys.[68]

---

61 Orpheus' Thracian background and general association with mystery cults are both relevant to his role in passage 1; see Schroeder 2012: 321.
62 For the connections between these passages, see, e.g.: Livrea 1973 ad *Arg.* 4.250; Paduano and Fusillo 1986 ad *Arg.* 4.247–252; Vian 2002: 3.156 ad *Arg.* 4.250; Clare 2002: 251–252; Cuypers 2004: 49.
63 Asper, in summarizing the AR narrator's pious self-presentation, judges this passage "perhaps the strongest first-person remark throughout the poem" (2008: 173).
64 See Schaaf 2014: 261–263. For this reason I have wondered if the narrator's motive could be dread of Medea's occult rites more than pious circumspection per se; for speculations in this vein, see: Schaaf 2014: 264–267; Dickie 1998: 53; Manuello 2012: 131 n. 33. There is also the practical (authorial) consideration that Hecataean rituals have already been described in elaborate detail in Book 3. Cf. Fusillo 1985: 374, who attributes the silence regarding Hecate's rites to Apollonius' discomfort with "la sfera magico-irrazionale e gli elementi fantastici" (see further 378). In a similar vein, Fantuzzi (2008b: 296–297) argues that Apollonius deploys the silence motif because of the irrelevance of this episode to the overarching plot, his interest in Medea's magic fading after its plot function has been fulfilled with the acquisition of the Fleece. Against these views, see Schaaf 2014: 263–264.
65 See, e.g., Strabo 10.3.10, 20; Paus. 2.30.2.
66 See Hornblower 2015 ad Lycoph. *Alex.* 77.
67 See Schroeder 2012: 315–316 with nn. 40, 42.
68 These silences represent another example of the frequent parallels between the outward and return journeys (e.g., the death of two pairs of Argonauts in quick succession, the navigation of two sets of mobile rocks, the two appearances of Apollo, the loss of Heracles and the failure to reunite with him, etc.), though in other respects the two voyages stand in tension (e.g., linearity vs. circuitousness). See on this phenomenon, e.g.: Händel 1954: 92; Beye 1982: 146–150; Hutchinson 1988: 128–129, 130–132, 133–134, 135, 137–139; Williams 1991: ch. 12; Köhnken 2003a: 209–210; Fantuzzi and Hunter 2004: 123–124.

Scholars agree that the narrator's silence in these passages contributes to our impression of his piety and religious authority,[69] but they differ as to which poetic precedents they emphasize for Apollonius' procedure. Morrison compares the Pindaric practice of rejecting or cutting short unseemly stories about gods and heroes, but despite superficial resemblances (e.g., cf. αἰδέομαι ... εἰπεῖν [*Nem.* 5.14] with ἅζομαι αὐδῆσαι [*Arg.* 4.250]), the motivations for these silences as well as the content so concealed are quite different.[70] Cuypers highlights the model of Herodotus, who several times in his Egyptian λόγος withholds theological details on the grounds that revealing them would be impious (οὐκ ὅσιον ποιεῦμαι, 2.86.1, 170.1), such as the identity of the god lamented at Bubastis (οὔ μοι ὅσιον ἐστὶ λέγειν, 2.61.1; cf. *Arg.* 1.921). At other points, the historian mentions the existence of a ἱρός λόγος that explains the rationale for a certain ritual, but he does not deign to explain it (e.g., 2.62.2), in one case offering that it would be improper for him to do so (οὐκ εὐπρεπέστερος ἐστὶ λέγεσθαι, 2.47.2).[71] In Apollonius, however, it is the rites themselves that must be kept secret (ἀρρήτους ... θέμιστας, *Arg.* 1.917), not the divinity to whom they are dedicated or the myth that lies behind them. For this reason, the closest parallel to the AR narrator's silences in Herodotus is the historian's refusal to reveal the particulars of the rituals that the Egyptians allegedly call the "Mysteries" (μυστήρια, 2.171.1), as well as those of their Greek equivalent in the Thesmophoria.[72]

Parallels in Alexandrian poetry have also been proposed. In the story of Acontius and Cydippe, the Callimachean narrator stops himself from telling an inappropriate myth about Hera (*Aet.* fr. 75.4–9 Pfeiffer, Harder):[73]

---

[69] E.g.: Hunter 1993: 101; Cuypers 2004: 49; Schaaf 2014: 69; Klooster 2007: 77, who also notes (n. 51) internal parallels with the concealment of some portion of Zeus' will by Phineus, one of the AR narrator's alter egos (see 238n41); cf. *Arg.* 1.919 with 2.425; 1.921 with 2.311.

[70] Morrison 2007: 282–284; see further Manuello 2011: 92; 2012: 131–132. Ironically, Morrison highlights this *Nemean* passage especially as a model for the AR narrator's pious silences (283), but the particular story that Pindar refrains from telling there—Telamon and Peleus' murder of their half-brother Phocus—is actually one that the AR narrator himself does not scruple to mention in the Catalog (*Arg.* 1.90–93; see McPhee, forthcoming c). This difference shows that, unlike the Pindaric speaker, the AR narrator's sense of religious propriety does not necessarily extend to heroic behavior.

[71] Cuypers 2004: 49. For a catalog and classification of these passages in Herodotus, see Mora 1981; the same author identifies further parallels in Attic drama in Mora 1983.

[72] See further 2.3.2, where Herodotus claims that he is not willing to relate (οὐκ εἰμὶ πρόθυμος ἐξηγέεσθαι) the stories he has heard about the gods; cf. *Arg.* 4.249 (μήτ' ἐμὲ θυμὸς ἐποτρύνειεν ἀείδειν). Herodotus also mentions the Samothracian Mysteries at 2.51.

[73] Adduced as a parallel by, e.g.: Fusillo 1985: 393 n. 36; Klooster 2007: 77; Morrison 2007: 294, 302. Fusillo also compares Theoc. *Id.* 3.50–51, which may have a connection to the Samoth-

```
    Ἥρην γάρ κοτέ φασι—κύον, κύον, ἴσχεο, λαιδρέ
5     θυμέ, σύ γ' ἀείσῃ καὶ τά περ οὐχ ὁσίη·
    ὤναο κάρτ' ἕνεκ' οὔ τι θεῆς ἴδες ἱερὰ φρικτῆς,
    ἐξ ἂν ἐπεὶ καὶ τῶν ἤρυγες ἱστορίην.
    ἦ πολυιδρείη χαλεπὸν κακόν, ὅστις ἀκαρτεῖ
    γλώσσης· ὡς ἐτεὸν παῖς ὅδε μαῦλιν ἔχει.
```

For they say that once upon a time Hera—dog, dog, refrain, my shameless soul! you would sing even of that which is not lawful to tell. It is a great blessing for you that you have not seen the rites of the dread goddess, or else you would have spewed up their story too. Surely much knowledge is a grievous thing for him who does not control his tongue; this man is really a child with a knife.

This passage draws an interesting connection between the concealment of potentially unseemly ἱεροὶ λόγοι and the secrecy demanded by the Mysteries in a way that recalls and combines some discrete elements from the Herodotean passages cited above (note the Herodotean tag ἱστορίην in line 7), while the address to the speaker's own θυμός and the device of the "spontaneous" break-off are reminiscent of Pindar.[74] Some of Callimachus' phrases find mild echoes in Apollonius,[75] and the relatively rare ἴστωρ at *Arg.* 4.248 may reflect Callimachus' ἱστορίην in particular. Nevertheless, Callimachus' tone is far less reverent,[76] and it is interesting that while the Callimachean narrator claims to know the story about Hera,[77] he presents himself as uninitiated in the Eleusinian Mysteries. The AR narrator maintains a solemn tone and implies that he knows, but should not say, what rites the Argonauts undertook in Samothrace and Paphlagonia; some scholars have even taken this passage to mean that the historical Apollonius was an initiate in the Samothracian Mysteries.[78]

---

racian Mysteries (see Hunter 1999 ad loc.), but has little in common with our Apollonian *loci* otherwise. See also Schroeder 2012: 324–326 on Callim. *Ia.* 9.

74 In addition, the mention of the Eleusinian Mysteries may allude to the *Homeric Hymn to Demeter*; see below.

75 μήτ' ἐμὲ θυμὸς ἐποτρύνειεν ἀείδειν (*Arg.* 4.249; ἀείδειν also at 1.921) ~ ἴσχεο, λαιδρέ | θυμέ, σύ γ' ἀείσῃ ... (*Aet.* fr. 75.5); τὰ μὲν οὐ θέμις (*Arg.* 1.921) ~ τά περ οὐχ ὁσίη (*Aet.* fr. 75.5).

76 Note the joke that, because of his big mouth, the narrator has actually benefitted from *not* being initiated into the Mysteries.

77 Apparently it is in circulation (cf. φασι, 4). If, as is likely, Callimachus is in fact referring to a literary source (such as *Il.* 14.294–296; see Harder 2012 ad loc.), we might compare *Arg.* 4.985 (discussed below).

78 See Schroeder 2012: 308 (with references in n. 3), 319, 322.

As Hunter notes, there is Archaic precedent for "adopting the conventional piety of the hymnal voice" by "ostentatiously refus[ing] to divulge secret rites" in the *Homeric Hymn to Demeter*,[79] in what is the most extensive passage to feature overt evaluative language in the narrator's own voice in the *HH* collection (473–482):[80]

  ἡ δὲ κιοῦσα θεμιστοπόλοις βασιλεῦσιν
  δεῖξεν, Τριπτολέμῳ τε Διοκλεῖ τε πληξίππῳ
475 Εὐμόλπου τε βίῃ Κελεῷ θ' ἡγήτορι λαῶν,
  δρησμοσύνην ἱερῶν, καὶ ἐπέφραδεν ὄργια καλά
  Τριπτολέμῳ τε Πολυξείνῳ ⟨τ'⟩, ἐπὶ τοῖς δὲ Διοκλεῖ,
  σεμνά, τά τ' οὔ πως ἔστι παρεξ[ίμ]εν οὔ[τε] πυθέσθαι
  οὔτ' ἀχέειν· μέγα γάρ τι θεῶν σέβας ἰσχάνει αὐδήν.
480 ὄλβιος ὅς τάδ' ὄπωπεν ἐπιχθονίων ἀνθρώπων·
  ὃς δ' ἀτελὴς ἱερῶν ὅς τ' ἄμμορος, οὔ ποθ' ὁμοίων
  αἶσαν ἔχει φθίμενός περ ὑπὸ ζόφῳ εὐρώεντι.

She went to the lawgiver kings, Triptolemos and horse-goading Diocles, strong Eumolpos and Keleos leader of hosts, and taught them the sacred service, and showed the beautiful mysteries to Triptolemos, Polyxenos, and also Diocles—the solemn mysteries which one cannot depart from or enquire about or broadcast, for great awe of the gods restrains us from speaking. Blessed is he of men on earth who has beheld them, whereas he that is uninitiated in the rites, or he that has had no part in them, never enjoys a similar lot down in the musty dark when he is dead.

The verbal parallels with Apollonius' passages are mainly negligible,[81] with the notable exception of a Homeric *dis legomenon*: the reference to "those mysteries" (ὄργια κεῖνα, *Arg.* 1.920) on Samothrace occurs in the same *sedes* as that to the "beautiful mysteries" (ὄργια καλά, *HH* 2.476) in Eleusis. ὄργια does not occur in the HEs, but it occurs twice in the *Homeric Hymn to Demeter*: in this pas-

---

79 Hunter 1993: 91 with n. 80. This passage is adduced as well by: Fusillo 1985: 393 n. 36; Manuello 2012: 131 n. 33.
80 Nünlist 2004: 37. The mystic injunction to silence may inform the presentation of the narrative earlier in the hymn, too; e.g., it could be the reason why the content of Iambe's words to Demeter are not specified (de Jong 2022b: 96–97).
81 ἄζομαι αὐδῆσαι (*Arg.* 4.250) ~ σέβας ἰσχάνει αὐδήν (*HH* 2.479); θέμιστας (*Arg.* 1.917) may reflect θεμιστοπόλοις βασιλεῦσιν (*HH* 2.473), given that these kings will begin to "administer θέμιστας" in a cultic as well as a regal sense after their induction into Demeter's Mysteries.

sage concerning the Eleusinian Mysteries and earlier in an internal prolepsis announcing their establishment (2.273). The term occurs just twice in the *Arg.* as well:[82] in the Samothracian episode and, tellingly, in a reference to the cult of Hecate (ἴστω νυκτιπόλου Περσηΐδος ὄργια κούρης, 4.1020)[83]—the same rites that had inspired the narrator's silence in passage 2.

Apollonius' use of this Homeric *dis legomenon* twice in his own work, once in one of his own deployments of the "pious silence" motif and once again in reference to the other goddess whose rites he keeps secret, strengthens the probability of a purposeful allusion to the *Homeric Hymn to Demeter*. If so, there may be a theological as well as literary point to these allusions: as mentioned above, Hecate had her own mystery cult on Samothrace, and the third-century BCE periegete Mnaseas of Patras identified three of the Μεγάλοι Θεοί with the Eleusinian triad of Demeter, Persephone, and Hades, though Mnaseas' work probably postdates Apollonius.[84] In this sense, the ὄργια κεῖνα, ὄργια καλά, and ὄργια κούρης might really all be the same. A hymnic intertext with passage 1 also makes sense given its hymnic-style dismissal of Samothrace and its gods as potential subjects of song with the third-person κεχάροιτο (1.920), comparable to the second-person χαῖρε of a hymn's Salutation.[85] But whatever one makes of these connections, the *Homeric Hymn to Demeter* vests Apollonius' pious silences concerning the Mysteries with a venerable Homeric authority.

2.3 *Apologies to the Gods*

A final device that I want to consider as an index of the AR narrator's piety occurs in those passages in which he begs a god's pardon for a perceived offense, a rhetorical move that paradoxically heightens rather than diminishes our estimation of his religiosity. For instance, the narrator expresses misgivings over a hyperbolic reference to a wound that the medicine god Paeëon himself could hardly heal—"if it is right for me to say this openly" (εἴ μοι θέμις ἀμφαδὸν εἰπεῖν, 4.1511).[86] Thanks to this aside, the narrator's irreverent exaggeration in fact

---

82 The cognate verb ὀργιάζω also occurs at *Arg.* 2.907, in reference to Bacchic cult.
83 Again, the phrase occurs in the same *sedes*. Here ἴστω may be playing with ἴστωρ at 4.248.
84 Mnaseas fr. 17 Cappelletto; see, e.g., Schroeder 2012: 319–320. As a reputed pupil of Eratosthenes of Cyrene, Apollonius' successor at the Library of Alexandria (though cf. Murray 2012), Mnaseas' floruit is probably later than Apollonius'. Cole (1984: 2–3) believes that Mnaseas (or the scholiast reporting his view) invented these *interpretationes graecae* himself, but if he did not, Apollonius could possibly have been aware of them.
85 *Arg.* 1.920 also recalls Hes. *Th.* 963–964.
86 The narrator evidently does not feel the need to excuse a similar hyperbole, comparing the speed of the Argo favorably to that of Poseidon's horses (1.1157–1158). In fact, partly on the

advertises his piety all the more powerfully.[87] That Apollonius traced this technique back to the *HH*s is suggested by the apology to Apollo at *Arg.* 2.708. This line alludes to *HH* 3.165, where the hymnist gently asks Apollo's pardon for seeming to stray from praising him (the proper Hymnic Subject) in favor of the Delian maidens.[88] I examine this passage from *Arg.* 2 in detail in the full treatment of Orpheus' hymn to Apollo in 4.4.

For now, I would like to focus on the narrator's apology to the Muses in the double-etiological passage that introduces the Phaeacian episode (4.982–992):

> ἔστι δέ τις πορθμοῖο παροιτέρη Ἰονίοιο
> ἀμφιλαφὴς πίειρα Κεραυνίῃ εἰν ἁλὶ νῆσος,
> ᾗ ὕπο δὴ κεῖσθαι δρέπανον φάτις—ἵλατε Μοῦσαι,
> 985 οὐκ ἐθέλων ἐνέπω προτέρων ἔπος—ᾧ ἀπὸ πατρὸς
> μήδεα νηλειῶς ἔταμε Κρόνος· οἱ δέ ἑ Δηοῦς
> κλείουσι χθονίης καλαμητόμον ἔμμεναι ἅρπην·
> Δηὼ γὰρ κείνῃ ἐνὶ δή ποτε νάσσατο γαίῃ,
> Τιτῆνας δ᾽ ἔδαε στάχυν ὄμπνιον ἀμήσασθαι,
> 990 Μάκριδα φιλαμένη. Δρεπάνη τόθεν ἐκλήϊσται
> οὔνομα Φαιήκων ἱερὴ τροφός· ὣς δὲ καὶ αὐτοὶ
> αἵματος Οὐρανίοιο γένος Φαίηκες ἔασιν.

> There is a fertile, expansive island at the entrance of the Ionian strait in the Ceraunian sea, under which is said to lie the sickle—forgive me, Muses, not willingly do I repeat my predecessors' words—with which Cronus ruthlessly cut off his father's genitals. Others, however, say it is the reaping scythe of indigenous Demeter. For Demeter once lived in that land and taught the Titans how to harvest the bountiful grain, out of devotion to Macris. Since then the divine nurse of the Phaeacians has been called by the name Drepane, and thus the Phaeacians themselves are descended from Uranus' blood.

---

basis of this simile, Clauss (1993: 181–183, 189, 196–197) has seen Poseidon's wrath as operative within this episode, which sets in motion the events leading to Heracles' departure from the heroic company.

87 For such hyperboles, see Headlam 1922 ad Herod. 2.90, who cites, among many other comparanda, *Il.* 17.398–399 (in narrator-text) and *HH* 5.149–152 (in character-text). For the apology, Morrison (2007: 282 with n. 45) points to Pindar as a model, perhaps with passages like *Pyth.* 3.2 in mind.

88 See 131n203.

Apollonius' immediate model for the apology to the Muses is a passage in Aratus in which the didactic speaker asks Artemis' pardon ("Ἄρτεμις ἰλήκοι, *Phaen.* 637) before relating another προτέρων λόγος (637), the story of her attempted rape by Orion.[89] Aratus' story, however, quickly becomes a tale of divine punishment of mortal hubris (641–644). By contrast, in the *Arg.*, the offending story is not given a morally edifying ending (e.g., Cronus' just punishment by his own son in turn), but only its vile climax is mentioned in passing. Many have thought that the point of Apollonius' inclusion of this ghastly αἴτιον here is to "correct" Callimachus (*Aet.* fr. 43.69–71) on two counts: the Cyrenian had cited the same myth, castration and all, to explain the name of Zancle (a Sicilian dialect word for "scythe"), and he had put this gruesome story in the mouth of Clio—one of the Muses themselves. In one fell swoop, Apollonius transfers the αἴτιον from Zancle to Drepane and reprimands Callimachus for attributing this indecorous tale to the Muses.[90] But likely as this allusion to the *Aetia* is, dialogue with (or correction of) Callimachus would not explain why the AR narrator imagines that the Muses should be offended by this story in the first place.

It has been thought that in this passage, as Cuypers put it, "the narrator piously apologizes to the Muses for telling a discrediting story about the gods."[91] But the Aratean model should make us pause: why should he apologize to the Muses rather than to one of the gods actually discredited by this story—Uranus or Cronus[92]—or even to the gods generally? The narrator's apostrophe to the Muses, together with the explicit reference to his poetic predecessors in προτέρων ἔπος,[93] suggests that the relevant impropriety is essentially literary in nature. On the basis of these considerations, I would advance an interpretation subtly different from that put forward by Cuypers: the narrator is not apologizing because the story is discreditable to the gods, but because he feels

---

89 See, e.g.: Livrea 1973 ad *Arg.* 4.984; Kidd 1997 ad loc.; Vian 2002: 3.112 n. 4. This Aratean passage is also alluding to *HH* 3.165; see Kidd loc. cit.

90 See, e.g., Harder 2012 ad Callim. *Aet.* fr. 43.70–71, with earlier bibliography. For such stories as violations of epic decorum (τὸ πρέπον), see Hunter 2008: 118.

91 Cuypers 2004: 47. Other explanations have relied more on gender stereotypes: the AR narrator is apologizing for bringing up such a grisly and sordid tale "in the presence of ladies," as it were.

92 Fränkel 1968 ad *Arg.* 4.984. Cf. Zyroff 1971: 54, who believes that the Muses would be offended because they are themselves descendants of Uranus and Cronus.

93 Klooster (2007: 73 n. 37) interprets προτέρων ἔπος as a "tale of olden days" (similarly Zyroff 1971: 54), but I think we should understand προτέρων to refer to earlier poets. The narrator does not feel compelled to mention the myth because it is set in times primordial—indeed, the story may not even be true, given the alternate αἴτιον offered in the following lines—but because it is hallowed by long tradition.

bound by tradition to mention a story that is *false*[94]—and its falsity is evidenced first and foremost by the fact that it *is* discreditable to the gods. To my mind, the key to understanding this passage is the insight that the narrator is not just choosing between two αἴτια for the name of Drepane here, but between two versions of the theogonic succession myth, and with it, two different attitudes toward mythological poetry. This passage demands to be contextualized in a long tradition of Greek literary criticism, stretching back at least to Xenophanes, that took archaic epic to task for presenting images of the gods engaged in immoral behavior. Among all the "false tales" (μύθους ... ψευδεῖς, Pl. *Resp.* 2.377d) that Homer, Hesiod, and the other poets proclaimed about the gods, these myths of dynastic succession in heaven are the first that Socrates condemns in the *Republic* (2.377e–378a). This story of genital mutilation was gruesome enough,[95] but more than that, it was morally offensive, in that it involved a son remorselessly (νηλειῶς, 986) injuring his own father (πατρός, 985).[96]

In Book 1, however, Orpheus' cosmo-theogonic song had envisioned a very different history of Mt. Olympus from that presupposed in the first αἴτιον. The bard begins with the differentiation of Gaia and Uranus from the primordial chaos (496), but he makes the first rulers of the universe the obscure Ophion and his wife, the Oceanid Eurynome (503–504). It is this king whom Cronus eventually expels from the throne of heaven "through force of hand" (βίῃ καὶ χερσίν, 505). The substitution of Ophion for Uranus successfully eliminates the most scandalous aspect of the Hesiodic succession myth, the son's maiming of his own father.[97] The character of Orpheus has often been understood as a stand-in for the narrator,[98] but nevertheless, the AR narrator never endorses

---

94 As Cuypers (2004: 47) notes, it is Herodotean to mention a story even when one disagrees with it.
95 Plato's Socrates refers to it only euphemistically as "how Cronus took revenge" on Uranus (ὅ τε αὖ Κρόνος ὡς ἐτιμωρήσατο αὐτόν, *Resp.* 377e–378a; adduced by Klooster 2011: 224 n. 70).
96 Plato makes this criticism explicit at *Euthyphr.* 6a, *Resp.* 2.378b.
97 By contrast, violence against serpentine monsters, such as Ophion's name suggests, typically requires no special justification in Greek myth (for Ophion as a reflex of Typhoeus, see Ogden 2013: 78–79). What is more, Cronus does not chain Ophion up in Tartarus, but the ousted ruling couple simply return to the Ocean (506). The end of Orpheus' song does allude to the destined conflict between Cronus and Zeus, but the bard tactfully stops short of this phase of his narrative (508–511). The specter of father-son conflict recurs at 4.800–804. There is nothing specifically "Orphic" about this version of the succession myth that would determine its selection here (see Iacobacci 1993: 91–92); rather, our poet has simply availed himself of a rare mythological variant for reasons of his own.
98 See 327n217.

the bard's cosmo-theogony *in propria persona*. It is telling, however, that the alternate αἴτιον under consideration in Book 4 features none other than the Titans coexisting peacefully with one of Cronus' Olympian daughters—a harmonious alternative, it would seem, to the violent generational struggles taken for granted by Homer and Hesiod. I am thus inclined to understand the apology to the Muses as related to their status as the traditional guarantors of poetic truth. As the daughters of Memory, they know what any devout Greek should realize anyway, that this προτέρων ἔπος of paternal castration in heaven is a μῦθος ψευδής,[99] and the AR narrator is accordingly embarrassed that his etiological instincts have impelled him to give this story oxygen.

The implications of this reading for the *Arg.*'s presentation of the gods are potentially far-reaching, but for present purposes, suffice it to say that this passage shows the AR narrator to be even more pious than interpreters have heretofore imagined. The specific device of narratorial apology to a god is not amply attested in the *HH*s, though Apollonius does allude to its one instantiation (*HH* 3.165) at *Arg.* 2.708.[100] Apollonius likewise seems to allude to the pious silence in the *Homeric Hymn to Demeter* in one of his own deployments of this topos, and his pious similes seem to interact with the *HH*s at both the level of verbiage[101] and motif, such as Artemis' riding from a river to meet Apollo.

3   Etiology

The Homeric-hymnic pedigree of the ubiquitous Apollonian motif of etiology may be surprising, since αἴτια are so strongly associated with Callimacheanism.[102] The *Arg.* includes some eighty etiologies, a type of "external prolepsis,"

---

99   This reading suggests a new interpretation of *Arg.* 4.991–992. In context, the phrase αἵματος Οὐρανίοιο γένος (992) recalls the Hesiodic plot point that when the blood from Uranus' castration fell to the earth, there emerged, among others, the Giants (*Th.* 183–187), whom the *Odyssey* presents as kin to the Phaeacians (7.205–206). But with the second αἴτιον, Apollonius suggests an alternative explanation for the Phaeacians' kinship with Uranus: they are descended from the Titans, the children of Uranus, who once inhabited their island.

100   Mentioned above, 251.

101   See nn. 45–48.

102   On etiology in the *Arg.*, see, e.g.: Valverde Sánchez 1989; Goldhill 1991: 321–333; Harder 1994: 21–29; Klooster 2014; Walter 2020: 120–134. For links with Callimachean etiological practice, see further 256n114 as well as, e.g.: Fraser 1972: 1.627–633; Hutchinson 1988: 93–96; DeForest 1994: 8.

or flash-forward beyond the time of the primary narrative,[103] in which some feature of the narrator's contemporary reality is explained with reference to events in the age of myth. Fusillo has provocatively labeled Apollonian etiology a "'betrayal' of Homeric epic"[104]—a dramatic turn of phrase, but one that accurately conveys just what "a *radical* departure from Homeric practise" it was to "poeticize aetiology in the epic *genre*."[105] The HEs contain no explicit examples of this practice,[106] and the *Iliad* even contains a passage that was understood in antiquity as something of an anti-etiology: the account of the destruction of the Achaean wall at the beginning of Book 12 was interpreted as a justification for the fact that this fortification did **not** leave a trace in the historical Troad.[107]

This divergence on the matter of etiology is related to deeper differences in the temporal frameworks of Homeric and Apollonian epic. With hardly a reference to the narrator's present time beyond the omnitemporal similes and some fleeting (and unfavorable) comparisons between the mythic heroes and "men as they are now,"[108] the HEs probably come closest of all the epics of Greco-

---

103 More rarely, Apollonius' αἴτια can also be analeptic; for examples, see Walter 2020: 126–128.
104 "L'eziologia come 'tradimento' dell'epos omerico" names the concluding subsection of Fusillo's discussion of etiology in the poem (1985: 136–142). By "betrayal," Fusillo means a fundamental generic transgression: etiology undermines the pastward orientation of epic and thus reduces the fluidity of the mythic narrative and sacrifices its pretense of distanced objectivity.
105 Klein 1975: 23–24 (italics original). Similarly, for Klein 1974: 228–229, Apollonian etiologizing participates in the *Arg.*'s paradoxical incorporation into epic of its own "countergenre," i.e. Callimachean etiological poetry. Cf. Williams 1991: 185–203, who considers Apollonian etiology as a novel extension of the Homeric preoccupation with κλέος.
106 Some HE passages have been read as etiological (see, e.g.: Codrignani 1958: 527–530; Fantuzzi 1996: 369; Nagy 2002: 89–90; Currie 2005: 53–54), but these are not flagged as such by the narrator. Cf. Walter 2020: 44–53, on a prominent counterexample of an (analeptic) αἴτιον in character-text (Agamemnon's story about *atê*). Cf. further the common heroic hope of leaving behind a tomb or reputation for future generations to learn of (Fusillo 1985: 137–138).
107 Harder (1994: 25–26) and Saïd (1998: 17, 19) both use this example to illustrate the difference between HE and Apollonian attitudes to etiology; see further Hunter 1993: 103–104. For this interpretation of the destruction of the Achaean wall in antiquity, see Scodel 1982: 33 n. 2; see further Porter 2011 for the implications of this view for notions of fiction in Homer. The permanent isolation of the Phaeacians from the outside world in the *Odyssey* (13.125–187) is analogous in several regards (Scodel 1982: 48–50); I would further compare the destruction of Cycnus' tomb at the end of the Hesiodic *Scutum* (472–480). For the concept of "anti-etiology," see McPhee 2023b: 185–186; cf. Harder (2012: 1.24), who uses the term "non-*aition*" for this phenomenon. For a few equivalent anti-etiologies in the *Arg.*, see Harder 1994: 27.
108 See *Il.* 5.302–304, 12.381–383, 12.447–449, 20.285–287, with Edwards 1991 *ad Il.* 19.387–391; van Wees 1992: 315 n. 9. For the term "omnitemporal," see 13*n*69.

Roman antiquity to fulfilling Bakhtin's conception of the "epic past" as "walled off absolutely from all subsequent times, and above all from those times in which the singer and his listeners are located."[109] Apollonius may begin his epic by emphasizing the antiquity of his subject, the παλαιγενέων κλέα φωτῶν (1.1),[110] but through its near-constant stream of αἴτια, his poem insists again and again on the enduring effects that the voyage of the Argo has had on the contemporary world.[111] Countless names, rituals, material monuments, and even natural phenomena are cast as the fruit of this heroic expedition, from the relatively trivial, such as the color of the pebbles on the beaches of Elba (4.654–658), to the consequential indeed, such as the Greek colonization of Libya.[112] So central is etiology to Apollonius' project that oftentimes the drive to incorporate Argonautic αἴτια appears to have determined the very shape of his plot.[113]

The sheer prominence of αἴτια in the *Arg.* makes it natural to associate Apollonian etiologizing with the example of Callimachus, who wrote his own four-book poem with this very title devoted exclusively to the mythical "causes" of contemporary institutions across the Greek world. Indeed, several passages in the *Arg.* have been plausibly interpreted as tributes to Apollonius' reputed mentor, and particularly in the matter of etiology.[114] I would not dispute the fact that in etiological passages, it is primarily the Callimachean facet of the AR narrator's voice that we are hearing, but I would like to contextualize this fact in light of a couple of additional points. First, there is a rich store of precedent for etiology in Greek poetry that forms part of the intertextual background of both

---

109 Bakhtin 1981: 15–16. For the applicability of Bakhtin's concept of the epic to Greco-Roman exemplars of the genre, see Nagy 2002: 80–91. In discussing HE temporality, Fusillo (1985: 137) cites the dictum of Goethe and Schiller that "the Epic poet presents the event as *perfectly past*" (in Calvert 1845: 379; italics original).
110 For the metageneric implications of this opening gesture, see, e.g.: Hunter 1993: 8, 105 with n. 19; 2008: 126–127; Clauss 2000: 11; Klooster 2007: 63, 2014: 524–525; Phillips 2020: 29–30; Stürner 2022: 59–61.
111 Hunter 1993: 105. For etiologies as links between past and present, see, e.g.: Fränkel 1957: 5; Hurst 1964: 235; Beye 1982: 75; Fusillo 1985: 116–117; Zanker 1987: 120–124; Fantuzzi and Hunter 2004: 92–93; Klooster 2007: 66, 2012: 60; Júnior 2021: 115–116.
112 See, e.g., Stephens 2003: 180–182.
113 See, e.g., *Arg.* 4.552–556 with the analysis of Caneva (2007: 75–76) and Klooster (2012: 62–63, 2013b: 168–169, 2014: 536–537). Fitch (1912) offers another fine demonstration of how the several αἴτια connected to Cyzicus "conditioned the narrative of Apollonius" (46); that is, the Cyzicus episode had to assume a certain (complex) shape in order to incorporate all of the traces of the Argonauts provided by Apollonius' sources. Cf. McPhee 2023b for the parallel role of αἴτια in shaping post-Homeric attempts to localize Odysseus' wanderings.
114 See: Albis 1995; Köhnken 2003a, 2008: 79 (in the latter place, building on the argument of Harder 1993: 108–109).

Apollonius' and Callimachus' deployment of this motif.[115] On this score, the opening paragraph of Páskiewicz's article on etiology in *Arg.* 2 is worth quoting in full:

> One of the most unHomeric features of Apollonius' poem are its many aitia, a type of subject absent from the Homeric epics, though well-established elsewhere. In non-epic poetry aitia appear in the Homeric hymns (e.g. *h. Dem.* on the origin of the Eleusinian mysteries), Pindar (e.g. *O.* 10 on the institution of the Olympic Games), tragedy (Euripides' plays often end with the foundation of some Attic cult, e.g. in *Hipp.* 1425 ff.) and very often in Hellenistic poetry, above all in Apollonius' contemporary Callimachus, who devoted an entire work in elegiac verse to the subject. Aitia are not lacking in earlier epic poetry, either, in Hesiod (e.g. *Aigimios* fr. 296, which explains the name Euboia, *Eoiai* fr. 233), Peisander of Cameirus (*Heracleia* fr. 7 Kinkel on the springs at Thermopylae) and Antimachus (*Thebais* fr. 35 on the cult of Demeter *Erinys*, frs. 44, 53).[116]

My second point flows directly from Páskiewicz's quotation: it is telling that he cites the *HH*s first of all in his survey of etiology in Greek poetry. Other than Hesiod,[117] the *Hymns* represent the earliest poetic corpus not only to feature etiology, but to make it a central poetic concern.[118] As Clay has argued, all of the major hymns are broadly etiological in nature, explaining how crises in the Olympian pantheon *in illo tempore*[119] precipitated the permanent reorder-

---

115 For etiology in earlier Greek poetry, see, e.g.: Codrignani 1958; Valverde Sánchez 1989: 37–42; Fantuzzi 1996: 369–370; Harder 2012: 1.24–25.
116 Páskiewicz 1988: 57.
117 We do not, with Páskiewicz, need to cite the *Aegimius* or even the *Ehoeae* to find etiology in Hesiod: the entire *Theogony* and certain passages of *Works and Days* (e.g., 109–201) possess general etiological significance, explaining the origin of the present-day order of the cosmos; we can also find therein etiologies for particular ritual usages, such as the Greek mode of sacrifice as explained in the Mecone episode (*Th.* 535–564). Etymological etiology is well-attested in the earliest Hesiodic poetry, too; see esp. Vergados 2020.
118 For etiologies in the *HH*s, see, e.g.: Codrignani 1958: 530–531; Lenz 1975: 16–17; Miller 1986: 25–26; Valverde Sánchez 1989: 39–40. Several of these are implicit; e.g., Borgeaud (1988: 101–102) plausibly connects the frightened reaction to Pan's appearance exhibited by the infant god's nurse (*HH* 19.38–39) to his role as the god of panic. Cf. also 7.53, which may be meant to explain the origin of dolphins, as in later-attested versions of this myth (e.g., Oppian *Hal.* 1.649–653).
119 This is Eliade's term for the mythical time of origins, when the deeds of gods and heroes inaugurated prevailing natural phenomena and cultural institutions by which the world is still configured today (see Eliade 1959: ch. 1).

ing of divine and human relations into those recognizable in the present day of the hymn's enunciation.[120] For instance, the *Homeric Hymn to Demeter* explains, inter alia, the origin of the seasons (2.398–403, 445–456)[121] and of the Eleusinian Mysteries (see esp. 270–274, 473–483); the *Hymn to Apollo*, the founding of an oracle to communicate the will of Zeus to mortals (3.287–293); etc. "The most aetiologically self-conscious of the *Homeric Hymns*," the major hymn dedicated to Hermes, is brimming with αἴτια, including the creation of that emblem of poetry itself, the lyre.[122] Moreover, the hymns contain many smaller-scale αἴτια for names, epichoric cults, inventions, and perhaps even local topographic features.[123] There is thus solid Homeric precedent for this innovative feature of Apollonius' epic in the *HH*s, which, indeed, have been recognized as a major influence on Callimachean etiologizing.[124]

We can go further still, for I would argue that there is positive evidence for the direct influence of the *HH*s' etiologizing on Apollonian practice. For instance, many etiologies in the hymns occur in character-text, taking the form of prophecies or promises (e.g., Delos' status as Apollo's cult site, 3.51–60, 84–88) or direct commands to mortals to found an institution (e.g., the foundation of the Eleusinian Mysteries: 2.270–274). Others, however, occur in narrator-text, and in some cases, the verbal formulations employed bear comparison with Apollonian *loci*. For example:

– Hecate, who had aided Demeter in the search for her daughter (*HH* 2.24–25, 51–62), embraces Persephone upon her return, and "**because of that** [or, "**from that time**"] the goddess **became** her attendant and servant" (ἐκ τοῦ οἱ πρόπολος καὶ ὀπάων ἔπλετ' ἄνασσα, 440). Apollonius uses precisely this for-

---

120   Clay 2006; this thesis is laid out at 15. Intriguingly, Tsakiris (2022: 68–69) interprets the Argonauts' neutralization of the Clashing Rocks, which opens up the sea lanes between East and West, as an equivalent reordering of the cosmos featured in the *Arg.* qua Homeric-style hymn; and indeed, alongside the Greek colonization of North Africa, this certainly is the major etiology connected to the Argonautic myth.
121   Strictly speaking, however, Persephone's return from the underworld is correlated with, but not explicitly said to cause, the advent of spring (see Foley 1994: 58–59, 99–100).
122   See Walter 2020: 70–88 (quotation at 70).
123   For names, see, e.g., *HH* 3.493–496, for Apollo's cult title Delphinius, or 19.47, for the etymology of the theonym Pan. For local cults, see 1D.1–3 with Càssola 1975a: 14–15 for an unidentified biennial festival, or Richardson 1974 ad 2.265–267 for the etiology of the annual mock battle (the βαλλητύς) held in Eleusis in honor of Demeter's nursling Demophon. For inventions, see 4.25, 111 (the lyre and fire-sticks), 5.12–15 (chariots and women's work), 20.2–7 (civilizational arts). For a landscape feature, see 3.382–383, which seems to explain the disposition of rocks in the stream of Telphusa.
124   See, e.g.: Bornmann 1968: xvi–xvii; Depew 1993: 62–63; Fantuzzi and Hunter 2004: 366.

mulation in one of his own etiologies, for the site at which Orpheus dedicates his lyre: "**For that reason**, Lyra **is the name of the place**" (ἐκ τοῦ δὲ Λύρη πέλει οὔνομα χώρῳ, *Arg.* 2.929).¹²⁵
– Apollo has the sun rot (πύθειν) the Delphic serpent's remains; "**hence the place is now called** Pytho, **and the people give** the god **the title** Pythios" (ἐξ οὗ νῦν Πυθὼ **κικλήσκεται**, οἳ δὲ ἄνακτα | Πύθιον ⟨αὖ⟩ **καλέουσιν ἐπώνυμον**, *HH* 3.372–373). Likewise, Apollonius explains a pair of names connected to Dionysus' travels back to Thebes from India: "[S]ince then, the local inhabitants **have called** the river **by the name** of Callichorus and the cave Aulion" (ἐξ οὗ Καλλίχορον ποταμὸν περιναιετάοντες | ἠδὲ καὶ Αὔλιον ἄντρον ἐπωνυμίην καλέουσιν, *Arg.* 2.909–910).¹²⁶
– Hermes stretches the hides of two slaughtered cows on a rock near the Alpheus, "as **even now** afterwards, a great length of time after these events, they have remained through many ages and unceasingly" (ὡς ἔτι νῦν τὰ μέτασσα πολυχρόνιοι πεφύασιν | δηρὸν δὴ μετὰ ταῦτα καὶ ἄκριτον, *HH* 4.125–126; see also ὡς ἔτι καὶ νῦν in line 508).¹²⁷ The phrase (εἰσ-)ἔτι νῦν is one of the commonest formulas marking etiology in the *Arg.* (1.1061, 1354; 2.526, 717, 850, 1214; 4.277, 480, 599, 1153, 1770; cf. 1.644, 825; 2.1145; 3.203, 312; 4.534).¹²⁸

In other cases, the fact that Apollonius alludes to specific αἴτια from the *HH*s when offering his own etiologies suggests his recognition of the hymns as an authoritative Homeric model for this practice. I discuss Apollonius' reworking of the αἴτιον for Apollo's worship under the title Delphinius (*HH* 3.493–496) in the analysis of the Thynias episode at 4.4.2. Here, I will examine in depth one

---

125   Notably, Persephone as queen of the dead features earlier in this very episode (*Arg.* 2.916).
126   For possible allusions in this passage to elements of Eleusinian cult, some of which featured in Rhapsodic Hymns (e.g., via the homonym Callichorus: see *HH* 2.272; Callim. *Hymn* 6.15; cf. also Callim. *Hec.* fr. 172 Hollis), see Schaaf 2014: 104–105; see further Massari 2017: 11 n. 3.
127   The passage is manifestly etiological, but what sort of relics or landmark is meant remains unclear. Given our ignorance concerning this etiology, I retain the manuscript reading ἄκριτον in favor of West's emendation ἄκριτοι, according to which the cowhides would be "in a fused mass."
128   Similar expressions occur at Callim. *Aet.* fr. 59.21 Pfeiffer, Harder; *Hymn* 3.77. For the related formula ἐξέτι κείνου ("ever since that time"), see Williams 1978 ad Callim. *Hymn* 2.47. The *Hermes* passage's (emphatic) deployment of the "long after" motif, noting the many centuries between "then" and "now" bridged by the αἴτιον, finds some parallel in Apollonian etiologies in which the narrator breaks off a digression because the ramifications of the Argonauts' deeds that he is tracing are so far removed from the time of his mythic narrative (4.1216, 1764; cf. 1.1309; see further Fusillo 1985: 377). Bornmann (1968: xvii) cites the *Hermes* passage as hymnic precedent for (Callimachus' use of) "il riferimento a reliquie ancora visibili come prova della veridicità del mito."

other example, which underlines Apollonius' debt to both Callimachean and *HH* etiologizing. One of the final αἴτια in the *Arg.* concerns the aeschrological rites dedicated to Apollo Aegletes at Anaphe (4.1719–1730):

> ῥέζον δ' οἷά κεν ἄνδρες ἐρημαίῃ ἐνὶ ῥέζειν
> 1720 ἀκτῇ ἐφοπλίσσειαν· ὃ δὴ σφεας ὁππότε δαλοῖς
> ὕδωρ αἰθομένοισιν ἐπιλλείβοντας ἴδοντο
> Μηδείης δμωαὶ Φαιηκίδες, οὐκέτ' ἔπειτα
> ἴσχειν ἐν στήθεσσι γέλω σθένον, οἷα θαμειὰς
> αἰὲν ἐν Ἀλκινόοιο βοοκτασίας ὁρόωσαι.
> 1725 τὰς δ' αἰσχροῖς ἥρωες ἐπεστοβέεσκον ἔπεσσιν
> χλεύῃ γηθόσυνοι· γλυκερὴ δ' ἀνεδαίετο τοῖσιν
> κερτομίη καὶ νεῖκος ἐπεσβόλον. ἐκ δέ νυ κείνης
> μολπῆς ἡρώων νήσῳ ἔνι τοῖα γυναῖκες
> ἀνδράσι δηριόωνται, ὅτ' Ἀπόλλωνα θυηλαῖς
> 1730 Αἰγλήτην Ἀνάφης τιμήορον ἱλάσκωνται.

> They sacrificed such things as men on a deserted shore could provide to sacrifice, so that when Medea's Phaeacian handmaids saw them pouring libations of water on the blazing brands, they could no longer contain the laughter in their breasts, for they had always seen lavish sacrifices of oxen in Alcinous' palace. The heroes enjoyed their jesting and scoffed at them with obscene language, and pleasant insults and scurrilous taunts were kindled among them. And so, from that jesting of the heroes, the women on the island hurl similar taunts at the men, whenever in their sacrifices they propitiate Apollo Aegletes, guardian of Anaphe.

Apollonius' entire Anaphe episode is in close dialogue with Callimachus' treatment thereof in the first book of his *Aetia*.[129] The passage relevant to the Anaphean sacrifices runs as follows (Callim. *Aet.* fr. 21 Pfeiffer, Harder):

> τόφρα δ' ἀνιήσουσα λόφον βοὸς ἔγρετο Τιτώ
>   Λαομεδοντείῳ] παιδὶ χροϊσσαμ[ένη
> 5]μετὰ δμωῇσι[
>   ]ξείνιον Ἀλκινο[ο

---

[129] For discussion, see, e.g.: Eichgrün 1961: 125–133; Hutchinson 1988: 87–88, 91–93; Albis 1995; Harder 2002: 217–223, 2019b: 19–22; Hunter 2015: 22–25; Klooster 2019; Murray 2019: 93–97, 101–103.

δ[ ] Φαιηκίδας, αἵ ῥα τ[
τερπ.... υ.. ισ.. τινος ἡδομέναις
χλεύ.. δει.... ος ἀπεκρύψαντο λα[
10   νῆστ[ι]ες ἐν Δηοῦς ἤμασι 'Ραριάδος

But when Tito [i.e., Eos], having slept with the son (of Laomedon), arose to set a chafing yoke on the neck of the ox ... among the slave women ... gift of (the wife of) Alcinoüs ... (and) the Phaeacian maids ... amused ... mocking ... had hidden ... fasting on the sacred days of the Rarian Demeter ...

That Apollonius alludes to this portion of Callimachus' Anaphe αἴτιον is demonstrated by his use of two Homeric *hapaxes* in his passage. One of these, ἐπεσβόλος ("scurrilous") at *Arg.* 4.1727 (a *hapax* from *Il.* 2.275), answers Callimachus' use of the cognate ἐπεσβολίη ("scurrility") in his line 11 (itself a *hapax* from *Od.* 4.159).[130] As Harder comments, "This kind of slightly oblique interaction between Callimachus and Apollonius agrees with the way in which they are carrying on an 'intertextual dialogue' all through the story of Anaphe."[131] The second *hapax* is the word χλεύη, "joke, jest," some form of which is discernible at the beginning Callim. fr. 21.9[132] and which Apollonius uses, likewise, at the beginning of *Arg.* 4.1726. This word does not appear in the HEs; before the Hellenistic period its only occurrence is at *HH* 2.202.[133]

Unfortunately, Callimachus' account is so fragmentary that it is difficult to determine how closely its plot matched Apollonius' or, conversely, that of an alternate version of the story preserved by the Augustan-era mythographer Conon (*Narr.* 49) and by Pseudo-Apollodorus (*Bib.* 1.9.26). These mythographers differ from each other on a few minor details, but they both depart from Apollonius' version on some substantial points. In their versions, when Apollo saves the Argonauts from a storm,[134] the heroes take anchor at Anaphe and

---

130   Newman (1998: 115–116) suggests that the use of these words derived from ἔπος βάλλω ("hurl words") may allude to an etymology for ἴαμβος from ἰὸν βάλλω ("shoot an arrow").
131   Harder 2012 ad Callim. *Aet.* fr. 21.11.
132   See Harder 2012 ad loc.
133   In other Hellenistic poetry, the word is used in an epigram of Aeschrion (*AP* 7.345.4) and in Lycoph *Alex.* 1386. Newman (1998: 115–116) connects the usage of this word in Apollonius, Callimachus, and the hymn. For the abusive connotations of the cognate verb χλευάζω, see Rosen 1988a: 54.
134   Cf. the mysterious shroud of darkness in Apollonius (4.1694–1698) and probably also Callimachus (fr. 18.8, 20). Both mythographers mention a flash of lightning in tandem with Apollo's shooting ([Apollod.]) or raising (Conon [as at *Arg.* 4.1709]) his bow. In Conon,

celebrate with sacrifices[135] and a feast—evidently this version envisions no scarcity of victims or wine. In Pseudo-Apollodorus, Medea's Phaeacian slave women then begin to jest with the Argonauts (ἔσκωπτον μετὰ παιγνίας),[136] apparently unprovoked. Conon explains the outbreak of this jesting in his rendition: Medea and her attendants had gotten drunk (μετὰ μέθην) amid the festivities, which are specified as an all-night celebration (ἐν τῇ παννυχίδι).[137] Conon also tells us that the men jeer right back, and thus that both sexes at Anaphe taunt each other at these sacrifices to this day,[138] whereas Pseudo-Apollodorus, like Apollonius, only mentions the women's ribaldry during these rites.

The matter must remain uncertain, but what clues we have suggest that it is Callimachus' version that Conon and Pseudo-Apollodorus are summarizing.[139] One considerable piece of external evidence is the fact that the only two Argonautic episodes included in Conon's miscellaneous assortment of fifty *Narratives* are precisely those that Callimachus had incorporated into the *Aetia*: the etiologies for the rites at Anaphe and for the Argonauts' anchor at Cyzicus (*Narr.* 41 ~ Callim. frr. 108–109 Pfeiffer, Harder).[140] In her commentary on this passage, Harder also (cautiously) notes several internal indications that point to a context for the fragment similar to that of the mythographers', and particularly Conon's. For instance, τόφρα in line 3 "suggests that the Argonauts

---

Anaphe does not simply appear to the Argonauts as a result, but actually emerges from the sea. It is tempting to think that this detail, which resonates strongly with the Egyptian cosmogonic myth of the primeval island arising from the sea, could go back to Callimachus' version. Stephens (2003: 209) has argued that Apollonius' Thera and Anaphe episodes allude to this Egyptian cosmogony, but Conon's version offers an even neater parallel. For Callimachus' possible allusions to this Egyptian myth elsewhere in his corpus, see Stephens 2003: ch. 2.

135   The word θυσίαις represents a very probable supplement in Conon's text by Henye.
136   Like Apollonius, Pseudo-Apollodorus does not specify whether Medea participates or not.
137   Text of Conon is taken from Brown 2002.
138   Likely this was Callimachus' view as well, per the phrasing of the question that launches this αἴτιον: "And why, goddesses, does a **man** at Anaphe [ἀνὴρ Ἀναφαῖος] sacrifice with insults?"
139   For this possibility, see, e.g., Knaack 1887: 1–5; cf. Pfeiffer 1922: 74–76; Wilamowitz 1924: 2.172 n. 1; and see further below. For his part, Pseudo-Apollodorus, who normally follows Apollonius for Argonautic material, deviates from him significantly in this section of his narrative in other ways as well, eliminating the entire Libyan episode and (against all geographic reason) setting the Talos episode after Anaphe rather than before it (Frazer 1921: 1.117 n. 4). Hunter (2015: 24 n. 70) notes that "Callimachus also seems to have taken his Argonauts directly from Corcyra to Anaphe, and there is no obvious trace of a stop in either Libya or Crete in his narrative."
140   Brown 2002: 339.

were doing something, presumably celebrating and sacrificing, and that in the meantime a new day began,"[141] à la Conon's παννυχίς. The fact that the women's mockery begins in line 5, immediately after this time indication, again, "would agree with its taking place at the end of a night of celebrations."[142] The words μετὰ δμῳῇσι in line 5 "suggest that Medea was the subject of these lines"[143]—I would note in this connection that Conon is the only ancient source to specify Medea's participation in the fun.[144]

This attempt at reconstructing the plot of Callimachus' Anaphe narrative may seem to have taken us far afield from Apollonius, but my essential purpose in pursuing this question is to make the point that Apollonius, by contrast, seems to have invented a new motivation for the ribaldry that sets the αἴτιον in motion. In the Callimachean version, it seems, no shortage of supplies hampered the Argonauts' celebration, and it was the festive atmosphere, if not the drunkenness of Medea (!) and her attendants, that occasioned the aeschrology. Apollonius appears to be alone in tracing the cause, so much more innocently, to water-libations, which appeared ridiculous to royal slaves accustomed to opulent offerings in Alcinous' palace. Why might the poet have preferred this version? Certainly Apollonius' variant is much the more decorous, perhaps as befits an epic treatment of the myth.[145] Apollonius does not specify Medea's participation in the ribaldry, let alone her or her slaves' drunkenness, and, uniquely, he makes sure that it is the men who begin the jeering (1725)—before that, the women's only impropriety is their inability to contain their laughter at the risible sight of the sacrifices (1723).[146]

I have discussed this problem at such length, however, in order to argue for a deeper motive: this change is part of a "two-tier allusion" that Apollonius is making to the *Homeric Hymn to Demeter* through the lens of Callimachus' own

---

141 Harder 2012 ad loc.
142 Ibid. ad lines 5–8.
143 Ibid. ad loc.
144 See further on this point McPhee 2021a: 248 n. 19.
145 For another possible case of Apollonius' maintenance of epic decorum, vis-à-vis the Argonauts' drunkenness on Lemnos, see Harder 2021: 229–230. From the *HH*s, we may compare the decorous treatment of Iambe's (traditionally lewd) humor in the *Homeric Hymn to Demeter*; see, e.g.: Richardson 1974 ad *HH* 2.202 f.; Brown 1997: 20; O'Higgins 2003: 44. The hymnist may also have chosen Iambe in conscious preference to Baubo (O'Higgins 2003: 38, 51–53), who plays an identical plot function in Eleusinian myth except that she cheers up the grieving goddess by exposing herself rather than by using ribald language. On this figure, see, e.g., Olender 1990.
146 This despite the fact that on present-day Anaphe, the AR narrator tells us, it is rather the women who aggress against the men (γυναῖκες | ἀνδράσι δηριόωνται, 1728–1729). For the possible significance of γέλως in this episode, see Chuvin 2003: 219–220.

allusion thereto.¹⁴⁷ Let us recall the Homeric *hapax* χλεύη that both Alexandrian poets use in their respective treatments. With this word, Callimachus is unmistakably alluding to the *Homeric Hymn to Demeter*, for not only is the word incredibly rare,¹⁴⁸ but he goes on to mention the "fasting on the sacred days of the Rarian Demeter" in the very next line (fr. 21.10).¹⁴⁹ Fasting and scurrility are precisely what we find combined in the original context in the hymn, which served as "almost the authorizing epic text for ritual mockery."¹⁵⁰ The goddess has just arrived in her disguise as an old nurse at the home of King Celeus of Eleusis and remains depressed by the loss of her daughter. "Diligent Iambe" ('Ιάμβη κέδν' εἰδυῖα, 195), who seems to be a δμωή herself,¹⁵¹ prepares a seat for Demeter and tries to brighten the goddess's mood (197–205):

ἔνθα καθεζομένη προκατέσχετο χερσὶ καλύπτρην·
δηρὸν δ' ἄφθογγος τετιημένη ἧστ' ἐπὶ δίφρου,
οὐδέ τιν' οὔτ' ἔπεϊ προσπτύσσετο οὔτέ τι ἔργῳ,
200 ἀλλ' ἀγέλαστος ἄπαστος ἐδητύος ἠδὲ ποτῆτος
ἧστο, πόθῳ μινύθουσα βαθυζώνοιο θυγατρός,
πρίν γ' ὅτε δὴ χλεύῃς μιν Ἰάμβη κέδν' εἰδυῖα
πολλὰ παρασκώπτουσ' ἐτρέψατο πότνιαν ἁγνήν
μειδῆσαι γελάσαι τε καὶ ἵλαον σχεῖν θυμόν·
205 ἣ δή οἱ **καὶ ἔπειτα μεθύστερον** εὔαδεν ὀργαῖς.

There she sat, holding her veil before her face, and for a long time she remained there on the seat in silent sorrow. She greeted no one with word or movement, but sat there unsmiling, **tasting neither food nor drink**, pining for her deep-girt daughter, until at last diligent Iambe **with ribaldry** and many a jest diverted the holy lady so that she smiled and laughed and became benevolent—Iambe who **ever since** has found favor with her moods.

The adverbial phrase καὶ ἔπειτα μεθύστερον (205) marks this passage as etiological,¹⁵² explaining why initiands into the Mysteries break their fast with ritual

---

147   For "two-tier allusions," see 29*n*147.
148   See 261*n*133.
149   As Harder (2012 ad loc.) points out, the epithet "Rarian" serves to identify Demeter's Eleusinian cult as the venue for this fasting; the plain of Rarium near Eleusis features prominently in the *HH* (2.450–456). For the use of a god's name to signpost an allusion to their *HH*, cf. Jackson 1990.
150   Hunter 2015 ad *Arg.* 4.1726.
151   Brown 1997: 18. Later sources make this status explicit; see Rotstein 2010: 173 n. 24.
152   Parker 1991: 8.

ribaldry.¹⁵³ It was probably in this connection that Callimachus brought up the Eleusinian fast days, because these concluded in a form of aeschrology just like that practiced at Anaphe.¹⁵⁴ Indeed, insofar as Iambe is the personification and eponym of ἴαμβος, Callimachus is essentially citing the Homeric account of the origin of aeschrology itself.¹⁵⁵

What Apollonius has done in his turn is to change the nature of the Argonauts' sacrifices to Apollo Aegletes the better to suit the context of this passage from the *HH*. In particular, we may compare the immediate sequel to the lines I have just quoted: Queen Metaneira offers the newly cheery Demeter some "honey-sweet wine" (μελιηδέος οἴνου, 206), but the goddess refuses on the grounds that it would not be proper (οὐ γὰρ θεμιτόν, 207; see also ὁσίης ἕνεκεν, 211) for her to drink red wine (οἶνον ἐρυθρόν, 208).¹⁵⁶ Instead, she requests and is served the Eleusinian ritual drink called κυκεών, specifying the ingredients as **water** mixed with barley and pennyroyal (ἄλφι καὶ ὕδωρ ... μείξασαν πιέμεν γληχῶνι, 208–209). Apollonius naturally dispenses with the distinctively Eleusinian ingredients of the κυκεών in his adaptation, but the substitution of water in place of wine¹⁵⁷ and the omission of any explicit reference to ani-

---

153 For Iambe and ritual aeschrology at Eleusis, see Richardson 1974: 22–23, 213–217. It is debated whether all of the rites implicitly etiologized in the hymn belong to the Eleusinian Mysteries, or if some could belong to the Thesmophoria; for the latter possibility, see Clinton 1992: 28–37, 96–99 (cf. Clinton 1986); Suter 2002: 4–7. In fact, aeschrology figured into many cults of Demeter; see, e.g., Olender 1990: 94–96.

154 And, indeed, at Lindos, the subject of the next αἴτιον and which Callimachus has already implicitly compared to the Anaphean rites (fr. 7.19–21).

155 On Iambe and her invention of ἴαμβος, see, e.g.: Fowler 1990: 18–19; Rotstein 2010: p. 120 and ch. 6. Other Hellenistic poets also seem to be aware of Iambe's metapoetic import as the πρώτη εὑρέτις of ἴαμβος. She figures prominently into Philicus' fragmentary *Hymn to Demeter* (*SH* 680.54–62), which was written in an iambic meter (stichic choriambic hexameters); Philicus thus implicitly traces the pedigree of his novel meter back to the Myth celebrated in his hymn, even as he emphasizes his own metrical innovation (*SH* 677). There is likely a similar programmatic significance in Herodas' allusions to Iambe (and her Orphic equivalent Baubo) in *Mimiambs* 1 and 6; see, e.g.: Stern 1979, 1981; Miralles 1992: 99; Piacenza 2014. For a different Iambe associated with Hipponax's initation as an iambic poet, see: Brown 1988; Rosen 1988b; Fowler 1990; for possible connections to the *Homeric Hymn*'s Iambe, see Ormand 2015: 46–54.

156 Lines 207 and 211 all but explicitly cast this scene as an etiology for the abstentions practiced in the actual Mysteries (Parker 1991: 8). For the prohibition on wine and for the drinking of the κυκεών, see Richardson 1974: 213, 224–226.

157 Bremmer (2005: 27) suggests that Apollonius preserves a genuine feature of the Anaphean cult: "The strange prominence of water ... in Apollonius' text is so striking that it must reflect a characteristic detail of the Anaphiote ritual." But if so, it is odd that wine features so prominently in Conon's telling; note also the (apparently normal) feast (εὐωχίαν) in Pseudo-Apollodorus' version. Moreover, as Bremmer himself recognizes (loc. cit.), Apol-

mal victims serve to assimilate the Argonauts' humble sacrifices at Anaphe with the solemn fasting at Eleusis[158]—both to be enlivened by the outbreak of playful aeschrology.[159] Apollonius' primary purpose may have been to "correct" Callimachus' account by more closely connecting the Anaphean rite to the origins of iambic abuse as given by the *Homeric Hymn to Demeter*,[160] but Apollonius' procedure here is also a wonderful illustration of the way that he looked not only to Callimachean etiology as a model for his own αἴτια, but also back to Callimachus' own sources of inspiration in the *HH*s. Indeed, given the programmatic potential of Apollonius' allusion to Callimachus' Anaphean αἴτιον—the second etiology in the entire *Aetia*, and one concerned with a substantial portion of the Argonautic myth[161]—we are perhaps entitled to discern here metacommentary upon the origins of literary etiology itself: Apollonius' own etiological practice is a Callimachean inheritance ultimately anchored, however, in the hymnic Homer.

4 Further Hymnic Techniques

Beyond the exceptions noted so far, the narrative technique of the *HH*s is substantially the same as that of the HEs.[162] They do, however, exhibit several minor departures from HE practice that intriguingly anticipate directions that Apollonius would explore more insistently; I would like to note a few of these

---

lonius likely drew this detail from *Od.* 12.362–363 (Odysseus' comrades' perverse sacrifice of the cattle of the Sun, using water in the absence of wine), though with a happy reversal in the ethical valence of this substitution; cf. Apollonius' innocuous reworking of the Thrinacian episode itself (Knight 1995: 219). See further n. 160 below.

158 Hunter (2015 ad *Arg.* 4.1719–1720) argues that "there is no reason to think that [the Argonauts] did not have a sheep to be killed (cf. 1593–1602)," but whether we assume the sacrifice of sheep or vegetarian offerings, there seems to be a contrast intended with the expensive βοοκτασία carried out in Alcinous' palace (1724).

159 These points of contact with the *Homeric Hymn to Demeter* have now been noted by Stürner 2022 ad 4.1721, 1725–1729, 1726.

160 It is also intriguing to contemplate the possible metapoetic significance of water vs. wine in this context. There is some precedent in Callimachus' own poetry for a preference for "poetic sobriety" (Harder 2019b: 29–31), which seems to have crystallized into the (later-attested) opposition of water- vs. wine-drinking as poetological symbols for alignment with or against Callimachean aesthetics (see: Kambylis 1965: 118–122; Crowther 1979: 5; Knox 1985: 107–112). If my reconstruction is correct, then Apollonius could be "out-Callimachus-ing" Callimachus, as it were, by replacing wine with water in his retelling of the Anaphe myth.

161 See 100n73, 126n185.

162 Nünlist 2004: 39.

here.[163] For instance, we may note the higher proportion of indirect speech in the hymns compared to the HEs, a change that, as Nünlist notes, "inevitably leads to greater salience of the narrator's controlling function."[164] Precisely the same observation has been made of the increased prominence of indirect speech in the *Arg*.[165] Another interesting example has to do with what Nünlist calls "confidence in the cooperation of their narratees." He explains:

> For they [the hymns] show a tendency to leave rather substantial "gaps" (*Leerstellen*) in the narrative, which the narratee is to fill in for himself or herself. An instructive, because "un-Homeric," example is a passage from the *Hymn to Hermes*: Apollo's actual discovery that his cattle have been abducted from Pieria, a corner-stone of the story, is left out of the narrative (between 183 and 184), but can be "reconstructed" from Apollo's speech to the old man in Onchestus (190–200).[166]

In fact, some of the gaps in the hymnic narratives are considerable—for instance, Demeter's motivation for becoming a nurse at Eleusis is never made explicit.[167] Similarly, Apollonius exploits such *Leerstellen* to a degree unthinkable in the HEs regarding major plot points, especially as regards character motivation (e.g., does Jason really plan to betray Medea as she alleges at 4.355–390?).[168]

Another device that Apollonius may have borrowed from the *HH*s is one very dear to his narrator's heart, the narratorial digression. Other than in exceptional contexts like the Catalog of Ships,[169] the HEs tend to put digressive material in the mouths of characters.[170] In contrast, the AR narrator is quite comfortable introducing digressions in his own voice, sometimes even retrospectively flagging a passage as digressive by means of a break-off formula.[171] The *HH*s

---

163   Clay (1997: 492) suggests that "the familiarity of the material" covered in their Myths and the "smaller scale" of the hymns "may have invited experimentation and innovation in both diction and narrative technique" vis-à-vis the HEs.
164   Nünlist 2004: 38; see also Nünlist 2007: 58, de Jong 2022b: 85 with n. 25.
165   See esp. Hunter 1993: 143–151.
166   Nünlist 2004: 39.
167   See, e.g.: Parker 1991: 8, 10–11; Foley 1994: 91, 98–103, 113–114; Clay 1997: 504; O'Higgins 2004: 39.
168   Byre 2002 is fundamental on this aspect of Apollonius' narrative technique.
169   E.g., the Thamyris digression at *Il*. 2.594–600. It is comically apt that this digression occurs in the entry for the Pylians, whose leader Nestor is famous for his geriatric digressions.
170   Nünlist 2009: 120.
171   See, e.g.: Fusillo 1985: 377; Cuypers 2004: 49.

are hardly riddled with digressions, but a pair of them in the *Homeric Hymn to Apollo* are particularly noticeable. One is an external analepsis on the birth of Typhoeus (3.305–355), the other an omnitemporal description of a certain rite observed at Onchestus, and this latter example is especially reminiscent of the AR narrator's practice. Apollo is traveling the Greek world in search of a suitable site at which to establish his oracle (229–239):

> ἔνθεν δὲ προτέρω ἔκιες, ἑκατηβόλ' Ἄπολλον,
> 230 Ὀγχηστὸν δ' ἷξες, Ποσιδήϊον ἀγλαὸν ἄλσος·
> ἔνθα νεοδμὴς πῶλος ἀναπνέει ἀχθόμενός περ
> ἕλκων ἅρματα καλά, χαμαὶ δ' ἐλατὴρ ἀγαθός περ
> ἐκ δίφροιο θορὼν ὁδὸν ἔρχεται· οἳ δὲ τέως μὲν
> κείν' ὄχεα κροτέουσιν ἀνακτορίην ἀφιέντες.
> 235 εἰ δέ κεν ἅρματ' ἀγῇσιν ἐν ἄλσεϊ δενδρήεντι,
> ἵππους μὲν κομέουσι, τὰ δὲ κλίναντες ἐῶσιν·
> ὣς γὰρ τὰ πρώτισθ' ὁσίη γένεθ'· οἳ δὲ ἄνακτι
> εὔχονται, δίφρον δὲ θεοῦ τότε μοῖρα φυλάσσει.
> ἔνθεν δὲ προτέρω ἔκιες, ἑκατηβόλ' Ἄπολλον ...

> From there you went on, far-shooting Apollo, and reached Onchestus, Poseidon's bright grove, where the new-broken colt takes breath from the burden of pulling a fine chariot: the driver, good as he is, jumps down from the car and walks, while they continue to rattle the empty vehicle along, having discarded their master. If the chariot gets smashed in the wooded grove, they take care of the horses but tip the chariot down and leave it; for so the rule was established in the beginning. They pray to the deity, and the chariot is kept as the god's property. From there you went on, far-shooting Apollo ...

I am tempted to call this interest in the details of a local cult,[172] apparently for their own sake,[173] Alexandrian avant la lettre.[174] The deployment of this digression in a travel catalog is particularly reminiscent of the ethnographic sections toward the end of *Arg.* 2: there the AR narrator digresses to describe the cus-

---

172 The hymnist's interest in this local cult is especially notable given the *HHs*' generally Panhellenic orientation (stressed, e.g., by Clay 2006: 9–11).
173 So, e.g., West 1975: 161: "When he gets to Onchestus, the poet cannot refrain from describing a curious ceremony to be seen there, although it has nothing to do with Apollo." But for other possible reasons for the digression, see Janko 1986: 54–55; Clay 2006: 59.
174 See 270n184.

toms of the various peoples of the Black Sea littoral whom the Argonauts pass by—without actually encountering any of them—as they approach Colchis.[175] It may thus be no coincidence that ἵππους ... κομέουσι at *HH* 3.236 finds a nice echo in an ethnographic digression on Amazonian religion at *Arg.* 2.1176 (ἵππους ... κομέουσαι),[176] though with a startling transformation from the original context: the Amazons would "tend to" their horses only in order to sacrifice them.[177] In part this allusion is playful (and xenophobic), but it may also make the literary-historical point that narratorial digressions on local cult practices are sanctioned by the august example of Homer himself.

I would adduce two further hymnic techniques that may have left their mark on Apollonius. The first is what Hopkinson calls the "antiquarian 'flashback,'"[178] in which the setting of the narrative in the ancient past is emphasized by noting what has *not yet* happened at that early point in mythological chronology. There is slight precedent for this device in *Il.* 20.216–218, but a much more notable example occurs, once again, in the *Homeric Hymn to Apollo*. During the god's travels, he arrives at Thebes (3.225–228):

225 Θήβης δ' εἰσαφίκανες ἕδος καταειμένον ὕλῃ·
     οὐ γάρ πώ τις ἔναιε βροτῶν ἱερῇ ἐνὶ Θήβῃ,
     οὐδ' ἄρα πω τότε γ' ἦσαν ἀταρπιτοὶ οὐδὲ κέλευθοι
     Θήβης ἂμ πεδίον πυρηφόρον, ἀλλ' ἔχεν ὕλη.

[You, Apollo] arrived at the site of Thebes, which was cloaked in vegetation, for no mortal yet dwelt in holy Thebes and there were not yet any paths or roads crossing the wheat-bearing Theban plain, but it was occupied by wild growth.[179]

As de Jong notes, this technique "was to have a great future in Apollonius of Rhodes and Callimachus."[180] Indeed, this οὐ πω ... οὐδέ πω structure recurs at *Arg.* 4.678–679, in a description of the primordial earth from which life arose,

---

175 See also the *HH* narrator's adverse, quasi-ethnographic comments about the Phlegyae as Apollo passes this tribe (*HH* 3.278–280).
176 Elsewhere in Homeric poetry, the collocation of ἵππος and κομέω occurs only at *Il.* 8.112.
177 The verb δαίτρευον implies that the Amazons eat the horses as well, as is typical in sacrifice.
178 Hopkinson 1984 ad Callim. *Hymn* 6.24.
179 This passage is well explained by Clay 2006: 58–59.
180 De Jong 2012: 51–52 (quotation at 52). Notably, Apollonius echoes this passage in recounting Cadmus' foundation of Thebes (ἐνὶ Θήβῃ ... εἰσαφίκανεν, *Arg.* 3.1178–1179; noted by Campbell 1981 ad loc.)—at Apollo's direction, of course (1181–1182).

and Apollonius happens to describe none other than Thebes itself as "still without towers" (ἀπύργωτος δ' ἔτι Θήβη, 1.736) in the ecphrasis of Jason's cloak.[181]

A second device that is naturally at home in hymnody is what Nünlist calls "eternal prolepsis," or the use of the future tense to describe the establishment of conditions that will persist, as it were, "world without end." For example, at *HH* 2.364–369, Hades promises Persephone that she will rule over the underworld—that is, from this moment forevermore; likewise, in exchange for allowing Apollo to be born on Delos, Leto promises the island that all people will bring hecatombs to Apollo's temple there (3.57–60, 87–88)—that is, from generation to generation ad infinitum; etc.[182] There is perhaps one good example of this unique variety of prolepsis in the *Arg.*, likewise in character-text: in gratitude for the elimination of Amycus, King Lycus promises to build temples to the Dioscuri, "which all sailors on the sea **will** behold from very far away and **seek** their favor" (τὸ μὲν μάλα τηλόθι πάντες | ναυτίλοι ἂμ πέλαγος θηεύμενοι ἱλάξονται, *Arg.* 2.807–808). Apollonius' use of eternal prolepsis here points to a function of his Mythic narrative that is utterly typical of the *HH*s, namely, that of furnishing the αἴτιον for a new addition to the ranks of the gods.[183]

5   Conclusion

Narratological studies of the *Arg.* rightly stress the novel features with which Apollonius has endowed his narrative vis-à-vis the precedent set by the HEs, but these innovations are typically viewed as Alexandrian mannerisms in line with trends discernible above all in his major contemporaries, Callimachus and Theocritus. In fact, many of these features have rich pedigrees in earlier Greek literature that often extend,[184] as we have seen, back to the *HH*s, which could have given Homer's blessing to a variety of devices alien to the *Iliad* and the *Odyssey*. In analyzing each potential instance of this phenomenon, I have traced parallels with the hymns in order to assess the likelihood that Apollonius is imitating them specifically in his deployment of these narrative devices. The evidence is not overwhelming in each instance, but the privileged

---

181   See also 1.508–509, 760, and particularly 4.261–266, which occurs in the antiquarian speech of Argus, another of the narrator's avatars.

182   Nünlist 2007: 61–62.

183   See further 4.649–653 with my analysis in the previous chapter (2.2.4).

184   Acosta-Hughes 2010b offers a salutary reminder of the degree to which "Hellenistic" devices and affectations can already be detected in Archaic and Classical poetry. See further on this score Hopkinson 1988: 7–8; Parsons 1993: 154–155.

status of the *HH*s within the *Arg.* makes the case for direct influence more probable. Moreover, certain allusions seem designed to underline Apollonius' debt to the hymns for specific devices. Thus his two uses of the Homeric *dis legomenon* ὄργια may point to the *Homeric Hymn to Demeter* as a model for his twin pious silences, and a two-tier allusion in his etiology for the ritual ribaldry on Anaphe may show that Apollonius regarded Callimachean etiologizing as an extrapolation of Homeric-hymnic practice specifically. But if this chapter proves anything, it is that the *HH*s did indeed supply Homeric precedent for many of the most "un-Homeric" features of Apollonius' narrative.

CHAPTER 4

Hymnic Moments within the Epic

In the previous chapter, I sought to establish that a great number of "un-Homeric" features in Apollonius' narrative do, in fact, find authorization in Homeric models so long as we are willing to expand the category of "Homeric" poetry to include the *HH*s. In some cases, the analysis focused on passages with a genuinely "hymnic" tone, such as Apollonius' series of pious similes. In others, the AR narrator's hymnic voice was discernible only beneath different layers representing other aspects of his complex personality, such as the scholarly-Callimachean mode that comes to the fore in his etiological passages. In this chapter, we will continue to see examples of the phenomena surveyed in chapter 3, such as the narrator's overtness or his demonstrations of piety, and I will continue to adduce precedents from the *HH*s where I think they are relevant. This chapter focuses, however, squarely on the phenomenon of the *Arg.*'s representation of hymnody itself—those narrative sequences in which gods and heroes are verbally invoked in prayer or celebration, whether by the AR narrator himself, his characters, or some indeterminate combination of the two. Apollonius' innovative approaches to representing hymnic praise, and the sheer frequency with which he does so, constitute one of the clearest ways in which the hymnic affiliation of the *Arg.* makes itself felt within his epic narrative.

Section 1 begins by analyzing the AR narrator's tendency to join in his characters' praise of a god by apostrophizing them in his own voice, in a device that I call "contagious hymnody." Section 2 moves on to study the hymnic subtext of some other of the poem's apostrophes, including other examples directed at gods, such as Eros and the Muses, but also some addressed to mortal characters, such as the Theran oecist Theras or the Argonauts themselves. I argue that in the context of a hymn dedicated to its own divinized heroes, this traditional epic device may gain new powers of suggestion, potentially intimating the addressee's present-day status as an immortalized cult hero.

Section 3 extends our analysis beyond narratorial apostrophizing to examine another typically Apollonian technique for representing hymnody, what I have termed "hymnic narratization": the AR narrator's predilection for favoring a god with Honorific epithets that are otherwise uncharacteristic of his poetic style when narrating that god's Invocation by one of his characters. Apollonius' technique is such that it is ultimately unclear whether these Honorifics are meant to suggest the invoking character's own words, in the manner of "free indirect discourse," or if they represent the narrator's own enthusiastic contributions to the hymnic atmosphere, in another species of "contagious hymnody"; the result of this uncertainty is a "metaleptic" blending together of the hymnic voices of narrator and character. Section 4 concludes this survey of hymnodic moments in Apollonius' narrative—and simultaneously provides a fitting coda for the whole of part 2—by bringing together the various strands of both this chapter and the last in a close reading of Apollonius' Thynias episode (*Arg.* 2.669–719), and especially its representation of Orpheus' hymn to Apollo. More than in any other part of the *Arg.*'s epic narrative, it is here that the AR narrator's hymnic voice truly shines through. Not coincidentally, it is also here that Apollonius most openly declares the literary heritage of the hymnic dimension of his narratorial persona by incorporating a prominent program of allusion to both the major Homeric and Callimachean *Hymns to Apollo*.

1 Contagious Hymnody

I begin with a technique that greatly contributes to the AR narrator's pious self-presentation, namely, the phenomenon of "contagious hymnody." By this term I intend to group together a variety of devices that, in narratological terms, feature metalepsis in a hymnic context. Metalepsis (μετάληψις, "sharing") is a phenomenon in which "the narrator enters ('shares') the universe of the characters or, conversely, a character enters ('shares') the universe of the narrator."[1] A common example of metalepsis is the device of apostrophe (ἀποστροφή): in apostrophizing their own characters, the narrator by definition "turns away" from their usual narratees and thus violates the ordinary boundaries separating the external narrator from the characters in their narrative.[2] My point in devising the term "contagious hymnody" is largely to underscore the AR narrator's tendency to intervene in his narrative in a markedly "hymnic" fashion when his characters are themselves invoking the gods. These interventions create the impression that our pious narrator is swept up in the religious fervor of his own narrative and wants personally to participate (μεταλαμβάνειν) in his characters' hymnody.

I will discuss other possible instances of this technique below, in my analyses of the phenomenon of "hymnic narratization" and of Orpheus' hymn to Apollo.

---

1 De Jong 2009: 89; her article gives many examples from both ancient and postmodern literature.
2 See de Jong 2009: 93–97. For other uses of the term ἀποστροφή in ancient scholarship, see Nünlist 2009: 114.

For now, I cite the most clear-cut examples of this technique in the *Arg.*: a pair of passages in which the AR narrator apostrophizes the same god whom one or more characters in the narrative is invoking. The use of an apostrophe at such a juncture produces a decidedly hymnic effect all on its own, even in the absence of Honorific epithets or other markers of hymnody.

1) The Phaeacian nymphs celebrate the wedding of Jason and Medea (4.1196–1200):

νύμφαι δ' ἄμμιγα πᾶσαι, ὅτε μνήσαιντο γάμοιο,
ἱμερόενθ' ὑμέναιον ἀνήπυον· ἄλλοτε δ' αὖτε
οἰόθεν οἶαι ἄειδον ἑλισσόμεναι περὶ κύκλον,
Ἥρῃ, σεῖο ἕκητι· σὺ γὰρ καὶ ἐπὶ φρεσὶ θῆκας
1200 Ἀρήτῃ πυκινὸν φάσθαι ἔπος Ἀλκινόοιο.

And all the nymphs together, whenever the men sang of marriage, sounded forth the lovely wedding song. But at other times they sang by themselves and danced in a circle, **in your honor, Hera**, because it was **you who put** the thought in Arete's mind to communicate Alcinous' wise words.[3]

2) Jason prays to Apollo amid the "shroud" of darkness on the Cretan Sea (4.1701–1710):[4]

αὐτὰρ Ἰήσων
χεῖρας ἀνασχόμενος μεγάλῃ ὀπὶ Φοῖβον ἀύτει,
ῥύσασθαι καλέων· κατὰ δ' ἔρρεεν ἀσχαλόωντι
δάκρυα· πολλὰ δὲ Πυθοῖ ὑπέσχετο, πολλὰ δ' Ἀμύκλαις,
1705 πολλὰ δ' ἐς Ὀρτυγίην ἀπερείσια δῶρα κομίσσειν.
Λητοΐδη, τύνη δὲ κατ' οὐρανοῦ ἵκεο πέτρας

---

3 Fränkel (1968 ad *Arg.* 3.861f.) suggests that in the case of 4.1199–1200, it is actually impossible to tell if it is the narrator who pronounces these words or if the nymphs are suddenly quoted in direct speech; see further his comments at 227–228; Klooster 2013a: 162. In my view, the adverb ἕκητι (1199), indicating why the nymphs are singing, belongs to the syntax of the previous sentence and thus signals that it is the narrator who addresses Hera in the second person here.

4 This passage represents Jason's prayer in indirect discourse, but the Anaphora of πολλά in lines 1704–1705 conveys the hymnic tone of his "actual" words (Hunter 1993: 140 n. 144; Albis 1996: 118) in a way that prepares for the contagious hymnody in the following lines; cf. *Arg.* 2.707–710 (discussed below).

ῥίμφα Μελαντείους ἀριήκοος, αἵ τ' ἐνὶ πόντῳ
ἧνται· δοιάων δὲ μιῆς ἐφύπερθεν ὀρούσας,
δεξιτερῇ χρύσειον ἀνέσχεθες ὑψόθι τόξον·
1710 μαρμαρέην δ' ἀπέλαμψε βιὸς περὶ πάντοθεν αἴγλην.

And Jason raised his hands and in a loud voice cried out to Phoebus, calling on him to save them, and the tears poured down in his distress. Many gifts he promised to bring to Pytho, many to Amyclae, and many to Ortygia—countless gifts. And **you, Son of Leto**, a ready listener, **came** swiftly down from the sky to the Melanteian rocks, which lie in the sea. And alighting on one of the twin peaks, **you raised** aloft in your right hand your golden bow, and that bow sent out a dazzling gleam in all directions.

As Fränkel observes, by intervening in the second person in his own voice, the narrator appears to participate personally in the praise of the god that he attributes to his characters.[5] I may note here in passing that the device of contagious hymnody would be put to good use, and much more extensively, by both Vergil and Ovid.[6]

Fränkel traces this technique back to the ending of Bacchylides' *Ode* 17, which similarly transitions from the description of the ululations and paean raised by Theseus' companions (125–129) to the narrator's own Prayer to Apollo (130–132).[7] The comparison is apt, but I believe that examples of contagious hymnody, including examples featuring apostrophe, already occur earlier in

---

5 Fränkel 1968 ad *Arg.* 3.861f.; see further: Herter 1944–1955: 281; Zyroff 1971: 101–102; Beye 1982: 18–19. For a different interpretation of the emotional dynamics of such passages, see Stürner 2022 ad 4.1702–1705, with my critique in McPhee 2023a: 43–44.

6 Scholars have particularly connected Vergil's Salian hymn (*Aen.* 8.285–304) to Orpheus' hymn to Apollo in the *Arg.* (e.g., Miller 2014: 447–450), which I discuss below. Another large-scale example in Ovid is the narrator's hymn to Bacchus at *Met.* 4.17–30, which grows directly out of a description of the god's Invocation by his Theban bacchants (see further 302n105). Many more passages in these authors (listed by Zyroff 1971: 494) rather correspond to the Callimachean practice of apostrophizing gods when aspects of their cults are mentioned, without explicit reference to a character's speech act (see 280n19): Verg. *Aen.* 6.18, 251; 8.84; 10.540; 11.7–8; Ov. *Met.* 4.754, 756; 15.731; see also Verg. *Aen.* 3.119, 371 (with Aeneas as internal narrator). These passages could represent a more oblique type of contagious hymnody, in that "the natural [i.e., presumable] invocation by the dedicator [or sacrificer, *vel. sim.*] is echoed in an apostrophe by the poet in the context of the narrative" (Eden 1975 ad Verg. *Aen.* 8.84f.). Verg. *Aen.* 7.389–391 imitates such passages as Callim. *Aet.* fr. 18.5–10 Pfeiffer, Harder and Apoll. Rhod. *Arg.* 4.1383–1387, on which see below in this section.

7 Fränkel 1968: 575, 1975: 452. For the question of whether Bacchyl. 17 is itself a paean or a dithyramb, see, e.g., Rutherford 2001: 98–99; Maehler 2004: 172–173.

the *HH*s. By "already occur earlier" I mean, first, that all of the hymns, as "Homeric" compositions, notionally ought to predate Bacchylides, at least from Apollonius' point of view,[8] and, second, that at least some of them actually must have predated him in historical fact—particularly the major *Homeric Hymn to Apollo*.[9] We may note the following passages:[10]

3) A group of goddesses attend to Leto at Apollo's birth (*HH* 3.119–122):

ἐκ δ' ἔθορε πρὸ φόωσδε· θεαὶ δ' ὀλόλυξαν ἅπασαι.
120 ἔνθα σέ, ἤιε Φοῖβε, θεαὶ λόον ὕδατι καλῷ
ἁγνῶς καὶ καθαρῶς, σπάρξαν δ' ἐν φάρεϊ λευκῷ,
λεπτῷ, νηγατέῳ· περὶ δὲ χρύσεον στρόφον ἧκαν.

Then the child leaped forth to the light, and all the goddesses raised a cry. Straightway, *ēïos* **Phoebus**, the goddesses washed **you** purely and cleanly with sweet water, and swathed **you** in a white garment of fine texture, new-woven, and fastened a golden band about **you**.[11]

4) The hymnist describes sounds that please Cybele, including those involved in her worship (*HH* 14.3–6):

---

8   For the question of Apollonius' attitude to the authorship of the hymns, see the introduction, 2.4.
9   Even analysts who would divide the poem into Delian and Pythian halves (if not Delian, Pythian, and Crisaean thirds: Wade-Gery 1936; Richardson 2010: 9–13; Faraone 2018) would date their present redaction to 523 BCE (e.g.: Burkert 1979: 59–60; Janko 1982: 112–113; West 2012: 241). The shorter *HH*s are more difficult to date; see the brief discussion of the date of the hymns in the introduction (2.1).
10 In addition to the passages cited here, de Jong (2009: 113) points to *HH* 3.544–546 and 7.55–59, in which "the absence of a capping formula makes it appear as if the narrator's salutation *chaire* responds directly to the speeches of Apollo and Dionysus respectively."
11 In the context of the plot, as Richardson (2010 ad *HH* 3.119) notes, "the ὀλολυγή (a women's ritual cry) marks the moment of relief after the tension of the birth"; for this practice, see further Frazer 1913: 46. The term also has a hymnic resonance, however, as the ὀλολυγή can be understood as the female equivalent to the male paean-cry (Deubner 1932: 24, 1941: 4 with n. 2; Calame 1997: 77–78), which, indeed, is suggested by the male hymnist's vocative address to the newborn god, ἤιε Φοῖβε (for the derivation of ἤιος from the ritual cry ἰή or ἰὴ ἰέ, see Janko 1994 ad *Il.* 15.365–366). For the combination of ὀλολυγή and παιάν, see, indeed, Bacchyl. 17.125–129 as well as Sappho fr. 44.31–33 LP, Xen. *An.* 4.3.19, Poll. *Onom.* 1.28–29 Bethe. The complementarity of the goddesses' cry and the hymnist's vocative is perceived by Miller 1986: 48; see also Clay 2006: 43.

ἦ κροτάλων τυπάνων τ' ἰαχὴ σύν τε βρόμος αὐλῶν
εὔαδεν ἠδὲ λύκων κλαγγὴ χαροπῶν τε λεόντων
5 οὔρεά τ' ἠχήεντα καὶ ὑλήεντες ἔναυλοι.
καὶ σὺ μὲν οὕτω **χαῖρε** θεαί θ' ἅμα πᾶσαι ἀοιδῇ.

She is well-pleased with the sound of rattles and of timbrels, with the voice of flutes and the outcry of wolves and bright-eyed lions, with echoing hills and wooded haunts. And so **hail to you** in my song and to all goddesses as well!

5) The nymphs sing of Pan's birth and introduction to Olympus (*HH* 19.27–49):

ὑμνεῦσιν δὲ θεοὺς μάκαρας καὶ μακρὸν Ὄλυμπον·
οἷόν θ' Ἑρμείην ἐριούνιον ἔξοχον ἄλλων
29 ἔννεπον, ὡς ...
48 καὶ σὺ μὲν οὕτω **χαῖρε**, ἄναξ, ἵλαμαι δέ σ' ἀοιδῇ·
αὐτὰρ ἐγὼ καὶ σεῖο καὶ ἄλλης μνήσομ' ἀοιδῆς.

They sing of the blessed gods and high Olympus and choose to tell of such a one as luck-bringing Hermes above the rest, how [he sired Pan and brought him to Olympus] ... And so **hail to you, lord**! I seek **your** favor with a song. And now I will remember **you** and another song also.

6) A hymn to Apollo, itself entirely in Du-Stil, describes how swans and bards sing of the god (*HH* 21):

Φοῖβε, σὲ μὲν καὶ κύκνος ὑπὸ πτερύγων λίγ' ἀείδει,
ὄχθῃ ἐπιθρώσκων ποταμὸν πάρα δινήεντα,
Πηνειόν· σὲ δ' ἀοιδὸς ἔχων φόρμιγγα λίγειαν
ἡδυεπὴς πρῶτόν τε καὶ ὕστατον αἰὲν ἀείδει.
5 καὶ σὺ μὲν οὕτω **χαῖρε**, ἄναξ, ἵλαμαι δέ σ' ἀοιδῇ.

Phoebus, of **you** even the swan sings with clear voice to the beating of his wings, as he alights upon the bank by the eddying river Peneus; and of **you** the sweet-tongued minstrel, holding his high-pitched lyre, always sings both first and last. And so **hail to you, lord**! I seek **your** favor with my song.

7) The nymphs who nursed Dionysus process behind their full-grown ward (*HH* 26.7–11):[12]

αὐτὰρ ἐπειδὴ τόνδε θεαὶ πολύυμνον ἔθρεψαν,
δὴ τότε φοιτίζεσκε καθ᾽ ὑλήεντας ἐναύλους,
κισσῷ καὶ δάφνῃ πεπυκασμένος· αἳ δ᾽ ἅμ᾽ ἕποντο
10 Νύμφαι, ὃ δ᾽ ἐξηγεῖτο· βρόμος δ᾽ ἔχεν ἄσπετον ὕλην.
καὶ σὺ μὲν οὕτω χαῖρε, πολυστάφυλ᾽ ὦ Διόνυσε ...

But when the goddesses had brought him up, the much-hymned god, then he began to wander continually through wooded haunts, thickly wreathed with ivy and laurel. And the Nymphs followed in his train with him for their leader; and the boundless forest was filled with their outcry. And so **hail to you, Dionysus, god of abundant clusters** ...

8) The Muses and Graces hymn Artemis as she dances at Delphi (*HH* 27.18–22):

αἳ δ᾽ ἀμβροσίην ὄπ᾽ ἰεῖσαι
ὑμνεῦσιν Λητὼ καλλίσφυρον, ὡς τέκε παῖδας
20 ἀθανάτων βουλῇ τε καὶ ἔργμασιν ἔξοχ᾽ ἀρίστους.
χαίρετε, τέκνα Διὸς καὶ Λητοῦς ἠυκόμοιο·
αὐτὰρ ἐγὼν **ὑμέων** τε καὶ ἄλλης μνήσομ᾽ ἀοιδῆς.

They [the Muses and Graces] utter their heavenly voice, singing how neat-ankled Leto bore children supreme among the immortals both in counsel and in deed. **Hail, children** of Zeus and rich-haired Leto! And now I will remember **you** and another song also.

In most of these passages (4–5, 7–8), an omnitemporal description of the god's worship in song immediately precedes the hymnist's own Salutation to the god,[13] in a device that de Jong calls "metaleptic fade-out."[14] The Salutation thus

---

12 The βρόμος in line 10 may include a processional hymn for the πολύυμνος (7) god.
13 Exceptions: passage 7 describes a recurrent situation in Dionysus' past rather than the present. In passages 4 and 7, there is not explicit mention of hymnody in the god's worship, though I would propose, at the risk of begging the question, that in these hymnic contexts its presence must be implied.
14 See de Jong 2009: 106–113. By this term she means a "type of metalepsis [that] features the merging of the world of the narrated and the world of the narrator at the end of narra-

seems to cap both the overarching poem itself qua hymn and the hymnic worship described in the foregoing narrative; the resultant mise-en-abyme aligns the present *HH* with a timeless hymnic tradition of recurrent songs in praise of the god. This device has a definite metaleptic effect, but probably the passage closest to the Apollonian examples quoted above is passage 3, in which, in the midst of a Mythic narrative, the narrative mode switches from Er-Stil to Du-Stil[15] in tandem with the mention of the attendant goddesses' ritual cry.[16] The same dynamic plays out in the Apollonian passages (1–2), in which the mentions of the nymphs' worship of Hera and of Jason's prayer to Apollo seem to trigger the narrator's own apostrophes to these deities.

One can hardly prove that Apollonius derived this technique, so foreign to HE practice, directly from the *HH*s. Indeed, for passage 2, at least, Apollonius' proximate influence is very likely Callimachus' own treatment of the Anaphe episode in the *Aetia*:[17]

9) As darkness envelops the Argo, Jason supplicates Apollo and reminds him that it was in obedience to his oracle that they launched the expedition (Callim. *Aet*. fr. 18.5–10):

5   ἀλλ' ὅγ' ἀνι]άζων ὃν κέαρ Αἰσονίδης
     σοὶ χέρας ἠέρ]ταζεν, Ἰήιε, πολλὰ δ' ἀπείλει
     ἐς Πυθὼ πέ]μψειν, πολλὰ δ' ἐς Ὀρτυγίην,
     εἴ κεν ἀμιχ₁θαλόεσσαν ἀπ' ἠέρα νηὸς ἐλάσσῃς·
     ]. ὅτι σήν, Φοῖβε, κατ' αἰσιμίην
10   πείσματ'] ἔλυσαν ἐκ[λ]ηρώσαντό τ' ἐρετμά ...

---

tives" (106). In effect, "the worlds of narrated and narrator merge, the metalepsis serving to bring together past and present and to show the continuity between myth and actuality" (107).

15   In this respect, cf. passage 6: here, too, the celebration of Apollo by swan and bard seems to coalesce with the hymnist's own vocative address to the god, but in this case, we cannot speak of a transition from Er-Stil into Du-Stil; this *HH* is, irregularly, cast entirely in Du-Stil.

16   Since this is the first vocative address to Apollo in the Myth proper, it is also possible to interpret it as a recognition that the newborn god has now emerged into the narrative as a full-fledged character: "Solange Apollon noch nicht geboren ist, wendet sich also der Dichter nicht mit unmittelbarer Anrufung ihm zu" (Altheim 1924: 434). I like this interpretation, but I would add that the hymnic undertone achieved by the juxtaposition of the ὀλολυγή with the epithet ἤιος (see 276n11) is suggestive of contagious hymnody.

17   Massimilla 1996 ad Callim. *Aet*. fr. 20.6–15 (= fr. 18 Pfeiffer, Harder).

> but the son of Aeson, troubled in his heart, lifted his hands to **you**, **addressed with *hie***, and promised solemnly to send many gifts to Pytho, and many to Ortygia, if **you would drive** the misty haze from the ship, ... that in accordance with the destiny decreed by **you, Phoebus**, they loosened the ropes and allotted the oars ...

Callimachus' technique is distinctive in that his internal narrator (the Muse Calliope) incorporates her apostrophe to Apollo within Jason's indirect statement, thus blending their voices together.[18] In passage 2, the AR narrator rather effects a transition from indirect speech (4.1701–1705) to an address to the god in his own voice (1706–1710)—just like the *HH* narrators in passages 5 and 8 above.[19] But despite these technical differences, *Aet.* fr. 18 is a fine example of contagious hymnody, and Apollonius unambiguously alludes to this fragment both in passage 2 and elsewhere in the *Arg*.[20] There is an intriguing possibility that in passage 9, Callimachus is himself imitating the device of contagious hymnody in passage 3 (ἤιε Φοῖβε, *HH* 3.120) with his use of the (cognate) epithet Ἰήιε paired with Φοῖβε;[21] it is also possible that Apollonius perceived this reworking.[22] Beyond that, all we can say is that there is indeed "Homeric" prece-

---

18 Harder 2012 ad Callim. *Aet.* fr. 18.6–13; Klooster 2013: 164. Apollonius himself adopts this procedure at *Arg.* 4.1383–1387; see also Verg. *Aen.* 7.389–391. For other apostrophes in Callimachus, see: Harder 2012 (loc. cit.); Klooster 2013a: 166–171.
19 The closest Callimachean parallels I have found for this procedure are a few passages in which the narrator apostrophizes a divinity when mentioning their festival, though without explicit reference to a speech act (*Aet.* fr. 67.5–6, 178.3–4, possibly 186.31; see further 275*n*6); cf. fr. 23, which juxtaposes a second-person address in character-text with a narratorial apostrophe, though in a reproachful context that suggests, if anything, a parody of hymnody. There are some passages in the hymns in which a switch to Du-Stil may correspond with a reference to a god's cult (*Hymn* 2.69, 98; cf. 4.300–313, 316–321); likewise, *Hymn* 3.136–142 is strikingly metaleptic, though neither in this case nor in the *Hymn to Delos* passages just cited can we speak of a "switch" into Du-Stil. Because of the abundance of apostrophe in Callimachus' oeuvre, and the lack of explicit reference to hymnody or prayer in most of these passages, I would hesitate to call any of them parallels for the precise variety of contagious hymnody identified in passages 1 and 2.
20 See, e.g., the notes in: Pfeiffer 1949; Massimilla 1996; and Harder 2012 ad loc. (fr. 18 Pfeiffer, Harder = fr. 20 Massimilla) as well as: Hutchinson 1988: 87–88; Clauss 1993: 77–79. Harder 1993 and Albis 1995 make convincing cases for Callimachean priority.
21 For the rough breathing mark on Ἰήιε, see, e.g., Harder 2012 ad loc. The apostrophe ἤιε Φοῖβε is also notable because this same formula constitutes the only apostrophe to a god in the HEs (at *Il.* 15.365, 20.152); see 108*n*106.
22 There is a faint connection between the epithet that the AR narrator employs at 4.1706 (Λητοΐδη) and the context of passage 3, which narrates Apollo's birth by Leto, but no firm evidence connects the two *loci*.

dent for contagious hymnody and that in these instances, Apollonius' procedure is closer on a technical level to that of the *HH*s than to Callimachus'.

2   Other Apostrophes

2.1   *Apostrophes to Mortals*

Apostrophe to a god is a natural venue for the exhibition of the AR narrator's hymnic voice, but the example of apostrophes to mortal characters provides a splendid illustration of the way that the generic affiliations of the *Arg.* qua epic hymn can breathe new life into the conventions of traditional epic. The HE narrator apostrophizes a limited group of characters with some frequency (Menelaus 7×, Patroclus 8×, Eumaeus 15×), as well as Apollo twice (*Il.* 15.365, 20.152) and Achilles (*Il.* 20.2) and Melanippus (*Il.* 15.582–583) once each.[23] Modern scholars have debated the purpose of these apostrophes, which seem so selectively employed and curiously distributed.[24] To the ancient scholiasts, however, the HE narrator's apostrophes reflect his emotional involvement in the narrative, signaling his sympathy or affection for the apostrophized character.[25] This interpretation is quite natural for a passage like *Il.* 16.786–789:

> ἀλλ' ὅτε δὴ τὸ τέταρτον ἐπέσσυτο δαίμονι ἶσος,
> ἔνθ' ἄρα τοι, Πάτροκλε, φάνη βιότοιο τελευτή·
> ἤντετο γάρ τοι Φοῖβος ἐνὶ κρατερῇ ὑσμίνῃ
> δεινός· ὁ μὲν τὸν ἰόντα κατὰ κλόνον οὐκ ἐνόησεν ...

> But when for the fourth time he [Patroclus] rushed on like a god, then for you, Patroclus, did the end of life appear; for Phoebus met you in the mighty combat, a terrible god. And Patroclus observed him not as he passed through the turmoil ...

All of the HE narrator's apostrophes to Patroclus occur in *Iliad* 16, the book devoted to the hero's tragic demise.

---

23   For a catalog of the apostrophes in both the HEs and the *Arg.*, see De Martino 1984–1985: 116–117.
24   For a survey of opinions, see, e.g.: Yamagata 1989: 91–92; de Jong 2009: 94–97; Klooster 2013a: 152–154.
25   For ancient citations, see Yamagata 1989: 91 n. 1.

The AR narrator's apostrophes, too, often seem to reflect his emotional reaction to his own narrative[26]—patently so in the case of an exclamation like "Father Zeus!" (Ζεῦ πάτερ, 4.1673), his tragic outburst in the Lemnian episode ("O wretched women, sad victims of insatiable jealousy!" [ὦ μέλεαι ζήλοιό τ' ἐπισμυγερῶς ἀκόρητοι, 1.616]), or his overwrought prayer to Eros at *Arg.* 4.445–449. I have also discussed above the impression of religious enthusiasm created by the device of contagious hymnody in the Book 4 apostrophes to Hera (4.1196–1200) and Apollo (4.1701–1710). There is, however, a notable difference between apostrophes in the HEs and the *Arg.*: whereas the HE narrator apostrophizes a god (Apollo) only twice,[27] the AR narrator apostrophizes divine subjects (6 or 7×)[28] more often than mortal ones (3 or 4×).[29] This difference in addressee matters when evaluating the metaleptic effect of the apostrophe, for apostrophes as ordinarily understood function to collapse the temporal divide between the narrator and his characters—"between the here-and-now of his performance and the there-and-then of his tale."[30] Unlike mortal characters, however, gods are deathless and really can be addressed in the narrator's present; divine apostrophes thus do less to erase the distance between past and present than to demonstrate the continuity between the two as bridged by the god's immortal existence.[31] HE apostrophes, in contrast, frequently emphasize precisely the mortality of their addressee; indeed, we have seen that ancient scholars considered the fact of Patroclus' fast-approaching death an important factor in motivating the HE narrator's sympathetic apostrophes to him in *Iliad* 16.[32]

---

26   Exceptions: the emotional valence, if any, of the Invocation of Apollo at 1.1–8 is unclear to me, and emotion is not easy to detect at 4.1763–1764 (if that passage really does feature an apostrophe; see below in this section).
27   See 108*n*106.
28   In addition to the apostrophes to Eros, Hera, Zeus, and Apollo, mentioned in the text, the introit apostrophizes Apollo (1.1–8; for various interpretations of this passage, see chapter 1), while the Envoi salutes the Argonauts in their capacity as divinized heroes (4.1773–1781). 2.708–710 is an ambiguous case, to be discussed below in section 4.3. I leave out of account here Appeals to the Muses, which, because metaliterary, I consider a distinct category; many interpreters similarly consider the Invocation of Apollo at 1.1 a claim to inspiration along the lines of a traditional Appeal to the Muses (see 1.1.3).
29   Besides the apostrophe to the Lemnian women (1.616), there are apostrophes in the Libyan episode to the Argonauts as a collective (4.1383–1387) and to Canthus (4.1485–1489). The case of Theras (4.1763–1764) is ambiguous because of a textual issue; see below.
30   Mackay 2001: 18; see further de Jong 2009: 96.
31   See, e.g., de Jong 2009: 95–96 (cf. Albis 1996: 118).
32   Apollonius imitates the pathetic Patroclus-type apostrophe in his address to Canthus, which similarly begins with a proleptic notice of his impending doom ("But you, Canthus, the Fates of Death seized in Libya" [Κάνθε, σὲ δ' οὐλόμεναι Λιβύῃ ἔνι Κῆρες ἕλοντο, 4.1485]); see, e.g.: Zyroff 1971: 150; Klooster 2013a: 161.

Now, if we remember that Apollonius embraces the reality of hero cult in the *Arg.*, and that the poem is itself framed as a hymn to its own heroized protagonists,[33] the foregoing analysis has important ramifications for our assessment of the AR narrator's apostrophes to human beings. These apostrophized characters may indeed have been mortal at the time of the story, but some of them, like the Argonauts, have since attained immortality. Accordingly, like gods, these heroes can now be conceived of as fully capable of being invoked at the present time of the narrator's enunciation, as the Salutation and Prayer to the Argonauts in the Envoi amply demonstrate (4.1773–1781). That is, in the context of an epic hymn like the *Arg.*, apostrophe to a hero is transformed from a literary mannerism into an actual address to a still-living divinity.[34]

This interpretation is supported, I would argue, by the noticeably "hymnic" tone of the AR narrator's apostrophe to the Argonauts as they port the Argo across the wasteland of the Syrtis for twelve days on end.[35] This feat is so impressive that the AR narrator defers all authority for the tale to the Muses (4.1381–1388):[36]

> Μουσάων ὅδε μῦθος, ἐγὼ δ' ὑπακουὸς ἀείδω
> Πιερίδων, καὶ τήνδε πανατρεκὲς ἔκλυον ὀμφήν,
> ὑμέας, ὦ πέρι δὴ μέγα φέρτατοι υἷες ἀνάκτων,
> ᾗ βίῃ, ᾗ ἀρετῇ Λιβύης ἀνὰ θῖνας ἐρήμους
> 1385 νῆα μεταχρονίην, ὅσα τ' ἔνδοθι νηὸς ἄγεσθαι,
> ἀνθεμένους ὤμοισι φέρειν δυοκαίδεκα πάντα
> ἤμαθ' ὁμοῦ νύκτας τε. δύην γε μὲν ἢ καὶ ὀιζὺν

---

33 As I argue particularly in chapter 2.
34 Cf. Eustathius' observation that in *Il.* 16.692–693 ("Then whom first, whom last did you slay, Patroclus, when the gods called you deathward?"), Homer is "both **exalting [Patroclus], like a divine character**, and at the same time showing him pity" (σεμνύνων τε αὐτὸν ἅμα ὡς θεῖόν τι πρόσωπον καὶ οἰκτιζόμενος, *Il.* 3.915.25–26 van der Valk; translation my own). See further: De Martino 1984–1985: 112; de Jong 2009: 96; Klooster 2013a: 154–158.
35 E.g., Pietsch (1999: 80) observes, "Der Ton hebt sich nach der Berufung auf die Musen zu hymnischem Preis der Helden." See further Klooster 2013a: 160. Cuypers (2004) considers the narrator's praise of the Argonauts generally as a hymnic/encomiastic feature of the poem.
36 This elaborate Alexandrian footnote may serve to underline the marvelous nature of the deed in question and does not necessarily imply serious skepticism on the narrator's part (Stinton 1976; Morrison 2007: 275; note πανατρεκές in line 1382). Nevertheless, this passage has sometimes been connected to the AR narrator's rational, scholarly persona (e.g., by Zyroff 1971: 56). On the ambiguous truth value of such elements of the narrative, see further McPhee, forthcoming b.

τίς κ' ἐνέποι, τὴν κεῖνοι ἀνέπλησαν μογέοντες;
ἔμπεδον ἀθανάτων ἔσαν αἵματος, οἷον ὑπέσταν
1390 ἔργον ἀναγκαίῃ βεβιημένοι.

> From the Muses comes this story, and I sing in obedience to the Pierides; and this account I heard in all accuracy: that you, O far mightiest sons of kings, by your strength and your valor lifted high the ship and everything that you brought in the ship on your shoulders and carried it over the desolate dunes of Libya for twelve whole days and as many nights. And yet who could recount the pain and suffering those men endured in their toil? They were assuredly of the blood of the immortals, such was the task they undertook when forced by necessity.

The second-person address begins with ὑμέας in line 1383, which also serves to introduce the content of the Muses' μῦθος in indirect speech via an accusative-infinitive construction. Yet despite this distancing style of presentation, the narrator immediately asserts himself, interrupting the indirect speech construction he has just set up with a vocative address to the Argonauts (ὦ πέρι δὴ μέγα φέρτατοι υἶες ἀνάκτων), which must be spoken in his own voice.[37] In part the vocative is necessary to identify the referent of the pronoun ὑμέας, since the narrator had not been apostrophizing anyone. But the rhetoric of the passage suggests that more is in play here: the decision to cast the indirect statement in the second person at all; the sudden switch from the Muses' focalization in indirect speech to the narrator's in a vocative address; the exuberant praise contained in the address; and the marked Anaphora in ᾗ βίῃ, ᾗ ἀρετῇ (1384)[38]—all of these features create an ecstatic effect suggestive of enthusiastic hymnody. The second-person address ends in line 1387 (note the third-person verbs and the distal demonstrative κεῖνοι, 1388), but the narrator's encomium continues

---

[37] The narrator's second-person address to the Argonauts would intrude again if we read ἄγεσθε in line 1385 (defended, e.g., by Hunter 2015 and Stürner 2022 ad loc.). This emendation would certainly heighten the confusion of voices that we hear in this passage, continuing the direct address to the Argonauts and introducing an effective juxtaposition with the *oratio obliqua* construction that resumes with the very next word, the accusative participle at the head of the following line (ἀνθεμένους, 1386).

[38] Noted by Hutchinson 1988: 136. Note also the repetition of νῆα ... νηός (1385) and the semantic redundancy of lines 1381–1382, which express essentially the same idea ("This story is the Muses', not mine") thrice in two lines. The phrase "twelve whole days and as many nights" (δυοκαίδεκα πάντα | ἤμαθ' ὁμοῦ νύκτας τε, 1386–1387) strikes me as rhetorically fulsome as well. See further Tsakiris 2022: 216 for the suggestion that ἀείδω ... ὑμέας recalls the Evocatory formulas of the *HH*s.

into line 1390: the Argonauts were not only "sons of kings" (υἶες ἀνάκτων, 1383);[39] to accomplish such a physically demanding task, they must also have been of divine descent (ἀθανάτων … αἵματος, 1389). This ontological upgrade, from princes to demigods, may in turn foreshadow the Argonauts' final transformation into a divinized "race of blessed heroes" (ἀριστήων μακάρων γένος, 4.1773) as revealed at the end of Book 4, in the next apostrophe addressed to them.[40]

A final passage that may reflect an interconnection between hero cult and apostrophe occurs near the very end of the poem—just ten lines before the apostrophe to the heroized Argonauts themselves in the Envoi. The AR narrator concludes the episode of Euphemus' dream with an external prolepsis tracing the colonial migrations of the hero's descendants from Lemnos to Sparta to the island of Calliste, which emerged from the clod that Triton had given him in Libya (4.1757–1761). The prolepsis closes with an etiology for the island's change of name before a break-off formula returns us to the main story of the Argonauts (1761–1764):

ἐκ δὲ λιπόντας
Σπάρτην Αὐτεσίωνος ἐὺς πάις ἤγαγε Θήρας
Καλλίστην ἐπὶ νῆσον, ἀμείψατο δ' οὔνομα Θήρης
ἐξ ἕθεν. ἀλλὰ τὰ μὲν μετόπιν γένετ' Εὐφήμοιο.

When they [the descendants of Euphemus] left Sparta, Theras, the noble son of Autesion, led them to the island of Calliste, and he changed the name to Thera after his own name. But these things happened long after Euphemus.

I have quoted the text of this passage as the manuscript tradition hands it down, but Wendel and Fränkel have drawn attention to the fact that the scholiast ad *Arg.* 4.1760–1764b paraphrases lines 1763–1764 as though the text contained an apostrophe to Theras: "The island of Calliste changed its name and was named Thera after you, Theras son of Autesion" (ἤλλαξε δὲ τὸ ὄνομα ἡ Καλλίστη νῆσος, καὶ ὠνομάσθη Θήρα ἀπὸ σοῦ, ὦ υἱὲ Αὐτεσίωνος Θήρα; translation my own).[41] These

---

39 Cf. Livrea (1973 ad loc.), who interprets ἀνάκτων as "divinità" precisely on the basis of ἀθανάτων at 1389. ἄναξ does frequently denote deities, but I should think that in the absence of contextual indicators pointing to gods, the reader will first interpret the term as referring to mortal kings.

40 Cuypers (2004: 47) and Klooster (2013a: 160) also connect these passages. For the relationship between heroic achievement and heroization, see 2.3.3.

41 See the *apparatus critici* ad loc. in Wendel 1935 and Fränkel 1961.

scholars have thus sensibly proposed that the scholiast's text read ἀμείψατο δ' οὔνομα, Θήρα, | ἐκ σέθεν, "It took its name from yours, Theras."[42]

Most editors since Fränkel have adopted this reading,[43] and Cuypers points out that a vocative Θήρα "allows a wordplay hinging on the formal identity of the vocative of his name and the name of the island called after him (*Thera*)."[44] Certainly there is wordplay here; indeed, this feature, together with the near-homeoteleuton in lines 1762–1763, is probably responsible for the uncertain state of the text.[45] I would only like to add that as a colony-founder (οἰκιστής), Theras would have received worship in his settlement.[46] More than a "mark of honour,"[47] this apostrophe could function as a subtle acknowledgment of Theras' continuing vitality as a cult hero down to the present day.[48] This evocation of hero cult in the case of Theras at 4.1763 would then pave the way for the hymnic Salutation to the Argonauts just ten lines later.

2.2 Other Hymnic Addresses

I transition from apostrophes addressed to mortals to a brief consideration of three of Apollonius' addresses to gods: the Appeals to the Muses that launch

---

42 Translation per Race 2008: 469 n. 200.
43 These include Livrea, Vian, Paduano and Fusillo, Glei and Natzel-Glei, Valverde Sánchez, Hunter, and Stürner.
44 Cuypers 2004: 48 n. 12. Cf. Hunter's notion (2015 ad *Arg.* 4.1762) that "Ap. encourages us to see that the words might suggest 'the excellent son of Autesion led them to the very beautiful island of Thera'" if we read Θήρας in line 1762 as the genitive form of Θήρα (the island) rather than the nominative of Θήρας (the man). For a similar wordplay in Callimachus, see Clauss 2019a: 80. This type of wordplay is the key to solving the riddle in *AP* 14.18, on which see: Luz 2013: 97; Gardella Hueso 2018: 7.
45 Hunter 2015 ad *Arg.* 4.1763–1764. The emendation considered here would introduce a sudden change of subject in the middle of line 1763, from Theras to the island of Thera. Such a change is hardly foreign to Apollonius' style, but it may have caused further confusion for copyists.
46 See the overview of hero cult in 2.1.
47 Hunter 2015 ad *Arg.* 4.1763–1764. Cf. Stürner (2022 ad 4.1762 f., 1763 f.) on the passage's hymnic character ("hymnischen Charakter").
48 Apollonius is consciously varying Pindar's account of the foundation of Cyrene by Euphemus' descendants in *Pythian* 4.3–64. Notably, the Theban poet highlights the oecist cult of Battus, the founder of Cyrene proper, in this ode's companion piece (*Pyth.* 5.93–95). Apollonius, having no reason to eulogize the defunct Battiad dynasty (Stephens 2003: 180), leaves the founding of Cyrene only implicit in his narrative and stops his historical prolepsis at an earlier founder figure (Hunter 2015 ad *Arg.* 4.1731–1764). For Apollonius' silence concerning the founding of Cyrene, see further Klooster 2019: 62–63, 64–65. Depending on the *Arg.*'s date, contemporary Cyrene may have been a Ptolemaic possession (Klooster 2013b: 166, 2014: 535; Murray 2019: 86–88).

Book 3 and 4 and the apostrophe to Eros at 4.445–449. The former passages instantiate a traditional epic device indeed, while the latter functions as a narratorial comment on the developing plotline in the episode of Apsyrtus' murder. But despite the metapoetic role that these passages play, scholars have singled out all three of them for comment on their strikingly hymnic style. They thus furnish yet further illustrations of the way that the AR narrator's hymnic voice can bleed over into the texture of his epic narrative.[49]

2.2.1 The Appeal to Erato in the Book 3 Introit

Arg. 3 begins with an "introit in the middle"[50] that signals a transition to an important new phase of the narrative, in which Medea and the love theme will loom large (3.1–5):

> Εἰ δ' ἄγε νῦν, Ἐρατώ, παρά θ' ἵστασο καί μοι ἔνισπε,
> ἔνθεν ὅπως ἐς Ἰωλκὸν ἀνήγαγε κῶας Ἰήσων
> Μηδείης ὑπ' ἔρωτι· σὺ γὰρ καὶ Κύπριδος αἶσαν
> ἔμμορες, ἀδμῆτας δὲ τεοῖς μεληδήμασι θέλγεις
> 5 παρθενικάς· τῷ καί τοι ἐπήρατον οὔνομ' ἀνῆπται.

> Come now, Erato, stand by my side and tell me how from here Jason brought the fleece back to Iolcus with the aid of Medea's love, for you have a share also of Cypris' power and enchant unwed girls with your anxieties; and that is why your lovely name has been attached to you.

The HEs never invoke a Muse by name, though one *HH* (31, *to Helius*) does provide Homeric precedent: "And now, O Muse **Calliope**, daughter of Zeus, begin to sing of glowing Helius, whom ..." (ἥλιον ὑμνεῖν αὖτε Διὸς τέκος ἄρχεο Μοῦσα, | **Καλλιόπη**, φαέθοντα, τὸν ..., 1–2). The hymnic tone of the Apollonian passage is mainly owed to lines 3–5, in which the AR narrator explains (γάρ, 3) his decision to invoke Erato of all Muses with reference to her specialty as the goddess of love poetry.[51] The poet maintains Du-Stil in lines reminiscent of the

---

49 I may note here as an aside that we should not be troubled if in these passages the AR narrator lavishes hymnic praise on divinities other than the Argonauts, the proper Hymnic Subjects of his poem, for the piety of a Greek hymnist is such that other worthy Subjects may also be praised in passing. For instance, before its primary Mythic narrative, the *Homeric Hymn to Aphrodite* pauses to list the attributes of Athena (5.8–15) and Artemis (16–20), to relate a Myth concerning Hestia's virginity (21–32), and finally to praise Zeus (36–37) and particularly Hera (40–44). The piety of the AR narrator is equally capacious.

50 To adapt a phrase from Conte 1992 ("proem in the middle").

51 See, e.g.: Zyroff 1971: 50; van den Eersten 2013: 52.

Attributive Section of a hymn.⁵² The theme of a god's acquisition of her or his τιμή is prominent in both Hesiod's *Theogony* and the *HHs*;⁵³ Hardie has shown that in these lines Apollonius particularly alludes to Hesiod's description of Aphrodite's τιμαί (203–205) and to his Hymnic Proem to the Muses (67).⁵⁴

To these insights, I would add only one further hymnic undertone that may be implicit in the AR narrator's Appeal to Erato. The explicit justification for her selection as the Muse of the second half of the poem is her association with love poetry, which is attested as early as Plato (*Phdr.* 259d).⁵⁵ Other sources, however, assign her to different domains of poetry, including dance and lyric,⁵⁶ but intriguingly, one anonymous epigram in the Palatine Anthology makes Erato the inventor of **hymnody** (ὕμνους ἀθανάτων Ἐρατὼ πολυτερπέας εὗρε, *AP* 9.504.6). This is but one of the several idiosyncratic associations between a Muse and a given sphere of poetry that appear exclusively in this epigram.⁵⁷ Consequently, I would not press this point further, but if the connection to hymnody presented in the epigram goes back to Apollonius' time, Erato might also have been a singularly appropriate Muse for the AR narrator to single out for invocation in this hymnic fashion within his epic hymn.

2.2.2 The Appeal to the Muse in the Book 4 Introit

Book 4 begins with another Appeal to the Muses, which thematizes Medea's mixed motivations for departing from Colchis aboard the Argo (4.1–5):⁵⁸

Αὐτὴ νῦν κάματόν γε, θεά, καὶ δήνεα κούρης
Κολχίδος ἔννεπε, Μοῦσα, Διὸς τέκος· ἢ γὰρ ἐμοί γε

---

52   Although Attributive Sections are generally cast in the omnitemporal present (for this term, see 13*n*69), the aorist verb ἔμμορες (4) constitutes no real exception, as it refers to the acquisition of a sphere of influence that continues to define the deity's activity eternally (Janko 1981: 12). Cf. the present-tense English translation: "for you **have** a share in ..."

53   For this theme in the *HHs*, see above all Clay 2006, whose argument is summarized in introduction, 2.1.

54   See Hardie 2009: 16–17.

55   See further, e.g., Ov. *Ars am.* 2.16, Plut. *Mor.* 746f., Ath. 13.555b (cf. Diod. Sic. 4.7.4, Ov. *Fast.* 4.195–196, Cornutus *Theol. Graec.* 14). For the role of etymology in assigning functions to the Muses, see Hardie 2009.

56   For sources, see the useful chart in *RE* 16.1 s.v. "Musai," coll. 727–730; note also that Erato's attribute in artistic representations is eventually the cithara or lyre (Taback 2002: 81, 87).

57   Taback 2002: 42–43. The closest precedent I can find for this idea is a potentially interesting juxtaposition of Erato's name with the word ὕμνους (in the generic sense of "song") in Stes. fr. 327 Finglass, though the text is corrupt.

58   For Medea's mixed motives here, Hunter 1987 is fundamental.

ἀμφασίη νόος ἔνδον ἑλίσσεται ὁρμαίνοντι,
ἠέ μιν ἄτης πῆμα δυσίμερον ἦ τό γ᾽ ἐνίσπω
5   φύζαν ἀεικελίην, ἧ κάλλιπεν ἔθνεα Κόλχων.

> Now, goddess, you yourself tell of the distress and thoughts of the Colchian girl, O Muse, daughter of Zeus, for truly the mind within me whirls in speechless stupor, as I ponder whether to call it the lovesick affliction of obsession or shameful panic, which made her leave the Colchian people.

This passage is less strikingly hymnic than the Book 3 introit, but we may note that here, uniquely, the Muse is dignified by an impressive series of three vocatives:[59] "goddess," "Muse," and "daughter of Zeus."[60] As with the Erato passage, I would only like to add the possibility of a further hymnic subtext, for which I have already argued in the introduction.[61] These first two Honorifics have often been connected to the opening words of the *Iliad* (μῆνιν ἄειδε, θεά, 1.1) and the *Odyssey* (ἔννεπε, **Μοῦσα**, 1.1). By the same token, I would propose that Διὸς τέκος is drawn from the Exordium of the *Homeric Hymn to Helius*, already quoted above in connection with the Erato-invocation: "And now, O Muse Calliope, **daughter of Zeus**, begin to sing of glowing Helius, whom ..." (ἥλιον ὑμνεῖν αὖτε **Διὸς τέκος** ἄρχεο Μοῦσα, | Καλλιόπη, φαέθοντα, τὸν ..., 1–2). Together, these three vocatives programmatically allude to all three of Apollonius' major Homeric models: the *Iliad* (θεά), the *Odyssey* (Μοῦσα), and the *HH*s (Διὸς τέκος).

2.2.3   The Apostrophe to Eros

My final example of a hymnic address to a deity occurs in the Apsyrtus episode, which is punctuated by an apostrophe to Eros that locates the ultimate cause of the murder of Medea's brother in the god's malign influence (4.445–449):

---

59   Scholars often assume that this Muse is Erato (e.g.: Zyroff 1971: 48; Campbell 1983: 2; Fusillo 1985: 367), and in fact there is good reason to suppose that Erato remains the Muse of 4.1: she had been invoked as the Muse of the *entire* second half of the poem, which involves bringing the Fleece back to Iolcus in Book 4 (3.2) through the love of Medea won in Book 3 (3.3) (Hunter 2015 ad *Arg.* 4.1–5). The narrator hedges his bets, however, by invoking an unnamed Muse, because he ostensibly does not know whether it was lovesickness (the especial domain of Erato) or panicked fear that caused Medea to abandon Colchis. The shift from Erato to an unnamed Muse who may or may not be Erato thus mirrors the complication of Medea's motivations in Book 4. Cf. De Martino 1984–1985: 109–110; Köhnken 2000: 56 n. 4.

60   Thus, e.g., Zyroff (1971: 50) says that our passage has "several of the traditional elements of prayer."

61   See 21–23 for a fuller explication of this argument.

445 σχέτλι᾽ Ἔρως, μέγα πῆμα, μέγα στύγος ἀνθρώποισιν,
ἐκ σέθεν οὐλόμεναί τ᾽ ἔριδες στοναχαί τε γόοι τε,
ἄλγεά τ᾽ ἄλλ᾽ ἐπὶ τοῖσιν ἀπείρονα τετρήχασιν.
δυσμενέων ἐπὶ παισὶ κορύσσεο, δαῖμον, ἀερθείς,
οἷος Μηδείῃ στυγερὴν φρεσὶν ἔμβαλες ἄτην.

> Cruel Love, great affliction, great abomination for humans; from you come deadly quarrels and groans and laments, and countless other pains besides these are stirred up. May it be against my enemies' children, O god, that you rise up and arm yourself, being such as when you cast abominable madness into the mind of Medea.

The tone of this passage is described as "tragic" as often as it is "hymnic,"[62] and appropriately so, as tragic choral odes hymning Eros represent an important group of intertexts.[63] As Zyroff has pointed out, this apostrophe systematically reverses the rhetoric of hymnody: Eros is invoked with hateful rather than Honorific epithets (445); an Attributive Section outlines his baleful rather than beneficial effects on humanity (446–446);[64] and the concluding Prayer is not a request for a boon but an apopemptic wish for harm to the children of the narrator's enemies (448–449). The effect is enhanced by the maintenance of the address over five lines and by the Anaphora of μέγα in line 445, which seems to be modeled on a line from the Hymnic Proem of Aratus' *Phaenomena* (15).[65] This apostrophe is often related to the invocation of Erato at the beginning of Medea's love story (*Arg.* 3.1–5).[66] The hymnic cast of both passages constitutes a further point of connection, but the negativized form assumed by this "hymn" to Eros reflects the bloody turn that this love story has taken.

---

62 Tragic: see, e.g.: Faerber 1932: 105 n. 3; Corbato 1955: 15; Natzel 1992: 104–105. Hymnic: see, e.g.: Zyroff 1971: 50–51; Livrea 1973 ad *Arg.* 4.445; Hunter 1993: 116 n. 68. Stoessl (1941: 110) rightly notes the passage's affiliations with both genres.

63 For such hymns, see Cerbo 1993. Soph. *Ant.* 781–800 and Eur. *Hipp.* 525–564 are particularly comparable, the former because it relates to strife among family (note σὺ καὶ τόδε νεῖκος ἀνδρῶν | ξύναιμον ἔχεις ταράξας, 793–794), the latter because it includes a negative wish regarding Eros (528–529), though not precisely an apopemptic prayer as in Apollonius (Hunter 2015 ad loc.). For other important intertexts, see the notes ad loc. in Hunter 2015.

64 Cf. the more positive tone in the description of Erato's powers at 3.3–5, in many ways the pointed opposite of the "Attributive Section" of this brief hymn to Eros (4.446–447).

65 See, e.g., Vian 2002: 3.166 ad *Arg.* 4.449; the echo enhances the hymnic tone of the passage (Hunter 1993: 116 n. 68). Note also the echo of στύγος (445) in στυγερήν (449).

66 E.g., Morrison 2007: 302–303.

3 Hymnic Narratization

I now turn from the topic of apostrophizing to another important device in the AR narrator's hymnic arsenal, namely, his exceptional deployment of multiple Honorific epithets in narrative contexts in which a god is invoked by a character. The piling-up of epithets, together with expansion via relative clause, is one of the most distinctive markers of the Greek hymnic style, especially within an Exordium.[67] The *Orphic Hymns*, which often consist of almost nothing but lists of epithets, take this tendency to an extreme,[68] but a milder form of the same mannerism is already in evidence in the *HH*s (note esp. *HH* 12.1–4, 27.1–3, 28.1–4).[69] With the exception of extraordinary passages like his apostrophe to Eros (*Arg.* 4.445–449), the AR narrator does not typically apply "ornamental" epithets to divinities (or, to a lesser extent, to other characters) with the high degree of frequency found in early Greek epic, a tendency that stems from Apollonius' more general aversion to an overly formulaic style.[70] But one significant exception to this rule occurs with marked consistency, namely, when the poem's mortal characters praise gods in a hymnic fashion, usually when invoking them in prayer or worship.[71] In some cases this praise is quoted directly, as in Mopsus' exuberant vision of Rhea's power and status on Olympus (1.1098–1102);[72] in other cases it is conveyed second-hand with an indirect speech construction, as in (the beginning of) Orpheus' hymn to Apollo (2.705–707).[73]

In most cases, however, the AR narrator's manner of conveying this sort of hymnic praise takes a rather more curious form, as in the following example.

1) Orpheus hymns Artemis as the Argonauts set sail from Pagasae (1.569–572):

---

67 Furley and Bremer 2001: 1.52–54.
68 As Athanassakis (1977: viii–ix) observes, these hymns "give the impression of being the work of a religious antiquary who had ready access to some sort of concordance from which he marshaled forth hosts of epithets which he then linked together as hexameters."
69 For accumulated epithets generally in the *HH*s, see Richardson 1974 ad *HH* 2.31.
70 For Apollonius' approach to formularity, see, e.g.: Ciani 1975; Fantuzzi 2008a. The comparative rarity of epithets in Apollonius vis-à-vis Homer has been observed by, e.g.: Parry 1971: 24–29; Beye 1982: 23; Vílchez 1986: 101; van den Eersten 2013: 10 (cf. 38).
71 van den Eersten 2013: 51.
72 Other cases of quoted hymnic praise include *Arg.* 1.411–412; 2.213–214, 258–260, 693; 3.467, 715–716, 986; 4.95–96, 382, 1019–1020, 1333, 1411–1414, 1597–1600.
73 More on Orpheus' hymn below. Other cases of hymnic praise conveyed using an indirect speech construction include 3.1211 and 4.145–148 (discussed below).

τοῖσι δὲ φορμίζων εὐθήμονι μέλπεν ἀοιδῇ
570 Οἰάγροιο πάϊς Νηοσσόον εὐπατέρειαν
Ἄρτεμιν, ἣ κείνας σκοπιὰς ἁλὸς ἀμφιέπεσκεν
ῥυομένη καὶ γαῖαν Ἰωλκίδα.

The son of Oeagrus played his lyre for them and in a well-composed song sang of Artemis Ship-Preserver, child of a great father, the goddess who watched over those peaks by the sea and protected the land of Iolcus.

It is helpful to analyze this passage with reference to Genette's three categories for the "states" that the representation of a character's speech may assume within a narrative.[74] The Apollonian narrator describes Orpheus as singing (μέλπεν), but he does not follow this verb up with a direct quotation of what Orpheus sang—a technique that would exemplify Genette's category of "reported speech."[75] Nor does the narrator follow the verb with an indirect speech construction summarizing the contents of Orpheus' song—Genette's category of "transposed speech."[76] Instead, μέλπεν simply takes an accusative direct object denoting the goddess about whom Orpheus is singing (Ἄρτεμιν).[77] These data would suggest that we are dealing with what Genette calls "narratized speech": Orpheus' speech is reduced to just another event in the narrative ("Orpheus sang of Artemis"), hardly different from the non-discursive events immediately preceding it (e.g., "Orpheus played his lyre").[78] In terms of speech act theory, we could say that the narrator minimizes the locutionary aspect of Orpheus' song (i.e., what the bard said) and focuses on the illocutionary (i.e., what he did, namely, sing).[79] But what is so peculiar about Apollonius' technique here is that the narrator appends to the goddess's name a pair of Honorific epithets (Νηοσσόον εὐπατέρειαν) and even a relative clause (ἣ ... Ἰωλκίδα) that differ markedly from the texture of the surrounding narrative, but which, crucially, *would be at home in the hymn that we can imagine Orpheus*

---

74 Genette 1980: 171–173.
75 This is the technique at *Arg.* 1.410–412.
76 This technique occurs at *Arg.* 1.885.
77 This device occurs at *Arg.* 1.1225 (Ἄρτεμιν ... μέλπεσθαι ἀοιδαῖς); 2.493 (κεκλόμενοι Μαντήιον Ἀπόλλωνα), 700 (ἐπικλείοντες Ἑώιον Ἀπόλλωνα).
78 Genette 1980: 170–171. De Jong (2004a: 114–115) calls this mode of speech representation a "speech-act mention," while de Bakker and de Jong (2022: 6–7) use the term "record of speech act" or "RSA." For the use of narratized speech in Apollonius' narrative, including a brief discussion of what I call "hymnic narratization," see now Klooster 2022: 106–107.
79 For these terms, see Chatman 1978: 161–166.

singing in this context. And yet we can be sure that Orpheus' words are not being quoted, for the accusative (as opposed to the vocative) case and the distal deictic adjective κείνας ("those") betray the distanced perspective of the narrator.

This technique for representing Orpheus' song to Artemis, which I here dub "hymnic narratization," is far from an anomaly in the *Arg*. Rather, the phenomenon I have just outlined could justly be called Apollonius' standard technique for narrating a character's Invocation (or Evocation) of a deity, as the following survey of comparable passages attests:[80]

2) The Argonauts and the Lemnian women offer celebratory sacrifices to the gods (*Arg*. 1.858–860):

> ἔξοχα δ' ἄλλων
> ἀθανάτων **Ἥρης υἷα κλυτὸν** ἠδὲ καὶ αὐτὴν
> 860 Κύπριν ἀοιδῇσιν θυέεσσί τε μειλίσσοντο.
>
> … and beyond all other immortals they propitiated **Hera's famous son** [*sc*. Hephaestus] and Cypris herself with songs and sacrifices.

3) The Argonauts supplicate Rhea-Cybele on Cyzicus (1.1123–1131):

> βωμὸν δ' αὖ χέραδος παρενήνεον· ἀμφὶ δὲ φύλλοις
> στεψάμενοι δρυΐνοισι θυηπολίης ἐμέλοντο,
> 1125 **Μητέρα Δινδυμίην πολυπότνιαν** ἀγκαλέοντες,
> ἐνναέτιν Φρυγίης, Τιτίην θ' ἅμα Κύλληνόν τε,
> οἳ μοῦνοι πολέων μοιρηγέται ἠδὲ πάρεδροι
> Μητέρος Ἰδαίης κεκλήαται, ὅσσοι ἔασιν
> Δάκτυλοι Ἰδαῖοι Κρηταιέες, οὕς ποτε νύμφη
> 1130 Ἀγχιάλη Δικταῖον ἀνὰ σπέος ἀμφοτέρῃσιν
> δραξαμένη γαίης Οἰαξίδος ἐβλάστησεν.
>
> Nearby they piled up an altar of stones and, wearing crowns of oak leaves, conducted their sacrifice around it [*sc*. a carved image of the goddess], as they called upon **the Dindymian Mother, the much-revered mistress**

---

[80] This list builds on that of Vian 2002: 3.152 ad *Arg*. 4.148, although his list also includes examples in indirect discourse (4.146–148) and quoted character-speech (1.1098–1102, 3.1035), which I would strictly distinguish on narratological grounds. Other scholars who have connected some of these passages include: Fränkel 1968 ad *Arg*. 3.861f.; Dickie 1990: 270 with n. 20; Hunter 1993: 140 n. 144, 2015 ad *Arg*. 4.146–148; Klooster 2022: 107.

who dwells in Phrygia, along with Titias and Cyllenus, who alone of the many Idaean Dactyls on Crete are called dispensers of destiny and ministers of the Idaean Mother. The nymph Anchiale once bore the Dactyls in the Dictaean cave while clutching the ground of Oaxus with both hands.

4) The Argonauts continue to worship Rhea-Cybele (1.1150–1151):

1150 καὶ τότε μὲν δαῖτ' ἀμφὶ θεᾶς θέσαν οὔρεσιν Ἄρκτων,
μέλποντες Ῥείην πολυπότνιαν.

Then they held a feast in honor of the goddess on Bear mountain and hymned **Rhea, the much-revered mistress.**

5) The Argonauts celebrate Polydeuces' victory over Amycus (2.161–163):[81]

Ὀρφείῃ φόρμιγγι συνοίμιον ὕμνον ἄειδον
ἐμμελέως· περὶ δέ σφιν ἰαίνετο νήνεμος ἀκτὴ
μελπομένοις· κλεῖον δὲ **Θεραπναῖον Διὸς υἷα.**

... and [they] sang a hymn to the accompaniment of Orpheus' lyre in beautiful harmony, and round about them the windless shore was charmed by their singing; and they celebrated **Zeus' son from Therapna.**

6) The Argonauts worship Apollo Heoïus (2.701–703):

ἀμφὶ δὲ δαιομένοις εὐρὺν χορὸν ἐστήσαντο,
καλὸν Ἰηπαιήον' Ἰηπαιήονα Φοῖβον
μελπόμενοι.

Around the burning offerings they formed a broad choral dance and chanted the beautiful **"Iêpaiêon, Phoebus Iêpaiêon."**[82]

---

[81] In fact, the Argonauts are here celebrating the still-mortal rather than the deified Polydeuces, but the passage contains other hymnic undertones besides the device currently under investigation; see 2.3.2. This hymnic subtext warrants the passage's inclusion in the present list.

[82] I analyze this passage as a debatable example of hymnic narratization in section 4.3 below.

7) The Argonauts build a shrine to Concord (2.715–719):[83]

715 λοιβαῖς εὐαγέεσσιν ἐπώμοσαν, ἦ μὲν ἀρήξειν
ἀλλήλοις εἰσαιὲν ὁμοφροσύνῃσι νόοιο,
ἁπτόμενοι θυέων· καί τ' εἰσέτι νῦν γε τέτυκται
κεῖσ' Ὁμονοίης ἱρὸν ἐύφρονος, ὅ ῥ' ἐκάμοντο
αὐτοὶ **κυδίστην** τότε **δαίμονα** πορσαίνοντες.

They swore an oath with holy libations as they laid hands upon the sacrifice, that they would forever aid one another in singleness of mind. And still to this day a shrine stands there to kindly Concord, which they themselves built at that time to honor **the most glorious goddess**.

8) The narrator describes the effects of Medea's Promethean drug (3.846–847):

τῷ εἴ κ' ἐννυχίοισιν ἀρεσσάμενος θυέεσσιν
Δαῖραν μουνογένειαν ἑὸν δέμας ἰκμαίνοιτο ...

If, after appeasing **the only-begotten Daira** with nocturnal sacrifices, a man should anoint his body with this drug ...

9) Medea harvests the sap of a flower to manufacture her Promethean drug (3.858–862):

τῆς οἵην τ' ἐν ὄρεσσι κελαινὴν ἰκμάδα φηγοῦ
Κασπίῃ ἐν κόχλῳ ἀμήσατο φαρμάσσεσθαι,
860 ἑπτὰ μὲν ἀενάοισι λοεσσαμένη ὑδάτεσσιν,
ἑπτάκι δὲ **Βριμὼ κουροτρόφον** ἀγκαλέσασα,
Βριμὼ νυκτιπόλον, χθονίην, ἐνέροισιν ἄνασσαν ...

Its sap, like the black juice of a mountain oak, she had collected in a Caspian shell to prepare the drug, after bathing herself seven times in ever-flowing streams, and calling seven times on **Brimo the youth-nourisher, Brimo the night-wanderer, the infernal goddess, queen of the nether dead** ...

---

83   See section 4.3 for this passage as an example of hymnic narratization despite the lack of a *verbum dicendi*.

10) Circe purifies Jason and Medea (4.700–702, 707–709):

700 τῶ καὶ ὀπιζομένη Ζηνὸς θέμιν Ἱκεσίοιο,
     ὅς μέγα μὲν κοτέει, μέγα δ' ἀνδροφόνοισιν ἀρήγει,
     ῥέζε θυηπολίην ...
707 ... αὖτις δὲ καὶ ἄλλοις
     μείλισσεν χύτλοισι **Καθάρσιον** ἀγκαλέουσα
     Ζῆνα, παλαμναίων τιμήορον ἱκεσιάων.[84]

Therefore, out of reverence for the ordinance of **Zeus, Protector of Suppliants—who mightily hates murderers, but mightily protects them—** she began making the sacrifice ... And again, with other libations she propitiated **Zeus**, invoking him as the **Purifier, defender of supplications by murderers.**

11) Medea bewitches the bronze giant Talos (4.1665–1669):

1665   ἀοιδῇσιν μειλίσσετο, μέλπε δὲ **Κῆρας**
        θυμοβόρους, Ἀίδαο θοὰς κύνας, αἵ περὶ πᾶσαν
        ἠέρα δινεύουσαι ἐπὶ ζωοῖσιν ἄγονται.
        τὰς γουναζομένη τρὶς μὲν παρακέκλετ' ἀοιδαῖς,
        τρὶς δὲ λιταῖς ...

She propitiated with songs and chanted the praises **of the heart-devouring Fates of Death, the swift hounds of Hades, who roam throughout the air and hunt down the living.** In her supplications she summoned them three times with songs, three times with prayers ...[85]

12) The Argonauts' ribaldry provides an etiology for an Anaphean ritual (4.1727–1730):

                    ἐκ δέ νυ κείνης
        μολπῆς ἡρώων νήσῳ ἔνι τοῖα γυναῖκες

---

84 For the alternate reading Παλαμναῖον, which would constitute a third epithet for Zeus here ("of Murderers"), see Vian 2002: 3.173–174 ad *Arg.* 4.709.
85 The manuscripts, and modern editors, are divided in whether to read μέλπε (Seaton, Mooney, Vian, Paduano and Fusillo, Dräger, Race, Hunter) or θέλγε (Fränkel, Livrea, Glei and Natzel-Glei, Stürner) in line 1665, but the former is favored by the parallel passages featuring hymnic narratization that use forms of μέλπω (1.569, 1151; 2.703; cf. 2.163).

ἀνδράσι δηριόωνται, ὅτ᾽ Ἀπόλλωνα θυηλαῖς
1730 Αἰγλήτην Ἀνάφης τιμήορον ἱλάσκωνται.

And so, from that jesting of the heroes, the women on the island hurl similar taunts at the men, whenever in their sacrifices they propitiate **Apollo Aegletes, guardian of Anaphe**.[86]

13) Euphemus has a prophetic dream (4.1731–1733):

ἀλλ᾽ ὅτε δὴ κἀκεῖθεν ὑπεύδια πείσματ᾽ ἔλυσαν,
μνήσατ᾽ ἔπειτ᾽ Εὔφημος ὀνείρατος ἐννυχίοιο
ἁζόμενος **Μαίης υἷα κλυτόν**.

But when, from that place too, they had loosed their cables in good weather, then Euphemus remembered that night's dream out of respect for **Maia's famous son**.[87]

Some of these passages are marked by greater degrees of hymnic expansion with epithets or relative clauses than are others, but all of them exhibit the same basic structural features:
a) The narrator is narrating a character's Invocation of a deity.
b) The Invocation is denoted by a declarative verb of singing, praying, calling upon, etc.
c) The verb takes the name of the divinity being invoked as its accusative direct object.
d) Appended to the divinity's name is at least one Honorific epithet, and in most cases, two or more.[88]
   i) In some cases, these epithets are supplemented by one or more relative clauses that give information that could be considered appropriate to a hymn (e.g., because they define the divinity's genealogy, domain, powers, etc.).

Item d in this list is the decisive element that enables us to recognize the phenomenon in question. Piled-up Honorifics are characteristic of divine Invo-

---

86 See further Stürner 2022: 15–16, who considers a hymnic tone to pervade the entire Anaphean episode.
87 This example is noteworthy because ἁζόμενος does not imply speech on Euphemus' part but rather his internal attitude of reverence toward Hermes, god of dreams.
88 In three cases, the name of the divinity (item c) is actually omitted; instead, the Honorific epithets (item d) serve to identify the deity periphrastically (1.859, 2.163, 4.1733).

cations in character-speech in the *Arg.*,[89] but for all the Apollonian narrator's piety, such epithets (to say nothing of Hymnic Relative clauses) are otherwise atypical of his style, as I demonstrate in detail in this book's appendix.

A comparison with the HE narrator is once again illuminating here. When Chryses prays to Apollo at the beginning of the *Iliad*, the narrator introduces his prayer in a way that almost exactly corresponds to the schema just outlined: "The old man prayed earnestly to the **lord Apollo, whom fair-haired Leto bore**" (πολλὰ δ' … ἠρᾶθ' ὁ γεραιὸς | Ἀπόλλωνι ἄνακτι, τὸν ἠύκομος τέκε Λητώ, *Il.* 1.35–36). Quoted out of context, these lines look like an example of narratized prayer (ἠρᾶθ') with a god as the (in this case, indirect) object; Apollo is dignified by the Honorific title ἄναξ and even a genealogical relative clause. As with Orpheus at *Arg.* 1.569–572, we could imagine that these Honorifics would have been appropriate to the address that Chryses "really" made to Apollo on this occasion. But if we keep reading, we find a direction quotation of Chryses' actual prayer beginning in the very next line: "Hear me, you of the silver bow, who …" (κλῦθί μευ, ἀργυρότοξ', ὅς …). It turns out that lines 35–36 had really served to introduce direct speech, which specify the exact words with which Chryses entreated Apollo; there is thus no sense that the Honorific epithet and relative clause in line 36 are somehow conveying the flavor of Chryses' prayer. Rather, these Honorifics are unambiguously attributable to the narrator, who speaks them *in propria persona*, as is in fact his wont: such *amplitudo* is a regular feature of the HE narrator's style.[90]

In Apollonius, by contrast, the situation is not so clear-cut. Scholars have interpreted the phenomenon of hymnic narratization in various ways, sometimes attributing primacy to the voice of the narrator, sometimes to that of the characters in question. Thus Hunter comments of passage 9, "The narrative imitates the piled epithets of an actual prayer,"[91] an assessment that seems to make the AR narrator "responsible" for these striking strings of Honorific epithets and relative clauses: he is mimicking the style of discourse in which his characters are engaged. This interpretation recalls Albis' notion of the AR narrator's "empathy" for his characters: the narrator often manipulates the style of his narration in order to mirror the experiences or emotions of his characters, thus effecting an "assimilation of poet and character that is ubiquitous in

---

89 See 291*n*72.
90 See, e.g.: Hoekstra 1981: 51–53, 81–89; Vivante 1982: *passim*.
91 Hunter 1989 ad *Arg.* 3.862. For a similar interpretation of passage 11, see Stürner 2022 ad *Arg.* 4.1666 (348–349).

the *Argonautica* and is one of the poet's essential narrative devices."[92] To use a term coined earlier in this chapter, these interpretations would classify hymnic narratization essentially as a type of contagious hymnody—as in the two apostrophes examined above (4.1196–1200, 1701–1710), the characters' action of invoking a god triggers a kind of hymnic reaction on the part of our pious narrator.[93]

Another interpretation is also possible, however, and elsewhere Hunter himself describes the narrator's technique as a "mingling of direct and indirect speech in the narrative of invocations," which creates the impression that "what [the character] 'actually said'" has been "transposed into narrative."[94] According to this interpretation, the Honorific epithets ultimately descend from the words that the characters themselves "really" used. Indeed, several scholars have taken this interpretation of these passages for granted. For example, Dickie summarizes passage 11: "Before Medea bewitches Talos she supplicates the Keres, invoking them thrice in incantation and prayer and appealing to them as the swift dogs of Hades ..."[95] Strictly speaking, it is the narrator who calls these death spirits "swift dogs of Hades," but Dickie appears to understand this device intuitively as a method of representing character-speech. On this interpretation, Apollonius' technique could be understood as a species of "free indirect discourse" (FID), which Bal defines as "a form of interference between narrator's text and actor's text" in which "signals of the personal language situation of the actor and of the (im)personal language situation of the narrator

---

92 Albis 1996: 95. See further Morrison 2007: 306–311, with additional references. Though Albis himself interprets hymnic narratization as an effect of the AR narrator's ἐνθουσιασμός, he seems to understand the technique as a species of free indirect discourse (for this term, see below), with the character's "original" wording determining that of the narrator's: "Apollonius' narrative persona is possessed, as it were, by his character. By not separating [the character's] speech into a direct quote, Apollonius creates the impression that he has lost some of his own identity and has become ἔκφρων" (1996: 35).

93 For this view, see esp. Klooster 2022: 107, who likens hymnic narratization to "a kind of apostrophe" and specifically cites 4.1196–1200, 1706–1709 as comparanda. For Fränkel (1968: 575 n. 259), by contrast, these two types of passages (i.e., what I call hymnic narratization and the two apostrophes featuring contagious hymnody) are in some senses opposite: in the former, the narrator seems to adopt the words of the character and maintains Er-Stil; in the latter, he participates in the character's praise of the god by adding his own voice in Du-Stil. Nevertheless, Fränkel recognizes that the *effect* of both techniques is similar ("mit einem ähnlichen Ergebnis").

94 Quotations from Hunter 2015 ad *Arg.* 4.1666 and ad 4.146–148, respectively; see also Vian 2002: 3.152 ad *Arg.* 4.148.

95 Dickie 1990: 269; see further ibid. 270 with n. 20; Paduano 1971: 52.

cross, without explicit reference to this."⁹⁶ FID is "free" in that it lacks an overt "tag" that identifies a section of the discourse as indirect speech. In English, this means that phrases like "She said that" will be absent, whereas in Greek, FID involves the omission of any of that language's various indirect speech constructions (e.g., a ὡς-clause, an accusative-and-infinitive construction, etc.).⁹⁷ Instead of these "tags," it is the switch from a narrator's usual diction and syntax to a style more appropriate to his or her characters that signals the presence of FID. The result is a striking merger between the narrator's more distanced style of narration and the words that the character in question is supposed to have used.

Which of these interpretations of hymnic narratization is correct? On examination, the evidence turns out to be ambivalent.⁹⁸ On the one hand, the FID interpretation is supported by such passages as 4.145–148, in which Medea invokes Sleep and Hecate as she begins to enchant the Colchian dragon:

145 τοῖο δ' ἑλισσομένοιο κατόμματον εἴσατο κούρη,
"Ὕπνον ἀοσσητῆρα, θεῶν ὕπατον, καλέουσα
ἡδείῃ ἐνοπῇ θέλξαι τέρας· αὖε δ' ἄνασσαν
νυκτιπόλον, χθονίην, εὐαντέα δοῦναι ἐφορμήν.

But as it was coiling, the girl rushed to look it in the eye, and in a sweet voice called **to her aid Sleep, highest of the gods, to enchant the monster,** and invoked **the queen of the underworld, the night-wanderer, to grant a favorable venture.**

---

96 Bal 2009: 54; for related terms and further bibliography, see: Prince 2003: 34–35; Keen 2015: 62. Cf. Fränkel 1968 ad *Arg.* 4.708 f., who comes close to identifying this technique as FID without using this critical vocabulary: he describes such passages as "sozusagen in indirekter Rede," commenting, "Zu einer grammatisch sauberen Sonderung dessen was der Dichter seinen Lesern berichtet, und dessen was eine epische Person ausspricht, fühlt sich dieser Stil nicht verpflichtet." See further his analysis at 575 n. 259.
97 For the relative difficulty of identifying FID in Ancient Greek, see de Bakker and de Jong 2022: 11.
98 E.g., we may consider the evidence furnished by the tenses used in the relative clauses that appear in some examples of hymnic narratization. In passage 1, the iterative imperfect tense of ἀμφιέπεσκεν (1.571) seems to assimilate an omnitemporal condition (Artemis' guardianship over Iolcus) to Orpheus' point of view in the past, a maneuver that strongly suggests FID. And yet in several other passages (3, 10, 11), such verbs are found in the perfect (κεκλήαται [1.1228]) or omnitemporal present tenses (ἔασιν [1.1228], κοτέει … ἀρήγει [4.701], ἄγονται [4.1667]), which could imply the temporal orientation of the narrator and thus reflect his "personal language situation."

This passage is often classed with the examples of hymnic narratization that I have listed above,[99] with which it does share notable characteristics. As in those passages, in narrating a character's calling upon a pair of deities, the narrator supplements each verb of Invocation (καλέουσα; αὖε) and, in Hypnus' case, the bare theonym of the invoked god ("Υπνον) with a series of Honorific epithets (θεῶν ὕπατον;[100] ἄνασσαν | νυκτιπόλον, χθονίην) that are uncharacteristic of his ordinary style but appropriate to the Prayer being described. But the placement of an infinitive following these epithets (θέλξαι; δοῦναι) marks an important formal difference: these Honorifics turn out to be incorporated into indirect speech constructions.[101] Are the comparable cases of hymnic narratization, then, simply instances of *free* indirect discourse? We might also cite as evidence a passage like 1.409–412:

αὐτὰρ Ἰήσων
410 εὔχετο κεκλόμενος πατρώιον Ἀπόλλωνα·
"κλῦθι ἄναξ, Παγασάς τε πόλιν τ' Αἰσωνίδα ναίων,
ἡμετέροιο τοκῆος ἐπώνυμον ..."

> Jason called on Apollo of his fathers and prayed: "Hear me, lord, you who dwell in Pagasae and the Aesonian city named for my father ..."

There are close correspondences between the initial narratization of Jason's prayer in the line introducing his speech (410) and the content of Jason's actual prayer as quoted in the succeeding verses—in particular, the narrator's epithet πατρώιον is effectively glossed by Jason's Invocation of Apollo in his epichoric aspect as lord of Aesonis, the city of which his father is the namesake. This early passage—the first prayer in the poem[102]—almost programmatically suggests

---

99 E.g.: Albis 1996: 34–35 with n. 51; Vian 2002: 3.152 ad *Arg.* 4.148; Hunter 2015 ad *Arg.* 4.146–148.
100 I understand ἀοσσητῆρα, "helper," not as an Honorific epithet for Sleep (who, I would think, is not usually or inherently a "helper"), but as part of the indirect command: Medea calls on Sleep "to be a helper and enchant the monster" (or "as a helper to enchant the monster," *vel sim.*). In the words of de Jong (2004a: 119), I would term ἀοσσητῆρα "a substantive used in predicative apposition and with a final nuance" (so also Harder 2012 ad Callim. *Aet.* fr. 18.4). εὐαντέα, "favorable," could be interpreted in the same way if it is taken with the preceding adjectives as an epithet for Hecate instead of with ἐφορμήν (see Hunter 2015 ad loc.). The construction is like that of 4.229–230 (Aeetes' Invocation of Zeus and Helius in indirect speech), which contains no hymnic elaboration.
101 I would interpret 3.1211 in the same way: Jason "invoked Hecate Brimo to be a helper in the contest" (Βριμὼ κικλήσκων Ἑκάτην ἐπαρωγὸν ἀέθλων [*sc.* εἶναι]).
102 Apollonius underlines this fact by modeling Jason's Invocation on the beginning of Chry-

that when the AR narrator mentions a character's speech act, his summaries cleave very close to their actual words.

On the other hand, in certain of the examples of hymnic narratization listed above, there is a disjunction between the description of the character's Invocation and the Honorifics that the narrator actually uses. For instance, in passage 9, Medea is said to call upon Hecate seven times (ἑπτάκι, 3.861), and there follows the longest string of epithets in the poem (Βριμὼ κουροτρόφον ἀγκαλέσασα | Βριμὼ νυκτιπόλον, χθονίην, ἐνέροισιν ἄνασσαν, 861–862). Anaphora of Βριμὼ within this series not only enhances the passage's "hymnic" atmosphere but gestures specifically toward the repetitious effect of calling on the goddess multiple times. Yet if we stop to count, Βριμὼ hardly occurs seven times in this series, and even adding up each of the epithets taken individually yields a total of only six (1. Βριμὼ; 2. κουροτρόφον; 3. Βριμὼ; 4. νυκτιπόλον; 5. χθονίην; 6. ἐνέροισιν ἄνασσαν)—one shy of Medea's seven addresses. It would have presumably been easy to add one further entry to this list ("Hecate" comes to mind) and thus render the parallel between Medea's sevenfold Invocation and the narration thereof more exact. But with this tantalizingly partial replication of Medea's prayer, it is as though the narrator has deliberately tried to mark the distorting effect that his mediation has on our access to the events of the narrative.[103] In this subtle way, he makes us aware of *his own* hymnic voice, through which Medea's Invocation is irrecoverably filtered.[104]

Ultimately, we cannot and do not need to decide one way or the other whether hymnic narratization is best understood as a type of FID or as a type of contagious hymnody in which the narrator himself adopts the hymnic style of the narratized Invocation—that is, whether the hymnic epithets and relative clauses reflect the "personal language situation" of the character invoking the deity or of the worshipful narrator caught up in praising the god.[105] In

---

ses' prayer to the same god near the opening of the *Iliad* (Hunter 1993: 84 n. 43). Chryses' Invocation likewise begins with the imperative κλῦθι (*Il.* 1.37) and names multiple of Apollo's local domains (37–38), including Chryse, of which Chryses himself is presumably the eponym (cf. Aesonis).

103   Likewise, note the repetition of τρίς, "three times," which occurs only *twice* at 4.1668–1669.
104   At a more general level, Apollonius can be seen to reflect on a basic problem with "transposed discourse": indirect speech, of which FID is a subspecies, purports to convey the gist of what a character "actually" said, but the exact degree of fidelity to the character's *ipsissima verba* is always unknowable. As per Chatman (1978: 201), with this device, the narrator "may equally summarize, epitomize, interpret, or otherwise alter the exact words of the quoted speaker"; see further, e.g.: Genette 1980: 171–172; Coulmas 1986: 3–6.
105   Ovid may reflect on this ambiguity in his own imitation of hymnic narratization at *Met.* 4.11–17. This passage makes clear that the list of epithets for Bacchus are those by which the Theban bacchants invoked the god (*pace* Syed 2004: 107): note the phrases *additur his*

another poem, this device might read unambiguously as FID, but the AR narrator's ἦθος as a pious singer of hymnic praise raises the possibility that it is his voice that we are hearing instead of or, perhaps, as well as, that of his characters.106 This ambiguity is itself another type of metalepsis, which de Jong calls the "blending of narrative voices": the voices of character and narrator cannot be distinguished.107

As a confirmation of this interpretation, we can compare the similar indeterminacy produced when hymnic narratization occurs in character-speech, as when Mopsus and Medea instruct Jason respectively to "propitiate the mother of all the blessed gods on her fine throne" (εὔθρονον ἱλάξασθαι | μητέρα συμπάντων μακάρων, 1.1093–1094) and to "appease Hecate, the only child of Perses" (μουνογενῆ δ' Ἑκάτην Περσηΐδα μειλίσσοιο, 3.1035). Are these characters using these hymnic Honorifics to suggest a sort of template that Jason could follow in his actual Invocation of these deities,108 or is their own piety affecting their language choices? After all, Mopsus is a seer and one of the crew's religious experts,109 while Medea is Hecate's own priestess.110 In the case of the

---

[sc. *nominibus*] (13) and *cum Lenaeo* (14). But Ovid then transitions from listing the epithets employed by the bacchants into a prominent example of contagious hymnody, as the narrator begins to hymn the god *in propria persona* (17–30). The Prayer of this hymn, however, is conceded back to the bacchants at the level of character-text, as their Invocation is at last reported in a direct quotation that is only introduced in line 31 (Fuhrer 1999: 365); thus Ovid does effect a kind of blending of the voices of narrator and characters after all.

106 I say "as well as" because there is an intermediate possibility: the AR narrator's piety could be taken to account for his decision to represent hymnic character-speech via FID with such frequency.

107 De Jong 2009: 99–106. By contrast, in the clear-cut examples of contagious hymnody we examined in section 1, the narrator unambiguously joins in *his own* voice in the hymnic praise of his characters.

108 In both cases, Jason's actual Invocation in the event is only paraphrased in indirect speech (1.1132–1133, 3.1211).

109 In addition to the quoted passage, see *Arg.* 2.922–923; 3.543–554, 938–947. Later in the quoted passage, Mopsus in fact goes on to pronounce upon Cybele's power in a sort of miniature hymn to the goddess (1.1098–1102).

110 There is perhaps a similar ambiguity in Eur. *Bacch.* 723–726, which Fränkel (1968 ad *Arg.* 3.861f.) has aptly compared to Apollonius' device of hymnic narratization. The context is a messenger's speech about the activities of the bacchants: "They, at the appointed hour, began to wave the thyrsus in their revelries, calling on **Iacchus, the son of Zeus, Bromius**, with united voice" (αἳ δὲ τὴν τεταγμένην | ὥραν ἐκίνουν θύρσον ἐς βακχεύματα, | Ἴακχον ἀθρόῳ στόματι τὸν Διὸς γόνον | Βρόμιον καλοῦσαι). Most likely the Honorifics included here represent FID, which adds some of the flavor of the Bacchic rites to the narrative, but as the messenger does evince sympathies toward the Dionysiac cult (711–712, 764, 769–774), his decision to include these Honorifics could be affected by his own attitude to the god.

AR narrator, too, the ambiguity produced by Apollonius' technique of hymnic narratization is an effect of character—to be specific, an effect only made possible by the hymnic dimension of the AR narrator's multifaceted voice.

I would like to conclude this discussion by cautiously suggesting a passage in the *HH*s that Apollonius might have taken as a model for the technique of hymnic narratization. It occurs near the beginning of the *Hymn to Pan* (19.1–7):

> Ἀμφί μοι Ἑρμείαο φίλον γόνον ἔννεπε, Μοῦσα,
> αἰγοπόδην δικέρωτα φιλόκροτον, ὅς τ' ἀνὰ πίση
> δενδρήεντ' ἄμυδις φοιτᾷ χορο⟨γ⟩ηθέσι νύμφαις,
> αἵ τε κατ' αἰγίλιπος πέτρης στείβουσι κάρηνα
> 5 Πᾶν' ἀνακεκλόμεναι, νόμιον θεὸν ἀγλαέθειρον
> αὐχμήενθ', ὃς πάντα λόφον νιφόεντα λέλογχεν
> καὶ κορυφὰς ὀρέων καὶ πετρήεντα κέλευθα.

> About Hermes' dear child tell me, Muse, the goat-footed, two-horned, rowdy, who roams about the wooded fields together with the dance-merry nymphs: along the precipitous crag they tread the summits, calling on **Pan, god of the pastures with splendor of rough hair, who has been assigned every snowy hill, the mountain peaks, and the rocky tracks.**

The first two lines offer a more or less typical Exordium: Pan is introduced as the Hymnic Subject under the periphrasis "Hermes' dear child" and is dignified by a series of three Honorific epithets (αἰγοπόδην, δικέρωτα, φιλόκροτον, 2); a Hymnic Relative pronoun then opens out into an Attributive Section detailing Pan's typical haunts and activities (2–3). But shortly after Pan's Evocation in line 1, we get a description of how Pan's attendant nymphs regularly invoke him in the wilderness. The verb used to denote their Invocation (or Evocation), ἀνακεκλόμεναι (5), is cognate to some of those that Apollonius himself uses to introduce hymnic narratization (ἀγκαλέοντες, *Arg.* 1.1125; ἀγκαλέσασα, 3.861; ἀγκαλέουσα, 4.708). Its direct object, the line-initial theonym "Pan," is once again dignified by three Honorific epithets (νόμιον θεόν, ἀγλαέθειρον, αὐχμήενθ', *HH* 19.5–6), as in a typical hymnic Exordium, before another Hymnic Relative clause delineates Pan's domains (6–7), again in the manner of the Attributive Section of a hymn.[111]

Ordinarily, I would hesitate to read too much into such a string of epithets or even a relative clause like those in lines 5–6, for as we saw with the Chry-

---

111 For this parallelism, see Thomas 2011: 159–160.

ses example above, these are typical features of the style of Homeric narrative. They are doubly appropriate within a hymn, and we have just seen the hymnist praise Pan in precisely this way in lines 1–3. But given that the narrator later transposes a full-scale hymn to Pan sung by these same nymphs in a way that strikingly blends together their voices with the hymnist' own,[112] it is tempting to view the Honorific epithets and the relative clause in lines 5–7 as mediating the hymn that the nymphs are actually supposed to sing to the pastoral god, in the manner of FID. In fact, we can take this interpretation further. The Exordial gestures of the hymn are repeated so precisely and in such close proximity to the hymn's actual Exordium, it is as though at the nymphs' Evocation, the hymn to Pan recommences. Thus from line 6 onward, the voice of the speaker and of the nymphs merge together: the timeless hymn of the nymphs unites with the particular hymn of the speaker. This effect, which we might call "metaleptic fade-in,"[113] is not quite like anything in Apollonius, but this experiment with different voices and levels of narration in narratizing hymnic speech remains a suggestive precursor for Apollonius' technique.

4 Orpheus' Hymn to Apollo: The Thynias Episode (*Arg.* 2.669–719)

The description of the Argonauts' worship of Apollo following his epiphany at the island of Thynias represents one of the most complex passages in the poem from a narratological point of view. I have saved analysis of this episode for last because it so beautifully brings together most of the narratorial traits and techniques that have been under consideration in part 2 of this study: the narrator's overtness and piety, his drive to etiology, and such devices as contagious hymnody, hymnic narratization, and allusive appeal to the precedent set by earlier Rhapsodic Hymns, both Homeric and Callimachean. Scholarship has especially focused on Orpheus' paean to Apollo (*Arg.* 2.701–716), but Apollonius' experiments with voice in representing this hymn can be appreciated properly only within the wider context of the entire episode, which amounts to a tour de force exploration of the various methods at a Greek poet's disposal for representing character-speech in narrative. After a brief summary of the episode and a lengthier consideration of the passage's hymnic intertexts, I present a survey of each of the speech acts contained therein, which culminates with an analysis of Orpheus' famous hymn.

---

112 See the discussion of the passage labeled 5 in 4.1, which is analyzed further on pp. 326–327.
113 Cf. the concept of metaleptic fade-out above, 278n14.

4.1 Summary of the Episode

Our episode follows the Argonauts' arduous navigation of the Clashing Rocks (2.533–606), Jason's πεῖρα testing his crew's morale (607–648), and virtually a full day and night's worth of rowing (649–668). In the twilight hour before dawn, the exhausted sailors row into the harbor of the desert island of Thynias (2.669–673).[114] Upon disembarking, the crew catches sight of Apollo as he makes one of his regular trips from Lycia to the land of the Hyperboreans (674–676); the verb ἐξεφάνη ("[he] appeared," 676) effectively glosses the ensuing scene as an epiphany (cf. φαάνθη, 687; φαανθείς, 693). There follows a description of the god partly focalized by the Argonauts, partly by the narrator, for the mortal onlookers quickly avert their gaze to the ground until Apollo has departed (676–684).[115] After some time, Orpheus—here as often playing the role of the crew's religious guide[116]—breaks the silence and bids the men raise an altar on the shore and sacrifice to Apollo under the new title Heoïus (Ἑώιος, "of the Dawn") because of his epiphany to them at daybreak (684–693).[117]

The Argonauts execute Orpheus' commands, constructing an altar (694–695), hunting quarry (providentially provided by Apollo) for the sacrifice (695–697), and finally burning the thigh pieces while invoking the god under his new title (698–700). During the offering, the Argonauts form a chorus around the altar and begin chanting the paean (701–703).[118] Orpheus then takes up his lyre

---

114 As Hunter (1986: 50 n. 2) notes, the episode is demarcated by symmetrical time-notices (669: ἦμος δ' οὔτ' ἄρ πω φάος ἄμβροτον; 720: ἦμος δὲ τρίτατον φάος ἤλυθε). The first (669–671) is especially significant because Apollo's appearance at dawn is key to the etiology for his new cult.

115 E.g., "No one dared to look directly into the **beautiful** eyes of the god" (οὐδέ τις ἔτλη | ἀντίον αὐγάσσασθαι ἐς ὄμματα καλὰ θεοῖο, 681–682) betrays the perspective of the narrator rather than the characters, who are explicitly not looking into the god's eyes (Phillips 2020: 94). For the description of Apollo here, see, e.g., Páskiewicz 1981: 157; Hunter 1986: 51, 52; 2009: 143–149; Belloni 1999; Green 2007 ad *Arg.* 2.678–680; Harder 2019b: 15–16.

116 For Orpheus' religious functions in the poem, see, e.g.: Busch 1993; Köhnken 2003b: 26; Scherer 2006: 117–124; Billault 2008: 203–205; Karanika 2010; Schaaf 2014: *passim*. The *Arg.* does not, in fact, make Orpheus "Apollo's son" (*pace* Páskiewicz 1981 ad *Arg.* 2.685ff.; see *Arg.* 1.23–25, and, in our passage, 2.703), but there is nevertheless a special appropriateness to Orpheus' leading the rites here, given the alternate genealogy that does assign him Apolline paternity (see, e.g., Bömer 1980 ad Ov. *Met.* 10.89) and given other myths that make him a zealous devotee of Helius-Apollo (see Hunter 1986: 53).

117 For the "hymnic" language of Orpheus' exhortation, see Bauer 2017: 66 (suggesting an allusion to *HH* 3.165 at *Arg.* 2.693); Vergados, forthcoming.

118 We should imagine that the Argonauts keep intoning the paean chant as Orpheus sings, per Miller 2014: 448; note the plural verb and the reference to "choral song" in the speech-capping line (χορείῃ μέλψαν ἀοιδῇ, 714).

and sings a hymn on the subject of Apollo's conquest of the Delphic serpent (703–714), in a section of the narrative I now quote in full:

> σὺν δέ σφιν ἐὺς πάις Οἰάγροιο
> Βιστονίῃ φόρμιγγι λιγείῃ ἦρχεν ἀοιδῆς·
> 705 ὥς ποτε πετραίῃ ὑπὸ δειράδι Παρνησσοῖο
> Δελφύνην τόξοισι πελώριον ἐξενάριξεν,
> κοῦρος ἐὼν ἔτι γυμνός, ἔτι πλοκάμοισι γεγηθώς—
> ἰλήκοις· αἰεί τοι, ἄναξ, ἄτμητοι ἔθειραι,
> αἰὲν ἀδήλητοι· τὼς γὰρ θέμις· οἰόθι δ' αὐτὴ
> 710 Λητὼ Κοιογένεια φίλαις ἐνὶ χερσὶν ἀφάσσει—
> πολλὰ δὲ Κωρύκιαι νύμφαι, Πλειστοῖο θύγατρες
> θαρσύνεσκον ἔπεσσιν, ἰὴ ἰὲ κεκληγυῖαι·
> ἔνθεν δὴ τόδε καλὸν ἐφύμνιον ἔπλετο Φοίβῳ.
> αὐτὰρ ἐπειδὴ τόν γε χορείῃ μέλψαν ἀοιδῇ ...

And among them the noble son of Oeagrus led off a clear song on his Bistonian lyre, telling how once upon a time beneath Parnassus' rocky ridge the god killed monstrous Delphyne(s) with his arrows, when he was still a naked boy, still delighting in his long locks—be gracious! Ever unshorn, lord, is your hair, ever unharmed, for such is right; and only Leto herself, Coeus' daughter, strokes it with her dear hands—and often did the Corycian nymphs, the daughters of Pleistus, encourage him with their words, as they shouted *iê ie*. From there arose this beautiful refrain for Phoebus. But when they had celebrated him with their choral song ...[119]

As the train of thought in this passage can be difficult to follow, I here present a brief analysis of just these lines.[120] Nine lines are devoted to Orpheus' hymn, and these are easily divisible into three subsections. In the first (705–707),

---

119 I have adapted Race's text and translation in several ways. First, I have placed parentheses around the 's' in the serpent's name, Delphyne(s) (706), for reasons that will become clear below. Second, I have reinterpreted αἰεί—ἀδήλητοι in lines 708–709 as a statement rather than a wish, as Race translates ("be gracious, lord, may your hair always remain unshorn, always unharmed"), though Race's interpretation finds support from a parallel with Tib. 2.5.121–122. Finally, I print the paean formula ἰὴ ἰέ in line 712 rather than Race's Ἰήιε, which looks like the vocative form of Apollo's epithet ἰήιος (hence Seaton's translation: "And often the Corycian nymphs, daughters of Pleistus, took up the cheering strain crying 'Healer'"; see also *Etym. Magn.* s.v. Ἰήιε). For the emendation ἰὴ ἰέ, with rough breathing marks, see the discussion of etymological wordplay below.

120 On this passage's train of thought, see, e.g.: Fränkel 1968 ad loc.; Hunter 1986: 56–57.

Orpheus' narrative is related in indirect speech, introduced by ὡς in line 705; the indefinite temporal adverb ποτε marks what follows as an external analepsis. But then ἰλήκοις at the head of line 708 signals a jarring transition into a second-person mode of address.[121] The eulogistic intent of line 707 had been to emphasize Apollo's youthfulness when he vanquished the dragon, for just as in the myth of baby Heracles' strangling the snakes, the juvenile vanquishing of a monster testifies all the more to the god's supernatural power.[122] As signs of Apollo's youth, line 707 points to his nakedness and to the fact that he was "still delighting in his long locks,"[123] πλόκαμοι being a symbol of youth because of the function of hair-cutting as a rite of passage for Greek boys. The adverb ἔτι, however, betrays an unduly mortal perspective on the god's aging: to say that Apollo was "still" rejoicing in his long locks implies that he would one day cut them, whereas Apollo is an eternal ephebe who will never come of age.[124] ἰλήκοις in the next line is intended to beg the god's pardon for this insinuation, and what follows are reassurances that Apollo's hair is never cut—indeed, only his

---

121 For ἰλήκοις as an allusion to *HH* 3.165, see 1.2.3.
122 Apollonius may have adapted this motif from the choral hymn to Pythian Apollo in Euripides' *Iphigenia in Tauris*, which employs even more marked Anaphora of ἔτι (1250–1251: ἔτι νιν ἔτι βρέφος, ἔτι φίλας | ἐπὶ ματέρος ἀγκάλαισι θρώσκων [Páskiewicz 1981 ad *Arg.* 2.704]; cf. *Arg.* 1.508 with 326n211 below). It may also be significant that the very next line of the choral ode reveals a transition from Er-Stil to Du-Stil (ἔκανες, ὦ Φοῖβε); with this "emotive effect" (Kyriakou 2006 ad loc.), cf. *Arg.* 2.708. Elsewhere, Apollonius also has Apollo shoot the giant Tityus "as a mighty youth, not yet fully grown" (βούπαις, οὔ πω πολλός, *Arg.* 1.760).
123 For a survey of interpretations of γυμνός, see Hunter 1986: 56–57. I agree with Hunter's own view that the adjective envisions Apollo as still being a naked babe-in-arms when he slays the Python, as in some other versions of the myth, but that the ambiguous use of the word κοῦρος in this line alludes to an alternate version in which Apollo is an ephebe at the time of the Pythonomachy.
124 Cf. Klooster's view that these lines express a mistaken assumption on Orpheus' part, borne from his temporal vantage point in remote antiquity: the mythical bard might have thought of Apollo's locks as "still" unshorn because Apollo was "still" a relatively young god at the time of the Argonautic expedition, whereas the narrator, writing with the benefit of many centuries of hindsight, is now in a position to know that Apollo is in reality an unaging ephebe and thus will never cut his locks (2011: 89–90, 2013a: 165, 2022: 109). I am skeptical, however, because sufficient time should have passed since the primordial Pythonomachy for Orpheus to realize that the god was not, in fact, going to continue to mature past adolescence (for the temporal setting of the Pythonomachy, see Clay 2006: 58). For Apollo's eternal youth and unshorn hair, see Williams 1978 ad Callim. *Hymn* 2.36, 38; for the possibility of an Apollonian allusion to these Callimachean lines, see Korenjak 1994: 21; Matteo 2007 ad loc. Manuello (2012: 129 n. 29) suggests that our passage evokes Apollo's traditional epithet ἀκερσεκόμης, "with unshorn hair." As it happens, this adjective occurs just once in the HEs (*Il.* 20.39) and once in the *HHs* (3.134), and there in a more contextually apropos passage set just after the god's birth.

mother can so much as stroke his hair, let alone cut it.¹²⁵ This brief digression on Apollo's hair constitutes the second subsection (708–710). The third subsection (711–713) returns us to the Pythonomachy narrative, which concludes, as often in the *Arg.*, on an etiological note. Line 714 offers a capping formula that formally marks the end of the Argonauts' choral song, including Orpheus' hymn.

The episode concludes with the establishment of a second new cult on the island. Following the song, the crew swears an oath over libations to maintain perpetual concord among themselves (715–717); the narrator then reveals that the Argonauts had also built a second altar to Concord (Ὁμονοία) "at that time" (τότε, 719).¹²⁶ The Argonauts stay two nights on Thynias before departing at dawn on their third day there (720–721), thus bringing the episode to a close.

4.2 Allusions to Apolline Hymns

This episode includes a hymn to Apollo and the inauguration of two cults, but its hymnic texture is enhanced even further by a persistent program of allusion to other hymns dedicated to Apollo, particularly those of Homer (*HH* 3) and Callimachus (*Hymn* 2).¹²⁷ It is noteworthy that both of these poems are Rhapsodic Hymns, given that we are certainly meant to imagine Orpheus leading the chorus of Argonauts in the performance of a paean, a type of Cultic Hymn specially associated with Apollo.¹²⁸ In fact, the narrator introduces Orpheus' song itself in strikingly Homeric-hymnic terms by using the line-final phrase ἦρχεν ἀοιδῆς (literally, "he began his song": 2.704). The narrator has effectively adapted into his third-person narration of Orpheus' song a variation of the most distinctive Evocatory formula employed in the Exordia of the *HH*s, ἄρχομ' ἀείδειν (literally, "I begin to sing"), even maintaining its metrical *sedes* at the end of

---

125 The "Leto alone" motif is reminiscent of *HH* 3.5. The family dynamic glimpsed here may afford another example of how the *HH*s influenced the later reception of the Homeric gods qua characters; see introduction, 4.3.

126 For connections between Apollo and Concord that may be relevant to their juxtaposition in this episode, see Hunter 1986: 53–54. On the importance of the timing of this incident (after the Symplegades episode and before the approach to Colchis begins in earnest), see Bauer 2017: 67–68, with earlier references.

127 In general on these allusions, see: Hunter 1986: 56–60; Bauer 2017; Vergados, forthcoming.

128 See Morrison 2007: 130 and esp. Bauer 2017. The strongest candidate that Bauer (65–66) raises for an allusion to a non-rhapsodic hymn to Apollo in this passage is Alcaeus' lost paean (fr. 307c Campbell), in which Apollo's travel to the land of the Hyperboreans spurs the people of Delphi to compose a (or invent the?) paean. See further 308n122 on a possible allusion to Eur. *IT* 1250–1252.

the verse.[129] In this narrative context, it makes far more sense for Orpheus to sing a paean than a Homeric-style hymn, but nevertheless, Apollonius' allusive realignment of Orpheus' song with the Rhapsodic Hymnic tradition suits his broader privileging of the *HH*s as models for the *Arg.* as a whole.[130]

We may begin analyzing the episode's allusions to earlier Apolline hymns by observing the overall shaping of its plot. At a general level, I would note that the instinct to erect an altar after witnessing a god's epiphany is alien to the HEs.[131] The *Iliad* and *Odyssey* tend to describe epiphanies with certain conventional elements, two of which are reproduced here: reactions in the natural world (*Arg.* 2.679–680) and the stupefied wonder produced in the mortal onlookers (681).[132] HE epiphanies typically feature minimal ecphrastic detail, however,

---

129 Matteo 2007 ad loc.; Vergados, forthcoming. Notably, Kahane (1994a: 127 with n. 16) even assumes that ἦρχεν ἀοιδῆς corresponds to ἄρχομ᾽ ἀείδειν as the actual wording we are to imagine Orpheus using in his song: "The narrator is appropriating words that, strictly speaking, belong to Orpheus." On this formula, see 11*n*58. Cf. Páskiewicz (1981 ad loc.), who compares the Prayer of *HH* 13.3 (ἄρχε δ᾽ ἀοιδῆς).

130 On this ambiguity in the portrayal of Orpheus' song, see further Phillips 2020: 86. For the effect of mise-en-abyme produced by Orpheus' song, see the discussion at the end of 4.4.3. The *HH*s themselves provide precedent for the framing of an inset choral hymn in parallel with the Rhapsodic Hymn that contains it; see, e.g., 109–110, on the song of the Delian maidens; 304–305, on the inset song of the nymphs in *HH* 19.

131 This fact would be especially significant if we could be sure that Apollonius invented the idea of Apollo's epiphany on Thynias in order to motivate the construction of this altar (e.g., Páskiewicz 1981: 157; Lachenaud 2010: 289 n. 210). Σ ad *Arg.* 2.684–687 tells us that Herodorus had traced the cult of Apollo Heoïus not to the god's sunrise epiphany, but to the Argonauts' arrival at Thynias at dawn ('Ηρόδωρος [*FGrH* 31 F 48] οὖν φησιν Ἑῷον Ἀπόλλωνα προσαγορεύεσθαι καὶ βωμὸν αὐτοῦ εἶναι ἐν τῇ νήσῳ, οὐ καθὸ ὄρθρου ἐφάνη αὐτοῖς, ἀλλὰ καθὸ οἱ Ἀργοναῦται ὄρθρου εἰς αὐτὴν κατέπλευσαν). It is unclear if the antithesis in this passage reflects Herodorus' original text or, as Blumberg (1931: 43) assumes, it has been added by the scholiast to contrast with Apollonius' version. In either case, however, it is perhaps likelier that Herodorus is rationalizing Apollo's epiphany out of the αἴτιον than that Apollonius is manufacturing it himself (Wilamowitz 1931: 1.23 n. 1; Fowler 2013: 223; Vergados, forthcoming), in which case Apollonius' version will have been the traditional one. For Apollonius' possible sources for this episode, see Thériault 1996: 29–31.

132 See Páskiewicz 1981: 157. For the conventions of HE epiphanies, see, e.g.: Pfister in *RE* Suppl. 4 s.v. "Epiphanie," coll. 282–283; Richardson 1974 ad *HH* 2.188–190. For Apollonius' reception of these conventions, see Fernández Contreras 1996. Many of these conventions recur in the *HH*s as well, and scholars have noted several precedents in the *Hymns* for details in our scene. For the Argonauts' averting their gaze, Páskiewicz (loc. cit.) aptly compares *HH* 5.181–182 (where n.b. ὄμματα καλ[ά], 181*). Páskiewicz (ad *Arg.* 2.680) also compares the action of the waves to the sea's reaction to Apollo's birth at *HH* 3.27–28. Bauer (2017: 66 with n. 54) suggests that our scene may owe something to Dionysus' terrifying epiphany in *HH* 7, as well as to the signs of Apollo's imminent advent at Callim. *Hymn* 2.1–7; on the latter score, see further Harder 2019b: 14.

and are deployed to serve concrete plot functions, such as encouraging a mortal character to take or refrain from some course of action (e.g., *Il.* 1.193–222, *Od.* 1.96–324).[133] The narrative pattern in the Thynias episode is much more characteristic of the *HH*s, in which epiphanies tend to be prominent, spectacular, and etiological in nature, often eventuating in the foundation of a new cult.[134] Thus, for instance, the passage describing Demeter's epiphany to Queen Metaneira is filled with sensuous detail, prophesies the establishment of Demophon's hero cult, and includes a command to the Eleusinians to establish a temple in the goddess's honor (*HH* 2.256–280).[135]

But the sequence of events in Apollonius is especially comparable to that at *HH* 3.388–544, a passage that explains how Apollo, having rid the land of the Python, recruits a priesthood for his newly established Delphic temple from a group of Cretan merchants sailing to Pylos.[136] The form that Apollo's epiphany takes in the hymn is quite different from that in Apollonius: the god jumps aboard the Cretan ship in the form of a dolphin and miraculously redirects their course to Crisa.[137] From there, however, we begin to see substantial parallels. The Cretan sailors, exhausted from their journey (460),[138] disembark and on the god's orders raise their own seaside altar to Apollo (490, 505).[139] Standing around the altar (492, 510),[140] they pray to the god under his new cult title Delphinius (Δελφίνιος, "of the Dolphin"), in recognition of the nature of

---

133 See de Jong 2018: 71, with earlier bibliography; for the difference with Apollonius here, see: Páskiewicz 1981: 157–158; Paduano and Fusillo 1986 ad *Arg.* 2.669–684.

134 On epiphanies in the *HH*s, see, e.g.: Pfister in *RE* Suppl. 4 s.v. "Epiphanie," coll. 288–290; Lenz 1975: 19–20; Sowa 1984: ch. 9; Parker 1991: 2; Platt 2011: 60–76; Petridou 2015: *passim*; de Jong 2018: 71–77. See further García 2002, who considers this theme as an index of the *Hymns*' cletic function in summoning the god's ritual presence.

135 See further Rives 2018: 73, who notes Anchises' initial desire to erect an altar to the disguised Aphrodite when he suspects that she might be a goddess (*HH* 5.100–102). It has been thought that these lines provide the etiology for an otherwise unattested cult of Aphrodite on Ida, but the hymn does not suggest that Anchises actually builds the altar (Clay 2006: 174 n. 73).

136 This resemblance is discussed by: Hunter 1986: 56; 1996: 143–144; Serafimidis 2016: 371 n. 1505; Noussia-Fantuzzi 2017: 256–257; Tsakiris 2022: 43 n. 120, 63–70; see further Faraone 2018: 25.

137 But see Belloni (1999: 235 n. 20) and Vergados (forthcoming) for parallels between these two epiphanies in terms of shared motifs of the god's radiance and the awe inspired in mortal onlookers.

138 Cf. *Arg.* 2.673.

139 The seaside altar is noted as a parallel by: AHS 1936: 262–263; Richardson 2010 ad *HH* 3.490–496; Bauer 2017: 66.

140 Cf. *Arg.* 2.701, where the Argonauts dance and sing around Apollo's altar. For the circular (as opposed to processional) choral performance of paeans, see Rutherford 2001: 63–65.

the epiphany that they had witnessed (493–496).[141] After feasting and pouring libations to the Olympians (497–499, 511–513),[142] the priests process to Delphi chanting the paean (500, 517), led by Apollo himself as he plays the lyre (514–517).[143] Finally, after showing them the temple, Apollo reassures his new priests that life will be easy for them there,[144] but he warns them against hubristic behavior (524–544).[145] These structural parallels are enhanced by several verbal correspondences between these passages, including the use of the term Ἰηπαιήων to designate the paean that the Cretan sailors (500, 517) and the Argonauts (*Arg.* 2.702) chant.[146] With the exception of the *Arg.* and its scholia, this word occurs nowhere else in extant Greek literature.[147] Finally, we should note that the Myth in Orpheus' hymn corresponds to the preliminary events of this very episode of the *HH*, namely, Apollo's conquest of the Delphic serpent (*HH* 3.300–374). Together, these evocations of the *Homeric Hymn to Apollo* suggest

141 Cf. the Argonauts' establishment of a new cult for Apollo under the title Heoïus for analogous reasons. For Apollonius' engagement with the *HH*'s "Delphinian" etymology for Delphi, see below.
142 Cf. *Arg.* 2.715, 717.
143 It is typical of Apollonius' "Göttertechnik" that whereas Apollo himself leads the chorus and instructs his priests in the *HH*, he remains distant in the *Argonautica* (see 142n249), and thus these duties devolve onto the mortal Orpheus as the crew's religious expert (Vergados, forthcoming; cf. Faraone 2018: 25).
144 Bauer (2017: 66–67) compares Apollo's promise of a steady stream of sacrificial victims for the Cretan priests' maintenance (*HH* 3.532–539) to the god's provision of game for the Argonauts to sacrifice on Thynias (*Arg.* 2.695–700).
145 Cf. the Argonauts' oath and erection of an altar to Concord (*Arg.* 2.714–719). Of course, just as Apollo's priests will indeed eventually succumb to hubris (see, e.g., Richardson 2010: 14–15, 151–152), so, too, the concord among the Argonauts will in fact fracture after the expedition; see 321n192.
146 Adduced by, e.g., Matteo 2007 ad loc., Nishimura-Jensen 2009: 7, Tsakiris 2022: 63–64. Oddly, a few scholars note the parallel with *HH* 3.272 (where Apollo is denoted by the epithet Ἰηπαιήων), but not the much stronger parallel with lines 500, 517: Mooney 1912 ad loc., Hunter 1986: 56, Vian 2002: 1.276 ad *Arg.* 2.703.
147 Ἰηπαιήων also occurs as an epithet for Apollo earlier in the hymn (272). At *Arg.* 2.702, Apollonius will have had his eye on *Il.* 1.472–474 as well; see also *Il.* 18.569–570. Another verbal echo concerns the lyre-playing of Apollo (ἦρχε δ' ἄρά σφιν ἄναξ Διὸς υἱὸς Ἀπόλλων | φόρμιγγ' ἐν χείρεσσιν ἔχων, ἐρατὸν κιθαρίζων, *HH* 3.514–515) and Orpheus (σὺν δέ σφιν ἐὺς πάϊς Οἰάγροιο | Βιστονίῃ φόρμιγγι λιγείης ἦρχεν ἀοιδῆς, *Arg.* 2.703–704). *Arg.* 2.726, slightly after the Thynias episode, echoes *HH* 3.403. Elsewhere Apollonius reworks other elements of the *Apollo* passage: the second of his "pious similes" adapts *HH* 3.510, 516–517 (see 240n46); the Argonauts' shoreside sacrifices to the Twelve Gods (*Arg.* 2.531–532) echoes *HH* 3.490, 508; and the description of Triton's human form at *Arg.* 4.1551–1552 resembles that of Apollo's similar disguise at Crisa (*HH* 3.449). N.b. as well that Phineus' thanksgiving to Apollo at *Arg.* 2.213–214 echoes the hymn's Salutation (*HH* 3.545), just after our passage. Most of these parallels are noted by Campbell 1981.

that the establishment of a new cult to Apollo Heoïus by Orpheus and the Argonauts is the newest in a series of cultic foundations inaugurated by Apollo himself and his crew of Cretan sailors at Delphi.[148]

Orpheus' hymn is a particular hotbed of Apolline allusivity, and we may begin the analysis thereof by considering the name that Apollonius chooses for the beast. Just by calling this serpent Delphyne(s) (706), Apollonius enters into a number of ancient debates over various mythological ζητήματα that intersect with the *Homeric Hymn to Apollo* and the Callimachean corpus in some fascinating ways.[149] In the *HH*, the dragon is unnamed; our first evidence for the name Delphyne(s) comes from a fragment of Callimachus and the third-century historian Meandrius.[150] Apollonius' choice of this rare name in favor of the commoner "Python" (Πύθων)[151] probably represents the influence of Callimachus,[152] but in one respect Apollonius parts company with his reputed mentor. Ancient authorities differed as to the serpent's sex, as evidently did Meandrius and Callimachus. The scholium that reports their opinions (Σ ad *Arg.* 2.705–711b) is less than lucid, but it definitely asserts that Meandrius endorsed the masculine tradition and thus called the snake Δελφύνης,[153] whereas Callimachus, preferring a dragoness, called her Δέλφυνα (or perhaps Δελφύνη) on

---

148 N.b. further Orpheus' promise of future sacrifice to Apollo if he grants the crew a safe return to Greece (689–691). This vow links the present sacrifices to Jason's similar promises at 1.415–419 and 4.1704–1705 (Páskiewicz 1981: 161), where Apollo's principal cult sites are specified. In effect, the new Argonautic cults of Apollo Actius, Heoïus, and Aegletes take their place alongside the god's venerable cults at Pytho, Amyclae, and Ortygia; see further McPhee 2017: 119; cf. Cusset 2018: 88–91. For the connections between the Thynias and Anaphe episodes, see Hunter 1986: 50, with earlier references.

149 For Apollonius' deployment of etymological allusions as a subtextual method of weighing in on mythological ζητήματα, with particular reference to the names of monsters, see McPhee, forthcoming d.

150 Callim. *Aet.* fr. 88 Pfeiffer, Harder; Meandrius *FGrH* 492 F 14a. Variants on this name, including Δελφίνη(ς) and Δελφίν, occur in some scholia (Σ ad Eur. *Phoen.* 232, 233; Tzetz. ad Lycoph. *Alex.* 207; paraphrase of Dion. Per. 437–446.10); Δελφύς (fem.) occurs in *Etym. Gud.* s.v. Ἑκατηβελέτης. Tzetzes actually cites Apollonius' line (2.706) with the reading Δελφίνην (PQ) or the unmetrical Δελφῖνα (H).

151 Simon. fr. 573 Campbell may have used this name (Fontenrose 1959: 15), but its first sure occurrences hail from the fourth century: Arist. fr. 637.16 Rose; Ephorus *FGrH* 70 F 31a, b; Theopomp. *FGrH* 115 F 80.31; Xenocrates fr. 225.14 Parenti. The name Python seems invariably masculine.

152 So, e.g., Harder 2012 ad Callim. *Aet.* fr. 88, 2019b: 15, though Harder is mistaken in thinking that Apollonius unambiguously embraces the feminine variant of the name.

153 Σ ad *Arg.* 2.705–711g, however, claims that Meandrius' serpent was female. Wendel (1935 ad loc.) seems correct in his assumption that this scholium is based on a misreading of Σ ad loc. b.

some unknown occasion;[154] he may, however, have sometimes conjured a male dragon in other works.[155] If Callimachus was "correcting" his prose source, he may have done so with the benefit of Homeric authority, as the *Homeric Hymn to Apollo* (our earliest account of the myth) makes its dragon unambiguously female.[156] But for his part, "Apollonius himself found a suitably playful way to remain learnedly agnostic," namely, by casting the serpent's name in the accusative case (Δελφύνην) and modifying it with the carefully chosen adjective πελώριος.[157] The accusative forms of a masculine Delphynes and a feminine Delphyne would both be Δελφύνην,[158] and the adjective πελώριος, since it can be treated as two-termination,[159] does not shed any light on the matter. Possibly by cultivating this ambiguity, Apollonius means to point up the contradiction between Callimachus and his source. In any event, this manner of foregrounding a mythological dilemma while reserving any judgment of his own is completely characteristic of Apollonian allusivity and of his "poetics of uncertainty."[160]

---

154 Δέλφυνα, with short alpha, occurs only in the Apollonius scholia. The feminine form Δελφύνη, with eta, occurs in the P scholium ad loc. (see Schafer 1813) as well as [Apollod.] *Bib.* 1.6.3, Dionys. Per. 442 (and Eust. ad loc.), John of Antioch fr. 21 Roberto (referring to a Delphic heroine), Tzetz. ad Ar. *Plut.* 213.7, and in various lexicographers.

155 For different understandings of the scholium, see Harder 2012 ad Callim. *Aet.* 4. fr. 88, who also offers many citations of the male and female variants of the myth. Fontenrose 1959: 14 n. 4, who offers further citations, argues that masculine adjectives and pronouns at Callim. *Hymn* 2.100–101, 4.91 show that in these passages, at least, Callimachus considers the serpent male, but I am not so sure. These may owe rather to the poet's use of the generic masculine noun ὄφις to denote the serpent (see Sancassano 1996: 49–50, 63); note that at *Hymn* 4.91–92, he uses the neuter, in agreement with θηρίον. Cf. *Dieg.* 2.24–25 (printed under *Aet.* 4 fr. 86 Pfeiffer, Harder) = fr. 89a.15–16 Harder, which uses the masculine term δράκων of the snake. It is possible that here we have a generic use of the masculine term to denote any member of the species; see, e.g., Dionys. Per. 441–442 (δράκοντος | Δελφύνης), Nicephorus Blemmydes *Conspectus geographiae* p. 461 col. 2 line 43 Müller (τῆς Δελφύνης τοῦ δράκοντος).

156 As Ogden (2013: 42) notes, the *Apollo* hymnist identifies the dragon as a δράκαινα (3.300) and even casts it as the nurse of Typhoeus (305–306).

157 See Fontenrose 1959: 14–15 n. 4; Ogden 2013: 42 (whence the quotation).

158 See Σ ad *Arg.* 2.705–711a (where a preference for a female dragon is declared).

159 E.g., Hes. *Theog.* 179 (πελώριον ... ἄρπην). Vian (2002: 1.276 ad *Arg.* 2.706) thinks Apollonius must have a male dragon in mind, because elsewhere he uses the unique feminine form πελωρίη at 4.1682 (see also Quint. Smyrn. 5.112), which would imply that he considers πελώριος three-termination; thus πελώριον at 2.706 must be masculine (so too Cusset 2018: 87 n. 10; Vergados, forthcoming). But Apollonius' penchant for using the same word in different ways in different places is well known; see also Matteo 2007 ad loc. As Matteo and others have noted (e.g., Hunter 1986: 59 n. 48), πελώριον may recall the serpent's label πέλωρ at *HH* 3.374.

160 To quote the subtitle of Byre 2002, who treats some much more significant examples of

The choice of the name Delphyne(s) in line 706 has a further dimension beyond the sex of the serpent: it strongly implies a derivation of the toponym Delphi (Δελφοί) from the name of the monster once resident there.[161] Since the description of the site of the future Delphi in line 705 borrows directly from the *Homeric Hymn to Apollo*,[162] Apollonius can be seen pointedly to distance himself from the etymology from δελφίς, "dolphin," endorsed by his own model in the *HH*. Elsewhere, however, Apollonius plays with another etymology in the hymn that involves the Delphic dragon. The hymnist derives Apollo's title Πύθιος and Delphi's poetic allonym Πυθώ from the fact that there the corpse of the slain beast "rotted" (πύθευ, 3.363; πύσει, 369; κατέπυσ', 371; πῦσε, 374). Apollonius mentions no rotting here, but he does affirm this tradition indirectly by transferring the motif to another dragon: at *Arg.* 4.1405, we hear of the "**festering** wounds" (πυθομένοισιν ... ἕλκεσι) of Ladon, the erstwhile guardian of the golden apples of the Hesperides,[163] piteously dispatched by Heracles' arrows the day before the Argonauts' own arrival at this Libyan oasis.[164] And yet earlier in Book 4, Apollonius points to an alternate derivation of Pytho from πυνθάνομαι ("learn by inquiry") via *figura etymologica*: Jason "went to holy **Pytho** to **inquire**" about his mission from the oracular god (Πυθώ | ἱρὴν πευσόμενος, *Arg.* 4.530–531).[165] Apollonius thus engages in a whole series of etymological word-

---

this phenomenon in Apollonius, like the future of Jason and Medea's relationship. We have already seen a similar example of this Apollonian tendency in the matter of Apollo's age at the time of the Pythonomachy; see 308n123; see also 317n175.

161 Hunter 1986: 56; Klooster 2007: 69 n. 24; Cusset 2018: 87 n. 10. This etymology is explicit in, e.g., Σ ad Eur. *Phoen.* 232, Tzetz. ad Lycoph. *Alex.* 207, Suda s.v. Δελφοί. For etymologizing in the Thynias episode, see now Vergados, forthcoming.

162 ὑπὸ δειράδι Παρνησσοῖο (*Arg.* 2.705) adapts δείραδα ... ὑπὸ Παρνησόν (*HH* 3.281–282); δειράς is a *hapax* in all the Homeric poems (Páskiewicz 1981 and Matteo 2007 ad loc.). The other model adduced by Matteo, Eur. *Phoen.* 206–207 (ὑπὸ δειράσι ... Παρνασοῦ), is closer to Apollonius' expression verbally but less apropos contextually.

163 The *Arg.* is the only source to name this dragon (Ogden 2013: 33–34, 153–154), and I wonder if, by evoking the name "Python" (Πύθων) via the etymon πύθω, Apollonius could in somewise be pointing to an analogous derivation of "Ladon" (Λάδων) from a form like λαθών (lit. "having escaped notice"); cf. Hesiod's description of this snake as dwelling "in the **hidden** places of the dark earth" (ἐρεμνῆς κεύθεσι γαίης, *Th.* 334). The actual derivation of "Ladon" may be Semitic; see, e.g., Astour 1964: 200; Korpel and de Moor 2017: 8.

164 The allusion is already flagged by the scholiast ad loc.; see further Ogden 2013: 38 and the notes of Hunter 2015 and Stürner 2022 ad loc. I am reminded of Campbell 1969: 281–282, who notes how Apollonius often "scatters the details given in the single Homeric passage over a wider stretch of the poem ... spreading out details so as to make the borrowings less obtrusive" (281–282).

165 Michalopoulos 2003: 172–173. A similar *figura etymologica* occurs in the same *sedes* in the

plays that respond to and vary the etymologizing found in the Python episode of the *Homeric Hymn to Apollo*.[166]

A final piece of potential etymologizing relates to Callimachus' treatment of the same episode in his own *Hymn to Apollo* (97–104).[167] Callimachus also offers an etiology for the paean-cry, which he traces to the Delphian population's shout of encouragement to Apollo, ἰὴ ἰὴ παιῆον, ἵει βέλος (*"Hië, Hië, Paeëon, shoot an arrow!"* 103)—that is, he interprets the cry as if from ἵει, παῖ, ἰόν ("Shoot, boy, an arrow!").[168] Similarly, perhaps, Apollonius alludes to Apollo's boyhood at 2.707[169] and has the Corycian nymphs[170] encourage the god in his archery (n.b. τόξοισι, 706) by shouting ἰὴ ἰέ (712), which gives rise to the famous refrain.[171]

---

oracle *ap.* Paus. 10.18.2. For these two etymologies, see, e.g., Eust. *Il.* 1.420.6–11 van der Valk, *Etym. Magn.* s.v. Πυθώ.

166 Alluding to an earlier text while offering competing etymologies is also a feature of Ovidian etymologizing; see O'Hara 1996: 268–273.

167 For connections between these passages and other relevant Callimachean *loci*, see, e.g.: Pfeiffer 1934: 11 n. 2; Páskiewicz 1981: 165; Kahane 1994a: 126–128; Vian 2002: 1.276 ad *Arg.* 2.703; Matteo 2007 ad *Arg.* 2.702. Euphorion seems to have connected the two passages, imitating both Callim. *Hymn* 2.98 and *Arg.* 2.702, 712 at fr. 116 Lightfoot (Páskiewicz 1981: 164). I have been noting other connections between our passage and other parts of Callimachus' *Hymn to Apollo* in the footnotes as they have become relevant, but here I will point especially to Williams 1978 ad Callim. *Hymn* 2.97–104 (an intriguing suggestion about the metapoetic significance of Callimachus' Python episode) and Matteo 2007 ad *Arg.* 2.687.

168 This translation is from Race 2008: 169 n. 58. On this and other etymologies, see, e.g., Rutherford 2001: 25–27. Callimachus could have believed that the etymology was already implicit in *HH* 3.357, describing Apollo's shooting the serpent with the words ἰὸν ἐφῆκε.

169 See 308n123.

170 These nymphs occur in a different context at Callim. *Aet.* fr. 75.56 Pfeiffer, Harder. On their function in Apollonius' *aition*, see Bauer 2017: 64, Phillips 2020: 88; cf. Cusset 2018: 94–95 on the homologous role of the people of Delphi in Callimachus' *Hymn*. Our punctilious poet could have replaced the Delphians from Callimachus' version because Delphi should not yet have been founded at the time of the Pythonomachy. Cf. Blumberg 1931: 43–44 ("dadurch wird die Handlung in göttliche Sphäre gehoben").

171 So already Σ ad loc. See further Apollonius' Late Republican Latin translator, Varro of Atax, who adds the phrase *te ... tendentem spicula* ("you [Apollo] as you were shooting arrows," my translation) to the Greek original in his adaptation of *Arg.* 2.711–712 (fr. 5 Blänsdorf). Varro thereby glosses the supposed etymology of *ieie* from ἵημι, "shoot" much more clearly than does Apollonius (Polt 2013: 629, O'Hara 2017: 56). This is not, however, the whole story of Varro's adaptation. The Roman poet also adds a second element to the nymphs' cry of *ieie*, namely, *o Phoebe* (~ *Arg.* 2.702). The pairing of *ieie* with this vocative address may suggest how the former could have given rise to one of Apollo's most unusual epithets: the cry ἰὴ ἰέ was interpreted in antiquity as a vocative of ἰήιος (Janko 1994 ad *Il.* 15.365–366). With the addition of *te* (referring to Apollo), Varro has cast these lines in Du-Stil (~ *Arg.* 2.708–710: Courtney 1993: 241), thus creating an interesting metaleptic effect when the nymphs also address Apollo.

Fränkel would go so far as to emend the transmitted text to the aspirated ἰή ἰέ to facilitate the allusion to this etymology,[172] though others have been less impressed by the connections between these passages.[173] They have in common the rare ἐφύμνιον in the same *sedes* (*Arg.* 2.713, Callim. *Hymn* 2.98); this term also occurs in one of Callimachus' likely sources for the paean etymology, Clearchus of Soli (fr. 64 Wehrli).[174] Both poets emphasize Apollo's youth and envision a drawn-out encounter, in contrast to the *HH*,[175] and each brings up Leto after describing the combat, though in different connections (*Arg.* 2.709–710, Callim. *Hymn* 2.103–104). It is notable, too, that Apollonius refers to the relatively obscure Pleistus River at *Arg.* 2.711 using the same form in the same *sedes* as Callimachus uses in another *Hymn* when mentioning the Pythonomachy (4.92).[176]

Together with the name Delphyne(s), it turns out that there are several strong Callimachean resonances in the passage, and especially in light of the Callimachean precedent, I would consider it legitimate to see subtle etymologizing of ἰή ἰέ from ἵημι ("shoot") in line 712, hinted at by τόξοισι several lines earlier. It is striking, however, that, absent Fränkel's emendation, Apol-

---

172 Fränkel 1961 in his apparatus ad loc.; he also suggests Ἰηπαιήον᾽ Ἰηπαιήονα as an emendation for line 702. Fränkel is followed by, e.g.: Páskiewicz 1981 ad *Arg.* 2.702–703; Paduano and Fusillo 1986 ad *Arg.* 2.701–713; Glei and Natzel-Glei 1996: 1.179; Valverde Sánchez 1996: 181 n. 309; Vian 2002: 1.276 ad *Arg.* 2.703.
173 See, e.g.: Wilamowitz 1924: 2.85; Blumberg 1931: 43–44; Eichgrün 1961: 168.
174 The etymology is also presupposed by Duris of Samos *FGrH* 76 F 79. Rutherford (2001: 26 n. 14) suggests that Ephorus (*FGrH* 70 F 31b) may have suppressed it because Apollo's boyhood did not fit into his rationalized version of the myth. See also Macrob. *Sat.* 1.17.20 and Hunter 1986: 59, who could be right that an etymology from ἵημι ("shoot") is already implicit in Timotheus (fr. 800 Campbell).
175 In the *Homeric Hymn to Apollo*, the god seems to be a young man (see 3.449–450), but his age is not stressed. Callimachus, conversely, implies that his Apollo is an infant (see *Hymn* 2.103–104 with Williams 1978 ad 103), as in one popular version of the myth. Apollonius seems to have a foot in both of these camps; see Hunter 1986: 56–57. As to the combat: the iterative imperfect θαρσύνεσκον (*Arg.* 2.712), together with the adverbial πολλά in the previous line, shows that Apollonius imagines an extended engagement, as in Callim. *Hymn* 2.101–102 (ἄλλον ἐπ᾽ ἄλλῳ | βάλλων ὠκὺν ὀιστόν); this version can be traced back to Simon. fr. 573 *PMG*. In the *HH*, by contrast, a single "strong arrow" (ἰόν ... | καρτερόν, 3.357–358) suffices to bring the monster down (Vergados, forthcoming).
176 The only earlier mention of the river is in Aesch. *Eum.* 27, as part of a prayer that recounts the history of the Delphic oracle—notably, without mentioning the Python. This Delphic river's name, suggestive of πλεῖστος, "greatest," may relate to an etymology connecting Apollo's name to πολύς (further activated by πολλά at the head of this same line); Apollonius plays on this etymology earlier at *Arg.* 1.759–760 (see Hunter 1986: 53 n. 22; 1993: 151 n. 186).

lonius hardly demands this interpretation of ἰὴ ἰέ.[177] We might equally assume that the Corycian nymphs encouraged Apollo with ecstatic, and semantically meaningless, cries of ἰὴ ἰέ,[178] which, after all, the Greeks considered suitable to chant before battle.[179] That is, an etymology from ἵημι is not necessary to understand the nymphs' cry. Apollonius' reticence in embracing Callimachus' etymology may, once again, stem from a reluctance to stake a firm position in a relevant philological debate: should the paean-cry have a rough breathing, per Callimachus, or a smooth breathing, as other authorities had it?[180] But however we resolve these specific problems of interpretation, Apollonius' extensive dialogue with earlier hymns to Apollo by Homer and Callimachus has the effect of placing Orpheus' composition in the same august tradition.

4.3 Representing Hymnic Speech

With this background in mind, we may now turn to the representation of speech in this episode. Orpheus' first speech, in which he proposes the erection of an altar to Apollo Heoïus, is given in direct quotation, complete with speech-introductory and capping formulas (685–694). The speech ends, notably, in an exuberant hymnic mode marked by Anaphora, which sets the tone for the scene to follow: "Be gracious, lord, be gracious, you who appeared to us" (ἀλλ' ἵληθι, ἄναξ, ἵληθι φααανθείς, 693).[181] In the description of the rites that follows, we encounter another method for representing character-speech: from each victim the Argonauts "piously burned two thighs on the holy altar, as they **invoked Apollo Heoïus**" (εὐαγέως ἱερῷ ἀνὰ διπλόα μηρία βωμῷ | καῖον, ἐπικλείοντες Ἑώιον Ἀπόλλωνα, 699–700).[182] This last phrase is an example of Genette's "narratized

---

177 Hunter (1986: 60) suggests that the Callimachean etymology might have been so well known that Apollonius could afford to be elliptical in alluding to it.

178 So Blumberg 1931: 43.

179 This is essentially the view of Ephorus of Cyme (*FGrH* 70 F 31b), who connects the origin of the paean to the Delphians' encouragement of Apollo in his battle with the Python, but without (apparently) positing an etymology for the cry. For the paean's military uses, see Rutherford 2001: 42–47.

180 For the debate, see Ath. 15.701d–e. This controversy is related to divided opinions on the paean's etymology: a derivation from ἵημι ("shoot") presupposes a rough breathing; from ἰάομαι ("heal") or ἰέναι ("go"), a smooth breathing. See, e.g., ΣA, bT ad *Il*. 15.365, Macrob. *Sat*. 1.17.16–20, *Etym. Magn*. s.v. Ἰήιε, Rutherford 2001: 25 n. 8. The debate is also adumbrated, notably, at Σ ad *Arg*. 2.702.

181 Apollonius has increased the religious fervor of his model (*Od*. 3.380 [ἀλλὰ ἄνασσ' ἵληθι], noted by Páskiewicz 1981 ad loc.) by doubling the imperative.

182 Note also the evaluative terms εὐαγέως and ἱερῷ, which suggest the AR narrator's religious expertise and create a "solemn, reverent tone" (Páskiewicz 1981 ad loc.). I would add that

speech": we are given no indication of the Invocation's content beyond the identity of its object, Apollo under his new title Heoïus.

This bare instance of narratized speech appears here as if to highlight by contrast the device we find next (2.701–703):

ἀμφὶ δὲ δαιομένοις εὐρὺν χορὸν ἐστήσαντο,
καλὸν Ἰηπαιήον' Ἰηπαιήονα Φοῖβον
μελπόμενοι.

Around the burning offerings they formed a broad choral dance and chanted the beautiful "Iêpaiêon, Phoebus Iêpaiêon."

Earlier in this chapter, I classified this passage as an example of hymnic narratization, but in fact, it can be analyzed in more ways than one, largely because of the semantic ambiguity of the word Ἰηπαιήων (or ἰηπαιήων) and the syntactic ambiguity of the use of the adjective καλός.[183] As noted above, other than in the *Arg.* and its scholia, Ἰηπαιήων occurs only in Apollo's major *HH*: once (3.272) as an "epith. for Apollo" (LSJ s.v. I) and twice to denote the "*hymn* sung to him" (LSJ s.v. II), in the expression ἰηπαιήον' ἀείδειν/ἄειδον (3.500, 517).[184] We have seen that these latter passages constitute important models for Apollonius' usage. Moreover, the same semantic range is observable in the Homeric use of the related term Παιήων/παιήων, which sometimes denotes the god (e.g., *Il.* 5.401; see also *Arg.* 4.1511), but which at other times denotes the paean sung in his honor; this latter usage is illustrated in another of Apollonius' models for this passage, *Il.* 1.473–474 (καλὸν ἀείδοντες παιήονα, κοῦροι Ἀχαιῶν, | μέλποντες ἑκάεργον).[185]

The question is, which usage is presupposed at *Arg.* 2.702? On the one hand, the hymnic repetition and the juxtaposition with the epithet Φοῖβος strongly

---

εὐαγής does not occur in the HEs, though this adverb in this *sedes* occurs twice in the *Homeric Hymn to Demeter* (2.274, 369; Matteo 2007 ad loc.).

183   In another of Apollonius' potential models—Orpheus' singing of an ἔλεγον ἰήϊον in his capacity as the Argo's boatswain (Eur. *Hypsipyle* fr. 752g.9 Collard and Cropp)—the adjective ἰήϊος is ambiguous in a different way: does this phrase mean "mournful plaint" or "hymn of thanks (for making landfall)"? See the note on this line in Collard and Cropp 2008.

184   Hunter (1986: 58) further compares Callim. *Hymn* 2.21 (ὁππόθ' ἰὴ παιῆον ἰὴ παιῆον ἀκούσῃ), which has a strikingly similar shape to *Arg.* 2.702; Harder (2019b: 15) notes also Callim. *Hymn* 2.97 (ἰὴ ἰὴ παιῆον ἀκούομεν).

185   See, e.g., Ford 2006: 287–291. παιήων in the sense "paean-song" is used in *HH* 3.518 as a synonym for ἰηπαιήων.

suggest that Ἰηπαιήων is functioning as an epithet, too: one would hardly say "chanting the paean-song, the paean-song" or place "Phoebus" in apposition in such a phrase. The interpretation of Ἰηπαιήων as an epithet would be consistent with other examples of hymnic narratization in the poem, in which strings of Honorific epithets often follow a verb of singing, invocation, etc., and as we have seen, in those cases it is difficult to be certain whether the epithets represent character-speech in FID or the narrator's own enthusiastic participation in the hymnody.

On the other hand, καλόν at the head of the verse permits another interpretation. Although it could be taken as an adverbial (or internal) accusative with μελπόμενοι (i.e., "beautifully chanting"),[186] there are good grounds for considering καλόν an adjective modifying the Argonauts' entire chant.[187] Whereas at *Iliad* 1.473 (καλὸν ἀείδοντες παιήονα), καλόν modifies the single word παιήονα, in the *Arg.* it may modify the entire phrase Ἰηπαιήον᾽ Ἰηπαιήονα Φοῖβον— hence Race's translation, "[they] chanted the beautiful 'Iêpaiêon, Phoebus Iêpaiêon.'"[188] To be sure, the Argonauts are not being directly quoted; this phrase rather stands in the accusative as the direct object of μελπόμενοι.[189] Nevertheless, with the repetition of Ἰηπαιήων and the adjoining epithet Φοῖβος, this phrase could represent the entire refrain in the Argonauts' "real" paean: "Hail to the Healing God, hail to the Healing God Phoebus."[190] Indeed, this understanding is probably what has led Race to place quotation marks around the phrase in his translation. On this interpretation, we effectively have an example of narratized speech whose "actual" wording is so re-constructible, because

---

186 As, e.g., at 4.1399 (ἐφίμερον ἀείδουσαι).

187 Line 713, which gives the etiology for the paean formula that the Argonauts chant at line 702, repeats the word καλόν (note also Φοίβῳ) from that line and uses it unambiguously as an adjective, modifying ἐφύμνιον ("refrain"). This usage suggests that Apollonius treats καλόν as adjectival in line 702 as well, where it modifies the words for which ἐφύμνιον in line 713 stands, that is, the chant Ἰηπαιήον᾽ Ἰηπαιήονα Φοῖβον (Hunter 1986: 56 n. 31; Matteo 2007 ad *Arg.* 2.702–703). *Arg.* 4.1197 presents a comparable case involving a ritual chant: the Phaeacian nymphs "sounded forth the lovely wedding song" (ἱμερόενθ᾽ ὑμέναιον ἀνήπυον). Here ἱμερόενθ᾽ is unambiguously adjectival. These parallels reduce the probability that καλόν might be modifying Φοῖβον, as many have thought (for references, see Matteo 2007 loc. cit.). See further Sappho fr. 44.32–33 LP, where ἐπήρατον ("lovely") modifies the substantive ὄρθιον ("high-pitched strain"), and cf. the more ambiguous use of καλόν at *Il.* 1.473.

188 We might compare such English expressions as, "He said a few quick Hail Marys."

189 Cf. ἰὴ ἰὲ κεκληγυῖαι below (712). As the direct object of the participle is an indeclinable exclamation, it could be "either direct speech or an internal accusative" (Kahane 1994a: 128 n. 18).

190 As Race (2008: 168 n. 58) translates Ἰηπαιήον᾽ Ἰηπαιήονα Φοῖβον.

of the more or less standardized form of the paean-chant, that it borders on direct quotation.[191]

Before turning to Orpheus' hymn, I would like to jump ahead to consider the end of the episode out of order, because it features another ambiguous example of hymnic narratization. The Thynias episode closes with the Argonauts' oaths of mutual goodwill (ὁμοφροσύνῃσι νόοιο, 716) and their establishment of a "shrine to kindly Concord" ('Ομονοίης ἱρὸν ἐύφρονος, 718), the goddess who personifies this Argonautic virtue. The oath, transposed with an infinitive construction (ἀρήξειν), is introduced with a verb of swearing (ἐπώμοσαν) and by the asseverative particles ἦ μέν (715–716), precisely on the model of *Il.* 1.76–77.[192] We thus get another brand of indirect speech in the episode's concluding αἴτιον (cf. the ὡς-clause used at 705). Earlier in this chapter, I listed the episode's final lines as an example of hymnic narratization: the Argonauts "themselves built [the shrine] at that time to honor **the most glorious goddess**" (ὅ ῥ' ἐκάμοντο | αὐτοὶ **κυδίστην** τότε **δαίμονα** πορσαίνοντες, *Arg.* 2.718–719). Unlike most examples of hymnic narratization, however, the verb in this instance, πορσαίνοντες, does not imply speech,[193] and in this context of building a shrine rather than directly invoking the goddess, it would be natural to assign the Honorific κυδίστην (and, perhaps, ἐύφρονος) to the reverential perspective of the AR narrator, who would once again involve himself personally in the Argonauts' act of worship. But Apollonius is using πορσαίνω, whose basic sense is "prepare" or "provide," in an extended sense denoting an act of care or an internal attitude of esteem[194]—hence the scholiast's gloss of τιμῶντες, "honoring."[195] For this reason, we could also view these Honorifics as focalized by the worshipful

---

191 See Bauer (2017: 61–62, 67) for similar interpretations of both our passage and the paean-song at *Il.* 1.472–474; see also Korenjak 1994: 20. For comparable deployments of the hymeneal chant, see Bion *Ep. Adon.* 88–89, Oppian *Cyn.* 1.341.

192 As noted by, e.g.: Campbell 1981 ad loc. In context, Calchas is extracting an oath from Achilles to support him when he counsels Agamemnon to return Chryseis; notably, perhaps, Achilles swears to do so by Apollo (86). The fact that Achilles' intervention ultimately proves disastrous for the Greek army may add an ominous note to the Argonauts' oath here: in fact, many of the crewmembers will later go on to kill each other after the expedition has concluded (see, e.g., Feeney 1991: 77 with n. 66; McPhee, forthcoming c: 180 n. 83; cf. Nishimura-Jensen 2009: 7 n. 19).

193 Perhaps for this reason, the scholiast ad *Arg.* 2.715–719b notes the alternate reading κιχλήσκοντες, "invoking."

194 LSJ s.v. πορσύνω III cites Pind. *Ol.* 6.33 for the meaning "treat with care, tend" and *Pyth.* 4.278 for the meaning "regard, esteem." For our passage, they gloss the verb with "honour, adore." Apollonius uses the verb in this sense again at 3.1124; see further Matteo 2007 ad loc.

195 We may compare *Arg.* 4.1733 as another example of hymnic narratization in which the

Argonauts, and possibly even reflecting a speech act related to the inauguration of the shrine.

But all of the mythological, philological, and narratological uncertainties we have encountered so far in this passage reach their height in the account of Orpheus' hymn. It may be useful to present this passage once again (703–714):

> σὺν δέ σφιν ἐὺς πάις Οἰάγροιο
> Βιστονίῃ φόρμιγγι λιγείης ἦρχεν ἀοιδῆς·
> 705 ὥς ποτε πετραίῃ ὑπὸ δειράδι Παρνησσοῖο
> Δελφύνην τόξοισι πελώριον ἐξενάριξεν,
> κοῦρος ἐὼν ἔτι γυμνός, ἔτι πλοκάμοισι γεγηθώς—
> ἱλήκοις· αἰεί τοι, ἄναξ, ἄτμητοι ἔθειραι,
> αἰὲν ἀδήλητοι· τὼς γὰρ θέμις· οἰόθι δ' αὐτὴ
> 710 Λητὼ Κοιογένεια φίλαις ἐνὶ χερσὶν ἀφάσσει—
> πολλὰ δὲ Κωρύκιαι νύμφαι, Πλειστοῖο θύγατρες
> θαρσύνεσκον ἔπεσσιν, ἰὴ ἰὲ κεκληγυῖαι·
> ἔνθεν δὴ τόδε καλὸν ἐφύμνιον ἔπλετο Φοίβῳ.
> αὐτὰρ ἐπειδὴ τόν γε χορείῃ μέλψαν ἀοιδῇ ...

And among them the noble son of Oeagrus led off a clear song on his Bistonian lyre, telling how once upon a time beneath Parnassus' rocky ridge the god killed monstrous Delphyne(s) with his arrows, when he was still a naked boy, still delighting in his long locks—be gracious! Ever unshorn, lord, is your hair, ever unharmed, for such is right; and only Leto herself, Coeus' daughter, strokes it with her dear hands—and often did the Corycian nymphs, the daughters of Pleistus, encourage him with their words, as they shouted *iê ie*. From there arose this beautiful refrain for Phoebus. But when they had celebrated him with their choral song ...

The narratological difficulties of this passage boil down to one simple question: who speaks? The conjunction ὡς in line 705 introduces the first subsection representing Orpheus' hymn (705–707) unambiguously as a transposition of the bard's narrative into indirect speech. Even here, however, the Anaphora of ἔτι in line 707 in two more or less redundant participial phrases (both emphasizing Apollo's youth) effects an "excited style" that would be at home in the hypothet-

---

verb indicates an attitude of reverence rather than speech (ἁζόμενος Μαίης υἷα κλυτόν, "out of respect for Maia's famous son").

ical hymn that Orpheus "actually" sang to Apollo.[196] Either some of Orpheus' "original" wording has shone through even in *oratio obliqua*, or possibly the AR narrator has allowed his own religious enthusiasm to color his transposition of the bard's narrative—a small example of contagious hymnody, in the terminology proposed earlier in this chapter. It is with the advent of ἰλήκοις in the next line, however, that real uncertainty as to the identity of the speaker sets in. It is clear, on any interpretation, that the switch from Er-Stil (705–707) to Du-Stil (708) constitutes a change in narrative mode that takes us out of indirect speech, but who exactly is begging the god's pardon for the faux pas of line 707?

One long-standing interpretation holds that in line 708, the AR narrator steps in to correct in his own voice the previous line's mistake, which is attributable either to Orpheus' actual hymn or to the narrator's own accidental distortion thereof in summarizing it.[197] Such a correction would suit the piety of Apollonius' narratorial persona; in particular, we have noted how phrases like τὼς γὰρ θέμις (709) contribute to our impression of his religious expertise,[198] and the AR narrator's apology to the Muses at 4.984 (with the cognate verb ἵλατε) has often been raised as a parallel.[199] Moreover, the hym-

---

[196] Hunter 1993: 150; see also Wifstrand 1929: 82. See 326n211 for a parallel from Orpheus' cosmogony.

[197] For the view that Orpheus errs and the narrator corrects him, see, e.g.: Páskiewicz 1981 ad *Arg.* 2.707; Beye 1982: 18–19 (comparing apostrophes from the *HH*s); Hunter 1986: 57; Busch 1993: 321 n. 46 (cf. 324 n. 53); Belloni 1999: 239; Matteo 2007 ad loc.; cf. Hutchinson 1988: 89–90, who reads the narrator's intervention as a parody of Orpheus' earnest prayer at 2.693. See further 308n124. Conversely, Fränkel (1968 ad loc.) doubts that Apollonius would attribute a theological error to the esteemed Orpheus (cf. Hunter 1993: 151) and adduces the tradition of poets correcting themselves, evident as early as Sappho fr. 105a LP. See further Callim. *Hymn* 2.38–40, a milder case of poetic self-correction in a strikingly similar context to which Apollonius may be alluding (again, see 308n124). For the idea that the AR narrator errs and corrects himself, see further: Wifstrand 1929: 82; Fusillo 1985: 384; Paduano and Fusillo 1986 ad loc.; Gummert 1992: 122–123; DeForest 1994: 81–82 (cf. Bauer 2017: 65 n. 49); Vian 2002: 1.210 n. 3; Manuello 2012: 129. Fränkel's position seems to be misunderstood by Green 2007 and Matteo 2007 ad loc. Finally, some have maintained that we cannot decide who erred, Orpheus or the narrator transposing his song (e.g., Albis 1996: 30; Cuypers 2004: 59); see further below.

[198] θέμις is perhaps a provocative word to use in this context given the myth that the Delphic oracle had previously been in the possession of Themis (e.g., Aesch. *Eum.* 2–4), the goddess who personifies this very concept.

[199] E.g.: Páskiewicz ad *Arg.* 2.707; Matteo 2007 ad loc. For the narrator's piety as displayed by his apology to the Muses, see the analysis in 3.2.3. The AR narrator uses the same verb (ἵλατε) again in his Salutation to the Argonauts (4.1773), where an apologetic tone may also be recognized (see 122n168).

nic mode of these lines would amplify the hint of hymnody found already in line 707: the narrator intervenes in a hymnic style suited to the narrative context.[200]

Another possibility, however, is that in line 708, Apollonius switches into direct speech, and it is in fact Orpheus who apologizes to Apollo.[201] Ancient scholars recognized HE precedent for the sudden switch from indirect to direct discourse (*Il.* 4.301–309, 15.346–349),[202] and Pseudo-Longinus lauds this technique as an effective "sort of outbreak of emotion" (ἐκβολή τις πάθους, 1.27.1), commenting, "This figure is useful, when a sudden crisis (ὀξὺς ὁ καιρὸς ὤν) will not let the writer wait, and forces him to change at once from one character to another."[203] It is entirely conceivable that Apollonius, a noted collector of Homeric curiosities, here imitates this rare procedure to achieve a comparable degree of πάθος after the "sudden crisis" constituted by the theological slight to the god in line 707. Moreover, the hymnic style of lines 708–710 is suited first and foremost to Orpheus' own "personal language situation" as he hymns Apollo; in fact, there are notable echoes in both verbiage and style between lines 708–710 and Orpheus' prayer to Apollo as given in direct speech at line 693 (ἀλλ' ἴληθι, ἄναξ, ἴληθι φαανθείς): Anaphora of ἴληθι (cognate to ἰλήκω) and the Honorific address ἄναξ (in the same *sedes*).[204] These resemblances might suggest we have Orpheus' direct speech in lines 708–710, too—though, to com-

---

200 The hymnic effect of these lines is achieved through direct Prayer to the god (ἰλήκοις); the use of Du-Stil (ἰλήκοις, τοι), including the Honorific vocative ἄναξ; Anaphora of forms of αἰεί paired with semantically redundant privative adjectives in ἀ- (in direct answer to the doubled ἔτι of the previous line: Phillips 2020: 95); and the genealogical epithet Κοιογένεια for Leto. For Anaphora of αἰεί in hymns, see Keyssner 1932: 39–45.

201 Hunter (1993: 151) admits the possibility that "an Alexandrian Orpheus" might err and then correct himself, and this interpretation is positively embraced by Green (2007 ad loc). As Wifstrand (1929: 82) notes, this understanding is also implicit in Ville de Mirmont (1894: 458), who quotes lines 707–710 as "dans le chant d'Orphée." For this interpretation, see further Goldhill 1991: 297–298. The remaining interpretative possibility—that the narrator errs and Orpheus corrects him—finds its champion in Korenjak 1994: 20–21, but such a configuration seems too postmodern to consider seriously, even in such an experimental Alexandrian epic.

202 See Fantuzzi 2008a: 223 with n. 7; Nünlist 2009: 104–105; de Jong 2022a: 46. For a modern interpretation of Demodocus' second lay along these lines, see 325n207. Incidentally, the same device is also found once in the *HHs* (4.524–527).

203 1.27.2: ἡ πρόσχρησις τοῦ σχήματος τότε, ἡνίκ' ἂν ὀξὺς ὁ καιρὸς ὢν διαμέλλειν τῷ γράφοντι μὴ διδῷ ἀλλ' εὐθὺς ἐπαναγκάζῃ μεταβαίνειν ἐκ προσώπων εἰς πρόσωπα.

204 Orpheus' prayer to the Hesperides at 4.1411–1421 betrays a similar hymnic style ("hymnischen Stil": Stürner 2022 ad loc.; see further Ibscher 1939: 135–136) and includes the phrase ἵλατ', ἄνασσαι in its opening line.

plicate the analysis yet further, one might equally argue that these similarities in expression rather reflect the AR narrator's well-known sympathy with the legendary bard.²⁰⁵

The third subsection (711–713) hardly resolves the matter. Here the Pythonomachy narrative begun in 705–707 continues, which may suggest that the narratorial digression of 708–710 has ended and that the transposition of Orpheus' hymn has resumed. Yet in the absence of a sure marker like another ὡς, we cannot be certain that these lines represent indirect speech; they might equally continue Orpheus' narrative in direct speech, if we think that the bard utters the previous lines.²⁰⁶ A third possibility is that in these lines, Apollonius imitates a distinctive narrative device found already in the *Odyssey*, in which a transposed narrative begins in a dependent construction that ultimately gives way to an independent construction essentially indistinguishable from narrator-text.²⁰⁷ The most famous example is Demodocus' second lay, on Aphrodite's affair with Ares: after an initial ὡς introducing the narrative in indirect discourse (he sings "how [ὡς] first they lay together in the house of Hephaestus secretly ..." *Od.* 8.268–269), almost one hundred lines pass with no further indications that this story is Demodocus', not the HE narrator's; we even get direct speech from the internal characters (292–294, 306–320, and dialogue from 329–358). Only the capping formula at line 367 ("This song the famous minstrel sang") reminds us that the foregoing narrative has been Demodocus' transposed speech. To that point, it is unclear whether the narrator is still transposing the bard's speech or if he has taken over the tale himself, and in this

---

205 See the discussion at the end of the present section.
206 Some scholars assert that line 713 cannot represent Orpheus' words because the deictic τόδε indicates that the etiology contained therein is addressed to the reader (Hunter 1993: 151 n. 185; Vian 2002: 1.210 n. 3; Matteo 2007 ad loc.; Vergados, forthcoming). This argument overlooks another possibility, however: if Orpheus is speaking, cannot τόδε ἐφύμνιον refer to the formula that the chorus of Argonauts are presently chanting (702; see further Phillips 2020: 87)? We have seen that etiology is an important part of the AR narrator's hymnic voice, but this motif is also appropriate to hymnody in general (Hunter 1993: 151) and to Orpheus' character in particular (Fusillo 1985: 59). The bard actually fashions two new *aitia* in this very episode (see 686–689 with Fränkel 1968 ad loc.), and a transparent etymology for "Delphi" is pointed up in lines that transpose his speech (705–706).
207 See de Jong 2009: 99–106 for a narratological account of this device (her third type of metalepsis, the "blending of narrative voices"). What follows is based on her analysis of Demodocus' second lay (99–101). De Bakker and de Jong (2022: 10) call this phenomenon "downshifting" (see also de Jong 2022a: 36–37, Klooster 2022: 108). Cf. Richardson 1990: 86, who interprets the abandonment of the dependent construction as betokening a switch to direct discourse, although he still finds that this technique has the effect of blending together the voices of narrator and character (on which, see below).

sense, their voices temporarily blend together.²⁰⁸ Notably, the capping formula at *Arg.* 2.714 uses a plural verb (μέλψαν) and makes reference to the "choral song" (χορείη ... ἀοιδῇ) that all the Argonauts, not just Orpheus, have been singing since line 701.²⁰⁹ It thus marks the end of an entire scene and does not necessarily imply that lines 711–713 represent the contents of Orpheus' hymn in the same way that *Od.* 8.367 does for Demodocus' lay.²¹⁰

It has been argued that Apollonius imitates the metaleptic technique from the *Odyssey* passage in transposing another of Orpheus' songs into indirect speech, namely, the pacifying cosmo-theogony that the bard performs in Book 1, which takes Demodocus' second lay as one of its primary models.²¹¹ In the case of Orpheus' hymn to Apollo, we might particularly point to another model, the *Homeric Hymn to Pan* (19),²¹² where the same device occurs within an internal hymn to the goat god sung by his attendant nymphs:²¹³ after an initial ὡς

---

208   So de Jong 2009: 100: "Due to the change from a dependent construction to an independent one, we can no longer determine whether we are hearing the primary narrator, 'Homer', or the reported narrator, Demodocus: their voices merge."

209   The vocabulary of line 714 picks up elements referring to both the Argonauts' chant (χορόν, 701; μελπόμενοι, 703) and Orpheus' song (ἀοιδῆς, 704) in order to mark the end of both elements of the performance.

210   Bauer (2017: 65) compares *Arg.* 1.512, where the end of Orpheus' cosmogonic song is clearly marked by ἦ (literally, "he spoke"); Apollonius' different procedure at 2.714 inclines him to think that in lines 711–713, by contrast, it is the narrator who speaks. But as Bauer himself acknowledges (64–65), scholars have discerned a blending of voices at 1.507–511 as well (see n. 211), so the difference between these passages is not as clear-cut as his argument assumes. Cf. Busch (1993: 317) and Korenjak (1994: 9), who argue that ἦ at 1.512 does reveal 1.507–511 to be a direct quotation of Orpheus' song. But this argument ignores epic precedent for the use of capping formulas to mark the end even of speeches transposed into *oratio obliqua*; see, e.g., the unambiguous cases in narrator-text at *HH* 2.316, 448, with Beck 2001: 67–73; see also Hes. *Op.* 69. This phenomenon occurs in character-text in the HEs at *Il.* 23.149; *Od.* 8.570 = 13.178.

211   See esp. Nelis 1992. At first the repeated conjunction ὡς keeps the mediation of Orpheus' cosmogonic song in indirect speech firmly in view (1.496, 499, 501 [2×], 503, 505; Hunter 1993: 148). The final sentences are not so introduced (507–511), however, so that it may be possible to see a blending of Orpheus' voice with that of the narrator in these lines (Hunter 1993: 149; Korenjak 1994: 9). Line 508 (Ζεὺς ἔτι κοῦρος, ἔτι φρεσὶ νήπια εἰδώς) furnishes a description of Zeus' youth closely parallel to 2.707 in Orpheus' hymn to Apollo (cf. 3.134) and even features some "hymnic" Anaphora—appropriately so, insofar as Orpheus' song constitutes a "Zeushymnos" (Bauer 2017: 64).

212   Cf. Beye 1982: 19: "The change from the indirect discourse of Orpheus' reported song to the poet's direct speech which is an apostrophe to the god is breathtaking. It is another technique which Apollonius has taken from the Homeric Hymns."

213   Cf. the Corycian nymphs from the inset Pythonomachy narrative, who correspond to the Argonauts themselves as they perform a paean and coin a new cult epithet in honor of Apollo (Walter 2020: 131; cf. Phillips 2020: 90–91).

introducing the narrative of Pan's birth in indirect discourse (29), the narrative continues right up to the Salutation that marks the conclusion of the *HH* itself (48) with no further indications of transposed speech—there is not even a capping formula this time.[214] Especially because the content of the nymphs' hymn is so congenial to the speaker's own hymnic agenda, their voices naturally blend, and the Salutation seems to cap both the internal and external hymns.[215] It turns out, then, that there is actually good Homeric precedent for Apollonius' distinctive procedure in this passage—that is, for the blending of the narrator's voice with that of an internal hymnist in transposed speech that transitions into an independent construction.

In the final analysis, like so many other issues of interpretation we have encountered in the Thynias episode, the matter of who is speaking in each of these lines is not finally resolvable.[216] The style and content of lines 708–713 suit both Orpheus and the AR narrator too well to make a determination, and there are Homeric and Apollonian precedents for construing either as speaker of these lines, or, indeed, to hear a blend of both their voices in lines 711–713. Our inability to disentangle character from narrator in this passage in fact reflects Orpheus' status as one of the AR narrator's most visible alter egos.[217] For example, Orpheus is given pride of place as the first Argonaut listed in the Catalog, and with one of the longest entries to boot (1.23–34);[218] his voice

---

214 Vamvouri Ruffy 2004: 149–150; de Jong 2009: 105; Hunzinger 2012: 51–52; cf. Thomas 2011: 163–165.
215 See above on "metaleptic fade-out" (278n14).
216 Hunter 1993: 151; Klooster 2011: 88–89.
217 For Orpheus as a narratorial alter ego, see, among others: Fränkel 1968 ad *Arg.* 1.23–34; Beye 1982: 14, 18–19; Fusillo 1985: 58–59, 362–363; Hopkinson 1988 ad *Arg.* 1.540; Busch 1993: 323–324; Hunter 1993: 127, 149; Korenjak 1994: 39–41; Kyriakou 1995: 190; Albis 1996: 29–30; Cuypers 2004: 58–59; Scherer 2006: 117; Asper 2008: 177–179; Billault 2008: 200–201; Manuello 2011: 89–91, 132; Klooster 2011: 91, 2012: 63; 2013b: 169–170; 2022: 108; Schaaf 2014: *passim* (summarized at 335); Serafimidis 2016: 372–376; Bauer 2017: 70–73; Phillips 2020: 56–61 (with some caveats); *pace* Köhnken's overly restrictive analysis of Orpheus' role in the poem (2003b: 23–27). Cf. Pavlock 1990: 31–33, who detects some irony in this sympathetic identification, and Murray 2018, who argues that the relationship between the narrator and Orpheus is in fact agonistic (now echoed by Vergados, forthcoming).
218 Billault (2008: 198) is right that Orpheus' importance is signaled both by his priority and by the considerable length of his entry, but he is mistaken that his is the longest in the Catalog: that honor goes to the Boreads (1.211–223), in the Catalog's final entry (as correctly noted by Köhnken 2003b: 25; cf. 2010: 145; cf. also Schollmeyer [2017: 36 n. 3], who similarly miscounts the length of the Heracles and Hylas entry [122–132]). Still, we could affirm, with Schollmeyer, that Orpheus receives the most lines in the Catalog of any single Argonaut.

and that of the narrator blend earlier at 1.507–511;[219] and his musical performances are often capable of metapoetic interpretation.[220] As to the present passage, although I disagree with those who would interpret the *Arg.* in toto as a hymn to Apollo,[221] the fact that the poem is a hymn (to the heroized Argonauts) that begins with an Invocation of Apollo does generate an unmistakable effect of mise-en-abyme.[222] Indeed, it has been argued that the verb ἦρχεν in line 704, marking the beginning of Orpheus' hymn to Apollo, should remind us of the poem's opening words (ἀρχόμενος σέο, Φοῖβε, 1.1).[223] By a similar token, the nymphs' cries of ἰὴ ἰέ within the Pythonomachy narrative (712) are themselves a hymnic refrain (ἐφύμνιον, 713) that mirrors the Argonauts' own choral paean-chant at 702.[224] In other words, at line 712, we have a hint of a hymn (the nymphs' refrain for Apollo) within a hymn (the Argonauts' refrain and Orpheus' hymn to Apollo) within a hymn (the AR narrator's hymn to the Argonauts, which begins with Apollo). In this passage, the AR narrator certainly seems interested in binding together past hymnic performances with his own in the present day.[225] It is only natural that the AR narrator would want to associate himself with the premier bard in the Greek mythological tradition;[226] and as a holy man, Orpheus is a particularly desirable model for the AR narrator's pious self-fashioning.

5   Conclusion

In a poem that presents itself as an "epic hymn," we could expect to find signs of hymnody in more than just the work's hymnic frame. In part 1, the poem's open acknowledgments of the institution of hero cult were correlated with the poem's status as a hymn dedicated to divinized heroes, and some of these pas-

---

219 See 326*n*211.
220 E.g., see Klooster (2011: 76–77; 2012: 63; 2013: 169–170; 2014: 538–539) and Murray (2018: 219–220) on *Arg.* 1.26–31 and Fränkel (1968: 623–625) on *Arg.* 1.494–515. See further 115*n*131.
221 See 1.1.5.
222 See esp. Bauer 2017.
223 Matteo 2007 ad loc.; Nishimura-Jensen 2009: 6. See also 310*n*129.
224 Paduano and Fusillo 1986 ad *Arg.* 2.701–713.
225 On the complex temporal dynamics of this passage, see, e.g.: Kahane 1994a: 126–128; Walter 2020: 129–134; Cusset 2021: 225–226. See further Noussia-Fantuzzi 2017: 257. Cf. Kampakoglou 2019: 147, who seems to misinterpret the passage as though the Argonauts here invent the paean-cry and Orpheus founds the genre.
226 See, as a comparandum, de Jong's comments on the effects of the HE narrator's self-identification with the blind bard Demodocus (2009: 100–101).

sages were interpreted as metapoetic reflections on the *Arg.*'s generic hybridity. The burden of part 2, conversely, has been to flesh out the hymnic voice of the narrator himself as an integral aspect of Apollonius' complex narratorial persona. In chapter 3, I have argued that Apollonius' hymnic voice can often be heard when the poet exploits narratorial strategies that have otherwise been associated primarily with other types of poetry beyond the realm of ἔπος, such as Callimachean etiology or Pindaric moralizing, for these devices can, in fact, claim the sanction of Homeric authority by way of the *HH*s. This chapter has surveyed numerous passages in which the hymnic voice takes center stage. In some of these passages, such as the introits in Books 3 and 4, we can observe hymnic transformations of standard epic conventions—in this case, the programmatic Appeal to the Muses. But in the instances of contagious hymnody and hymnic narratization, the AR narrator exhibits a striking tendency toward metalepsis, or blurring the boundaries between his own hymnic voice and that of his characters. This tendency reaches its apex in the Thynias episode, where I have argued it is impossible to disentangle the voices of the characters and the narrator; both seem to join in hymning Apollo. In the last analysis, this blending of voices suggests that the portrait of Apollonius' hymnic narrator that we have been sketching is ultimately a portrait of Orpheus himself, projected from the level of the story to that of the narration. Indeed, given the generic affiliations of the two major songs that Orpheus performs in the poem, an "epic" cosmo-theogony and a hymn to Apollo, Orpheus might emblematize the hybrid identity of the *Arg.* itself as an epic hymn. It only remained for an anonymous poet of the Imperial era to literalize this conceit in penning the *Orphic Argonautica*, in which Orpheus really does become the poem's homodiegetic narrator.

One issue that the analysis to this point has only brushed up against here and there is the relationship between the narrator's hymnic voice and the characterization of his Hymnic Subjects, the Argonauts. For instance, I have argued that the apostrophe to the Argonauts in Libya (4.1381–1388) represents a hymnic development of the epic-style apostrophe to mortals that anticipates the Argonauts' heroization as revealed in the poem's Envoi. Nevertheless, a critical question remains: does the fact that the *Arg.* is a hymn to the Argonauts bear on the question of their portrayal as actors in the narrative, particularly in view of their often problematic brand of heroism? I have already had occasion in a footnote to quote Cuypers' observation, "Congruous with his aim of 'hymning' the Argonauts …, the narrator shows a strong awe for the gods and for the heroes of the past about whom he narrates, and an outspoken disapproval of those who oppose either."[227] Cuypers is right that, with only a few (outsized) exceptions,

---

227 Cuypers 2004: 61.

the AR narrator typically presents his Hymnic Subjects almost in hagiographic terms and hardly ever criticizes them outright. And yet for anyone acquainted with the bibliography on the poem, I need hardly point out that countless scholars have heard in the *Arg.* a "further voice," as it were, one that criticizes the heroes—above all their leader Jason—and often quite vociferously at that. I can hardly hope to resolve the question of the Argonauts' heroism here, but its connection with heroization and hymnody, along with the potential political subtext of these complex issues, are two of the major questions that will preoccupy us in the conclusion to this study.

Conclusion

I proceed first by summarizing the primary results of this inquiry and then by indicating some directions in which future research might fruitfully be conducted (section 1). I finish in section 2 by offering some preliminary thoughts as to how this study relates to two broader topics in Apollonian criticism: the long-standing question of the Argonauts' heroism and the more recent interest in situating the *Arg.* within its Ptolemaic context.

1 Major Findings and Directions for Future Research

In the course of this study I have had occasion to comment upon a good number of passages in the *Arg.*, and I hope to have shared many new insights in the process. The following three items, however, represent this book's most important contributions to Apollonian scholarship.

1. **Apollonius' Use of the *HH*s**

    The programmatic allusions to the hymns at both the beginning and end of the *Arg.*,[1] the metapoetic import of several passages in the poem,[2] the sheer variety of functions that allusion to the hymns can play in the *Arg.*,[3] and the likelihood that Apollonius traced some of his most distinctive narrative devices back to these poems[4]—all this evidence supports this book's fundamental thesis, namely, that the *HH*s should be placed alongside the HEs among Apollonius' primary poetic models. In keeping with larger trends in the Hellenistic reception of Homer, Apollonius shows an especial interest in the atypical features of the *HH*s. We have encountered multiple instances in which he employs *hapax* or *dis legomena* from the *HH*s that do not occur in the HEs,[5] and when adapting the formulas that characterize

---

1 See chapter 1, esp. 1.1.1, 1.1.4, 1.2.1–2.3.
2 See 2.3.
3 See introduction, section 4, and *passim*.
4 See, e.g., the discussion of etiology in 3.3.
5 See 45–46 (on σκαλμός); 46n221 (on πυρεῖον); 51n239 (on τύπανον); 53 (on ῥικνός); 249–250 (on ὄργια); 261, 264 (on χλεύη); 315n162 (on δειράς); 318n182 (on εὐαγής); and McPhee 2021a: 250–252 (on βρίμη); see also 131 with n. 203 (on ἰλήκω, which occurs in the *Od.*, but which Apollonius has taken from *HH* 3). Another example has recently been identified by Tsakiris 2022: 31 n. 94 (μεταρίθμιος, occurring at *Arg.* 1.205 and *HH* 26.6). For a notable *tris legomenon* from the *HH*s, see 312 (on Ἰηπαιήων).

the *HH*s' Exordia and Envois—their most unvarying structural elements—he systematically opts for the most exceptional usages that, nevertheless, still find precedent in the hymnic collection.[6] The natural inference from these data is that Apollonius (or, more cautiously, the implied author of the *Arg.*) paid such regard to the *HH*s because of their perceived Homeric authority, which in turn authorized the poem's departures from the conventions of the HEs on a number of points.[7]

2. **The Genre of the *Arg.***

I have argued that the hymnic frame of the *Arg.* casts the poem as a Homeric-style hymn dedicated to its own protagonists, the Argonauts, in their capacity as cult heroes divinized after death. Although the introit is ingeniously engineered to facilitate several possible interpretations on a first-time reading, the Envoi retrospectively clarifies the status of the poem as a hymn to the Argonauts and enables a reinterpretation of the introit consistent with this insight. The epic narrative, too, is revealed anew as corresponding to the central section of a hymn (the *Laudatio*), which in this case takes the form of a Myth—the Argonauts' quest for the Golden Fleece—that has been extended to the length of four epic books.[8] The result of this procedure is a poem that unites the two branches of hexametric poetry attributed in antiquity to Homer, his epics and hymns, into a hybrid "epic hymn" that evinces features of both of these genres. This merger of epic and hymnody finds its logical justification in the duality of the Greek concept of the hero, who is at once a mythical figure whose deeds are commemorated in epic verse and a cult figure whose worship includes, inter alia, celebration in hymns. Accordingly, Apollonius departs from the precedent of the HEs in acknowledging the institution of hero cult repeatedly in the *Arg.*, and often in ways that are capable of metapoetic interpretations that relate to the poem's generic duality. The logic underpinning Apollonius' merger of epic and hymnody finds parallel exemplification in contemporary poets and predecessors, and in fact a precursor in the *HH*s themselves, the *Hymn to Heracles the Lionhearted*, might have served as a principal model for Apollonius' experiment.[9]

3. **The Apollonian Narrator's Hymnic Voice**

The AR narrator's persona is a complex construct that combines a variety of influences, including the HEs, Pindar, Herodotus, Callimachus, and

---

6 See 1.4.
7 See esp. chapter 3.
8 See chapter 1 and the introductory section of chapter 2.
9 See chapter 2.

more. One of these voices directly corresponds to the *Arg.*'s generic affiliations with hymnody, namely, the AR narrator's "hymnic voice," and part 2 of this book constitutes a study of this aspect of Apollonius' narratorial persona. Chapter 3 demonstrates that many of the narrative techniques that distance the *Arg.* from the HEs in fact find precedent in the *HH*s or are bolstered by allusions thereto. For instance, the AR narrator's personal intrusions into his own narrative are particularly reminiscent of the major *Homeric Hymn to Apollo*; his pious self-presentation is built upon recollections of devices from the *HH*s, like "pious silences" concerning mystery cults, and gains from redeployments of hymnic phraseology in new contexts, as in his "pious similes"; and Apollonius may signal his debt to the *HH*s in the matter of etiology through, inter alia, a two-tiered allusion to Callimachus' *Aetia* and the *Homeric Hymn to Demeter* in his Anaphe episode. Chapter 4 examines passages in which the narrator either engages in hymnic speech himself or portrays his characters as doing so. The most interesting result of this portion of the study is that Apollonius enhances the AR narrator's pious self-presentation through the use of two techniques, "contagious hymnody" and "hymnic narratization," both of which are precedented in the *HH*s. What these devices have in common is the potential for metalepsis, or the breaking down of the barrier that normally separates the epic narrator from his characters, thus creating the impression that the pious AR narrator enthusiastically joins in the religious celebrations of his Subjects.

These findings, especially as regards the construal of the poem's hybrid genre, have the potential to reshape our basic understanding of the *Arg.* itself, and I hope that by illuminating the fundamental trilateral relationship between the *Arg.*, the HEs, and the *HH*s, I have provided the necessary backdrop against which future studies of Apollonius' allusions to Homer's *Hymns* can be contextualized—for a great deal of work remains to be done on the subject of "Apollonius' *Argonautica* and the *Homeric Hymns*." Here, I would like to lay out some of the avenues of inquiry that seem like the natural next steps following the present study.

The raw material for future research into Apollonian intertextuality with the *HH*s is conveniently assembled in Campbell's *Echoes and Imitations*, which records a huge number of intertexts that unfortunately found no place for analysis here.[10] Many of these intertexts will have been fortuitous, but many others likely constitute purposeful allusions whose significance awaits interpretative

---

10   See Campbell 1981: 119–122.

unpacking. I have tried to indicate something of the promise that these intertexts hold for interpreters of the *Arg.* in the introduction, section 4, but this book constitutes but an inkling of the rich vein of scholarship that we have to look forward to. More comprehensive study of the intertexts that Campbell has assembled also has the potential to unlock insights into the state of the collection of *HH*s as Apollonius knew them. We have already seen in this study that Apollonius appears to allude to a considerable range of *HH*s, without at all limiting himself to just the major ones.

Yet even more than the rather small-scale engagements with the *HH*s in localized contexts, I would be particularly keen to see new literary-interpretative essays that read entire scenes or that conduct character studies or thematic analyses in light of the models provided by the hymns. Several existing articles furnish rubrics here,[11] and I hope that this book has also contributed something toward this effort through its investigation of the thematic significance of the *Arg.*'s opening allusion to the *Homeric Hymn to Selene* (introduction, 4.6) and of the role of the *Homeric Hymn to Heracles* as a model for the *Arg.* qua "epic hymn" (2.4.4–2.5). This kind of work would also enrich the study of the reception of the *HH*s among, for instance, the Roman poets, whose receptions of the hymns were often self-consciously mediated by their intervening receptions in their Hellenistic forebears,[12] including Apollonius.[13]

Theocritus' hymnic *Idylls* and especially Callimachus' *Hymns* have come up numerous times in this study, both to serve as intertextual comparanda and because in many cases, they seem to be participants in a genuine allusive dialogue with the *Arg.* This fact reveals the need to take the Rhapsodic Hymns of the Hellenistic period into fuller account: if the *Arg.* does indeed postdate these works by his contemporaries, as has been my working assumption throughout this study, then Apollonius' reception of the *HH*s inevitably must have been filtered through their earlier receptions of the same. Theocritus and Callimachus also present further evidence for the state of the *HH* collection in third-century Alexandria, and as we saw in 2.4, both poets' oeuvres include smaller-scale antecedents for the mixture of epic and hymnody that defines Apollonius' *Arg.*

Finally, I would note that a full-scale study concerning Apollonius' reception of Hesiod, that other great Archaic hexameter poet, remains a desideratum, as Vox noted already over twenty years ago.[14] Hesiod enjoyed a high regard in the

---

11 See: Pace 2004; Clayton 2017; McPhee 2021a; Vergados, forthcoming.
12 For examples, see Faulkner, Vergados, and Schwab 2016: 3–4 with n. 13.
13 See already on this score Clauss 2016a.
14 Vox 2002: 156 n. 16.

Hellenistic period,[15] and unlike with the *HH*s, we happen to know that Apollonius engaged the Hesiodic poems in his scholarly work as well as in his poetry.[16] More work has been done on Apollonian allusion to Hesiod than to the *HH*s,[17] and Hesiod's portrayal of the Age of Heroes in the *Works and Days* has surfaced more than once as a key reference point in the present investigation.[18] Nevertheless, it would be gratifying to see further systematic studies investigating Apollonius' reception of specific literary predecessors.[19]

2   Final Reflections

2.1   *The Ptolemaic Context*

Over the last thirty years, the sociopolitical context of Apollonius' composition of the *Arg.* in third-century BCE Alexandria as a Ptolemaic court poet has attracted increasing scholarly interest.[20] Here, I would like to contribute to this scholarly conversation by expanding upon an idea that Hitch already presented *in nuce* in her article on hero cult in the *Arg.*, namely, that "[the Argonauts'] process of immortalization would have resonated with the ongoing deification of the Ptolemaic rulers during their lifetimes."[21] It is certainly tempting to connect the increasing divinization of the Ptolemies to Apollonius' transfiguration of the model furnished by the "secular" HEs, which emphasize their heroes' mortality, into an epic hymn dedicated to its own divinized protagonists. Before expanding on this idea, I here present a brief overview of the Ptolemaic ruler cult, which took different forms as a direct corollary to the Ptolemies' dual status as βασιλεῖς in the Macedonian tradition and as the new Pharaohs of Egypt.[22]

---

15   See, e.g., Reitzenstein 1931: 41–52.
16   See 20.
17   Several articles by Clauss (1990, 2000, 2016b) represent important steps toward a Hesiodic reading of the *Arg.* See further, e.g.: Campbell 1981: 117–119; Newman 1986: 95; Roth 2004; Mason 2016. See now, too, Tsakiris 2022: 71–77 for the *Arg.*'s place on the mythological timeline that (per Clay 2006: 15) bridges Hesiod's *Theogony*, the *HH*s, and the HEs.
18   See 1.2.4, and 2.2.3.
19   I would note that, to my knowledge, a systematic study even of the use that Apollonius made of Euripides' *Medea* has yet to appear. For his reception of Pindar's fourth *Pythian Ode*, see: Manuello 2011; Kampakoglou 2019: chh. 3, 9.
20   Particular milestones include: Hunter 1993: ch. 6; Stephens 2003: ch. 4; Mori 2008.
21   Hitch 2012: 133 n. 7; see further 158.
22   In what follows, I attempt to summarize a great deal of work on the combination of Hellenistic ruler cult and Pharaonic ideology that defined the religious role of the Ptolemaic dynasts. On this subject, see, e.g.: Bulloch 1984: 212–214; Koenen 1993; Hölbl 2001: ch. 3; Pfeiffer 2008, 2016.

To begin with, the Ptolemies inaugurated ruler cults in line with trends in the broader Hellenistic world.[23] The focal point of these Greek-facing cults was the cult of Alexander the Great instituted by Ptolemy I Soter in Alexandria, where the dead king was worshipped as something like the national god of the Ptolemaic state.[24] The importance of this cult is illustrated by the fact that the annual tenure of the "eponymous" priest of Alexander was used to identify the year for purposes of dating in official documents. During his own lifetime, Ptolemy II Philadelphus expanded this cult to incorporate himself and his second wife and sister Arsinoe II as the "Sibling Gods" (Θεοὶ Ἀδελφοί). Each living royal couple thereafter followed suit, so that the cult of Alexander effectively became a cult of the Lagid dynasty.[25] Furthermore, several members of the Ptolemaic family enjoyed independent cult worship. For instance, after their deaths, Philadelphus deified his father Soter and his mother Berenice I as the "Savior Gods" (Θεοὶ Σωτῆρες), who would only be incorporated into the Alexander cult under Ptolemy IV Philopator; the cult of Soter included the provision of lavish quadrennial games in Alexandria, the Ptolemaea, which provided the occasion of Philadelphus' legendarily opulent grand procession.[26] Of the several independent cults for Ptolemaic queens and other Ptolemaic women, the most notable was that dedicated to Arsinoe II, who enjoyed crossover appeal among both Greeks and Egyptians largely independent from her attachment to Philadelphus as one of the Sibling Gods.

In addition, the Ptolemies actively collaborated with the ancient Egyptian religious traditions that regarded the Pharaoh as the spiritual son and "living image" of Amun-Ra on earth. Before the Ptolemies, the Pharaoh was not regarded as a living god per se, but the office itself was divine, as every Pharaoh stepped anew into the role of Horus, the falcon-headed god of kingship. In this role, he mediated between gods and humankind and maintained cosmic order (Maat) through the central role he played in the conduct of religious rites; in death, the Pharaoh was assimilated with Osiris, god of the underworld.[27]

---

23 For Hellenistic ruler cult generally, see, e.g., Chaniotis 2003. That developments in Greek religion rather than Egyptian theology provided the main impetus for the Ptolemaic ruler cult is underlined by, e.g.: Fraser 1972: 214; Walbank 1991: 108–110.

24 For Alexander's divinity during his own lifetime, see, e.g., the summary in *ThesCRA* 2.167–171.

25 *ThesCRA* 2.173 notes that the Ptolemies were the first of the Diadochi to institute ruler cult as a dynastic practice and institutionalized method of ideological legitimation. See further on this cult, e.g., Fraser 1972: 213–226.

26 On this procession, see, e.g.: Rice 1983; Thompson 2000.

27 See, e.g., Frankfort 1948: ch. 10.

CONCLUSION

A paradigm shift began to take shape in the wake of the death of Arsinoe II, when Philadelphus had her image installed as a "temple-sharing goddess" (σύν-ναος θεά) in all the temples of Egypt to receive worship alongside the shrine's primary god. Beginning under Ptolemy III at the latest, each living royal couple was likewise installed as θεοὶ σύνναοι throughout the country and thereby received worship as Egyptian gods.

As this overview suggests, the ruler cult expanded over time from the post-mortem deification of Alexander and Soter to the worship of the living king under Philadelphus, while the Pharaoh transformed from a mediator between gods and humankind to a living god himself, coworshipped in every major temple in Egypt. Greek literature of this period provides a tantalizing glimpse into the contemporary discourse surrounding the ontological status of the Ptolemies, as poets and intellectuals tried to make sense of these new and shifting phenomena in terms of traditional Greek religion. Two historians of Egypt in the court of Ptolemy I offer intriguing reflections on the office of the Pharaoh in describing the earliest origins of the institution. First, Hecataeus of Abdera claims that the earliest Pharaohs were gods (Diod. Sic. 1.26.1, 1.44.1),[28] but he describes them as "gods, they say, who were terrestrial, having once been mortals, but who, by reason of their sagacity and the good services which they rendered to all men, attained immortality."[29] Hecataeus is here tapping into another Hellenistic discourse keenly interested in the connection between kingship and divinity, namely, Euhemerism, which held that the gods had originally been historical kings and queens who only later came to be deified in commemoration of their great achievements or public benefactions.[30] Second, in the chronicle attributed to the Egyptian priest Manetho, the earliest Pharaohs were the gods themselves, followed by a group that the author refers to as "the dead demigods" (νέκυες ἡμίθεοι)—an evident attempt at rendering the Greek concept of the cult hero.[31]

Beside these prose writers we might set a poem like Theocritus' encomium for Ptolemy II Philadelphus (*Id.* 17), which plays with several competing possi-

---

28 For Diodorus' adaptation of Hecataeus' work, see, e.g., Murray 1970: 144–150; Murray considers 1.44.1 Diodorus' own insertion into the material he borrowed from the Abderite (see his table at 146). For further attestations of the idea that the first Pharaohs were gods, see Hdt. 2.144.2, Diog. Laert. 1.2, Athenagoras *Leg.* 28.

29 [sc. θεοὺς] ἐπιγείους γενέσθαι φασίν, ὑπάρξαντας μὲν θνητούς, διὰ δὲ σύνεσιν καὶ κοινὴν ἀνθρώπων εὐεργεσίαν τετευχότας τῆς ἀθανασίας (Diod. Sic. 1.13.1).

30 In fact, Murray (1970: 151) argues that Hecataeus preceded and influenced Euhemerus.

31 See Waddell 1940: 5 n. 5. Cf. Hdt. 2.50.3, who had claimed that the Egyptians do not worship heroes.

bilities for locating the king within the Greek chain of being: is he man, hero, or god?[32] Thus, for instance, the poem begins (1–8):

> Ἐκ Διὸς ἀρχώμεσθα καὶ ἐς Δία λήγετε Μοῖσαι,
> ἀθανάτων τὸν ἄριστον, ἐπὴν μνασθῶμεν ἀοιδᾶς·
> ἀνδρῶν δ' αὖ Πτολεμαῖος ἐνὶ πρώτοισι λεγέσθω
> καὶ πύματος καὶ μέσσος· ὁ γὰρ προφερέστατος ἀνδρῶν.
> 5 ἥρωες, τοὶ πρόσθεν ἀφ' ἡμιθέων ἐγένοντο,
> ῥέξαντες καλὰ ἔργα σοφῶν ἐκύρησαν ἀοιδῶν·
> αὐτὰρ ἐγὼ Πτολεμαῖον ἐπιστάμενος καλὰ εἰπεῖν
> ὑμνήσαιμ'· ὕμνοι δὲ καὶ ἀθανάτων γέρας αὐτῶν.

> With Zeus let us begin, Muses, and with Zeus you should end whenever we are minded to sing, since he is best of the immortals; but of men let Ptolemy be mentioned first and last and in the middle, since of men he is the most excellent. Past heroes, the sons of demigods, found skillful poets to celebrate their fine deeds, but my skill in praise will make a hymn for Ptolemy: hymns are an honor given even to the immortals themselves.

Philadelphus is first identified as a man (ἀνδρῶν) in lines 3 and 4, but in the context of an analogy with Zeus. He is implicitly likened to the heroes in lines 5–8, but the poem is emphatically characterized as a "hymn" through the *figura etymologica* in line 8 (ὑμνήσαιμ'· ὕμνοι), with a direct comparison to the hymns offered to the immortal gods.[33] This kaleidoscopic effect continues virtually throughout the poem, as Theocritus likens Ptolemy to various gods (58–76, 128–134) and heroes (53–57, 118–120) and dwells at length on the deification of his parents, the previous king and queen (13–52, 121–128). Finally, he concludes the poem with another twist, saluting Ptolemy in an Envoi modeled on those of the *HH*s and identifying the king explicitly as a latter-day demigod (135–137):

> 135 χαῖρε, ἄναξ Πτολεμαῖε· σέθεν δ' ἐγὼ ἶσα καὶ ἄλλων
> μνάσομαι ἡμιθέων, δοκέω δ' ἔπος οὐκ ἀπόβλητον
> φθέγξομαι ἐσσομένοις· ἀρετήν γε μὲν ἐκ Διὸς αἰτεῦ.

> Farewell, lord Ptolemy! I shall make mention of you just as much as of the other demigods, and I think my account will not be rejected by future generations. As for virtue, you should request that from Zeus.

---

32 See Hunter 2003: 93–96; Heerink 2010, esp. 385–394; Prioux 2012: 135–138.
33 For the dual valence of ὕμνος in the Hellenistic period, see 2.3.2.

CONCLUSION

Like Manetho and Hecataeus, Theocritus in his own way presents a range of modes for conceptualizing the place of the Ptolemaic Pharaohs within the traditional Greek hierarchy of gods, heroes, and mortals.

The fuzziness of these speculations and innuendos about the nature of the Pharaoh and of the contemporary Pharaohs, the Ptolemies, show that the leap from hero cult to ruler cult was not far to make. Indeed, modern scholars have often seen Hellenistic ruler cult as an outgrowth of the heroization of living persons,[34] especially since in this period, "gottgleiche und heroische Ehren für Könige existierten jetzt nebeneinander ... Im Kult der Herrscher und Politiker war die Trennung zwischen Götter- und Heroenkult beseitigt."[35] Indeed, I might note in this connection that in Alexandria, Alexander was worshipped both as a state god and with hero cult as the city's οἰκιστής.[36] Thus Koenen observes, apropos of Callimachus' role in promoting the divinity of the Ptolemaic family, "The hero of old was the thing closest to a divine king on earth."[37] As scholars have interpreted the apotheoses of Heracles or the Dioscuri in Alexandrian poetry as nods to the Ptolemaic ruler cult,[38] so we might interpret the Argonauts' decidedly un-Homeric heroization as premonitions of the same. It is suggestive, moreover, that in raising this analogy, both Apollonius and, as we have seen, Theocritus would have recourse to the venerable tradition of the *HH*s, the oldest body of religious poetry in the Greek canon,[39] endowed with the authority of Homer himself.

But is there any positive evidence in the *Arg.* that suggests that Apollonius was alive to the possible connections between his heroization of the Argonauts and the Ptolemaic ruler cult? I believe that there is, though Apollonius presents it in characteristically subtle fashion. The first case occurs early in the poem, in the Catalog: the Argonaut Nauplius is introduced according to a genealogy that

---

34 See, e.g.: Hölbl 2001: 92; Currie 2005: 9–11, with earlier bibliography. For ruler cult's earlier roots in the Greeks' godlike view of kings, visible already in Homer and Hesiod, see, e.g., Habicht 2017: 3–10.

35 Schuller and Leschhorn in *ThesCRA* 2.151. For the erosion of the distinction between divine and heroic honors for historical personages, especially rulers and other politicians, see further Leschhorn 1984: 339–343.

36 Leschhorn 1984: 204–212; see further Fraser 1972: 212; Habicht 2017: 36. A good discussion of the fate of Alexander's body can be found in Erskine 2002. Bérard (1982: 91) comments that the use of a prince's remains to legitimate the current ruler's authority hearkens back to Archaic institutions of hero cult.

37 Koenen 1993: 114.

38 See, e.g., Sens 1997: 23, with further citations.

39 Excepting the hymns attributed to mythical figures like Orpheus, Musaeus, etc., if Apollonius credited their authenticity.

stretches back seven generations to "**divine** Danaus" (θείοιο ... Δαναοῖο, 1.133). In the epic *Kunstsprache*, θεῖος is a formulaic epithet used of certain extraordinary individuals, rather than a recognition of true divine status;[40] it is interchangeable with other formulas meaning "godlike," like ἀντίθεος or δαίμονι ἶσος. Indeed, Apollonius implies that he will make just such regular use of the epithet by applying it again to Neleus, the father of Periclymenus (and Nestor), just twenty-five lines later (Νηλῆος θείοιο, 1.158). In fact, however, Apollonius uses the epithet but sparingly; the only other mortals to whom he applies it are the Argonauts, in a Hesiodic phrase that I have argued foreshadows their heroization (1.970, 2.1091),[41] and Orchomenus, the eponymous founder of the city in Boeotia (2.1186). The rarity of these usages, together with Apollonius' general avoidance of purely "ornamental" epithets,[42] argues for their significance. Neleus and Orchomenus could both be considered "divine" in their capacity as city-founders, who regularly received hero cult in their settlements.[43] But what of Danaus?

Danaus is a fascinating choice of figure to receive this epithet, because for the Greek rulers of Egypt, his fabled flight with his fifty daughters provided an important mythological link between Egypt and Greece. He was, moreover, crowned the king of Argos, the city from which the (Macedonian) Ptolemies traced their descent and hence their "Greekness."[44] Accordingly, Danaid ancestry played an important role in Ptolemaic self-fashioning[45] and was exploited to this end more than once in the poetry of Callimachus, as Stephens and others have shown.[46] Given Danaus' identification with the Ptolemies, the application of the epithet θεῖος to the original Greco-Egyptian king may hint at the divinity of his present-day descendants and counterparts.[47] It is also notable that as the ancestor of the nautical Nauplius, Danaus is made a forerunner (and forefather) of the Argonauts—especially since, in some traditions, Danaus was

---

40 See, e.g.: Bieler 1967: 9–13; Buraselis in *ThesCRA* 2.164.
41 See 2.2.3.
42 See, e.g., Fränkel 1968: 636 (§ I.42), 639 (§ I.81).
43 Neleus' city, Pylos, is mentioned together with him (1.132); for his foundation thereof, see Hes. *Cat.* fr. 31.5–6 Most, Diod. Sic. 4.68.6.
44 For a concise summary of the Ptolemaic claim to Argive descent, see Bulloch 1985: 12–13.
45 See Acosta-Hughes and Stephens 2012: 168–170.
46 See: Stephens 2002: 247–250; 2003: 8–9, 99; 2015: 238; Acosta-Hughes and Stephens 2012: 185–187; see also Harder 2012: 2.400–401, Kampakoglou 2016, Boychenko 2017, Manakidou 2017: 188–191 and *passim*.
47 Note also the epithet ἰσόθεος (4.1513) applied to Perseus, another Ptolemaic ancestor, with Hunter 2015 ad loc.

himself the inventor of the penteconter, an innovation demanded by the need to accommodate his fifty daughters in their flight from Egypt to Argos.⁴⁸

The other instance of a possible allusion to Ptolemaic ruler cult that I have identified occurs in the portion of the Libyan episode concerned with Triton (4.1537–1622). When the Argonauts cannot find passage out from Lake Triton to the sea, they make an offering of one of the tripods given them by Apollo to the "indigenous divinities" (δαίμοσιν ἐγγενέταις, 1549), whereupon Triton himself meets them "in the guise of a young man" (αἰζηῷ ἐναλίγκιος, 1551).⁴⁹ He offers them a clod of earth, in a gesture that invests the historical Greek claim to Cyrenaica with divine backing,⁵⁰ and introduces himself as King Eurypylus, son of Poseidon (1558–1561). Euphemus accepts the clod, and, addressing Triton as "hero" (ἥρως, 1564), asks for directions to Apis (Ἀπίδα, 1564), an old name for the Peloponnesus. The god gives the directions, but once the Argonauts have boarded their ship, he disappears with the tripod into the lake; thus they recognize his divinity and sacrifice a sheep to him over the stern of the Argo.⁵¹ Triton then reemerges in his true form as a marine god and guides the ship to the outlet to the sea; altars to Poseidon and Triton remain in the "harbor of Argo" (Ἀργῷος ... λιμήν, 1620) as etiological traces of these events.

Knight has already noted some of the religious undertones of this scene in which a god appears in the guise of a "hero": "The only god to appear disguised as a human being, Triton, chooses the form of a young man (4.1551), making himself as similar as possible to the Argonauts and thereby further blurring the distinction between the Argonauts and the gods they honour."⁵² Indeed, the equivalence is enhanced by the fact that Triton and Euphemus are half brothers, both sons of Poseidon (1.179–181).⁵³ We may justly see in this blurring of the boundaries between hero and god another hint of the Argonauts' own destined heroization, but certain elements in the scene raise the possibility of Ptolemaic connection as well.

---

48 See Jacoby 1904: 41–42 on the Parian chronicle (*FGrH* 239 A 9) and Eust. *Il.* 1.60.37–61.1 van der Valk; see further Σ ad Aesch. *PV* 853a. For more on Apollonius' framing of Danaus as a forerunner for both the Argonauts and the Ptolemies, see McPhee 2021b: 184–188.
49 For a possible allusion to the major *Homeric Hymn to Apollo* here, see 312*n*147.
50 See, e.g., Stephens 2003: 180–182.
51 For the reworking of a detail from the longer *Homeric Hymn to the Dioscuri* here, see 175*n*152.
52 Knight 1995: 277; see further Hitch 2012: 155–156. The mutual exchange of guest gifts further flattens the ontological difference between Triton-Eurypylus and the Argonauts (Mori 2008: 154–155).
53 As noted already by Σ ad Pind. *Pyth.* 4.36c, 61 Drachmann.

A major pointer in this direction is Apollonius' designation of the Peloponnesus by the name "Apis." This usage invests the scene with Egyptian undertones, for already in Aeschylus there is evidence for the identification of this eponymous Argive hero with the Egyptian bull god of the same name.[54] Apollonius had played on this Egyptian resonance already toward the beginning of Book 4 in Argus' reference to the "Apidanian Arcadians" (Ἀρκάδες Ἀπιδανῆες, 4.263), in a speech that insistently blurs the distinction between Greek and Egyptian.[55] Notably, in that same speech, "Triton" is twice given as an earlier name for the Nile (4.260, 269).[56] Already in Pindar a god (identified as Triton only in the scholia) appears to the Argonauts by Lake Triton in the guise of Eurypylus, son of Poseidon (*Pyth.* 4.33–34),[57] but Apollonius seems to have seized on the Egyptianizing potential of this idea. He makes the god's identity as Triton explicit[58] and adds the detail that Eurypylus is the ruler of the Libyan coastland (ἀνάσσω | παρραλίης, *Arg.* 4.1559–1560). Apollonius thereby alludes to the myth that regarded Eurypylus or Triton himself (Diod. Sic. 4.56.6) as an early king of Libya.[59] In light of the episode's subtle Egyptian connections, Triton's presentation as a god either disguised as or identified with an early North African[60] king may constitute an allusion to the tradition, already encountered above, that the first kings of Egypt, too, were gods—as, indeed, were her contemporary rulers, the Ptolemies. If so, Triton-Eurypylus' resemblances to both the Argonauts and the Ptolemies would mutually reinforce a potential allusion to the heroization of the former and the deification of the latter.

---

54 See Saïd 1993: 168–169, 175 on Aesch. *Supp.* 117, 128, 260–270; this identification is explicit in Aristippus *BNJ* 317 F 1 (*ap.* Clem. Al. *Strom.* 1.21.106.4–5), Apollod. *Bib.* 2.1.1, August. *De civ. D.* 18.5; see further: Stambaugh 1967: 70–71; 1972: ch. 7; Stephens 1998: 176; Massimilla 2005: 14; Kampakoglou 2016: 124–125.
55 See Stephens 2003: 190; McPhee 2021b: 183.
56 This allonym for the Nile may be related to a theory that connects the waters of Lake Triton to a westerly source for the Nile; see Priestley 2014: 126–127.
57 The scholiast ad *Pyth.* 4.37 claims that this detail was Pindar's innovation. Apollonius combines the Pindaric story of the clod with an alternate version featuring Triton and the tripod (see, e.g., Ottone 2002: 235).
58 See Jackson 1993: 54, who notes that Triton's epiphany to the Argonauts in his true form is Apollonius' own invention.
59 Some sources may imply that Eurypylus is but an assumed identity or allonym for Triton, but others seem to view him as a real and distinct personage; see, e.g., Ottone 2002: 285–288. For a possible depiction of Eurypylus on a fourth-century votive relief sculpture from Euesperides, see Ferri 1976: 15–16.
60 For the possibility that in Apollonius the Triton episode serves as an αἴτιον for the Greek presence not just in Cyrenaica, but in the entire "continent" of Libya, including Egypt, see Stephens 2003: 181–182.

It is hardly incontrovertible, but it turns out that there is some evidence that Apollonius drew a parallel between the Argonauts' divinization and that of the Ptolemies. But even if he does not directly allude to Ptolemaic ruler cult, the prominence with which Apollonius brings hero cult into the poem—into its very generic fabric, and in a marked departure from the HEs—must have resonated with the contemporary reality that some select individuals could and did transcend the limits of ordinary humanity, as is evidenced first and foremost by the deification of the royal family. To this extent at least, ruler cult provides an important context in which to understand Apollonius' unusual emphasis on the divinity of his epic heroes.

2.2   Heroization and Heroism

I have spent a great deal of this study, above all in chapter 2, discussing the Argonauts' heroization, as distinct from the question of their heroism, a topic that has long dominated Apollonian studies, especially with regard to the Argo's captain, Jason.[61] As Klein once remarked, "There is perhaps no more complex question in Hellenistic literature than this: in what does the heroism of the *Argonautica* reside?"[62] I can hardly resolve this problem here, but approaching it from the point of view of the heroization theme does present some of the pertinent issues in a fresh light.

To begin with, all but Jason's most ardent defenders would admit that in certain scenes, his behavior is presented in a critical light. The banner example is the moral low point of the narrative (*Arg.* 4.410–481): Jason's deadly ambush of Apsyrtus, lured to his doom by his own sister Medea, on a holy island (ἱερῆς ... νήσου, 458) and, indeed, in the very portico of the temple of Artemis (469–471).[63] This "wicked murder" (κακῷ ... ὀλέθρῳ, 450) provokes the explicit condemnation of the narrator in his apostrophe to Eros (445–451) as well as the wrath of the Furies and of Zeus himself (475–476, 557–561, 585–588, 700–717).[64] As commentators have observed, the scene of the murder is marked by an apparently ironic use of religious terminology and

---

61   For an overview of the enormous bibliography in this area, see Glei 2008: 6–12.
62   Klein 1974: 229.
63   The narratee is invited to sympathize with Apsyrtus through the second-person address at 4.428–429 (Byre 1991: 225). Williams (1991: 113–114, 271) argues that the winter torrent simile at 4.460–461 underscores Jason's impiety in this scene by recalling his contrastingly virtuous service to Hera at the Anaurus (3.66–74).
64   In one respect, the impious murder functions as a plot device, as the need for expiation allows Apollonius to take the Argonauts westward; see 4.552–561. The motif of Zeus' wrath may even be meant to justify the detour to Libya; see 4.1225–1227 with Fränkel 1968 ad loc.; Stürner 2022: 22.

the ennobling epithet ἥρως.[65] The hapless Apsyrtus is dubbed a "hero" (ἥρως, 471) as he breathes his last breath, slaughtered like a sacrificial ox (468). Jason then attempts to expiate the murder—ineffectively, as we soon learn—with the gruesome ritual of μασχαλισμός (477–479):

ἥρως δ' Αἰσονίδης ἐξάργματα τάμνε θανόντος,
τρὶς δ' ἀπέλειξε φόνου, τρὶς δ' ἐξ ἄγος ἔπτυσ' ὀδόντων,
ἣ θέμις αὐθέντῃσι δολοκτασίας ἱλάεσθαι.

The **hero** Jason cut off the extremities of the dead man, licked up some of his blood three times and three times spat out the **pollution** through his teeth, **which is the proper way for killers to expiate treacherous murders.**

In the meantime, the rest of the Argonauts engage the crew of Apsyrtus' ship in a battle—really, a massacre—that Jason evidently misses while busy burying Apsyrtus' corpse (480–491).[66] I need hardly explain why critics have felt that Jason comes off as less than a true "hero" in this sequence, and the juxtaposition of the pious formula ἣ θέμις, which so often marks the AR narrator's religious expertise,[67] with words for "pollution" (ἄγος), "killers" (αὐθέντῃσι), and "treacherous murders" (δολοκτασίας) is deeply ironic.[68]

I would propose that a similar type of irony is in evidence on one of the early occasions in which the AR narrator foreshadows the Argonauts' destined heroization. The Argonauts' two landings on Cyzicus are each associated with a different sort of rock that is rendered holy through its association with the heroes.[69] On their first landing, the Argonauts discard their anchor stone, which the area's Ionian colonists later dedicate to Athena Jasonia (1.955–960). When the Argonauts first depart from Cyzicus, they proceed with favorable winds at first, but soon their progress is reversed (1.1015–1022):

---

65   For other potentially ironic deployments of ἥρως, see, e.g., Köhnken 1965: 45 n. 2 on *Arg.* 2.967; Daniel-Müller 2012: 104–105 on *Arg.* 1.781.
66   Race 2008: 367 n. 56.
67   See 238n40.
68   See, e.g.: Hutchinson 1988: 96 n. 15, 127; Newman 2008: 437; van den Eersten 2013: 11–13. Cf. Cuypers 2004: 52, who seems as though she has to fight to resist the natural urge to see irony here: "In the last example, the emphasis on religious observance is particularly remarkable: the killing of Apsyrtus and the mutilation of his corpse are not beyond reproach. The narrator, however, insists on evaluating his heroes' behaviour in a positive way." I see a similar irony in *Arg.* 4.701.
69   See 159.

1015 ἡ δ' ἔθεεν λαίφεσσι πανήμερος· οὐ μὲν ἰούσης
     νυκτὸς ἔτι ῥιπὴ μένεν ἔμπεδον, ἀλλὰ θύελλαι
     ἀντίαι ἁρπάγδην ὀπίσω φέρον, ὄφρ' ἐπέλασσαν
     αὖτις εὐξείνοισι Δολίοσιν. ἐκ δ' ἄρ' ἔβησαν
     αὐτονυχί· Ἱερὴ δὲ φατίζεται ἥδ' ἔτι πέτρη,
1020 ᾗ πέρι πείσματα νηὸς ἐπεσσύμενοι ἐβάλοντο.
     οὐδέ τις αὐτὴν νῆσον ἐπιφραδέως ἐνόησεν
     ἔμμεναι ...

The ship sped under sail all day long, but when night came on the rushing wind no longer remained steady, but contrary storm winds seized the ship and carried it back, until they reached once again the hospitable Doliones. That same night they disembarked, **and the rock is still called Sacred rock, around which they hastily cast the ship's cables.** But no one took care to notice that it was the same island ...

This αἴτιον for the name of Sacred Rock is jarring, given the events that are about to unfold as a direct consequence of the Argonauts' second landing at Cyzicus.[70] Indeed, the etiology is flanked on either side by hints of the horror to come: the epithet "hospitable" for the Doliones (εὐξείνοισι Δολίοσιν, 1018) and the notice of the heroes' ignorance concerning their whereabouts (1021–1022) foreshadow the Argonauts' tragic slaughter of their erstwhile hosts in the confusion of the ensuing nighttime battle (1022–1052). Only at dawn do the two sides "recognize their deadly and irrevocable mistake" (ὀλοὴν καὶ ἀμήχανον εἰσενόησαν | ἀμπλακίην, 1053–1054).

Unlike the murder of Apsyrtus, the Argonauts' ξενοκτονία at Cyzicus is unwitting and, accordingly, less morally problematic.[71] Nevertheless, the national calamity that the Argonauts' return precipitates—commemorated "to this day" (ἔτι, 1047; ἔτι νῦν, 1075) in the hero cult afforded their Dolionian victims (1047–1048, 1070–1077)—sits ill at ease with the sacrality that the crew's arrival confers upon the site of their second landing, or, in retrospect, even upon the

---

70   The scholiast ad loc. was evidently bothered by precisely such considerations and thus tries to explain away ἱερή as a euphemism (cited approvingly by Fusillo 1985: 119, Valverde Sánchez 1989: 173). But why should this rock's epithet be so interpreted when real sacrality evidently attaches to the Argonauts' discarded anchor stone? Moreover, the parallel that the scholiast proposes for such a euphemistic usage of ἱερός is inapt: epilepsy was not called the "sacred" disease euphemistically, but because it was thought to come from the gods; see Nikitinski 1996: 129–131.

71   But for parallels between these episodes, see Durbec 2008: 69–70.

anchor stone associated with their first landing. The awkwardness of this juxtaposition points up a troubling facet of heroization in the *Arg.*: it is not, apparently, inconsistent with the commission of grave errors (ἁμαρτίαι), as in the Cyzicus episode, or even of sacrilegious and perfidious murder, as in the Apsyrtus episode.[72] In chapter 2, I argued that the *Arg.* presupposes the common notion that heroes merited their heroization through their completion of great labors (ἄεθλοι), but the Cyzicus and Apsyrtus episodes raise a different problem with a long history in Greek theological speculation on hero cult: what is the relationship, if any, between the receipt of heroic honors and the normative value of the hero's actions in life?

Greek hero cult has often been compared to the Christian cult of the saints, but it is also a commonplace of scholarship on the subject to note a crucial difference between these conceptions: "To qualify as a saint, one had to behave in an exemplary fashion and to be a paragon for other believers. To qualify as a hero in ancient Greece, one had to be extreme, in every sense of the term, in life or death; virtue was not necessarily a qualification."[73] This generalization is true so far as it goes: Aristotle cites this idea as a popular notion about apotheosis in his day,[74] and it is a simple matter to find examples of cult heroes who were downright despicable human beings in life.[75] From this perspective, problematic behavior is no obstacle to the Argonauts' heroization.

Nevertheless, we should not overlook a frequent countervailing desire in the Greek religious imagination to league the hero with moral right. Thus in the myth of the Five Ages in the *Works and Days*, whose framework Apollonius adopts in the *Arg.*,[76] Hesiod's characterization of the heroes of the fourth age as "more just and superior" (δικαιότερον καὶ ἄρειον, 158) to their predecessors in the Bronze Age may imply that their blessed afterlife constitutes in some measure a reward for their goodness in life;[77] and the heroes' righteousness stands out all the more sharply in view of the destined degeneracy of the Iron Age

---

72 Cf. Jason and Medea's misuse of the "sacred" robe of Hypsipyle (πέπλον ... ἱερὸν Ὑψιπυλείης, 4.423) to commit a treacherous kin-murder.

73 Ekroth 2009: 121; see further, e.g.: Nilsson 1967: 189–190; Parker 2011: 104.

74 "Hence if, **as men say**, surpassing virtue changes men into gods ..." (ὥστ᾿ εἰ, **καθάπερ φασίν**, ἐξ ἀνθρώπων γίνονται θεοὶ δι᾿ ἀρετῆς ὑπερβολήν, *Eth. Nic.* 1145.22–23). The context makes clear that by ἀρετῆς ὑπερβολή Aristotle means an amoral state that transcends the human distinctions between good and evil (see Gigon and Nickel 2001: 505).

75 E.g., Ekroth (2009: 140 n. 1) adduces the Megarians' worship of Tereus (Paus. 1.41.9), a man who raped, imprisoned, and mutilated his sister-in-law and unwittingly consumed his own son's flesh.

76 See 2.2.3.

77 Jones 2010: 6.

that succeeds them (174–201). The moral dimension of heroization becomes clearer in Pindar, who explicitly reserves the Island of the Blessed for the righteous (*Ol.* 2.68–83, fr. 133 Race; we owe this latter fragment to an approving quotation from Plato [*Meno* 81b]). These Pindaric passages reflect a wider discourse in the Classical and Hellenistic periods that regarded heroization or deification as a reward, often in explicitly moral terms.[78] And after heroization, heroes could continue to be connected with morality; Aristophanes, for instance, likely reflects popular religious belief when the titular chorus of his *Heroes* claim to punish the wicked and, presumably, reward the good (fr. 322 Henderson).[79]

Apollonius' Argonauts often appear as righteous avengers of the wicked and as benefactors of humanity,[80] but they occasionally commit transgressions as well, both unwitting and intentional. Jason's moral integrity and heroic mettle fall under particular suspicion in numerous passages, as Apollonius hints at the possibility that he may become the scoundrel of Euripides' *Medea*[81]—and yet his personal heroization is vouchsafed by the reference to the cult of Athena Jasonia at Cyzicus, of all places, at *Arg.* 1.960.[82] Likewise, Medea's individual fate is specified as the eternal bliss of Elysium (4.811–815), despite her violations of the patriarchal norms of the Greek family in Book 3 and her betrayal of her own brother to death in Book 4. As I have said, the Greeks generally did not demand absolute purity of their heroes, and it is telling that, as we saw in chapter 2, the only hymn in the Homeric collection to countenance its deified Subject's preapotheosis career as a mortal hero (in strikingly epic terms) frankly admits his moral failings. The *Homeric Hymn to Heracles* summarizes the hero's labors thus (15.4–6):

ὃς πρὶν μὲν κατὰ γαῖαν ἀθέσφατον ἠδὲ θάλασσαν
5 πλαζόμενος πομπῇσιν ὑπ' Εὐρυσθῆος ἄνακτος
πολλὰ μὲν αὐτὸς ἔρεξεν ἀτάσθαλα, πολλὰ δ' ἀνέτλη.

---

78 I also discuss this discourse in 2.3.3.
79 Aristophanes' Heroes call themselves the dispensers of good and ill (ἡμεῖς ἐσμεν οἱ ταμίαι | τῶν κακῶν καὶ τῶν ἀγαθῶν, 3–4), but the fragment as it stands only lists some of the punishments that they dole out.
80 Book 2 especially promotes this view of the heroes: note their punishment of Amycus, their liberation of Phineus from the Harpies' harassment, their neutralization of the Symplegades, and the aid that they lend to two sets of brothers stranded abroad, the Deimachids and the Phrixids.
81 For Euripides' *Medea* as one possible "sequel" to the *Arg.*, see the nuanced discussion of Byre 2002: chs. 3–4.
82 See 159.

> Formerly he roamed the vast land and sea at the behest of King Eurystheus, **committing many reckless deeds himself** and enduring many.[83]

Even an acknowledgment of Heracles' (many!) "reckless deeds," it seems, is not incompatible with the hymnist's eulogistic agenda. Likewise, through the ironic juxtapositions analyzed here, Apollonius seems positively to draw attention to the failure of his heroes to live up to the idealized image that one strain of Greek thought projected onto the recipients of hero cult.[84] Catullus, we may note, would make much the same point in a more potent and concentrated form in his celebrated epyllion (c. 64), which simultaneously extols the superiority of the Heroic Age to the Iron Age while demonstrating that it suffered from the same ethical lapses that characterize the present day.[85]

At this point, we can perhaps see how the question of heroization and heroism impinges upon the *Arg.*'s potential connections with the Ptolemaic ruler cult. As Newman has shown, a critical reading of an unheroic Jason could have had subversive political implications in third-century Alexandria;[86] we can imagine how much more subversive such a reading could become if we extend this analysis to encompass the issues of heroization and ruler cult. To put the matter in extreme terms: the Argonauts and their morally checkered leader especially are not "heroes" but ordinary human beings like you or me—or, indeed, like the Ptolemaic dynasts and all the rest who appropriate divinity for themselves; the theme of hero cult and the hymnic format of the *Arg.* are just so much window dressing, mere lip service, meant to disguise their fundamental moral and ontological equivalence to "men as they are now." More charitably (and plausibly, I would think), we could say that Apollonius presents his heroes in a realistic light as flawed individuals whose occasional mistakes and transgressions nevertheless pale in comparison before their extraordinary achieve-

---

83   I follow Athanassakis 2004 in translating ἀτάσθαλα with "reckless deeds"; Evelyn-White 1914 ("deeds of violence") and West 2003a ("suffering") both downplay the moral import of this weighty word, evidently uncomfortable with the hymn's attribution of such deeds to Heracles "himself" (αὐτός, 6).

84   Whereas the AR narrator is evidently concerned to present the gods in a favorable light, he does not show the same concern for his heroes; see 247n70.

85   For this interpretation of Catullus c. 64, see, e.g., Konstan 1977, 1993; for this connection between Hesiod, Apollonius, and Catullus see Clauss 2000: 23–25.

86   See Newman 2008: 439–441, whose account is rather fanciful (because based on the ancient biographical tradition) but illustrative of the subversive potential of certain readings of the *Arg.*

ments, which fully justify their heroization.[87] Such a view could leave open the possibility of divinization for the great women and men of the Hellenistic present, whose accomplishments similarly raise them above the inevitable imperfections of their human station and closer to that of the gods.[88]

---

[87] Cf. Jackson's view that "Jason is, in fact, *not* a hero of non-human proportions at all, but a man, with all man's qualities and faults" (1992: 155; emphasis original).

[88] For the idea that the *Arg.* leaves room in its divine economy for new deities, like the Ptolemies, see Clauss 2016b: 150–151.

APPENDIX

Divine Epithets in the *Argonautica*

In this appendix, I detail the AR narrator's standard practices for applying epithets to deities in order to contextualize the striking departures from the norm constituted by his technique of "hymnic narratization," in which gods receive Honorific epithets or relative clauses when a character is described as invoking them.[1] The AR narrator often uses the bare name of a god without any ornamentation:[2] "Nor was their going forth unnoticed by **Athena**" (οὐδ' ἄρ' Ἀθηναίην προτέρω λάθον ὁρμηθέντες, 2.537); "but all those things had been accomplished by **Zeus**' designs" (τὰ δὲ πάντα Διὸς βουλῇσι τέτυκτο, 2.154); etc.[3] The narrator deploys a handful of theonym-epithet pairings of a type common in early Greek epic, such as "Apollo Phoebus" (Ἀπόλλων Φοῖβος, 1.759) or "early-rising Dawn" (ἠριγενὴς Ἠώς, 3.1224, 4.981),[4] but for the most part, he uses a single such epithet or phrase independently as a substitute for the god's name. For example, Apollo is frequently designated simply by "Phoebus," beginning from the opening line of the poem (1.1, 536; 2.506, 847; 4.529, 1493, 1550, 1702, 1717);[5] Dawn can appear solely as "the early-riser" (2.450, 3.824); and so on.[6] In some cases, this

---

1 I discuss hymnic narratization in 4.3. I make no attempt here at a rigorous definition of the term "epithet," but generally I have in mind those adjectives, nouns, and phrases, whether used alone as a "periphrastic denomination" for a given entity or whether modifying or set in apposition to it, that indicate an inherent or recurrent quality or that delineate some aspect of that entity's identity. For a survey of definitions and interpretations of the epithet, ancient and modern, see Vivante 1982: chs. 20–21; for ancient definitions, see also Bécares Botas 1985 s.v. ἐπίθετος. For divine epithets in Homer, see Dee 2001.
2 Furley and Bremer (2001: 1.53) refer to the god's "first name" in such cases.
3 In several passages, it is striking just how little the narrator seeks to vary a god's name across a series of repeated occurrences. E.g., the name "Ares" occurs three times in as many lines at 2.989–991, twice in the same case and *sedes*; in the Olympian colloquy at 3.6–111, the narrator uses the names "Hera" (8, 10, 23, 55, 77, 83, 106) and "Athena" (8, 10, 17, 30, 111) over and over with hardly a single variation (they are θεαί at line 100), even if we include variants in character-speech (11, 79); etc. But cf. 352n8.
4 Note also "Zeus son of Cronus" (Κρονίδῃ Διΐ, 2.524; Διὸς Κρονίδαο, 4.520; Κρονίδαο Διός, 4.753), "Pallas Athena" (Ἀθηναίη Παλλάς, 3.340); "Enyalius Ares" (Ἐνυαλίου ... Ἄρεος, 3.1366), "Muse, daughter of Zeus" (Μοῦσα, Διὸς τέκος, 4.2), and "Leto's son Apollo" (Ἀπόλλωνος ... Λητοΐδαο, 4.612).
5 "Phoebus" also occurs at 2.713, in a narratologically complex passage; see 4.4.3.
6 Apollo also appears simply as "Leto's son" (1.66, 144, 439; 2.181, 674, 698; 4.1706; cf. 2.771, in indirect speech), "the Far-shooter" (Ἑκήβολος: 1.88; Ἕκατος: 1.958, 2.518, 4.1747), and perhaps as "Paeëon" (4.1511), though Homeric scholarship recognized a separate deity under this title in Homer and Hesiod (Hunter 2015 ad loc.). Likewise Aphrodite appears as "Cypris" (1.615,

technique of "periphrastic denomination" (ἀντονομασία, *pronominatio*)⁷ seems to be motivated by a desire for lexical *variatio*,⁸ but for the most part, this technique serves to furnish the poet with a handy set of alternative appellatives and circumlocutions for designating the gods, just as with mortal characters (e.g., Jason is frequently Αἰσονίδης; the Argonauts are frequently ἥρωες, ἀριστῆες, νέοι, or Μινύαι; etc.).

Otherwise, the narrator's use of divine epithets generally falls into only a few, limited categories:

a) Identifying the particular cultic aspect of the god that is relevant to the context, as when, for example, the Argonauts sacrifice to "Apollo of Embarkation" before departing on their journey.⁹

　　i) Frequently such epithets denote an epichoric aspect of the deity relevant to a particular setting (e.g., Pelias, King of Iolcus, disrespects "Pelasgian Hera" specifically, 1.14).¹⁰

　　850, 860, 1233; 3.3, 37, 80, 90, 127; 4.918) and "Cytherea" (1.742); Athena, as "Pallas" (1.723) and under the periphrases "the Itonian goddess" (1.721), "Zeus' daughter" (2.547), and "the Tritonian goddess" (3.1183); Rhea-Cybele, as "the mountain goddess" (1.1119); Dionysus, in an etymologizing gloss, as "Zeus' Nysean son" (Διὸς Νυσήιον υἷα, 2.905, 4.1134); Artemis, as "Leto's daughter" (2.938, 3.878, 4.346) and "Zeus' daughter" (4.334); Zeus, as "son of Cronus" (2.1083, 4.1643); Hera, as "Zeus' wife" (3.922; 4.753, 959, 967, 1152); and the Muses, as the "Pierides" (4.1382). For Leto as "Coeus' daughter" (Κοιογένεια, 2.710), see the analysis of Orpheus' hymn in 4.4.3. I have not included in this list periphrases of a "contextual" type, whether representing embedded focalization (e.g., "his father," i.e., Apollo vis-à-vis Aristaeus, 2.519) or anaphoric reference (e.g., "the goddess," i.e., Hera, just mentioned two verses earlier: 4.648).

7　　De Jong (2001: xvi) defines this technique as "a reference to a character not by proper name but by a form of indirect description (e.g., 'father' or 'master' instead of 'Odysseus')."

8　　E.g., in the Aristaeus digression, Apollo's unadorned name (Ἀπόλλων, 2.502) is varied with "Phoebus" (Φοίβῳ, 506), "the god" (θεός, 508), "the Far-shooter" (Ἑκάτοιο, 518), and "[Aristaeus'] father" (πατρός, 519) in less than twenty lines. See also, e.g., 2.432–433 (in indirect speech).

9　　Thus Iphias is a priestess specifically of "city-protecting Artemis" (1.312); the Argonauts raise altars to Apollo under the titles of Actius (1.404), Embasius (1.404), Ecbasius (1.966, 1186), and Neossos (2.927), all in littoral, seafaring contexts; the Ionian colonists of Cyzicus possess a temple to Athena Jasonia, mentioned in an etiological context (1.960); Poseidon Genethlius (2.3) is a relevant title in its genealogical context, and may designate Poseidon as an ancestral god of the Bebrycians (Cuypers 1997 ad loc.); Jason and the Boreads call on Apollo Manteius at the bidding of the seer Phineus (2.493); the refugee Phrixus set up an altar to "Zeus, Protector of Fugitives" (4.119); Circe purifies Jason and Medea out of reverence for the ordinance of "Zeus, Protector of Suppliants" (4.700); on Phaeacia Demeter is "indigenous" (4.986–987); and Medea sets up altars in the precinct of "Apollo Nomius" (4.1218; for the local salience of this cult on Phaeacia, see 176n156). "Zeus the king" at 1.731 is a special case; here the epithet serves to situate the scene within the chronology of myth, at a time after Zeus' ascension to power (cf. 1.508–511).

10　　Thus Hera is also Imbrasian (1.187); Athena is Itonian (1.551, 721, 768) and Minoan (4.1691);

b) In a few cases the epithet suggests a character's focalization[11] or motivation.[12]
c) As descriptors for physical phenomena that are identified with a deity (e.g., "radiant Dawn").[13]
d) In etiologies explaining the origin of the epithet in question.[14]
e) As markers of moments of high drama or gravity.[15]

Zeus is Genetaean (2.1009); and Aphrodite is once "the goddess who rules over Eryx" (θεὰ Ἔρυκος μεδέουσα, 4.917). Another epithet that should probably fall into this category occurs at 1.410, where Jason calls on "Apollo of his fathers" (πατρώιον Ἀπόλλωνα) at Pagasae, that is, from within his own ancestral territory. Cf. Apollo's epithet "Lycoreian" (4.1490), which the scholiast ad loc. connects to Delphi, though Apollonius uses it in a Libyan context. Whatever its true significance, the epithet appears to be connected to an acrostic, ΛΥΚΕ (1489–1492), identified by Danielewicz 2005: 332. Athena's epithet "Tritonian" (1.109, 3.1183) presents another interesting case: it is apparently chosen in both of the cited passages to connect the goddess to the Triton River in Boeotia (Race 2008: 12 n. 20), but in Book 4 the narrator rather sets Athena's birth by Lake Triton in Libya (4.1309–1311; cf. 1495). In addition, "Tritonian" rather than "Itonian" is the manuscript reading at 1.768 and a variant at 1.551, 721; if read in any of these passages, the epithet would presumably refer to yet another Triton River in Thessaly, Jason's homeland and the starting point of the Argonautic expedition. For these various "Tritonian" connections, see Kirk 1985 ad *Il.* 4.513–516; and cf. Paus. 8.26.6 for an Arcadian claimant to being Athena's Triton River. Finally, cf. also "Thracian" Boreas, whose epithet appears even in contexts where the wind's northerly source is not obviously pertinent (1.214, 1300; 2.427; 4.1484).

11 Thus Cybele is the "amenable goddess" (ἀνταίη δαίμων, 1.1141) as she heeds the Argonauts' sacrifices; Hades is "hateful" to Medea as she remembers all of life's pleasures (στυγεροῖο ... Ἀίδαο, 3.810); Hecate is "the dread goddess" in her terrifying epiphany that Jason is not to look upon (δεινὴ θεός, 3.1213); "mother earth," strikingly enough, represents the filial perspective of the earthborn men (γαῖαν | μητέρα, 3.1374–1375); the Furies are "terrible" to Circe as she attempts to placate their anger (σμερδαλέας ... Ἐρινύας, 4.714; note that purpose clauses inherently represent character focalization: de Jong 2004a: 118); and Night is a "giver of rest from labors" as it comes to the weary Argonauts (εὐνήτειρα | νὺξ ἔργων, 4.1058–1059).

12 Thus Hera's status as "Zeus' wife" (Ἥρη, Ζηνὸς ἄκοιτις) is relevant at 1.997 because it suggests her motivation for preparing a trial for Heracles, namely, her abhorrence of her husband's bastard (Levin 1971: 100 n. 3).

13 Eos is "radiant" at 1.519 (αἰγλήεσσα ... Ἠώς) and "light-brining" at 4.885 (φαεσφόρος ... Ἠώς). See n. 10 above on "Thracian Boreas."

14 The derivation of the epithet is in each case clear from context but is explained with varying degrees of explicitness: Aristaeus Agreus and Nomius (2.507; see Levin 1969), Zeus Icmaeus (2.522), Apollo Heoïus (2.700), and Apollo Aegletes (4.1716).

15 Thus when Jason and Medea murder Apsyrtus, "the all-subduing, pitiless Fury" (πανδαμάτωρ ... νηλειὴς ... Ἐρινύς, 4.475–476) takes notice. The same explanation holds true for "Zeus himself, king of the gods" (αὐτόν ... Ζῆνα, θεῶν βασιλῆα, 4.557–558).

The comparatively few divine epithets that fall outside the norms of usage outlined here are generally well suited to their contexts,[16] and in some cases they seem to be chosen to generate unique effects,[17] including irony.[18] Only a very few epithets are not immediately significant in context,[19] and one example thereof is probably due to textual corruption.[20]

16 Often such epithets have something of an explanatory purpose or serve to emphasize important points in the narrative. Thus Iris is "swift" (ὠκέα Ἶρις, 2.286) when she intervenes just in the nick of time to stop the Boreads from slaying the Harpies; when the Argonauts erect a shrine to "kindly Concord" (Ὁμονοίης ... εὔφρονος, 2.718), εὔφρονος may be meant as a cultic epithet; Eros is "greedy" (μάργος Ἔρως, 3.120) as he beats Ganymede in a game of dice; Hephaestus is "the craftsman" (τεχνήεις Ἥφαιστος) at 3.229, in a catalog of his Colchian handiwork; "Apollo of the golden sword" (χρυσαόρῳ Ἀπόλλωνι, 3.1283) is motivated by the god's comparison with the sword-wielding Jason (Race 2008: 317 n. 110); "man-destroying Ares" (Ἄρηος ... φθισιμβρότου, 3.1357) occurs in a martial context; the Loves—if we choose to personify them (Feeney 1991: 83)—are "bold" when they urge Medea on in her scheme to help Jason (θρασέες ... Ἔρωτες, 3.687); at 3.765, they are "tireless" as they perturb her through the night (ἀκάματοι ... Ἔρωτες); and Terpsichore is "beautiful" in an erotically-charged passage (εὐειδής ... Τερψιχόρη, 4.895–896).

17 Thus the epithet pairing "Uranus' son Cronus" (Οὐρανίδης ... Κρόνος, 2.1232) constitutes an allusion to Pind. *Pyth.* 3.4, which uses the same phraseology in referring to the same myth of Chiron's parentage; this is the only other *locus* where these words are paired in this way. At 4.1552, the epithet "wide-ruling Triton" (Τρίτων εὐρυβίης) seems to be chosen to connect with Triton's alias when he approaches the Argonauts, Eurypylus (1561). For the epithets applied to the Muse in the Book 4 introit, see introduction, 2.4, and 4.2.2.2.

18 Thus Hephaestus is dubbed "resourceful" at 1.851 (Ἡφαίστοιο ... πολυμήτιος), though it is in fact the god's wife who is actually exhibiting μῆτις in this episode (note 1.802, where, however, the text is uncertain; cf. Cusset 2015: 138). He is likewise Cypris' "lame husband" (πόσις ἀμφιγυήεις) at 3.37, in a scene that seems designed to make us think of Demodocus' second lay (see, e.g., Knight 1995: 224–225), which stresses Hephaestus' besting of the physically much more impressive Ares.

19 Thus Selene is "the Titanian goddess, the Moon" at 4.54–55 (Τιτηνίς ... θεά ... Μήνη); Dionysus is the "Nysean king" (ἄναξ ... Νυσήιος, 4.431), in an evident attempt to vary his name at 4.424; Persephone appears as "Demeter's mighty daughter" (Δηοῦς | θυγατέρ' ἰφθίμην, 4.896–897; see McPhee 2021a: 258); and the smith god is styled as "lord Hephaestus" at 4.956–958 (ἄναξ ... Ἥφαιστος, with considerable hyperbaton). Note also Apollonius' mannerism, inherited from early Greek epic (e.g., in the formula θεὰ γλαυκῶπις Ἀθήνη [*Il.* 1.206, 2.166, etc.]), of applying a rather superfluous θεά to the names of his goddesses (van den Eersten 2013: 19). Thus Athena is "the goddess Athena" at 1.226, and she is "the Itonian goddess Athena" at 1.768. Likewise Hera is "the goddess Hera" at 4.241–242, 781, and "goddess" is added superfluously also at 1.996. Both the "Muses" and the "Graces" are "goddesses" at 2.511 and 4.425, respectively; a singular Muse is a goddess at 4.1.

20 In many editions, Zeus appears as "mighty" at 3.158 (μεγάλοιο Διός). It has long been recognized that the epithet μεγάλοιο would have no special relevance here (Gerhard 1816: 78; Mooney 1912 ad loc.; Platt 1914: 27–28; Ardizzoni 1958 ad loc.; cf. Campbell 1994 ad loc.; van den Eersten 2013: 24), and the AR narrator's conservative use of divine epithets would tell

Notably, Apollonius' procedure in applying epithets to mortal characters generally agrees, mutatis mutandis,[21] with the practices I have just outlined, except that the AR narrator actually tends to be more sparing in his application of epithets to gods than to mortals.[22] For instance, the narrator once refers to "the Minyan son of Athamas" (Μινυήιον υἷ' Ἀθάμαντος, 4.117), identifying him two lines later as "the Aeolid Phrixus" (Αἰολίδης ... Φρίξος). The point of these genealogical epithets is not immediately apparent in context,[23] but they add a degree of rhetorical *amplitudo* to this mention of Phrixus that most Apollonian divinities never enjoy. One major reason for this difference in treatment of gods and mortals must be the narratee's greater familiarity with the former than with the latter. Especially on a mortal character's first appearance (or reappearance after some time), they may receive multiple epithets or even a relative clause as a means of introducing or identifying them: for example, "the son of Aeneus, the hero Cyzicus, whom Aenete bore, the daughter of noble Eusorus" (ἥρως Αἰνήιος υἱός ... Κύζικος, ὃν κούρη δίου τέκεν Εὐσώροιο | Αἰνήτη, 1.948–950). Apparently "Ancaeus, the bold son of Lycurgus" (Ἀγκαῖος Λυκοόργοιο θρασὺς υἱός, 2.118) is so identified to avoid confusion with the crew's other "Ancaeus, whom Astypalaea bore to Poseidon by the waters of the Imbrasus" (Ἀγκαίῳ ... ὃν Ἰμβρασίοισι παρ' ὕδασιν Ἀστυπάλαια | τίκτε Ποσειδάωνι, 2.865–867).[24] By contrast, the AR narrator seems to assume that his narratees are already familiar with the major gods and thus gives them no elaborate introduction; they appear in his narrative relatively unadorned as "Zeus," "the Far-Shooter," "Cypris," and so on.[25] But my essential point is this: under no circumstances, outside the

---

against such a seemingly unmotivated usage. On the other hand, Levin's (1963) proposal to read μεγάλοιο θεοῦ on the basis of Π[20] is more consistent with Apollonian technique: this periphrasis for "Zeus" at the end of the passage would vary the mention of the god in the same capacity at the beginning of the passage (3.114; Hunter 1989 ad *Arg*. 3.158, *pace* Vian 2002: 2.158). Moreover, διὲκ μεγάλοιο could be appreciated as a typically Apollonian *variatio in imitando* of the Homeric διὲκ μεγάροιο, which is in fact the reading of the *codd*. Reitzenstein's (1900: 607) conjecture, μεγάλοιο θέων (or θέειν), would introduce a contradiction into Apollonius' narrative (Levin 1963: 108).

21 I include this caveat because, for instance, mortal characters differ from gods in that they lack particular "aspects" that an epithet can serve to identify, and Apollonius rarely needs to explain the origin of a human being's epithet or metonym (though cf. 1.229–233, 3.245–246).

22 See further van den Eersten 2013: 50. For an exhaustive account of Apollonius' applications of epithets to his heroes, with a view to their traditionality or divergence from Archaic usages, see Vílchez 1986.

23 Perhaps they serve to heighten the epic atmosphere of this climactic scene, in which the Fleece is finally acquired.

24 Hübscher 1940: 60.

25 Minor divinities do, however, receive these sorts of "introductory" epithets, in some cases

extraordinary case of hymnic narratization, would the narrator refer to a goddess in the style of "Artemis Ship-Preserver, child of a great father, the goddess who watched over those peaks by the sea and protected the land of Iolcus" (1.570–572), *vel sim.*

> expanded by relative clauses. Thus the sea god Glaucus is introduced to the narrative as "the wise interpreter of divine Nereus" (Νηρῆος θείοιο πολυφράδμων ὑποφήτης, 1.1311); Cyrene's son is styled "clever Aristaeus, who discovered the keeping of bees and the oil of the olive, gained with much labor" (Ἀρισταίοιο περίφρονος, ὅς ῥα μελισσέων | ἔργα πολυκμή- τοιό τ' ἀνεύρατο πῖαρ ἐλαίης, 4.1132–1133); and the Libyan heroines receive a full three lines of introduction (4.1309–1311).

Glossary of Hymnic Terminology

In order to facilitate precise analysis, it has been necessary in this study to employ a fair number of technical terms that denote specific formal features of Greek hymns or that otherwise relate to hymnody. For convenience, a list of this terminology with brief definitions is provided here. A good many of these have been culled from a number of different sources,[1] while others are of my own devising. Terms marked with an asterisk (*) are defined in other entries in the glossary. Hymnic terms that are defined in this glossary are capitalized throughout in order to mark them out as technical usages.

Anaphora The repetition of a word, especially at the beginning of successive clauses,[2] as in, "**Often** [Pan] runs through the long white mountains, and **often** he drives the wild creatures through the glens, killing them" (*HH* 19.12–13).[3] This device creates an enthusiastic effect that is especially at home in hymnody.

Appeal to the Muses The term by which I denote the requests for the Muses' assistance that begin both the Homeric epics and many *Homeric Hymns*, in order to avoid confusion with the term Invocation*.

Attributes All the materials that hymnists use to describe a deity in the present tense (e.g., their "appearance, possessions, haunts and spheres of activity"[4]), typically placed in the hymn's central section (the *Laudatio**) as an "**Attributive Section**"; contrast Myth*.

Charis (χάρις) The "relationship ... of reciprocal pleasure and goodwill"[5] that the hymnist tries to establish with the god by means of the hymn. A good deal of common hymnic diction refers to this hoped-for bond between god and mortal (e.g., χαῖρε, πρόφρων, ἰανθείς, γηθόσυνος).

---

1 I have drawn especially on: Bremer 1981; Janko 1981; Race 1982a, 1992; Furley and Bremer 2001; Calame 2005; Hall 2012: ch. 3. For further discussion and bibliography, see introduction, 2.2.
2 "Anaphora" is often used loosely to designate any sort of repetition (e.g., Richardson 2010 ad *HH* 4.373–374).
3 πολλάκι δ' ἀργινόεντα διέδραμεν οὔρεα μακρά, | πολλάκι δ' ἐν κνημοῖσι διήλασε θῆρας ἐναίρων. On this example, see Germany 2005: 190 with n. 9. Another possible example from the hymns is *HH* 24.4, where, however, the text is uncertain; see AHS 1936 and Olson 2012 ad loc. Generally, however, Anaphora is probably more common in Cultic Hymns*; see, e.g., Fehling 1969: 169, 173, 174–176.
4 Janko 1981: 11.
5 Race 1982a: 8.

Contagious Hymnody My term for a range of poetic devices that give the impression that the narrator himself is swept up in religious fervor as he describes his own characters' Invocation (or Evocation) of a divinity. E.g., a narrator might be paraphrasing a hymn in indirect speech before he addresses the god in his own voice, as if he were joining in his character's worship of the deity. On one interpretation, Hymnic Narratization* could also be understood as a subtype of Contagious Hymnody.[6]

Cultic Hymns Most Greek hymns were "Cultic," in that their performance accompanied religious rituals such as processions (προσόδια) or were associated with particular cults, such as the paean (παιάν) for Apollo and related deities.[7] These hymns are characterized by different stylistic conventions from those of Rhapsodic Hymns* like the *Homeric Hymns*, such as a preference for Du-Stil* and a more personal tone.

Du-Stil and Er-Stil Two hymnic styles. In the former, the god is spoken *to*, in the second person; in the latter, the god is spoken *of*, in the third person. The *Homeric Hymns* tend to maintain Er-Stil except in the Envoi*, which is typically marked by a sudden switch into Du-Stil.

Envoi The conclusion of a hymn, which typically consists of a combination of the following: a Salutation*, a Prayer*, and (in the *Homeric Hymns*) the Poet's Task*.

Evocation See Invocation*.

Evocatory Verb See Invocation*.

Exordium The material at the beginning of a hymn up to the Hymnic Relative*; component parts typically include the Evocation* (sometimes accomplished by means of an Appeal to the Muses*) and one or more Honorific* epithets appended to the name of the god.

Honorific I employ this term for a range of epithets, appositive phrases or periphrases, and descriptive relative clauses or participial phrases whose use is designed to honor and delight a god in a hymn.[8] They are frequently deployed throughout a hymn, but they are virtually requisite in the Exordium* and Salutation*; for example, "I will never stop singing **far-shooting** Apollo, **wielder of the silver bow, whom fine-haired Leto bore**" (*HH* 3.177–178).[9]

Hymnic Narratization My term for a device common in Apollonius in which the Evocation* or Invocation*

---

6   See 4.1.
7   Moreover, most "literary hymns" (i.e., those embedded in non-hymnic literary genres) tend to imitate Cultic Hymns, such as those featured in the choruses of Attic drama (see, e.g.: Fränkel 1931: 3–11; Bremer 1981: 213 n. 67) or in lyric poetry (see Danielewicz 1974).
8   For a useful delineation of typical epithets used in hymns, see Bremer 1981: 195.
9   ἐγὼν οὐ λήξω ἑκηβόλον Ἀπόλλωνα | ὑμνέων ἀργυρότοξον, ὃν ἠΰκομος τέκε Λητώ.

of a god is "narratized" (i.e., a character's speech act is mentioned but not represented in either direct or indirect speech), but in which the god nonetheless receives one or more Honorifics* characteristic of actual hymnody. On one interpretation, this device could be understood as a type of Contagious Hymnody*.[10]

Hymnic Proem (προοίμιον)   A hymn that is sung before an epic performance, as the *Homeric Hymns* are believed to have functioned, or a hymnic prelude that is integrated into the beginning of an epic poem (e.g., Hes. *Op.* 1–10). By this somewhat cumbersome phrase I mean to avoid confusion with the common use of the term "proem" to refer to any introductory section of an epic poem (or other work of literature).

Hymnic Relative   The device, usually a relative clause with the Hymnic Subject as its antecedent, by which the *Homeric Hymns* transition from their Exordium* into the *Laudatio**.

Hymnic Subject   The divinity to whom the hymn is dedicated.

Ich-Du   This term refers to the tendency in addresses to the god to juxtapose first-person and second-person verbs and pronouns. Race explains the effect of one example of this technique thus: "This climactic juxtaposition of the god (second person) and man (first person) dramatizes the desire of the hymnist to bring together god and man in common delight."[11]

introit   The term I will be using (uncapitalized) to designate the introductory section of an epic poem, in order to avoid confusion with the term Proem*. Cf. also Exordium*.

Invocation and **Evocation**   The formal beginning of a hymn's Exordium*, in which the god to be honored (the Hymnic Subject*) is named. In an Invocation, this naming is achieved with a vocative address to the god in Du-Stil*, but the *Homeric Hymns* regularly feature the Evocation of the god as the third-person object of a first-person **Evocatory Verb** of singing, telling, commemorating, etc. (e.g., ἀείσομαι, ἄρχομ' ἀείδειν, μνήσομαι) in Er-Stil*. In some cases, the Evocation is accomplished instead by an Appeal to the Muses* (e.g., ἔννεπε, Μοῦσα).

Laudatio (εὐλογία)   The central section of a hymn, whose rhetorical function is to prepare for the petition in the Prayer* by winning the god's favor. In the *Homeric Hymns*, the *Laudatio* may take the form of a past-tense narrative taken from the god's life (Myth*), a present-tense description of the god's attributes (Attributive Section*), or a composite of the two.[12]

---

10   See 4.3.
11   Race 1982a: 13 n. 28.
12   For other terms by which scholars have designated this part of a hymn, see Furley and Bre-

Myth A narrative in the central section of a hymn (the *Laudatio**) that recounts the deity's birth or deeds, characterized by past tenses; contrast Attributes*. The Myth may be recounted quickly or over hundreds of verses. Contrast Attributive Section*.

Poet's Task Janko's term for a frequent element in the Envoi* of the *Homeric Hymns* in which the poet promises to remember the god as he transitions to another song. This formula is a key piece of evidence supporting the hypothesis that the *Homeric Hymns* were sung as Hymnic Proems* before the recitation of epic lays in rhapsodic performance.

Prayer A request to the deity in the hymn's Envoi*. In the *Homeric Hymns*, the verb that constitutes the petition is always imperatival, but other hymns use verbs in the optative mood as well.

Proem, Proemial Hymn See Hymnic Proem*.

Prolongation The transition out of a Mythic* narrative (set in the past) and back to the present tense before the Envoi*.

Rhapsodic Hymns* A general term for the genre of hexameter hymns exemplified by the *Homeric Hymns*, so called because of their likely recitation as Hymnic Proems* in rhapsodic performances. The term is also used for later compositions, such as Callimachus' *Hymns*, that more or less subscribe to the same formal conventions.[13] Contrast Cultic Hymns*.

Salutation An address to the deity in the vocative case in the Envoi* of the hymn, coupled with a **Salutatory Verb**. In the *Homeric Hymns*, this verb is almost always a form of χαῖρε or ἵληθι, but Cultic Hymns* also use imperatival verb forms requesting the god's attention (e.g., κλῦθι) or presence (e.g., ἵκεο, ἐλθέ, φάνηθι).[14]

Subject See Hymnic Subject*.

---

mer 2001: 1.51. Probably Bremer's term "argument" is preferable in describing the central section of Greek hymns generally (1981: 196); by this term he refers to any line of reasoning, which could be narrativized or not, intended to predispose the god to granting the hymnist's petition. He classifies four typical arguments: 1) *da quia dedi*; 2) *da ut dem*; 3) *da quia dedisti*; 4) *da quia hoc dare tuum est*. But as the HHs generally prefer to win the god's favor through straightforward praise rather than the explicit articulation of such logically worked out arguments, I prefer the term *Laudatio* for the present study. Cf. 14n76.

13 For these conventions and particularly the structural elements of a Rhapsodic Hymn*, see introduction, section 2.

14 Menander Rhetor gives the label κλητικὸς ὕμνος to hymns that request the god's presence (1.2.2 Race).

Bibliography

Texts and Translations[1]

Athanassakis, Apostolos N. 2004 [1977]. *The Homeric Hymns*. 2nd ed. Baltimore: Johns Hopkins University Press.

Bekker, Immanuel. 1833. *Apollonii Sophistae Lexicon Homericum*. Berlin: Reimer.

Bernabé, Alberto. 1987. *Poetae epici graeci: Testimonia et fragmenta*. Vol. 1. Leipzig: K.G. Saur.

Bernabé, Alberto. 2004. *Poetae epici graeci: Testimonia et fragmenta*. Vol. 2.1. Leipzig: K.G. Saur.

Bernabé, Alberto. 2017. *Himnos homéricos*. Madrid: Abada.

Bethe, Erich. 1900–1937. *Pollucis Onomasticon*. 3 vol. Leipzig: Teubner.

*Campbell, David A. 1982–1993. *Greek Lyric*. 5 vol. Cambridge, MA: Harvard University Press.

*Collard, Christopher, and Martin Cropp. 2008. *Euripides. Fragments*. 2 vol. Cambridge, MA: Harvard University Press.

*Couvreur, P. 1901. *Hermiae Alexandrini in Platonis Phaedrum scholia*. Paris: Émile Bouillon.

*Erbse, Hartmut. 1950. *Untersuchungen zu den attizistischen Lexika*. Berlin: Akademie-Verlag.

Evelyn-White, Hugh G. 1914. *Hesiod, the Homeric Hymns and Homerica*. Cambridge, MA: Harvard University Press.

Fränkel, Hermann. 1961. *Apollonii Rhodii Argonautica*. Oxford: Clarendon.

*Gerber, Douglas E. 1999. *Greek Elegiac Poetry from the Seventh to the Fifth Centuries BC*. Cambridge, MA: Harvard University Press.

Gronovius, Jakob. 1698. *Manethonis Apotelesmaticorum libri sex*. Leiden: Frederik Haarung.

Harder, Annette. 2012. *Callimachus. Aetia*. 2 vol. Oxford: Oxford University Press.

*Hilgard, A. 1901. *Grammatici graeci*. Vol. 1.3. Leipzig: Teubner.

Hollis, Adrian. 2009 [1990]. *Callimachus. Hecale*. 2nd ed. Oxford: Oxford University Press.

Köchly, Hermann. 1858. *Manethonis Apotelesmaticorum qui feruntur libri VI*. Leipzig: Teubner.

---

1 Items marked with an asterisk represent the editions from which texts and translations have been taken throughout the book. See further the Note on Texts, Translations, and Abbreviations (XIII–XIV). Items cited both as critical texts and as commentaries are included both here and under "Secondary Scholarship."

Lachenaud, Guy. 2010. *Scholies à Apollonios de Rhodes*. Paris: Les Belles Lettres.
Lightfoot, J.L. 2014. *Dionysius Periegetes. Description of the Known World*. Oxford: Oxford University Press.
Lloyd-Jones, Hugh, and Peter Parsons. 1983. *Supplementum Hellenisticum*. Berlin: De Gruyter.
*Most, Glenn W. 2006. *Hesiod. Theogony, Works and Days, Testimonia*. Cambridge, MA: Harvard University Press.
*Mozley, J.H. 1936 [1934]. *Valerius Flaccus. Argonautica*. Rev. ed. Cambridge, MA: Harvard University Press.
*Murray, A.T. 1995 [1919]. *Homer. Odyssey*. 2 vol. Rev. George E. Dimock. Cambridge, MA: Harvard University Press.
*Murray, A.T. 1999 [1924]. *Homer. Iliad*. 2 vol. Rev. William F. Wyatt. Cambridge, MA: Harvard University Press.
*Paton, W.R. 2014 [1916]. *The Greek Anthology: Books 1–5*. Rev. Michael A. Tueller. Cambridge, MA: Harvard University Press.
*Paton, W.R. 1917. *The Greek Anthology: Book 9*. Cambridge, MA: Harvard University Press.
*Perry, Ben Edwin. 1952. *Aesopica*. Urbana: University of Illinois Press.
Powell, J.U. 1925. *Collectanea alexandrina*. Oxford: Clarendon.
*Race, William H. 1997. *Pindar*. 2 vol. Cambridge, MA: Harvard University Press.
*Race, William H. 2008. *Apollonius Rhodius. Argonautica*. Cambridge, MA: Harvard University Press.
*Race, William H. 2019. *Menander Rhetor; [Dionysius of Halicarnassus]. Ars rhetorica*. Cambridge, MA: Harvard University Press.
*Scheer, Eduard. 1908. *Lycophronis Alexandra*. Vol. 2: *Scholia continens*. Berlin: Weidmann.
Seaton, R.C. 1912. *Apollonius Rhodius. The Argonautica*. London: Heinemann.
*Spengel, Leonhard von. 1854. *Rhetores graeci*. Vol. 2. Leipzig: Teubner.
*Vian, Francis. 1987. *Les Argonautiques Orphiques*. Paris: Les Belles Lettres.
*Waddell, W.G. 1940. *Manetho*. Cambridge, MA: Harvard University Press.
*Wendel, Carl. 1935. *Scholia in Apollonium Rhodium vetera*. Berlin: Weidmann.
West, M.L. 1998 [1971]. *Iambi et elegi graeci ante Alexandrum cantati*. 2 vol. 2nd ed. Oxford: Clarendon.
West, M.L. 2003a. *Homeric Hymns, Homeric Apocrypha, Lives of Homer*. Cambridge, MA: Harvard University Press.
*West, M.L. 2003b. *Greek Epic Fragments: From the Seventh to the Fifth Centuries BC*. Cambridge, MA: Harvard University Press.

Secondary Scholarship

Abbamonte, Giancarlo. 2008. "Apollonio Rodio 2, 264–265 e Omero A 4–5: Ancora un esempio di *epos* filologico." *SIFC* 6.1: 113–122.

Accorinti, Domenico, and Pierre Chuvin, Eds. *Des Géants à Dionysos: Mélanges de mythologie et de poésie grecques offerts à Francis Vian*. Alessandria: Edizioni dell'Orso.

Acosta-Hughes, Benjamin. 2010a. *Arion's Lyre: Archaic Lyric into Hellenistic Poetry*. Princeton: Princeton University Press.

Acosta-Hughes, Benjamin. 2010b. "The Prefigured Muse: Rethinking a Few Assumptions on Hellenistic Poetics." In Clauss and Cuypers: 81–91.

Acosta-Hughes, Benjamin, and Christophe Cusset. 2012. "Callimaque face aux *Hymnes Homériques*." In Bouchon, Brillet-Dubois, and Le Meur-Weissman: 123–133.

Acosta-Hughes, Benjamin, and Susan A. Stephens. 2012. *Callimachus in Context: From Plato to the Augustan Poets*. Cambridge: Cambridge University Press.

Adkin, Neil. 2019. "An Acrostic in Apollonius of Rhodes (*Arg.* 3.1008–1011)." *Mnemosyne* 72: 1–7.

Agosti, Gianfranco. 2016. "Praising the God(s): *Homeric Hymns* in Late Antiquity." In FVS: 221–240.

Albersmeier, Sabine, ed. 2009. *Heroes: Mortals and Myths in Ancient Greece*. Baltimore: Walters Art Museum.

Albinus, Lars. 2000. *The House of Hades: Studies in Ancient Greek Eschatology*. Aarhus: Aarhus University Press.

Albis, Robert V. 1995. "Jason's Prayers to Apollo in *Aetia* 1 and the *Argonautica*." *Phoenix* 49.2: 104–109.

Albis, Robert V. 1996. *Poet and Audience in the Argonautica of Apollonius*. Lanham, MD: Rowman & Littlefield.

Alcock, Susan E. 1997. "The Heroic Past in a Hellenistic Present." *Hellenistic Constructs: Essays in Culture, History, and Historiography*. Ed. Paul Cartledge, Peter Garnsey, and Erich Gruen. Berkeley: University of California Press. 20–34.

Allen, T.W., and E.E. Sikes. 1904. *The Homeric Hymns*. London: Macmillan.

Allen, T.W., W.R. Halliday, and E.E. Sikes (= AHS). 1936. *The Homeric Hymns*. 2nd ed. of Allen and Sikes. Oxford: Clarendon.

Aloni, Antonio. 1980. "*Prooimia, Hymnoi,* Elio Aristide e i cugini bastardi." *QUCC* 4: 23–40.

Aloni, Antonio. 1989. *L'aedo e i tiranni: Ricerche sull'Inno omerico a Apollo*. Rome: Ateneo.

Aloni, Antonio. 2001. "The Proem of Simonides' Plataea Elegy and the Circumstances of Its Performance." In Boedeker and Sider: 86–105.

Altheim, Franz. 1924. "Die Entstehungsgeschichte des homerischen Apollonhymnus." *Hermes* 59.4: 430–449.

Altman, William H.F. 2022. "Reading Xenophon's *Cyropaedia*." *AncPhil* 42.2: 335–352.

Álvarez Espinoza, Nazira. 2018. "Medea y la heroicidad femenina en las *Argonáuticas*." *Revista de Lenguas Modernas* 29: 93–113.

Ambühl, Annemarie. 2005. *Kinder und junge Helden: Innovative Aspekte des Umgangs mit der literarischen Tradition bei Kallimachos*. Leuven: Peeters.

Andersen, Øivind, and Dag T.T. Haug, Eds. 2012. *Relative Chronology in Early Greek Epic Poetry*. Cambridge: Cambridge University Press.

Antonaccio, Carla. 1993. "The Archaeology of Ancestors." *Cultural Poetics in Archaic Greece: Cult, Performance, Politics*. Ed. Carol Dougherty and Leslie Kurke. New York: Oxford University Press. 46–70.

Antonaccio, Carla. 1994. "Contesting the Past: Hero Cult, Tomb Cult, and Epic in Early Greece." *AJA* 98.3: 389–410.

Antonaccio, Carla. 1995. *An Archaeology of Ancestors: Tomb Cult and Hero Cult in Early Greece*. Lanham, MD: Rowman & Littlefield.

Ardizzoni, Anthos. 1958. *Le Argonautiche: Libro III*. Bari: Adriatica.

Ardizzoni, Anthos. 1967. *Le Argonautiche: Libro I*. Rome: Ateneo.

Ardizzoni, Anthos. 1970. "Note sul testo di Apollonio Rodio e Callimaco." *GIF* 22.2: 40–46.

Asheri, David, Alan Lloyd, and Aldo Corcella. 2007. *A Commentary on Herodotus Books I–IV*. Ed. Oswyn Murray and Alfonso Moreno, with Maria Brosius. Oxford: Oxford University Press.

Astour, Michael C. 1964. "Greek Names in the Semitic World and Semitic Names in the Greek World." *Journal of Near Eastern Studies* 23.3: 193–201.

Athanassakis, Apostolos N. 1977. *The Orphic Hymns: Text, Translation and Notes*. Atlanta: Scholars Press.

Athanassakis, Apostolos N. 2004 [1976]. *The Homeric Hymns*. 2nd ed. Baltimore: Johns Hopkins University Press.

Avallone Riccardo. 1953. "Catullo e Apollonio Rodio." *Antiquitas* 8.3–4: 8–75.

Bakhtin, M.M. 1981. *The Dialogic Imagination: Four Essays*. Trans. Caryl Emerson and Michael Holquist. Austin: University of Texas Press.

Bakker, Egbert J. 2005. *Pointing to the Past: From Formula to Performance in Homeric Poetics*. Washington, DC: Center for Hellenic Studies.

Bakker, Mathieu de, and Irene de Jong. 2022. "Introduction: Narratological Theory on Speech." *SAGN* 5: 1–30.

Barber, E.A., with an appendix by G. Giangrande. 1968 [1954]. "Hellenistic Poetry." *Fifty Years (and Twelve) of Classical Scholarship*. Rev. ed. Oxford: Blackwell. 267–291.

Barchiesi, Alessandro. 1999. "Venus' Masterplot: Ovid and the Homeric Hymns." *Ovidian Transformations: Essays on the Metamorphoses and its Reception*. Ed. Philip Hardie, Alessandro Barchiesi, and Stephen Hinds. Cambridge: Cambridge Philological Society. 112–126.

Barchiesi, Alessandro. 2001. "Genealogie letterarie nell'epica imperiale: Fondamentalismo e ironia." *L'histoire littéraire immanente dans la poésie latine*. Ed. Ernst August Schmidt, François Paschoud, Claudia Wick, and Lavinia Gilli Milić. Geneva: Fondation Hardt. 315–354.

Barnes, Michael H. 2003. *Inscribed Kleos: Aetiological Contexts in Apollonius of Rhodes*. Diss. University of Missouri.

Barrigón, Carmen. 2000. "La désignation des héros et héroïnes dans la poésie lyrique grecque." In Pirenne-Delforge and Suárez de la Torre: 1–14.

Barron, John P. 1984. "Ibycus: *Gorgias* and Other Poems." *BICS* 31.1: 13–24.

Barthes, Roland. 1977. *Image Music Text: Essays Selected and Translated by Stephen Heath*. London: Fontana.

Bassett, Samuel Eliot. 1938. *The Poetry of Homer*. Berkeley: University of California Press.

Bassino, Paola. 2019. *The Certamen Homeri et Hesiodi: A Commentary*. Berlin: De Gruyter.

Bauer, Martin M. 2017. "Der Dichter und sein Sänger: Orpheus und Apollonios im Paian (Apollonios Rhodios 2, 669–719)." *A&A* 63: 58–77.

Baumbach, Manuel. 2012. "Borderline Experiences with Genre: The Homeric *Hymn to Aphrodite* between Epic, Hymn and Epyllic Poetry." In Baumbach and Bär: 135–148.

Baumbach, Manuel, and Silvio Bär, Eds. 2012. *Brill's Companion to Greek and Latin Epyllion and Its Reception*. Leiden: Brill.

Baumeister, August. 1860. *Hymni Homerici*. Leipzig: Teubner.

Bécares Botas, Vicente. 1985. *Diccionario de terminología gramatical griega*. Salamanca: Ediciones Universidad de Salamanca.

Beck, Deborah. 2001. "Direct and Indirect Speech in the *Homeric Hymn to Demeter*." *TAPhA* 131: 53–74.

Beecroft, Alexander. 2011. "Blindness and Literacy in the *Lives* of Homer." *CQ* 61.1: 1–18.

Beekes, Robert. 2010. *Etymological Dicitonary of Greek*. 2 vols. Leiden: Brill.

Belloni, Luigi. 1995. "Ultimi accordi alla spinetta (Apoll. Rhod. *Arg.* IV 1773–1781)." *Studia classica Iohanni Tarditi oblata*. Vol. 1. Ed. Luigi Belloni, Guido Milanese, Antonietta Porro. Milan: Vita e Pensiero. 171–185.

Belloni, Luigi. 1996. "Esordio e finale delle *Argonautiche*: Reminiscenze di una *performance* in Apollonio Rodio." *Aevum(ant)* 9: 135–149.

Belloni, Luigi. 1999. "Un'icona di Apollo (Apoll. Rhod. *Argon.* 2.669–684)." *Prometheus* 25.3: 231–242.

Belloni, Luigi. 2017. "Sulla rotta degli Argonauti: Diacronia di un *genos* (Apoll. Rhod. 1.536–585; 4.1773 ss.)." *Prometheus* 43: 89–96.

Benveniste, Émile. 1969. *Le vocabulaire des institutions indo-européennes*. 2 vol. Paris: Minuit.

Bérard, Claude. 1982. "Récupérer la mort du prince: Héroïsation et formation de la cité." In Gnoli and Vernant: 89–105.

Berg, Robert M. van den. 2016. "The *Homeric Hymns* in Late Antiquity: Proclus and the *Hymn to Ares*." In FVS: 203–219.

Berkowitz, Gary. 2004. *Semi-Public Narration in Apollonius' Argonautica*. Leuven: Peeters.

Beye, Charles Rowan. 1964. "Homeric Battle Narrative and Catalogues." *HSCPh* 68: 345–373.

Beye, Charles Rowan. 1969. "Jason as Love-hero in Apollonios' *Argonautika*." *GRBS* 10.1: 31–55.

Beye, Charles Rowan. 1982. *Epic and Romance in the Argonautica of Apollonius*. Carbondale: Southern Illinois University Press.

Beye, Charles Rowan. 2006. *Ancient Epic Poetry: Homer, Apollonius, Virgil; with a chapter on the Gilgamesh Poem*. 2nd ed. Wauconda, IL: Bolchazy-Carducci.

Bieler, Ludwig. 1935. Θεῖος Ἀνήρ: *Das Bild des "göttlichen Menschen" in Spätantike und Frühchristentum*. Darmstadt: Wissenschaftliche Buchgesellschaft.

Biffis, Giulia. 2021. "Lycophron's Cassandra: A Powerful Female Poetic Voice." *HG* 26: 35–58.

Billault, Alain. 2008. "Orphée dans les *Argonautiques* d'Apollonios de Rhodes." Φιλευριπίδης: *Mélanges offerts à François Jouan*. Ed. Danièle Auger and Jocelyne Peigney. Nanterre: Presses universitaires de Paris. 197–207.

Bing, Peter. 1990. "A Pun on Aratus' Name in Verse 2 of the *Phainomena*?" *HSCPh* 93: 281–285.

Bing, Peter. 2008 [1988]. *The Well-Read Muse: Present and Past in Callimachus and the Hellenistic Poets*. Rev. ed. Ann Arbor: Michigan Classical Press.

Bing, Peter. 2009. *The Scroll and the Marble: Studies in Reading and Reception in Hellenistic Poetry*. Ann Arbor: University of Michigan Press.

Bloomer, W. Martin. 1993. "The Superlative *Nomoi* of Herodotus's *Histories*." *CA* 12.1: 30–50.

Blumberg, Karl Wilhelm. 1931. *Untersuchungen zur epischen Technik des Apollonios von Rhodos*. Diss. Universität Leipzig.

Boedeker, Deborah, and David Sider, Eds. 2001. *The New Simonides: Contexts of Praise and Desire*. Oxford: Oxford University Press.

Boedeker, Deborah. 2001. "Paths to Heroization at Plataea." In Boedeker and Sider: 148–163.

Boesch, Georg. 1908. *De Apollonii Rhodii elocutione*. Diss. Humboldt-Universität zu Berlin.

Bömer, Franz. 1958. *P. Ovidius Naso. Die Fasten*. Vol. 2 (Komm.). Heidelberg: Winter.

Bömer, Franz. 1980. *P. Ovidius Naso. Metamorphosen*. Vol. 5 (*Buch X–XI*). Heidelberg: Winter.

Bona, Giacomo. 1978. "Inni omerici e poesia greca arcaica: A proposito di una recente edizione e di un convegno." *RFIC* 106: 224–248.

Booth, Wayne C. 1983 [1961]. *The Rhetoric of Fiction*. 2nd ed. Chicago: University of Chicago Press.

Borgogno, Alberto. 2002. "Le Muse di Apollonio Rodio." *RPL* 5: 5–21.

Bornmann, Fritz. 1968. *Callimachi Hymnus in Dianam*. Florence: Nuova Italia.

Borthwick, E.K. 1970. "P. Oxy. 2738: Athena and the Pyrrhic Dance." *Hermes* 98.3: 318–331.

Bouchon, Richard, Pascale Brillet-Dubois, and Nadine Le Meur-Weissman, Eds. 2012. *Hymnes de la Grèce antique: Approches littéraires et historiques*. Lyon: Maison de l'Orient et de la Méditerannée.

Bowersock, Glen Warren, Walter Burkert, and Michael C.J. Putnam, Eds. 1979. *Arktouros: Hellenic Studies Presented to Bernard M.W. Knox on the Occasion of His 65th Birthday*. Berlin: De Gruyter.

Bowie, E.L. 2000. "The Reception of Apollonius in Imperial Greek Literature." *HG* 4: 1–10.

Boyancé, Pierre. 1964. "La science d'un *quindecemvir* au Ier siècle ap. J.C." *REL* 42: 334–346.

Boychenko, Leanna Lynn. 2013. *Callimachus' Book of Hymns: Poet, Narrator, Voice*. Diss. Yale University.

Boychenko, Leanna Lynn. 2017. "Callimachus' *Bath of Pallas* and the Greco-Egyptian Danaids." *HG* 21: 161–180.

Braund, David C. 1994. *Georgia in Antiquity: A History of Colchis and Transcaucasian Iberia, 550 BC–AD 562*. Oxford: Clarendon.

Braund, David C. 1996. "The Historical Function of Myths in the Cities of the Eastern Black Sea Coast." *Sur les traces des Argonautes. Actes du 6e symposium de Vani (Colchide), 22–29 septembre 1990*. Besançon: Université de Franche-Comté. 11–19.

Bravo, Jorge J., III. 2009. "Recovering the Past: The Origins of Greek Heroes and Hero Cults." In Albersmeier: 10–29.

Brelich, Angelo. 1958. *Gli eroi greci: Un problema storico-religioso*. Rome: Ateneo.

Bremer, J.M. 1981. "Greek Hymns." *Faith, Hope and Worship: Aspects of Religious Mentality in the Ancient World*. Ed. H.S. Versnel. Leiden: Brill. 193–215.

Bremer, J.M. 1987. "Full Moon and Marriage in Apollonius' *Argonautica*." *CQ* 37.2: 423–426.

Bremmer, Jan N. 2005. "Anaphe, Aeschrology and Apollo Aigletes: Apollonius Rhodius 4.1711–1730." In Harder and Cuypers: 18–34.

Bremmer, Jan N. 2006. "The Rise of the Hero Cult and the New Simonides." *ZPE* 158: 15–26.

Brioso Sánchez, Máximo. 1995. "Las musas y el poeta: Su problemática relación en Apolonio de Rodas." *Fortunatae* 7: 51–62.

Brioso Sánchez, Máximo. 2003. "El concepto de divinidad en las *Argonáuticas* de Apolonio de Rodas." *Mitos en la literature griega helenística e imperial*. Ed. Juan Antonio López Férez. Madrid: Ediciones Clásicas. 15–54.

Broeniman, Clifford Scott. 1989. *Thematic Patterns in the Argonautica of Apollonius Rhodius: A Study in the Imagery of Similes*. Diss. University of Illinois at Urbana-Champaign.
Brown, Christopher G. 1988. "Hipponax and Iambe." *Hermes* 116.4: 478–481.
Brown, Christopher G. 1997. "Iambos." *A Companion to the Greek Lyric Poets*. Ed. Douglas E. Gerber. Leiden: Brill. 11–88.
Brown, Malcolm Kenneth. 2002. *The Narratives of Konon*. Munich: K.G. Saur.
Brumbaugh, Michael. 2019. *The New Politics of Olympos: Kingship in Kallimachos' Hymns*. Oxford: Oxford University Press.
Bruss, Jon Steffen. 2004. "Lessons from Ceos: Written and Spoken Word in Callimachus." *HG* 7: 49–69.
Bulloch, A.W. 1977. "Callimachus' Erysichthon, Homer and Apollonius Rhodius." *AJPh* 98.2: 97–123.
Bulloch, A.W. 1984. "The Future of a Hellenistic Illusion: Some Observations on Callimachus and Religion." *MH* 41: 209–230.
Bulloch, A.W. 1985. *Callimachus. The Fifth Hymn*. Cambridge: Cambridge University Press.
Bulloch, Anthony, Erich S. Gruen, A.A. Long, and Andrew Stewart, Eds. 1993. *Images and Ideologies: Self-definition in the Hellenistic World*. Berkeley: University of California Press.
Bundy, Elroy L. 1972. "The 'Quarrel between Kallimachos and Apollonios' Part I: The Epilogue of Kallimachos's *Hymn to Apollo*." *CSCA* 5: 39–94.
Burgess, Jonathan S. 2001. *The Tradition of the Trojan War in Homer and the Epic Cycle*. Baltimore: Johns Hopkins University Press.
Burkert, Walter. 1979. "Kynaithos, Polycrates, and the *Homeric Hymn to Apollo*." In: Bowersock, Burkert, and Putnam: 53–62.
Burkert, Walter. 1985. *Greek Religion: Archaic and Classical*. Trans. John Raffan. Oxford: Blackwell.
Burkert, Walter. 1987. "The Making of Homer in the Sixth Century B.C.: Rhapsodes versus Stesichoros." *Papers on the Amasis Painter and His World*. Malibu: J. Paul Getty Museum. 43–62.
Burstein, Stanley Mayer. 1976. *Outpost of Hellenism: The Emergence of Heraclea on the Black Sea*. Berkeley: University of California Press.
Busch, Stephan. 1993. "Orpheus bei Apollonios Rhodios." *Hermes* 121.3: 301–324.
Byre, Calvin S. 1991. "The Narrator's Addresses to the Narratee in Apollonius Rhodius' *Argonautica*." *TAPhA* 121: 215–227.
Byre, Calvin S. 1996. "Distant Encounters: The Prometheus and Phaethon Episodes in the *Argonautica* of Apollonius Rhodius." *AJPh* 117.2: 275–283.
Byre, Calvin S. 1997. "On the Departure from Pagasae and the Passage of the Planctae in Apollonius' *Argonautica*." *MH* 54.2: 106–114.

Byre, Calvin S. 2002. *A Reading of Apollonius Rhodius' Argonautica: The Poetics of Uncertainty*. Lewiston: Edwin Mellen.

Cairns, Francis. 1979. "Self-Imitation within a Generic Framework: Ovid, *Amores* 2.9 and 3.11 and the *renuntiatio amoris.*" *Creative Imitation and Latin Literature*. Ed. David West and Tony Woodman. Cambridge: Cambridge University Press. 121–141.

Cairns, Francis. 2007 [1972]. *Generic Composition in Greek and Roman Poetry*. Rev. ed. Ann Arbor: Michigan Classical Press.

Calame, Claude. 1997 [1977]. *Choruses of Young Women in Ancient Greece: Their Morphology, Religious Role, and Social Function*. Trans. Derek Collins and Janice Orion. Lanham, MD: Rowman & Littlefield.

Calame, Claude. 2005. "Relationships with the Gods and Poetic Functions in the *Homeric Hymns.*" *Masks of Authority: Fiction and Pragmatics in Ancient Greek Poetics*. Trans. Peter M. Burk. Ithaca: Cornell University Press. 19–35.

Calame, Claude. 2011. "The *Homeric Hymns* as Poetic Offerings: Musical and Ritual Relationships with the Gods." In Faulkner: 334–357.

Calvert, George H., trans. 1845. *Correspondence between Schiller and Goethe, from 1794 to 1805*. New York: Wiley and Putnam.

Calzascia, Sonja Caterina. 2015. *Il carme 64 di Catullo e le Argonautiche di Apollonio Rodio*. Bologna: BraDypUS.

Cameron, Alan. 1995. *Callimachus and His Critics*. Princeton: Princeton University Press.

Campbell, M. 1969. "Critical Notes on Apollonius Rhodius." *CQ* 19.2: 269–284.

Campbell, M. 1971. "Further Notes on Apollonius Rhodius." *CQ* 21.2: 402–423.

Campbell, M. 1973. "Notes on Apollonius Rhodius, *Argonautica* II." *RPh* 47: 68–90.

Campbell, M. 1976. Review of Livrea 1973. *Gnomon* 48.4: 336–340.

Campbell, M. 1977. "Βώσεσθε Again." *CQ* 27.2: 467.

Campbell, M. 1981. *Echoes and Imitations of Early Epic in Apollonius Rhodius*. Leiden: Brill.

Campbell, M. 1983a. *Studies in the Third Book of Apollonius Rhodius' Argonautica*. Hildesheim: Georg Olms.

Campbell, M. 1983b. "Apollonian and Homeric Book Division." *Mnemosyne* 36.1/2: 154–156.

Campbell, M. 1994. *A Commentary on Apollonius Rhodius Argonautica III 1–471*. Leiden: Brill.

Caneva, Stefano. 2007. "Raccontare nel tempo: Narrazione epica e cronologia nelle *Argonautiche* di Apollonio Rodio." *Il lavoro sul mito nell'epica greca: Letture di Omero e Apollonio*. Ed. Stefano Caneva and Victoria Tarenzi. Pisa: ETS. 67–132.

Caneva, Stefano. 2010a. "Da Crono agli eroi: Ordine e disordine, violenza e *homonoia* nelle *Argonautiche* di Apollonio Rodio." *Come bestie? Forme e paradossi della violenza tra mondo antico e disagio contemporaneo*. Ed. Valeria Andò and Nicola Cusumano. Caltanissetta: Salvatore Sciascia. 165–188.

Caneva, Stefano. 2010b. "*Argonautiques* IV.257–293: De l'Égypte devenue texte au texte qui devient monde." *Monde du texte, texte du monde*. Ed. Isabelle Millat-Pilot. Grenoble: J. Millon. 49–66.

Cantilena, Mario. 1982. *Ricerche sulla dizione epica. 1. Per uno studio della formularità degli Inni Omerici*. Rome: Ateneo.

Capra, Andrea, and Matteo Curti. 1995. "Semidei Simonidei: Note sull'elegia di Simonide per la battaglia di Platea (P. Oxy. 3965 frr. 1–2+2327 fr. 6+27 col.i)." *ZPE* 107: 27–32.

Carey, Chris. 2009. "Genre, Occasion and Performance." *The Cambridge Companion to Greek Lyric*. Ed. Felix Budelmann. Cambridge: Cambridge University Press. 21–38.

Carspecken, John Frederick. 1952. "Apollonius Rhodius and the Homeric Epics." *YClS* 13: 33–143.

Casabona, Jean. 1966. *Recherches sur le vocabulaire des sacrifices en grec, des origines à la fin de l'époque classique*. Aix-en-Provence: Editions Ophrys.

Casali, Sergio. 2021. "Intertestualità autoriflessiva nei poeti ellenistici e romani." *La letteratura latina in età ellenistica*. Ed. Luigi Galasso. Rome: Carocci. 165–190.

Casevitz, M. 1984. "Temples et sanctuaires: Ce qu'apprend l'étude lexicologique." *Temples et sanctuaires: Séminaire de recherche 1981–1983*. Ed. G. Roux. Lyon: GIS—Maison de l'Orient. 81–95.

Càssola, Filippo. 1975a. *Inni Omerici*. 6th ed. Milan: Fondazione Lorenzo Valla.

Càssola, Filippo. 1975b. "Note sul primo epigramma omerico e su Era ninfa." *Studi triestini di antichità in onore di Luigia Achillea Stella*. Trieste: EUT. 215–219.

Celoria, Francis. 1992. *The Metamorphoses of Antoninus Liberalis: A Translation with a Commentary*. London: Routledge.

Cerbo, Ester. 1993. "Gli inni ad Eros in tragedia: Struttura e funzione." *Tradizione e innovazione nella cultura greca da Omero all'età ellenistica: Scritti in onore di Bruno Gentili*. Vol. 2. Ed. Roberto Pretagostini. Rome: GEI. 645–656.

Cerri, Giovanni. 2007. "Apollonio Rodio e le Muse *hypophetores*: Tre interpretazioni a confronto." *QUCC* 85.1: 159–165.

Chaniotis, Angelos. 2003. "The Divinity of Hellenistic Rulers." *A Companion to the Hellenistic World*. Ed. Andrew Erskine. Malden, MA: Blackwell. 431–445.

Chatman, Seymour. 1978. *Story and Discourse: Narrative Structure in Fiction and Film*. Ithaca: Cornell University Press.

Chuvin, Pierre. 1991. *Mythologie et géographie dionysiaques: Recherches sur l'œuvre de Nonnos de Panopolis*. Clermont-Ferrand: Adosa.

Chuvin, Pierre. 2003. "Anaphé, ou la dernière épreuve des Argonautes." In Accorinti and Chuvin: 215–221.

Ciani, Maria Grazia. 1975. "Ripetizione 'formulare' in Apollonio Rodio." *Bollettino dell' Istituto di Filologia Greca* 2: 191–208.

Clack, Jerry. 1982. *An Anthology of Alexandrian Poetry*. Pittsburgh: Classical Association of the Atlantic States.

Clare, R.J. 1996. "Catullus 64 and the *Argonautica* of Apollonius of Rhodes: Allusion and Exemplarity." *PCPhS* 42: 60–88.
Clare, R.J. 2000. "Epic Itineraries: The Sea and Seafaring in the *Odyssey* of Homer and the *Argonautica* of Apollonius Rhodius." *The Sea in Antiquity*. Ed. G.J. Oliver, R. Brock, T.J. Cornell, and S. Hodkinson. Oxford: Archaeopress. 1–12.
Clare, R.J. 2002. *The Path of the Argo: Language, Imagery and Narrative in the Argonautica of Apollonius Rhodius*. Cambridge: Cambridge University Press.
Clarke, Michael. 1999. *Flesh and Spirit in the Songs of Homer: A Study of Words and Myths*. Oxford: Clarendon.
Clausing, Adolf. 1913. *Kritik und Exegese der homerischen Gleichnisse im Altertum*. Diss. Albert-Ludwigs-Universität Freiburg.
Clauss, James J. 1986. "Lies and Allusions: The Addressee and Date of Callimachus' Hymn to Zeus." *CA* 5.2: 155–170.
Clauss, James J. 1989. "Two Curious Reflections in the Argonautic Looking-Glass (*Argo*. 1.577 and 603)." *GIF* 41: 195–207.
Clauss, James J. 1990. "Hellenistic Imitations of Hesiod *Catalogue of Women* fr. 1, 6–7 M.-W." *QUCC* 36.3: 129–140.
Clauss, James J. 1991. "A Mythological Thaumatrope in Apollonius Rhodius." *Hermes* 119.4: 484–488.
Clauss, James J. 1993. *The Best of the Argonauts: The Redefinition of the Epic Hero in Book 1 of Apollonius' Argonautica*. Berkeley: University of California Press.
Clauss, James J. 1997. "Conquest of the Mephistophelian Nausicaa: Medea's Role in Apollonius' Redefinition of the Epic Hero." *Medea: Essays on Medea in Myth, Literature, Philosophy, and Art*. Ed. James Clauss and Sarah Iles Johnston. Princeton: Princeton University Press. 149–177.
Clauss, James J. 2000. "Cosmos without Imperium: The Argonautic Journey through Time." *HG* 4: 11–32.
Clauss, James J. 2012. "The Argonautic *Anabasis*: Myth and Hellenic Identity in Apollonius' *Argonautica*." *Mythe et pouvoir à l'époque hellénistique*. Ed. C. Cusset, N. Le Meur-Weissman, and F. Levin. Leuven: Peeters. 417–437.
Clauss, James J. 2016a. "The Hercules and Cacus Episode in Augustan Literature: Engaging the *Homeric Hymn to Hermes* in Light of Callimachus' and Apollonius' Reception." In FVS: 55–78.
Clauss, James J. 2016b. "*Heldendämmerung* Anticipated: The Gods in Apollonius' *Argonautica*." *The Gods of Greek Hexameter Poetry: From the Archaic Age to Late Antiquity and Beyond*. Ed. James Clauss, Martine Cuypers, and Ahuvia Kahane. Stuttgart: Franz Steiner. 135–151.
Clauss, James J. 2019a. "The Near Eastern Background of Aetiological Wordplay in Callimachus." *HG* 24: 65–96.
Clauss, James J. 2019b. "Cross-Pollination among Artists across Time: A Response to Annette Harder." *Aevum(ant)* 19: 43–56.

Clauss, James J., and Martine Cuypers, Eds. 2010. *A Companion to Hellenistic Poetry.* Malden, MA: Wiley-Blackwell.

Clay, Jenny Strauss. 1997. "The Homeric Hymns." *A New Companion to Homer.* Ed. Ian Morris and Barry Powell. Leiden: Brill. 489–507.

Clay, Jenny Strauss. 2006 [1989]. *The Politics of Olympus: Form and Meaning in the Major Homeric Hymns.* 2nd ed. London: Bristol Classical Press.

Clay, Jenny Strauss. 2011. "The *Homeric Hymns* as Genre." In Faulkner: 232–253.

Clayton, Barbara Leigh. 2017. "Heracles, Hylas, and the *Homeric Hymn to Demeter* in Apollonius's *Argonautica*." *Helios* 44.2: 133–156.

Clinton, Kevin. 1986. "The Author of the *Homeric Hymn to Demeter*." *OAth* 16: 43–49.

Clinton, Kevin. 1992. *Myth and Cult: The Iconography of the Eleusinian Mysteries.* Stockholm: Svenska Institutet i Athen.

Codrignani, Giancarla. 1958. "L'*aition* nella poesia greca prima di Callimaco." *Convivium* 26: 527–545.

Cohen, Beth. 1998. "The Nemean Lion's Skin in Athenian Art." *Le bestiaire d'Héraclès: IIIe rencontre héracléenne.* Ed. Corinne Bonnet, Colette Jourdain-Annequin, and Vinciane Pirenne-Delforge. Liège: Centre international d'étude de la religion grecque antique. 127–139.

Coldstream, J.N. 1976. "Hero-Cults in the Age of Homer." *JHS* 96: 8–17.

Cole, Susan Guettel. 1984. *Theoi Megaloi: The Cult of the Great Gods at Samothrace.* Leiden: Brill.

Cole, Spencer. 2008. "Annotated Innovation in Euripides' *Ion*." *CQ* 58.1: 313–315.

Collins, John Francis. 1967. *Studies in Book One of the Argonautica of Apollonius Rhodius.* Diss. Columbia University.

Connolly, Andrew. 1998. "Was Sophocles Heroised as Dexion?" *JHS* 118: 1–21.

Conte, Gian Biagio. 1986. *The Rhetoric of Imitation: Genre and Poetic Memory in Virgil and Other Latin Poets.* Ed. with foreword by Charles Segal. Ithaca: Cornell University Press.

Conte, Gian Biagio. 1992. "Proems in the Middle." *YClS* 29: 147–159.

Consigny, Scott. 2001. *Gorgias: Sophist and Artist.* Columbia: University of South Carolina Press.

Cook, J.M. 1953. "The Cult of Agamemnon at Mycenae." Γέρας Αντωνίου Κεραμοπούλλου. Athens: Myrtide. 112–118.

Cook, Erwin. 1999. "'Active' and 'Passive' Heroics in the *Odyssey*." *CW* 93.2: 149–167.

Corbato, Carlo. 1955. *Riprese callimachee in Apollonio Rodio.* Trieste: Istituto di filologia classica.

Corradi, Michele. 2007. "Apollonio Rodio e il 'comando burbanzoso' di Omero alla dea." *La cultura letteraria ellenistica: Persistenza, innovazione, trasmissione.* Ed. Roberto Pretagostini and Emanuele Dettori. Rome: Quasar. 71–86.

Cosgrove, Matthew R. 2011. "The Unknown 'Knowing Man': Parmenides, B1.3." *CQ* 61.1: 28–47.
Costantini, Michel, and Jean Lallot. 1987. "Le προοίμιον est-il un proème?" *Le texte et ses représentations*. Paris: Presses de l'École Normale Supérieure. 13–27.
Couat, Auguste. 1882. *La poésie alexandrine sous les trois premiers Ptolémées (324–222 av. J.-C.)*. Paris: Hachette.
Coulmas, Florian. 1986. "Reported Speech: Some General Issues." *Direct and Indirect Speech*. Ed. Florian Coulmas. Berlin: De Gruyter. 1–28.
Courtney, Edward. 1993. *The Fragmentary Latin Poets*. Oxford: Clarendon.
Crowther, N.B. 1979. "Water and Wine as Symbols of Inspiration." *Mnemosyne* 32.1: 1–11.
Crump, M. Marjorie. 1931. *The Epyllion from Theocritus to Ovid*. Oxford: Basil Blackwell.
Curiazi, Dalilia. 1979. "Choliamb. Fragm. Novum." *Museum Criticum* 13–14: 333–336.
Currie, Bruno. 2005. *Pindar and the Cult of Heroes*. Oxford: Oxford University Press.
Cusset, Christophe. 2001. "Apollonios de Rhodes, lecteur de la tragédie classique." *Lectures antiques de la tragédie grecque*. Lyon: Université Jean Moulin. 61–76.
Cusset, Christophe. 2013. "Souffrance et vaillance: Sur un acrostiche méconnu au chant III des *Argonautiques* d'Apollonios de Rhodes." *REG* 126.2: 623–633.
Cusset, Christophe. 2015. "Héphaïstos comme figure de création dans les *Argonautiques* d'Apollonios de Rhodes." *D'Alexandre à Auguste: Dynamiques de la creation dans les arts visuels et la poésie*. Ed. Pascale Linant de Bellefonds, Évelyne Prioux, and Agnès Rouveret. Rennes: Presses universitaires de Rennes. 135–141.
Cusset, Christophe. 2017. "Apollonios de Rhodes et Ératosthène de Cyrène: Bibliothécaires et poètes à Alexandrie." *The Library of Alexandria: A Cultural Crossroads of the Ancient World*. Ed. Christophe Rico and Anca Duncan. Jerusalem: Polis Institute. 141–162.
Cusset, Christophe. 2018. "La présence de Delphes dans la poésie hellénistique." *Delphes et la littérature d'Homère à nos jours*. Ed. Jean-Marc Luce. Paris: Classiques Garnier. 77–99.
Cusset, Christophe. 2021. "Etymology as a Poetic Resource among the Poets of Alexandria." *Ancient and Medieval Greek Etymology: Theory and Practice 1*. Ed. Arnaud Zucker and Claire Le Feuvre. Berlin: De Gruyter. 213–228.
Cuypers, M.P. 1997. *Apollonius Rhodius Argonautica 2.1–310: A Commentary*. Diss. Universiteit Leiden.
Cuypers, M.P. 2004. "Apollonius of Rhodes." *SAGN* 1: 43–62.
Cuypers, M.P. 2005. "Interactional Particles and Narrative Voice in Apollonius and Homer." In Harder and Cuypers: 35–69.
D'Aleo, Alessia. 2012. "Butes in Eryx: Constructions and Religious Interpretation of an *Oikistes* between Hellenes, Phoenicians, and Natives." *Mediterraneo Antico* 15.1–2: 71–82.

D'Alessio, Giovan Battista. 2000. "Le *Argonautiche* di Cleone Curiense." *La letteratura ellenistica: Problemi e prospettive di ricerca*. Ed. Roberto Pretagostini. Rome: Quasar. 91–112.

Danek, Georg. 2009. "Apollonius Rhodius as an (anti-)Homeric Narrator: Time and Space in the *Argonautica*." *Narratology and Interpretation: The Content of Narrative Form in Ancient Literature*. Ed. Jonas Grethlein and Antonios Rengakos. Berlin: De Gruyter. 275–291.

Daniel-Müller, Bénédicte. 2012. "Une épopée au féminin: La question des genres dans le livre III des *Argonautiques* d'Apollonios de Rhodes." *Gaia* 15: 97–120.

Danielewicz, Georgius. 1974. "De elementis hymnicis in Sapphus Alcaei Anacreontisque Carminibus Obviis Quaestiones Selectae." *Eos* 62: 23–33.

Danielewicz, J. 2005. "Further Hellenistic Acrostics: Aratus and Others." *Mnemosyne* 58.3: 321–334.

Davies, M., and P.J. Finglass. 2014. *Stesichorus: The Poems*. Cambridge: Cambridge University Press.

De Marco, Vittorio. 1963. "Osservazioni su Apollonio Rodio I 1–22." *Miscellanea di Studi Alessandrini in Memoria di Augusto Rostagni*. Ed. Leonardo Ferrero, Carlo Gallavotti, Italo Lana, Antonio Maddalena, Arnaldo Momigliano, and Michele Pellegrino. Turin: Bottega d'Erasmo. 350–355.

De Martino, Francesco. 1980. "Ἄλλη ἀοιδή (in coda all'inno omerico *Ad Apollo*, 545–546)." *AC* 49.1: 232–240.

De Martino, Francesco. 1984–1985. "Note apolloniane." *AFLB* 27–28: 101–117.

de Polignac, François. 1995 [1984]. *Cults, Territory, and the Origins of the Greek City-State*. Trans. Janet Lloyd. Chicago: University of Chicago Press.

DeBrohun, Jeri Blair. 2007. "Catullan Intertextuality: Apollonius and the Allusive Plot of Catullus 64." *A Companion to Catullus*. Ed. Marilyn B. Skinner. Malden, MA: Blackwell. 293–313.

Dee, James H. 2001. *Epitheta Deorum apud Homerum: The Epithetic Phrases for the Homeric Gods: A Repertory of the Descriptive Expressions for the Divinities of the Iliad and the Odyssey*. 2nd ed. Hildesheim: Olms-Weidmann.

DeForest, Mary Margolies. 1994. *Apollonius' Argonautica: A Callimachean Epic*. Leiden: Brill.

Del Corno, Dario, ed., Maria Maletta, trans., and Francesco Tissoni, comm. 1999. *Nonno di Panopoli. Le Dionisiache*. Vol. 2: *Canti 13–24*. Milan: Adelphi.

Delage, Émile. 1930. *La géographie dans les Argonautiques d'Apollonios de Rhodes*. Bordeaux: Feret.

Delcourt, Marie. 1953. "La légende de Kaineus." *RHR* 144.2: 129–150.

Deneken, F. 1884–1890. "Heros." *Ausführliches Lexikon der griechischen und römischen Mythologie*. Ed. W.H. Roscher. Vol. 1. Leipzig: Teubner. 2441–2589.

Depew, Mary. 1993. "Mimesis and Aetiology in Callimachus' *Hymns*." *HG* 1: 57–77.

Depew, Mary. 2000. "Enacted and Represented Dedications: Genre and Greek Hymn." *Matrices of Genre: Authors, Canons, and Society.* Ed. Mary Depew and Dirk Obbink. Cambridge, MA: Harvard University Press. 59–79.

Depew, Mary. 2004. "Gender, Power, and Poetics in Callimachus' Book of *Hymns*." *HG* 2: 117–137.

Desideri, Paolo. 1967. "Studi di storiografia eracleota, I: Promathidas e Nymphis." *SCO* 16: 366–416.

Deubner, Ludwig. 1932. *Attische Feste.* Berlin: Akademie-Verlag.

Deubner, Ludwig. 1941. "*Ololyge* und Verwandtes." *Abhandlungen der Preußischen Akademie der Wissenschaften* 1: 3–28.

Dickey, Eleanor. 2007. *Ancient Greek Scholarship.* Oxford: Oxford University Press.

Dickie, Matthew. 1990. "Talos Bewitched: Magic, Atomic Theory and Paradoxography in Apollonius *Argonautica* 4.1638–1688." *Papers of the Leeds International Latin Seminar: Sixth Volume.* Ed. Francis Cairns and Malcolm Heath. Leeds: Francis Cairns. 267–296.

Dickie, Matthew. 1998. "Poets as Initiates in the Mysteries: Euphorion, Philicus and Posidippus." *A&A* 44: 49–77.

Diggle, James. 1970. *Euripides. Phaethon.* Cambridge: Cambridge University Press.

Dihle, A. 1987. "Dionysos in Indien." *India and the Ancient World: History, Trade and Culture Before A.D. 650.* Ed. Gilbert Pollet and P.H.L. Eggermont. Leuven: Departement Oriëntalistiek. 47–57.

Dihle, A. 2002. "Zu den Fragmenten eines Dionysos-Hymnus." *RhM* 145.3/4: 427–430.

Dimock, G.E., Jr. 1956. "The Name of Odysseus." *Hudson Review* 9.1: 52–70.

Dodds, E.R. 1960. *Euripides. Bacchae.* 2nd ed. Oxford: Clarendon.

Domaradzki, Mikolaj. 2012. "Theological Etymologizing in the Early Stoa." *Kernos* 25: 125–148.

Dougherty, Carol. 1993. *The Poetics of Colonization: From City to Text in Archaic Greece.* Oxford: Oxford University Press.

Dova, Stamatia, Cathy Callaway, and George A. Gazis, Eds. 2023. *Homer in Sicily.* Siracusa: Parnassos Press.

Dover, Kenneth J. 1971. *Theocritus: Select Poems.* Bristol: Bristol Classical Press.

Dover, Kenneth J. 1989 [1978]. *Greek Homosexuality.* 2nd ed. Cambridge, MA: Harvard University Press.

Dräger, Paul. 2002. *Apollonios von Rhodos: Die Fahrt der Argonauten.* Stuttgart: Reclam.

Drögemüller, Hans-Peter. 1956. *Die Gleichnisse im hellenistichen Epos.* Diss. Universität Hamburg.

Du Quesnay, Ian M. Le M. 1977. "Vergil's Fourth *Eclogue*." *Papers of the Liverpool Latin Seminar, 1976: Classical Latin Poetry, Medieval Latin Poetry, Greek Poetry.* Ed. Francis Cairns. Leeds: Francis Cairns. 25–99.

Du Quesnay, Ian M. Le M. 1979. "From Polyphemus to Corydon: Virgil, *Eclogue* 2 and the *Idylls* of Theocritus." *Creative Imitation and Latin Literature.* Ed. David West and Tony Woodman. Cambridge: Cambridge University Press. 35–69.

Dué, Casey. 2001. "Achilles' Golden Amphora in Aeschines' *Against Timarchus* and the Afterlife of Oral Tradition." *CPh* 96.1: 33–47.

Dufner, Christina Marie. 1988. *The Odyssey in the Argonautica: Reminiscence, Revision, Reconstruction.* Diss. Princeton University.

Duncan, Anne. 2001. "Spellbinding Performance: Poet as Witch in Theocritus' Second *Idyll* and Apollonius' *Argonautica.*" *Helios* 28.1: 43–56.

Durbec, Yannick. 2008. "Several Deaths in Apollonius Rhodius' *Argonautica.*" *Myrtia* 23: 53–73.

Dyck, Andrew R. 1989. "On the Way from Colchis to Corinth: Medea in Book 4 of the *Argonautica.*" *Hermes* 117:4: 455–470.

Dyer, Robert. 1975. "The Blind Bard of Chios (*Hymn. Hom. Ap.* 171–176)." *CPh* 70.2: 119–121.

Eagleton, Terry. 2008 [1983]. *Literary Theory: An Introduction.* Anniversary ed. Minneapolis: University of Minnesota Press.

Eden, P.T. 1975. *A Commentary on Virgil: Aeneid VIII.* Leiden: Brill.

Edmunds, Lowell. 2001. *Intertextuality and the Reading of Roman Poetry.* Baltimore: Johns Hopkins University Press.

Edmunds, Lowell. 2011. "Isocrates' *Encomium of Helen* and the Cult of Helen and Menelaus at Therapnē." *Electronic Antiquity* 14.2: 21–35.

Edwards, Anthony T. 1985. "Achilles in the Underworld: *Iliad, Odyssey,* and *Aethiopis.*" *GRBS* 26.3: 215–227.

Edwards, Mark W. 1987. *Homer: Poet of the Iliad.* Baltimore: Johns Hopkins University Press.

Edwards, Mark W. 1991. *The Iliad: A Commentary.* Vol. 5 (*Books 17–20*). Cambridge: Cambridge University Press.

Eersten, Aniek van den. 2013. "To this well-nightingaled vicinity? Epithets in Apollonius Rhodius' *Argonautica.*" Diss. Universiteit van Amsterdam.

Ehrhardt, Norbert. 1995. "*Ktistai* in den *Argonautika* des Apollonios Rhodios: Beobachtungen zur Entwicklung von Gründungstraditionen in Kyzikos, Kios, Herakleia Pontike und Sinope." *Studien zum antiken Kleinasien III.* Bonn: Habelt. 23–46.

Eichgrün, Egon. 1961. *Kallimachos und Apollonios Rhodios.* Diss. Freie Universität Berlin.

Ekroth, Gunnel. 2002. *The Sacrificial Rituals of Greek Hero-Cults in the Archaic to the Early Hellenistic Periods.* Liège: Centre international d'étude de la religion grecque antique.

Ekroth, Gunnel. 2007. "Heroes and Hero-Cults." *A Companion to Greek Religion.* Ed. Daniel Ogden. Malden, MA: Blackwell. 100–114.

Ekroth, Gunnel. 2009. "The Cult of Heroes." In Albersmeier: 120–143.

Ekroth, Gunnel. 2015. "Heroes—Living or Dead?" *Oxford Handbook of Ancient Greek Religion*. Ed. Esther Eidinow and Julia Kindt. Oxford: Oxford University Press. 383–396.

Eliade, Mircea. 1959 [1949]. *Cosmos and History: The Myth of the Eternal Return*. Trans. Willard R. Trask. New York: Harper.

Erbse, Hartmut. 1953. "Homerscholien und hellenistische Glossare bei Apollonios Rhodios." *Hermes* 81.2: 163–196.

Erskine, Andrew. 2002. "Life after Death: Alexandria and the Body of Alexander." *G&R* 49.2: 163–179.

Evans, Stephen. 2001. *Hymn and Epic: A Study of Their Interplay in Homer and the Homeric Hymns*. Turku: Turun Yliopisto.

Faber, Riemer A. 2017. "The Hellenistic Origins of Memory as Trope for Literary Allusion in Latin Poetry." *Philologus* 161.1: 77–89.

Fantuzzi, Marco. 1980. "La contaminazione dei generi letterari nella letteratura greca ellenistica: Rifiuto del sistema o evoluzione di un sistema?" *L&S* 15: 433–450.

Fantuzzi, Marco. 1988. *Ricerche su Apollonio Rodio: Diacronie della dizione epica*. Rome: Ateneo.

Fantuzzi, Marco. 1989. "La censura delle Simplegadi: Ennio, *Medea*, fr. 1 Jocelyn." *QUCC* 31.1: 119–129.

Fantuzzi, Marco. 1996. "Aitiologie (in der griechischen Dichtung)." *Der neue Pauly. Altertum*: Vol. 1. Ed. Hubert Cancik and Helmuth Schneider. Stuttgart: Metzler. 369–371.

Fantuzzi, Marco. 2001. "Heroes, Descendants of *Hemitheoi*: The Proemium of Theocritus 17 and Simonides 11 W^2." In Boedeker and Sider: 232–241.

Fantuzzi, Marco. 2008a [2001]. "'Homeric' Formularity in the *Argonautica* of Apollonius of Rhodes." In Papanghelis and Rengakos: 221–241.

Fantuzzi, Marco. 2008b. "Which Magic? Which Eros? Apollonius' *Argonautica* and the Different Narrative Roles of Medea as a Sorceress in Love." In Papanghelis and Rengakos: 287–310.

Fantuzzi, Marco, and Richard Hunter. 2004 [2002]. *Tradition and Innovation in Hellenistic Poetry*. English ed. Cambridge: Cambridge University Press.

Faerber, Horst. 1932. *Zur dichterischen Kunst in Apollonios Rhodios' Argonautica: Die Gleichnisse*. Diss. Universität Bonn.

Faraone, Christopher A. 1997. "Salvation and Female Heroics in the Parodos of Aristophanes' *Lysistrata*." *JHS* 117: 38–59.

Faraone, Christopher A. 2016. "On the Eve of Epic: Did the Chryses Episode in *Iliad* 1 Begin Its Life as a Separate Homeric *Hymn*?" *Persistent Forms: Explorations in Historical Poetics*. Ed. Ilya Kliger and Boris Maslov. New York: Fordham University Press. 397–428.

Faraone, Christopher A. 2018. "Seaside Altars of Apollo Delphinios, Embedded Hymns, and the Tripartite Structure of the *Homeric Hymn to Apollo*." *G&R* 65.1: 15–33.

Farnell, Lewis Richard. 1921. *The Hero Cults and Ideas of Immortality*. Oxford: Clarendon.
Farrell, Joseph. 2003. "Classical Genre in Theory and Practice." *New Literary History* 34.3: 383–408.
Faulkner, Andrew. 2008. *The Homeric Hymn to Aphrodite: Introduction, Text, and Commentary*. Oxford: Oxford University Press.
Faulkner, Andrew. 2010a. "Callimachus and His Allusive Virgins: Delos, Hestia, and the *Homeric Hymn to Aphrodite*." *HSCPh* 105: 53–63.
Faulkner, Andrew. 2010b. "The Homeric *Hymn to Dionysus*: P. Oxy. 670." *ZPE* 172: 1–2.
Faulkner, Andrew, ed. 2011a. *The Homeric Hymns: Interpretative Essays*. Oxford: Oxford University Press.
Faulkner, Andrew. 2011b. "Introduction." In Faulkner 2011a: 1–25.
Faulkner, Andrew. 2011c. "The Collection of *Homeric Hymns*: From the Seventh to the Third Centuries BC." In Faulkner 2011a: 175–205.
Faulkner, Andrew. 2015. "The Silence of Zeus: Speech in the *Homeric Hymns*." In Faulkner and Hodkinson: 31–45.
Faulkner, Andrew, Athanassios Vergados, and Andreas Schwab (= FVS), Eds. 2016. *The Reception of the Homeric Hymns*. Oxford: Oxford University Press.
Faulkner, Andrew, and Owen Hodkinson, Eds. 2015. *Hymnic Narrative and the Narratology of Greek Hymns*. Leiden: Brill.
Feeney, D.C. 1987. "Following after Hercules, in Virgil and Apollonius." *PVS* 18: 47–85.
Feeney, D.C. 1991. *The Gods in Epic: Poets and Critics of the Classical Tradition*. Oxford: Clarendon.
Fehling, Detlev. 1969. *Die Wiederholungsfiguren und ihr Gebrauch bei den Griechen vor Gorgias*. Berlin: De Gruyter.
Felson, Nancy. 2011. "Children of Zeus in the *Homeric Hymns*: Generational Succession." In Faulkner: 254–279.
Fernández Contreras, Maria Ángeles. 1996. "Elementos formales en las epifanías de Apolonio de Rodas." *Excerpta philologica* 6: 19–33.
Ferri, S. 1976. "Fenomeni ecologici della Cirenaica costiera nel II millennio a. C. Nuovi dati archeologici su gli Argonauti a Euesperide." *QAL* 8: 11–17.
Finkelberg, Margalit. 1995. "Odysseus and the Genus 'Hero.'" *G&R* 42.1: 1–14.
Fish, Stanley. 1980. *Is There a Text in this Class? The Authority of Interpretive Communities*. Cambridge, MA: Harvard University Press.
Fitch, Edward. 1912. "Apollonius Rhodius and Cyzicus." *AJPh* 33.1: 43–56.
Floyd, Edwin D. 1969. "The Singular Uses of Ἡμέτερος and Ἡμεῖς in Homer." *Glotta* 47: 116–137.
Foley, Helene P., ed. 1994. *The Homeric Hymn to Demeter: Translation, Commentary, and Interpretative Essays*. Princeton: Princeton University Press.
Foley, John Miles, ed. 2005. *A Companion to Ancient Epic*. Malden, MA: Blackwell.

Fontenrose, Joseph. 1959. *Python: A Study of Delphic Myth and Its Origins*. Berkeley: University of California Press.

Fontenrose, Joseph. 1978. *The Delphic Oracle: Its Responses and Operations, with a Catalogue of Responses*. Berkeley: University of California Press.

Ford, Andrew. 1992. *Homer: The Poetry of the Past*. Ithaca: Cornell University Press.

Ford, Andrew. 2002. *The Origins of Criticism: Literary Culture and Poetic Theory in Classical Greece*. Princeton: Princeton University Press.

Ford, Andrew. 2006. "The Genre of Genres: Paeans and *Paian* in Early Greek Poetry." *Poetica* 38.3/4: 277–295.

Ford, Andrew. 2011. *Aristotle as Poet: The Song for Hermias and Its Context*. Oxford: Oxford University Press.

Foster, Andrew. 2007. "*Sema Polyphemou*: A Case of Paraleipsis in the *Argonautica* of Apollonius Rhodius." *CB* 83.2: 247–264.

Foucault, Michel. 1984. *The Foucault Reader*. Ed. Paul Rabinow. New York: Pantheon.

Fowler, Alastair. 1982. *Kinds of Literature: An Introduction to the Theory of Genres and Modes*. Oxford: Clarendon Press.

Fowler, Don. 1997. "On the Shoulders of Giants: Intertextuality and Classical Studies." *MD* 39: 13–34.

Fowler, R.L. 1987. *The Nature of Early Greek Lyric: Three Preliminary Studies*. Toronto: University of Toronto Press.

Fowler, R.L. 1990. "Two More New Verses of Hipponax (and a Spurium of Philoxenus)?" *ICS* 15: 1–22.

Fowler, R.L. 2000–2013. *Early Greek Mythography*. 2 vol. Oxford: Oxford University Press.

Fränkel, Hermann. 1957. "Das Argonautenepos des Apollonios." *MH* 14.1: 1–19.

Fränkel, Hermann. 1968. *Noten zu den Argonautika des Apollonios*. Munich: Beck.

Fränkel, Hermann. 1975. *Early Greek Poetry and Philosophy*. Trans. Moses Hadas and James Willis. Oxford: Blackwell.

Frankfort, Henri. 1948. *Kingship and the Gods: A Study of Ancient Near Eastern Religion as the Integration of Society and Nature*. Chicago: University of Chicago Press.

Fraser, P.M. 1972. *Ptolemaic Alexandria*. 3 vol. Oxford: Clarendon.

Frazer, J.G. 1913. *Pausanias's Description of Greece*. Vol. 5. London: Macmillan.

Frazer, J.G. 1921. *Apollodorus. The Library*. 2 vol. London: Heinemann.

Friedländer, P. 1914. "Das Proömium der *Theogonie*." *Hermes* 49.1: 1–16.

Fröhder, Dorothea. 1994. *Die dichterische Form der Homerischen Hymnen: Untersucht am Typus der mittelgrossen Preislieder*. Hildesheim: Georg Olms.

Fuhrer, Therese. 1999. "Der Götterhymnus als Prahlrede: Zum Spiel mit einer literarischen Form in Ovids *Metamorphosen*." *Hermes* 127.3: 356–367.

Furley, William. 1995. "Praise and Persuasion in Greek Hymns." *JHS* 115: 29–46.

Furley, William D., and Jan Maarten Bremer. 2001. *Greek Hymns: Selected Cult Songs from the Archaic to the Hellenistic Period*. 2 vol. Tübingen: Mohr Siebeck.

Fusillo, Massimo. 1985. *Il tempo delle Argonautiche: Un'analisi del racconto in Apollonio Rodio*. Rome: Ateneo.

Fusillo, Massimo. 1994. "El sueño de Medea." *Revista de Occidente* 158–159: 92–102.

Gainsford, Peter. 2003. "Where does the Proem of the *Odyssey* End?" *Theatres of Action: Papers for Chris Dearden*. Ed. John Davidson and Arthur Pomeroy. Auckland: Polygraphia. 1–11.

Galinsky, G. Karl. 1972. *The Herakles Theme: The Adaptations of the Hero in Literature from Homer to the Twentieth Century*. Oxford: Basil Blackwell.

Gantz, Timothy. 1993. *Early Greek Myth: A Guide to Literary and Artistic Sources*. Baltimore: Johns Hopkins University Press.

García, John F. 2002. "Symbolic Action in the Homeric Hymns: The Theme of Recognition." *CA* 21.1: 5–39.

Gardella Hueso, Mariana. 2018. "Un enigma sobre el enigma: Safo de Lesbos y el acertijo de la carta." *Cuadernos de filosofía* 71: 5–18.

Garson, R.W. 1972. "Homeric Echoes in Apollonius Rhodius' *Argonautica*." *CPh* 67.1: 1–9.

Garvie, A.F. 2009. *Aeschylus. Persae*. Oxford: Oxford University Press.

Gassner, Jakob. 1972. *Kataloge im römischen Epos: Vergil, Ovid, Lucan*. Diss. Ludwig-Maximilians-Universität München.

Gemoll, Albert. 1886. *Die homerischen Hymnen*. Leipzig: Teubner.

Genette, Gérard. 1980 [1972]. *Narrative Discourse: An Essay in Method*. Trans. Jane E. Lewin. Ithaca: Cornell University Press.

George, Edward V. 1977. "Apollonius, *Argonautica* 4.984–985: Apology for a Shameful Tale." *Rivista di Studi Classici* 25: 360–364.

Gercke, Alfred. 1889. "Alexandrinische Studien." *RhM* 44: 127–150.

Germany, Robert. 2005. "The Figure of Echo in the *Homeric Hymn to Pan*." *AJPh* 126.2: 187–208.

Giangiulio, Maurizio. 1981. "Deformità eroiche e tradizioni di fondazione: Batto, Miscello e l'oracolo delfico." *ASNP* 11: 1–24.

Giangrande, G. 1967. "'Arte Allusiva' and Alexandrian Epic Poetry." *CQ* 17.1: 85–97.

Giangrande, G. 1968. "On the Use of the Vocative in Alexandrian Epic." *CQ* 18.1: 52–59.

Giangrande, G. 1970. "Hellenistic Poetry and Homer." *AC* 39.1: 46–77.

Giangrande, G. 1971. Review of Bornmann 1968. *CR* 21.3: 354–357.

Giangrande, G. 1977. "Aspects of Apollonius Rhodius' Language." *Papers of the Liverpool Latin Seminar, 1976: Classical Latin Poetry, Medieval Latin Poetry, Greek Poetry*. Ed. Francis Cairns. Leeds: Francis Cairns. 271–291.

Giaquinta, Irene. 2021. "Hypsipyle from Euripides to Apollonius Rhodius: New Perspectives Regarding Female Power in Hellenistic Poetry." *HG* 26: 121–138.

Gigon, Olof, trans., and Rainer Nickel, ed. 2001. *Aristoteles. Die Nikomachische Ethik*. Düsseldorf: Artemis & Winkler.

Gildersleeve, B.L., and C.W.E. Miller. 1903. "The Vocative in Apollonios Rhodios." *AJPh* 24.2: 197–199.
Gillies, Marshall M. 1928. *The Argonautica of Apollonius Rhodius: Book III*. Salem, NH: Ayer.
Glei, Reinhold F. 2008 [2001]. "Outlines of Apollonian Scholarship 1955–1999." In Papanghelis and Rengakos: 1–28.
Glei, Reinhold, and Stephanie Natzel-Glei. 1996. *Apollonios von Rhodos: Das Argonautenepos*. 2 vol. Darmstadt: WBG.
Gnoli, Gherardo, and Jean-Pierre Vernant, Eds. 1982. *La mort, les morts dans les sociétés anciennes*. Cambridge: Cambridge University Press.
Goldhill, Simon. 1991. *The Poet's Voice: Essays on Poetics and Greek Literature*. Cambridge: Cambridge University Press.
Goldhill, Simon. 2010. "Cultural History and Aesthetics: Why Kant is No Place to Start Reception Studies." *Theorising Performance: Greek Drama, Cultural History and Critical Practice*. Ed. Edith Hall and Stephe Harrop. London: Duckworth. 56–70.
González, José M. 2000. "*Musai Hypophetores*: Apollonius of Rhodes on Inspiration and Interpretation." *HSCPh* 100: 268–292.
Goodwin, Charles J. 1891. *Apollonius Rhodius: His Figures, Syntax, and Vocabulary*. Diss. Johns Hopkins University.
Gow, A.S.F. 1942. "The Twenty-Second *Idyll* of Theocritus." *CR* 56.1: 11–18.
Gow, A.S.F. 1952. *Theocritus*. 2 vol. 2nd ed. Cambridge: Cambridge University Press.
Graziosi, Barbara. 2002. *Inventing Homer: The Early Reception of Epic*. Cambridge: Cambridge University Press.
Green, Peter. 1988. "The Armchair Epic: Apollonius Rhodius and the Voyage of Argo." *Southern Humanities Review* 22: 1–15.
Green, Peter. 2007 [1997]. *The Argonautika*. Expanded ed. Berkeley: University of California Press.
Grethlein, Jonas. 2008. "Memory and Material Objects in the *Iliad* and the *Odyssey*." *JHS* 128: 27–51.
Griffin, Jasper. 1977. "The Epic Cycle and the Uniqueness of Homer." *JHS* 97: 39–53.
Griffin, Jasper. 1980. *Homer on Life and Death*. Oxford: Clarendon.
Griffiths, F.T. 1976. "Theocritus' Silent Dioscuri." *GRBS* 17: 353–367.
Grillo, Antonino. 1988. *Tra filologia e narratologia: Dai poemi omerici ad Apollonio Rodio, Ilias Latina, Ditti-Settimio, Darete Frigio, Draconzio*. Rome: Ateneo.
Groddeck, Gottfried Ernst. 1786. *Commentatio de hymnorum Homericorum reliquiis*. Göttingen: Dieterich.
Guinee, David A. 1999. *The Roman Argonautica: Valerius Flaccus and the Epic Tradition*. Diss. University of Michigan.
Gummert, Peter H. 1992. *Die Erzählstruktur in den Argonautika des Apollonios Rhodios*. Frankfurt am Main: Peter Lang.

Guthrie, W.K.C. 1950. *The Greeks and Their Gods*. Boston: Beacon.
Gutzwiller, Kathryn J. 1981. *Studies in the Hellenistic Epyllion*. Königstein: Hain.
Haacke, August. 1842. *Commentationis de elecutione Apollonii Rhodii particula*. Diss. Martin-Luther-Universität Halle-Wittenberg.
Habicht, Christian. 2017 [1956]. *Divine Honors for Mortal Men in Greek Cities: The Early Cases*. Trans. John Noël Dillon. Ann Arbor: Michigan Classical Press.
Hack, Roy Kenneth. 1929. "Homer and the Cult of Heroes." *TAPhA* 60: 57–74.
Hadas, Moses. 1932. "Apollonius Called the Rhodian." *Classical Weekly* 26.6: 41–54.
Hadjittofi, Fotini. 2008. "Callimachus' Sexy Athena: *The Hymn to Athena* and the *Homeric Hymn to Aphrodite*." *MD* 60: 9–37.
Hadzisteliou Price, Theodora. 1973. "Hero-Cult and Homer." *Historia* 22.2: 129–144.
Hadzisteliou Price, Theodora. 1979. "Hero Cult in the 'Age of Homer' and Earlier." In Bowersock, Burkert, and Putnam: 219–228.
Hägg, Robin, ed. 1999. *Ancient Greek Hero Cult*. Stockholm: Åström.
Hall, Alexander E.W. 2012. *'To the Beguiling Dance of the Gods': Genre and the Short Homeric Hymns*. Diss. University of Wisconsin–Madison.
Hall, Alexander E.W. 2013. "Dating the *Homeric Hymn to Selene*: Evidence and Implications." *GRBS* 53: 15–30.
Hall, Alexander E.W. 2021. "The Evolving Arrangement of the *Homeric Hymns*." *Poems without Poets: Approaches to Anonymous Ancient Poetry*. Ed. Boris Kayachev. Cambridge: Cambridge Philological Society. 13–31.
Hall, Alexander E.W. 2023. "Rhapsody in Siracusa: Sicily and the *Homeric Hymns*." In Dova, Callaway, and Gazis: 77–91.
Hall, Jonathan M. 1999. "Beyond the *Polis*: The Multilocality of Heroes." In Hägg: 49–59.
Händel, Paul. 1954. *Beobachtungen zur epischen Technik des Apollonios Rhodios*. Munich: Beck.
Harder, M. Annette. 1992. "Insubstantial Voices: Some Observations on the *Hymns* of Callimachus." *CQ* 42.2: 384–394.
Harder, M. Annette. 1993. "Aspects of the Structure of Callimachus' *Aetia*." *HG* 1: 99–110.
Harder, M. Annette. 1994. "Travel Descriptions in the *Argonautica* of Apollonius Rhodius." *Travel Fact and Travel Fiction: Studies on Fiction, Literary Tradition, Scholarly Discovery and Observation in Travel Writing*. Ed. Zweder von Martels. Leiden: Brill. 16–29.
Harder, M. Annette. 2002. "Intertextuality in Callimachus' *Aetia*." *Callimaque: Sept exposés suivis de discussions*. Geneva: Fondation Hardt. 189–233.
Harder, M. Annette. 2012. *Callimachus. Aetia*. 2 vol. Oxford: Oxford University Press.
Harder, M. Annette. 2019a. "Sons and Fathers in the Catalogue of Argonauts in Apollonius' *Argonautica* 1.23–233." *Eugesta* 9: 1–25.
Harder, M. Annette. 2019b. "Aspects of the Interaction between Apollonius Rhodius and Callimachus." *Aevum(ant)* 19: 9–34

Harder, M. Annette. 2021. "Before the Canon: The Reception of Greek Tragedy in Hellenistic Poetry." *Reception in the Greco-Roman World: Literary Studies in Theory and Practice*. Ed. Marco Fantuzzi, Helen Morales, and Tim Whitmarsh. Cambridge: Cambridge University Press. 219–240.

Harder, Annette, and Martine Cuypers, Eds. 2005. *Beginning from Apollo: Studies in Apollonius Rhodius and the Argonautic Tradition*. Leuven: Peeters.

Hardie, Alex. 2009. "Etymologising the Muse." *MD* 62: 9–57.

Hardie, Philip. 2006. "Virgil's Ptolemaic Relations." *JRS* 96: 25–41.

Hardie, Philip. 2013. *"Redeeming The Text*, Reception Studies, and the Renaissance." *Classical Receptions Journal* 5.2: 190–198.

Hardwick, Lorna. 2003. *Reception Studies*. Oxford: Oxford University Press.

Harmon, D.P. 1973. "Nostalgia for the Age of Heroes in Catullus 64." *Latomus* 32.2: 311–331.

Harrison, S.J. 2007. *Generic Enrichment in Vergil and Horace*. Oxford: Oxford University Press.

Harrison, Thomas. 2002. *Divinity and History: The Religion of Herodotus*. Oxford: Oxford University Press.

Harvey, A.E. 1955. "The Classification of Greek Lyric Poetry." *CQ* 5.3–4: 157–175.

Haslam, Michael W. 1993. "Callimachus' *Hymns*." *HG* 1: 111–125.

Hasluck, F.W. 1910. *Cyzicus*. Cambridge: Cambridge University Press.

Haubold, Johannes. 2001. "Epic with an End: An Interpretation of *Homeric Hymns* 15 and 20." *Homer, Tragedy, and Beyond: Essays in Honour of P.E. Easterling*. Ed. Felix Budelmann and Pantelis Michelakis. London: Society for the Promotion of Hellenic Studies. 23–41.

Hawes, Greta. 2014. *Rationalizing Myth in Antiquity*. Oxford: Oxford University Press.

Headlam, Walter. 1922. *Herodas. The Mimes and Fragments*. Ed. A.D. Knox. Cambridge: Cambridge University Press.

Heath, Malcolm. 2000. "Do Heroes Eat Fish? Athenaeus on the Homeric Lifestyle." *Athenaeus and His World: Reading Greek Culture in the Roman Empire*. Ed. David Braund and John Wilkins. Exeter: University of Exeter Press. 342–352.

Heerink, Mark. 2010. "Merging Paradigms: Translating Pharaonic Ideology in Theocritus' *Idyll* 17." *Interkulturalität in der Alten Welt. Vorderasien, Hellas, Ägypten und die vielfältigen Ebenen des Kontakts*. Ed. Robert Rollinger et al. Wiesbaden: Harrassowitz. 383–408.

Heiserman, Arthur. 1977. *The Novel before the Novel: Essays and Discussions about the Beginnings of Prose Fiction in the West*. Chicago: University of Chicago Press.

Henrichs, Albert. 1983. "The 'Sobriety' of Oedipus: Sophocles *OC* 100 Misunderstood." *HSCPh* 87: 87–100.

Henrichs, Albert. 1993. "Gods in Action: The Poetics of Divine Performance in the *Hymns* of Callimachus." *HG* 1: 127–147.

Hensel, Ludwig. 1908. *Weissagungen in der alexandrinischen Poesie*. Diss. Justus-Liebig-Universität Gießen.

Herington, John. 1985. *Poetry into Drama: Early Tragedy and the Greek Poetic Tradition*. Berkeley: University of California Press.

Herter, Hans. 1944–1955. "Bericht über die Literatur zur hellenistischen Dichtung seit dem Jahre 1921. II. Teil: Apollonios Rhodios." *Bursians Jahresbericht über die Fortschritte der Altertumswissenschaft* 285: 213–410.

Heubeck, Alfred, Stephanie West, and J.B. Hainsworth. 1988. *A Commentary on Homer's Odyssey, Volume I: Introduction and Books I–VIII*. Oxford: Clarendon.

Hinds, Stephen. 1987. *The Metamorphosis of Persephone: Ovid and the Self-Conscious Muse*. Cambridge: Cambridge University Press.

Hinds, Stephen. 1998. *Allusion and Intertext: Dynamics of Appropriation in Roman Poetry*. Cambridge: Cambridge University Press.

Hitch, Sarah. 2012. "Hero Cult in Apollonius Rhodius." *HG* 16: 131–162.

Hoekstra, A. 1969. *The Sub-Epic Stage of the Formulaic Tradition: Studies in the Homeric Hymns to Apollo, to Aphrodite and to Demeter*. Amsterdam: North-Holland.

Hoekstra, A. 1981. *Epic Verse Before Homer: Three Studies*. Amsterdam: North-Holland Publishing.

Hölbl, Günther. 2001 [1994]. *A History of the Ptolemaic Empire*. Trans. Tina Saavedra. London: Routledge.

Holub, Robert. 1995. "Reception Theory: School of Constance." *The Cambridge History of Literary Criticism, Volume 8: From Formalism to Poststructuralism*. Ed. Raman Selden. Cambridge: Cambridge University Press. 319–346.

Hopkinson, N. 1984. *Callimachus. Hymn to Demeter*. Cambridge: Cambridge University Press.

Hopkinson, N. 1988. *A Hellenistic Anthology*. Cambridge: Cambridge University Press.

Hopkinson, Neil, ed. and comm., and Francis Vian, trans. 1994. *Nonnos de Panopolis. Les Dionysiaques*. Vol. 8: *Chants XX–XXIV*. Paris: Les Belles Lettres.

Hornblower, Simon. 2015. *Lykophron. Alexandra*. Oxford: Oxford University Press.

Horsfall, Nicholas. 1988. "Camilla, o i limiti dell'invenzione." *Athenaeum* 66: 31–51.

Horsfall, Nicholas. 1990. "Virgil and the Illusory Footnote." *Papers of the Leeds International Latin Seminar*. Vol. 6. Ed. Francis Cairns and Malcolm Heath. Leeds: Francis Cairns. 49–63

Hosty, Matthew. 2013. *An Edition with Commentary of the Batrachomyomachia*. Diss. St. John's College, Oxford.

de Hoz, María Paz. 1998. "Los himnos homéricos cortos y las plegarias cultuales." *Emerita* 66.1: 49–66.

Hübscher, P. Adalgott. 1940. *Die Charakteristik der Personen in Apollonios' Argonautika*. Diss. Universität Freiburg in der Schweiz.

Hughes, Dennis D. 1999. "Hero Cult, Heroic Honors, Heroic Dead: Some Developments in the Hellenistic and Roman Periods." In Hägg: 167–175.

Hunter, Richard. 1986. "Apollo and the Argonauts: Two notes on Ap. Rhod. 2, 669–719." *MH* 43: 50–60.

Hunter, Richard. 1987. "Medea's Flight: The Fourth Book of the *Argonautica*." *CQ* 37.1: 129–139.

Hunter, Richard. 1989. *Apollonius of Rhodes: Argonautica Book III*. Cambridge: Cambridge University Press.

Hunter, Richard. 1991. "Greek and Non-Greek in the *Argonautica* of Apollonius." Ἑλληνισμός: *Quelques jalons pour une histoire de l'identité grecque: Actes du Colloque de Strasbourg, 25–27 Octobre 1989*. Ed. S. Saïd. Leiden: Brill. 81–99.

Hunter, Richard. 1992. "Writing the God: Form and Meaning in Callimachus, *Hymn to Athena*." *MD* 29: 9–34.

Hunter, Richard. 1993. *The Argonautica of Apollonius: Literary Studies*. Cambridge: Cambridge University Press.

Hunter, Richard. 1995. "The Divine and Human Map of the *Argonautica*." *SyllClass* 6: 13–27.

Hunter, Richard. 1996. *Theocritus and the Archaeology of Greek Poetry*. Cambridge: Cambridge University Press.

Hunter, Richard. 1999. *Theocritus: A Selection*. Cambridge: Cambridge University Press.

Hunter, Richard. 2000. "εἰς ἔτος ἐξ ἔτεος γλυκερώτεραι: The *Argonautica* after Hermann Fränkel." In Pretagostini: 63–77.

Hunter, Richard. 2003. *Theocritus: Encomium of Ptolemy Philadelphus*. Berkeley: University of California Press.

Hunter, Richard. 2005. "Generic Consciousness in the *Orphic Argonautica*?" In Paschalis: 149–168.

Hunter, Richard. 2006a. *The Shadow of Callimachus: Studies in the Reception of Hellenistic Poetry at Rome*. Cambridge: Cambridge University Press.

Hunter, Richard. 2006b. Review of Vamvouri Ruffy 2004. *JHS* 126: 161–162.

Hunter, Richard. 2008 [2001]. "The Poetics of Narrative in the *Argonautica*." In Papanghelis and Rengakos: 115–146.

Hunter, Richard. 2009. *Critical Moments in Classical Literature: Studies in the Ancient View of Literature and its Uses*. Cambridge: Cambridge University Press.

Hunter, Richard. 2014. *Hesiodic Voices: Studies in the Ancient Reception of Hesiod's Works and Days*. Cambridge: Cambridge University Press.

Hunter, Richard. 2015. *Apollonius of Rhodes: Argonautica Book IV*. Cambridge: Cambridge University Press.

Hunter, Richard, and Therese Fuhrer. 2002. "Imaginary Gods? Poetic Theology in the *Hymns* of Callimachus." *Callimaque: Sept exposés suivis de discussions*. Geneva: Fondation Hardt. 143–187.

Hunzinger, Christine. 2012. "À qui l'aède raconte-t-il l'histoire du dieu? Figures du narrataire dans les *Hymnes homériques*." In Bouchon, Brillet-Dubois, and Le Meur-Weissman: 37–58.

Hurst, André. 1964. "Le retour nocturne des Argonautes." *MH* 21.4: 232–237.

Hurst, André. 1967. *Apollonios de Rhodes, manière et coherence: Contribution à l'étude de l'esthétique alexandrine*. Rome: Institut suisse de Rome.

Hutchinson, G.O. 1988. *Hellenistic Poetry*. Oxford: Clarendon.

Hutchinson, G.O. 2008. *Talking Books: Readings in Hellenistic and Roman Books of Poetry*. Oxford: Oxford University Press.

Hutchinson, G.O. 2013. "Genre and Super-Genre." *Generic Interfaces in Latin Literature: Encounters, Interactions and Transformations*. Ed. Theodore D. Papanghelis, Stephen J. Harrison, and Stavros Frangoulidis. Berlin: De Gruyter. 19–34.

Iacobacci, Gabriella. 1993. "Orfeo Argonauta: Apollonio Rodio 1, 494–511." *Orfeo e l'Orfismo*. Ed. Agostino Masaracchia. Rome: GEI. 77–92.

Ibscher, Rolf. 1939. *Gestalt der Szene und Form der Rede in den Argonautika des Apollonios Rhodios*. Diss. Ludwig-Maximilians-Universität München.

Ilgen, Karl David. 1796. *Hymni Homerici cum reliquis carminibus minoribus Homero tribui solitis et Batrachomyomachia*. Halle: Libraria Hemmerdeana.

Jackson, Steven. 1990. "Apollonius of Rhodes and the Corn-goddess: A Note on *Arg.* 4.869–876." *LCM* 15.4: 53–56.

Jackson, Steven. 1993. *Creative Selectivity in Apollonius' Argonautica*. Amsterdam: Hakkert.

Jackson, Steven. 1995. "Apollonius of Rhodes: Author of the *Lesbou Ktisis*?" *QUCC* 49.1: 57–66.

Jackson, Steven. 1999. "Apollonius of Rhodes: The Asopid Dichotomy." *SIFC* 3.2: 137–142.

Jacoby, Felix. 1904. *Das Marmor Parium*. Berlin: Weidmann.

James, A.W. 1981. "Apollonius Rhodius and His Sources: Interpretative Notes on the *Argonautica*." *Corolla Londiniensis* 1: 59–86.

Janko, R. 1979. "Βώσεσθε Revisited." *CQ* 29.1: 215–216.

Janko, R. 1981. "The Structure of the *Homeric Hymns*: A Study in Genre." *Hermes* 109.1: 9–24.

Janko, R. 1982. *Homer, Hesiod and the Hymns: Diachronic Development in Epic Diction*. Cambridge: Cambridge University Press.

Janko, R. 1986. "The *Shield of Heracles* and the Legend of Cycnus." *CQ* 36.1: 38–59.

Janko, R. 1994. *The Iliad: A Commentary*. Vol. 4: *Books 13–16*. Cambridge: Cambridge University Press.

Janko, R. 2012. "πρῶτόν τε καὶ ὕστατον αἰὲν ἀείδειν: Relative Chronology and the Literary History of the Early Greek Epos." In Andersen and Haug: 20–43.

Jebb, Richard Claverhouse. 1883. *Sophocles: The Plays and Fragments*. Vol. 1. Cambridge: Cambridge University Press.

Johnston, Sarah Iles. 1999. *Restless Dead: Encounters between the Living and the Dead in Ancient Greece*. Berkeley: University of California Press.

Johnston, Sarah Iles. 2015. "The Greek Mythic Story World." *Arethusa* 48.3: 283–311.

Jones, Christopher P. 2010. *New Heroes in Antiquity: From Achilles to Antinoos*. Cambridge, MA: Harvard University Press.

Jong, Irene J.F. de. 1993. "Studies in Homeric Denomination." *Mnemosyne* 46.3: 289–306.

Jong, Irene J.F. de. 2004a [1987]. *Narrators and Focalizers: The Presentation of the Story in the Iliad*. 2nd ed. Bristol: Bristol Classical Press.

Jong, Irene J.F. de. 2004b. "Homer." *SAGN* 1: 13–24.

Jong, Irene J.F. de. 2009. "Metalepsis in Ancient Greek Literature." *Narratology and Interpretation: The Content of Narrative Form in Ancient Literature*. Ed. Jonas Grethlein and Antonios Rengakos. Berlin: De Gruyter. 87–115.

Jong, Irene J.F. de. 2012. "The *Homeric Hymns*." *SAGN* 3: 39–53.

Jong, Irene J.F. de. 2014. *Narratology and Classics: A Practical Guide*. Oxford: Oxford University Press.

Jong, Irene J.F. de. 2018. "The *Homeric Hymns*." *SAGN* 4: 64–79.

Jong, Irene J.F. de. 2022a. "Homer." *SAGN* 5: 33–55.

Jong, Irene J.F. de. 2022b. "The *Homeric Hymns*." *SAGN* 5: 77–99.

Júnior, Fernando Rodrigues. 2020. "Μοῦσαι ὑποφήτορες: A relação entre o narrador e as Musas nos três prólogos das *Argonáuticas* de Apolônio de Rodes." *Conexão Letras* 15.24: 107–119.

Kahane, Ahuvia. 1994a. "Callimachus, Apollonius, and the Poetics of Mud." *TAPhA* 124: 121–133.

Kahane, Ahuvia. 1994b. *The Interpretation of Order: A Study in the Poetics of Homeric Repetition*. Oxford: Clarendon.

Kaibel, G. 1887. "Sententiarum Liber Quartus." *Hermes* 22.4: 497–514.

Kambylis, Athanasios. 1965. *Die Dichterweihe und ihre Symbolik: Untersuchungen zu Hesiodos, Kallimachos, Properz und Ennius*. Heidelberg: Winter.

Kampakoglou, Alexandros. 2016. "Danaus βουγενής: Greco-Egyptian Mythology and Ptolemaic Kingship." *GRBS* 56: 111–139.

Kampakoglou, Alexandros. 2019. *Studies in the Reception of Pindar in Ptolemaic Poetry*. Berlin: De Gruyter.

Kampakoglou, Alexandros. 2021. "Modern Trends in the Study of Theocritus." *Brill's Companion to Theocritus*. Ed. Poulheria Kyriakou, Evina Sistakou, and Antonios Rengakos. Leiden: Brill. 1–38.

Karanika, Andromache. 2010. "Inside Orpheus' Songs: Orpheus as an Argonaut in Apollonius Rhodius' *Argonautica*." *GRBS* 50: 391–410.

Katz, Joshua T. 2013. "The Hymnic Long Alpha: Μούσας ἀείδω and Related Incipits in Archaic Greek Poetry." *Proceedings of the 24th Annual UCLA Indo-European Conference*. Ed. Stephanie W. Jamison, H. Craig Melchert, and Brent Vine, with Angelo Mercado. Bremen: Hempen. 87–101.

Kearns, Emily. 1989. *The Heroes of Attica*. London: Institute of Classical Studies.

Kearns, Emily. 1992. "Between God and Man: Status and Function of Heroes and Their Sanctuaries." *Le sanctuaire grec*. Ed. Jean Bingen. Vandœuvres: Fondation Hardt. 65–99.

Kearns, Emily. 1998. "The Nature of Heroines." *The Sacred and the Feminine in Ancient Greece*. Ed. Sue Blundell and Margaret Williamson. London: Routledge. 74–86.

Keith, Alison. 1999. "Versions of Epic Masculinity in Ovid's *Metamorphoses*." *Ovidian Transformations: Essays on the Metamorphoses and its Reception*. Ed. Philip Hardie, Alessandro Barchiesi, and Stephen Hinds. Cambridge: Cambridge Philological Society. 214–239.

Kelly, Adrian. 2014. "Hellenistic Arming in the *Batrachomyomachia*." *CQ* 64.1: 410–413.

Kerekes, Pavlos. 1913. "Οἱ τρόποι τῶν Ἀργοναυτικῶν τοῦ Ἀπολλώνιου τοῦ Ῥοδίου." *Egyetemes Philologiai Közlöny* 37: 385–408.

Keyssner, Karl. 1932. *Gottesvorstellung und Lebensauffassung im griechischen Hymnus*. Stuttgart: W. Kohlhammer.

Kidd, Douglas. 1997. *Aratus. Phaenomena*. Cambridge: Cambridge University Press.

Kirk, G.S. 1985. *The Iliad: A Commentary*. Vol. 1: *Books 1–4*. Cambridge: Cambridge University Press.

Klein, Theodore M. 1974. "The Role of Callimachus in the Development of the Concept of Counter-Genre." *Latomus* 33: 217–231.

Klein, Theodore M. 1975. "Callimachus, Apollonius Rhodius, and the Concept of the 'Big Book.'" *Eranos* 73: 16–25.

Kleywegt, A.J. 2005. *Valerius Flaccus, Argonautica, Book 1: A Commentary*. Leiden: Brill.

Klinger, Friedrich. 1964. *Studien zur griechischen und römischen Literatur*. Zurich: Artemis.

Klooster, Jacqueline. 2007. "Apollonius of Rhodes." *SAGN* 2: 63–80.

Klooster, Jacqueline. 2011. *Poetry as Window and Mirror: Positioning the Poet in Hellenistic Poetry*. Leiden: Brill.

Klooster, Jacqueline. 2012. "Apollonius of Rhodes." *SAGN* 3: 55–76.

Klooster, Jacqueline. 2013a. "Apostrophe in Homer, Apollonius and Callimachus." *Über die Grenze: Metalepse in Text- und Bildmedien des Altertums*. Ed. Ute E. Eisen and Peter von Möllendorff. Berlin: De Gruyter. 151–173.

Klooster, Jacqueline. 2013b. "Argo was Here: The Ideology of Geographical Space in the *Argonautica* of Apollonius of Rhodes." *The Ideologies of Lived Space in Literary Texts, Ancient and Modern*. Ed. Jacqueline Klooster and Jo Heirman. Ghent: Academia Press. 159–173.

Klooster, Jacqueline. 2014. "Time, Space, and Ideology in the Aetiological Narratives of Apollonius Rhodius' *Argonautica*." *Von Ursachen sprechen: Eine aitiologische Spurensuche.* = *Telling Origins: On the Lookout for Aetiology*. Ed. Christiane Reitz and Anke Walter. Hildesheim: Georg Olms. 519–543.

Klooster, Jacqueline. 2018. "Apollonius of Rhodes." *SAGN* 4: 80–99.
Klooster, Jacqueline. 2019. "The Thera Episode in *Argonautica* IV Reconsidered in Light of the Poetic Interaction between Apollonius and Callimachus." *Aevum(ant)* 19: 57–75.
Klooster, Jacqueline. 2022. "Apollonius of Rhodes." *SAGN* 5: 100–119.
Knaack, Georg. 1887. *Callimachea*. Szczecin: Herrcke & Lebeling.
Knauer, Georg Nicolaus. 1964. *Die Aeneis und Homer: Studien zur poetischen Technik Vergils, mit Listen der Homerzitate in der Aeneis*. Göttingen: Vandenhoeck & Ruprecht.
Knight, Virginia. 1995. *The Renewal of Epic: Responses to Homer in the Argonautica of Apollonius*. Leiden: Brill.
Knox, Bernard M.W. 1968. "Silent Reading in Antiquity." *GRBS* 9.4: 421–435.
Knox, Peter E. 1985. "Wine, Water, and Callimachean Polemics." *HSCPh* 89: 107–119.
Koenen, Ludwig. 1993. "The Ptolemaic King as a Religious Figure." In Bulloch et al.: 25–115.
Koenen, Ludwig. 1994. "Greece, the Near East, and Egypt: Cyclic Destruction in Hesiod and the *Catalogue of Women*." *TAPhA* 124: 1–34.
Kofler, Johann. 1890. "Die Gleichnisse bei Apollonios Rhodios." *Jahresbericht des f.b. Privat-Gymnasiums am Seminarium Vincentinum in Brixen* 15: 1–58.
Köhnken, Adolf. 1965. *Apollonios Rhodios und Theokrit: Die Hylas- und die Amykosgeschichten beider Dichter und die Frage der Priorität*. Göttingen: Vandenhoeck & Ruprecht.
Köhnken, Adolf. 2000. "Der Status Jasons: Besonderheiten der Darstellungstechnik in den *Argonautika* des Apollonios Rhodios." *HG* 4: 55–68.
Köhnken, Adolf. 2003a. "Apoll-Aitien bei Kallimachos und Apollonios." In Accorinti and Chuvin: 207–213.
Köhnken, Adolf. 2003b. "Herakles und Orpheus als mythische Referenzfiguren ('Identifikations-' bzw. 'Integrationsfigur') im hellenistischen Epos." *Literarische Konstituierung von Identifikationsfiguren in der Antike*. Ed. Barbara Aland, Johannes Hahn, and Christian Ronning. Tübingen: Mohr Siebeck. 19–27.
Köhnken, Adolf. 2008 [2001]. "Hellenistic Chronology: Theocritus, Callimachus, and Apollonius Rhodius." In Papanghelis and Rengakos: 73–94.
Köhnken, Adolf. 2010. "Apollonius' *Argonautica*." In Clauss and Cuypers: 136–150.
Koller, Hermann. 1956. "Das kitharodische Prooimion: Eine formgeschichtliche Untersuchung." *Philologus* 100: 159–206.
Konstan, David. 1977. *Catullus' Indictment of Rome: The Meaning of Catullus 64*. Amsterdam: Hakkert.
Konstan, David. 1993. "Neoteric Epic: Catullus 64." *Roman Epic*. Ed. A.J. Boyle. London: Routledge. 59–78.
Korenjak, Martin. 1994. "Orpheus bei Apollonios Rhodios." Dipl.-Arb. Innsbruck.

Korenjak, Martin. 2009. "ΛΕΥΚΗ: Was bedeutet das erste 'Akrostichon'?" *RhM* 152.3/4: 392–396.

Korpel, Marjo, and Johannes de Moor. 2017. "The Leviathan in the Ancient Near East." *Playing with Leviathan: Interpretation and Reception of Monsters from the Biblical World*. Ed. Koert van Bekkum et al. Leiden: Brill. 1–18.

Kowerski, Lawrence M. 2008. "A Competition in Praise: An Allusion to Simon. fr. 11 W^2 in Theoc. *Id.* 22.214–223." *Mnemosyne* 61.4: 568–585.

Kraup, Per. 1948. "Verwendung von Abstrakta in der direkten Rede bei Homer." *C&M* 10: 1–17.

Krevans, N. 2000. "On the Margins of Epic: The Foundation-Poems of Apollonius." *HG* 4: 69–84.

Kroll, Wilhelm. 1924. *Studien zum Verständnis der römischen Literatur*. Stuttgart: J.B. Metzler.

Kronenberg, Leah. 2018a. "Seeing the Light, Part I: Aratus's Interpretation of Homer's *LEUKĒ* Acrostic." *Dictynna* 15: 1–11.

Kronenberg, Leah. 2018b. "Seeing the Light, Part II: The Reception of Aratus's *LEPTĒ* Acrostic in Greek and Latin Literature." *Dictynna* 15: 1–32.

Kühlmann, Wilhelm. 1973. *Katalog und Erzählung: Studien zu Konstanz und Wandel einer literarischen Form in der antiken Epik*. Diss. Albert-Ludwigs-Universität Freiburg.

Kurke, Leslie. 2000. "The Strangeness of 'Song Culture': Archaic Greek Poetry." *Literature in the Greek and Roman Worlds: A New Perspective*. Ed. Oliver Taplin. Oxford: Oxford University Press. 58–87.

Kyriakou, Poulheria. 1995. *Homeric Hapax Legomena in the Argonautica of Apollonius: A Literary Study*. Stuttgart: Franz Steiner.

Kyriakou, Poulheria. 2006. *A Commentary on Euripides' Iphigenia in Tauris*. Berlin: De Gruyter.

Lane Fox, Robin. 2008. *Travelling Heroes: Greeks and their Myths in the Epic Age of Homer*. London: Allen Lane.

Lardinois, André. 1997. "Modern Paroemiology and the Use of *Gnomai* in Homer's *Iliad*." *CPh* 92.3: 213–234.

Larson, Jennifer. 1995. *Greek Heroine Cults*. Madison: University of Wisconsin Press.

Larson, Jennifer. 2001. *Greek Nymphs: Myth, Cult, Lore*. Oxford: Oxford University Press.

Larson, Jennifer. 2007. *Ancient Greek Cults: A Guide*. Routledge: New York.

Lawall, Gilbert. 1966. "Apollonius' *Argonautica*: Jason as Anti-Hero." *YClS* 19: 121–169.

Lefkowitz, Mary R. 2008. "Myth and History in the Biography of Apollonius." In Papanghelis and Rengakos: 51–71.

Lehnus, Luigi. 1997. "Ipotesi sul finale dell'*Ecale*." *ZPE* 117: 45–46.

Lennox, P.G. 1980. "Apollonius, *Argonautica* 3, 1 ff. and Homer." *Hermes* 108.1: 45–73.

Lenz, Ansgar. 1980. *Das Proöm des frühen griechischen Epos: Ein Beitrag zum poetischen Selbstverständnis*. Bonn: Habelt.

Lenz, Lutz. 1975. *Der homerische Aphroditehymnus und die Aristie des Aineias in der Ilias*. Bonn: Habelt.

Leschhorn, Wolfgang. 1984. *Gründer der Stadt: Studien zu einem politisch-religiösen Phänomen der griechischen Geschichte*. Stuttgart: Franz Steiner.

Lévêque, Pierre, and Annie Verbanck-Piérard. 1992. "Héraclès: Héros ou dieu?" *Héraclès: D'une rive à l'autre de la Méditerranée: Bilan et perspectives*. Ed. Corinne Bonnet and Colette Jourdain-Annequin. Brussels: Institut Historique Belge de Rome. 43–65.

Levin, Donald Norman. 1962. "Apolloniana Minora." *TAPhA* 93: 154–163.

Levin, Donald Norman. 1963. "Zeus's Orchard without Zeus's Palace." *CPh* 58.2: 107–109.

Levin, Donald Norman. 1969. "Two Epithets of Aristaeus." *Hermes* 97.4: 498–501.

Levin, Donald Norman. 1971. *Apollonius' Argonautica Re-Examined, 1: The Neglected First and Second Books*. Leiden: Brill.

Liberman, Gauthier. 2002. *Alcée: Fragments*. 2 vol. Paris: Les Belles Lettres.

Lightfoot, J.L. 1999. *Parthenius of Nicaea: The Poetical Fragments and the Ἐρωτικὰ Παθήματα*. Oxford: Clarendon.

Lightfoot, J.L. 2014. *Dionysius Periegetes: Description of the Known World*. Oxford: Oxford University Press.

Lindner, Ruth. 1994. *Mythos und Identität: Studien zur Selbstdarstellung kleinasiatischer Städte in der römischen Kaiserzeit*. Stuttgart: Franz Steiner.

Livrea, Enrico. 1966. "Il proemio degli *Erga* considerato attraverso i vv. 9–10." *Helikon* 6: 442–475.

Livrea, Enrico. 1972. "Una tecnica allusiva apolloniana alla luce dell'esegesi omerica alessandrina." *SIFC* 44: 231–243.

Livrea, Enrico. 1973. *Apollonii Rhodii Argonauticon Liber Quartus*. Florence: La Nuova Italia.

Livrea, Enrico. 1979. "Da Pagasai a Lemnos." *SIFC* 51: 146–154.

Livrea, Enrico. 1983. Review of Vian and Delage 1981 [= 2002.3]. *Gnomon* 55.5: 420–426.

Llanos, Pablo Martín. 2017a. "Ficción de *performance* original en el exordio de *Argonáuticas* de Apolonio de Rodas." *Synthesis* 24.1: 1–13.

Llanos, Pablo Martín. 2017b. "Alusiones hímnicas en el exordio de *Argonáuticas* de Apolonio de Rodas: Tradiciones renovadas e innovaciones tradicionales." *Circe* 21.1: 1–15.

Lloyd, G.E.R. 1966. *Polarity and Analogy: Two Types of Argumentation in Early Greek Thought*. Cambridge: Cambridge University Press.

Lloyd-Jones, Hugh. 1984. "A Hellenistic Miscellany." *SIFC* 3.2: 52–71.

Lozynsky, Yuriy. 2014. *Ancient Greek Cult Hymns: Poets, Performers and Rituals*. Diss. University of Toronto.

Ludwich, Arthur. 1908. *Homerischer Hymnenbau nebst seinen Nachahmungen bei Kallimachos, Theokrit, Vergil, Nonnos und Anderen.* Leipzig: S. Hirzel.

Luz, Christine. 2013. "What Has It Got in Its Pocketses? Or, What Makes a Riddle a Riddle?" *The Muse at Play: Riddles and Wordplay in Greek and Latin Poetry.* Ed. Jan Kwapisz, David Petrain, and Mikołaj Szymański. Berlin: De Gruyter. 83–99.

Lye, Suzanne. 2012. "Rewriting the Gods: Religious Ritual, Human Resourcefulness, and Divine Interaction in the *Argonautica.*" *HG* 16: 223–247.

Lye, Suzanne. 2016. *The Hypertextual Underworld: Exploring the Underworld as an Intertextual Space in Ancient Greek Literature.* Diss. University of California, Los Angeles.

Lyne, R.O.A.M. 2005. "Horace *Odes* Book 1 and the Alexandrian Edition of Alcaeus." *CQ* 55.2: 542–558.

Lyons, Deborah. 1997. *Gender and Immortality: Heroines in Ancient Greek Myth and Cult.* Princeton: Princeton University Press.

Lyons, John. 1977. *Semantics.* 2 vol. Cambridge: Cambridge University Press.

Mackay, Elizabeth Anne. 2001. "The Frontal Face and 'You': Narrative Disjunction in Early Greek Poetry and Painting." *AC* 44: 5–34.

Mackie, C.J. 1998. "Achilles in Fire." *CQ* 48.2: 329–338.

Maehler, H. 2004. *Bacchylides: A Selection.* Cambridge: Cambridge University Press.

Malkin, Irad. 1987. *Religion and Colonization in Ancient Greece.* Leiden: Brill.

Malkin, Irad. 1993. "Land Ownership, Territorial Possession, Hero Cults, and Scholarly Theory." *Nomodeiktes: Greek Studies in Honor of Martin Ostwald.* Ed. Ralph M. Rosen and Joseph Farrell. Ann Arbor: University of Michigan Press. 225–234.

Malten, Ludolf. 1910. "Ein Alexandrinisches Gedicht vom Raube der Kore." *Hermes* 45.4: 506–553.

Manakidou, Flora P. 2017. "Past and Present in the Fifth *Hymn* of Callimachus: Mimesis, Aitiology and Reality." *HG* 21: 181–210.

Manuello, Patrick. 2011. "La trattazione del mito argonautico nella *Pitica* IV di Pindaro e in Apollonio Rodio." *Digressus* 11: 74–152.

Manuello, Patrick. 2012. "Alcuni interventi diretti di Apollonio Rodio nelle *Argonautiche.*" *Gaia* 15: 121–142.

Marg, Walter. 1976. "Kampf und Tod in der *Ilias.*" *WJA* 2: 7–19.

Martin, Richard P. 2005. "Epic as Genre." In Foley: 9–19.

Martindale, Charles. 1993. *Redeeming the Text: Latin Poetry and the Hermeneutics of Reception.* Cambridge: Cambridge University Press.

Martindale, Charles, and Richard F. Thomas, Eds. 2006. *Classics and the Uses of Reception.* Malden, MA: Blackwell.

Maslov, Boris. 2012. "The Real Life of the Genre of *Prooimion.*" *CPh* 107.3: 191–205.

Mason, H.C. 2016. "Jason's Cloak and the *Shield of Heracles.*" *Mnemosyne* 69: 183–201.

Massari, Pietro. 2017. "Il fulmine e il Caucaso in Apollonio Rodio." *Poesia e prosa di età ellenistica. In ricordo di Roberto Pretagostini.* Ed. Mauro Tulli. Pisa: Serra. 11–19.

Massimilla, Giulio. 1994. "L'invocazione di Callimaco alle Cariti nel primo libro degli *Aitia* (fr. 7, 9–14 Pf.)." *Proceedings of the 20th International Congress of Papyrologists*. Ed. Adam Bülow-Jacobsen. Copenhagen: Museum Tusculanum. 322–325.

Massimilla, Giulio. 1996–2010. *Aitia*. 2 vol. Pisa: Giardini.

Massimilla, Giulio. 2005. "Considerazioni su PSI inv. 1923." *Comunicazioni dell'Istituto papirologico "G. Vitelli"* 6: 13–18.

Mastronarde, Donald J. 2003. "Iconography and Imagery in Euripides' *Ion*." *Oxford Readings in Classical Studies: Euripides*. Ed. Judith Mossman. Oxford: Oxford University Press. 295–308.

Matteo, Rocchina. 2002. "Note apolloniane." *ARF* 4: 155–165.

Matteo, Rocchina. 2007. *Apollonio Rodio: Argonautiche Libro II*. Lecce: Pensa.

Matthews, Victor J. 1996. *Antimachus of Colophon*. Leiden: Brill.

Mazzarino, Santo. 1989 [1947]. *Fra Oriente e Occidente: Ricerche di storia greca arcaica*. Milan: Rizzoli.

McKeown, J.C. 1987. *Ovid. Amores*. Leeds: Francis Cairns.

McLennan, G.R. 1977. *Callimachus. Hymn to Zeus*. Rome: Ateneo & Bizzarri.

McNelis, Charles. 2003. "Mourning Glory: Callimachus' Hecale and Heroic Honors." *MD* 50: 155–161.

McNelis, Charles, and Alexander Sens. 2011. "Trojan Glory: *Kleos* and the Survival of Troy in Lycophron's *Alexandra*." *Trends in Classics* 3.1: 54–82.

McPhee, Brian D. 2017. "Numbers and Acrostics: Two Notes on Jason's Prayer at Pagasae in Apollonius' *Argonautica*." *Akropolis* 1: 111–120.

McPhee, Brian D. 2018. "Phineus' Perpetual Night: Ovid, *Metamorphoses* 7.2–4, and Apollonius, *Argonautica* 2.178–497." *Hermathena* 195: 55–69.

McPhee, Brian D. 2021a. "Power Divine: Apollonius' Medea and the Goddesses of the *Homeric Hymns*." *HG* 26: 245–270.

McPhee, Brian D. 2021b. "The Argo, Danaus, and Sesostris: On Allusions to Two First-Ship Traditions in Apollonius' *Argonautica*." *YAGE* 5: 166–195.

McPhee, Brian D. 2022. "Off to Scythia: Apollonius *Arg.* 1, 307–311, and Ananius fr. 1 West." *RFIC* 150.2: 352–378.

McPhee, Brian D. 2023a. Review of Stürner 2022. *AAHG* 76.1: 42–47.

McPhee, Brian D. 2023b. "What Became of the Sicilian Cyclopes? And Other Monstrous Homeric Problems." In Dova, Callaway, and Gazis: 179–201.

McPhee, Brian D. 2023c. "The Odysseus Gene: A Case of Reverse-Genealogical Characterization in Ovid's *Metamorphoses* (11.312–315, 344–345)." *Ankara Sosyal Araştırmalar Dergisi* 1.2: 171–187.

McPhee, Brian D. Forthcoming, a. "Lame Snakes and Limping Iambics: Apollonius' *Canobus* and Its Nicandrian Reception." *Hellenistic Literature in Fragments*. Ed. Manolis Pagkalos and Manolis Spanakis.

McPhee, Brian D. Forthcoming, b. "Ethnography in the Past Tense: The Amazons in Apollonius' *Argonautica*." *Time, Tense and Genre in Ancient Greek Literature*. Ed. Connie Bloomfield-Gadêlha and Edith Hall. Oxford: Oxford University Press.

McPhee, Brian D. Forthcoming, c. "Uncool in a Crisis: Apollonius' Tragic Telamon (A.R. 1.1280–1344)." *HG* (forthcoming): 163–187.

McPhee, Brian D. Forthcoming, d. "Etymological Allusion as Mythological Commentary: The Case of Apollonius' Sirens." Forthcoming in *MD*.

Mehmel, Friedrich. 1934. *Valerius Flaccus*. Diss. Universität Hamburg.

Merkel, R., and Heinrich Keil. 1854. *Apollonii Argonautica*. Leipzig: Teubner.

Meyer, Herbert. 1933. *Hymnische Stilelemente in der frühgriechischen Dichtung*. Düsseldorf: Triltsch.

Michaelis, Julius Johann. 1875. *De Apollonii Rhodii fragmentis*. Diss. Martin-Luther-Universität Halle-Wittenberg.

Michalopoulos, Andreas N. 2003. "Working on an Established Etymological Background: Ovid and his Hellenistic Predecessors." *Etymologia: Studies in Ancient Etymology*. Ed. Christos Nifadopoulos. Münster: Nodus. 165–175.

Mikalson, Jon D. 1991. *Honor Thy Gods: Popular Religion in Greek Tragedy*. Chapel Hill: University of North Carolina Press.

Miller, Andrew M. 1979. "The 'Address to the Delian Maidens' in the *Homeric Hymn to Apollo*: Epilogue or Transition?" *TAPhA* 109: 173–186.

Miller, Andrew M. 1986. *From Delos to Delphi: A Literary Study of the Homeric Hymn to Apollo*. Leiden: Brill.

Miller, John F. 2014. "Virgil's Salian Hymn to Hercules." *CJ* 109.4: 439–463.

Minchin, Elizabeth. 1999. "Describing and Narrating in Homer's *Iliad*." *Signs of Orality: The Oral Tradition and its Influence in the Greek and Roman World*. Ed. E. Anne Mackay. Leiden: Brill. 49–64.

Mineur, W.H. 1984. *Callimachus. Hymn to Delos*. Leiden: Brill.

Minton, William W. 1970. "The Proem-hymn of Hesiod's *Theogony*." *TAPhA* 101: 357–377.

Miralles, Carles. 1992. "La poetica di Eroda." *Aevum(ant)* 5: 89–113.

Mirto, Maria Serena. 2011. "Il nome di Achille nelle *Argonautiche* tra intertestualità e giochi etimologici." *RFIC* 139.2: 279–309.

Montana, Fausto. "Hellenistic Scholarship." *History of Ancient Greek Scholarship: From the Beginnings to the End of the Byzantine Age*. Ed. Franco Montanari. Leiden: Brill. 132–259.

Montiglio, Silvia. 2005. *Wandering in Ancient Greek Culture*. Chicago: University of Chicago Press.

Mooney, George W. 1912. *The Argonautica of Apollonius Rhodius*. London: Longmans, Green, and Co.

Mora, Fabio. 1981. "I silenzi erodotei." *Studi storico-religiosi* 5: 209–222.

Mora, Fabio. 1983. "Il silenzio religioso in Erodoto e nel teatro ateniese." *Le regioni del silenzio: studi sui disagi della comunicazione*. Ed. Maria Grazia Ciani. Padua: Bloom. 54–76.

Moran, William Stephen. 1975. "Μιμνήσκομαι and 'Remembering' Epic Stories in Homer and the *Hymns*." *QUCC* 20: 195–211.

Moreau, Alain. 1994. *Le mythe de Jason et Médée: Le va-nu pied et la sorcière*. Paris: Les Belles Lettres.

Moreau, Alain. 2000. "Les transformations du périple des Argonautes: Un miroir des progrès de la colonisation grecque." *Euphrosyne* 28: 325–334.

Mori, Anatole. 2007. "Acts of Persuasion in Hellenistic Epic: Honey-Sweet Words in Apollonius." *A Companion to Greek Rhetoric*. Ed. Ian Worthington. Malden, MA: Blackwell. 458–472.

Mori, Anatole. 2008. *The Politics of Apollonius Rhodius' Argonautica*. Cambridge: Cambridge University Press.

Morris, Ian. 1988. "Tomb Cult and the 'Greek Renaissance': The Past in the Present in the 8th Century BC." *Antiquity* 62: 750–761.

Morrison, A.D. 2007. *The Narrator in Archaic Greek and Hellenistic Poetry*. Cambridge: Cambridge University Press.

Morrison, A.D. 2020. *Apollonius Rhodius, Herodotus and Historiography*. Cambridge: Cambridge University Press.

Most, Glenn W. 1981. "On the Arrangement of Catullus' *Carmina Maiora*." *Philologus* 125.1: 109–125.

Moulton, Carroll. 1973. "Theocritus and the Dioscuri." *GRBS* 14: 41–47.

Murnaghan, Sheila. 2007. Review of Martindale and Thomas 2006. *BMCR* 2.19.

Murray, Jackie. 2004. "The Metamorphoses of Erysichthon: Callimachus, Apollonius, and Ovid." *HG* 7: 207–242.

Murray, Jackie. 2005a. *Polyphonic Argo*. Diss. University of Washington.

Murray, Jackie. 2005b. "The Constructions of the Argo in Apollonius' *Argonautica*." In Harder and Cuypers: 88–106.

Murray, Jackie. 2012. "Burned after Reading: The So-called List of Alexandrian Librarians in *P. Oxy.* x 1241." *Aitia* 2: 1–16.

Murray, Jackie. 2018. "Silencing Orpheus: The Fiction of Performance in Apollonius' *Argonautica*." *HG* 23: 201–224.

Murray, Jackie. 2019. "Quarreling with Callimachus: A Response to Annette Harder." *Aevum(ant)* 19: 77–106.

Murray, Oswyn. 1970. "Hecataeus of Abdera and Pharaonic Kingship." *JEA* 56: 141–171.

Naber, S.A. 1906. "Ad Apollonium Rhodium." *Mnemosyne* 34.1: 1–39.

Nagy, Gregory. 1974. *Comparative Studies in Greek and Indic Meter*. Cambridge, MA: Harvard University Press.

Nagy, Gregory. 1982. "Hesiod." *Ancient Writers: Greece and Rome*. Vol. 1. Ed. T. James Luce. New York: Charles Scribner's Sons. 43–72.

Nagy, Gregory. 1990a. *Pindar's Homer*. Baltimore: Johns Hopkins University Press.
Nagy, Gregory. 1990b. *Greek Mythology and Poetics*. Ithaca: Cornell University Press.
Nagy, Gregory. 1999 [1979]. *The Best of the Achaeans: Concepts of the Hero in Archaic Greek Poetry*. Rev. ed. Baltimore: Johns Hopkins University Press.
Nagy, Gregory. 2002. "Reading Bakhtin Reading the Classics: An Epic Fate for Conveyors of the Heroic Past." *Bakhtin and the Classics*. Ed. R. Bracht Branham. Evanston, IL: Northwestern University Press. 71–96.
Nagy, Gregory. 2005. "The Epic Hero." In Foley: 71–89.
Nagy, Gregory. 2008. *Homer the Classic*. Washington, DC: Center for Hellenic Studies.
Nagy, Gregory. 2010. *Homer the Preclassic*. Berkeley: University of California Press.
Nagy, Gregory. 2011. "The Earliest Phases in the Reception of the *Homeric Hymns*." In Faulkner: 280–331.
Nagy, Gregory. 2012. "Signs of Hero Cult in Homeric Poetry." *Homeric Contexts: Neoanalysis and the Interpretation of Oral Poetry*. Ed. Franco Montanari, Antonios Rengakos, and Christos Tsagalis. Berlin: De Gruyter. 27–71.
Natzel, Stephanie A. 1992. *Κλέα γυναικῶν: Frauen in den Argonautika des Apollonios Rhodios*. Trier: Wissenschaftlicher Verlag.
Nelis, Damien P. 1991. "Iphias: Apollonius Rhodius, *Argonautica* 1.311–316." *CQ* 41.1: 96–105.
Nelis, Damien P. 1992. "Demodocus and the Song of Orpheus: Ap. Rhod. *Arg*. 1, 496–511." *MH* 49.3: 153–170.
Nelis, Damien P. 2001. *Vergil's Aeneid and the Argonautica of Apollonius Rhodius*. Leeds: Francis Cairns.
Nelis, Damien P. 2005a. "Apollonius of Rhodes." In Foley: 353–363.
Nelis, Damien P. 2005b. "The Reading of Orpheus: The *Orphic Argonautica* and the Epic Tradition." In Paschalis: 169–192.
Nelson, Thomas J. 2023. *Markers of Allusion in Archaic Greek Poetry*. Cambridge: Cambridge University Press.
Newman, John K. 1986. *Classical Epic Tradition*. Madison: University of Wisconsin Press.
Newman, John K. 1998. "Iambe/Iambos and the Rape of a Genre: A Horatian Sidelight." *ICS* 23: 101–120.
Newman, John K. 2008 [2001]. "The Golden Fleece: Imperial Dream." In Papanghelis and Rengakos: 413–444.
Ní Mheallaigh, Karen. 2020. *The Moon in the Greek and Roman Imagination: Myth, Literature, Science and Philosophy*. Cambridge: Cambridge University Press.
Niedergang-Janon, Florence. 2002. *Mythes et représentations dans les Argonautiques d'Apollonios de Rhodes*. Diss. Université Paris Nanterre.
Nikitinski, Oleg. 1996. *Kallimachos-Studien*. Frankfurt am Main: Peter Lang.
Nilsson, Martin P. 1967 [1955]. *Geschichte der griechischen Religion*. 3rd ed. Vol. 1. Munich: Beck.

Nisbet, R.G.M., and Niall Rudd. 2004. *A Commentary on Horace: Odes Book III*. Oxford: Oxford University Press.

Nishimura-Jensen, Julie Mariko. 1996. *Tragic Epic or Epic Tragedy: Narrative and Genre in Apollonius of Rhodes' Argonautica*. Diss. University of Wisconsin–Madison.

Nishimura-Jensen, Julie Mariko. 2000. "Unstable Geographies: The Moving Landscape in Apollonius' *Argonautica* and Callimachus' *Hymn to Delos*." *TAPhA* 130: 287–317.

Nishimura-Jensen, Julie Mariko. 2009. "The Chorus of Argonauts in Apollonius of Rhodes' *Argonautica*." *Phoenix* 63.1–2: 1–23.

Nock, Arthur Darby. 1944. "The Cult of Heroes." *Harvard Theological Review* 37.2: 141–174.

Nock, Arthur Darby. 1972. *Essays on Religion and the Ancient World*. 2 vol. Ed. Zeph Stewart. Cambridge, MA: Harvard University Press.

Noegel, Scott. 2004. "Apollonius' *Argonautika* and Egyptian Solar Mythology." *CW* 97.2: 123–136.

Norden, Eduard. 1956. *Agnostos Theos: Untersuchungen zur Formengeschichte religiöser Rede*. Stuttgart: Teubner.

Norden, Eduard. 1957. *P. Vergilius Maro Aeneis Buch VI*. 4th ed. Stuttgart: Teubner.

Noussia-Fantuzzi, Maria. 2017. "'Lyric' Atmosphere in Apollonius Rhodius and Callimachus (with an Analysis of Theocritus 18)." *TC* 9.2: 248–280.

Nünlist, René. 2004. "The *Homeric Hymns*." *SAGN* 1: 35–42.

Nünlist, René. 2007. "The *Homeric Hymns*." *SAGN* 2: 53–62.

Nünlist, René. 2009. *The Ancient Critic at Work: Terms and Concepts of Literary Criticism in Greek Scholia*. Cambridge: Cambridge University Press.

Nuttall, A.D. 1992. *Openings: Narrative Beginnings from the Epic to the Novel*. Oxford: Clarendon.

Nyberg, Lars. 1992. *Unity and Coherence: Studies in Apollonius Rhodius' Argonautica and the Alexandrian Epic Tradition*. Lund: Lund University Press.

Obbink, Dirk. 2001. "The Genre of *Plataea*: Generic Unity in the New Simonides." In Boedeker and Sider: 65–85.

Ogden, Daniel. 2013. *Drakōn: Dragon Myth and Serpent Cult in the Greek and Roman Worlds*. Oxford: Oxford University Press.

O'Hara, James J. 1996. "Vergil's Best Reader? Ovidian Commentary on Vergilian Etymological Wordplay." *CJ* 91.3: 255–276.

O'Hara, James J. 2007. *Inconsistency in Roman Epic: Studies in Catullus, Lucretius, Vergil, Ovid and Lucan*. Cambridge: Cambridge University Press.

O'Hara, James J. 2017 [1996]. *True Names: Vergil and the Alexandrian Tradition of Etymological Wordplay*. Expanded ed. Ann Arbor: University of Michigan Press.

O'Higgins, Laurie. 2003. *Women and Humor in Classical Greece*. Cambridge: Cambridge University Press.

Olender, Maurice. 1990. "Aspects of Baubo: Ancient Texts and Contexts." *Before Sexuality: The Construction of Erotic Experience in the Ancient Greek World*. Ed. David

M. Halperin, John J. Winkler, and Froma I. Zeitlin. Princeton: Princeton University Press. 83–113.

Olson, S. Douglas. 2012. *The Homeric Hymn to Aphrodite and Related Texts*. Berlin: De Gruyter.

Opelt, Ilona. 1978. "Gefühlswörter bei Homer und in den *Argonautika* des Apollonios Rhodios." *Glossa* 56.3/4: 170–190.

Ormand, Kirk. 2015. "Toward Iambic Obscenity." *Ancient Obscenities: Their Nature and Use in the Ancient Greek and Roman Worlds*. Ed. Dorota Dutsch and Ann Suter. Ann Arbor: University of Michigan Press. 44–70.

Ottone, Gabrielle. 2002. *Libyka: Testimonianze e frammenti*. Tivoli: TORED.

Pace, Cristina. 2004. "Il tizzone sotto la cenere: Apoll. Rh. 3.275 ss. e l'*Inno omerico a Hermes*." *La cultura ellenistica. L'opera letteraria e l'esegesi antica*. Ed. Roberto Pretagostini and Emanuele Dettori. Rome: Quasar. 95–111.

Paduano, Guido. 1971. "L'episodio di Talos: Osservazioni sull'esperienza magica nelle *Argonautiche* di Apollonio Rodio." *SCO* 19–20: 46–67.

Paduano, Guido, and Massimo Fusillo. 1986. *Apollonio Rodio: Le Argonautiche*. Milan: Rizzoli.

Paduano Faedo, Lucia. 1970. "L'inversione del rapporto poeta-Musa nella cultura ellenistica." *ASNP* 39.3/4: 377–386.

Palombi, Maria Garza. 1985. "Apollonio e il *dodecathlon*." *Prometheus* 11: 126–136.

Palombi, Maria Garza. 1993. "Mito e storia in due episodi delle *Argonautiche* di Apollonio Rodio." *Prometheus* 19: 154–168.

Papanghelis, Theodore D., and Antonios Rengakos, Eds. 2008 [2001]. *Brill's Companion to Apollonius Rhodius*. 2nd ed. Leiden: Brill.

Papathomopoulos, Manolis. 1968. *Antoninus Liberalis. Les Métamorphoses*. Paris: Les Belles Lettres.

Parker, Robert. 1983. *Miasma: Pollution and Purification in Early Greek Religion*. Oxford: Clarendon.

Parker, Robert. 1991. "The *Hymn to Demeter* and the *Homeric Hymns*." *G&R* 38.1: 1–17.

Parker, Robert. 1996. *Athenian Religion: A History*. Oxford: Clarendon.

Parker, Robert. 2005. "ὡς ἥρωι ἐναγίζειν." *Greek Sacrificial Ritual, Olympian and Chthonian*. Ed. Robin Hägg and Brita Alroth. Stockholm: Åström. 37–45.

Parker, Robert. 2011. *On Greek Religion*. Ithaca: Cornell University Press.

Parry, Milman. 1971. *The Making of Homeric Verse: The Collected Papers of Milman Parry*. Ed. Adam Parry. Oxford: Clarendon.

Parsons, Peter. 1993. "Identities in Diversity." In Bulloch et al.: 152–170.

Paschalis, Michael, ed. 2005. *Roman and Greek Imperial Epic*. Herakleion: Crete University Press.

Páskiewicz, T.M. 1981. *A Commentary on the Second Book of the Argonautica by Apollonius of Rhodes*. Diss. Hertford College, Oxford.

Páskiewicz, T.M. 1988. "Aitia in the Second Book of Apollonius' *Argonautica*." *ICS* 13.1: 57–61.

Pavese, C.O. 1991. "L'inno rapsodico: Analisi tematica degli *Inni omerici*." *L'inno tra rituale e letteratura nel mondo antico. Atti di un colloquio, Napoli 21–24 ottobre 1991.* Ed. Albio Cesaro Cassio. Rome: GEI. 155–178.

Pavese, C.O. 1993. "L'inno rapsodico: Indice tematico degli *Inni omerici*." *AION(filol)* 15: 21–36.

Pavlock, Barbara. 1990. *Eros, Imitation, and the Epic Tradition*. Ithaca: Cornell University Press.

Pease, Arthur Stanley. 1955–1958. *M. Tulli Ciceronis De Natura Deorum*. 2 vol. Cambridge, MA: Harvard University Press.

Perrotta, Gennaro. 1931. "Il carme 64 di Catullo e i suoi pretesi originali ellenistici." *Athenaeum* 9.2, 3: 177–222, 370–409.

Perrotta, Gennaro. 1978 [1926]. "La chiusa del *Tolomeo*." *Poesia ellenistica: Scritti minori*. Vol. 2. Rome: Ateneo. 180–186.

Peschties, Eric. 1912. *Quaestiones philologicae et archaeologicae de Apollonii Rhodii Argonauticis*. Diss. Albertus-Universität Königsberg.

Petridou, Georgia. 2015. *Divine Epiphany in Greek Literature and Culture*. Oxford: Oxford University Press.

Petrovic, Ivana. 2012. "Rhapsodic Hymns and Epyllia." In Baumbach and Bär: 149–176.

Petrovic, Ivana. 2013. "Never-Ending Stories: A Perspective on Greek Hymns." *The Door Ajar: False Closure in Greek and Roman Literature and Art*. Ed. Farouk F. Grewing, Benjamin Acosta-Hughes, and Alexander Kirichenko. Heidelberg: Winter. 203–227.

Petzl, Georg. 1969. *Antike Dikussionen über die beiden Nekyiai*. Meisenheim an Glan: Hain.

Pfeiff, Karl Arno. 2002. *Homerische Hymnen*. Ed. Gerd von der Gönna and Erika Simon. Tübingen: Stauffenburg.

Pfeiffer, Rudolf. 1922. *Kallimachosstudien: Untersuchungen zur Arsinoe und zu den Aitia des Kallimachos*. Munich: Hueber.

Pfeiffer, Rudolf. 1934. *Die neuen ΔΙΗΓΗΣΕΙΣ zu Kallimachosgedichten*. Munich: Bayerischen Akademie der Wissenschaften.

Pfeiffer, Rudolf. 1949–1951. *Callimachus*. 2 vol. Oxford: Clarendon.

Pfeiffer, Rudolf. 1968. *History of Classical Scholarship from the Beginnings to the End of the Hellenistic Age*. Oxford: Clarendon.

Pfeiffer, Stefan. 2008. *Herrscher- und Dynastiekulte im Ptolemäerreich: Systematik und Einordnung der Kultformen*. Munich: Beck.

Pfeiffer, Stefan. 2016. "The Ptolemies: Hellenistic Kingship in Egypt." *Oxford Handbooks Online*. DOI: 10.1093/oxfordhb/9780199935390.013.23.

Pfister, Friedrich. 1909–1912. *Der Reliquienkult im Altertum*. 2 vol. Giessen: Töpelmann.

Phillips, E.D. 1953. "Odysseus in Italy." *JHS* 73: 53–67.
Phillips, Tom. 2018. "Polyphony, Event, Context: Pindar, *Paean* 9." *Textual Events: Performance and the Lyric in Early Greece*. Ed. Felix Budelmann and Tom Phillips. Oxford: Oxford University Press. 189–209.
Phillips, Tom. 2020. *Untimely Epic: Apollonius Rhodius' Argonautica*. Oxford: Oxford University Press.
Phinney, Edward Sterl, Jr. 1963. *Apollonius Rhodius*. Diss. University of California, Berkeley.
Piacenza, Nicola. 2014. "Eronda e la musa giambica ipponattea: per l'interpretazione del *Mimiambo* 1 (con un excursus sulle *Siracusane* di Teocrito)." *Annali Online di Ferrara. Lettere* 9.2: 167–187.
Pietsch, Christian. 1999. *Die Argonautika des Apollonios von Rhodos: Untersuchungen zum Problem der einheitlichen Konzeption des Inhalts*. Stuttgart: Franz Steiner.
Pike, D.L. 1984. "Pindar's Treatment of the Heracles Myths." *AC* 27: 15–22.
Pirenne-Delforge, Vinciane. 2008. "Le lexique des lieux de culte dans la *Périégèse* de Pausanias." *Archiv für Religionsgeschichte* 10: 143–178.
Pirenne-Delforge, Vinciane, and Emilio Suárez de la Torre, Eds. 2000. *Héros et héroïnes dans les mythes et les cultes grecs*. Liège: Centre international d'étude de la religion grecque antique.
Platt, Arthur. 1914. "On Apollonius Rhodius." *JPh* 33: 1–53.
Platt, Verity. 2011. *Facing the Gods: Epiphany and Representation in Graeco-Roman Art, Literature and Religion*. Cambridge: Cambridge University Press.
Poli, Silvia, ed., and Franco Ferrari, introd. 2010. *Inni Omerici*. Turin: UTET.
Pompella, Giuseppe. 2002. *Apollonii Rhodii Lexicon*. Hildesheim: Olms-Weidmann.
Porter, James I. 2008. "Reception Studies: Future Prospects." *A Companion to Classical Receptions*. Ed. Lorna Hardwick and Christopher Stray. Malden, MA: Blackwell. 469–481.
Porter, James I. 2011. "Making and Unmaking: The Achaean Wall and the Limits of Fictionality in Homeric Criticism." *TAPhA* 141.1: 1–36.
Preininger, Johann. 1976. *Der Aufbau der Argonautika des Apollonios Rhodios*. Diss. Universität Graz.
Preller, L. 1894. *Griechische Mythologie*. Vol. 1: *Theogonie und Goetter*. 4th ed. Ed. Carl Robert. Berlin: Weidmann.
Pretagostini, Roberto, ed. 2000. *La letteratura ellenistica: Problemi e prospettive di ricerca*. Rome: Quasar.
Price, Simon. 2005. "Local Mythologies in the Greek East." *Coinage and Identity in the Roman Provinces*. Ed. Christopher Howgego, Volker Heuchert, and Andrew Burnett. Oxford: Oxford University Press. 115–124.
Priestley, Jessica. 2014. *Herodotus and Hellenistic Culture: Literary Studies in the Reception of the Histories*. Oxford: Oxford University Press.

Prince, Gerald. 2003. *A Dictionary of Narratology*. Rev. ed. Lincoln: University of Nebraska Press.

Prioux, Évelyne. 2012. "Représenter les dieux, représenter les rois: Hymnes, *enkômia* et entre-deux." In Bouchon, Brillet-Dubois, and Le Meur-Weissman: 135–150.

Pritchett, W. Kendrick. 1979. *The Greek State at War*. Vol. 3. Berkeley: University of California Press.

Pulleyn, Simon. 1997. *Prayer in Greek Religion*. Oxford: Clarendon.

Race, William H. 1982a. "Aspects of Rhetoric and Form in Greek Hymns." *GRBS* 23.1: 5–14.

Race, William H. 1982b. *The Classical Priamel from Homer to Boethius*. Leiden: Brill.

Race, William H. 1985. "Pindar's Heroic Ideal at *Pyth.* 4.186–187." *AJPh* 106.3: 350–356.

Race, William H. 1992. "How Greek Poems Begin." *YClS* 29: 13–38.

Ransom, Christopher N. 2014. "Back to the Future: Apollonius' *Argonautica* 1.553–558 Chronological Play and Epic Succession." *Mnemosyne* 67: 639–645.

Rawles, Richard. 2018. *Simonides the Poet: Intertextuality and Reception*. Cambridge: Cambridge University Press.

Redondo, J. 2000. "Non-Epic Features in the Language of Apollonius Rhodius." *HG* 4: 129–154.

Reich, Franz, and H. Maehler. 1991. *Lexicon in Apollonii Rhodii Argonautica*. Amsterdam: Hakkert.

Reinhardt, Karl. 1960. *Tradition und Geist: Gesammelte Essays zur Dichtung*. Göttingen: Vandenhoeck & Ruprecht.

Reinhardt, Karl. 1961. *Die Ilias und ihr Dichter*. Göttingen: Vandenhoeck & Ruprecht.

Rengakos, Antonios. 1993. *Der Homertext und die hellenistischen Dichter*. Stuttgart: Franz Steiner.

Rengakos, Antonios. 1994. *Apollonios Rhodios und die antike Homererklärung*. Munich: Beck.

Rengakos, Antonios. 2002. "The Hellenistic Poets as Homeric Critics." *Omero tremila anni dopo*. Ed. Franco Montanari and Paola Ascheri. Rome: Edizioni di Storia e Letteratura.

Rengakos, Antonios. 2004. "Die *Argonautika* und das 'kyklische Gedicht': Bemerkungen zur Erzähltechnik des griechischen Epos." *Antike Literatur in neuer Deutung*. Ed. Anton Bierl, Arbogast Schmitt, and Andreas Willi. Munich: Saur. 277–304.

Rengakos, Antonios. 2008. "Apollonius Rhodius as a Homeric Scholar." *Brill's Companion to Apollonius Rhodius*. In Papanghelis and Rengakos: 243–266.

Rice, E.E. 1983. *The Grand Procession of Ptolemy Philadelphus*. Oxford: Oxford University Press.

Richardson, N.J. 1974. *The Homeric Hymn to Demeter*. Oxford: Clarendon.

Richardson, N.J. 2010. *Three Homeric Hymns: To Apollo, Hermes, and Aphrodite*. Cambridge: Cambridge University Press.

Richardson, N.J. 2015. "Constructing a Hymnic Narrative: Tradition and Innovation in the Longer *Homeric Hymns*." In Faulkner and Hodkinson: 19–30.

Richardson, Scott. 1990. *The Homeric Narrator*. Nashville: Vanderbilt University Press.

Richey, Elizabeth. 2008. *Apollonius' Argonautica: A Landscape of Nymphs*. Diss. Indiana University, Bloomington.

Rieu, E.V. 1959. *Apollonius of Rhodes. The Voyage of Argo*. Harmondsworth: Penguin.

Rijksbaron, Albert. 2002. *The Syntax and Semantics of the Verb in Classical Greek: An Introduction*. 3rd ed. Chicago: University of Chicago Press.

Rijksbaron, Albert. 2009. "Discourse Cohesion in the Proem of Hesiod's *Theogony*." *Discourse Cohesion in Ancient Greek*. Ed. Stéphanie Bakker and Gerry Wakker. Leiden: Brill. 241–265.

Rives, James B. 2018. "Cult Practice, Social Power, and Religious Identity: The Case of Animal Sacrifice." *Juden, Christen, Heiden? Religiöse Inklusion und Exklusion in Kleinasien bis Decius*. Ed. Stefan Alkier and Hartmut Leppin. Tübingen: Mohr Siebeck.

Robert, Carl. 1921. *Die griechische Heldensage* = Preller, Ludwig, ed. *Griechische Mythologie*, Vol. 2.3.1: *Die Argonauten. Der thebanische Kreis*. Berlin: Weidmann.

Robinson, David M. 1905. "Greek and Latin Inscriptions from Sinope and Environs." *AJA* 9.3: 294–333.

Rodríguez Moreno, Inmaculada. 2000. "Le héros comme μεταξύ entre l'homme et la divinité dans la pensée grecque." In Pirenne-Delforge and Suárez de la Torre: 91–100.

Rohde, Erwin. 1925 [1894]. *Psyche: The Cult of Souls and Belief in Immortality among the Greeks*. Trans. W.B. Hillis. London: Paul, Trench, Trubner.

Rohrbach, Hans Hermann. 1960. *Kolonie und Orakel: Untersuchungen zur sakralen Begründung der griechischen Kolonisation*. Diss. Ruprecht-Karls-Universität Heidelberg.

Roller, Lynn E. 1981. "Funeral Games for Historical Persons." *Stadion* 7: 1–18.

Roloff, Dietrich. 1970. *Gottähnlichkeit, Vergöttlichung und Erhöhung zu seligem Leben: Untersuchungen zur Herkunft der platonischen Augleichung an Gott*. Berlin: De Gruyter.

Romeo, Alessandra. 1985. *Il proemio epico antico: Quattro capitoli*. Rome: Gangemi.

Rose, Amy R. 1984. "Three Narrative Themes in Apollonios' Bebrykian Episode (*Argonautika* 2, 1–163)." *WS* 18: 115–135.

Rose, Herbert Jennings. 1937. "The 'Oath of Philippus' and the *Di Indigetes*." *HThR* 30.3: 165–181.

Rosen, Ralph M. 1988a. *Old Comedy and the Iambographic Tradition*. Atlanta: Scholars Press.

Rosen, Ralph M. 1988b. "A Poetic Initation Scene in Hipponax?" *AJPh* 109.2: 174–179.

Rosenmeyer, Patricia A. 2004. "Girls at Play in Early Greek Poetry." *AJPh* 125.2: 163–178.

Rosenmeyer, Thomas G. 1992. "Apollonius *lyricus*." *SIFC* 10: 177–198.

Ross, David O., Jr. 1975. *Backgrounds to Augustan Poetry: Gallus, Elegy and Rome*. Cambridge: Cambridge University Press.

Rossbach, Otto. 1901. "Verschollene Sagen und Kulte auf griechischen und italischen Bildwerken." *Neue Jahrbücher für das klassische Altertum, Geschichte und deutsche Literatur und für Pädagogik* 7.1: 385–417.

Rossi, Luigi Enrico. 1968. "La fine alessandrina dell'*Odissea* e lo ζῆλος Ὁμηρικός di Apollonio Rodio." *RFIC* 96: 151–163.

Rossi, Luigi Enrico. 2000. "La letteratura alessandrina e il rinnovamento dei generi letterari della tradizione." In Pretagostini: 149–161.

Rostropowicz, Joanna. 1990. "Das Heraklesbild in den *Argonautika* des Apollonios Rhodios." *Acta Classica Univ. Scien. Debrecen.* 26: 31–34.

Roth, Peter. 2004. "Apollonios Rhodios zwischen Homer und Hesiod: Beobachtungen zum Argonautenkatalog." *Ἐγκύκλιον Κηπίον (Rundgärtchen): Zu Poesie, Historie und Fachliteratur der Antike*. Ed. Markus Janka. Munich: Saur. 43–54.

Rotstein, Andrea. 2010. *The Idea of Iambos*. Oxford: Oxford University Press.

Roux, Jean-Paul. 1999. *Montagnes sacrées, montagnes mythiques*. Paris: Fayard.

Roux, R. 1949. *Le problème des Argonautes: Recherches sur les aspects religieux de la légende*. Paris: de Boccard.

Rudhardt, Jean. 1978. "A propos de l'hymne homérique à Déméter." *MH* 35.1: 1–17 (= Foley 1994: 198–211 [English trans.]).

Rudhardt, Jean. 1992 [1958]. *Notions fondamentales de la pensée religieuse et actes constitutifs du culte dans la Grèce classique*. 2nd ed. Paris: Picard.

Russel, D.A. 1964. *'Longinus'. On the Sublime*. Oxford: Clarendon.

Rusten, Jeffrey S. 1982. *Dionysius Scytobrachion*. Wiesbaden: Springer Fachmedien.

Rutherford, Ian. 2001. *Pindar's Paeans: A Reading of the Fragments with a Survey of the Genre*. Oxford: Oxford University Press.

Rutherford, Richard. 2005. *Classical Literature: A Concise History*. Malden: Blackwell.

Saïd, Suzanne. 1993. "Tragic Argos." *Tragedy, Comedy and the Polis: Papers from the Greek Drama Conference, Nottingham, 18–20 July 1990*. Ed. Alan H. Sommerstein, Stephen Halliwell, Jeffrey Henderson, and Bernhard Zimmermann. Bari: Levante. 167–189.

Saïd, Suzanne. 1998. "Tombes épiques d'Homère à Apollonios." *Nécropoles et Pouvoir: Idéologies, pratiques et interprétations*. Ed. Sophie Marchegay, Marie-Thérèse Le Dinahet, and Jean-François Salles. Lyon: Maison de l'Orient. 9–20.

Sancassano, Marialucia. 1996. "Il lessico greco del serpente: Considerazioni etimologiche." *Athenaeum* 84: 49–70.

Sansone, David. 2000. "Iphigenia in Colchis." *HG* 4: 155–172.

Schaaf, Ingo. 2014. *Magie und Ritual bei Apollonios Rhodios: Studien zu ihrer Form und Funktion in den Argonautika*. Berlin: De Gruyter.

Schein, Seth L. 1984. *The Mortal Hero: An Introduction to Homer's Iliad*. Berkeley: University of California Press.

Scheinberg, Susan. 1979. "The Bee Maidens of the *Homeric Hymn to Hermes*." *HSCPh* 83: 1–28.
Schellert, Maximilian. 1885. *De Apollonii Rhodii comparationibus*. Diss. Martin-Luther-Universität Halle-Wittenberg.
Schelske, Oliver. 2011. *Orpheus in der Spätantike: Studien und Kommentar zu den Argonautika des Orpheus: Ein literarisches, religiöses und philosophisches Zeugnis*. Berlin: De Gruyter.
Schenck zu Schweinsberg, Julia-Maria. 2017. *Der pseudohomerische Hermes-Hymnus: Ein interpretierender Kommentar*. Heidelberg: Winter.
Scherer, Burkhard. 2006. *Mythos, Katalog und Prophezeiung: Studien zu den Argonautika des Apollonios Rhodios*. Stuttgart: Franz Steiner.
Schollmeyer, Jonas. 2017. "Genealogie als intertextuelles Spiel: Zur Charakterisierung Admets im Katalog der Argonauten bei Apollonios Rhodios (1,49 f.)." *Philologus* 161.1: 35–46.
Schmakeit, Iris Astrid. 2003. *Apollonios Rhodios und die attische Tragödie: Gattungsüberschreitende Intertextualität in der alexandrinischen Epik*. Diss. Rijksuniversiteit Groningen.
Schmid, Wolf. 2009. "Implied Author." *Handbook of Narratology*. Ed. Peter Hühn, John Pier, Wolf Schmid, and Jörg Schönert. Berlin: De Gruyter. 161–173.
Schmidt, Martin. 1976. *Die Erklärungen zum Weltbild Homers und zur Kultur der Heroenzeit in den bT-Scholien zur Ilias*. Munich: Beck.
Schroeder, Chad Matthew. 2012. "'To Keep Silent is a Small Virtue': Hellenistic Poetry and the Samothracian Mysteries." *HG* 16: 307–334.
Schwinge, Ernst-Richard. 1986. *Künstlichkeit von Kunst: Zur Geschichtlichkeit der alexandrinischen Poesie*. Munich: Beck.
Scodel, Ruth. 1982. "The Achaean Wall and the Myth of Destruction." *CPh* 86: 33–50.
Scodel, Ruth. 2008. *Epic Facework: Self-Presentation and Social Interaction in Homer*. Swansea: Classical Press of Wales.
Seaford, Richard. 1994. *Reciprocity and Ritual: Homer and Tragedy in the Developing City-State*. Oxford: Clarendon.
Seaton, R.C. 1890. "On the Imitation of Homer by Apollonius Rhodius." *JPh* 19: 1–13.
Seaton, R.C. 1914. Review of Mooney 1912. *CR* 28.1: 15–19.
Sens, Alexander. 1992. "Theocritus, Homer, and the Dioscuri: *Idyll* 22.137–223." *TAPhA* 122: 335–350.
Sens, Alexander. 1994. "Hellenistic Reference in the Proem of Theocritus, *Idyll* 22." *CQ* 44.1: 66–74.
Sens, Alexander. 1997. *Theocritus: Dioscuri (Idyll 22)*. Göttingen: Vandenhoeck & Ruprecht.
Serafimidis, Christina. 2016. *Ererbte Waffen: Homerische Wörter aus dem Sachbereich 'Kampf und Krieg' in den Argonautika des Apollonios Rhodios*. Frankfurt am Main: Peter Lang.

Shackle, R.J. 1915. "Some Emendations of the *Homeric Hymns*." *CR* 29.6: 161–165.
Sharrock, Alison. 2018. "How Do We Read a (W)hole?: Dubious First Thoughts about the Cognitive Turn." *Intratextuality and Latin Literature*. Ed. Stephen Harrison, Stavros Frangoulidis, and Theodore D. Papanghelis. Berlin: De Gruyter. 15–31.
Sider, David. 2001. "Fragments 1–22 W²: Text, Apparatus Criticus, and Translation." In Boedeker and Sider: 13–29.
Sider, David. 2010. "Greek Verse on a Vase by Douris." *Hesperia* 79.4: 541–554.
Sistakou, Evina. 2001. "Παράδοση και νεοτερικότητα στον κατάλογο των Αργοναυτών (Απολλ. Ρόδ. *Αργ*. 1.23–233)." *Hellenica* 51.2: 231–264.
Sistakou, Evina. 2007. "Cyclic Stories? The Reception of the *Cypria* in Hellenistic Poetry." *Philologus* 151.1: 78–94.
Sistakou, Evina. 2008a. *Reconstructing the Epic: Cross-Readings of the Trojan Myth in Hellenistic Poetry*. Leuven: Peeters.
Sistakou, Evina. 2008b. "Beyond the *Argonautica*: In Search of Apollonius' *Ktisis* Poems." In Papanghelis and Rengakos: 311–340.
Sistakou, Evina. 2012. *The Aesthetics of Darkness: A Study of Hellenistic Romanticism in Apollonius, Lycophron and Nicander*. Leuven: Peeters.
Sistakou, Evina. 2016. *Tragic Failures: Alexandrian Responses to Tragedy and the Tragic*. Berlin: De Gruyter.
Smith, Janet M. 2001. "Firmer Foundations? A Note on the *ktiseis* of Apollonius Rhodius." *Essays in Honor of Gordon Williams: Twenty-five Years at Yale*. Ed. Elizabeth Tylawsky and Charles Weiss. New Haven: Henry R. Schwab. 263–281.
Snodgrass, A.M. 1977. *Archaeology and the Rise of the Greek State*. Cambridge: Cambridge University Press.
Snodgrass, A.M. 1980. *Archaic Greece: The Age of Experiment*. Berkeley: University of California Press.
Snodgrass, A.M. 1982. "Les origins du culte des héros dans la Grèce antique." In Gnoli and Vernant: 107–119.
Snodgrass, A.M. 1988. "The Archaeology of the Hero." *AION(archeol)* 10:19–26.
Solmsen, Friedrich. 1961. "Greek Philosophy and the Discovery of the Nerves." *MH* 18.3–4: 150–197.
Solmsen, Friedrich. 1982. "Achilles on the Islands of the Blessed: Pindar vs. Homer and Hesiod." *AJPh* 103.1: 19–24.
Solomon, Elizabeth Melpomene. 1998. *Jason the Great? Reminiscences of Alexander in Apollonius' Argonautica*. Diss. University of Georgia.
Sourvinou-Inwood, Christiane. 1995. *'Reading' Greek Death to the End of the Classical Period*. Oxford: Oxford University Press.
Sourvinou-Inwood, Christiane. 2005. *Hylas, the Nymphs, Dionysos and Others: Myth, Ritual, Ethnicity*. Stockholm: Åström.
Sowa, Cora Angier. 1984. *Traditional Themes and the Homeric Hymns*. Chicago: Bolchazy-Carducci.

Spaltenstein, François. 2002. *Commentaire des Argonautica de Valérius Flaccus (livres 1 et 2)*. Brussels: Latomus.

Spentzou, Efrossini. 2002. "Stealing Apollo's Lyre: Muses and Poetic ἆθλα in Apollonius' Argonautica 3." *Cultivating the Muse: Struggles for Power and Inspiration in Classical Literature*. Ed. Efrossini Spentzou and Don Fowler. Oxford: Oxford University Press. 93–116.

Stafford, Emma. 2005. "Vice or Virtue? Herakles and the Art of Allegory." *Herakles and Hercules: Exploring a Graeco-Roman Divinity*. Ed. Louis Rawlings and Hugh Bowden. Swansea: Classical Press of Wales. 71–96.

Stafford, Emma. 2010. "Herakles between Gods and Heroes." *The Gods of Ancient Greece: Identities and Transformations*. Ed. Jan N. Bremmer and Andrew Erskine. Edinburgh: Edinburgh University Press. 228–244.

Stafford, Emma. 2012. *Herakles*. London: Routledge.

Stambaugh, John E. 1967. "Aristeas of Argos in Alexandria." *Aegyptus* 47.1/2: 69–74.

Stambaugh, John E. 1972. *Satraps under the Early Ptolemies*. Leiden: Brill.

Stanzel, Karl-Heinz. 1999. "Jason und Medea: Beobachtungen zu den Gleichnissen bei Apollonios Rhodios." *Philologus* 143: 249–271.

Stenzel, Julius. 1908. *De ratione, quae inter carminum epicorum prooemia et hymnicam Graecorum poesin intercedere videatur*. Diss. Uniwersytet Wrocławski.

Stephens, S.A. 1998. "Callimachus at Court." *HG* 3: 167–185.

Stephens, S.A. 2002. "Egyptian Callimachus." *Callimaque: Sept exposés suivis de discussions*. Geneva: Fondation Hardt. 235–270.

Stephens, S.A. 2003. *Seeing Double: Intercultural Poetics in Ptolemaic Alexandria*. Berkeley: University of California Press.

Stephens, S.A. 2011. "Remapping the Mediterranean: The Argo Adventure in Apollonius and Callimachus." *Culture in Pieces*. Ed. Dirk Obbink and Richard Rutherford. Oxford: Oxford University Press. 188–207.

Stephens, S.A. 2015. *Callimachus. The Hymns*. Oxford: Oxford University Press.

Stephens, S.A. 2018. *The Poets of Alexandria*. London: Bloomsbury.

Stern, Jacob. 1979. "Herodas' *Mimiamb* 6." *GRBS* 20: 247–254.

Stern, Jacob. 1981. "Herodas' *Mimiamb* 1." *GRBS* 22: 161–165.

Stewart, Selina. 2010. "'Apollo of the Shore': Apollonius of Rhodes and the Acrostic Phenomenon." *CQ* 60.2: 401–405.

Stinton, T.C.W. 1976. "*Si credere dignum est*: Some Expressions of Disbelief in Euripides and Others." *PCPhS* 22: 80–89.

Stoessl, Franz. 1941. *Apollonios Rhodios: Interpretationen zur Erzählungskunst und Quellenverwertung*. Bern: Haupt.

Stürner, Stephanie. 2022. *Die Argonauten in Afrika: Einleitung, Übersetzung und Kommentar zur Libyenepisode der Argonautika des Apollonios von Rhodos (A.R. 4,1223–1781)*. Berlin: De Gruyter.

Suter, Ann. 2002. *The Narcissus and the Pomegranate: An Archaeology of the Homeric Hymn to Demeter*. Ann Arbor: University of Michigan Press.

Svenbro, Jesper. 1993. *Phrasikleia: An Anthropology of Reading in Ancient Greece*. Ithaca: Cornell University Press.

Syed, Yasmin. 2004. "Ovid's Use of the Hymnic Genre in the *Metamorphoses*." *Rituals in Ink*. Ed. Alessandro Barchiesi, Jörg Rüpke, and Susan Stephens. Stuttgart: Franz Steiner. 99–113.

Taback, Natalie. 2002. *Untangling the Muses: A Comprehensive Study of Sculptures of Muses in the Greek and Roman World*. Diss. Harvard University.

Tarditi, Giovanni. 1989. "Le muse e le Chariti tra fede del poeta ed *ethos poietikon*." *Aevum(ant)* 2: 19–45.

Thalmann, William G. 2011. *Apollonius of Rhodes and the Spaces of Hellenism*. Oxford: Oxford University Press.

Theodorakopoulos, Elena-Maria. 1998. "Epic Closure and Its Discontents in Apollonius' *Argonautica*." *HG* 3: 187–204.

Thériault, Gaétan. 1996. *Le culte d'Homonoia dans les cités grecques*. Lyon: Maison de l'Orient méditerranéen.

Thomas, Oliver. 2011. "The *Homeric Hymn to Pan*." In Faulkner: 151–172.

Thomas, Richard F. 1982. "Catullus and the Polemics of Poetic Reference (Poem 64.1–18)." *AJP* 103.2: 144–164.

Thomas, Richard F. 1986. "Virgil's *Georgics* and the Art of Reference." *HSCPh* 90: 171–198.

Thompson, Dorothy J. 2000. "Philadelphus' Procession: Dynastic Power in a Mediterranean Context." *Politics, Administration and Society in the Hellenistic and Roman World*. Ed. Leon Mooren. Leuven: Peeters. 365–388.

Thomson, D.F.S. 1997. *Catullus*. Toronto: University of Toronto Press.

Tissoni, Francesco. 2000a. *Cristodoro: Un'introduzione e un commento*. Alessandria: Edizioni dell'Orso.

Tissoni, Francesco. 2000b. "Cristodoro e Callimaco." *Acme* 53.1: 213–218.

Toohey, Peter. 1992. *Reading Epic: An Introduction to the Ancient Narratives*. London: Routledge.

Torres-Guerra, José B. 2003. "Die Anordnung der *Homerischen Hymnen*." *Philologus* 147.1: 3–12.

Tralau, Johan. 2008. "The Revolt of Images: Mutual Guilt in the *Parodos* of Sophokles' *Antigone*." *GRBS* 48.3: 237–257.

Tress, Heather van. 2004. *Poetic Memory: Allusion in the Poetry of Callimachus and the Metamorphoses of Ovid*. Leiden: Brill.

Tsakiris, Manolis. 2022. *Epic in Uncharted Waters: The Genres of Apollonius Rhodius' Argonautica*. Diss. University of Edinburgh.

Tzifopoulos, Yannis Z. 2000. "Hermes and Apollo at Onchestos in the *Homeric Hymn to Hermes*: The Poetics and Performance of Proverbial Communication." *Mnemosyne* 53.2: 148–163.

Ustinova, Yulia. 2009. *Caves and the Ancient Greek Mind: Descending Underground in the Search for Ultimate Truth*. Oxford: Oxford University Press.

Valk, M. van der. 1964. *Researches on the Text and Scholia of the Iliad, Part Two*. Leiden: Brill.

Valk, M. van der. 1976. "On the Arrangement of the *Homeric Hymns*." *AC* 45: 419–445.

Valverde Sánchez, Mariano. 1989. *El aition en las Argonáuticas de Apolonio de Rodas: Estudio literario*. Murcia: Universidad de Murcia.

Valverde Sánchez, Mariano. 1996. *Apolonio de Rodas. Argonáuticas*. Madrid: Gredos.

Vamvouri Ruffy, Maria. 2004. *La fabrique du divin: Les Hymnes de Callimaque à la lumière des Hymnes homériques et des Hymnes épigraphiques*. Liège: Centre international d'étude de la religion grecque antique.

van Wees, Hans. 1992. *Status Warriors: War, Violence and Society in Homer and History*. Amsterdam: Gieben.

van Wees, Hans. 2006. "From Kings to Demigods: Epic Heroes and Social Change, c. 750–600 BC." *Ancient Greece: From the Mycenaean Palaces to the Age of Homer*. Ed. Sigrid Deger-Jalkotzy and Irene S. Lemos. Edinburgh: Edinburgh University Press. 363–379.

Vasilaros, Georgios. 2004. *Ἀπολλωνίου Ῥοδίου Ἀργοναυτικά Α'*. Athens: Κέντρον Ἐρεύνης τῆς Ἑλληνικῆς καὶ Λατινικῆς Γραμματείας.

Venzke, Helmut. 1941. *Die orphischen Argonautika in ihrem Verhältnis zu Apollonios Rhodios*. Berlin: Junker und Dünnhaupt.

Verdenius, W.J. 1972. "Notes on the Proem of Hesiod's *Theogony*." *Mnemosyne* 25.3: 225–260.

Vergados, Athanassios. 2013. *A Commentary on the Homeric Hymn to Hermes*. Berlin: De Gruyter.

Vergados, Athanassios. 2020. *Hesiod's Verbal Craft: Studies in Hesiod's Conception of Language and its Ancient Reception*. Oxford: Oxford University Press.

Vergados, Athanassios. Forthcoming. "Etymology and the Rewriting of the *Homeric Hymn to Apollo* in Apollonius Rhodius 2.669–719." *Ancient Greek Theories and Practices of Etymology*. Vol. 2. Ed. Arnaud Zucker and Claire Le Feuvre. Berlin: De Gruyter.

Vian, Francis. 1987. *Les Argonautiques Orphiques*. Paris: Les Belles Lettres.

Vian, Francis, ed. and comm., and Émile Delage, trans. 2002 [1974–1981]. *Apollonios de Rhodes: Argonautiques*. 3 vol. Rev. ed. Paris: Les Belles Lettres.

Vílchez, Mercedes. 1985. "Estructura literaria y métrica en la poesía de catálogo helenística." *Habis* 16: 67–94.

Ville de Mirmont, H. de la. 1894. *Apollonios de Rhodes et Virgile: La mythologie et les dieux dans les Argonautiques et dans l'Énéide*. Paris: Hachette.

Ville de Mirmont, H. de la. 1895. "Le navire Argo et la science nautique d'Apollonios de Rhodes." *Revue international de l'enseignement* 30: 230–285.

Vivante, Paolo. 1982. *The Epithets in Homer: A Study in Poetic Values.* New Haven: Yale University Press.
Vox, Onofrio. 1999. "Noterelle di epica ellenistica." *Rudiae* 11: 161–172.
Vox, Onofrio. 2002. "Dionigi Alessandrino e Apollonio Rodio: cornici innodiche." *Lexis* 20: 153–170.
Wade-Gery, H.T. 1936. "Kynaithos." *Greek Poetry and Life: Essays Presented to Gilbert Murray on His Seventieth Birthday.* Oxford: Clarendon. 56–78.
Walbank, Frank W. 1991–1992. "The Hellenistic World: New Trends and Directions." *SCI* 11: 90–113.
Walbank, Frank W. 1992 [1981]. *The Hellenistic World.* Rev. ed. Cambridge, MA: Harvard University Press.
Walter, Anke. 2020. *Time in Ancient Stories of Origin.* Oxford: Oxford University Press.
Walther, Richard. 1894. *De Apollonii Rhodii Argonauticorum rebus geographicis.* Diss. Martin-Luther-Universität Halle-Wittenberg.
Weinberg, Florence M. 1986. *The Cave: The Evolution of a Metaphoric Field from Homer to Ariosto.* New York: Peter Lang.
Wellauer, Augustus. 1828. *Apollonii Rhodii Argonautica.* 2 vol. Leipzig: Teubner.
Wendel, Carl. 1932. *Die Überlieferung der Scholien zu Apollonios von Rhodos.* Berlin: Weidmann.
Werner, Erika. 2013. "Os hinos 'rapsódicos' de Calímaco: Tradição e inovação." *Hellenistica.* Ed. Joao Angelo Oliva Neto, Alexandre Pinheiro Hasegawa, Fernando Rodrigues Junior, Breno Battistin Sebastiani. São Paulo: Humanitas. 117–165.
West, M.L. 1966. *Hesiod. Theogony.* Oxford: Clarendon.
West, M.L. 1970. "The Eighth Homeric Hymn and Proclus." *CQ* 20.2: 300–304.
West, M.L. 1975. "Cynaethus' *Hymn to Apollo.*" *CQ* 25.2: 161–170.
West, M.L. 1978. *Hesiod. Works and Days.* Oxford: Clarendon.
West, M.L. 1993. "Simonides Redivivus." *ZPE* 98: 1–14.
West, M.L. 1999. "The Invention of Homer." *CQ* 49.2: 364–382.
West, M.L. 2001. "The Fragmentary Homeric Hymn to Dionysus." *ZPE* 134: 1–11.
West, M.L. 2011. "The First *Homeric Hymn* to Dionysus." In Faulkner: 29–43.
West, M.L. 2012. "Towards a Chronology of Early Greek Epic." In Andersen and Haug: 224–241.
West, M.L. 2013. *The Epic Cycle: A Commentary on the Lost Troy Epics.* Oxford: Oxford University Press.
West, Stephanie. 1965. "Apollonius Rhodius 4, 1773." *Hermes* 93.4: 491.
Wheeler, Graham. 2002. "Sing, Muse …: The Introit from Homer to Apollonius." *CQ* 52.1: 33–49.
Whitley, James. 1988. "Early States and Hero Cults: A Re-Appraisal." *JHS* 108: 173–182.
Whitley, James. 1994. "The Monuments That Stood before Marathon: Tomb Cult and Hero Cult in Archaic Attica." *AJA* 98.2: 213–230.

Whitley, James. 1995. "Tomb Cult and Hero Cult: The Uses of the Past in Archaic Greece." *Time, Tradition, and Society in Greek Archaeology: Bridging the 'Great Divide.'* Ed. Nigel Spencer. London: Routledge. 43–63.

Widzisz, Marcel. 2007. Review of Currie 2005. *CR* 57.2: 275–277.

Wifstrand, Albert. 1929. "Kritische und exegetische Bemerkungen zu Apollonios Rhodios." *Bulletin de la Société Royale des Lettres de Lund 1928–1929*. Lund: Gleerup. 73–107.

Wilkins, E.G. 1920. "A Classification of the Similes in the *Argonautica* of Apollonius Rhodius." *Classical Weekly* 14.21: 162–166.

Willcock, M.M. 1995. *Victory Odes: Olympians 2, 7, 11; Nemean 4; Isthmians 3, 4, 7*. Cambridge: Cambridge University Press.

Williams, Frederick. 1978. *Callimachus. Hymn to Apollo: A Commentary*. Oxford: Clarendon.

Williams, Mary Frances. 1991. *Landscape in the Argonautica of Apollonius Rhodius*. Frankfurt am Main: Peter Lang.

Wilson, Donna F. 2002. "Lion Kings: Heroes in the Epic Mirror." *Colby Quarterly* 38.2: 231–254.

Winkler, John J. 1985. *Auctor & Actor: A Narratological Reading of Apuleius's Golden Ass*. Berkeley: University of California Press.

Wilamowitz-Moellendorff, Ulrich von. 1895. "Hephaistos." *NAWG* 217–245.

Wilamowitz-Moellendorff, Ulrich von. 1924. *Hellenistische Dichtung in der Zeit des Kallimachos*. 2 vol. Berlin: Weidmann.

Wilamowitz-Moellendorff, Ulrich von. 1931. *Der Glaube der Hellenen*. 2 vol. Berlin: Weidmann.

Wimsatt, W.K., Jr., and M.C. Beardsley. 1946. "The Intentional Fallacy." *Sewanee Review* 54.3: 468–488.

Wolf, Friedrich August. 1985. *Prolegomena to Homer, 1795*. Trans. Anthony Grafton, Glenn W. Most, and James E.G. Zetzel. Princeton: Princeton University Press.

Wolff, Nadège. 2020. "Nuit et féminité dans les *Argonautiques* d'Apollonios: Vers l'émergence d'un héroïsme (au) féminin?" *Féminités hellénistiques: Voix, genre, représentations*. Edd. C. Cusset, P. Belefant, C.-E. Nardone. Leuven: Peeters. 53–83.

Wünsch, Richard. 1904. "Ein Dankopfer an Asklepios." *Archiv für Religionswissenschaft* 7: 95–116.

Wray, David. 2000. "Apollonius' Masterplot: Narrative Strategy in *Argonautica* 1." *HG* 4: 239–265.

Yamagata, Naoko. 1989. "The Apostrophe in Homer as Part of the Oral Technique." *BICS* 36: 91–103.

Zanetto, Giuseppe. 1996. *Inni Omerici*. Milan: BUR.

Zanker, Graham. 1977. "Callimachus' Hecale: A New Kind of Epic Hero?" *Antichthon* 11: 68–77.

Zanker, Graham. 1979. "The Love Theme in Apollonius Rhodius' *Argonautica*." *WS* 13: 52–75.

Zanker, Graham. 1987. *Realism in Alexandrian Poetry: A Literature and Its Audience*. London: Croom Helm.

Ziogas, Ioannis. 2013. *Ovid and Hesiod: The Metamorphosis of the Catalogue of Women*. Cambridge: Cambridge University Press.

Zissos, Andrew. 2008 *Valerius Flaccus' Argonautica Book 1*. Oxford: Oxford University Press.

Zumbo, Antonino. 1978. "Ψεύδη della tradizione e sistemazione di miti, ovvero Ap. Rh. *Arg.* 4.1130 sgg. e Call. *Iov.* 5 sgg., 32–38, 46–51." *Scritti in onore di Salvatore Pugliatti*. Vol. 5. Milan: Giuffrè. 1035–1041.

Żybert, Emilia. 2009. "Simaetha Versus Medea: Examples of *oppositio in imitando* in Apollonius Rhodius' *Argonautica*." *Eos* 96: 79–92.

Zyroff, Ellen Slotoroff. 1971. *The Author's Apostrophe in Epic from Homer to Lucan*. Diss. Johns Hopkins University.

Index of Greek Terms

ἄεθλος 191, 193–197, 225–227, 346
ἀλεξίκακος 194
ἀλυκτοπέδῃσι 32
ἀλωή 36n170
ἀνδροκτασία 179
ἀριστεία 72n334, 188, 227
ἄρχω, ἄρχομαι 11n58, 58, 62–63, 64–65, 89–90, 91–104, 105, 107, 113, 114, 117–118, 141, 143, 147n10, 309, 328

δειράς 315n162
δεῦνος 37n175

εὐαγής 318n182

ἤιος 108n106, 276n11, 279n16, 280
ἡρῷον 160n83
ἥρως 148–149, 151, 153, 156, 174n147, 178–179, 185, 341, 344, 352

θέμις 238, 246, 323, 344

ἱερόν 159, 160, 176n156, 187
ἰὴ ἰέ (or ἰὴ ἰέ) 276n11, 307n119, 316–318, 319n184, 320n189, 328
ἰήιος (or ἰήιος) 280, 307n119, 316n171, 319n183
Ἰηπαιήων (or Ἰηπαιήων) 312, 317n172, 319–320
ἵλημι, ἱλάομαι, ἱλήκω 14, 118n148, 119, 122n168, 125n180, 126n185, 127, 131, 134, 143, 144, 182, 323–324

κλέος 122, 132, 146n8, 151, 179, 180, 183–184, 187–188, 190–191, 196, 206, 211n303, 227, 255n105
κλυτός 122n166, 196, 206
κυδαίνω 182–183
κυδρός 33–34

λεπτότης 71

μάκαρ 127–128, 133–137, 172
μνήσομαι 10, 58, 59, 88, 90n29, 100n72, 107, 109, 117–118, 123–124, 139, 141, 143, 200, 223

νήπιος 234, 235
νόστος 119, 213–214, 224
νώνυμνος 190–191

ὀλολυγή 275, 276n11, 279n16
ὄργια 249–250

παλαιγενής 12, 58, 59n274, 72n332, 74, 109, 140, 146n7–8, 182, 188, 256
παμφαίνω 33
προοίμιον 17, 91–92, 104, 109, 189
πυρεῖον 46n221

ῥικνός 53

σηκός 160n83
σκαλμός 45–46
συνοίμιος 188–189
σχέτλιος 235
Σωτήρ 173n142, 174–175

τιμή 6, 14, 159n79, 174n150, 288
τύπανον 51n239

ὕμνος 10, 184–189, 190–191, 202, 338

φῶς 65–66, 69, 71–72, 136n232, 207

χαίρω 14, 125n180, 127, 143, 147n10, 209n295, 250, 276n10
χάρις 10, 122, 132, 209n295
χλεύη 261, 264

ὦ 128, 237

Index Locorum

Aelian Dionysius
Attic Lexicon
   α 76 Erbse   127n188

Aelius Theon
Prog.
   p. 109.20–26 Spengel
                                  154n51

Aeschylus
Eum.
   2–4   323n198
   27   317n176
   736–738   50
Pers.
   205–210   75
   938 with Σ   167
Suppl.
   117   342n54
   128   342n54
   260–270   342n54

Aesop
   111 Perry   36n169

Alcaeus
   fr. 307c Campbell   309n128

Alcman
   fr. 48 Campbell   107n96

Ananius
   fr. 1 West   240n45, 244n58

Andromachus the Elder
   GDRK 62.169–174   131n203

Anthologia Palatina
   2.378   58n268, 146n8
   6.225   34n165, 149n14
   7.254.1   206n280
   7.345.4   261n133
   9.24   71n327
   9.485   154n53
   9.504.6   288
   11.275   3n9
   14.18   286n44

Antoninus Liberalis
Met.
   23   44

[Apollodorus]
Bib.
   1.6.3   39n186, 44n208
   1.9.26   261–262

Apollonius of Rhodes
Argonautica
   1.1   12, 68–69, 71–72, 74,
                                 87, 89, 93, 100n71–
                                 72, 102, 105, 107, 108,
                                 115n132, 122n166,
                                 136n232, 146, 182, 188,
                                 196, 207, 211n303,
                                 234n15, 256, 282n28,
                                 328
   1.1–2   4, 30, 66, 67–77, 83,
                                 91, 101, 103, 104–106,
                                 109–110, 111, 113–114,
                                 139–141, 206n282,
                                 234, 237
   1.1–4   57, 86, 93, 102, 140,
                                 215
   1.1–8   119, 282n26
   1.1–22   83, 86–87, 93, 140,
                                 214
   1.2   59, 87–88, 145, 223
   1.2–4   213n311
   1.3   102
   1.5   68–69, 98n62, 99,
                                 102
   1.5–8   101–102
   1.5–17   86, 93, 99, 102, 215
   1.8   68–69, 87, 93,
                                 96n57, 100n71, 102,
                                 139n240, 141–142,
                                 234n15
   1.14   116n138
   1.16–17   213, 217
   1.18   58n270, 187
   1.18–19   190
   1.18–20   95
   1.18–22   86, 234n15
   1.20   113, 234, 237n35

Argonautica (cont.)

1.20–22	118*n*147, 187, 196*n*247, 213, 217, 218, 219, 220, 223	1.496–500	74
		1.503–505	253
		1.506–511	253*n*97
		1.507–512	326*n*210, 328
1.21	213*n*310	1.508	308*n*122, 326*n*211
1.21–22	218, 223	1.508–509	270*n*181
1.22	58*n*270, 70, 93, 120, 234	1.515	111
		1.536–541	115, 240
1.23	223, 235	1.548	55*n*258, 137*n*236
1.23–34	327	1.548–549	134–135, 171, 196
1.23–233	220	1.569–572	291–293, 298
1.25	117*n*143	1.570–579	111
1.26–31	111, 328*n*220	1.583–591	158
1.59	95, 187*n*206	1.587	182
1.59–64	157*n*68	1.587–588	162*n*90
1.81	219*n*330	1.608	54
1.90–93	247*n*70	1.616	282
1.101–104	157*n*68	1.644–648	157*n*68
1.122	150*n*21	1.648–649	235*n*23
1.122–131	221	1.669	53
1.122–132	327*n*218	1.675–696	54
1.123	235	1.736	270
1.130	217	1.740–741	111
1.133	340	1.759–760	317*n*176
1.135	235	1.759–762	114
1.141	180, 183, 184*n*186	1.760	270*n*181, 308*n*122
1.146–150	221–222	1.781	344*n*65
1.158	340	1.851	54
1.205	331*n*5	1.858–860	293
1.211–223	327*n*218	1.885	292*n*76
1.229–233	74*n*340	1.896	59
1.234–4.1772	220	1.915–921	245
1.287	183*n*182	1.920	120*n*157, 147*n*10, 250
1.307–311	68, 115*n*134, 240	1.955–960	344
1.308	244	1.959–960	159
1.323	217	1.960	347
1.362	102*n*82	1.966	159*n*75
1.375–376	182*n*179	1.970	171–172, 340
1.379	45–46	1.981	216*n*320
1.388	182*n*179	1.988	159*n*75
1.389	45–46	1.992	194*n*240
1.409–412	301	1.996–997	55
1.410–412	292*n*75	1.997	192*n*231, 194, 211*n*303
1.415–419	313*n*148	1.1012	194
1.419	240*n*46	1.1015–1022	344–345
1.443–447	180	1.1019	159
1.447	183	1.1022–1054	345
1.494–515	328*n*220	1.1030–1039	160*n*81
1.496	253	1.1040–1047	160*n*81, 179

INDEX LOCORUM

Argonautica (cont.)

1.1048	159, 179, 182	
1.1058–1062	160	
1.1063–1069	160n81	
1.1070–1077	345	
1.1098–1102	291, 303n109	
1.1099	212–213	
1.1071–1076	160	
1.1075	159, 162n89	
1.1075–1076	160n81	
1.1093–1094	303	
1.1123–1131	293–294	
1.1125	304	
1.1132–1133	303n108	
1.1139	51n239	
1.1148–1149	159n75	
1.1150–1151	294	
1.1151–1152	158n74	
1.1157–1158	250n86	
1.1165	160n83	
1.1182–1184	46	
1.1220	110, 235n23	
1.1225	292n77	
1.1226–1229	241n47	
1.1285–1286	55n260	
1.1292	183n182	
1.1304	160n82	
1.1305–1308	182n179	
1.1309	259n128	
1.1317	216	
1.1317–1320	172, 193	
1.1317–1325	165n109	
1.1319	36n169	
1.1319–1320	192n231	
1.1322–1323	161n84	
1.1324–1325	176	
1.1325	110	
1.1345–1357	165n109	
1.1346	161n84	
1.1348–1357	172n138, 176	
2.1–129	238n39	
2.1–163	76	
2.38–40	186	
2.40–43	187	
2.159	187n205	
2.161	188–189	
2.161–163	186–187, 294	
2.162	111	
2.164–176	188	
2.198	53	
2.209–211	216	
2.213	128	
2.213–214	107, 312n147	
2.216–217	116	
2.262–300	188	
2.278	29	
2.298–300	194	
2.311	247n69	
2.423–424	54–55	
2.425	247n69	
2.468–489	47, 48	
2.477–479	47–48	
2.479–480	47	
2.493	292n77	
2.504–505	149n14	
2.506–507	176	
2.508–509	47n227, 177	
2.531–532	46, 116n138, 312n147	
2.533–668	306	
2.598–603	117n143	
2.628–630	213n309	
2.655–657	160n83	
2.658	160	
2.669–719	116–117, 273, 305–328	
2.693	306n117	
2.700	292n77	
2.701–703	294	
2.705–707	291	
2.705–714	29	
2.707–710	274n4	
2.708	131, 144, 237, 251, 254	
2.708–710	115n132, 282n28	
2.715–719	295	
2.726	312n147	
2.735	162n87	
2.743	162n87	
2.752–758	187	
2.754–756	188n208	
2.763	216	
2.772	111	
2.774–798	195	
2.780–783	160n82	
2.780–785	166	
2.784–785	167n115	
2.786–791	167	
2.792–798	167n119	
2.806–810	174n150, 187	
2.807	160n83	

Argonautica (cont.)

2.807–808	270	3.32–35	50
2.835–840	181	3.64–65	116
2.841–850	181–184	3.66–74	343n63
2.842	161, 184	3.69	29
2.843	182, 183n184	3.115–116	177
2.845	184	3.115–117	34–37
2.846	161	3.134	326n211
2.847	161, 182	3.200–209	74n344
2.848	182	3.245–246	73n336
2.850	161, 182	3.307–313	73n336
2.852	182n176	3.320–326	195n244
2.892–893	190	3.336	215n317
2.905	37, 38, 40, 42n198	3.348–349	213n309
2.906	42n198	3.390	216
2.907	250n82	3.402	134, 136
2.907–908	162n87	3.464–466	178n162
2.909–910	259	3.467	74n345
2.911–929	162	3.478	74n345
2.912–913	168	3.533	73
2.916	259n125	3.535–536	54
2.922–923	303n109	3.540–543	54
2.929	259	3.543–554	303n109
2.946–954	168n122	3.549–550	54–55
2.955–956	168	3.669	74
2.967	344n65	3.714–716	74
2.982	190n221	3.757–758	239
2.985–995	195n244	3.846–847	295
2.989–991	351n3	3.858–862	295
2.1047–1067	195	3.861	304
2.1091	171–172, 340	3.861–862	302
2.1093–1096	216n318	3.862	68n313
2.1172–1173	195n244	3.865	74n347
2.1176	269	3.865–866	74
2.1181	163n95	3.876–886	52, 68, 241
2.1186	340	3.877	244n59
2.1210	42n197	3.878	52, 53n249
2.1211	39n185	3.897	52
2.1214–1215	37, 38, 39–40	3.898–899	52
2.1223	134	3.938–947	303n109
2.1246–1259	74	3.948–956	244n60
2.1248–1249	32n157	3.1000–1001	194n238
2.1249	32	3.1001–1002	177
2.1272–1274	163	3.1029–1041	158n72
2.1273–1274	179	3.1035	74n345, 303
3.1–5	287–288, 290	3.1069	59
3.2–3	289n59	3.1085–1095	74n340
3.3	68	3.1087–1088	74n346
3.6–111	351n3	3.1100–1101	194n238
		3.1110–1111	59

INDEX LOCORUM 417

Argonautica (cont.)

3.1124	321n194	4.530–531	315
3.1178–1179	269n180	4.539–541	164, 224
3.1191–1192	61n282	4.540	43n203
3.1194–1223	158n72	4.552–556	256n113
3.1211	240n45, 291n73, 301n101, 303n108	4.552–561	343n64
		4.557–561	174, 343
		4.580–594	174
3.1228–1230	73n336, 232n48	4.585–588	343
3.1240–1244	241–242	4.611–618	114
3.1273	160n82	4.649–653	174n150, 175–176, 270n183
3.1283	68n312		
4.1–5	21–23, 288–289	4.654–658	256
4.54–55	74	4.678–679	269
4.54–65	71, 73	4.700–709	296
4.57–58	177	4.700–717	343
4.59–61	73	4.701	344n68
4.68–69	186n200	4.708	304
4.131	74	4.800–804	253n97
4.145–148	291n73, 300	4.805	55
4.150	111	4.810	163n94
4.205	183n182	4.811	163, 177
4.220–221	73n336	4.811–815	225n355, 347
4.229–230	301n100	4.867–879	150n19
4.231–232	213n309	4.869–879	177
4.244–252	245	4.891–899	41
4.259–281	38	4.892	41n195
4.260	342	4.894	111
4.261–266	270n181	4.898	52
4.263	342	4.912–919	165
4.264	74	4.917–918	55–56
4.268	74n346	4.982–992	251–254
4.269	242	4.984	134, 323
4.282–283	38n180	4.984–985	131n203
4.303–304	194n237	4.985	248n77
4.355–390	267	4.1001–1003	194n237
4.361	70n329	4.1014	134n222
4.383	59	4.1020	74n345, 250
4.410–481	343–344	4.1027–1028	183n182
4.423	346n72	4.1041	219n330
4.430–434	177	4.1131	163
4.431	37n175	4.1131–1134	37n176
4.434	194n238	4.1132–1133	176n157
4.445–449	282, 287, 289–290, 291	4.1134	37, 38, 43
		4.1134–1138	41–42
4.451	235n23	4.1135–1136	43n205
4.479	134n222	4.1139	163
4.480–491	344	4.1140	163
4.507–521	194n237	4.1142–1143	184n189
4.526–536	116	4.1153	163

Argonautica (cont.)

4.1153–1154	159n78	4.1673	282
4.1196–1200	274, 282, 299	4.1682	314n159
4.1197	320n187	4.1694–1698	261n134
4.1206–1216	194n237	4.1694–1730	100, 112
4.1216	259n128	4.1701–1710	274–275, 280, 282, 299
4.1218	176n156	4.1704–1705	313n148
4.1225–1227	343n64	4.1705	240n46
4.1280–1289	191n223	4.1706	236n31
4.1285	160n83	4.1719–1730	260–266
4.1305–1307	189–191, 195, 196	4.1727–1730	296–297
4.1307	197	4.1731–1733	297
4.1309	149n14	4.1733	321n195
4.1309–1311	33	4.1747	112n120
4.1316	149n14	4.1749	183n182
4.1319–1321	216n319, 217–218, 223	4.1757–1761	285
4.1322	149n14	4.1761–1764	285–286
4.1323	149n14	4.1763–1764	165n105, 282n26, 282n29
4.1331	43n205		
4.1333	33–34, 134, 149n14	4.1764	259n128
4.1347	34, 149n14	4.1765–1772	118
4.1358	149n14	4.1770–1772	118, 133n217
4.1359–1360	217–218, 223	4.1773	118n149, 119, 126, 127, 128, 131, 133–137, 138n238, 140, 145, 172, 182n180, 196, 285, 286, 323n199
4.1381–1388	283–285, 329		
4.1383–1387	275n6, 280n18, 282n29		
4.1395	219n330		
4.1399	320n186	4.1773–1774	119n153, 128
4.1405	315	4.1773–1775	84, 119, 120n156, 121n162, 124, 132, 157, 165, 190, 197, 199, 207, 237
4.1411	128, 134, 237		
4.1411–1421	324n204		
4.1414	128		
4.1472–1477	161n84, 165n109	4.1773–1777	195–197
4.1476	182n179	4.1773–1781	4, 30, 83, 118–119, 146, 205–206, 220, 224, 282n28, 283
4.1485	282n32		
4.1485–1489	282n29		
4.1489–1492	352n10	4.1774	119, 120, 129, 131
4.1511	250, 319	4.1774–1775	127
4.1513	340n47	4.1775	122n166, 137n235
4.1537–1622	341–342	4.1775–1776	119, 126n181, 224
4.1547–1550	116	4.1775–1781	120, 236n31
4.1551–1552	312n147	4.1776–1778	119
4.1593–1602	46–47	4.1778–1781	119
4.1620–1622	127n188	4.1781	119n151
4.1636–1693	194	Σ ad *Arg.* 1.1–4a	91–93, 101
4.1641–1642	171	Σ ad *Arg.* 1.1–4b	97n58
4.1665	111	Σ ad *Arg.* 1.587	158n69
4.1665–1669	296	Σ ad *Arg.* 1.1019	159n78, 345n70
4.1668–1669	302n103	Σ ad *Arg.* 1.1039	160n81

INDEX LOCORUM 419

Argonautica (*cont.*)
Σ ad *Arg.* 1.1040–1041
    160n81
Σ ad *Arg.* 1.1126–1131a
    168
Σ ad *Arg.* 2.162–163 187
Σ ad *Arg.* 2.684–687 310n131
Σ ad *Arg.* 2.702 318n180
Σ ad *Arg.* 2.705–711a 314n158
Σ ad *Arg.* 2.705–711b 313
Σ ad *Arg.* 2.705–711g 313n153
Σ ad *Arg.* 2.712–713 316n171
Σ ad *Arg.* 2.715–719b 321
Σ ad *Arg.* 2.780–783a–b
    166
Σ ad *Arg.* 2.843 182n179
Σ ad *Arg.* 2.844–847a
    161n85
Σ ad *Arg.* 2.848–850b
    161n85
Σ ad *Arg.* 2.911–914 162n87
Σ ad *Arg.* 2.1273 179n167
Σ ad *Arg.* 3.1–5c 97n58
Σ ad *Arg.* 3.114–117a 36
Σ ad *Arg.* 3.114–117b 36n168
Σ ad *Arg.* 4.1760–1764b
    285

Epigrams
  fr. 50 SH 3n9, 44–45
  fr. 13 Powell 3n9
Foundation of Rhodes
  fr. 11 Powell 50n236

Aratus
1 92–93
1–18 104, 113
2 103
15 290
16 120n157, 135n227
16–18 93
96–136 171
637 131n203, 252
641–644 252
783–787 71
Σ ad *Phaen.* 16 135n227

Aristophanes
Pax
  406–411 75

Heroes
  fr. 322 Henderson 347
Σ ad Ar. *Vesp.* 819 160n83

Aristotle
Eth. Nic.
  1145.22–23 346

Athenaeus
1.22b 19

Bacchylides
3.96–98 122n166
13.228–231 122n166
17.125–129 276n11
17.125–132 275

Batrachomyomachia
1–8 98–99

Bion
Ep. Adon.
  88–89 321n191

Callimachus
Aetia
  fr. 1.21–22 Pfeiffer 98n64
  fr. 7.13–14 Pfeiffer 126n185
  fr. 7.19–21 265n154
  fr. 7.22–26 Pfeiffer 113n126
  fr. 7.25 Pfeiffer 99–100
  fr. 18.5–10 275n6, 279–280
  fr. 18.8 Pfeiffer 261n134
  fr. 18.9 Pfeiffer 100n71
  fr. 20 Pfeiffer 261n134
  fr. 21 Pfeiffer 260–266
  fr. 23 Pfeiffer 280n19
  fr. 37 Pfeiffer 34n164
  fr. 43.69–71 252
  fr. 59.21 Pfeiffer 259n128
  fr. 67.5–6 Pfeiffer 280n19
  fr. 75.4–9 Pfeiffer 247–248
  fr. 75.56 Pfeiffer 316n170
  fr. 88 Pfeiffer 313
  fr. 108–109 Pfeiffer 262
  fr. 112 Pfeiffer 121n161
  fr. 178.3–4 280n19
  fr. 186.31 280n19
  Dieg. 2.24–25 314n155

420   INDEX LOCORUM

Epigrams
2.2	59
24.1–2	176n154
35.1	44n210

Hecale
fr. 74.10 Hollis	53n251
fr. 80.3–5 Hollis	199–200
fr. 81–83 Hollis	200
fr. 172 Hollis	259n126
Dieg. 11.5–7	200

Hymns
1.4–5	23n115
1.4–10	37
1.32–54	41n196
1.58	74n346
1.87–88	25
1.91–94	125n180
1.94–96	209n297
2.1–7	310n132
2.21	319n184
2.26–27	25
2.36–38	308n124
2.38–40	323n197
2.69	280n19
2.70	240n45
2.97	319n184
2.97–104	316–317
2.98	280n19
2.100–101	314n155
2.113	120
3.77	259n128
3.110–112	241n47, 244n59
3.111	52n248
3.136–142	280n19
3.170–176	242n49
3.266	129n199
4.79–85	47n228
4.81	48n229
4.91–92	314n155
4.92	317
4.118	128n193
4.160–190	25
4.300–321	280n19
4.325	128n193
4.326	120n157, 128n193
5.60–65	242n49
6.15	259n126
6.121–127	129n199
fr. 384.30 Pfeiffer	160n82
fr. 602 Pfeiffer	34n165, 149n14

Catullus
64	348
64.21–22	137
64.22–23	135
64.22–24	125–126
64.23	136
64.24	200n257
64.382–396	137

Certamen Homeri et Hesiodi
16 West	23n114
18 West	23n114

Clearchus of Soli
fr. 64 Wehrli	317

Cleon of Curium
Arg.
fr. 339 *SH*	158n69

Conon
Narr.
41	262
49	261–263

Corinna
fr. 664b *PMG*	72n333

Corpus Inscriptionum Graecarum
4162	169n123

Deiochus of Cyzicus
FGrH
471 F 5	159n75
471 F 8b	160n81

Diodorus Siculus
1.2.4	192n230
1.13	192n230, 337
1.15.7	8
1.26.1	337
1.44.1	337
3.57.5	68n307
3.66.3	8
3.71.3	37n175
3.72.1–2	37n175
4.2.4	8
4.56.6	342
4.81.2–3	176n156
4.82.5–6	176n156

INDEX LOCORUM   421

Dionysius the Periegete
1–3	90
447	131n203
1181–1186	121n163

Dionysius Thrax
Σ Dion. Thrax p. 451.6–7 Hilgard
    154

Domitius Callistratus
FGrH
433 F 2	168

Duris of Samos
FGrH
76 F 79	317n174

Empedocles
fr. 12.2 DK	191n223
fr. 45 DK	69n319

Ephorus of Cyme
FGrH
70 F 31b	317n174, 318n179

Epica adespota
fr. 10 Davies	127n188

Epigoni
fr. 1	63n294

Etymologicum Magnum
s.v. Ἰήιε	307n119
s.v. Νυκτέλιος	37, 40

Euphorion
fr. 116 Lightfoot	316n167

Euripides
Bacch.
1–23	42n98
519–525	42n201
723–726	303n110

Hipp.
525–564	290n63

Hippolytus Veiled
fr. 446	192n228

Hypsipyle
fr. 752g.9	319n183
fr. 752k.17–21	180n172

IT
1250–1251	308n122, 309n128

Med.
6	216n321

Phoen.
206–207	315n162

Rhes.
962–973	155

Eustathius
Il.
3.915.25–26 van der Valk
    283n34

Gospel of John
1:4	69n319

Heliodorus
Aeth.
3.2	154n53

Heraclitus
B 5 DK	153

Herodas
1	265n155
4.1–9	120n157
6	265n155

Herodorus
FGrH
31 F 48	310n131

Herodotus
1.90.2	75
2.3.2	247n72
2.47.2	247
2.50.3	337n31
2.51	247n72
2.61.1	247
2.62.2	247
2.86.1	247
2.170.1	247
2.171.1	247
3.5	38
3.5.3	39n184
5.75.2	174n147
7.188–191	158n74

Hesiod
Theogony
1	113n123
1–115	17, 141
33	137n235
36	113n123
67	288
77–79	223n345
79–80	22n110
100	72n333
179	314n159
183–187	254n99
201–202	34n63
203–205	288
235	163n94
334	315n63
521	32
522	32n157
535–564	257n117
924–929t	50
949	177
954–955	192n231, 209n297
963–964	147n10, 250n85
988–991	165
995–996	216n321

Works and Days
1–10	17, 92
10	113, 237n35
69	326n210
109–201	257n117
156–173	169–170
158	346
159–160	135, 171, 205
171	136, 172
174–201	347
379	163n95

Catalog of Women
fr. 22.26–33 Most	206n282
fr. 155.64–65 Most	169n124
fr. 159–160 Most	176n156

Shield of Heracles
472–480	255n107

Hesychius
s.v. Βῶρμον	167

Homer
Iliad
alternate *incipit*	107–108
1.1	21, 22, 61, 97, 108, 120, 289
1.1–2	12
1.1–7	86n8
1.3–4	179
1.4	213n310
1.8	99
1.8–9	108n105
1.21	108n105
1.35–37	298
1.37	108n105
1.37–38	243, 302n102
1.42	108n105
1.44–53	108n105
1.76–77	321
1.234–237	182n179
1.458–474	238
1.472–474	312n147, 321n191
1.473	320
1.473–474	319
1.594	54
1.605–608	59
2.275	261
2.506	242n48
2.550–551	149
2.594–600	267n169
2.670	163n95
2.783	39m85
2.830–834	180n173
3.236–244	202
3.243–244	173
4.301–309	324
5.199	242n48
5.302–304	170n127, 255n108
5.401	319
5.638–642	173n143
5.639	211
6.60	191
6.132	43n203
6.133	37, 40
7.228	211
8.112	269n176
9.97	146n7
9.189	71, 146
9.410–416	180
9.413	151, 183n183, 205
9.524	71, 146
9.527	146n7
10.360	29

INDEX LOCORUM 423

Iliad (cont.)
11.60 64n299
11.328–335 180n173
12.23 135n226, 170–171
12.70 191
12.322–328 180n169
12.381–383 170n127, 255n108
12.447–449 170n127, 255n108
13.227 191
14.70 191
14.294–296 248n77
15.346–349 324
15.365 108n106, 280n21, 281
15.582–583 281
16.435–438 23n115
16.688 238
16.692–693 283n34
16.786–789 281
17.398–399 251n87
18.117 173n143
18.117–119 150n21
18.239 64n299
18.429–441 55
18.484 64n299
18.567–572 240n46
18.569–570 312n147
20.2 281
20.9–10 241n47
20.39 308n124
20.152 108n106, 280n21, 281
20.216–218 269
20.232–235 34–37
20.285–287 170n127, 255n108
23.149 326n210
24.1–5 150n20
24.804 162n88
ΣbT ad *Il.* 1.3 179n165
ΣA ad *Il.* 9.246 19
Σ Genevese ad *Il.* 21.319
 19–20

Odyssey
1.1 12, 21, 97, 120, 289
1.1–5 210–211, 213–215
1.1–21 86n8
1.2 219
1.3–4 217n325
1.9 213
1.10 21n107, 96n57, 99
1.14 176n154
1.338 187
3.380 318n181
4.159 261
4.271 210n300
4.561–569 150, 163n94, 191–192
4.724 211
4.814 211
5.120 176n154
5.206–224 176
6.100–101 52
6.102–103 242
6.123–124 241n47
7.205–206 254n99
7.256–258 176
8.73 71, 146
8.79–81 116n136
8.223–225 173n143
8.268–367 325–326
8.293 54n253
8.429 185
8.462 59
8.499 95
8.570 326n210
10.516–534 158n72
11.15–47 158n72
11.77 182n179
11.267 211
11.300–304 150, 173
11.601–604 150, 206n282
12.15 182n179
12.69–72 213n311
12.259 214n313
12.362–363 265n157
13.125–187 255n107
13.178 326n210
16.101 69
21.363–365 131n203
23.244–246 59n272
23.296 119n151
23.306–307 210n300
23.335–337 176
24.11 150n20
ΣT ad *Od.* 8.499 95
Homeric Hymns
1 7n34
1A.2–7 236n31
1A.6 42
1A.8 39n184
1A.9–10 37–40

Homeric Hymns (cont.)

1A.9–11	38n180	2.477	150n19
1A.9–14	40n192	2.490–495	131n208
1A.13–14	39	3	236–237
1C.5	32n156	3.1	88–89, 91, 107, 109, 139, 143, 237
1D.1–3	258n123	3.2	241n47
1D.8	143	3.5	309n125
1D.8–9	106n93, 127	3.14	128, 237
1D.8–10	123–124, 143	3.16	240n46
1D.8–12	125n180	3.19	237
2.1	89	3.27–28	310n132
2.1–2	131n208	3.40	240n45
2.1–3	13	3.51–60	258
2.5–6	52	3.57–60	270
2.6–8	41n195	3.84–88	258
2.7	39	3.87–88	270
2.17	39–41	3.111	46n221
2.24–25	258	3.119–122	276
2.51–62	258	3.120	108m106, 280
2.63	59n272	3.134	308n124
2.88–89	59n272	3.156	110
2.113	72n332	3.156–161	109–111, 113, 130
2.153	150n19	3.160	72n333, 109, 113, 237
2.195–205	264	3.161	110, 185, 187n205
2.202	261	3.162–164	110
2.206–211	265	3.165	120n157, 127, 143, 144, 237, 251, 252n89, 254, 306n117
2.233–291	177		
2.256–280	311		
2.263–267	150	3.165–176	18, 130–133
2.270–274	258	3.166–178	237
2.272	259n126	3.169	131
2.273	250	3.172	18
2.274	318n182	3.173	131
2.316	326n210	3.177–178	358
2.328	54n257	3.179	128
2.364–369	270	3.179–181	240n45
2.369	318n182	3.207–208	237
2.385	240n45	3.216–246	120n156, 236
2.398–403	258	3.225–228	269
2.417	41n195	3.229–239	268
2.425	52	3.230	242n48
2.431	52, 53n249, 241n47	3.236	269
2.425–429	41n195	3.272	312n147, 319
2.440	258	3.250	19
2.445–456	258	3.277–282	120n156, 236
2.448	326n210	3.278–280	269n175
2.450–456	264n149	3.281–282	315n162
2.473–482	249, 258	3.287–293	258
2.474	150n19	3.290	19

INDEX LOCORUM

Homeric Hymns (cont.)

3.296	150n19	5.8–44	287n49
3.300–306	314n156	5.12–15	258n123
3.300–374	29, 312	5.33	54–55
3.305–355	268	5.58–63	34n163
3.308–325	50	5.58–67	64n298
3.317	53	5.68–74	241n47
3.341	19–20	5.97–100	241n47
3.357	316n168	5.100–102	311n135
3.357–358	317n175	5.149–152	251n87
3.363–369	68n309	5.181–182	310n132
3.363–374	315	5.202–206	35–37
3.372–373	259	5.208	36n171
3.374	314n159	5.256–273	47–48
3.382–383	258n123	5.264	48
3.388–544	311	5.292	56
3.403	312n147	5.293	89, 185
3.449–450	317n175	6.5–15	34, 64n298
3.490	312n147	6.19–21	15, 16
3.493–496	258n123, 259	6.20	123
3.500	319	7	310n132
3.508	312n147	7.1–2	88–89, 91, 139–140, 143
3.510	240n46, 312n147	7.2	123n171
3.514–515	312n147	7.42	46
3.516–517	240n46, 312n147	7.53	257n118
3.517	319	7.55–59	276n10
3.518	319n185	7.58–59	123–124, 128–129, 143
3.526	128		
3.544–546	276n10	8	7, 111n119
3.545	312n147	9	243–244
4.1	143	9.1	143
4.17–18	25, 61n282	9.3–4	18
4.25	258n123	9.5	240n45
4.69	59n272	9.7	135n227
4.87–94	44	9.9	89, 185
4.111	258n123	10.1–2	12
4.111–113	46	10.4	7, 127n188
4.125–126	259	10.4–5	56
4.128–129	46	10.5	123
4.136	46	12.1–4	291
4.187–212	44	13.3	122, 123n173, 310n129
4.190	44n211	14.2	143
4.508	259	14.3	51n239
4.524–527	324n202	14.3–6	276–277
5	7	14.6	135n227
5.1	12, 143	15	174, 206–226 *passim*
5.1–2	140	15.1	201n258
5.7	54–55	15.1–2	55
5.8–15	50	15.4–6	145n3, 347–348

Homeric Hymns (cont.)

16	174, 207	28.5–6	33
16.2–4	207n285	28.14	59n272
17	174, 207	29	111, 131n208, 138n238, 236n31
17.1	143	30.4–16	236n31
17.2–4	207n285	31	207n284
17.5	221n336	31.1	62–63
18.10–12	126n180	31.1–2	22, 61, 143, 287, 289
18.11	89, 185	31.2	64n299
19.1	143	31.2–7	61
19.1–7	304–305	31.4	62n287
19.12–13	357	31.5–6	62n298
19.15	29	31.5–7	62n299
19.27–49	277	31.8	61
19.29–48	326–327	31.8–16	61
19.38–39	257n118	31.9	242n48
19.47	258n123	31.9–13	64
19.48	127n186	31.10–12	73
20.1	143	31.12–13	64n299
20.2–7	258n123	31.14	63
20.8	127n186, 143, 209n297	31.14–16	61n282
21	111–112, 236n31, 277	31.16	62
21.1	113–114, 143	31.17–19	65–66
21.5	127n186	31.18	72, 89, 187
22.7	127	31.18–19	15, 22, 171n133
23.4	127n186, 143	32	207n284
24	111, 236n31	32.1	22, 61, 62–63
24.4	357n3	32.1–2	61, 143
24.5	123	32.2	58n270, 63, 234n15
25	112–113, 131n208	32.2–6	64
25.1	89, 113–114, 143	32.3–13	61
25.6	123n173	32.4	64
26.3–5	43	32.7	62
26.4	43n205	32.7–8	64n298
26.5	39n187	32.9	63–64
26.6	43n205, 331n5	32.10	64n298
26.7–11	278	32.11	62
26.8–10	39n187	32.11	61
26.11	128	32.14–16	61–62
26.11–13	129	32.16	64n298
27	244n59	32.17–18	64n298
27.1–3	291	32.17–20	57–58, 65–66
27.18–22	278	32.18	71n329, 72, 89
27.21	135n227	32.18–19	4, 67–77, 85, 88, 91, 94, 104–106, 113, 171n133
28	50		
28.1	33	32.18–20	15, 22
28.1–4	291	32.19	58n270, 59, 187
28.4–5	33		

INDEX LOCORUM

Homeric Hymns (cont.)

33	174, 186n201, 201, 203n268, 207
33.1	62, 143, 175
33.4–5	207n285
33.5–6	175
33.6–17	207n285
33.9	175n151
33.10–11	47
33.18	221n336

Horace
Odes

1.9–11	107n99
3.3.9–10	225n360

Ibycus

fr. 282.47–48 Campbell

	122n166
fr. 289 Campbell	36n168

Inscriptiones Graecae

14.2012A38–39	69n319

Isocrates

9.70	192
10.64–65	155n61

Istrus
FGrH

334 F 38 [51]	192

Juba
FGrH

275 F 97	37n175

Little Iliad

fr. 1	12–13

[Longinus]
Subl.

1.27.1–2	324
9.11–15	23n114

Lucian
True Story

2.20	23n114

Lycophron
Alex.

721	182n181
929	182n181
1189–1213	183
1213	182n181
1386	261n133

[Manetho]

6.751–754	121n163, 122n168

Meandrius
FGrH

492 F 14a	313

Mimnermus

fr. 11.3 West	216n321

Mnaseas of Patras

fr. 17 Cappelletto	250

Moero

fr. 1.7–8 Powell	36–37

Nicander

Σ ad Nic. *Alex.* 130	19

Nonnus
Dion.

21.109	43n206
21.193–195	43n206
29.272	43n206
35.362	43n206

Paraphrase

4.4–5	69n319

Nymphis
FGrH

432 F 3	167n115
432 F 5	167
432 F 9b	167n115

Ovid
Met.

2.687–707	44
4.11–30	302n105
4.17–30	275n6
4.754–756	275n6
5.319–331	39n186

Met. (cont.)		4.78–168	99
7.365	103	4.176	96n54
15.731	275n6	4.176–177	117n143
		4.184	171n134
Oppian		4.184–187	180n170
Hal.		4.194–200	117n143
1.649–653	257n118	4.204–211	117n143
1.652–654	69n319	4.211	171n134
2.385	32	5.93–95	286n48
Cyn.		5.94–95	136n230
1.341	321n191	6.10–17	122n166
		9.59–65	176n156
Orion of Thebes		11.7	149n14
s.v. φώς	69n318	*Nem.*	
		1.62–63	210n301
Orphic Argonautica		1.70	193
1–6	100–101	2.1–3	17
461	164	3.22	225n360
1161–1162	191n223	5.14	247
1186–1202	40n192	8.50–51	186n200
		9.53–55	122n166
Parmenides		10.55–59	173
fr.14.3 DK	69	10.83–90	173
		11.22–25	23n115
Pausanias		*Isthm.*	
1.41.9	346n75	4.37–39	132n214
2.26.6	42	4.55–56	210n301
10.18.2	315n165	4.55–60	225n360
		4.57–58	209n297
Pindar		*Paean*	
Ol.		7b	18n93
1.82–84	155n60	15	154
1.90–93	155n60	18	154n54
2.2	151	fr. 133	192, 347
2.68–80	192, 347	Σ ad Pind. *Pyth.* 4.36c	341n53
3.19–20	59n272	Σ ad Pind. *Pyth.* 4.37	342n57
		Σ ad Pind. *Pyth.* 4.61	341n53
10.76–79	186n200	Σ ad *Pyth.* 4.313a–b	96n54
14.4	74n340	Σ ad *Nem.* 2.1c	19, 132n210
Pyth.			
3.2	251n87	**Pherecydes of Athens**	
3.4	354n17	FGrH 3 F 54	38n181
4.3–64	286n48		
4.12	171n134	**Philicus**	
4.13	136n232	fr. 677 *SH*	265n155
4.33–34	342	fr. 680.54–62 *SH*	265n155
4.69	74n340		
4.70–71	99	**Plato**	
4.70–78	113n126	*Cra.*	
4.71–78	99	397c–d	75

INDEX LOCORUM 429

Euthyphr.
  6a   253n96
Leg.
  958e   149
Meno
  81b   347
Phd.
  60d   23n114
Phdr.
  243a–b   155n61
  259d   288
Resp.
  377d–378b   253
  540b–c   170
  607a   185
Symp.
  208c–e   180n173

Pollux, Julius
Onom.
  1.28–29   276n11
  4.54–55   167

Promathidas of Heraclea
FGrH
  430 F 3   161n85, 181n175
  430 F 4   162n86

Quintus of Smyrna
  5.112   314n159
  6.464   161n85
  7.39–41   69n319

Sappho
  fr.1.8–9 LP   52n428
  fr. 44.31–33 LP   276n11, 320n187
  fr. 105a LP   323n197

Seneca
Dial.
  10.13.2   23n114

Servius
  ad Verg. G. 1.14   176n156

Silius Italicus
  1.1   147n10
  17.651–654   147n10

Simonides
  fr. 11.14–28 W^2 203–206
  fr. 11.31 W^2 174n147
  fr. 11.32 W^2 205
  fr. 11.33–34 W^2 205n276
  fr. 573 *PMG*   317n175
  fr. 558 *PMG*   205
  fr. 559 *PMG*   205n278

Sophocles
Ant.
  781–800   290n63
Colchian Women
  fr. 345 Radt   36n168
OT
  1099   177n158

Statius
Achil.
  190–191   146n5

Stesichorus
  fr. 327 Finglass   288n57

Strabo
  9.2.10   160n83

Suda
  s.v. συνοίμιον   189

Theocritus
Id.
  1.61   185
  1.123–125   243
  3.50–51   247n73
  16.2   186n198
  16.50   186n198
  16.103   186n198
  17   338–339
  17.1   92–93
  17.8   186
  17.46–50   165n108
  17.135–136   16n82
  17.135–137   124–125
  22   186n201, 188n210
  22.1   185, 202
  22.1–22   201
  22.4   186, 202
  22.6–22   175

Id. (cont.)

22.23	207n283
22.26	186, 202
22.27–135	203
22.33	46n221
22.135	186, 202
22.135–213	202
22.214	186
22.214–215	120
22.214–223	122n166, 135n227, 201–203
22.218	131n206
22.221	204
22.223	131n206
24	123n173, 138n237, 220n332
24.1	201n258
26.33	120n157
26.35	120n157

Ep.

2.2	185

Theognis

1–4	106–107, 112n121, 113n125
5–11	107n95
243–252	151
1345–1348	36n168

Thucydides

3.104.4–6	17, 18, 237
5.11.1	155

Tibullus

2.5.121–122	307n119

Tzetzes

praef. ad Lycoph. *Alex.* p. 3.27–4.1 Scheer
  18

Valerius Flaccus

Arg.

1.5–7	97–98
1.352–483	222n342
2.10	164
5.82–89	162n86
5.98–100	162n91

Varro of Atax

fr. 5 Blänsdorf	316n171

Vergil

Aen.

1.1	13
3.119	275n6
3.371	275n6
6.18	275n6
6.251	275n6
7.389–391	275n6, 280n18
8.84	275n6
8.285–304	275n6
10.540	275n6
11.7–8	275n6

Vita Homeri

2.8–9	9
2.9	23n114
9.3	19

Xenophon

An. 4.3.19	276n11

Index Rerum

Acamas   64n299
Acastus   217
Acheron   165n108
Acherusia   162n87, 190
Achilles   55n260, 146n5, 150n20, 154n53, 155, 162n87, 163, 164, 177, 180–181, 183n183, 203–206, 210, 211, 212, 225n355, 281, 321n192
acrostics   71, 94, 150n20, 352n10
Aea   *see* Colchis
Aeacus   154
Aeetes   53, 54, 73, 76, 163n95, 186n199, 193n235, 241–242, 301n100
Aegaeon   160n83
Aegina   118
Aeneas   34, 48, 275n6
Aeschylus   32–33
Aesonis   301
Aethalides   157n68
Aetolia   222n337
Agamemnon   136n116, 191n223, 255n106, 321n192
Agamestor   161, 169, 182, 184
aition   *see* etiology
Alcaeus   107
Alcestis   155
Alcinous   263, 266n158
Alcmene   208
Alexander the Great   179n167, 336–337, 339
Alexandria; *see also* Ptolemies
    avant-garde poetics   25–26, 71, 94, 120–121, 141, 144, 156, 179, 199, 233, 268, 270
    cults of Alexander   336, 339
    Museum   97n61, 103n83
    philological scholarship   7–8, 19–20, 105, 107, 185
    Royal Library of   3, 28, 105, 250n84
Alexandrian footnote   30, 39n185, 235, 283n36
Alpheus   46, 259
allusion
    memory as a trope for   59–60
    theory of   20n104, 27–31, 67, 76, 77, 136
    tool for characterization   51–53

alter egos, narratorial   95n50, 96n54, 138n239, 238, 247n69, 253, 270n181, 325, 327
Amazons   168, 173n141, 195n244, 269
Amnisus   241
Amphiaraus   157n68, 180
Amphipolis   155
Amun-Ra   336
Amyclae   313n148
Amycus   76, 167n119, 186, 194, 221n336, 227, 238n39, 270, 294, 347n80
Anaphe   68, 100, 112, 116, 260–266, 271, 279, 296, 313n148, 333
anaphora   125–126, 210, 274n4, 284, 290, 302, 308n122, 318, 322, 324, 326n211
anastrophe   128
Anaurus   343n63
Ancaeus (son of Lycurgus)   355
Ancaeus (son of Poseidon)   355
Anchises   34n163, 35, 36, 311n135
Anthemoessa   41n195, 72n334
anti-etiology   255
Antigonus   45n212
antiquarian "flashback"   269–270
Apellicon of Teos   107–108
Apis   341–342
Aphrodite   4n19, 34, 35, 36, 50, 54–56, 64n298, 115, 165, 288, 311n135, 351–356 *passim*
Apollo   44, 47n227, 67, 68–69, 72–76, 83, 84, 89, 91–118 *passim*, 119, 131, 138, 141, 142–143, 159n75, 161, 162, 176n157, 177, 181–182, 185n192, 187, 234n15, 236–237, 239n44, 240, 241n47, 242n48, 243, 244, 246n68, 251, 254, 258, 259, 260–261, 265, 268, 269, 270, 273, 274, 275, 276, 277, 279, 280, 281, 282, 291, 294, 298, 301, 305–328, 329, 341, 351–356 *passim*
Apollodorus (pupil of Aristarchus)   19–20
Apollonius of Rhodes
    Alexandrian, as an   39, 49
    alleged quarrel with Callimachus   3n9, 44n209
    Against Zenodotus   3
    career   3, 94, 97n61, 103n83

dating   24–25, 84n5, 192, 198–199, 250
lost works   3, 20, 147n9
ostensible rationalism   246n64, 283n36
philological scholarship   3, 20, 43–44, 71n329, 77, 95–96, 105, 131, 150, 164, 179, 190–191, 237, 244, 313, 318, 335
Samothracian Mysteries, and the   248
Apollonius' *Argonautica*
  episodic narrative   26
  first edition (προέκδοσις)   84n5
  "hymnic frame"   4, 5, 57, ch. 1 *passim*, 146, 226, 328, 331, 332
  "love theme"   70–71, 287
  narrator   110, chs. 3–4 *passim*, 333
  performance   83, 84n6, 94–96, 104–105, 109–111, 121n162, 122, 129, 132, 206
  pessimism   227
  reception of the Homeric epics   2–5, 21, 51, 77, 144, 198, 222, 310n132, 331, 332
  scholia   91n30
apologies to the gods   122n168, 233, 250–254, 323–324
apopemptic prayer   290
apostrophe   96n57, 107, 108n106, 118n148, 119, 128n193, 131–132, 143, 183, 199, 206n281, 234, 235, 236, 252, 272, 273, 274–275, 279, 280, 281–290, 291, 299, 323, 329, 343
apotheosis   9, 36n169, 150, 165n108, 168, 172–177, 186–188, 192–193, 195, 202–203, 211n307, 212, 220, 224, 227, 336–339, 342, 343, 346, 347; *see also* immortalization
appeal to the Muses   11, 12, 21, 61, 63, 93, 96, 97, 98, 108, 113, 120, 142, 143, 204–205, 234, 235, 282n28, 286–289, 329
Apsyrtus   178n163, 218, 219n330, 287, 289, 343–344, 345, 346, 353n15
Aratus   150n20
Arcadia, Arcadians   74, 342
Ares   351–356 *passim*
Arete   134n222, 185n193
Aretias   195
Argo   45, 46–47, 53, 115n134, 134–135, 159, 171, 174, 182n179, 187, 188, 196–197, 250n86, 256, 279, 283, 288, 341

Argonauts   4, 32, 46, 54–55, 68, 74, 75, 83, 85–86, 93, 100, 105, 106, 114, 115, 116, 118–122, 125–126, 129, 132, 133–143, 148, 156, 157, 158, 160, 162, 164, 167n119, 168, 171–177, 178, 179, 180, 182, 186–189, 190–191, 193–197, 199–200, 206, 211n307, 214–220, 223, 226–227, 231, 237, 239, 240, 244–246, 248, 261–266, 269, 272, 282n28, 283–285, 286, 287n49, 291, 293, 294, 295, 296, 305, 306, 312, 313, 320, 321, 323n199, 325n206, 326, 328, 329, 330, 331, 332, 335, 340–342, 343–348, 351–356 *passim*
Argos   180, 340
Argus, son of Phrixus   38, 54, 74, 215n317, 270n181, 342; *see also* Phrixids
Ariadne   177, 194n238
Aristaeus   163, 176, 216, 351–356 *passim*
Aristarchus   20n100, 119n151
Aristophanes of Byzantium   107, 119n151
Aristotle   146n4
Arsinoe II   68n307, 336–337
Artemis   52–53, 55, 68, 69n321, 76, 239n44, 241, 242, 243–244, 252, 254, 278, 287n49, 291–293, 300n98, 343, 351–356 *passim*
Asclepius   42, 174, 207
Athena   33–34, 39, 50–51, 55, 115, 159, 287n49, 344, 347, 351–356 *passim*
Athens, Attica, Athenians   7, 62n284, 149, 153n38, 155, 161n85, 192, 199–200
Atossa   75
attributive section (of a *HH*)   13–14, 51n239, 61–62, 88, 207n285, 243–244, 288, 290, 304
Aulis   158n73
Ausonian (Tyrrhenian) Sea   174
Autolycus   169

bacchants   275n6, 302n105, 303n110
Bacchus   *see* Dionysus
Bacchylides   120n159
"barbarians"   73–76, 194n237
Battus (mythological character)   44–45
Battus (oecist)   136n230, 286n48
Baubo   263n145, 265n155
Bebrycia, Bebrycians   72n334, 167n119, 186–188, 203n267, 238n39, 352n9

INDEX RERUM   433

Berenice I   165n108, 336
bird-signs   54–55
birds of Ares   195
Bithynia   161n85
Black Sea   68, 194, 269
Boeotia, Boeotians   161n85, 340, 352n10
book culture   94n43
Boreads   72n334, 182n179, 188, 194, 327n218, 352n9, 354n16
Boreas   351–356 passim
Borimus   166–168
Bosporus   194n237
Brasidas   155
Bronze Age (Hesiodic)   171, 346
Bubastis   247
Butes   55–56, 165

Cadmus   269n180
Caeneus   157n68
Calais   see Boreads
Calchas   321n192
Callichorus   259
Callimachus of Cyrene
    Aetia   23n115
    alleged quarrel with Apollonius   see Apollonius of Rhodes
    court poet, as   340
    Hecale   121n162
    Hymns   8, 24, 25, 47–48, 50, 94n47, 237, 334
    poetics   25–26, 93n37, 94n47, 102n82, 232, 233, 236, 254–266 passim, 270–271, 272, 329, 332
Calliope   11n59, 22, 61, 280, 287, 289
Calliste   see Thera
Calypso   176
Campania   41
Canthus   282n29, 282n32
Caria   40n189, 41n193
Casius, Mt.   38n181
Cassandra   183
catalog, epic   119, 149, 179, 219–223, 227, 235, 236n31, 247n70, 267, 268, 327, 339, 354n16
catasterism   186–187
Caucasus   32–33, 38
Celeus   264
Ceraunian Mountains   38n181
Chalciope   54

Charites   see Graces
childhood   26, 36
Chios   18, 131–132, 202, 237
Chiron   158n69, 354n17
choral song   109, 115, 306, 309, 310n130, 325n206, 326, 328
Chryses   243, 298, 301n102, 304–305
Chryseis   321n192
Circe   174, 213n311, 296, 352n9, 353n11
Cius, Cians   161n84, 176
Clarus   240, 244
Clashing Rocks   117n143, 160, 194, 213n311, 258n120, 306, 309n126, 347n80
Cleite   160n81
Clio   252
Clytius   178n161
Colchian serpent   300
Colchis, Colchians   32, 53, 73–75, 163, 164, 194n237, 216, 219n330, 288, 289n59, 309n126
collective security   52
colonization   75–76, 155, 159, 161, 165n106, 169, 181–182, 194, 256, 258n120, 285–286, 339, 344
color (imagery)   35n166
Concord   117n142, 295, 309, 312n145, 321, 354n16
contagious hymnody   272, 273–281, 282, 299, 302, 305, 323, 329, 333
Coronis   42
correction, allusive   29n147, 37, 44, 136, 183n183, 222n342, 252, 266, 314, 316n170
Corycian Cave   316, 318, 326n213
Crete, Cretans   36, 72n334, 194, 274, 311, 312, 313
Crisa   311, 312n147
Croesus   75
Cronus   252–254, 354n17
Cyanean Rocks   see Clashing Rocks
Cybele   51n239, 158n74, 276, 293–294, 303, 351–356 passim; see also Rhea
Cycnus   255n107
Cynaethus   7n38, 19, 132n210
Cyprus   7, 34, 55–56
Cyrene (city)   136n230, 194n239, 286n48, 341, 342n60
Cyrene (nymph)   47n227, 177, 355n25
Cyrnus   151

Cyzicus (place)   158n74, 159, 160n81, 162n89, 179, 192n231, 193n235, 194, 256n113, 262, 293, 344–346, 347, 352n9
Cyzicus, King   160, 166n112, 178n163, 216n320, 355
cultic hymns   6, 10, 11, 14, 26, 111, 120, 127, 236n27, 309, 357n3

Danaus   340–341
Dawn   *see* Eos
Deianeira   225
deification   *see* apotheosis
Deimachids   168–169, 347n80
Delian maidens   109–111, 130–132, 236, 251, 310n130
Delos   240, 258, 270, 313n148
Delphi, Delphians   115n132, 116n136, 154n53, 240, 244n59, 278, 309n128, 311, 312, 313, 315, 316, 317n176, 318n179, 323n198, 325n206, 352n10
Delphic serpent, the   29, 37n173, 259, 307, 308, 309, 311, 312, 313–317, 325, 328
Delphyne(s)   *see* Delphic serpent
Demeter   48, 150, 177, 240n45, 249–250, 254, 258, 264–265, 311, 352n9
Demodocus   95, 110, 185, 213n311, 238, 324n202, 325–326, 328n226, 354n18
Demophon   150, 177, 258n123, 311
Deucalion   74n346
Dexion   192
diachronic method   30, 83–85, 332
Diadochi   336n25
Didymarchus   45n212
digression   41, 47, 110, 114, 117, 157n68, 164, 168n122, 238, 242n48, 259n128, 267–269, 309, 325, 352n8
Dindymum, Mt.   51n239
Dionysius Scytobrachion   8, 37n175, 68n307
Dionysius the Periegete   147
Dionysus   37–44, 106n93, 123–124, 128–129, 162n87, 163, 177, 185n192, 250n82, 259, 275n6, 278, 302n105, 303n110, 310n132, 351–356 *passim*
Dioscuri   47, 131n208, 150, 173–176, 185, 187–188, 195n245, 201–203, 205, 207, 212, 221–222, 270, 339; *see also* Polydeuces
Dipsacus   160, 169
direct speech   274n3, 291, 292, 293n80, 298, 299, 302n105, 318, 321, 324, 325

Dolionians   159–160, 162n89, 166, 169, 179, 345
Dolopians   158n69
Dolops   158, 162n89, 164–165, 169
domain (of a god)   103n83, 242–243, 297, 301n102, 304
downshifting   325n207, 327
Draco   153n38
du-Stil   11, 14, 111, 120, 139n240, 236, 277, 279, 280n19, 287, 299n93, 308n122, 316n171, 323, 324n200

eagle   36–37
earthborn men (Colchis)   353n11
earthborn men (Cyzicus)   192n231, 193n235, 194
Egypt, Egyptians   38–40, 67–68, 74, 247, 261n134, 335–337, 340–342
Elba   256
Electryon   154n54
Eleusis, Eleusinians   150, 240n45, 258n123, 264, 311
Eleusinian Mysteries   248–250, 258, 259n126, 264–266
Elpenor   182n179
Elysium   133, 150, 152, 163, 164, 205, 225n355, 347
empathy (of a narrator for their characters)   110, 196n247, 298, 325
Endymion   71, 177
Eos   59n272, 61, 64n299, 351–356 *passim*
Epic Cycle   2n5, 19n98, 63n294, 149, 162n87, 203n267, 227n363
epic hymn   22, 140, 143, 147, 178, 180, 189, 191, 197, 198, 203, 206–207, 212, 218, 220, 226, 231–232, 281, 283, 288, 328, 329, 332, 334, 335
Epimenides   146n4
epinician   186, 187n205
epiphany   6, 9, 68, 116–117, 152, 162, 174, 175n152, 305, 306, 310, 311–312, 341, 342n58, 353n11
epyllion   26, 138n237, 199–200, 201n258, 348
Erato   22n110, 287–288, 289n59, 290
Eratosthenes of Cyrene   250n84
Erechtheus   149
Erichthonius   50n236
Eridanus (Po)   174

INDEX RERUM 435

Eros 4n19, 34, 36n170, 50, 115, 272, 282, 287, 289–290, 291, 343, 354n16
er-Stil 11, 14, 120, 139, 143, 147n10, 279, 299n93, 308n122, 323
Erysichthon 47, 48
Eryx 55–56, 165
eternal prolepsis 270
ethnography 45n213, 74n344, 75, 232, 238n40, 268–269
etiology 26, 46, 51n239, 74, 112n120, 118, 133n217, 156, 158, 159, 160n81, 162, 163, 164, 166, 172n138, 174–175, 179, 183n184, 184n186, 186, 192, 238, 251–254, 254–266, 270, 271, 272, 285, 305, 306, 309, 310n131, 311, 316, 320n187, 321, 325n206, 329, 331n4, 333, 341, 345, 352n9, 353
etymology 33n160, 37, 38n181, 41, 48, 69, 103, 127, 162n89, 175, 191, 211n303, 257n117, 258n123, 261n130, 286, 288n55, 301, 312, 315–318, 325n206, 338, 351n6
Euboea 42–43
Euhemerism 37n175, 68n307, 176n156, 192, 336
Eumaeus 131n203, 281
Euphemus 285, 286n48, 297, 341
Euripides 335n19, 347
Eurynome 253
Euryphaessa 61, 62n287, 64n298–299
Eurypylus see Triton
Eurystheus 209n294, 215n317, 216–217, 219n330, 224
evocation (of a hymned divinity) 11, 12, 62, 88, 139, 143, 175, 223, 284n38, 293, 304, 305, 309

free indirect discourse (FID) 272–273, 299–300, 301, 302, 303, 305, 320
funerary rites 42, 160, 162n88, 166–167, 181, 238n40
Furies 343, 351–356 *passim*

Gaia 61, 74, 163, 186, 236n31, 253, 353n11
Ganymede 34–37, 177, 354n16
generic hybridity 22, 83, 120, 122, 140, ch. 2 *passim*, 231–232, 329, 332, 333
Giants 186, 192n231, 254
Glaucus (Lycian hero) 180n169
Glaucus (sea god) 172, 193, 195, 355n25
Golden Apples 173n142, 315

Golden Fleece 213, 224n350, 246n64, 289n59, 332, 355n23
Graces 34n163, 126n185, 244n59, 278, 354n19
Greek (ethnicity) 73–76, 340, 342
Gyrton 157n68

Hades (god) 37, 41n193, 52–53, 250, 270
Hades (underworld) 150n20, 152, 157n68, 162n86–87, 165n108, 179, 181, 270, 336
Haemonia see Thessaly
Halys 245
hamadryad see nymphs
hapax/dis legomena 32, 33, 46, 51n239, 53, 77, 131, 144, 184–189, 211, 249–250, 261, 264, 271, 308n124, 312, 315n162, 318n182, 319, 331
Harmodius and Aristogeiton 155
Harpies 188, 194, 347n80, 354n16
Hebe 209n294, 225
Hecale 53n251, 159n77, 199–200, 212
Hecataeus of Abdera 8n39, 192n230, 337
Hecate 52, 68n313, 74n345, 158n72, 241, 245–246, 250, 258, 300–301, 302, 303, 353n11
Hector 155, 162n88, 183
Hecuba 205n278
Helen 155
Helius 59n272, 61–77, 103n83, 207n284, 242n48, 301n100, 306n116
Hephaestus 50n236, 53–54, 209n297, 351–356 *passim*
Hera 42–43, 50, 53, 55, 115, 116, 117n143, 163, 164, 192n231, 215n316, 225n355, 247–248, 279, 282, 287n49, 343n63, 351–356 *passim*
Heraclea Pontica 161, 181, 183n184, 184
Heracles 55, 110, 150, 157n68, 162, 164, 165n109, 166–168, 172–173, 174, 178n161, 183n182, 184n188, 186, 192–195, 206–212, 216–217, 219–220, 221n335, 222–226, 246n68, 250n86, 308, 315, 327n218, 339, 348, 353n12
Herodotus 232, 248, 253n94, 332
heroes
  Age of Heroes 45, 134, 135, 149, 155, 156, 169–172, 198, 205, 335, 337, 346, 348
  cult 85–86, 129, 133–137, ch. 2 *passim*, 272, 283, 285–286, 328, 332, 335, 339, 340, 343–348

heroism 77, 156n63, 329–330, 331, 343–349
heroization *see* immortalization
heroines 149n14; *see also* Herossae, Libyan
Hermes 4n19, 42, 44–45, 46, 131n208, 158n69, 258, 259, 297
Herossae, Libyan 33–34, 149n14, 190n220, 217–218, 355n25
Hesiod 6, 20n103, 45n212, 49, 76, 112–113, 149n16, 174n150, 222n341, 238, 253–254, 334–335, 340, 348
Hesperides 128, 315, 324n204
Hestia 55, 106, 287n49
Hiero II 186n198
Hippolyta 162
Hipponax 265n155
Homer
 biographical traditions 9, 18, 23n114, 111, 131, 155, 202, 237, 244
 epics 6, 49–51
 theological critiques of 253–254
 narratorial style ch. 3 *passim*
 "sun poet," as 71n327
Homeridae 19, 132–133
Homeric Hymns
 as mythological sources 32–45
 attribution to Homer 18–24
 collection 6–9, 60n280, 129n197, 207n284, 334
 dating 7, 56, 58–60, 64n299, 206n282, 276
 narratorial style 26, ch. 3 *passim*
 performance 16–17, 96, 104–105, 109–111, 129, 206n282
 reception 5, 19–20, 23–26, 44n207, 49–51
 rhetorical structure 9–16, 119–120, 139
Homonoia *see* Concord
honorifics 11, 12, 21, 33, 114, 127, 140, 272, 274, 289, 290, 291, 292, 297–298, 299, 301, 302, 303, 304, 305, 320, 321, 324, 351
Horae 34
Horus 39, 67, 336
Hydrophoria 112n120, 118n148, 129n199, 133n217
Hylas 4n19, 165n109, 167, 172n138, 176, 327n218

hymnic long alpha 22n111
hymnic narratization 242n52, 272, 273, 291–305, 319, 320, 321, 329, 333, 351, 356
hymnic relative 12, 61, 62, 87–88, 140, 145, 298, 304
Hyperboreans 306, 309n128
Hyperion 61, 73
Hypnus 300–301
Hypsipyle 59, 346n72

Iambe 249n80, 263n145, 264–265
ich-du juxtaposition 126
Idmon 161, 166n112, 180–184, 227
imitatio cum variatione see *oppositio in imitando*
immortalization 133, 134, 136, 137, ch. 2 *passim*, 272, 282n28, 283, 285, 328, 329, 330, 332, 335, 339, 341, 342, 343–349; *see also* apotheosis
Ida, Mt. 311n135
implied author 20, 332
India 37n175, 40n189, 259
indirect speech 216, 267, 274n4, 280, 284, 291, 292, 293n80, 299, 300, 301, 303n108, 308, 321, 322–323, 325, 326, 327
Ino 43n206, 163n95
intention, authorial 27–28, 30
interpretatio graeca 39, 67–68, 250n84; *see also* syncretism
interpretive community 28, 30
intertextuality 27–31, 106
invocation (of a hymned divinity) 9, 11, 83, 85, 100, 118n148, 128, 141n246, 143, 240n45, 242, 272, 273, 274, 282n26, 283, 290, 291, 293, 297–298, 299, 301, 302, 303, 304, 319, 320, 328, 351
Iolcus 224, 289n59, 300n98, 352
Ionia, Ionians 159, 344, 352n9
Iphias 352n9
Iron Age (Hesiodic) 76n353, 135, 346–347, 348
Iris 215n316, 354n16
Isis 67, 69n321
Islands of the Blessed 133, 136, 152, 172, 205, 347
Italy 41

INDEX RERUM 437

Jason 46, 50, 51–53, 54, 68, 69n321, 71, 73, 76–77, 99, 102, 112n120, 115n134, 116, 117n143, 155, 158n72, 159, 163, 164, 166n112, 175n152, 178, 179, 183n182, 184n189, 186n199, 190, 193, 197n250, 214n312, 215–217, 219, 224, 225n355, 239n44, 240, 241, 244, 267, 270, 274, 279, 280, 296, 301, 303, 306, 313n148, 314n160, 315, 343–344, 346n72, 347, 348, 351–356 passim

Keres 299

Ladon 315
Laius 161n85
Lamidae 43n206
laudatio 9, 12, 13–14, 140, 143, 227, 332
Leda 221–222
Leerstellen 267
Lemnos, Lemnians 53–54, 194n239, 263n145, 282, 286, 293
Leto 128, 236, 270, 276, 280n22, 309, 317, 324n200, 351–356 passim
Leucothea see Ino
Libya 33–34, 39, 46–47, 149n14, 173, 189–190, 256, 258n120, 262n139, 282n28, 285, 315, 329, 341–342, 352n10
Lilybaeum, Cape 55–56, 165
Lindos 265n154
Lucan 51
Lycia 240, 306
Lycurgus 37, 40n190
Lycus 166–168, 187, 188n208, 194, 216, 270
Lynceus 173n142
Lyra 162, 163n97, 259

Macaera 192n228
Macris 41–43, 159n78, 163, 164
Magnesia 158
Maia 4n19
Manetho 337
Marathon 206n282
Marathonian bull 199
Mariandynians 166–168, 187, 188n208, 194–195
Mecone 257n117

Medea 50, 51–53, 54–55, 59, 68, 69n321, 71–72, 73, 76–77, 111n114, 134n222, 155, 159n78, 163, 164, 178n162, 184n189, 224, 225n355, 239, 241, 244, 246n64, 262–263, 267, 274, 287, 288, 289–290, 295, 296, 299, 300–301, 302, 303, 314n160, 343, 346n72, 347, 351–356 passim
Mediterranean 194
Megara, Megarians 161n85, 346n75
Megara (wife of Heracles) 224
Melanippus 281
Meleager 146n7
Meles river 18, 244
Memory see Mnemosyne
Mene see Selene
Menelaus 149–151, 163n94, 174n147, 191–192, 203n269, 205, 281
Merops 180n173
metabasis see poet's task
metalepsis 273, 278–279, 280n19, 282, 303, 305, 316n171, 325–327, 329, 333
Metaneira 265, 311
metapoetry 59, 71n327, 95n48, 111n114, 115, 120, 123, 128–129, 148, 179–197 passim, 200, 226, 235, 265n155, 266, 287, 316n167, 328, 329, 331, 332
metempsychosis 157n68, 192
mimesis 94, 105, 110
Minos 194n238
Minotaur 194n238
Minyae 74n340, 352
mise-en-abyme 111, 184n190, 188, 235, 279, 310n130, 328
Mnemosyne 183, 254
model as code (Conte) 45n214
monstrosity 76
moon see Selene
Mopsus 162, 291, 303
multiple allusion 29, 34
Musaeus 103n86, 339n39
Muses 21–22, 66, 70, 103n86, 108, 113, 131n208, 137n235, 183–184, 223n345, 232, 237, 244n59, 251–254, 272, 278, 280, 283–284, 287–289, 323, 351–356 passim; see also appeal to the Muses
Mysia, Mysians 46, 110, 167, 172, 193

myth (central narrative of a *HH*)   13–14, 33, 41, 43, 47, 61–62, 64*n*299, 88, 93, 114, 120, 133*n*217, 140, 143, 145, 188, 203*n*272, 207, 208*n*287, 209*n*292, 212, 221*n*334, 223, 224, 225–226, 227, 265*n*155, 267*n*163, 270, 279, 287*n*49, 312, 332

Naples   165*n*105
narratee   235, 267, 273, 343*n*63, 355
narratized speech   292, 298, 301, 302, 318–319, 320; *see also* hymnic narratization
Nauplius   339–340
Nausicaa   51–52, 59, 242
Nausithous   178*n*163
Neleus   340
Neoptolemus   154*n*53
Nereids   158*n*74, 215*n*316
Nestor   267*n*169, 340
Nicander   45*n*212
Night   353*n*11
Nile   38–39, 342
Nonnus   43*n*206, 50*n*236, 147*n*10
nurses of Dionysus   37, 40*n*190, 41*n*193, 42–43, 163*n*95, 278
nymphs   41*n*193, 43, 47–48, 149*n*14, 160, 168*n*122, 176, 177, 241*n*47, 242*n*49, 274, 277, 278, 279, 304–305, 310*n*130, 316, 318, 320*n*187, 326–327, 328
Nysa ad Maeandrum   41*n*193
Nysa (mythological locale)   37–44

Ocean   39*n*188, 62, 253
Oceanids   39*n*188, 52
Odysseus   149*n*16, 176, 210–211, 214*n*312, 256*n*113
Oechalia   225*n*355
Olympia   46, 155*n*60
Olympus, Mt.   34*n*164, 53, 173, 208, 212–213, 220, 225, 253, 277, 291
omnitemporal present tense   13–14, 243, 255, 268, 278, 288*n*52, 300*n*98
Onchestus   242*n*48, 268
Ophion   253
oppositio or *variatio in imitando*   29, 34*n*163, 38*n*180, 55, 71, 72*n*332, 90*n*29, 135*n*229, 146*n*6, 234*n*15, 244*n*60, 265*n*157, 269, 354*n*20

optative (in prayer)   119, 120–121, 126, 143*n*252
Orchomenus   74*n*340, 340
Orion   252
Orpheus   72*n*334, 74, 95*n*50, 96*n*54, 100, 111*n*114, 112*n*121, 115, 117*n*143, 128, 131, 138*n*239, 149*n*16, 162, 182*n*179, 186–188, 223, 237, 238, 246*n*61, 251, 253–254, 259, 273, 275*n*6, 291–293, 298, 300*n*98, 305–328, 329, 339*n*39
Orphic Argonautica   329
Orphic Hymns   101, 291
Ortygia   *see* Delos
Osiris   67, 69*n*321, 336
overt narrator   26, 233–237, 249, 272, 305
Ovid   5, 49, 50*n*236–237, 316*n*166

paean   95*n*48, 115, 240*n*46, 275, 276*n*11, 305, 306, 309, 310, 311*n*140, 312, 316–318, 319–321, 326*n*213, 328
Paeëon   250, 319, 351*n*6
Pagasae   115, 117*n*143, 164, 196, 224, 240, 291
Pamphilus   45*n*212
Pan   243, 257*n*118, 258*n*123, 277, 304–305, 326–327
Pandia   61–62, 64*n*298
Paphlagonia   246, 248
Paraebius   47–48
Parthenius (river)   241
Parthenope   165*n*105
Patroclus   180*n*173, 281, 282
Pausanias the Regent   205*n*276
Peleus   55, 137, 154*n*53, 247*n*70
Pelias   85, 91, 99, 102, 116*n*138, 160*n*82, 213, 214*n*312, 215–217, 224*n*350, 352
Pelion, Mt.   128*n*193
Peloponnesus   341–342
Pelops   155*n*60
Periclymenus   340
periphrastic denomination   352
Persephone   4*n*19, 37, 39, 41, 44, 52–53, 68*n*313, 131*n*208, 162*n*86, 250, 258, 259*n*125, 270, 354*n*19
Perses   74*n*345
Perseus   216, 340*n*47
Persia, Persians   75, 158*n*74, 205
Phaeacia, Phaeacians   163, 194*n*237, 251–254, 255*n*107, 262–263, 274, 320*n*187, 352*n*9
Phaethon   165

INDEX RERUM 439

Pharaoh   102*n*82, 192*n*230, 335–337, 339
Phasis   179
Phemius   95, 110, 213*n*311
Phineus   53, 54–55, 107, 116, 188, 194, 216, 238, 247*n*69, 312*n*147, 347*n*80, 352*n*9
Phlegyae   269*n*175
Phlogius   169*n*123
Phocus   247*n*70
Phoenicia   38
Phoenix   146*n*7
Phrixids   195*n*244, 216, 219*n*330, 347*n*80; *see also* Argus, son of Phrixus
Phrixus   160*n*83, 163*n*95, 352*n*9, 355
Phyllis   160
piety (narratorial)   237–254, 272, 273, 287*n*49, 298, 299, 303, 305, 318*n*182, 323, 328, 333, 344
"pious silences"   244–250, 333
"pious similes"   239–244, 254, 272, 312*n*147, 333
Pindar   120*n*159, 173, 232, 239, 248, 329, 332, 335*n*9
Planctae   *see* Wandering Rocks
Platea   203–206, 212
Pleistus   317
poet's task   14–15, 16, 22, 60, 88, 89, 104, 106, 121–126, 143, 185, 200, 205
Polydeuces   72*n*334, 186–189, 227, 294; *see also* Dioscuri
Polyphemus (Argonaut)   161*n*84, 165*n*109, 178*n*161, 182*n*179
Polyxena   162*n*87
Polyxo   53–54
Poseidon   117*n*143, 127, 141*n*248, 250*n*86, 341–342, 351–356 *passim*
Pothus   34*n*163
prayer   9, 14, 15, 83, 84, 85, 93, 101, 114, 119–129, 132, 133, 134, 137, 138, 143, 157, 172, 174–175, 196, 197, 199, 209, 220, 242, 243, 272, 275, 283, 290, 298, 299, 301, 302, 324*n*200
Priolas   160*n*82, 166–168
Proclus   7
proem, hymnic   16–17, 60, 66, 85, 91–96, 100–101, 104–114, 121, 140–142, 185, 189, 205, 206, 211, 223*n*245, 288, 290
prolongation (*HH* narrative technique)   13–14, 133*n*217, 203*n*272, 209*n*292
Prometheum   295

Prometheus   32–33, 74
Proteus   163*n*94
Ptolemies   25, 67–68, 69*n*321, 102*n*82, 156*n*63, 286*n*48, 331, 335–343, 348, 349*n*88
Ptolemy I Soter   336–337
Ptolemy II Philadelphus   124, 186, 336–338
Ptolemy III Euergetes   337
Ptolemy IV Philopator   336
Pylos, Pylians   267*n*169, 311, 340*n*43
Pythagoras   157*n*68
Pytho   *see* Delphi
Python   *see* Delphic serpent

Rarium   264
rationalization, mythological   37*n*175, 42*n*202, 68*n*307, 116*n*139, 176*n*156, 192, 310*n*131, 317*n*174, 337
reader (interpretive construct)   30–31
reception (Jaussian)   49
red herrings   86, 104, 141, 197
re-reading   30, 83–84, 86, 139, 142, 143, 188, 197, 332
rhapsodes   7, 16, 95–96, 104–105, 109–110, 132–133
rhapsodic hymns   6, 10, 11, 13, 24, 26*n*131, 60, 111, 120, 121, 127*n*188, 133, 138*n*239, 139, 143, 147*n*9, 201, 212, 226, 259*n*126, 305, 309, 310, 334
Rhea   43*n*206, 51*n*239, 291, 293–294, 351–356 *passim*; *see also* Cybele
Rhodanus (Rhone)   174
Rhodes   50*n*236, 103, 163*n*95
ruler cult   25, 156*n*62, 335–343, 348–349

sacrifice   9*n*46, 46–47, 50*n*236, 52, 75*n*348, 116, 153, 158, 159, 162, 163, 175*n*152, 179, 183, 202, 242*n*51, 262–263, 265–266, 306, 309, 312*n*144, 318, 341, 352
Salamis (Cyprus)   7, 56
Salii   275*n*6
salutation   14, 15, 55–56, 83, 85, 119, 120*n*157, 121, 122*n*168, 125, 126*n*185, 127, 131, 133, 134, 137, 138, 143, 145, 157, 172, 196, 197, 199, 205, 209, 220, 250, 278, 283, 286, 312*n*147, 323*n*199, 327, 338
Samothrace   246, 248, 250
Samothracian Mysteries   245, 248–250
Sarpedon   180*n*169

Scipio Africanus 147n10
Selene 59n272, 61–77, 105, 177, 207n284, 354n19
Semele 42
Serbonis (lake) 38
Sesostris 74n346
Set 39
Sicily 55, 165, 252
similes 52, 68, 114, 115, 160n82, 186–187, 191n223, 239, 250n86, 255, 343n63, 354n16; *see also* "pious similes"
Sinai Peninsula 38
Sinope 168–169
Sintians 54
Sirens 41, 55, 165
Sleep *see* Hypnus
Smyrna 18, 244
Socrates 253
song culture 94
Sparta, Spartans 155, 174, 205, 222n337, 285
speech act theory 292
sphragis 103, 130–133, 237
"spontaneous" break-off 248, 267
Stesichorus 155n61
Sthenelus 162, 169
Stoechades 174n150
Stymphalian birds 195
sun *see* Helius
super-genre 6n27, 10n52
Symplegades *see* Clashing Rocks
syncretism 67–68, 76, 161n85; *see also* interpretatio graeca
Syrtis 189, 283
system reference 10, 30, 45, 57, 60, 87–88, 104

Talos 72n334, 171, 194, 262n139, 296, 299
Tartarus 253n97
Teichoscopia 202
Telamon 247n70
Telphusa 258n123
Tereus 346n75
Terpsichore 354n16
Thamyris 267n169
Thebes 42, 161n85, 183, 206n282, 208n290, 225n355, 259, 269–270, 275n6, 302n105
Themis 323n198
Theocritus 24, 25, 237n35, 270, 334

Thera 165n105, 261n134, 272, 285–286
Therapna 173–174, 186, 187
Theras 165n105, 272, 282n29, 285–286
Theseus 157n68, 193n235, 194n238, 199–200, 275
Thesmophoria 247
Thessaly 100n72, 352n10
Thetis 55, 137, 154n53, 158n74, 163, 177, 180
Thrace, Thracians 37, 40, 246n61
threnody 166–167, 191
Thrinacia 265n157
Thynia 46, 72n334
Thynias 68, 73, 115n131–132, 116–117, 273, 305–328 *passim*, 329
Thyrsis 185, 243
Tiphys 182n176, 188
Tiresias 210n301
Titans 73–74, 254
Titias (Mariandynian) 166–168
Tityus 308n122
tombs 152, 156n62, 158, 160, 161, 162, 164, 173, 174, 180–184, 227, 255n106–107
Triptolemus 150n19
Triton (god) 175n152, 178n163, 285, 312n147, 341–342, 354n17
Triton (lake) 33–34, 47, 341–342, 352n10
Triton (river) 352n10
Trojan War 135n227, 202, 203–206
Trophonius and Agamedes 150n19
Troy, Troad, Trojans 135n226, 170–171, 173n143, 179n167, 183, 185n193, 191n223, 203, 210n300, 255
Twelve Gods 46, 312n147
two-tier allusion 4n19, 24–25, 29, 90, 126, 131, 215, 263, 333
Tyndareus 174
Typhoeus 37, 38–39, 44, 186, 253n97, 268, 314n156

Uranus 61, 74, 252–254, 354n17

Valerius Flaccus 97n61
Vergil 239n44

Wandering Rocks 55
White Island 150n20, 155n61
Wolf, Friedrich August 16–17, 185
world-building 45–48, 157, 164, 169, 177

INDEX RERUM

Xenophanes 253
Xerxes I 75

Zancle 252
Zenodotus 3, 179n165
Zetes *see* Boreads
Zeus 6, 33, 34–37, 38, 41n196, 42–43, 52, 62, 63, 76, 92–93, 104, 106, 117, 131n208, 136, 150, 159n77, 163n95, 172, 173–175, 177, 183, 186, 191–192, 200, 224n350, 238, 247n69, 253n97, 258, 282, 287n49, 301n100, 326n211, 338, 343, 351–356 *passim*
Zerynthus 246